MUSLIMS IN DIALOGUE

The Evolution of A Dialogue

MUSLIMS IN DIALOGUE

The Evolution of A Dialogue

Edited By
Leonard Swidler

The Edwin Mellen Press
Lewiston/Queenston/Lampeter

Library of Congress Cataloging-in-Publication Data

Muslims in dialogue : the evolution of a dialogue / edited by Leonard
  Swidler.
      p.   cm.
    Includes bibliographical references.
    ISBN 0-88946-499-5
    1. Islam--Relations--Christianity. 2. Christianity and other
  religions--Islam. 3. Islam--Relations. I. Swidler, Leonard J.
  BP172.M83   1992
  297'.1972--dc20

                                                              92-9459
                                                                 CIP

This is volume 3 in the continuing series
Religions in Dialogue
Volume 3 ISBN 0-88946-499-5
RD Series ISBN 0-88946-379-4

A CIP catalog record for this book
is available from the British Library.

The Edwin Mellen Press   The Edwin Mellen Press
        Box 450   Box 67
   Lewiston, New York   Queenston, Ontario
      USA 14092   CANADA L0S 1L0

               The Edwin Mellen Press, Ltd.
                 Lampeter, Dyfed, Wales
               UNITED KINGDOM SA48 7DY

          Printed in the United States of America

RELIGIONS IN DIALOGUE

Religion can be described as "an explanation of the ultimate meaning of life – based on the notion of the transcendent – and how to live accordingly." A comprehensive ideology, such as Marxism, can also function as a religion. The difference is that an ideology is not based on the notion of the transcendent – that is, that which "goes beyond" the ordinary (which we grasp with our senses and discursive rational minds) – however it may be perceived and described. Religions, and ideologies, thus are the most all-embracing of human structures, fitting all aspects of life within their "explanations of the ultimate meaning of life and how to live accordingly."

Being so all-embracing, religions, and ideologies, have also tended to be absolutistic and exclusivistic. If some persons or institutions did not agree with our "explanation of the ultimate meaning of life...," they were simply judged wrong and dealt with in a manner ranging from simple indifference through conversion, hostility and violence, to war and even genocide.

In a world poised on the brink of the third millennium after the birth of that Jew who thought of himself as the bringer of peace, such attitudes toward those who differ from us in that all-embracing paradigm through which we perceive, interpret and act on the world, religion (or its functional equivalent, ideology), are no longer viable. Tens of millions of us travel all over the world every year, our economies are increasingly globally interlinked, persons of every culture and religion are daily guests in our homes through radio and television.

We can no longer ignore "The Others," but we can close our mind and spirits to them, look at them with fear and misunderstanding, come to resent them, and perhaps even hate them, leading to hostility and eventually war and death. Today nuclear or ecological, or other, catastrophic devastation lies just a little way further down the path of monologue. It is only by struggling out of the self-centered monologic mindset into dialogue with "The Others" as they really are, and not as we have projected them in our monologues, that we can avoid such cataclysmic disaster.

It is to that end that this series of volumes on religions, and ideologies, in dialogue is conceived: To help move us out of the Age of Monologue into the Age of Dialogue.

Leonard Swidler
Temple University

CONTENTS

INTRODUCTION

THE EVOLUTION OF A DIALOGUE
Leonard Swidler iii

MUSLIM-CHRISTIAN DIALOGUE: MUSLIM PERSPECTIVES

1. ISLAM AND CHRISTIANITY: DIATRIBE
   OR DIALOGUE 1
   Isma'il Ragi al Faruqi

2. THE DIALOGICAL RELATIONSHIP BETWEEN
   CHRISTIANITY AND ISLAM 37
   Hasan Askari

3. INTERRELIGIOUS DIALOUGE AND THE
   ISLAMIC "ORIGINAL SIN" 49
   Khalid Duran

4. MAHMUD MUHAMMAD TAHA AND THE CRISIS IN
   ISLAMIC LAW REFORM: IMPLICATIONS FOR
   INTERRELIGIOUS RELATIONS 59
   Abdullahi Ahmed An-Na'im

5. MUSLIMS AND NON-MUSLIMS 87
   Khalid Duran

6. POSSIBILITIES AND CONDITIONS FOR A BETTER
   UNDERSTANDING BETWEEN ISLAM AND THE WEST 111
   Mohamed Talbi

7. ISLAM AND SOCIOECONOMIC DEVELOPMENT:
   REFLECTIONS INSPIRED BY MOHAMED TALBI 155
   Khalid Duran

CHRISTIAN-MUSLIM DIALOGUE: CHRISTIAN PERSPECTIVES

8. CHRISTIAN DIALOGUE WITH NON-CHRISTIANS 169
   Leonard Swidler

9. ON CHRISTIANS AND JEWS...AND MOSLEMS 173
   George H. Tavard

10. TOWARD A THEOLOGICAL UNDERSTANDING OF ISLAM 177
     Richard H. Drummond

11. ISLAMIC-CHRISTIAN DIALOGUE: APPROACHES TO THE
     OBSTACLES 203
     P. Jacques Lanfry

12. THE DOCTRINAL BASIS COMMON TO CHRISTIANS
     AND MUSLIMS AND DIFFERENT AREAS OF
     CONVERGENCE IN ACTION 225
     Maurice Borrmans

13. CHRISTIANITY AND WORLD RELIGIONS: DIALOGUE
     WITH ISLAM 249
     Hans Küng

14. HANS KÜNG'S THEOLOGICAL RUBICON 273
     Paul F. Knitter

15. CHRISTIAN-MUSLIM DIALOGUE: A REVIEW OF
     SIX POST-VATICAN II CHURCH-RELATED
     DOCUMENTS 283
     John Renard

MUSLIM DIALOGUE WITH JEWS AND CHRISTIANS

16. BASES AND BOUNDARIES OF JEWISH, CHRISTIAN,
     AND MOSLEM DIALOGUE 311
     Zalman Schachter

17. BASES AND BOUNDARIES FOR INTERFAITH DIALOGUE:
     A CHRISTIAN VIEWPOINT 327
     Monika Konrad Hellwig

18. NEW PERSPECTIVES FOR A JEWISH-CHRISTIAN-MUSLIM
     DIALOGUE 345
     Mohammed Arkoun

19. JESUS IN JEWISH-CHRISTIAN-MUSLIM DIALOGUE 353
     Fathi Osman, Zalman Schachter,
     Gerard S. Sloyan and Dermot A. Lane

20. THE QUR'AN AND THE CONTEMPORARY MIDDLE EAST 377
     Kenneth Cragg

21. THE LACK OF JEWISH-ARAB DIALOGUE IN ISRAEL
     AND THE SPIRIT OF JUDAISM: A TESTIMONY 389
     Haim Gordon

MUSLIM DIALOGUE WITH HINDUS

22. THE BASIS FOR A HINDU-MUSLIM DIALOGUE AND
STEPS IN THAT DIRECTION FROM A MUSLIM
PERSPECTIVE..403
    Riffat Hassan

23. EXPLORING THE POSSIBILITY OF A HINDU-MUSLIM
DIALOGUE...425
    Kana Mitra

MUSLIM DIALOGUE ON HUMAN RIGHTS

24. ON HUMAN RIGHTS AND THE QUR'ANIC PERSPECTIVE...................445
    Riffat Hassan

25. RELIGIOUS LIBERTY: A MUSLIM PERSPECTIVE.........................465
    Mohamed Talbi

26. A BUDDHIST RESPONSE TO MOHAMED TALBI.........................483
    Masao Abe

27. RELIGIOUS FREEDOM IN EGYPT: UNDER THE
SHADOW OF THE ISLAMIC *DHIMMA* SYSTEM............................489
    Abdullahi Ahmed An-Na'im

28. RELIGIOUS LIBERTY AND HUMAN RIGHTS IN THE SUDAN.............513
    Khalid Duran

INTRODUCTION

THE EVOLUTION OF A DIALOGUE

Leonard Swidler[*]

Dialogue as the term is used today to characterize encounters between persons and groups with different religions or ideologies is something quite new under the sun. In the past when different religions or ideologies met it was mainly to overcome, or at least to teach, the other, because each was completely convinced that it alone held the secret of the meaning of human life.

In recent times more and more sincerely convinced persons of different religions and ideologies have slowly come to the conviction that they did not hold the secret of the meaning of human life entirely unto themselves, that in fact they had something very important to learn from each other. As a consequence they approached their encounters with other religions and ideologies not primarily in the teaching mode – holding the secret of life alone – but *primarily* in the learning mode – seeking to find more of the secret of the meaning of life. That is dialogue.

---

[*] Leonard Swidler (Catholic) has an STL in Catholic Theology, University of Tübingen and a Ph.D. in history and philosophy, University of Wisconsin. Professor of Catholic Thought and Interreligious Dialogue at Temple University since 1966, he is author or editor of over 50 books and 130 articles, and Co-founder (1964) and Editor of the *Journal of Ecumenical Studies*. His books include: *Dialogue for Reunion* (1962), *The Ecumenical Vanguard* (1965), *Jewish-Christian Dialogues* (1966), *Buddhism Made Plain* (co-author, 1984), *Toward a Universal Theology of Religion* (1987), *Bursting the Bonds*: *A Jewish-Christian Dialogue on Jesus and Paul* (1990), *After the Absolute: The Dialogical Future of Religious Reflection* (1990).

I. The "Journal Of Ecumenical Studies"

This book is about the entrance of one of the world's major religions Islam, into dialogue. It is a very special approach to that slow, painful, at times quite reluctant move to dialogue; it is a particular "empirical" approach that will trace that hesitant journey to dialogue through the pages of the *Journal of Ecumenical Studies* (JES). Gathered here are almost all the articles dealing with Islam that appeared in JES or books spun off from it over the past generation.

Bringing these essays together in a single book will serve several purposes: One, it will present in "empirical" fashion the development of the entrance of Islam into dialogue; two, as such, it will provide strong encouragement, for the progress made in these two decades will be apparent to the reader; three, and most important, these essays are still extraordinarily pertinent today. They will act as a primer for both Muslim and non-Muslim to enter into the dialogue of Islam with the rest of the world's religions and ideologies.

The entrance of Islam into the dialogue in the pages of JES occurred in the first issue of 1968. This of course was not the first time any Muslim engaged in dialogue with non-Muslims. However, it does mark the period when Islam began to enter onto the more public stage of dialogue. It is interesting to note that the *Journal of Ecumenical Studies* began[1] with the

---

[1]   The first issue appeared in 1964, but plans for it began already in 1961 when my wife Arlene suggested that since there was no journal devoted to ecumenical dialogue in America, perhaps we should start one. We had just returned the previous year from Germany where we both had spent three years working on the research for my dissertation on the German Protestant-Catholic ecumenical movement known as the "Una Sancta Movement." We enlisted the participation of a Presbyterian scholar, Elwyn Smith, from Pittsburgh Theological Seminary (we were both teaching at the Catholic university in Pittsburgh, Duquesne University) to serve as Co-editor and began to gather Associate Editors from among Protestant, Catholic and Orthodox Christian scholars from around the world.

Father Henry Koren, Director of the Duquesne University Press, heard of our efforts and offered to publish JES. We were hesitant at first, fearful of official Catholic restrictions, but Father Koren and I then met with Bishop John J. Wright, Catholic bishop of Pittsburgh, who graciously said that Father Koren would serve as the official "Censor librorum" for the Catholic articles, and Father Koren said that he would read them over after they were printed. These conversations, which took place after the Fall, 1962 session of Vatican Council II – the first session – allayed our fears. Shortly thereafter the Catholic "Index of Forbidden Books" and the whole Counter-Reformation Catholic apparatus of censorship disappeared.

subtitle "Catholic-Protestant-Orthodox," which disappeared already in the second volume (1965). The very next issue, the first in 1966, Rabbi Arthur Gilbert became an Associate Editor of JES and all during the years of Vatican II (1962-65) and afterwards JES carried many articles dealing with Jewish-Christian dialogue.

In that first 1968 issue I wrote an editorial on Christian dialogue with non-Christians, arguing for the necessity thereof. When I read that brief essay today I am slightly surprised that I still agree with it entirely, and that more than twenty years later it is still "out in front" of the great majority of religious, ideological thinkers today–which is discouraging–but whose theme is being sounded by a rising crescendo of religious and ideological scholars today–which is encouraging.

That issue also contained for the first time articles by a Hindu and a Muslim. The latter was Isma'il Ragi al Faruqi, a Palestinian-born Muslim who was to join the Temple University Religion Department (where I was then–and now am–teaching and editing JES). The following year Isma'il became an Associate Editor of JES. Faruqi was a traditionally orthodox Muslim (he and his wife Lois were tragically murdered in 1986 by an American Black whom he had befriended and converted to Islam while in prison), a highly knowledgeable Islamicist who did an immense amount to break open Islam to dialogue.

It was Isma'il's very traditional orthodoxy that allowed him to accomplish this so effectively. His often highly skeptical religious confreres trusted him implicitly not to "give away" anything Islamic, and hence were open to being coaxed into joining the dialogue, although most often rather defensively.

It was not easy, however, to find Muslim Islamicist scholars who were willing to enter openly into dialogue with critical-thinking non-Muslim religious scholars. Modern critical-thinking, religiously knowledgeable and committed Muslims open to interreligious dialogue seemed to be in extremely short supply in the world. It seems that they began to appear–or develop–in the last decade or so. This fact is reflected in the appearance of only a single additional JES article by a Muslim until 1977–and it must be remembered that JES had been judged in a worldwide survey of all the institutions devoted to ecumenism and interreligious dialogue as far and away the most valuable publication to them in any language.

A perusal of the many hundreds of book reviews during these years and the even more hundreds of articles summarized in JES dealing with interreligious dialogue corroborates the dearth of Muslims involved in interreligious dialogue. However, in the past dozen years, despite, or perhaps ironically partly because of Khomeini, Muslim scholars have been increasingly participating in interreligious dialogue. This has also begun to happen on the grass-roots level as well.

II. Sources Of The Dialogue:
Dialogue Of The Abrahamic Religions

I would like to look at why this evolution of Muslim dialogue has occurred, starting with the underlying reasons. Since the impetus for dialogue in the contemporary world in general has come, and continues to come, mainly from Christians, and then secondly from Jews, the encounter among these religions is the obvious place to begin to look for reasons for the rise of dialogue. The need for dialogue between Islam and Hinduism and even Buddhism is underlined almost daily in the newspaper reports of mutual hostility and killings. But it is the encounter of the three Abrahamic religions that have been the motor driving Islam toward dialogue.[2]

---

[2] For a brief history of perhaps the longest-lived, most organized Trialogue, see the report by Eugene Fisher, "Kennedy Institute Jewish-Christian-Muslim Trialogue," *Journal of Ecumenical Studies*, 19, 1 (Winter 1982), pp. 197-200. This trialogue, consisting of approximately twenty Jewish, Christian, and Muslim scholars, was sponsored by the Kennedy Institute of Ethics, Georgetown University. It started in 1978 and ran until 1984, meeting twice a year for three days each time.

In April, 1989, another ongoing trialogue, this time international, sponsored by the *Journal of Ecumenical Studies* and the National Conference of Christians and Jews, held its first, very successful three-day meeting; the second, equally successful, was held in January, 1990, and the third in January, 1991...and on into the future.

A dialogue between Muslims and Hindus has been launched, but unfortunately on a relatively small scale to date. One such dialogue between Riffat Hassan and Kana Mitra was sponsored by the *Journal of Ecumenical Studies* in 1985 and was published in Leonard Swidler, ed., *Religious Liberty and Human Rights in Nations and Religions* (Philadelphia & New York: Ecumenical Press & Hippocrene Books, 1986), pp. 109-142, and is reproduced here. A miniature dialogue between Islam and Buddhism also took place at the same conference between Mohammad Talbi and Masao Abe and was likewise published in *ibid.* and is reproduced here.

As a prolegomenon it is important to list at least some of the major elements these three Semitic or Abrahamic religions have in common.

1) They all come from the same Hebraic roots and claim Abraham as their originating ancestor: the historical, cultural and religious traditions all flow out of one original source, an *Urquelle*.

2) All three traditions are religions of ethical monotheism, that is, they all claim there is one, loving, just, creator God who is the Source, Sustainer, and Goal of all reality and that S/He expects all human beings, as images of God, to live in love and justice; in other words, belief in the One God has ethical consequences concerning oneself, other persons, and the world. This is a *common* heritage of the three Abrahamic religions, which is by no means shared by all elements of the other major world religions.

3) The three traditions are all historical religions, that is, they believe that God acts through human history, that God communicates through historical events, through particular human persons, preeminently Moses, Jesus, and Muhammad. Historical events, like the exodus, crucifixion, and *hijrah*, and human persons do not at all play the same central role in many other world religions, as, for example, in Hinduism and Taoism.

4) Judaism, Christianity, and Islam are all religions of revelation, that is, they are persuaded that God has communicated, has revealed, something of God's own self and will in special ways through particular persons, but for the edification, for salvation – or said in another way, for the humanization, which is also the divinization – of all humankind. In all three religions this revelation has two special vehicles: prophets and scriptures.

> a. Clearly in Judaism the men prophets Isaiah, Amos, Hosea, Jeremiah, and the women prophets Miriam and Huldah, etc., are outstanding "mouthpieces" of Yahweh (*prophetes* in Greek, one who speaks for another), and the greatest of all the prophets in Judaism is Moses. For Christianity Moses and the other prophets are God's spokespersons – but also numbered among the Christian prophets are Anna (Lk. 2:36-8), and the two daughters of Philip (Eusebius, *Eccl. Hist.* III.31), and most of all Jesus – though most Christians later came to claim something beyond prophethood for him. For Islam all these Jewish and Christian prophets are also authentic prophets, God's revealing voice in the world – and to that list they add Muhammad, the Seal of the Prophets.

    b. For these three faiths God's special revelation is also communicated in "The Book," the "Bible." For Jews the Holy Scriptures are the Hebrew Bible, for Christians it is the Hebrew Bible and the New Testament, and for Muslims it is those two plus the Qur'an, which is corrective and supplemental to them. For Muslims, Jews and Christians have the special name "People of the Book."

There are many more things that the three Abrahamic faiths have in common, such as the importance of convenant, of law and faith, of the community (witness in the three traditions the central role of the terms "People," "Church," and "Ummah," respectively). But just looking at the list of commonalties already briefly spelled out will provide us with an initial set of fundamental reasons why it was eventually perceived as imperative for Jews, Christians and Muslims to engage in serious, ongoing dialogue.

    First, if Jews, Christians and Muslims believe that there is only one, loving, just God in whose image they are and whose will they claim to try to follow, they need to face the question of why there are three different ways of doing that – obviously that question can be faced only in dialogue.

    Second, if Jews, Christians and Muslims believe that God acts through human history, that God communicates through historical events and particular human persons, they need to face the question of whether all religiously significant historical events and persons are limited to their own histories – put colloquially: Do Jews, Christians and Muslims really believe that they have God in their own historical boxes, or that, by their own principles, God transcends all limitations, including even their sacred historical events and persons?

    Third, If Judaism, Christianity and Islam believe that God communicates, reveals, Her/Himself to humans not only through things, events, and human persons in general, but also in special ways through particular events and persons, they are going to have to face the question of whether God's will as delivered through God's spokespersons, i.e., prophets, and the recording in writing of their teachings and kindred material in what is known as Holy Scriptures, is limited to their own prophets and scriptures. Concretely, Jews will have to reflect on whether Jesus and the writings of his first – Jewish – followers (the so-called New Testament) have something to say about God's will for humankind to non-Christians (and themselves?). Jews and Christians will have to reflect on whether the prophet Muhammad and his "recitation," i.e., "Qur'an," have something to say about God's will for humankind to non-Muslims (including themselves?!). Muslims of course already affirm the importance of the Jewish and Christian prophets and scriptures.

Obviously these questions, and others of serious importance to the ultimate meaning of life, can be addressed only in dialogue among Jews, Christians and Muslims.

Once this is recognized, however, it also immediately becomes clear that all the questions just listed which challenge the absoluteness and exclusivity of the three Abrahamic traditions' claims about having all the truth, about God being found only in the boxes of their history, prophets, scriptures, and revelation, also apply to the non-Abrahamic religions and ideologies, such as Hinduism, Buddhism and Marxism.

III. Different Dialogues – Different Goals

Pragmatically, however, one cannot engage in dialogue with all possible partners at the same time. Moreover, all the goals of one dialogue with a certain set of partners can never be fulfilled by another set of dialogue partners. For example, the goal of working toward denominational unity between the Lutheran Church in America an the American Lutheran Church would never have been accomplished if Catholics had been full partners in that dialogue with Lutherans. Or again, Jews and Christians have certain items on their mutual theological agenda, e.g., the Jewish claim that the Messiah has not yet come, that will not be adequately addressed if Muslims are added as full partners. And so it goes with each addition or new mix of dialogue partners.

There is a special urgency about the need for Christians to dialogue among themselves to work toward the goal of some kind of effective, visible Christian unity: the absurdity and scandal of there being hundreds of separate churches all claiming "one foundation, Jesus Christ the Lord," is patent. The need for intra-Jewish dialogue I will leave to my Jewish sisters and brothers to inform me about in specifics, but it nevertheless appears apparent in general. However, for Christians dialogue with Jews has an extraordinarily high priority that cannot be displaced, and where it has not been both initiated and continued, it needs to be undertaken with all possible speed and perseverance. If nothing else, the twentieth-century Holocaust of the Jews within the heart of Christendom makes this dialogue indispensable.

Nevertheless, there is something like – though not precisely – a relationship of parent and offspring which compels Jews and Christians to enter into dialogue with Muslims. Furthermore, there are today all the external reasons for Jewish-Christian dialogue with Islam that flow from the reality of the earth now being a global village and the unavoidable symbiotic relationship between the Judeo-Christian industrialized West and the partly oil-rich, relatively non-industrialized Islamic world.

IV. Expectations from the Trialogue

A special word of caution to Jews and Christians entering into dialogue with Muslims is in order. They will be starting such a venture with several disadvantages: 1) the heritage of colonialism, 2) ignorance about Islam, 3) distorted image of Muslims, and 4) culture gap.

The vast majority of Muslims trained in Islamics are non-Westerners, which means they very likely come from a country that was until very recently a colony of the West. Many Muslims are still traumatized by Western colonialism and frequently identify Christianity, and to a lesser extent, Judaism, with the West. Jewish and Christian dialogue partners need to be aware of this and move to diffuse the problem.

Jews and Christians will need to make a special effort to learn about Islam beyond what was required for them intelligently to engage in the Jewish-Christian dialogue, for in the latter they usually knew at least a little about the partner's religion. With Islam they will probably be starting with a negative quantity compounded from sheer ignorance and massive misinformation.

Most often the current Western image of a Muslim is a gross distortion of Islam. Indeed, it is frequently that of some kind of inhuman monster. But the Khomeini distortion of Islam is no more representative of

Islam than the Rev. Ian Paisley of Northern Ireland is of Christianity in general or Richard Nixon was of the pacifist Quaker tradition.

Most difficult of all is the fact that a huge cultural gap exists between the great majority of Muslims and precisely those Jews and Christians who are open to dialogue. In brief: Islam as a whole has not yet really experienced the "Enlightenment" and come to terms with it, as has much of the Judeo-Christian tradition, although obviously not all of it. Only a minority of Muslim Islamics scholars will share the "deabsolutized" understanding of truth needed to be able and want to enter into dialogue with "the other," that is, to converse with the religiously "other" primarily to learn religiously from her or him–which means that many efforts at dialogue with Muslims will in fact be prolegomena to true interreligious dialogue. Frequently such attempts will be not unlike "dialogue" with many Orthodox Jews or evangelical Christians – or with Catholics before Vatican II.

But the prolegomena must be traversed in order to reach authentic dialogue. In this case surely the words of the Vatican and Pope Paul VI apply to all Christians and Jews, who "must assuredly be concerned for their separated brethren...making the first approaches toward them....dialogue is *demanded* nowadays...by the pluralism of society, and by the maturity man has reached in this day and age."[3] It is toward that end all Christians and Jews must strive, first among themselves, then with each other, and then with their quasi "offspring," Islam.

V. Muslim Critical Thinkers

Despite the facts of the cultural gap and that only a minority of Muslim Islamicists have a "deabsolutized" view of truth, there are today many more of them than is usually recognized. Often, however, they live outside the Muslim world. Let me recall a personal experience exemplifying why: An Egyptian Muslim Islamicist spent a number of years studying and teaching in America. At that time he made his own the historical-critical mentality and was very open to interreligious dialogue. We spoke quite specifically about a "dialogic" article he wished to write for the *Journal of*

---

[3] *Ecclesiam suam*, no. 78, quoted in Austin Flannery, *Vatican Council II* (Collegeville, MN: Liturgical Press, 1975), p. 1003.

Ecumenical Studies. Suddenly, for family reasons, he had to return to Egypt and shortly thereafter took a position teaching Islamics at a university in Saudi Arabia. After two years of correspondence and coaxing he wrote in despair that he could not write the article we had worked out together so long as he was in the Arabian world; the intellectual atmosphere was just too restrictive for him to be able to think the thoughts he would have to in order to write the article.[4]

This point was made poignantly by Fazlur Rahman: "Free thought and thought are synonymous, and one cannot hope that thought will survive without freedom....Islamic thought, like all thought, equally requires a freedom by which dissent, confrontation of views, and debate between ideas is assured."[5]

Professor Rahman, who until his death in 1988 was for many years at the University of Chicago, knew well whereof he spoke. He was the Minister of Education of the newly created Pakistan from 1947 to 1957, and from 1962 to 1968 he was Director of a newly formed Islamic Research Institute (established by President Ayub Khan).

> But even as the institute was a little less than halfway through to the initial stage of its goal, it became the victim of a massive attack of the combined forces of the religious right and the opposition politicians. I resigned in September 1968 and the Ayub Khan government fell six months later, and, although this group of progressive scholars has done its best to maintain itself, it has since been overwhelmed by the forces of reaction.[6]

Nevertheless, critical thinking among Muslim Islamicists has broken through. The Yugoslavian Muslim Smail Balic wrote that,

> In regard to research into the real occasions for the individual revelations of the Qur'an and the consequent legal philosophy, not enough is done seriously to distinguish the time-bound elements from the enduring. The knowledge that the Qur'an is

---

[4] The Muslim scholar in question was Fathi Osman who taught with me at Temple University in 1975-76, during which time he wrote the review article on Christology that was published in JES in 1977 and is reproduced here. He recently returned to the United States, and joined the Jewish-Christian-Muslim trialogue sponsored by JES and the NCCJ – and is again his former liberated self, even more deeply mature as a critical-thinking, dialogue-oriented committed Muslim scholar.

[5] Fazlur Rahman, *Islam* (New York: Doubleday, 1968), p. 125.

[6] *Ibid.*

in part also a collection of time-related documents from the early history of Islam has not yet been able to move beyond pure theory.[7]

The Indian Muslim Asaf A. A. Fyzee stated that,

> For me it is clear that we cannot "go back" to the Qur'an. Rather, we must go forward with it. I want to *understand* the Qur'an as the Arabs of the time of the Prophet did only in order *to interpret it anew*, in order to apply it to my living conditions and to believe in it insofar as it speaks to me as a human person of the twentieth century.[8]

The Professor of Arabic Language and Islamic Culture at the University of Paris and Temple University, Philadelphia, Pennsylvania, Muhammad M. Arkoun, severely criticized at a Christian-Muslim dialogue in Bonn in 1981 the kind of dialogue wherein the conservative and fundamentalist elements of each side simply reenforced each other; rather, he wanted modern critical scholarly thought brought to bear on both religions and their dialogue: "For this reason I demand in what concerns me a critically new reading of the Scripture (Bible, Gospels, Qur'an) and a philosophical critique of exegetical and theological reason."[9] Professor Arkoun recently argued this point even more forcefully and with great stress on the need to study religions together:

> In this context where struggling ideologies are at work, it seems totally romantic, irrelevant, and useless to engage in debates between religions about traditional faiths, values, or dogmas. Positive and efficient initiatives should be taken in the field of education: primary and secondary schools, universities, the mass media, nongovernmental organizations and other private and public institutions, so as to promote a new teaching of history, *comparative* cultures, *comparative* religions, *comparative* philosophies and theologies, *comparative* literature and law.[10]

After spelling out in some detail how this comparative study should be carried out with the aid of modern critical scholarly tools, Arkoun concluded:

---

[7] Smail Balic, *Ruf vom Minareth* (Berlin, 1979), p. 90.

[8] Cited in Rotraud Wielandt, *Offenbarung und Geschichte im Denken moderner Muslime* (Wiesbaden: F. Steiner, 1971), p. 159.

[9] Cited in M. S. Abdulla, ed., *Der Glaube in Kultur, Recht und Politik* (Mainz: Hase & Koehler, 1982), p. 142.

[10] Mohammad Arkoun, "New Perspectives for a Jewish-Christian-Muslim Dialogue," *Journal of Ecumenical Studies*, 25, 3 (Summer, 1989).

This is, in very short allusive terms, my proposal as a
Muslim scholar – not to contribute, I repeat to an encounter
that would mean that we think and work within the framework
of *I and we vs. you and them* but to the creation of a new space
of intelligibility and freedom. We need to be emancipated
from inherited traditions not yet studied and interpreted with
controlled methods and cognitive principles.

Muslims are currently accused of being closed-minded,
integrists, fundamentalists, prisoners of dogmatic beliefs. Here
is a liberal, modern, humanist, Muslim proposal. I await the
response of Jews, Christians, and secularists to my invitation to
engage our thoughts, our endeavors, and our history in the
cause of peace, progress, emancipation, justice through
knowledge, and shared spiritual values.[11]

One of the most thoroughgoing exponents of the historical-critical
method's being indispensable to ascertaining the correct meaning of the
foundation of Islam, the Qur'an, was Fazlur Rahman. He clearly argued that
the text can be understood only in context:

The Qur'an is the divine response, through the Prophet's
mind, to the moral-social situation of the Prophet's Arabia....It
is literally God's response through Muhammad's mind (this
latter factor has been radically underplayed by the Islamic
orthodoxy) to a historic situation (a factor likewise drastically
restricted by the Islamic orthodoxy).[12]

Like Asaf Fyzee, Rahman too wished to get to the original meaning of
he Qur'an so it can be applied, *mutatis mutandis*, now:

There has to be a two-fold movement: First one must
move from the concrete case treatments of the Qur'an – taking
the necessary and relevant social conditions of that time into
account – to the general principles upon which the entire
teaching converges. Second, from this general level there must
be a movement back to specific legislation, taking into account
the necessary and relevant social conditions now obtaining.[13]

This is very much like the "two-pole" theology of many contemporary
Christian theologians (e.g., Hans Küng and Edward Schillebeeckx). From
this there follows another logical step – again like that of many progressive
Christian theologians, and similarly criticized from the respective bastions of

---

[11] *Ibid.*

[12] Rahman, *Islam.*, pp. 5, 8.

[13] *Ibid.*, p. 20.

orthodoxy – namely, that "the tradition will therefore be more an object of judgment of the new understanding [of the Scripture] than an aid to it."[14]

Moreover, Rahman rejected the notion that, "any significant interpretation of the Qur'an can be absolutely monolithic...the Prophet's companions themselves sometimes understood certain Qur'anic verses differently, and this was within his knowledge."[15] Further, "It is obviously not necessary that a certain interpretation once accepted must continue to be accepted; there is always both room and necessity for new interpretation, for this is, in truth, an ongoing process."[16]

It is precisely this last point that was raised to the level of a critical hermeneutical methodological principle in dealing with the Qur'an by Ustaz Mahmud Muhammad Taha from the Sudan. Taha was an engineer and a sufi mystic who worked tirelessly for the reform of Islam both inwardly and outwardly. He was tragically executed at age 75 in January of 1985 in a final outburst of violence by General Nimieri before his overthrow a number of weeks later. However, Taha's thought continues in his followers, such as the jurist Abdullahi Ahmed An Na'im.

Taha argued that the shift from the earlier revelation of principles in Mecca to the later one in Medina is essentially reversible. The Mecca principles are fundamentally open, liberal, liberating principles, whereas the Medina principles are specific and restrictive. The shift was made because in the concrete circumstances – both the external ones and the then internal capabilities of the Muslims – the Mecca principles could not yet be implemented in all their openness. They were the ideal, on the way to which Medina was but a way station; it is now time for the Muslims to leave the Medina way station and move forward toward fulfilling the liberating Mecca ideal. This in brief is the heart of the teaching of Taha, filled out with Qur'anic citations and argumentation of course.[17]

---

14 *Ibid.*, p. 7.

15 *Ibid.*, p. 144.

16 *Ibid.*, p. 145.

17 See Abdullahi Ahmed An Na'im [transliterated here as El Naiem], "A Modern Approach to Human Rights in Islam: Foundations and Implications for Africa," in Claude Welch and Ronald Meltzer, eds., *Human Rights and Development in Africa* (Albany: State University of

Mohammed Talbi of the University of Tunisia at Tunis has for years been active both nationally and internationally in dialogue with Christians, receiving the Lukas Prize for his contributions to interreligious dialogue from the Protestant Theological Faculty of the University of Tübingen in May, 1985 (the funding for the Lukas Prize comes from the son of Rabbi Lukas, who had been a student at Tübingen). Representative of Talbi's self-critical, yet Islamically-committed, thought are his reflections on "Religious Liberty: A Muslim Perspective":

> In short, from the Muslim perspective that is mine, our duty is simply to bear witness in the most courteous way that is most respectful of the inner liberty of our neighbors and their sacredness. We must also be ready at the same time to listen to them in truthfulness. We have to remember, as Muslims, that a *hadith* of our Prophet states: "The believer is unceasingly in search of wisdom; wherever he finds it he grasps it." Another saying adds: "Look for knowledge everywhere, even as far as in China." And finally, it is up to God to judge, for we, as limited human beings, know only in part. Let me quote: "To each among you We prescribed a Law and an Open Way. And if God had enforced His Will, He would have made of you all one people. But His plan is to test you in what He hath given you. So strive as in a race in all virtues. The goal of you all is to God. Then will He inform you of that wherein you differed" (Qur'an, V, 51)....

> At the heart of this problem we meet the ticklish subject of apostasy...the Qur'an argues, warns and advises, but never resorts to the argument of the sword. That is because that argument is meaningless in the matter of faith. In our pluralistic world our modern theologians must take that into account.

> We can never stress too much that religious liberty is not an act of charity or a tolerant concession towards misled persons. It is a fundamental right of everyone. To claim it for myself implies *ipso facto* that I am disposed to claim it for my neighbor too.[18]

New York Press, 1984), pp. 75-89; "Religious Freedom in Egypt: Under the Shadow of the Islamic *Dhimma* System," Swidler, *Religious Liberty and Human Rights*, pp. 43-62 – the latter is reproduced here. El Naiem has translated into English Taha's fundamental work *The Second Message of Islam* (Omdurman, 1967), but because El Naiem was also imprisoned for years, the English translation was published only in 1987 with the Syracuse University Press.

[18] From a lecture given at a conference sponsored by the *Journal of Ecumenical Studies* at Temple University, November 3-8, 1985: "Religious Tolerance and Human Rights within the International Community, within Nations and within Religions." An earlier version had been delivered at the Second World Congress on Religious Liberty in Rome, September 3-4, 1984.

Hasan Askari, formerly Chairperson of the Sociology Department of Muslim University of Aligarh, India, and recently a Fellow at the Center for the Study of Islam and of Christian-Muslim Relations, Selly Oak Colleges, Birmingham, U.K., has long espoused authentic interreligious dialogue, placing at the base of which a deabsolutized understanding of truth:

> One who does not allow for alternatives within one's own religious tradition may not allow for more than one religious approach....[But we must] hesitate to absolutise any of the approaches within one or other plurality as the only true approach....All religions, and all approaches within each one of them, are relative to the Absolute Truth [God]....The worst of all defiance is to be locked up within one's own tradition and refuse to embrace each and every one, whatever his or her race and creed.[19]

Likewise deeply involved as critical-thinking committed Muslims in interreligious dialogue not only with Christians but also with Jews – and others – are the Moroccan Khalid Duran (long at the Deutsches Orient Institut at Hamburg and more recently at Temple University, the American University and the University of California, Irvine),[20] and the Pakistani/American Riffat Hassan (now at the University of Louisville in Kentucky).[21] Duran has been active for years in Jewish-Christian-Muslim trialogue, first in England, then in Germany, and now in the United States, whereas Hassan has been active in the trialogue in America since 1979, and has recently established an ongoing Christian-Muslim dialogue in her native Pakistan.

Published as "Religious Liberty: A Muslim Perspective," in Swidler, *Religious Liberty*, pp. 181, 187, and reproduced here.

[19] Hasan Askari, "Within and Beyond the Experience of Religious Diversity," John Hick and Hasan Askari, eds., *The Experience of Religious Diversity* (Hants, England: Gower, 1985), pp. 191, 217. See also his 1972 article in JES, reproduced here.

[20] See, e.g., Khalid Duran, "Muslim Openness to Dialogue," Leonard Swidler, ed., *Toward a Universal Theology of Religion* (Maryknoll, NY: Orbis Books, 1987), pp. 210-217; "Religious Liberty and Human Rights in the Sudan," Swidler, *Religious Liberty*, pp. 61-78, both reproduced here.

[21] See, e.g., Riffat Hassan, "On Human Rights and the Qur'änic Perspective," *Journal of Ecumenical Studies*, 19, 3 (Summer, 1982), pp. 51-65; "The Basis for a Hindu-Muslim Dialogue and Steps in that Direction from a Muslim Perspective," Swidler, *Religious Liberty*, pp. 125-142, both of which are reproduced here.

With such dialogue partners, and others not here mentioned, authentic dialogue, and not just prologomena thereto, between Islam and other religions is possible – and actual.

However, important as this scholarly level dialogue is – and it is extremely important, for these scholars are the shapers of the shapers of opinion – the dialogue must also be translated onto the middle and grass-root levels. I hope that this primer of *Muslims In Dialogue* will help to promote that dialogue on all levels, the scholarly, middle and grass roots.

I urge the reader to begin to make use of the work of these pioneer scholars in dialogue, both through their writings, and even in person. I urge you to begin, or continue, the work of dialogue with sensitivity for your "other" sister and brother and persevere in it, for it will not only contribute to a cessation of hostilities and a resolution of tensions, but also to a deepening and enriching of your own inner and communal life.

MUSLIM-CHRISTIAN DIALOGUE:
MUSLIM PERSPECTIVES

ISLAM AND CHRISTIANITY: DIATRIBE OR DIALOGUE*

Isma'il Ragi A. Al Faruqi**

This is not the place to review the history of Christian-Muslim relations. This history may now be read in the erudite works of Norman Daniel.[1] The reading is sad and agonizing. The conclusion which may be safely drawn from this history is that Christianity's involvement with the Muslim World was so full of misunderstanding, prejudice, and hostility that it has warped the Western Christian's will and consciousness. "Would to God Christianity had never met Islam!" will reverberate in the mind of any student patient enough to peruse that history.[2] On the other side, Muslim-Christian

---

* *Journal of Ecumenical Studies*, 5:1 (Winter, 1968).

** Isma'il R. al Faruqi (Muslim) was born in Palestine in 1921. He studied philosophy at the American University of Beirut, Indiana University and Harvard University. His doctoral dissertation was on the metaphysical status of the good. He studied Islam at Cairo and other centers of Muslim learning, and Christianity at the Faculty of Divinity, McGill University. He taught at the Institute of Islamic Studies, McGill University; the Central Institute of Islamic Research, Karachi; the Institute of Higher Arabic Studies of the League of Arab States, Cairo University; and al Azhar University, Cairo, and, between 1964 and 1968 was Associate Professor of Religion at Syracuse University, developing a program of Islamic Studies. From the fall of 1968 he was Professor in the Department of Religion at Temple University until his death in 1986.

[1] *Islam and the West: The Making of an Image* (Edinburgh: The University Press, 1960); *Islam, Europe and Empire* (Edinburgh: The University Press, 1966).

[2] In considering that history one must take account of the following facts: The first missionaries which Islam sent to Christendom were met with swords drawn and were massacred at Dhat al Talh in 629 A.C. From that moment, however, a section of Christendom which might be called "Semitic Christianity" welcomed the Muslims, gave them protection, listened to and were converted by, or simply tolerated them. These Christians were for the

most part Arab or Semitic, though not necessarily Arabic speaking, and a fair number were Copts, whether Abyssinian or Egyptian. The Abyssinian state, Christian and theocratic, previously welcomed and protected the Muslim refugees from Mecca and was regarded as a friend by the Muslims ever since. With the rise of the Islamic state and the entry of Islam onto the stage of history, a much older division began to resume its shape: the division of Christianity itself into Eastern and Western, Semitic and Hellenic.

Though they had abandoned most of the so-called "heretical" doctrines of the ancestors, submitted themselves to the main pronouncements of the synods and councils and acquiesced to the theological, christological and ecclesiological tenets of catholic Christianity, the Semitic Christians cooperated with the Muslims. Despite the fact that the innate appeal of Islam, its examplars in life and action, and the continuous exposure to its civilizing and cultural power had taken their toll of converts from their ranks, these Christians have survived in considerable numbers fourteen centuries of living under the political rule of Islam. Islamically acculturated they certainly are; but not converted. They constitute a living monument of Christian-Muslim co-existence, of mutual tolerance and affection, of cooperation in civilization and culture building. Their interreligious *modus-vivendi* is an achievement in which the whole human race may take rightful pride.

On the other hand, Western Christians, embittered by a military defeat initially brought about by their own intolerance to allow the Islamic call to be heard, nursed their resentment and laid in wait. For three centuries, sporadic fighting erupted between the two camps without decisive advantage to either party. In the eleventh century, the Western Christians thought the time had come to turn the tables of history. The Crusades were launched with disastrous consequences to Christian-Muslim and Muslim-Christian relations. Christian executions, forced conversions or expulsion of the Muslims from Spain followed the political defeat of the Muslim state. For eight centuries, Islam had been the faith not only of immigrant Arabs and Berbers but of native Spaniards who were always the majority. The "Inquisition" made no differentiation; and it brought to an end one of the most glorious chapters in the history of interreligious living and cooperation.

Modern times brought a story of continuous aggression and tragic suffering beginning with the pursuit and obliteration of Islam from Eastern Europe where the Ottomans had planted it, to the conquest, fragmentation, occupation and colonization of the whole Muslim World except the impenetrable interior of the Arabian Peninsula. Muslims remember with bitterness that this is the period when Christendom changed the script of Muslim languages in order to cut off their peoples from the Islamic tradition and sever their contact with the heartland of Islam; when it cultivated and nursed Hindu and Buddhist reaction against the progress of Islam in the Indian sub-continent; when it invited the Chinese to dwell and to oppose Islam in Malaysia and Indonesia; when it encouraged the Greeks in Cyprus and the Nile Valley, the Zionists in Palestine and the French in Algeria; when, as the holder of political and economic power within the Muslim World, Christendom discouraged, retarded or impeded by every means possible the awakenings, renaissance and self-enlightenment processes of Muslim societies; when, controlling the education of Muslims, it prescribed for it little beyond the purpose of producing clerks for the colonialist administration.

Equally, modern times witnessed the strongest movement of Christian proseletization among Muslims. Public education, public health and welfare services were laid wide open to the missionary who was accorded the prestige of a colonial governor, and who entered the field with pockets full of "rice" for the greedy, of intercession with the colonialist governor for the enterprising, and of the necessities of survival for the sick and the needy.

Throughout this long history of some fourteen centuries of Christian-Muslim relations, the researcher can hardly find one good word written or spoken about Islam by Christians. One must admit that a number of Semitic Christians, of Western Christian Crusade-annalists or of relations have been determined by the Qur'an.[3] Doctrinally, therefore, these relations have seen no change. Throughout their history, and despite the

---

merchants and travellers may and did say a few good words about Islam and its adherents. Samplings of this were given by Thomas Arnold in his *The Preaching of Islam* (reprinted by Sh. Muhammad Ashraf, Lahore, 1961), especially the conclusion. Modern times have seen a number of scholars who conceded that Muhammad's claims were candid, that Islamic religious experience was genuine, and that underlying the phenomenon of Islam, the true and living God had been and still is active. But these are isolated statements even in the life of those who made them, not to speak of the deluge of vituperation and attack upon Islam, Muhammad and the Muslims which fill practically all Christian writing about the world of Islam. Moreover, whatever little may be found belongs to Christians as individual persons. Christianity as such, i.e., the bodies which speak in its name, be they Catholic, Protestant or Greek Orthodox, has never recognized Islam as a genuine religious experience. The history of academic Western Christian writing on the subject of Islam is a history of service to the world of scholarship, though one of misunderstanding and falsification. As a librarian seeking to collate manuscripts, establish texts and analyze historical claims, the Christian scholar has done marvellous work which earned him the permanent gratitude of scholars everywhere. But as an interpreter of the religion, thought, culture and civilization of Islam, he has been – except in the rarest of cases – nothing less than a misinterpreter and his work, a misrepresentation of its object. (See the scathing analysis of A. L. Tibawi, "English-Speaking Orientalists: A Critique of Their Approach to Islam and Arab Nationalism," *The Muslim World*, Vol. LIII, Nos. 3, 4 [July, October], 1963, pp. 185-204, 298-313.) Vatican II conceded that "the Moslems...adore one God, living and enduring, merciful and all-powerful, Maker of heaven and earth and Speaker to men...they prize the moral life and give worship to God..." though it carefully equated these characteristics not with actual salvation but with the mere inclusion within "the plan of salvation." (*The Documents of Vatican II*, ed. Walter M. Abbott, S.J., New York, Guild Press [An Angelus Book], 1966, p. 663.) Little rewarding as this concession becomes when conjoined with the earlier statement that "whosoever..., knowing that the Catholic Church was made necessary by God through Jesus Christ, would refuse to enter her or to remain in her could not be saved" (*ibid.*, pp. 32-33), anything similar to it has yet to come from the World Council of Churches – indeed from any Protestant church, synod or council of churches.

[3] Before the Hijrah to Madinah and the establishment of the first Islamic polity, the revelation of Muhammad, i.e., the Qur'an, defined the religious relation of Islam and Christianity. To the Jews, it asserted, God sent Jesus, a prophet and apostle born of Mary by divine command. He was given the Evangel, taught to relieve the hardships of Jewish legalism and to exemplify the ethic of love, humility and mercy. Those of his followers who remained true to his teaching are blessed. Those who associated him with God, invented trinitarianism and monkery and falsified the Evangel, are not. The former the Qur'an described in terms reserved for the friends of God: "The Christians are upright; they recite the revelations of God during the night hours and prostrate themselves in worship. They believe in God and in the Day of Judgment. They enjoin the good, forbid evil and compete in the performance of good works. Those are certainly righteous" (Qur'an, 3:113). "And you will find among the People of the Book the closer to you those who said that they were Christians; for many of them are priests and ascetics and are humble" (Qur'an, 5:82). "In their hearts, We planned compassion and mercy" (Qur'an, 57:27). Parallel to this lavish praise of some Christians, stands the Qur'an's castigation of the others. "Some Christians said: The Messiah is the Son of God, thereby surpassing in unbelief the unbelievers of old....They have taken their priests

political hostilities, the Muslims revered Jesus as a great prophet and his faith as divine religion. As for the Christians, the Muslims argued with them in the manner of the Qur'an. But when it came to political action, they gave them the benefit of the doubt as to whether they followed the Christianity of Jesus or of the Church. Muhammad and 'Umar's wager for a Christian victory over the Zoroastrians, the Meccan Muslim's choice of, welcome and protection by Christian Abyssinia and Muhammad's personal waiting upon the Christian Abyssinian delegates to Madinah, the Prophet's covenant with the Christians of Najran, 'Umar's convenant with the Archbishop of Jerusalem and his refusal to hold prayer on the premises of the Church of the Holy Sepulchre lest later Muslims might claim the place, the total cooperation of the Umawis and 'Abbasis with their Christian subjects, and of the Umawis of Cordova with Christians who were not their subjects – all these are landmarks in a record of cooperation and mutual esteem hardly paralleled in any other history. Some persecution, some conversion under influences of all sorts, some aggression, some doctrinal attacks going beyond the limits defined by the Qur'an, there were, without a doubt. The Muslims in all places and times were not all angels! But such were scattered cases

---

and monks for gods, as well as the Messiah, son of Mary, whereas they were commanded never to worship but one God beside Whom there is none else" (Qur'an, 9:30). "O People of the Book! Do not go to extremes in your religion and never say anything on behalf of God except the truth. Jesus, the Messiah, the son of Mary, is only a prophet of God, a fulfillment of His command addressed to Mary....So believe in God and in His prophets and do not hold the trinitarian view....God is the one God. May He be exalted above having a son. To Him belongs everything in heaven and earth" (Qur'an, 4:171). As for what Muslim attitude towards Christians should be, the Qur'an prescribed: "Say: O People of the Book! Let us now come to agreement upon a noble principle common to both of us, namely, that we shall not worship anyone but God, that we shall never associate aught with Him, and that we shall not take one another for lords beside God. And if they turn away, then say: Remember, as for us, we do submit to God....We believe in that which has been revealed to us and that which has been revealed to you and our God and your God is One. It is to Him that we submit" (Qur'an, 3:64; 29:47). From this we may conclude that Islam does not condemn Christianity but reproaches some devotees of it whom it accused of deviating from the true path of Jesus. Every sect in Christianity has accused the other sects of the same. Yet, Christianity has never recognized Islam as a legitimate and salutary movement. It has never regarded Islam as part of its own tradition except to call Muhammad a cardinal in rebellion against the Pope because of his jealousy for not being elected to the office, and Islam a "de relicta fide catholica" (*Islam and the West*, pp. 83-84).

whose value falls to the ground when compared with the overwhelming spread of history which has remained true to this Qur'anic position.

I. The Present Problem

Perhaps nothing is more anachronistic – indeed absurd – than the spectacle of the Western Christian missionary preaching to Muslims the Western figurization of the religion of Jesus. The absurdity is twofold: First, the West, whence the missionary comes and which sustains him in his effort, has for decades stopped finding meaning in that figurization which is the content of mission. Indeed, in the missionary himself, that figurization determines but one little portion of his consciousness, the remainder falling under the same corroding secularism, materialism and skeptical empiricism so common in Western thought and culture. Second, the missionary preaches this figurization to Muslims who, in North Africa and the Near East, were thrice Christians. They were Christians in the sense of preparing, through the spiritualization and interiorization of the Semitic religion, for the advent of Jesus. It was their consciousness and spirit which served God as human substrate and historical circumstance for that advent. Naturally, they were the first to "acknowledge" Jesus and to believe in him as crystallization of a reality which is themselves. They were Christians in the second sense of the Western figurization of Christianity when, having fallen under the dominion of Byzantium, they flirted with that figurization and in fact adopted all its doctrinal elements regardless of whether or not they officially joined the churches of Western Christianity. After living with this figurization a while, they welcomed and embraced Islam. But they remained, even as Muslims, Christians in the sense of holding the realization of the ethic of Jesus as the *conditio sine qua non* of Islamicity and of realizing a fair part of the Jesus-ethic in their personal lives. The comedy in evidence today is that the missionary is utterly unaware of this long experience of the Muslim with Jesus Christ.

This Western missionary, whether *monastes* or other, has associated himself with, and often played the role of colonial governor, trader, settler, military, physician and educator. In the last two decades, after the Muslim countries achieved independence, he found for himself the role of development expert. Expertise in poultry breeding, neurological surgery or industrial management, and the crying need of the Muslim as yet underdeveloped countries were callously taken as God-sent occasions to evangelize, thus stirring within the Muslim a sense of being exploited and producing still more bitterness. Besides, such an expert-missionary is often sponsored by, if not the direct employee of, the aiding agency of the Western government; and a fair harmonization of his tactics and purposes with those of that government were safely presupposed. The Western World knows of no Christian who, moved by the Sermon on the Mount, came to live among Muslims as a native, who made their burden his burden, their hopes and yearnings his hopes and yearnings. Albert Schweitzer, the idol of the modern West in Christian self-giving to the natives of Africa, was as unchristian as to condemn all the Africans' search for liberty;[4] indeed, publicly to request President Eisenhower to prevent a United Nations debate on Algeria. The Africans ought to be helped and their suffering relieved, this saint of the twentieth century commanded his fellow Christian whites – but as our colonial subjects! Moreover, where it dissociated itself from imperialism and was purely religious, Western Christian mission to the Muslim World was never a mission of Jesus, but a mission of the Western figurization of Christianity arrogantly asserted in words, hardly ever exemplified in deeds. Modern Christendom has produced a Mrs. Vester who really gave and, fortunately, is still giving of her life to the orphans of Jerusalem.[5] There probably were and still are other isolated individuals of this caliber. Nonetheless, the persistent effort needed to establish an ethically respectable relation with Muslim society has been neglected. Since it has brought hardly any significant conversions and aggravated the alienation of the two world communities, and since the Muslims, as well as Muslim World Christians, regard it as pouring ideological salt into political wounds inflicted by the Crusades and a century of colonization, the mission chapter of Christian history, as we have so far known it, had better be closed, the hunt called off,

[4] Albert Schweitzer, *Out of My Life and Thought*, tr. C. T. Campion (New York: Mentor Books, 1955), pp. 147-148.

[5] See Bertha Spafford Vester's article "Jerusalem, My Home" in *National Geographic Magazine* (December, 1964), pp. 826-847.

the missionaries withdrawn and the mission-arm of the Catholic Church and of the World Council of Churches liquidated.

To say all this is not to advocate isolation. In fact, isolation is impossible. The world is simply too small, and our lives are utterly interdependent. Not only our survival, but even our well-being and happiness depend on our cooperation. Mere diplomatic courtesy or casual coalescence of political interests will not suffice. No genuine and effective cooperation can proceed without mutual esteem and respect, without agreement on purposes, final objectives and standards. If it is to last through the generations and withstand the excruciating travails that it must and will face in the construction of a viable world-ecumene, cooperation must be firmly based on a communion of faith in ultimate principles, on communion in religion.

There is yet a more important and logically prior consideration why isolation is neither possible nor desirable. In Islam as well as in Christianity, and probably in all other religions, the man of religion does not, in his religious claim, assert a tentative hypothesis, nor *a* truth among other truths, or *a* version of the truth among other possible versions, but *the* truth. This is so much part of religious experience and of the claim resting on such experience that to deny it is to caricature the religion as a whole. Neither Islam nor Christianity can or will ever give it up. Certainly this is exclusivism; but *the* truth is exclusive. It cannot run counter to the laws of identity, of contradiction, of the excluded middle. Unlike science which works with probabilities, religion works with certainties. Religious diversity is not merely a religious problem. If the religion in question lays claim to *the* truth, contrary or diverse claims are intellectual problems which cannot be ignored. In the absence of evidence to the contrary, the exclusivist claim is as much *de jure* as it is *de facto*.

In our day and age, exclusivism casts a bad smell. Having worked with probabilities for three hundred years, as scientists or the audience of scientists, and – as philosophers or the audience of philosophers – with skeptical notions of the truth for over half a century, we contract our noses whenever an exclusive claim to the truth is made. As men of religion, I hope we all have the strength of our convictions, and feel neither offended nor shamed by what our faiths claim. On the other hand, there is something shameful about exclusivism, just as there is about mission. That is to lay one's claim with authority, to refuse to listen to or silence criticism, and to hold tenaciously to one's claim in face of evidence to the contrary. We regard the exclusivist in science stupid, and even insane, for running in the face of evidence. Such opprobrium equally belongs to the man of religion guilty of the same offence against the truth. Resistance to evidence, however, is not a necessary quality of religion, nor of the man of religion. It falls within the realm of ethics of knowledge. True, religious theses are not as easily demonstrable as those of science; and the man of religion appears often to flout the evidence when it would be more just to say that he is not yet convinced thereby. But where the evidence is significant or conclusive, to flout it is a deficiency of the man. Though its object is religious or moral, exclusivism is epistemological and hence not subject to moral considerations. On the other hand, although its object is epistemological, fanaticism is moral.

Islam and Christianity cannot therefore be impervious to each other's claims, for just as it is irrefutably true that each lays claim to *the* truth and does so candidly, it is irrefutably true that the truth is one, that unless the standpoint is one of skepticism, of two diverse claims to *the* truth, one or both must be false! In the awareness that the standpoint of religion is that of a claim to *the* truth, none but the most egotistic tribalism or cynicism would sit content with its grasp of *the* truth while diverse claims to *the* one and the same truth are being made just as candidly by others. The man of religion, however, is moral; and in Christianity and Islam, he is so *par excellence*. He must therefore go out into the world, teach *the* truth which his religious experience has taught him and in the process refute the contrary claims. In Islam as well as in Christianity, the man of religion is not a tribalist nor a cynic; and his personal relation to other men, if not the fate itself of other men, weighs heavily in the outcome of his own fate. Hence, both the Muslim and the Christian are intellectually and morally bound to concern themselves with the religious views of each other, indeed of all other men. To concern oneself with the convictions of another man is to understand and to learn these convictions, to analyze and criticize them and to share with their adherents one's own knowledge of the truth. If this is mission, then Islam and Christianity must missionize to the ends of the earth. I realize the equivocation of the term, and I suggest that the word "mission" itself be dropped from our vocabulary and the term "dialogue" be used to express the man of religion's concern for men's convictions.

"Dialogue" then is a dimension of human consciousness (as long as that consciousness is not skeptical), a category of the ethical sense (as long as that sense is not cynical). It is the altruistic arm of Islam and of Christianity, their reach beyond themselves. Dialogue is education at its widest and noblest. It is the fulfillment of the command of reality to become known, to be compared and contrasted with other claims, to be acquiesced in if true, amended if inadequate, and rejected if false. Dialogue is the removal of all barriers between men for a free intercourse of ideas where the categorical imperative is to let the sounder claim to the truth win. Dialogue disciplines our consciousness to recognize the truth inherent in realities and figurizations of realities beyond our usual ken and reach. If we are not fanatics, the consequence cannot be anything but enrichment to all concerned. Dialogue, in short, is the only kind of inter-human relationship worthy of man! Vouching for Islam and, unless my reading of Christianity has completely deceived me, for Christianity as well, dialogue is of the essence of the two faiths, the theater of their eventual unity as the religion of God, the religion of truth.[6]

We must say it boldly that the end of dialogue is conversion; not conversion to my, your or his religion, culture, mores or political regime, but to *the* truth. The conversion that is hateful to Islam or to Christianity is a conversion forced, bought or cheated out of its unconscious subject. Conversion as conviction of the truth is not only legitimate but obligatory – indeed, the only alternative consistent with sanity, seriousness

---

[6] By their abuse, the Crusades and the last two centuries of Christian mission have spoilt the chances of the Muslim masses entering trustfully into such common endeavor. For the time being, the grand dialogue between Muslims and Christians will have to be limited to the intelligentsia where, in the main, propaganda does not convince and material influences produce no Quislings. This limitation is tolerable only so long as the Muslim World is underdeveloped and hence unable to match measure for measure – and thus neutralize – the kilowatts of broadcasters, the ink and paper of publishers and the material bribes of affluent Christendom.

and dignity. Moreover, the mutual understanding between Islam and Christianity which we yearn for is not merely the conceptual, descriptive knowledge of Islam texts and manuscripts achieved by the *Orientalistik* discipline, nor of the Christian tradition achieved by the Muslim and older discipline of "*Al Milal wa al Nihal*" where the elements constitutive of Christianity are simply listed as in a series. It is primarily an understanding of the religion in the sense of faith and ethos, of apprehending the moving appeal of its categories and values, of their determining power. Religious facts may be studied scientifically like any specimens of geology. But to understand them religiously is to apprehend them as life-facts whose content is this power to move, to stir and to disturb, to command and to determine. But to apprehend this power is to be determined by it, and to do so is precisely to attain religious conviction – in short, conversion, however limited or temporary. To win all mankind to *the* truth is the highest and noblest ideal man has ever entertained. That history has known many travesties of this ideal, that man has inflicted tremendous sufferings upon his fellowmen in the pursuit of it are arguments against man, not against the ideal. They are the reasons why dialogue must have rules. Dialogue according to rule is the only alternative becoming of man in an age where isolation – were it ever possible – implies being bypassed by history, and non-cooperation spells general disaster. Granted, the rules must be critical and their presuppositions the fewest and simplest.

II. Methodology of Dialogue

Granted then that dialogue is necessary and desirable, that its final effect should be the establishment of truth and its serious, free, candid and conscious acceptance by all men, we may now move on to the specific principles of methodology which guarantee its meaningfulness and guard against its degeneration into propaganda, brainwashing or soul-purchasing. These are the following:

1. No communication of any sort may be made *ex cathedra*, beyond critique. No man may speak with silencing authority. As for God, He may have spoken with silencing authority when man was an infant, and infant man may have accepted and submitted. To mature man, however, His command

is not whimsical and peremptory. He argues for, explains and justifies His command, and is not offended if man asks for such justification. Divine revelation is authoritative, but not authoritarian; for God knows that the fulfillment of His command which issues from rational conviction of its intrinsic worth is superior to that which is blind. Fully aware of his moral freedom, modern man cannot be subjected; nor can he subject himself to any being without cause; nor can such cause be incomprehensible, irrational, esoteric or secret.[7]

2. No communication may violate the laws of internal coherence mentioned earlier. Paradox is legitimate only when it is not final, and the principle overarching thesis and antithesis is given. Otherwise, discourse will issue in unintelligible riddles.

3. No communication may violate the laws of external coherence; that is to say, man's religious history. The past may not be regarded as unknowable, and historiography assumed to stand on a par with either poetry or fiction. Historical reality is discoverable by empirical evidence, and it is man's duty and greatness to press ever forward towards the genuine understanding and reconstruction of his actual past. The limits of evidence are the only limits of historical knowledge.

4. No communication may violate the law of correspondence with reality, but should be open to corroboration or refutation by reality. If the laws of nature are not today what they were before Einstein or Copernicus, it is not because there are no laws to nature, nor because reality is unknowable, but because there is a knowable reality which corroborates the new insights. The psychic, ethical and religious sensitivities of the people, of the age, are part of this reality; and man's knowledge of them is most relevant for the Muslim-Christian dialogue we are about to begin.

---

[7] The Qur'an tells us that Abraham, the paragon of faith in the one true God, asked God to show him evidence of His power to resurrect the dead. When God asked, "Have you not believed?" Abraham retorted, "Indeed, but I still need to see evidence so as to put my heart at rest" (Qur'an, 2:260). Likewise, the Qur'anic discourse with the Meccans concerning their religion and Islam was a rational one, replete with "evidence" and with the retort, "Say, Bring forth your evidence [against God's] if you are truthful" (Qur'an, 2:111; 21:24; 27:64; etc.). On a number of occasions, the Qur'an speaks of "the evidence of God," "the proof of God" which it goes on to interpret in rational terms (see for example, Qur'an, 4:173; 12:24; 23:118; 28:32).

5.   Dialogue presupposes an attitude of freedom vis-à-vis the canonical figurization. Jesus is a point at which the Christian has contact with God. Through him, God has sent down a revelation. Just as this revelation had to have its carrier in Jesus, it had to have a space-time circumstance in the historical development of Israel. Equally, Muhammad, the Prophet, is a point at which the Muslim has contact with God Who sent a revelation through him. Muhammad was the carrier of that revelation, and Arab consciousness and history provided the space-time circumstance for its advent. Once the advent of these revelations was complete, and men began to put their faith there in numbers and confronted new problems calling for new solutions, there arose the need to put the revelation in concepts for the ready use of the understanding, in precepts for that of the intuitive faculties, and in legal notions and provisions for the guidance of behavior. The revelations were "figurized." Simultaneously, as is natural in such cases, different minds created different figurizations because they had different perceptions of the same reality. This latter pluralism is not a variety of the object of faith, the content revealed *an sich*, but of that object or content *in percipi*, i.e., as it became the object of a perception that is intellectual, discursive, intuitive and emotional all at once. Within each religion, the object of faith which is also the content of the revelation was, in itself, all one and the same. Although the figurizations of the revelation were many, that of which they were the figurization was one. Jesus is one; the God who sent him, and the divine revelation with which he was sent, each and every one of these was one, not many. When, as objects of human knowledge, they were conceptualized and perceptualized, they became many. The same is of course true in the case of the figurization of Islam.

The pluralistic variety of men, of their endowments and talents, their needs and aspirations, and the peculiarities of their varying environments and historical circumstances produced a great array of figurizations in both religions. Undoubtedly, some of them were, some others were not, and still others were more or less inspired. There were differences in the accuracy of figurization, in the adequacy of conceptualization and perceptualization, and outrightly in the truthfulness and veracity of the representation. That is all too natural. Disputation and contention arose and lasted for many centuries;

they continue to our present day. In the case of Christianity, it became evident that one of the figurizations surpassed in the mind of the majority all other figurizations. It must then be, the community concluded, an identical copy of the content revealed. Since this content is holy and is the truth, the thinkers of the community reasoned, all other figurizations are "heresies" inasmuch as any departure from the Holy is anathema, and any variance from the Truth is falsehood. Slowly but surely, the "other" figurizations were suppressed, and the chosen figurization stood as "the dogma," "the catholic Truth." In the case of Islam, the general religious and ethical principles revealed in the Qur'an were subjected to varying interpretations, and a large array of schools produced differing figurizations of law and ethics. As in the case of Jesus, the life of the Prophet was the subject of numerous figurizations. In order to bolster its authority and add to its faith in its own genuineness, each school projected its own thought onto his own person. Consensus finally eliminated the radical figurizations and preserved those which, in the judgment of the community, contained all the essentials. Later Muslims sanctified this figurization of the fathers, solemnly closed the gates of any creative interpretation however orthodox, and practically, though not theoretically, hereticated every departure from what they had made canonical.

Being human conceptualizations and preceptualizations of reality, the figurizations of Islam and Christianity are necessarily tinged with the particularism of space-time. It is quite possible, therefore, that some later generation might find some aspect of the holy content in the old figurization dimmed by time or distance; that the said content might need to be rediscovered therein; that some other generation might find new figurizational items which express to them that content or some part thereof more vividly. Certainly this is what happened in the Reformation, which brought in its wake revivification of many an aspect of the divine revelation of Jesus and released new as well as dormant energies in the service of the holy. This is also what happened in the Taymiyan (fourteenth century) and Wahhabi (eighteenth century) reforms in Islam.

Would such a re-presentation or rediscovery necessitate the Christian's and the Muslim's going out, as it were, of their own figurizations?

14

out of their "catholic" truths? Not *simpliciter*. For there is no *a priori* or wholesale condemnation of any figurization. But we should never forget that, as a piece of human work, very figurization is capable of growing dim in its conveyance of the holy, not because the holy has changed, but because man changes perspectives. Truth, goodness and value, God and the divine will for man as such, are always the same. But His will in the change and flux of individual situations, of the vicissitudes of history – and that is precisely what the figurization had been relational to – must be changing in order that the divine will for man be always the same. To question the figurization is identically to ask the popular question: What is God's will in the context of our generation? of our historical situation? indeed, in the context of our personal individuation? The dimness of the figurization must be removed at all costs; its meanings must be rediscovered and its relevance recaptured.

There are those who argue that the figurization can and should never be transcended. Some of these do not recognize the humanity of the figurization. Others insist that piety and morality are rediscoverable only in the figurization itself. To seek the ever-new relevance of the divine imperative is for them to relate the figurization of the fathers to the new situations of human life and existence. That that is not a barren alternative is proved for them by numerous movements within the Christian tradition, and by a number of juristic interpretations of the sharīʻah, in the Islamic tradition. Whether or not the present needs can be met by such means cannot be decided beforehand, and must be answered only after the needs themselves have been elaborated and the relating attempted. We can say at this stage, however, that a considerable degree of freedom *vis-à-vis* the figurization is necessary to insure the greatest possible tolerance for the issues of the present to voice their claim.

6. In the circumstances in which the Muslims and Christians find themselves today, primacy belongs to the ethical questions, not the theological. When one compares the canonical figurization of Christianity with that of Islam, one is struck by the wide disparateness of the two traditions. While Christianity regards the Bible as endowed with supreme authority, especially as it is interpreted with "right reason" – that is to say, in loyalty to the central tenets of the figurization according to the Protestant

school, or in loyalty to the tradition of the Church as understood by its present authorities, according to the Catholic – Islam regards the Bible as a record of the divine word but a record with which the human hand had tampered, with holy as well as unholy designs. Secondly, while Christianity regards God as man's fellow, a person so moved by man's failure that He goes to the length of sacrifice for his redemption, Islam regards God primarily as the Just Being whose absolute justice – with all the reward and doom for man that it enjoins – is not only sufficient mercy, but the only mercy coherent with divine nature. Whereas the God of Christianity acts in man's salvation, the God of Islam *commands* him to do that which brings that salvation about. Thirdly, while Christianity regards Jesus as the second person of a triune God, Islam regards him as God's human prophet and messenger. Fourthly, while Christianity regards space-time and history as hopelessly incapable of embodying God's kingdom, Islam regards God's kingdom as truly realizable – indeed as meaningful at all – only within the contexts of space-time and history. Fifthly, while Christianity regards the Church as the body of Christ endowed with ontic significance for ever and ever, Islam regards the community of faith as an instrument mobilized for the realization of the divine pattern in the world, an instrument whose total value is dependent upon its fulfillment or otherwise of that task.

This list is far from complete. But it does show that the pursuit of dialogue on the level of theological doctrine is marred by such radical differences that no progress may be here expected without preliminary work in other areas. Since it is at any rate impossible for this generation of Muslims and Christians to confront one another regarding all facets of their ideologies at once, a choice of area for a meager start such as this is imperative. Priority certainly belongs to those aspects which are directly concerned with our lives as we live them in a world that has grown very small and is growing smaller still. The Muslim-Christian dialogue should seek at first to establish a mutual understanding, if not a community of conviction, of the Muslim and Christian answers to the fundamental ethical question, What ought I to do? If Muslims and Christians may not reach ready appreciation of each other's ideas or figurizations of divine nature, they may yet attempt to do the will of that nature, which they both hold to be one. To seek "God's way," i.e., to understand, to know, to grasp its relevance for every occasion, to anticipate its judgment of every moral deed – that is the prerequisite whose satisfaction may put the parties to the dialogue closer to mutual self-understanding. Even if theories of God's nature, of His revelation, of His kingdom, and of His plans for man's destiny were to be regarded as objects of faith beyond critique, certainly the ethical duties of man are subject to a rational approach. Neither Christianity nor Islam precludes a critical investigation of the ethical issues confronting modern man in the world. The proximity of these issues to his life, his direct awareness of them as affecting his own life as well as that of mankind give immediacy to the investigation, and they assign the prerogatives of competence and jurisdiction to his personal and communal judgment in the matter. The relevance of the issues involved to world problems pressing him for an answer furnishes the investigation with a ready testing ground.

Moreover, ethical perceptions are different from the perceptions of theoretical consciousness where to miss is to perceive unreality. Difference in ethical perception is that of the brother who does not see as much, as far or as deep as the other. This is a situation which calls for the involved midwifery of ethical perception. Here, there is no question of error and falsehood, as every perception is one of value and difference consists in perceiving more or less of the same. Neither is the question one of an acquiescent profession of a propositional fact. It is rather one of determination of the perceiving subject by the value that is beheld; and for such perception to be itself, it must be the perception of the man, just as for his realization of the will of God to be itself, i.e., moral, that realization has to be his own free and deliberate act. On the purely theological level, when the impulse to make others heretical is at work, tolerance can mean either contemptuous condescension, conversion, or compromise with the truth. In ethical perception, on the other hand, disagreement is never banished or excommunicated; and heretication defeats its own purpose. Tolerance and midwifery – which are precisely what our small world needs – are the only answer. Their efforts are in the long run always successful; and, at any rate, they are in the Muslim's opinion the better as well as the "Christian" view.

III. Themes for Dialogue

Looking upon the contemporary ethical reality of Muslims and Christians, three dominant facts are discernible:

First, the modern Muslim and Christian regard themselves as standing in a state of innocence. Whatever their past ideas and attitudes may have been, both of them agree that man's individuation is good, that his life of person and in society is good, that nature and cosmos are good. Fortunately, modern Christian theologians too have been rejoicing in their rediscovery of God's judgment of creation "that it was good."[8] The ideological import of this re-discovery is tremendous. Man has rehabilitated himself in creation. He has found his place in it and re-presented his destiny to himself as one of engagement in its web of history. He is in God's image, the only creature with consciousness and spirit, unto whom the command of God has come, and upon whom the will of God on earth depends for realization as that will is, in itself, a will to a morally perfected world. Certainly, God could have created the world already perfect, or necessarily perfectible by the workings of natural law. But He created this world, "where rust and moth consume and where thieves break through and steal,"[9] i.e., a world where His will, or value, is not yet realized, that in the free realization of it by man, the moral values may be realized which could not be realized otherwise. Hence, this world is good, despite its imperfection; and man occupies therein the especially significant – indeed cosmic – station of the bridge through which the ethical elements of divine will enter the realm of creation. It is not surprising that a rediscovery of such momentum causes a great deal of joy, a feeling of self-confidence in the great task ahead. Gone are the sordid obsessions with the innate depravity, the intrinsic futility, the necessary fallenness and cynical vacuity of man and of the world. Modern man affirms his life and his world. Recognizing the imperativeness as well as the moving appeal of God's command, he accepts his destiny joyfully and presses forth upright into the thick of space-time where he is to make that will real and actual.

---

[8] Genesis 1:18, 21.

[9] Matthew 6:19.

Secondly, the modern Muslim and Christian are acutely aware of the necessity and importance of recognizing God's will, of recognizing His command. This acknowledgment is the substance, the content or "meat" of their acknowledgment of God. "Recognition of God's command," "ethical perception" and "the act of faith" are mutually convertible and equivalent terms. Such acknowledgment is indubitably the first condition; for it is absurd to seek to realize the divine will in the world without a prior acknowledgment of its content, just as it is absurd to seek to realize what ought to be done without the prior recognition of what is valuable. How is one to recognize that which ought to be done in any given situation – which must be one among a number of possible alternatives – without the standard or norm with which the realizability in the alternatives of that which ought to be can be measured and ascertained? Indeed, if any axiology-free program of action could ever be envisaged, the agent thereof would not be a moral subject, but an automaton of duties. To be moral at all, the act must imply a free choice; and this is a choice in which consciousness of the value, or of its *matériel* as the spatio-temporal concretization thereof, plays the crucial part. All this notwithstanding, and however absolutely indispensable and necessary the acknowledgment of God's command and will may be, it is only a condition, a *conditio sine qua non* to be sure, but still a condition. Philosophically stated, this principle is that of the priority of the study of values to duties, of axiology to deontology. The act of faith, of acknowledgment, recognition and acquiescence, is the first condition of piety, of virtue and felicity. But woe to man if he mistakes the condition of a thing for the thing itself! The act of faith neither justifies nor makes just. It is only an entrance ticket into the realm of ethical striving and doing. It does no more than let us into the realm of the moral life. There, to realize the divine imperative in the value-short world, to transfigure and to fill it with value, is man's prerogative as well as duty.

Thirdly, the modern Muslim or Christian recognizes that the moral vocation or mission of man in this world has yet to be fulfilled, and by him; that the measure of his fulfillment thereof is the sole measure of his ethical worth; that in respect to this mission or vocation all men start out in this world with a carte blanche *on which noting is entered except what each individual earns with his own doing or not-doing.* In the discharge of his mission in space-time, no man is privileged and every man is an equal conscript. For the command of the one God is also one, for all men without discrimination or election; and His justice is absolute.[10]

IV. Dialectic of the Themes with the Figurizations

A. Modern Man and the State of Innocence

The notion of original sin, of the fallenness of man, appears from the perspective of contemporary ethical reality to have outlived its meaningfulness.

1. Sin is, above all, a moral category; it is not ontological. For modern man, there is no such a thing as sin of creation, of nature, of man as such, no sin as entry into existence or space-time. Physical death is perhaps the deepest mystery of the process of space-time; it is certainly a disvalue, but it is not moral, and therefore not sin, nor the consequence of sin.

2. Moral sin is not hereditary; neither is it vicarious, or communal, but always personal, always implying a free choice and a deliberate deed on the part of a moral agent in full possession and mastery of his powers. The actual involvement, or the "attraction," to which the free moral agent may be subject by merely being a member of his family, of his community, of his religio-cultural group, is not denied. Modern man is also aware that sin is an evil act the ontic consequences of which – whether material or psychological – diverge in space-time *ad infinitum*, affecting in some measure the being and lives of other people. He is equally aware that such consequences are not moral precisely because they are ontic, i.e., necessary,

---

[10] Certainly God may and does grant His grace to whomsoever He chooses; but such grace is never a category of the moral life, a credit which can be taken for granted or "counted upon" by any man. It remains a category of God's disposition of human destinies, never an attribute of men's lives. The gratuitous gift is not a thing earned, by definition; and that which is not earned cannot figure on God's scale of justice – equally by definition.

There is yet another divine grace which is not quite gratuitous. It is called "grace" by equivocation; for it is a good thing which God grants freely but not whimsically, and which He does only in deserving cases. Such grace is really "a lift" on the road of ethical perceiving and living, accorded to those who are really persevering and hard-pressing forward towards the goal. Specifically, it is the gift of a sharper cognition of, or of a more total determination by the goal and no more. It is earned.

involving no choice on the part of the person whom they affect. Moreover, modernity has removed the hitherto necessary connection between existence and membership in the family, community or religio-cultural group. It was this strict necessity of the connection, characteristic of ancient societies, which, though partially, had induced the fathers to represent sin as a necessary and universal category. The modern Muslim and Christian no more hold a man as member of a group and as subject to the fixations operative in that group except as the result of a decision that man makes for himself. This is particularly true of those societies which have achieved a high degree of internal mobility, especially true of Western society. But the fact is that the whole world is moving in that direction and the day is not far when, from the perspective of the now-forming world community, the universalization of education and the termination of the age of societal isolation, it will be relatively easy to move from one culture to another.

3. Sin is not only a doing, whether introverted, as when the doing is strictly within the person's soul directly affecting neither his body nor anything else outside his soul, or extroverted, as when the doing is spatial involving his body, the souls and bodies of others, or nature. Such doing is only the spatio-temporal consequence of sin. Sin is primarily a perceiving. Here lies its locus and genesis, i.e., in perception. Its effect is in intent and doing. Accordingly, it can be counteracted only in the faculties of perception and its solution must therefore be in education. It is obvious that retaliation and retribution are by themselves inadequate to meet sin wherever it may take place. That forgiveness is equally inadequate becomes clear when we consider that by releasing the ethical energies of the sinner from frustration at his own misdeed, the spiritual power of forgiveness can cure only the sinner with strong ethical sensitivities. For it takes a sinner genuinely frustrated by his own moral failure to respond to its moving appeal. The rest – and the rest is surely the great majority – remain untouched by its power, if not encouraged and confirmed in their sinfulness. Education, on the other hand, ministers to everybody's need. It is universal in its application as all men stand to benefit from its fruits. Admittedly, forgiveness does have an intrinsic power which acts on all perceiving subjects moving them to emulate the forgiver. Like love, courtesy and respect, it is

"contagious." But it is forever personal, its activity and effect are always erratic; whereas education is always subject to deliberation, to critique and to planning.

4. It is within the realm of perception that the modern Muslim and Christian can make sense out of the Christian figurization's notion of sin. From this perspective, sin is man's propensity to ethical misperception. It is an empirical datum whose ubiquitousness is very grave and disturbing. Nonetheless, it is not necessary. The general propensity to ethical misperception is counterbalanced by the propensity to sound ethical perception which is at least as universal as its opposite. Indeed, there is far more value in the world than there is disvalue, far more virtue than sin. If by nature man falls in error in his cognition of the ethical, of value, it is equally by nature, if not by a stronger nature, that he is driven to keep on looking and trying despite the faltering. "Man by nature desires to know" the true, the good and the beautiful (said Aristotle); and "man is doomed to love the good" and pursue the true and the beautiful (said Plato). While his soul yearns for, seeks and pursues value, man's natural "will to live" keeps him on his feet, and his "will to do" propels him forward despite the setbacks of sin. True, man is by nature inclined to moral complacency, but he is equally inclined to the life of danger. And while modern man is certainly resolved in favor of the latter, our reason tells us that we should encourage him all the more because the life of danger holds the greater promise. Man may and certainly will err in ethical perception. But he is not hopeless; nor are his misperceptions – his sins – incorrigible. His fate, blest or unblest, devolves in the first place upon him alone.

If this is convincing to both, the dialogue must move on towards revivifying the figurization – recapturing whatever truth there is in it. We may hence expect it to bring out the following point. Ethical misperception, in all its varieties, is that which we ought to guard against, to avoid and to combat in ourselves, in the others and in all men. Indubitably, we must become fully aware of the enemy, of his tactics and defences, of his nature and constitution, if we are to fight him successfully. In the mind of the general, a very prominent place is occupied by "the enemy." It was such genuine awareness on the part of the fathers that induced them to put sin in man's flesh, in the passions for the lower values of pleasure and comfort, of life and power, in the overhasty realization of value, the surmounting of man's cosmic station, in the arrogant pride that the ethical job of man on earth has already been done and finished. In this sense everyone is susceptible to sin as every man has his temptations, his weak moments when his ethical perception is dimmed and his moral vigor is dull and slow to act. To be always conscious of this disposition, i.e., to keep it constantly in mind as the negative object of the moral struggle, is the peculiar merit of the fathers' emphasis on sin.

Unlike the fathers, therefore, the modern Christian and Muslim cannot think of sin as the predicament out of which there can be no hope of deliverance save by a non-human, divine act. Even if, in the interest of final victory in man's moral struggle, we overestimate the enemy, victory must certainly be possible if it is to be an objective and the struggle is to be sustained despite the eventual setbacks. Were we to grant that sin is necessary but keep in mind its meaning as ethical misperception, we would be contradicted by the fact that man has in fact perceived rightly when he perceived God's past revelations as genuine. This inconsequence may not be removed except by adding another fantastic assumption nihilating man's responsibility for genuine perception, *viz.*, predestination to right perception. But that is a pure fabrication; that perception which is not the person's perception is not perception.

Finally, the dialogue must move towards a clear answer to the ethical question. If we keep our balance, we will recognize that the right mental and emotional attitude to sin is to keep it in consciousness in order to avoid and to surmount it. The road hitherto is and can be only education, the axiological *anamnesis* which causes the man to see for himself, to perceive value and expose his own ethos to determination by it. The teacher in general, whether mother, father or elder, teacher by concepts, or by example, is precisely the helper who helps man perceive rightly and thereby surmount the sinful misperceptions. Education is the unique processus of salvation. No ritual of water, therefore, or ablutions or baptism, of initiation or confirmation, no acknowledgment of symbols or authority, no confession or contrition, can by themselves do this job for man. Every person must do it for himself, though he may be assisted by the more experienced; and everybody can.

B. *Justification as Declaring or Making Good*

Looking at the figurization created by the fathers, the contemporary Muslim and Christian observe that its notion of justification as a declaring or making good the person who has acknowledged the figurization does not accord with contemporary reality. Here three considerations are in order. First, where ethical misperception has been the fact or the rule, no confession of any item in the figurization will transform misperception into perception. Even the confession of God as conceived of in the figurization does not constitute the "entrance ticket" we mentioned earlier, the *sine qua non* of salvation. What will do so is the confession of the content of divine will, of value itself. For it is the *materiale* values themselves, not the concepts and theories of "God" or "divine will" as enunciated or elaborated by the figurization, that move the human soul, that can be realized once they are known, and that must be known in order to be realized.

Second, education, as we have defined it, is a long and continuous growth which has no divisions admitting of the representation of its processes as a before and an after. Neither is the realm of values (the will of God) divided into two parts such that only the attainment of one, rather than the other, may be said to constitute, or begin, ethical living. Genuine perception, therefore, as well as genuine value-realization, is with the child as well as with the mature elder, though the objects (values and their relations) discerned may belong to different orders of rank. Salvation or, rather, an amount of it may be the work of the "faithful" of any religion as that of the "faithless" – the *goyim* or *barbaroi* of any faith without regard to the figurization to which they subscribe. The child must then be "justified" as much as the adult, the "sinner" as much as the "saved," provided he perceives that which his yet-undeveloped, or little-developed faculties enable him to perceive. Value-perception is a continuous growth process. It does not admit of a moment of justification before which there was no growth at all and then, by divine fiat, it has come to be. Third, perception of genuine value is only the beginning of the process of felicitous achievement. Beyond

24

it yet lies the longest and hardest part of the road, the realization in space-time of that which had been correctly perceived.

Another meaning of confession is conversion. It consists of a new openness of mind and heart to the determining power of the divine, of value. It is the state of fulfillment of the admirably stated first command of Jesus, namely, to love God with all one's mind, all one's heart and all one's power.[11] This is certainly a radical transformation, for it entails a deliberate willingness to seek the good and to submit to its determination rather than to evil's. As the first step of faith, however, it must stand below the act of confession as perception of value at all. All it recognizes is the value of submission to value which is also a prerequisite but more fundamental, more elemental, than the first. It can also refer to an attitude that comes after perception of the whole, or a large part of the realm of value. In this case, it is of momentous significance if we regard the ethical phenomenon as necessarily broken into perception and action, as separate successive stages between which the devil and his temptations may intervene. This view rests upon the groundless assumption that ethical perception is formalistic and, hence, discursive and intellectual (Kant's "practical reason" trying to subdue and to discipline an erratic "*Willkür*"). The establishment of ethical perception as emotional *a priori* intuition (Scheler, Hartmann) has recaptured the unity of the ethical phenomenon as perception and action at the same time, and proved the Socratic formula "knowledge = virtue" once again true.

There is yet another sense, recognized and well-emphasized by the figurization of Christianity, in which faith and its confession can constitute a real achievement. This is the sense in which the confession of faith, i.e., the subject's conviction that he is now reconciled to God and accepted by the community, means the liberation of his ethical energies for self-exertion in God's cause. Since the state of sin is by definition the undesirable state of being, and faith is the consciousness of this undesirability at all levels, the solemn confession of faith becomes the resolution not to relapse into that which has so far been rightly perceived as undesirable. Psychologically

---

[11] Matthew 22:37; Mark 12:30; Luke 10:27.

speaking, assurance of the acceptance by God and the community of this resolution as something serious and significant, has the good effect of removing whatever fixity misperception may have developed in the moral subject and releasing his energies towards value-realization, *as if* a new page had been turned in his book-of-life. Though this must remain a mere "as-if," it is a powerful moment psychologically. In a person of ethically sensitive nature, the consciousness of sin may possess that person to the point of frustrating his determination by the good, his will to right perception and right action. In such a person, the phenomena of repentance, confession, reconciliation and acceptance can not only release pent up energies but create new ones and orient them towards the good to which they can then rush with a great surge. But, as we have said earlier in connection with the psychological effect of salvation upon the subject, we must remember that such responses and effects are the prerogative of the few, just as great sin equally belongs to the few. The majority, however, remains as little determined by the one as by the other. In the mediocre measure that the majority can have either the cause (sin) or the effect (justification), the advantage of the confession of faith must perforce be equally mediocre.

There is a sense, therefore, though a unique one indeed, in which the act of faith carries an ontic relation to man and cosmos, which is its capacity to infuse into the psychic threads of the subject new determinants and thus bring about a new momentum as it deflects the causal threads from the courses they would have taken had these new determinants not entered the scene. This "plus" of determination is as ontically real as any natural determination since both of them equally produce the same result, namely, the deflection of causal threads to ends other than those to which they would lead otherwise. But we should guard against ever confusing the nature of this "plus." It is certainly not a *justifacti*, a making just, for, ontologically speaking, the deflection of causal threads which constitutes the moral deeds have not yet taken place though it has become a real possibility. Nor is it a declaring just in the forensic sense that, whereas the same person remains the same, the scales of justice that pronounced him sinful have just been tipped in his favor by the fact of solemn confession. Such would be literally a case of "cheating." Nor, finally, is justification a considering of the sinful as innocent, ethically speaking. For it is neither a category of God's thought, nor one of the man's deeds which belong to history and can never be undone. It is only a psychic release in the justified sinner, whose real value is not intrinsic but derivative of that of the values which the newly released energies may, or may not, realize.

C. Redemption as Ontic Fait Accompli

Thirdly, looking at the figurizations of the fathers, the modern Muslim and Christian recognize that redemption is not a *fait accompli* inasmuch as the filling of space-time with realized value is not yet, but has still to be done by man; that it is man's works, his actualization of divine will on earth as it is in heaven, that constitutes redemption. Were redemption a *fait accompli* in this sense, i.e., were the ethical job or duty of man towards God done and finished, his cosmic status, and hence his dignity, would be impaired. In that case, morality itself falls to the ground. Salvation must flow out of morality, not *vice versa*. The only morality that can flow out of accomplished salvation necessarily robs man's life and struggle in space-time of its gravity, its seriousness and significance. True, the already-saved man is not free to lead any life and must live like a person unto whom God had accomplished salvation. Such a man will therefore be under the obligation of gratitude for the salvation done. Far from underrating the order of rank of the ethical value of gratitude, the modern Muslim and Christian find any ethic in which gratitude is the determining cornerstone inadequate to confront space-time, to govern the plunging of oneself into the thick of tragedy-laden existence, to guide man's efforts for transformation of the universe into one fully realizing the will of God. Historically speaking, and in the figurizations of Christianity and Islam, the ethic of gratitude that emerged out of the notion of redemption as a *fait accompli* devaluated space-time as an unfortunate, insignificant interlude, the end of which was eagerly awaited. In the perspective of such an ethic, the fulcrum of life and existence is clearly shifted outside of space-time, which becomes no longer the "body" and theater in which the will of God is constantly prayed to be and should be done. That is all in addition to the superciliousness and complacency which the carrying around of one's title to paradise generates. If, on the other hand, redemption is remembered – and affirmed – to be the doing of man's cosmic vocation, the realization of value in space-time, then the assumption of redemption as accomplished salvation must be the greatest sin.

This consideration need not blind us to the fact, hinted at in the foregoing section, that redemption does achieve an ontically real accomplishment: namely, the release of energies and the infusion of determinants which would not have become real otherwise, and the actualization of ends other than those to which the un-increased determinants and energies would have led. But the "plus" of determination, the pent-up energies released by the redemptive act of faith are not bound to produce any given ends. As a rule, they will go to reinforce those applications of energies, or those causal nexus at which the moral subject has already been working; and the act of faith presupposes that what has been discerned is the genuine truth, goodness and beauty. But the application of the new energy to the pursuit of what has been rightly discerned is not necessary. That is why sin is possible even after redemption – a fact which the figurization which understands redemption as a being-done of man's ethical vocation cannot recognize or affirm except through the inconsequence of paradox. Thus, it takes something more than redemption in the sense of forgiveness and release of ethical energies to achieve salvation in the sense of ethical felicity, of realizing value in space-time, of deflecting its threads towards value-realization, the bringing about of the *matériaux* of value and of filling the world therewith.

In giving us the notions of justification and redemption, therefore, the canonical figurizations gave us merely a prolegomenon to ethical salvation. These notions provide a cure for those who need it and these are of two kinds: the hypersensitive person, whose consciousness of his past ethical shortcomings and misperceptions has prevented him from trying again; the hypochondriac, who dwells on his sad state of affairs so strongly and so long that he forgets that there is a task yet to be performed, however bad his past may have been, and that his complaining will not perform that task. Just like the man who has been so sick that he has lost the sense of life and can think only of death, and who will lead a superficial life if he were to come to a sudden cure, so the moral hypochondriac, upon redemption, would hardly exert himself morally, or know what to exert himself for, as his ethical vision has been warped by the long illness. Such a man will never recover from the event of his cure, of his redemption. He will never pass to the sanity, sobriety and gravity of facing space-time with its crying need for God, for value.

Both these types are rare; mankind is neither made of ethical geniuses and heroes, nor of hypochondriacs. For the majority of men, redemption remains an event of especial significance only inasmuch as it is the perception of that which ought to be and, in this capacity, it is an actual embarkation on the ethical road, a prolegomenon to real felicity. Valuable and necessary as it may be, it constitutes no salutory merit and those who have achieved it have achieved only the beginning. They are not the elect in any sense, and neither is their salvation guaranteed. What they achieve is not only possible, but actual for every man; all men must come to it sooner or later by nature as they begin consciously to live under the human predicaments of desiring knowledge and of loving the good. Far from furnishing ground for a new "election," a new particularism, and a new exclusivism, redemption in the only sense in which it makes sense, namely value-perception and value-realization, is truly universalist in that it expresses modalities of ethical living which are actual in all human beings. Ethical salvation, on the other hand, i.e., the actualization of divine will or moral value, is a progressive achievement open to all men by birth; and it is judged and measured on the scale of an absolute justice that knows no alternative to or attenuation of the principle "Better among you is the more righteous," for "whoso doeth good an atom's weight will see it then, and whoso doeth ill an atom's weight will see it then."[12]

V. Prospects

This has been a sample dialogue between Islam and Christianity. It has anchored itself in a common reality and paid the tribute due to the canonical figurizations. Beyond the latter, however, it has moved towards reconstructing religious thought consonantly with its own experience of reality and without violating any of the necessary conditions of dialogue.

---

[12] Qur'an, 99:7-8.

However hard the results may have been on the Islamic and Christian figurizations, they can be claimed and asserted by the modern Christian as a continuation of that same loyalty to Jesus which produced the Christian figurization, and *mutatis mutandis* in the case of the modern Muslim. The novelty is that in asserting them the Christian is joined by the Muslim, and their communion will undoubtedly open limitless vistas of common religious and moral ideas for further exploration. As to whether the Christian is likely to enter into dialogue and follow this course in our generation, I am pessimistic.

A. The Catholic Church

On the Catholic side, we can safely take the record of Vatican II not only as representative, but as determining the future for at least this generation. As regards the issues taken up by the foregoing dialogue, Catholic Christianity is still to be heard from. As far as I know, Vatican II has not even attempted to discuss such issues, let alone re-present them as objects of a critical Christian-Muslim dialogue. It has stopped the calling of non-Christians by bad names. But that is too modest a contribution. Modern man takes the prerequisites of politeness, courtesy and mutual respect for granted, and he is not moved to admiring trance by an assertion or defence of them. As far as the Muslim is concerned, such defence is fourteen centuries late.[13]

As a matter of fact, Vatican II left much to be desired that is of far greater importance. Besides joining the Muslims to the devotees of most archaic religions, the statement – "the plan of salvation also includes those who acknowledge the Creator...the Moslems...[and] those who in shadows and images seek the unknown God" – merely subsumes them under the call of God.[14] The universality of the call is not an actual but an ought-universality, and hence it does not yield the desired universalism at all. If

---

[13] "Call men unto the path of your Lord through wisdom and becoming preaching. Argue with men gently....Tell My worshippers to limit themselves to the comelier words....Do not contend with the People of the Book except with arguments yet more considerate and gentle....Those are the servants of God who...when the ignorant dispute with them respond with 'Peace'" (Qur'an, 16:125; 17:53; 29:46; 25:63).

[14] *The Documents of Vatican II*, p. 35.

God called all men, it goes without saying that the Muslims are included. To exclude them is tantamount to counting them among the trees. If this is an advance over the former position where the Muslim was regarded as a subhuman, it is an advance which stinks by virtue of this relation. Moreover, the same document has stressed that of the pious among those who "do not know the gospel of Christ or His Church" only those may "attain to everlasting salvation" who do so "through no fault of their own."[15] The Muslim who has been thrice Christian is therefore excluded. The judgment – "whatever goodness or truth is found among them is looked upon by the Church as a preparation for the Gospel"[16] – may be as old and classical as Eusebius to which the text proudly refers. Condescending? Indeed! Do I see progressivism at the apex of which stands Christianity as the archetype of religion and the other religions as faltering approximations? Yes; but wait for the explanation of this religious diversity and imperfect approximations outside of Christianity! "Often men, deceived by the Evil One, have become caught up in futile reasoning and have exchanged the truth of God for a lie, serving the creature rather than the Creator"!!![17] The non-Christians do not even know God; neither do they serve Him! This is utterly out of tune with the twentieth century. Name-calling will not do. It is amazing that despite this low esteem of those who are not Christians, Vatican II agrees with my plea to seek mutual understanding and cooperation on the ethical level, "to make common cause...on behalf of all mankind...of safeguarding and fostering social justice, moral values, peace and freedom."[18] As a Muslim who has been thrice Christian, I applaud and stretch forth my hand in the hope that my Sermon-on-the-Mount ethic my prove contagious.

B. The Protestants

Unlike the case of Catholics, no pronouncement is vested with decisive authority for Protestants. Their position would have to be surmised

---

[15] *Ibid.*

[16] *Ibid.*

[17] *Ibid.*

[18] *Ibid.*, p. 663.

from the writings of those who regard themselves as the spiritual thinkers of their community. I therefore propose to do no more than plumb one thinker on this matter who, many Protestants will probably agree, stands on the frontier of Christian theology. That is the late Paul Tillich.

In his *Christianity and the Encounter of the World Religions*, Tillich repudiated the neo-orthodox approach which refuses even to acknowledge the existence of such a problem as man's religions pose for Christianity.[19] He criticized the progressivist explanation of the religions of the world and refuted the circular arguments of those theologians who, assuming Christianity to be the *typos* of religion, measure man's religions with its rod.[20] He spoke of an original universalism of the early church meaning thereby Christianity's adoption of elements from other religions and their subjection to the particularist idea of Jesus as the Christ.

Though commendable, this idea is hardly adequate to meet the issue of interreligious confrontation.[21] The problem is not one of approving of or adopting that which agrees or can be made to agree with us but of what to do with that which contradicts us, that which stands on the other side of us. On this issue Tillich suggests the possibility of self-criticism in light of the difference with other religions. Appropriately, he entitled his concluding lecture "Christianity Judging Itself in the Light of Its Encounters with the World Religions." No more promising title can be found than this. But before he let his audience rise to cheer, Tillich dissolved the whole promise as he defined the basis of any future self-judgment of Christianity. "There is only one point," he said, "from which the criteria can be derived and only one way to approach this point. The point is the event on which Christianity is

---

[19] (New York: Columbia University Press, 1963), p. 45.

[20] Such as Ernst Troeltsch, Rudolph Otto, Adolph Harnack, etc. *Ibid.*, p. 43.

[21] *Ibid.*, pp. 34-37. There is historical spuriousness in Tillich's claim that Christianity turned "radically exclusive and particularistic as the result of the first encounter...with a new world religion," namely, Islam (*ibid.*, pp. 38-39). In fact, Christianity was radically exclusive at Nicaea and at every other post-Nicene council. This characteristic was probably developed much earlier than Nicaea. Even if Tillich's claim were true, it constitutes a poor apology. The astounding novelty however is Tillich's claim that Christianity's self-consciousness with respect to the Jews and hence, Christian anti-Semitism, were the result of "the shock of the encounter with Islam."

based, and the way is the participation in the continuing spiritual power of this event, which is the appearance and reception of Jesus of Nazareth as the Christ, a symbol which stands for the decisive self-manifestation in human history of the source and aim of all being."[22] Evidently, the basis is not God, nor the will of God, but the Christian figurization of God. But loyalty to figurization produces footnotes and commentaries, not knowledge; and Christianity, if based upon such a principle, will learn nothing at all.

Here Tillich has failed in our fifth methodological principle, viz., freedom vis-à-vis the canonical figurization. It seems as if Tillich, despite the depth and breadth of his vision, is telling the Muslim: Assuming the Council of Nicaea consisted of God as chairman, His angels and prophets as members, and that it did unanimously and under express divine command decide for all eternity what it did decide, what use can we make of what you or any other religion has to offer? The Muslim retort is that it is precisely here in the Nicene Council that the dialogue will have to start, if at all, assuming that the council is still on and deliberating. Consisting of men with holy as well as unholy motives and presided over by a pagan emperor interested in the political unity of the Empire more than in the truth, the council is either closed and hence only of didactic value to modern man, or open and modern man may participate therein as constituent member.[23] It was precisely at Nicaea that the split of Christianity into Eastern and Western formally began, not in the meaning usually attached to these terms as denoting the Roman Catholic Church and the Greek Orthodox Church, or

---

[22] Ibid., p. 79.

[23] The accounts of the tactics used in the Council or thereafter in order to implement or defeat its decision by the parties involved were far from inspiring any awe or silencing authority. "Intrigues and slanders of the lowest kind," wrote Harnack, "now began to come into play, and the conflict was carried on sometimes by means of moral charges of the worst kind, and sometimes by means of political calumnies. The easily excited masses were made fanatical by the coarse abuse and execrations of the opponents, and the language of hate which hitherto had been bestowed on heathen, Jews and heretics, filled the churches. The catchwords of the doctrinal formulae, which were unintelligible to the laity and indeed even to most of the bishops themselves, were set up as standards, and the more successful they were in keeping up the agitation the more surely did the pious-minded turn away from them and sought satisfaction in asceticism and polytheism in Christian garb" etc., etc. (A. Harnack, History of Dogma, tr. by Neil Buchanan [New York: Dover Publications, Inc., 1961], Vol. IV, p. 61).

the Churches of the West as distinguished from those of the East, but in the older sense of a Semitic Christianity of so-called "heretic" churches of the East and a Christianity figurized under terms supplied by Hellenistic consciousness. Only at "Nicaea" can the dialogue with Islam, the heir of that Eastern Christianity which was hereticated at Nicaea, be resumed.

In the last lecture of his career, "The Significance of the History of Religions for the Systematic Theologian,"[24] Tillich did not progress beyond the foregoing position. He called "Religion of the Concrete Spirit" the "telos" or the "inner aim" which the history of religions "is to become." This is composed of three elements: "the sacramental basis" which is "the universal...experience of the Holy within the finite"; the "critical movement against the demonization of the sacramental"; and the "ought-to-be...the ethical or prophetic element [which] becomes moralistic and finally secular" without the other two.[25] One can hardly miss the parochial representation of Western Christianity in this scheme where the first element is the Jesus-event, the second the Reformation, and the third, the secular moralistic humanism of modern times. And we must, in addition, overlook Tillich's lack of information, at least regarding Islam, evident in his generalization that "the universal religious basis is the experience of the Holy within the finite."[26]

Having defined these elements, Tillich then tells us that they always struggle against one another; but that when integrated within the Religion of the Concrete Spirit, they struggle as one organic whole against the domination of each.[27] "Kairoi" or "moments...in which the Religion of the Concrete Spirit is actualized fragmentarily can happen here and there."[28] But "the whole history of religions" is "a fight for the Religion of the Concrete

---

[24] Published together with a number of other lectures by Tillich, and statements of friends at a memorial service dedicated to him, under the title, *The Future of Religions* (New York: Harper and Row, 1966), pp. 80-94.

[25] *Ibid.*, p. 86.

[26] *Ibid.*

[27] *Ibid.*, pp. 86-88.

[28] *Ibid.*, p. 89.

Spirit, a fight of God against religion within religion."[29] In this continuing world struggle of God against the demonic forces, "the decisive victory" was "the appearance of Jesus as the Christ."[30] "The criterion" of victory, or of the presence of the Religion of the Concrete Spirit is "the event of the cross. That which has happened there in a symbolic way, which gives us the criterion, also happens fragmentarily in other places, in other moments, has happened and will happen even though they are not historically or empirically connected with the cross."[31] Tillich even suggests the re-use of the symbol "Christus Victor" in this view of the history of religions.[32] How do we know that what happened in the *kairos* of Muhammad or of the Reformation was "a fragmentary event of the cross" unless it is assumed that all religious moments are *kairoi* of the same? But if this is assumed beforehand, what novelty did the minor premise bring? Obviously, this is the same circular reasoning Tillich had criticized in Troeltsch and Otto, however disguised the terms.

Tillich's "last word" was his answer to the question of the meaning of the history of religions "to the religion of which one is the theologian." "Theology," he claimed, "remains rooted in its experiential basis. Without this, no theology at all is possible." Thus, in loyalty to the canonical figurization, Tillich persistently refused to recognize any sacrament-free consciousness as religious. Straightjacketed by his own self-imposed limitation to the experience of the Christian figurization, the Christian theologian is to spend the rest of time "formulat[ing] the basic experiences which are universally valid [sic! the experience of the Holy in the finite is anything but universal] in universally valid statements."[33]

How can such an attempt see anything in the religions of man but fragmentary realizations of the Christian experience? Can it be said that

---

[29] *Ibid.*, p. 88.

[30] *Ibid.*

[31] *Ibid.*, p. 89.

[32] *Ibid.*, p. 88.

[33] *Ibid.*, p. 94.

such an attitude enables the Christian to understand the other faiths of other men, let alone produce a fruitful dialogue with the men of other faiths?

As for his systematic theology, its pages run counter to every one of the ethical insights we have attributed to modern man. One might conclude that if Tillich were still alive, he would not carry the dialogue a single step forward. Surprisingly, however, this conclusion is not true. For just before he died, he read the sections of this paper entitled "Methodology of Dialogue," "Themes for Dialogue" and "Dialectic of the Themes with the Figurizations" and wrote in a letter to the author: "I...read your manuscript and thought it was an excellent basis for any discussion between Christianity and Islam. You bring out the points of difference with great clarity and sharpness. Not in order to let them stay where they are, but in order to show that behind the different figurizations there is, especially in the present moment, a common ground and a common emergency. I believe that with this presupposition in mind, a discussion could be very fruitful."

This was a surprise. It recaptures my lost optimism.

THE DIALOGICAL RELATIONSHIP BETWEEN CHRISTIANITY AND ISLAM[*]

· Hasan Askari[**]

It is sometimes easier to reflect with the aid of poetic metaphors, particularly when one has to tread the difficult space between two massive traditions. Where the conceptual finds the door solidly barred against all entry, the symbolic carves its way in. Where the theologian is confident within his boundaries, the poet takes the risk and leaps beyond. Rumi, the Persian Sufi poet, once said:

> O for a friend to know the sign,
> And mingle all his soul with mine.

With the help of these two line, let us reflect on the "friend," the "sign," and the mingling of "all his soul with mine." Is there any common sign between Christians and Muslims? Would they become friends? And would their souls mingle?

There are certain difficulties in the way. Dialogue is sometimes misunderstood by Muslims as a masked attempt at syncretism. The suspicion is not always without basis. The Muslim immediately becomes self-conscious

---

[*] *Journal of Ecumenical Studies*, 9:3 (Summer, 1972).

[**] Syed Hasan Askari (Muslim) holds a Ph.D in sociology, specializing in symbolism and the sociology of religion. His numerous publications in English include "Modernity and Faith" in *Islam and the Modern Age*, Jamia Nagar, Delhi, 1970. Dr. Askari has been Chair of the Department of Sociology of the Muslim University of Aligarh, India and a Fellow at the Center for the Study of Islam and Christian-Muslim Relations, Selley Oak Colleges, Birmingham, U.K.

of the differences that lie between Christianity and Islam. He often fails to notice the deep and vast changes the Christian faith, in its interpretation and expression, has been undergoing in almost every century. The notion of an evolving and expanding faith is somehow alien to the Muslim mind. It is however strange that evolution is often considered as betrayal and perversion of the original dogma. Herein lies, I suppose, that most serious disparity between the Christian and Muslim attitudes to questions of faith. Secondly, the political experience of Christianity, recently in the form of imperialism, hampers on both sides the openness and trust necessary for an informal encounter. Thirdly, the cultural experience of Christianity, particularly in the shape of science and technology, is usually looked upon as a threat to Islamic civilization. The Christian-Western influence is held responsible for secularization of culture and institutions. The intermingling of academic and religious traditions by Muslims is another aggravating factor. One often comes across an intriguing mixture of fantasy with fact, inquiry with apology. It appears that, more than the primary and fundamental differences in the dogmatic frame, the differences in historical experience and cultural development are responsible for incommunication and mistrust among Christians and Muslims.

But equally grave are certain features in the Christian situation. Many a complex issue owe their origin to the scientific traditions as well. The speech of religion is being determined after the model of the speech of science. The process of secularization has already taken command paving the way for the priority of "word of man" over "Word of God." Above all, the entire theory of communication on which most of the theologians and philosophers rely is a historicist theory through and through. We are told that the first revolution in communication was brought about by scientific invention and mechanical engineering, and the heroes of this revolution were Thomas Edison and Alexander Graham Bell. At the heels of this revolution came another, the consequence of the theory of cybernetics headed by Norbert Wiener and Dichter. It was the discovery of the unity of communication and control. All communication to the giant computers seems to take place in an imperative mood. Wiener is afraid that this process might be reversed with immense consequences for the human civilization: The process of *from man to machine* might soon become *from machine to man*. A corrective against the cybernetic threat becomes imperative. The foundations of a third revolution have to be explored. The forces of monologue engendered by cybernetics should be countered by a dialogical revolution. Camus, Buber, Marcel, and Erich Fromm seem to be the prophets of this third revolution. The end of human communication is not to *command* but to *commune*. Dialogue should confront the forces of monologue. Alienation and anxiety are to be fought with the instruments of "love" and "intersubjectivity." "There is a third attitude (of dialogue) which the Catholic should adopt *at this period* in this history of the world, an attitude characterized by study of contacts which the Church ought to maintain with humanity," says Pope Paul VI (*Ecclesiam suam* III).

From mechanics to cybernetics the forces of monologue become clearer, stronger, wider. The twentieth century is considered to be the point at which man is most threatened, lonely, driven to despair and insanity. It is to this challenge that the forces of dialogue should respond. Interreligious dialogue is therefore urgent and imperative.

My protest against this mode of formulation is that it makes dialogical consciousness in matters of religion a question of historical need. It seems to rest on history as creed. It might be misunderstood as implying that the monologue-dialogue confrontation is a challenge of this epoch only. It is not realized that human communication can fall into a monologue, and can rise into dialogue, irrespective of any epoch or culture. The sickness of monologue is as ancient as the remedy of dialogue. The threat of monologue, in every age, is both complete and incomplete. The revolution of dialogue is likewise both finished and unfinished. It is only the historicist attitude that gives to both a false finality.

One might not be aware that acceptance of history as creed is in fact acceptance of the cybernetic revolution that history might act as a giant computer issuing messages to man, the great invisible machine recoiling on us all. Dialogue in service of this machine is another monologue in disguise. The very talk of dialogue, as history being the master, is a fulfillment of the cybernetic threat. All dialogical consciousness might then turn into its very opposite, and might return to man the very loneliness that he had intended to shake off. Man becomes a sacrament unto himself, and this pure monological existence. Let us look into the matter in detail.

The distinguishing trait of a monological self is its insistence on autonomy. It feels, thinks, speaks, and acts as an autonomous being. It resists, attacks, destroys anything that either qualifies or threatens this autonomy. Ontologically, there is no other for such an existence, no inter-existence, only existence, no speech, only language, no future, only time, no neighbourhood, only home, no family, only individuals, no children, only issues. Thus, monologue is a monstrous existence that sweeps the social and the cultural worlds, without conditions, without limits. One should suspect that the feeling that one is in dialogue might be a form of reminiscence of the bygone society wherein the monological forces were not predominant. Both speech and prayer, work and sacrifice, turn into dead rituals under the stamp of a monological era. Other evidence of monological existence is the destruction and irrelevance of all addressees. Either there is a frank admission of this destruction or a helpless postponement of the question of the addressee to some distant future. Phrases like politics for future, art for future, are quite self-revealing. This is more manifest in the realm of science and technology. Science does not address any particular person: it is an address to all and to none. The particular listener, the concrete addressee, is absent in science. Science, like play, creates a group, a team, a code, a heritage of principles. In order to be true to itself, science should not have any concrete addressee. Science thrives in general principles and truths, in methods that could be used without any essential, emotional relationship between the users. Under the impact of the monological era, religion might also attempt to imitate the preoccupation of science with general and abstract truths. Religion might thus be drawn into a false position of being a rival to science. The co-presence of science and religion, in our age, with their highly articulate and confident representatives, is hazardous and crucial. There are dangers of mutual falsification.

The only way to confront monologue is to free religion from this sense of being a rival to science by keeping in view the specific form of religious speech. Religion is made of the hazards and crises of being personally addressed. Here, address is not a general formulation, nor an abstract truth, but a promise or a threat to our entire being. Either as affirmation or denial, it has grave and abiding consequences. We are familiar in our scriptures with such calls as, "O Noah," "O Abraham," "O Moses," "O Jesus," and "O Mohammed." God addresses in particular. When He says "O Mankind," it is not a general address, it is again specific: God confronted with Man. Each address is thus an opening or a chasm, an uplifting or an abyss. Something is always at stake in thus being addressed. The response is equally crucial. In turn, man says "O God," and alters his being accordingly. Monological autonomy is instantly destroyed. A divine companionship comes to birth. Existence now becomes inter-existence. Each man becomes a neighbour. "O Mankind" and "O Man" are God's calls of confrontation and concern. "O Lord of the Worlds" and "O My God" are man's expressions of alienation and belonging. Perhaps God also takes the risk in addressing man. The speech of religion is therefore a unity of these tensions and risks. It rests on the universal forms of tension and anxiety, and is not exhausted in only one or another period of history. It uses the medium of language, subject to change and development, but does not become its subordinate. With the aid of symbols and allegory, religious speech transcends the limitations that history and social organization impose on language. The word of man dies several times in history, but the Word of God remains alive and eternal. They refer to the temporal and the eternal components of human speech. The "Word of God," apart from its divinity and infallibility, is also a critique of the word of man. Dialogue rests on their inter-relationship and distinction.

With this introduction we turn to the particular issue of Christianity and Islam, how they constitute a dialogical whole, how their differences and what they share are essential to their dialogical authenticity.

Is there any common "sign" between Christianity and Islam? Would Christians and Muslims become "friends"? Would their souls "mingle"?

These are not primarily questions of fact, event, or probability. These are methodological questions. They are not intended to explore the *where* of the "sign," the *when* of the "friendship," and the *what* of the "mingling." They are intended to *create* dialogical consciousness in both Christianity and Islam, and to enable one to *feel* the dialogical bond between them. No other two faiths on this planet share so much of the other. Each has a viewpoint for the other, not an external viewpoint, but one which is internal to their creeds and claims. Each has something to say to the other. The misfortune is that their speech so far has been a monologue. It was not intended thus.

The kind of relationship laid down in the Quran between Christians and Muslims is fundamentally a dialogical relationship. From chapter to chapter the Quran engages the Christians in discussion, and all the time insists that Jesus is an integral part of the Muslim faith. The Quran thus involves Christians in the new faith of Islam, and reminds Muslims that Christians have a special relationship with them. The real dialogue between religions was, however, started by the Quran. Its recognition of the People of the Book – the believers in God spread all over the earth, the Sabeans and the Jews – was a dialogical recognition. In all such Quranic discourses it is difficult to miss the deep feeling of Christianity and Islam being present to each other. One is aware of the other's presence. One is aware of strong disagreements. One is aware of deep sharing. What else could signify this deep sharing more than the fact that Jesus is the common center between Christians and Muslims? He is the word, speech, meaning, and occasion of the dialogical relationship between them. He is the common "Sign."

This most difficult statement raises a series of uncertainties both in the minds of Christians and Muslims. The source of uncertainty is, however, located within the viewpoint of each creed. For the Muslim, Christ is a sign among other signs. But the Quran takes care to emphasize the uniqueness of Christ as Sign. He is the Word of God. He is unlike any other sign the Quran speaks about – the heavens and the earth, the day and night, the sun and moon, thunder and lightning, life and death, the different stages of man's life, his mating and his food, his cattle and his children, the early hours of the morning, the death and still nights, the winter and summer, the dry and thirsty earth, the refreshing and life-giving rain, the ships sailing amidst vast waters, and the storm and the safe approach to shore. All these the Quran calls "aiyat," signs. Is Jesus a similar sign? Other signs are referred to in order to remind man of his being and his world, to invoke in him the feeling and the presence of god. But Jesus, in my view, lives as a Sign in a different realm, the realm of the deep relation between God and man. The Sign refers to how ambiguous and how difficult is the sphere of this relationship, how deeply man can deceive himself in the name of God, how truth could be used to destroy truth, how the most elaborate and confident theologies could become a wall between God and man. It is here, in this realm, that Christ lives on in history as a sure reminder, as an unmistakable warning. Christ appears then a Sign *outside* and *against* all creed-based testimonies of truth, love, and suffering. All creeds, even the best of them, might turn their truths into a monologue. To me, personally, Christ as Sign of God liberates man from the dead circle of monological religion and restores unto him his genuine dialogical existence.

Monological religion might give a sense of security, a feeling of certitude, a confidence in the finality of dogmatic beliefs. It is in the nature of all monological consciousness that it gives to its owner the feeling of self-sufficiency and self-adequacy. Hence, it destroys the listener, the other. This is obvious in situations of man-to-man communication. But its seriousness is not clear when we turn to communication between God and man. As all monological speech destroys the listener, so all monological religion might tend to neglect God as Listener. One of the Arabic names God is *as-samih,* one who listens. The Muslim has to repeat seventeen times during his prescribed prayers the self-reminding clause: "God listens to one who praises (Him)." Most of us tend to forget that while we discourse on religion, while we talk *about* God, as we discuss the formulations of faith and different systematizations of creeds, God is always present listening to what we utter about Him. It is again not always remembered that God is free. It is this awareness of *the listening of a free God* that lends to the religious mind its tension, anxiety, and fear. It is then that man becomes free from his monological speech, and having become free, feels anxious and afraid. It is in this state that man's speech to God becomes prayer (praise), and God's speech to man, Blessing and Grace.

As God is Absolute, we can never, in life or beyond death, comprehend His Being. What He allows us to know of Him is His Revelation. The highest form of the knowledge of God is to admit that He is unknowable. What we know of Him is equal to what we do not know of Him. He is both Manifest and Hidden. To the Hidden Being of God we bow in humility and silence. No words can express this awareness of the

Hidden God. Silence itself becomes the profoundest form of religious speech. To the Manifest Being of God, we bow in prayer and praise. Even in prayer and praise, there is an element of silence. There is a vast abyss after every word we speak before God. Night, death, nothingness are the expressions of the Hidden Day; life, and existence are the symbols of the Manifest God. Silence and speech, meditation and prayer, submission and praise are the reflection in man of the Absolute, equally Hidden and Manifest. The Hidden partakes of the Manifest, and the Manifest partakes of the Hidden. The Hidden is revealed in the Manifest, and the Manifest is always on the verge of being Hidden. Silence and prayer are likewise interrelated. One of the great differences between speech in general and speech in religion is that in the latter the element of silence and prayer is even present. There is always a surrender of speech in every speech, and there is deep awe about words even if they are of praise. It is in this dichotomy that religious speech maintains its dialogical character.

When we say that Christ is symbol *par excellence* of the dialogical relationship between God and man, we mean that Christ reminds us not to regard as "fetish" the revealed word, the revelation in terms of human speech, the "book" as such, the commandments in themselves. Human speech, the word spoken by man, does receive the divine light and becomes the scripture. But when Christ is addressed as the Word of God, here the Person is addressed, here the Person is the Word. Here is no book as such, but the Life of Christ. Even the revealed word, the scripture, as it is made of the finite stuff of the speech of man, may fall short of the real Intent and Being of God. The scripture may even tend to substitute the revelation for God. The very revealed word may become a barrier between man and God. But the Person of Christ having become the Word questions the complacency of the believer in the revealed word, and keeps him in perpetual openness before his Lord. It is the wisdom of the Quran, its *hikma*, that Christ is called the Word of God. The Quran keeps the two forms of revelation – the revelation in words, and the revelation as a Person – in constant tension. Both are held in such a relationship that one is made to check the idolatory of the other. It is in this mode that Christ is present in the Quran, as a warning, as a Sign, against the tendency (with men in general) of the very word, the revelation as such, becoming an idol. When the Quran rejects the Incarnation of God in Christ, it corrects the idolatry of the Person as Word of God, and this it does by establishing the supremacy of Speech ("Kalam") as Revelation. But when the Quran narrates the events of life of Jesus, and refers to the manner in which the Jews had flouted the revealed truth of God, it invokes the supremacy of the Person of Christ as Word of God ("Kalama").

It is in this capacity of the Word of God as Person that Christ is in each faith, and yet outside. He stands between. He is the redeemer of the monological man with his monological faith. By believing in Christ, a Muslim has to be aware of the monological traps within his own faith. The truth is that Christianity and Islam constitute one complex of faith, one starting with the Person, and another with the Word. Their separateness does not denote two areas of conflicting truths, but a dialogical necessity.

Is there any common "sign" between Christians and Muslims? Answer: Only "friends" would know.

A sign is not a technical truth nor a new discovery in one or another discipline. Technical truths and new discoveries can be known and shared without persons necessarily becoming friends. It is very significant that for the possession and communication of knowledge, as we understand it today, friendship is not required. Total strangers and enemies can share technical information. But in matters spiritual, to know is to be in a new relationship with one who shares that knowledge. To know is to belong. Friendship is presupposed in common religious knowledge. Unity is had when a religious sign is shared. Once having known Christ is to belong together. It is true that the Christian and the Muslim attitudes to Christ are not similar. They are *different*, not conflicting. A common religious sign must be differently apprehended. It is the very ambiguity, richness, of the religious sign that gives rise to different and even opposed interpretations and understandings. But those who know Christ as Love do not dispute about his Being. They are silent. They are humble. They love one another. They all know the mystery of his Being, but do not become impatient about it. They all know that it is the love of Christ that creates their mutual humanity, their suffering in togetherness, their submission to God. The Sign precedes their consciousness as humanity, creates it, and uplifts it as prayer and sacrifice to

God. Are humanity and love mere horizontal and uniform expressions of mundane peace and tolerance among men? Perhaps not. Humanity is worth having only as an act of sacrifice before God. Hence, the humanity in us all has the tragic potentiality of being annihilitated by God inasmuch as it is mere pride and self-love. Humanity as an offering to God is the beginning of love and friendship between mankind. Here, the sign that inspires love, and love are one. Here, "sign" and "friend" mean one thing – one cannot be had without the other. Two persons torn by mutual hatred cannot possibly know and share the sign of Christ. To know is to discover the common ground of existence. To know is to love. If there is a common "sign" between Christians and Muslims, they *are* friends. The question is not to create this belonging but to discover it. And the discovery is immediate as soon as both drop their respective monologues.

To drop the monologue is to immediately discover the other. Confrontation follows. Most of us fear it. Most of us like to remain inside the fortress of the monologue. To discover the other is to discover the very core of our being. Most of us are afraid of this. We even use the best of our beliefs and loyalties to keep away from that core. The discovery of the other, of our own being, is both soothing and painful, more the latter. The other is pain, a sting, a bite, but a pain in our very being, of it. It is right in the middle of this pain and anxiety that a Divine Sign is known. It is known, not in the ordinary way, but in its act of sharpening the frontiers of otherness, of heightening anxiety, of deepening confrontation. It is here that a Sign is both Love and Suffering. Christ alienated man, and also reconciled him. It is here that crisis and salvation merge and mingle. Upheld by God, forsaken by God, are the names of the same Love.

Hence, "friendship" in relation to "sign" is not without pain and crisis. But pain and crisis, in this realm, are without hate and fear. Its first challenge is the deepening and sharpening of the differences. Christians and Muslims, when they accept "common sign" and "friendship" between them, have to undergo the deep pain and crisis of being *other* in relation to each other. This is essential, paramount, desirable. They have to resist the temptation of drowning this crisis for the sake of political and social challenges. The argument of common humanity, common heritage, common predicament in the world, and common spirituality should not be allowed to blunt the primary crisis which is essential to all deeply religious friendships."

Being committed to a common "sign" and being "friends," the primary crisis and pain will lead us, by and by, to discover the futility, the relativity, the *worldliness* of our theological and religious standpoints. Thrown in front of God, facing this deep, vast Absolute, Christians and Muslims will undergo the second pain, far acuter, wider and sharper than the first. This is Second Suffering. It is here that God meets man, and man meets Christ. It was in this state that Mohammed heard the Word of God.

It is by the aid of the aforesaid symbolic structures that Christians and Muslims might help one another in transcending their differences, not so much in their creeds, but in their crisis-consciousness regarding faith and God. But within the Christian situation there are dangers, as we notice in our times, of secularizing and demythologizing the Cross, of according a false finality to the suffering and tragedies of the world, of drawing the Cross into a parallel position with other symbols of tragedy and alienation. Here, the Muslim recalls his witnessing – there is no God but God – and might remind his Christian brother that there is no Cross but the Cross of Jesus.

INTERRELIGIOUS DIALOGUE AND THE ISLAMIC "ORIGINAL SIN"*

Khalid Duran**

I. Muslim Openness to Dialogue

Ever since I went to Europe some nine years ago, I have hardly been pursuing theology or the study of religion – certainly not in any systematic way and not as a university discipline. After leaving the Islamic Research Institute in Islamabad and taking up assignments in Europe, I became more and more restricted to the field of political science, a development probably indicative of the state of affairs, if not the state of mind, in the Muslim world at large – and this not just because of the rise of fascism in countries such as Pakistan, Iran, and Sudan, but also because we are still fighting national wars of liberation. In Afghanistan we have been set back some thirty or forty

---

* In Leonard Swidler, ed., *Toward a Universal Theology of Religion* (Maryknoll, NY: Orbis Books, 1987). This is a response to Hans Küng's essay on p. 249.

** Khalid Duran (Muslim), was born in Germany to a Moroccan father and Spanish mother; was educated in Spain, Pakistan, and Germany (political science and sociology at the Universities of Bonn and Berlin); and became an Associate Professor in the Islamic Research Institute in Pakistan in 1968, where he also taught at Islamabad University. He has been a research scholar since 1978 at the Deutsches Orient-Institut in Hamburg, Germany, at its Egypt-Libya-Sudan desk. A frequent lecturer in European and American institutions and at interfaith conferences, he was a founding member of the Committee for Christian-Muslim Dialogue for the biannual Protestant *Kirchentag* in West Germany. In 1985 the Deutsches Orient-Institut, Hamburg, published his *Islam und politischer Extremismus: Einführung und Dokumentation*. He has been Visiting Professor of Islamics at Temple University (1987), American University (1988), University of California Irvine (1989) and the Freie Universität Berlin.

years, in the sense that once again we have to fight against premodern European-style colonialism, with a racialist tinge, animated by a missionary zeal and the crusading spirit of once-upon-a-time – the difference being one of nomenclature. This time the crusade is undertaken in the name of Marxism-Leninism, but *la mission civilisatrice* remains the same as in former days in Algeria and elsewhere.

It might be felt that this is not exactly the topic for which we have come together, but these facts need to be mentioned, because too often complaints are heard about a lack of openness to dialogue among Muslims, or of a lack of interest, or even of a lack of sense for interfaith enterprises. The problem in the Muslim community, however, is in fact quite different. As a result of recent events in the Muslim world, Western Europe is being flooded with intellectuals from Muslim countries. If one wants to meet the true elite of Iran, Afghanistan, Pakistan, or Turkey – come to France, Germany, England, the Netherlands, Italy, or Spain. Besides many a religious leader, numerous intellectuals of the highest caliber who are deeply involved in religion are to be found there. There is no question of any resistance to or even hesitation about interreligious dialogue – not even where Israelis are involved! That is not at all an issue. But how can one expect Muslim thinkers to sit down for interfaith talks or to take part in dialogue experiments when all their energies are absorbed in a struggle against the most ruthless dictatorship at home or in an outright battle for survival against an expanding colonial empire?

Let me give just one typical example. Several weeks ago some Christian friends paid me a surprise visit while I was hosting Dr. Sa'ed, a former vice-rector of Kabul University. All the outstanding former Afghan newspaper editors, writers, and poets as well as former ministers, now refugees in Germany, had assembled to meet him. Dr. Sa'ed speaks German, English, and French fluently. Although he is a chemical engineer by training, my Christian friends discovered to their amazement that his first degree had been in theology and that he was a very profound Sufi – or "Hassidic" Muslim, if you wish. Immediately they started to complain to me: "Khalid, why do you keep these pearls hidden from us? These are exactly the Muslim partners we have always been longing for!" Of course, I had not shielded those precious gems from interreligious dialogue, but Dr. Sa'ed was on his way to Paris, where he has subsequently opened an office of Afghan resistance, while other friends have been busy finding the means to maintain that office. As said before, this is just one example illustrating the point.

Inasmuch as I am neither an Afghan, nor an Iranian, nor Pakistani, Sudanese, Turk, Palestinian, nor Lebanese, I am always being urged by groups of exiles and laborers from those countries in Europe to act on their behalf as a spokesman for religious affairs, particularly where interreligious dialogue is concerned. This has earned me an honorary chairmanship of half a dozen national associations and clubs, a burden almost impossible to cope with. It has led, inter alia, to the creation of a budding Islamic Academy in Hamburg in response to an appeal by the former Turkish prime minister, Bulent Ecevit. Among my Jewish and Christian partners in dialogue, however, the impression persists that Muslims, on the whole, are not eager for dialogue, that their reluctance is simply too strong, their resentment too deep. The contrary, in fact, is true, but the historical phase we are passing through is not propitious for such an exercise.

These complaints come most frequently from Christian theologians who used to be enthusiastic about the Iranian movement called Mujahidin-e Khalq, because at one stage that movement produced a large amount of religious literature and these Christian friends started dreaming of a universal theology of liberation. However, when the first seminar with exiled priests from Argentina was convened, there were among the Iranians present none who were competent to speak on religious matters. The trained ones had all gone back to Iran to fight the fascist regime, and had been killed in the process. Some of my friends sometimes wonder why I wear this typically Shi'ite Iranian ring on my finger. It belonged to a brilliant young scholar of religion who left German comfort to fight Khomeini in Iran–and was executed. This is the situation we find ourselves in. We are simply under duress–and even that is an understatement.

Nonetheless, as the Muslim co-chairman of the "Standing Conference of Jews, Christians, and Muslims in Europe," I manage every year in March to bring a dozen or two really competent Muslim students from various countries together to participate in the annual "Students' Week" trialogue.

Despite a host of shortcomings, I still consider this to be one of the most noteworthy experiments in trialogue. From these and other experiences it is clear that we all have much to learn from each other.

I do not wish to claim that I have "grown old" in what some friends have started to call the "dialogue business," but I do concede to Hans Küng the advantage of being a newcomer to the dialogue with Islam, or the Jewish-Christian-Muslim trialogue. This enables him to enter the fray with a "naivety" that is at times disarming – just as it can also be refreshing. Much of what he calls "new findings" appear almost like ancient history to us "old-timers in the field," if I am allowed to say that – and I say it without any animus. In fact, his "new findings" sum up what we have been working at in various dialogue bodies over the last twenty years and more. This does not detract from the value of his "popularization" of those positions, however. After all, where are the Christians, outside such conference halls as this, who know that some wise men in the Christian church have at last accepted Muhammad as a kind of prophet?

When I say "a kind of prophet," I recall a radio talk I had many years ago with the Jewish thinker Pinchas Lapide, who exclaimed: "Muhammad was recognized by Jewish scholars as early as the eleventh century as a prophet on a par with the non-Jewish biblical prophets, such as Job." If Lapide's statement were a matter of common knowledge, it would seem that all the problems have been solved long ago and all that is left to do is joint celebration – one day Shabbat, another day Iftari, then Christmas, and so on. But where are the Jews, apart from such rare scholars as Lapide, who know about such a Jewish recognition of Muhammad as *a* prophet?

This, of course, is a general problem applying to most of the other "new findings" as well. Hence, although valuing the modest but important advances made in such specialized meetings as this, I also value highly, and personally am involved in, searching for the means to have them reach to the grassroots level. As a matter of fact, in Germany we have been singularly successful in this by making use of biannual Protestant mass meetings called "Church Days" (*Kirchentage*), at which we reach tens of thousands of young Christians eager for dialogue with Islam. If I am allowed a bit more "self-glorification," I should like to mention that I initiated a "Committee for

Christian/Muslim Dialogue" at the Protestant "Church Days," a committee that has developed into an important institution and had a tremendous impact, especially in Hannover in 1983, and even more so in Düsseldorf in 1985.

Muslim View of Jesus

Before making my basic observation regarding some of Prof. Küng's statements, I believe a corrective comment is in order. Such a procedure is characteristic of the initial stages of dialogue where much time is consumed with an exchange of information and clarification of each other's positions. Prof. Küng states that the portrait of Jesus in the Qur'ān is very different from the portrait of Jesus in the Gospels, for Jesus not only confirms the Law, as the Qur'ān records, but also counters all legalism with radical love, which extends even to his enemies; that is why he was executed – and this the Qur'ān fails to recognize. I find it difficult to identify with this reading of his.

The image I as a Muslim have of Jesus is in fact more or less that which Küng projects here as a gospel understanding. Muslims recognize Jesus as the greatest prophet next to Muhammad, and yet they see Muhammad's mission as more akin to that of Moses. Moses and Muhammad each brought a new law – not so Jesus, who came to recall the spirit underlying the law. For this reason many of the mystic saints of Islam see their role in relation to Muhammad as similar to the role of Jesus in relation to Moses. They combat legalism by trying to imbue the law with notions of love, and they very much see themselves in the tradition of Jesus – to the extent sometimes of precipitating their own doom. Nothing could be more rewarding for them than being crucified, though few of them seem ever to have had the privilege of ending in exactly the same way as Jesus did, as recorded in the Gospels.

For Muslims, Jesus is an extreme, a heartrending as well as heartwarming example, but one who is to be imitated only under the most extraordinary circumstances – unlike Muhammad, who is for Muslims primarily the good exemplar, for all times and climes. So the real difference is that for Muslims Jesus lacks the catholicity Muhammad has. Jesus is of utmost importance, but more for special occasions – not all year round.

Perhaps we can understand this more fully by realizing that Christians, according to the quranic image of them, are extremists in that they take love, patterned on the radical love of Jesus, to the extremes of world-renunciation and extraordinary forms of penitence. Apparently the many Christian hermits who relished Arabian abodes during the time of the Prophet were seen as something like "drop-outs," good-natured cranks, loveable as friends or "sages," but mostly somewhat "off-track." In the Muslim daily prayer (*Al-Fatihah*, the "Muslim Paternoster"), Muslims ask God to lead them on the straight path – which elsewhere has been explained as the Aristotelian *via media*, the golden mean between a Jewish extreme of materialist this-worldliness and a Christian extreme of spiritualist other-worldliness. This is a traditional explanation for "those on whom there is the wrath of God" (the Jews) and "those who go astray" (the Christians). Had Hans Küng said that Muslims overgeneralize in their extreme images of Jews and Christians, I could have agreed with him. But he is on weak ground when he says that the Qur'an fails to recognize Jesus as the apostle of radical love and the antilegalist par excellence. There is an enormous literature in Muslim tradition celebrating Jesus as precisely that. Admittedly much of those materials owe their inspiration to the Christian background of numberless converts, but the source stimulus was provided by the Qur'an itself.

Trialogue and the Thrust toward Unity

Let this be enough of corrective statements. I should like to concentrate on one major point in Hans Küng's paper; it is an issue that has proved bedeviling to myself and many of my coreligionists. Prof. Küng implicitly states that Islam is a great faith because it means submission to God, but that it needs to be liberated from the oppressiveness of legalism – though surely not from law. I fully agree that we Muslims suffer from legalism. Our "sacred law," the *shari'ah*, in its present stagnated form as it was handed down to us from seventh-century Arabia, has certainly become oppressive under the changed circumstances of the twentieth-century pluralist world community. It no longer suits the needs and standards of what we call the emerging universal civilization of a global society.

If our Christian friends take upholders of the *shari'ah* as their partners on the Muslim side, then there can simply be no consensus on the question of human rights. The *shari'ah* that is now being reinforced by atavistic Islam is a petrified law, and the oil dollars that go into its present worldwide propagation tend only to further petrify it. One might think that this position is very much in line with what Küng is saying. But there is one important difference. He tends to think of the *shari'ah* as a nonbiblical element, the murkier Arabian side of Islam. I believe this is only partially true. I see the *shari'ah* more like the product of Jewish traditions, as a biblical legacy – and I do not feel at all comfortable with this particular linkage. Although it no doubt endows Jews, Christians, and Muslims with common notions that allow us to become more familiar with one another, it also bogs me down as a Muslim in my religious development – and I would almost say in my spiritual edification as well.

Interreligious dialogue often proceeds on the assumption that there is a core of religious heritage to start with, a kind of family tree representing Judaism, Christianity, and Islam. It is somehow assumed that because these three traditions have so much in common, they could provide the starting point for dialogue on a universal scale. It is as if some of us believed that charity begins at home, or that it is easier first to reconcile family members before arriving at a deeper understanding with outsiders, which in this case would mean Buddhists, Hindus, and others. In fact, such notions are especially strong among Muslims. First, there are the ringing verses of the Qur'an that speak of a common platform, calling Jews and Christians to join Muslims on the basis of a common denominator – that is, belief in the one and only God. (Incidentally, these appeals give evidence that Christian monotheism is very well recognized in the Qur'an, despite the "uneasiness" created by such symbols as the Trinity.) Then there is the designation "people of the book" for Jews and Christians, which affords them a special status in the Muslim worldview; they are seen as standing in the prophetic tradition on which Islam bases its self-understanding.

All this, however, is mere surface. Beneath it we discern the historical development of incipient Islam as a religious community part. Even a cursory acquaintance with Islam renders it clear that there are two levels of understanding the word "Islam": a primary one, which refers to the prophetic tradition of Judaism, in which Jesus is included, and a secondary one, which designates a new community, the followers of Muhammad, the new prophet – so to say, an alternative to the two previous attempts (Judaism and Christianity) that seemed no longer workable. The history of that evolution need not detain us here. What deserves to be emphasized is the fact that the separation of these two meanings of the term "Islam" has never been fully resolved.

For "official" Islam, for the religious establishment associated with government and power, the emergence of Islam as a new and superior community was never in doubt. This "communal Islam" of history was sure of its mission to dominate the world. With a broad spectrum of Islamic theology, however, especially where it merges into the mystic currents that proved at times overwhelming, the primary meaning often reasserted itself, at least in the form of a question as to what had become of it or what relevance it still held. After all, it was very much there, enshrined in the quranic revelation, and could not be brushed aside so easily. Added to this was sometimes a third meaning, when Islam was understood not only in its abstract literal meaning, but even in a futuristic sense, as an ideal toward which all of us must strive together – Jews, Christians, and Muslims (in the "communal" sense).

Thus we are confronted with at least one tradition within the Islamic heritage that is strongly motivated by a desire for religious unification, by a longing to break down communal barriers and bring humankind together through belief in one God, which goes back to the initial vision of Muhammad when he conceived of himself not as the founder of something new, but as the reaffirmer of the prophetic tradition. It would be patently wrong to relegate this tendency solely to the realm of Islamic mysticism, which derived much of its inspiration from external sources. Rather we should ask whether this openness to "foreign" elements was not prompted by the very revelation of the Qur'an itself. This is an age-old discussion on which many learned tomes have been written. But is has rarely been related to the phenomenon of the many syncretist movements, sects, and new faiths that sprang from the soil of Islam and that always emphasize the unifying aspect. Here is a tradition that makes Islam appear as the motivator of religious unification per se–all the fervid communalism of Muslim fundamentalists notwithstanding.

For this brand of Muslim thought, interreligious dialogue is highly attractive. It is as if the followers of the other faiths had finally seen the point and had come around to a demand that is as old as the revelation of the Qur'an in history. Obviously this poses dangers of a special kind, for in this way interreligious dialogue may quickly "degenerate" into what is precisely not the purpose of our coming together here–the deepening of each of us in our own foundations through the stimulating process of learning from the other.

II. Jewish/Christian Origins and Islamic "Original Sin"

Much of this is due to Islam's indebtedness to the Jewish/Christian tradition, although more in the "communal" than in the "syncretist" form. For many Muslim scholars of religion, especially those falling within the restrictive fold of fundamentalism, Muhammad's anchorage in the world of ideas propounded by Jewish-Christianity will hardly be a matter of dispute. But it does not do justice to another fundamental concern of Muslim thought, which is the emancipation from a Jewish/Christian tradition that ties Muslims down to a narrow geographico-historical confine.

The quranic view of religious history is obviously an evolutionary one that sees prophethood as culminating with Muhammad, after whom humanity needs no further direct intervention from on high: humanity can now stand on its own feet. The prophetic quality has become a common property, manifesting itself in saints and reformers until it is to be shared by large masses of "friends of God," to use Sufi eschatological terminology. This presupposes, however, outgrowing the historical molds that revelation, of necessity, had to assume in its historical unfoldings. For this development the Jewish/Christian childhood of Islam may certainly prove helpful–provided it is finally outgrown. Otherwise it could be retarding as well.

This is precisely my overall reaction to Hans Küng's paper. In the final analysis I feel obstructed by being time and again tied down to that particular past. I accept that those bridges are important, but I am not fond of being reminded of the crossings I have made. It was not so pleasant. In many ways I feel freer with Buddhists and Hindus. Moreover, I notice that the interreligious dialogue in India seems to be making more headway. When Muslims meet Buddhists and Hindus, there is not so much past history they have to come to terms with. The historical bitterness between Hindus and Muslims is not reflected in their holy scriptures. Therefore they can straightaway proceed to more essential issues with a philosophical approach.

At the meetings of the "Standing Conference of Jews, Christians, and Muslims in Europe" we hold daily services – one day Jewish, another day Christian, then Muslim. Everybody participates in each service. At one such occasion I had selected a passage from the Qur'an and asked an Egyptian participant to read it in the Arabic original. While chanting, the man fell in love with his own voice and read beyond that passage dealing with Abraham and the other biblical prophets. He read and read until he came to a passage that says Muslims should never trust Jews or take them as friends. The Yugoslav Muslim I had chosen to read the text in German was a formalist who read not only what I had indicated beforehand, but also up to the point where the Egyptian had ended his recitation. There were some thirty Jews in the hall. They told me later on that they realized very well what had happened, and they now realized that dialogue was more difficult than they had previously thought.

Some of us Muslims, too, felt that God could have made it easier for us by dispensing with those many references to the biblical past in the Qur'an and allowing us to start with a clean slate. To me this Jewish/Christian legacy appears sometimes as if it were our "original sin," and it is extremely difficult for us Muslims to free ourselves of it. In the form of the *shari'ah*, this legacy is altogether tragic. Contrary to what both some of my Christian friends and some of my Muslim friends say, only a minor part of the *shari'ah* derives from the Qur'an or the example of the Prophet. A large portion of it is Hebraic, biblical, particularly where it conflicts with our present-day notions of human rights.

MAHMUD MUHAMMAD TAHA AND THE CRISIS IN ISLAMIC LAW REFORM: IMPLICATIONS FOR INTERRELIGIOUS RELATIONS[*]

Abdullahi Ahmed An-Na'im[**]

[*] *Journal of Ecumenical Studies,* 25:1, (Winter, 1988)

[**] Abdullahi Ahmed An-Na'im (Muslim) headed the Dept. of Public Law of the Faculty of Law at the University of Khartoum from 1979 to 1985, where he is an Associate Professor of Law, on leave from 1985 to 1989. During 1985-87, he was a Visiting Professor of Law at the School of Law, University of California at Los Angeles. From August, 1987, to July 1988, he has been a Fellow at the Woodrow Wilson International Center for Scholars at the Smithsonian Institution in Washington, DC, and he will be a Visiting Professor of Law at the College of Law, University of Saskatchewan, Sasketoon, during 1988-89. He has been an attorney in the Sudan since 1977 and a member of the Sudanese Bar Association. He is a Board Member (1986-88) of the International Third World Legal Studies Association and a member of the Foundation for the Establishment of an International Criminal Court and International Criminal Law Commission, U.N. Affiliate Conferences. He holds an LL.B. from the University of Khartoum, both a graduate LL.B. and a diploma in criminology (M.A.) from the University of Cambridge, and a Ph.D. in law from the University of Edinburgh (1976). He also attended the International Institute of Human Rights in Strasbourg, France, in the summer of 1981. He has published an Arabic *Sudanese Criminal Law* (Omdurman: Huriyah Press, 1986), and the English translation and an introduction for Muhamoud Mohamed Taha's *The Second Message of Islam* (Syracuse University Press, 1987). He has published more than a dozed articles on legal and human-rights topics, including "Religious Freedom in Egypt: Under the Shadow of the *Dhimma System,*" in L. Swidler, ed., *Religious Liberty and Human Rights in Nations and Religious* (Ecumenical Press, 1986); "Christian-Muslim Relations in the Sudan: Peaceful Co-existence at Risk," in K. Ellis, ed., *Vatican Islam, and the Middle East* (Syracuse University Press, 1987); and "Islamic Law, International Relations, and Human Rights: Challenge and Response," in *Cornell International Law Journal,* vol. 20, no. 2 (1987). He has also participated in numerous conferences, symposia, and seminars in the Middle East and throughout the U.S.A., as well as lectured in the U.S.A. and West Germany.

Introduction

A fundamental problem facing both Muslims and non-Muslims who wish to engage one another in serious interreligious dialogue has been the traditional Muslim position that all non-Muslims perforce will be second-class citizens in any state where the Muslims obtain political power. A similar domineering attitude prevailed until just a few decades ago in Roman Catholicism, making it almost impossible for Catholics to enter into dialogue with non-Catholics until Vatican II (1962-54).[1] Similarly, dialogue with orthodox Marxists from countries under Communist control today still suffers from a like disability. Clearly, an essential question for dialogue with Islam, then, is whether full equality between Muslims and non-Muslims can be reconciled with the major sources of Islam, the Qur'an and *sunna*. If so, how? It is these two extremely difficult but essential questions that will be addressed in this article.

Despite the apparent growing demand for Islamization – the total application of Islamic law to every aspect of public as well as private life – in many Muslim countries, and perhaps because of that, there is also growing awareness of the crisis in Islamic law reform that is explained and discussed in this article. As demands for Islamization force politicians to adopt supposedly "Islamic" policies and implement allegedly "Islamic" laws throughout the Muslim world problems with these policies and deficiencies in these laws immediately come to the forefront. When we resort to the early Muslim jurists, we find that those techniques are inadequate and incapable of resolving the problems or supplementing the deficiencies.

It is true that Muslims believe that Islam, as contained in its fundamental sources, namely the Qur'an and *sunna* traditions of the Prophet, is perfect and infallible. It does not follow from this belief, I submit, that the *shari'a*, which is in fact no more than the interpretation and application of those fundamental sources by the early Muslims, is also perfect and infallible. This basic distinction between Islam and historical *shari'a* is vital to the

---

[1] See Leonard Swidler, *The Ecumenical Vanguard* (Pittsburgh: Duquesne University Press, 1965), for a detailed documentation and discussion of largely foiled pre-Vatican II Catholic attempts at intra-Christian – to say nothing of interreligious – dialogue.

success of the process of modern Islamization. If historical *shari'a* is to be held as sacred and permanent as Islam itself, Muslims cannot change those principles of *shari'a* that are no longer valid and viable.

For better and for worse, Muslims have already accepted the nation-state as the framework for their governmental organization and international relations.[2] This framework presupposes certain constitutional principles, especially the principle of equality of all citizens of the state in terms of their public civil rights. Moreover, as members of the international community and signatories to international human-rights instruments, Muslim states are bound to maintain such equality among their citizens without discrimination on grounds of gender, religion or belief.[3] Yet, as will be demonstrated in this article, *shari'a* does not conceive of women and non-Muslims as full citizens of an Islamic state. It is imperative, I believe, that the process of Islamization should not be allowed to violate these fundamental constitutional and human-rights obligations.

This article is concerned with the prospects of reconciling Islamic law with current standards of constitutionalism and human rights. In particular, we shall attempt an assessment of the reform methodology developed by the late Sudanese Muslim reformer, *Ustadh* (revered teacher) Mahmud Muhammed Taha, because it seems to offer the best prospects for humane and intelligent Islamization that satisfies the Muslim need for self-determination while fully guaranteeing constitutional and human rights.

---

[2] See, generally, James P. Piscatori, *Islam in a World of Nation-States* (New York: Cambridge University Press, 1987).

[3] Except for Saudi Arabia, all Muslim states that were independent at the time supported the Universal Declaration of Human Rights in 1948: G. A. Res. 217A (III), U.N. Doc. A/180, at 71 (1948). All Muslim states that have become independent since then have endorsed the Declaration. Moreover, Muslim states have also endorsed other relevant resolutions of the General Assembly of the United Nations, such as the Declaration on the Elimination of All Forms of Intolerance and of Discrimination Based on religion or Belief: U.N. GAOR Supp. (51), U.N. Doc. A/RES/36/55 (1982). Furthermore, many Muslim states are signatories to specialized human-rights instruments, including the International Covenant on Civil and Political Rights and the International Covenant on Economic, Social, and Cultural Rights: G.A. Res. 2200 (XXI), U.N. Doc. A/6316 (1966), respectively. The principle of nondiscrimination on grounds of gender, religion, or belief is fundamental to all the international obligations that Muslim states have undertaken under these instruments.

In view of the common mistaken identification of *shari'a* with Islam itself, modern Muslim scholars tend to prefer to address their criticism to Islamic *fiqh*, the jurisprudence of the early Muslim jurists, rather than *shari'a*.[4] As we shall see below, however, the problems are deeper, in that they pertain to the very nature of the Qur'an and *sunna* as sources of law to be understood in historical context. Superficial and apologetic treatment of the issues in terms of *fiqh* rather than *shari'a* may appeal to popular Muslim sentiments, but it does not resolve the problems authoritatively and finally for the purposes of concrete Islamization. During the previous historical Muslim experience, the problem may have been the rigidity of theory and, as a consequence, the divergence of subsequent practice from the early model and its theoretical articulation in *shari'a*. When we consider the prospects of the modern application of *shari'a*, argued *Ustadh* Mahmud, we find that there are very serious problems with the early model itself as well as with the basic assumptions of all former theoretical articulations.

With particular awareness of the need for reform and sensitivity to the serious implications of premature implementation, *Ustadh* Mahmud Muhammad Taha has proposed a comprehensive theory for modern Islamization. As a result of his opposition to what he perceived to be misconceived and premature Islamization in the Sudan, *Ustadh* Mahmud was executed in Khartoum on January 18, 1985.[5] Although he believed that the public law of *shari'a* provided a comprehensive and satisfactory body of principles and rules for government in the early Islamic historical context, he also maintained that some of those principles and rules are no longer valid in the modern context. What distinguishes *Ustadh* Mahmud from other modern Muslim writers who call for reform and modernization, in my view, is his exceptional courage and conceptual clarity in facing the real issues and proposing sufficient, albeit novel and controversial, answers.

In order to appreciate his proposed methodology for safeguarding the constitutional and human rights of women and non-Muslims within any

---

[4] See, e.g., Kemal Faruki, *The Evolution of Islamic Constitutional Theory and Practice* (Karachi and Dacca: National Publishing House, 1971), pp. 81-82, 84-85.

[5] On the circumstances of his trial and execution, see my article, "The Islamic Law of Apostasy and Its Modern Applicability: A Case from the Sudan," *Religion*, vol. 16 (1986), pp. 197-224.

national Islamization process, we need to emphasize certain aspects of the nature and development of *shari'a* and to recognize the limitations of traditional Islamic law reform. This will be done in the first two sections of the article. The following three sections of the article will survey the life and work of *Ustadh* Mahmud, explain the main features of his proposed reform technique, and assess the realistic prospects of its implementation. In conclusion, the article will emphasize the significance of this man's work for interreligious relations, not only within any particular nation-state but also in the wider international context.

Aspects of the Nature and Development of Shari'a

Without going into a detailed discussion of the development and content of *shari'a* in general,[6] we can briefly note the following. First, there is the historical context within which the first Islamic state, which came to be taken as the model state under *shari'a*, was established. For the first thirteen years of his mission, the Prophet propagated the faith and laid down the moral principles of Islam through divine revelation, the Qur'an, and his own personal example, which came to be known as *sunna*, in Mecca from 610 to 622. In the face of continuing persecution and mounting hostility, the Prophet and his companions had to migrate to Medina, another town in western Arabia, where the brotherhood of the migrants and their supporting hosts was welded into the first integrated Muslim community. The treaty or charter among the two segments of the Muslim community, on the one hand, and the Jewish and Christian tribes of the Medina area, on the other hand, constituted the basis of the first Muslim state.[7] The precedent of equality and security for the Jewish and Christian participants of that initial charter is, of course, very significant in terms of the future reform of the status of non-Muslims under Islamic law. Nevertheless, it must be noted that those

---

[6] On this broad and somewhat controversial subject, see, e.g., Joseph Schacht, *An Introduction to Islamic Law* (Oxford: Clarendon Press, 1964): N. J. Coulson, *A History of Islamic Law* (Edinburgh: Edinburgh University Press, 1964): and Ahmad Hasan, *Early Development of Islamic Jurisprudence* (Islamabad: Islamic Research Institute, 1970).

[7] Fazlur Rahman, *Islam* (London: Weidenfeld and Nicholson, 1966), pp. 11-19; and Montgomery Watt, *Islamic Political Thought* (Edinburgh: Edinburgh University Press, 1968), p. 406.

communities had to pledge submission to Muslim sovereignty and to the Prophet as the absolute rule of the state.[8]

When the Jewish tribe of *Banu Qurayiza* violated the terms of the accord by siding with forces invading Medina, the Prophet repudiated the charter and severely punished the Jewish tribe.[9] As a result of this development, the status of non-Muslims within the first Islamic state was drastically altered. Qur'anic revelation, *sunna*, and other practice subsequent to that incident came to be taken as the authoritative sources of *shari'a* on the status of non-Muslims in general. It is important for our purposes here to note the historical context of the change.

Second, we need to note the nature of the sources from which *shari'a* was developed by the founding jurists. The original sources of *shari'a* were the Qur'an and *sunna* of the Prophet. On the basis of *sunna* authority, *ijma'*, the consensus of the Muslim community, was also accepted as a source of *shari'a*. In their efforts to articulate and tabulate the law, the leading Muslim jurists of the eighth and ninth centuries applied *qiyas*, analogy, to resolve new problems according to established precedent. They also exercised *ijtihad*, independent juristic reasoning, according to the view of the best interest of the community. Due to the accumulation of precedents, including established interpretation of the Qur'an and *sunna*, room for innovation was gradually narrowing until it was deemed to have been exhausted around the beginning of the tenth century. This phenomenon, known as the closing of the gates of *ijtihad*, marked the end of the era of establishing distinctive schools of jurisprudence.[10] Subsequent jurists such as the Ibn Taimiyya attempted to challenge some of the assumptions of the formative era of *shari'a* jurisprudence but only by reasserting the absolute authority of the

---

[8] For an English translation of the Medina charter, see Watt, *Islamic Political Thought*, pp. 130-134.

[9] Ibn Hisham, *As-sira an-Nabawiya* (The Biography of the Prophet), 2nd ed. (Cairo 1955), pp. 214-233. The episode is also discussed in numerous works such as Sayyid Ameer Ali, *The Spirit of Islam* (London: Methuen and Co., 1922), pp. 72-82; Montgomery Watt, *Muhammad: Prophet as Statesman* (New York: Oxford University Press, 1961), pp. 166-175; and Bernard Lewis, *The Arabs in History* (New York: Harper and Row, 1960), pp. 40ff.

[10] Schacht, *Introduction to Islamic Law*, pp. 69-75; Coulson, *History of Islamic Law*, pp. 62, 80-81, 84-85.

interpretations and practices of the first few generations of Muslims (*as-salaf*).[11]

With respect to the basic sources of *shari'a*, namely, the Qur'an and *sunna*, we need to note the following. Although the Qur'an was recorded very early, leaving no room for significant controversy over its text, disagreement over the interpretation of that text has always been unavoidable. As to the *sunna*, which was recorded much later,[12] there has been controversy over the authenticity of its texts as well as disagreement over their interpretation and relationship to the Qur'an. Despite the efforts of leading compilers of the *sunna*, challenges to the authenticity of some reports of the Prophet's actions and words continue to the present day because of allegations of fabrication to support political and intellectual positions. The very fact that these compilation were prepared 200 years later out of oral traditions that were no doubt affected by political events and ideological and jurisprudential debates of the time seems to lend support to charges of fabrication.[13] At best, the compilers must have run the risk of disregarding some authentic *sunna* for lack of appropriate corroboration – thereby, in some cases, as it were, throwing out the baby with the bath water. Nevertheless, the *sunna* is generally accepted as the second source of the law, often used to explain and restrict or extend the meaning of the first source itself, the Qur'an.

Thirdly, there is the role of *naskh*, abrogation, in the development of *shari'a*. Working out of the above mentioned sources, with an increasingly narrowing scope of *ijtihad*, the jurists employed the principle of *naskh*, the assumption that subsequently revealed verses of the Qur'an and subsequent *sunna* must have repealed or restricted the legal effect of earlier verses of the

---

[11] On the methods and views of Ibn Taimiyya, see Erwin I.J. Rosenthal, *Political Thought in Medieval Islam* (New York: Cambridge University Press, 1962), pp. 245-249; and Omar A. Farruk, *Ibn Taimiyya on Public and Private Law in Islam* (Beirut: Khayats, 1966).

[12] The compilers of what are now accepted by the majority of Muslims as authentic *sunna* are Bukahri (d. 869), Muslim (d. 874), Ibn Da'ud (d. 888), Ibn Maja (d. 886), Trmidhi (d. 892), and Nasa'i (d. 915).

[13] Rahman, *Islam*, pp. 63-66.

Qur'an and *sunna*.[14] This was a vital and logical process for reconciling apparent contradictions and deducing integrated and coherent legal principles and rules. Since any reformative effort will have to deal with the problem of reconciling apparently contradictory texts of the Qur'an and *sunna*, especially in the realm of public and constitutional law, the question of *naskh* is a fundamental component of both the crisis in Islamic law reform and its proposed resolution.

Moreover, and of special interest for the purposes of the present article, we have to understand the role and limitations of *ijtihad* within the framework of *shari'a*. Given the established and fixed nature of the two basic sources, namely, the Qur'an and *sunna*, modern Muslim writers have demanded the reopening of the gate of *ijtihad*, that is to say, they call for the resumption of independent juristic reasoning.[15] To understand why this approach will not achieve the desired objective of resolving some of the fundamental problems noted below, we now turn to a brief consideration of *ijtihad* and its limitations.

The Role of Ijtihad

Ijtihad is primarily based on several *sunna* in which the Prophet approved the use of this method in supplementing the Qur'an and *sunna* as sources of *shari'a*. According to a generally accepted *sunna*, for example, the Prophet is reported to have asked Ma'adh ibn Jabal, when he appointed him governor for Yemen in southern Arabia, "How would you govern?" Ma'adh replied, "I will decide it in accordance with the *sunna* of the Messenger of God [the Prophet]." "What if you find nothing on the issue in the *sunna*? asked the Prophet; and Ma'adh responded that he would then exercise his own independent judgment (*ajtihidu ra'iy*). The Prophet is reported to have

---

[14] On this technique and its application in *shari'a*, see e.g., Mustafa Zaid, *An-Naskh fi 'l-Qur'an al-karim* (Abrogation in the Glorious Qur'an), 2 vols. (Beirut, 1971); and K. I. Semann, "Al-Nasikh wa al-Mansukh, Abrogation and Its Application in Islam" *Islamic Quarterly* 5 (April-July, 1959): 11.

[15] See, e.g., Wael B. Hallaq, "Was the Gate of Ijtihad Closed?" *International Journal of Middle East Studies*, vol. 16, no. 1 (1984), p.3.

approved this.[16] Similar *sunna* texts are reported with reference to 'Ali ibn 'Abi Talib and other provincial governors appointed by the Prophet.

The same order of sources is also supported by the logic of religious law, with the Qur'an as the literal word of God ranking at the top, followed by the *sunna* as the example set by the perfect Muslim, the Prophet. Only in the absence of a clear and definite ruling in both the Qur'an and *sunna* would it be open for the human reasoning of the believer to presume to supplement the rules of *shari'a*.

By the same logic, it seemed obvious to the leading jurists that *ijtihad* should not be open to every believer. To ensure that there is no applicable clear and definite text of the Qur'an and *sunna*, the purported *mujtahid* – one who claims to exercise *ijtihad* – must not only memorize the Qur'an and *sunna* but also master the established techniques of interpretation and deduction of principles and rules. To this end, the jurists sought to lay down, in great detail, the qualifications and requirements for practicing *ijtihad*. A *mujtahid* must therefore lean the Qur'an and *sunna* by heart, be well versed in the arts and techniques of the Arabic language in which those sources were expressed, and be knowledgeable in early Islamic history, etc. Moreover, since *ijtihad* was considered to be a religious function, the person must be a devout Muslim of impeccable character and moral standing.

However, although one concedes the reasonableness of these qualifications and requirements in the historical context of previous *ijtihad*, the following considerations should be taken into account in relation to the modern exercise of ijtihad. First, the requirement of memorizing the Qur'an and *sunna* may have been imperative in the largely oral tradition of early Islam, but it ceases to be compelling in the modern context with the wide availability of indexed sources and even computerized access and cross-reference. Second, personal piety and moral standing can hardly be verified by formal qualifications. It may have been possible to form a somewhat sound judgment on such subjective qualifications in the small and close-knit

---

[16] A full translation of the *sunna* may be found in Duncan B. MacDonald, *Development of Muslim Theology, Jurisprudence, and Constitutional Theory* (Russel & Russell, 1965; orig.-London: Routledge, 1903), p. 86. See also Majid Kadduri, "Nature and Sources of Islamic Law," *The George Washington Law Review, vol. 22, no. 1 (1953), p.11.*

community of scholars in the few leading centers of learning of the Middle East in the eighth and ninth centuries. Such subjective judgment, I would submit, is neither possible nor desirable today, with the potential for manipulating the mass media to distort and misrepresent facts for the benefit of vested interest and political expediency.

For these and other related reasons, it would not be desirable, in my view, to designate certain individuals or institutions as having an exclusive monopoly on the exercise of modern *ijtihad*. It must remain open to every Muslim to offer her or his views and interpretations, leaving it to them to accept or reject such views and interpretations. Instead of prior censorship by official or formal institutions, which are liable to manipulation or abuse, the personal credibility of the particular person and the validity of her or his views are best left to popular judgment. This obviously presupposes freedom of thought and expression to facilitate scholarly debate and scientific investigation. Unfortunately, the *shari'a* notion of apostasy and its harsh penal and other consequences, to be explained below, severely restrict freedom of thought and expression.

Believers and ideologues of all traditions have always claimed the prerogative of defining the boundaries of their faith or ideology to the exclusion of people who claim commitment to, but express views which are perceived to be inconsistent with, the same belief or ideology. With the separation of state and church in the West, the consequences of apostasy in Christianity, for example, have been confined to the psychological and social spheres. Alleged apostates or heretics may suffer the psychological pressure of social isolation and spiritual deprivation, but their legal rights to personal safety and security of property are not affected. This is not yet the position under *shari'a*, as the fate of *Ustadh* Mahmud himself clearly illustrates. According to all the established schools of Islamic jurisprudence, as accepted by the vast majority of Muslims today, an apostate must be put to death, his property confiscated, and his Muslim wife divorced from him, regardless of her wishes.[17] As recently as 1985, the ruling of a Sudanese Court of Appeal

---

[17] If apostasy is committed by a woman, she would suffer all the "civil" consequences under *shari'a:* her property would be confiscated and her marriage annulled. However, there is some disagreement among the jurists as to whether she may be executed for the offense. On the

purported to apply *shari'a* not only by sentencing *Ustadh* Mahmud to death but also by ordering the burning of his books and prohibiting the propagation of his views in the future.[18] A similar fate and consequences face anyone who expresses unpopular or unorthodox views in purported exercise of *ijtihad.* What is left of the freedom of thought and expression if a man who claims to be a Muslim is executed because his views are perceived by a court of law, or even the vast majority of Muslims, to be heretical!

In addition to this most serious obstacle facing freedom of thought and expression under *shari'a*, there remains the problem of the limitations of *ijtihad* itself. According to both its textual authority and original logic, orthodox *ijtihad* cannot be exercised in matters governed by clear and definite texts of the Qur'an or *sunna.* According to historical Islamic jurisprudence, jurists may have some room for interpretation within the limits of a clear and definite text of the Qur'an and/or *sunna,* but they may not exercise *ijtihad* to develop alternative rules in any matter on which clear and definite texts can be found. Thus, any rule of *shari'a* that is based on clear and definite texts of the Qur'an and/or *sunna,* as is the case with some of the rules discriminating against women and non-Muslims, cannot be changed or modified through the use of orthodox *ijtihad.*

Therefore, it would seem necessary that a revolutionary approach be developed and applied if the problems of *shari'a* explained below are to be resolved. As H. A. R. Gibb rightly said, "Every scientific argument must also take the same course and reach the same conclusion, unless you change the same postulates or invent new tools."[19] Before discussing the basic premise of the particular revolutionary approach proposed by *Ustadh* Mahmud, it may be helpful to give some background information on his life and work.

---

question, see Rudolph Peters and Gert J.J. DeVires, "Apostasy in Islam," *Die Welt des Islams,* vol. 17 nos. 1-4 (1976-77), p. 5.

[18] See An-Na'im, "Islamic Law of Apostasy," pp. 208ff.

[19] H. A. R. Gibb, *Muhammadanism: An Historical Survey,* 2nd ed. (New York: Oxford University Press, 1962), p. 91. Gibb made the same point in *Modern Trends in Islam* (Chicago: University of Chicago Press, 1947), p. 124.

The Man and His Movement

Ustadh Mahmud was born in the town of Rufa'a, on the Blue Nile in central Sudan, around 1909.[20] After the death of his mother in 1915, and his father in 1920, he was raised, together with his two sisters and one brother, by relatives in a nearby village. Since Rufa'a was one of the early centers of civil, as distinguished from traditional religious, education, *Ustadh* Mahmud went to modern civil schools until he graduated in civil engineering from the Gordon Memorial College (later to become the University of Khartoum) in 1936. Nevertheless, in accordance with the traditions of religious families at the time, the young *Ustadh* Mahmud received early instruction in the Qur'an, but he did not finish learning it by heart at that stage.

His professional career started with a short period of government service with the Sudan Railway Department. During the late 1930's and early 1940's, he became involved with the emerging nationalist struggle for independence from colonial Anglo-Egyptian rule. This led to difficulties with his employer, the colonial government, and resignation to go into private practice, with the intention of devoting more time and energy to political activities.

He was not happy, however, with the political activities of Sudanese intellectuals who were willing to act as mouthpieces for the traditional sectarian leadership at the time.[21] In dissatisfaction with the available options, *Ustadh* Mahmud established, with some colleagues, *al-Hizb al-Jamhuri* (the Republican Party) in October, 1945. He was elected the Party's first leader. His political activities led to his imprisonment by the British colonial authorities in 1946 for refusing to sign a bond to cease publishing pamphlets demanding independence. After his release without signing that bond, he was rearrested in the same year, tried, and sentenced to two years' imprisonment for his leading role in the so-called Rufa'a revolt of 1946. It

---

[20] This is the estimate of his date of birth given by *Ustadh* Mahmud himself. No official records of birth dates were kept at the time.

[21] Most intellectual activists joined the political parties established by the two main Islamic sects in the Sudan: the *Ansar* (Mahdists) and the *Khatmiya* sects. It is remarkable that the same two sects and their hereditary leadership continue to dominate Sudanese party politics to the present day. The current government is a combination of the two parties of these two sects.

was during this second prison term, that the subsequent three years of self-imposed religious seclusion (*khalwa*) in the Muslim *Sufi* (mystic) tradition, that he underwent a profound religious experience and emerged, in 1951, with his integrated theory for what he described as the Evolution of Islamic Legislation (*tatwir At-tashri' Al-islami*).

From 1951 till his execution in January, 1985, *Ustadh* Mahmud continued to propagate his views, assisted by his growing circle of followers, who became known as *al-Jamhuriun* (the Republicans). Although retaining its name and most of its membership, the political party of 1945 was transformed into a religious ideological organization following its general conference of 1951, with some of the founding members gradually opting out in favor of action with the main political parties of the time. Since its transformation, the organization centered around the figure of *Ustadh* Mahmud in the traditions of the classic *Sufi* fraternities rather than adopt the structure and methods of a political party or organization as such. Although feeling a special affinity and sharing a basic orientation with classic Islamic *Sufism*, *Ustadh* Mahmud and his followers were critical of what they regarded to be the degenerate contemporary successors of the early masters and their fraternities. Following the dissolution of all political parties by the *coup d'etat* of May 25, 1969, the organization adopted the name of *al-Ikwan al-Jamhuriun* (the Republic Brothers). They were able to continue to operate until 1983 because they were never a political party in the usual sense of the term.

Because of the novelty of his proposed methodology for reform and the challenge he posed to the traditional Islamic leadership in the Sudan, *Ustadh* Mahmud was often charged with apostasy by his political opponents. However, since the secular legal system that used to prevail in the country did not provide for the punishment of this *shari'a* offense, these charges were ineffective in silencing *Ustadh* Mahmud and his followers. In 1968, for example, the *shari'a* High Court of Khartoum ruled that *Ustadh* Mahmud was a apostate from Islam. Because the court's jurisdiction was confined to family-law matters, and it had no power to enforce any criminal or civil sanctions, the ruling remained a dead letter until it was invoked to support

Ustadh Mahmud's conviction and execution in 1985.[22] This criminal trial and execution of *Ustadh* Mahmud for his views was only possible because of the 1983 transformation of the legal system under former President Numairi of the Sudan.[23]

The revolutionary religious nature of the work of *Ustadh* Mahmud was reflected in his own lifestyle and organizational methods. While drawing from his civil education and knowledge of modern sciences, *Ustadh* Mahmud was a profoundly religious man. Living and teaching in the tradition of Islamic *Sufi* masters, he emphasized the values of simplicity of lifestyle and genuine humble piety. His organization of the Republicans also reflected private discipline, *adab*, and informal structure of the classic *Sufi* fraternities. Nevertheless, the group departed from that tradition in several ways that they regarded as significant in terms of the content and purpose of their approach. First, their activities were characterized by much greater involvement in the public and political affairs of the community and the country at large. To this end, they had very specific and highly publicized views on all the public issues of the day, whether local, national, or international. For example, their advocacy of peace and normal relations with the state of Israel since the 1950's was well known. Second, and in accordance with their advocacy of equality for women, the Republican sisters played a very prominent role in the leadership of the group and participated fully in all its activities.

As these two examples clearly show, the group was willing to live its views in day-to-day practice, however unpopular those views and the policies they generated may have been. In this regard, the group was trying to live up to the standards set by its founder and leader who took consistency of thought and action to be the essence of the religious life. As he repeatedly emphasized, a believer's obligation is to act in accordance with what she or he perceived to be her or his immediate duty, without worrying about the

---

[22] In January, 1985, the Special Criminal Court of Appeal relied on that 1968 decision in confirming the conviction for apostasy and the death sentence on *Ustadh* Mahmud. See An Na'im, "Islamic Law of Apostasy," p. 209.

[23] Former President Numairi was overthrown on April 6, 1985, seventy-six days after the execution of *Ustadh* Mahmud. However, the *shari'a* laws introduced by Numairi in 1983 remain in force in the Sudan to the present.

consequences. In accordance with the *Sufi* principle that God is the only real actor in the universe, *Ustadh* Mahmud took every single incident or encounter of the day, however minor or apparently insignificant, as a crucial test of his faith and religious integrity. As a believer in God's providence and mercy, he maintained, one should not worry about the apparently or initially unpleasant consequences, because the real or ultimate consequences are bound to be good.

When the ultimate test came, *Ustadh* Mahmud stood firm on this principle and suffered death rather than recant his views.[24] In accordance with his best judgment, he felt bound to oppose Numairi's premature, misconceived, and distorted Islamization. It was therefore *Ustadh* Mahmud's immediate duty to oppose, without worrying about the consequences that, he believed, are bound to be good so long as he was true to the discipline of the immediate moment, *adab al-waqt*. This discipline also accounts for the more significant aspect of the life and work of *Ustadh* Mahmud, namely, the willingness and ability to live throughout his life in accordance with his convictions. His death may have provided a more dramatic illustration of his courage and the strength of his convictions, but it was his day-to-day living in accordance with this principle that was much more difficult and impressive.

The theological and philosophical aspects of the life and work of *Ustadh* Mahmud will no doubt receive the attention of more competent authors. For the purposes of the present article, however, we are concerned with some of the constitutional and human-rights implications of his reform methodology.

---

[24] Representatives of President Namairi's regime sought to spare *Ustadh* Mahmud's life in exchange for some token submission and withdrawal of opposition to Numairi's Islamization. *Ustadh* Mahmud rejected their mediation, preferring to die rather than compromise his principles. At the same time, capital charges against the Rev. Phillip 'Abbas Ghabush and over seventy of his supporters were dropped when they signed a letter of submission and apology to Namairi.

The Evolution of Islamic Legislation

As explained above, the crisis in Islamic law reform is due to the fact that the traditional reform techniques are no longer adequate. Since certain aspects of the problematic *shari'a* principles are based on clear and definite texts of the Qur'an and *sunna*, they are not open to reform through the exercise of orthodox *ijtihad*. The specific techniques of *ijma'*, consensus, and *qiyas*, analogy, are no more promising because they follow established precedents based on the same objectionable principles. In any case, these two techniques are also restricted by the same limitation of orthodox *ijtihad* because *ijma'* and *qiyas* are invalid if they contradict any clear and definite text of the Qur'an or *sunna*. More general arguments that seek to resolve the problems through reinterpretation and restriction of some of the texts or raising doubts with respect to certain *sunna* will also fail because they cannot avoid or circumvent some clear and definite texts of the Qur'an itself. To illustrate this point, we will take two examples here, the rights and status of women and of non-Muslims. It is with respect to these specific issues that the superiority of the evolutionary principle can best be appreciated.

Because of certain clear and definite texts of the Qur'an itself, aside from *sunna* that may, however unreasonably, be challenged by some scholars, women and non-Muslims can never be regarded as equal, *in every respect*, to Muslim males under *shari'a*. Any attempt to achieve such complete legal equality through traditional techniques will fail, I would suggest, in view of the following verses of the Qur'an.

In relation to the status of women, verse 34 of chapter 4 of the Qur'an has been translated af follows:[25]

> Men are the protectors and maintainers of women, because God has given the one more (strength) than the other, and because they support them from their means. Therefore the righteous women are devoutly obedient, and guard in (the husband's) absence what God would have them guard. As to those women on whose part ye fear disloyalty and ill-conduct, admonish them (first), (next) refuse to share their beds, (and last) beat them (lightly); but if they return to obedience, seek

[25] This and the following translations of verses of the Qur'an are taken from Abdullah Yusuf Ali, *The Holy Qur'an* (Qatar National Printing Press, n.d.), except verse 106 of chapter 2, quoted below.

not against them means (of annoyance): For God is Most High, Great (above you all).

This verse sets two main principles in relation to the status and rights of women. There is, first, men's general *qawama*, translated above as protection and maintenance but also having the sense of general guardianship. The corresponding duty of devout women is to submit and be loyal and obedient. Secondly, men may discipline, to the extent of beating if necessary, women who are *nashiz*, disloyal and ill-behaved. These two main principles, and related *sunna* of the Prophet, have been taken as the basis for a wide variety of rules signifying women's inferior status and restricting their access to general high-ranking executive and judicial office. Other verses requiring women to be veiled and confined to the home are also used to support restrictions and limitations on women.[26]

No argument would be allowed, within the framework of traditional reform techniques of *shari'a*, to change the basic status of women as subject to men's guardianship and discipline or release them of the duty to stay out of sight, whether at home or under the veil. These restrictions have already been the consensus, *ijma'*, of Muslims since the earliest times. As such, there is no precedent for analogy, *qiyas*, to the contrary. Again, since the question has been settled by clear and definite texts of Qur'an and *sunna*, there is no room for exercising *ijtihad*, in the traditional sense, in a way that would either abolish guardianship, with the consequent male power to discipline disobedient women, or release women from general confinement to the home.

The position of non-Muslims is similar in that their inferior status is entrenched by clear and definite verses of the Qur'an. Verses 5 and 29 of chapter 9, for example, have been translated as follows:

> But when the forbidden months are past, then fight and slay the Pagans wherever ye find them, and seize them, beleaguer them, and lie in wait for them in every stratagem (of war); but if they repent, and establish regular prayers and practice regular charity, then open the way for them: For God is Oft-forgiving, Most Merciful.

---

[26] Such as verses 33 and 53 of chapter 33 of the Qur'an. The immediate context of these verses speaks of the Prophet's women, but it is obvious – and universally accepted – that what applies to the Prophet's women in this regard applies, *a fortiori*, to all other Muslim women.

Fight those who believe not in God nor the Last Day, nor hold that forbidden by God and His Apostle, nor acknowledge the Religion of Truth (even if they are) of the People of the Book, until they pay the *jizya* with willing submission, and feel themselves subdued.

On the basis of the second verse and early Muslim practice,[27] the People of the Book are offered the status of *dhimma*; that is, they are guaranteed Muslim protection and freedom to practice their own religion in private, in exchange for payment of *jizya* and submission to Muslim rule. As such, *dhimmis*, those living within the Muslim state under a status of *dhimma*, lack the basic competence to hold positions of authority over Muslims. Several verses of the Qur'an that provide that Muslims shall not take People of the Book as guardians and protectors, *awliya'*, have also been employed to support this basic principle.[28]

The choices open to unbelievers, as defined by *shari'a*,[29] are more limited – either embrace Islam, or be killed unless granted temporary safe conduct, *aman,* to be within Muslim territory for a limited period of time and for a specific purpose.[30] Again, verses of the Qur'an which provide that Muslims shall not take unbelievers as guardians and protectors, *awliya,* are used to deny to an unbeliever who is permitted to stay within a Muslim state access to positions of authority over Muslims.[31] As in the case of women, neither consensus nor analogy nor orthodox *ijtihad* can possibly change the

---

[27] For this early practice, see, e.g., Daniel C. Dennett, *Conversion and the Poll Tax in Early Islam* (Cambridge, MA: Harvard University Press, 1950).

[28] E.g., verses 51 and 57 of chapter 5. See the *Ahl al-Kitab, Dhimma, and Djizya* in H. A. R. Gibb and J. H. Kramer, eds., *Shorter encyclopedia of Islam* (Leiden: E. J. Brill, 1953), pp. 16-17, 75-76, and 91-92, respectively.

[29] There is some controversy over whether Hindus, Buddhists, etc., are to be treated as believers or unbelievers. See *Abu Yusuf, Kitab al-Karaf* (Cairo: Maktaba Salafiya, 1382 Hijri), pp. 128-132, 191-217; *Islamic Jurisprudence: Sharfi'i's Risala,* tr. Majid Kadduri (Baltimore: The Johns Hopkins Press, 1961), pp. 58-59, 265-266; and *The Islamic Law of Nations: Shaybani's Siyar,* tr. Majid Kadduri (Baltimore: The Johns Hopkins Press, 1966), pp. 142-154, 224, 275-283. See also Muhammad Hamidullah, *The Muslim Conduct of State,* 3rd ed. rev. (Lahore: Sh. Muhammad Ashaf, 1953), pp. 106-112, 322-331.

[30] Ibn Rushd, *Bidayat al-Mujtahid,* vol 1 (Cairo: Maktabat al-Khanji, n.d.), pp. 308-309; and Majid Kadduri, *War and Peace in the Law of Islam* (Baltimore: The Johns Hopkins Press, 1956), pp. 170-174. On the status of unbelievers in general, see *Kafir* and *Shirk* in Gibb and Kramer, *Shorter Encyclopedia,* pp. 205-206 and 542-544, respectively.

[31] Such as verse 28 of chapter 3 and verse 144 of chapter 4 of the Qur'an.

fundamental status of non-Muslims established by these clear and definite verses of the Qur'an.

Modern Muslim traditional reform efforts have attempted to improve the status of women, especially in family law, and sought to rationalize and restrict the inferior status of non-Muslims. None of these efforts, however, has suggested a way for achieving the necessary degree of reform, namely, achieving *complete legal equality* for women and non-Muslims under *shari'a*. The uncircumventable barrier facing all traditional reform techniques of *shari'a* is the fact that the inequality of women and non-Muslims is entrenched by clear and definite texts of the Qur'an itself. This is, in my view, the genuine crisis facing Muslim law reform.

It is with reference to this particular crisis that the revolutionary technique proposed by *Ustadh* Mahmud is best appreciated. However drastic it may appear to be, this technique would seem to be the only way to break the deadlock. Briefly stated,[32] this technique is based on the fundamental proposition that both the Qur'an and the *sunna* should be seen as containing two messages: the primary and permanent message of the Mecca stage, and the subsidiary and traditional message of the Medina stage. Both messages were revealed in the Qur'an to the Prophet Muhammad, who is the final Prophet in accord with Muslim belief. In view of persistent and violent rejection by the Meccans of the fundamental principles of justice and equality contained in the Mecca message, Islam implemented, as its First Message, the principles of relative justice and equality, which were more appropriate to the concrete circumstances of the seventh century. Now that humanity has achieved sufficient advances through human endeavor as guided by God, including the application of the First Message, it is now appropriate, urged *Ustadh* Mahmud, to implement the primary and permanent message, which would be, in chronological order of implementation, the Second Message of Islam. According to this logic, certain aspects of the Qur'an and *sunna*, revealed and uttered during the

---

[32] *Ustadh* Mahmud's views are best stated in his own publications in Arabic, which may be obtained from Mr. Abdel Mutalab Bala Zahran, P.O. Box 1151, Omdurman, The Sudan. An English translation of his main book, *The Second Message of Islam,* prepared and introduced by the present author, was published by Syracuse (NY) University Press in June, 1987.

subsequent stage of Medina, should be seen as of transitional, not permanent, application. When it is appropriate to do so, the transitional aspects of *shari'a* should be replaced by the fundamental principles of the Qur'an and *sunna* of the earlier Mecca period. In other words, Islamic legislation should be elevated from one level of the Qur'an and *sunna* to another higher level of the same Qur'an and *sunna*.

On examining the Qur'an in these terms, one finds that all the verses quoted and referred to above as the basis of restrictions on women and non-Muslims were, in fact, revealed in Medina, not Mecca. The *sunna* simply reiterated and explained the Qur'an of both periods and may also be classified in the same way. In contrast, the Qur'an and *sunna* of the Mecca period provided for complete equality and freedom for both women and non-Muslims. In relation to women, the Qur'an in Mecca emphasized the equality of men and women as a matter of religion and in the sight of God.[33] For non-Muslims, the Qur'an revealed in the same period provided for complete freedom of choice and conscience.[34] If these Qur'anic principles are to have the force of law now, as suggested by *Ustadh* Mahmud, all discrimination against women and non-Muslims will have to be eliminated.

The same shift proposed by *Ustadh* Mahmud can also be used to reinterpret the above texts of the Medina period. For example, the verse of men's guardianship, *qawama*, over women will cease to have the force of law because the rationale for such *qawama*, as provided by the same verse, is no longer valid. The verse justified *qawama* and its consequences on the grounds that men protect and provide for women. Since women no longer need protection and provision by individual men, the rationale for *qawama* ceases to be valid. Protection for both men and women is guaranteed through the rule of law. As to material provision, we perceive the growing economic independence of women. It may be noted here that the technique of linking a legal principle to its rationale is well established in Islamic jurisprudence. The proposal of *Ustadh* Mahmud makes it possible to use the

---

[33] See, e.g., verse 164 of chapter 6, verse 17 of chapter 40, and verse 38 of chapter 38.

[34] See, e.g., verse 29 of chapter 18 and verses 21-24 of chapter 88.

technique in a way that removes all legal restrictions on the legal rights of women and non-Muslims.

On the question of the future enactability of the Mecca texts, *Ustadh* Mahmud used to argue in terms of verse 106 of chapter 2 of the Qur'an: "None of Our revelations do We abrogate or cause to be postponed unless (until) We substitute something better or similar: Knowest thou not that God hath power over all things?"[35] He maintained that the "better or similar" revelation is that which is more appropriate for implementation in the concrete circumstances of the time. In this sense, that part of the Qur'an which was revealed during the Mecca stage, he argued, is now the better revelation in the same way that the part revealed in the Medina stage was the better one in the seventh century. In both case, abrogation and enactment are done by God, acting through the Prophet. It is true that the Prophet is no longer with us in person, but his personal example and techniques for acquiring religious knowledge remain.

The acquisition of religious insight through the imitation of the exact example of the Prophet is crucial to understanding *Ustadh* Mahmud's position. He claimed that he did not develop his methodology through purely rational and objective study of Islamic jurisprudence but, rather, through intuitive religious knowledge out of his profound religious experience of 1946-51. In other words, although he emphasized that he is not a prophet who received revelation – the Prophet Muhammad being the final Prophet – *Ustadh* Mahmud also claimed that his theory was derived from the Qur'an and from the living example of the Prophet as educational techniques and sources of original knowledge.

---

[35] A key word in the original Arabic text of the verse is the one equivalent to the word "postpone" in this translation. In his own Arabic writing, *Ustadh* Mahmud wrote the word as *"nunsi'ha"*; in the Arabib alphabet, *"hamza"*. When written in this way, the word is translated as "cause it to be postponed." See Taha, *Second Message,* p. 40. Some translators of the Qur'an, such as Yusuf Ali, cited in note 25, above, write the word as *"nunsyha"* and, in the Arabic alphabet, *"ya."* In this manner of writing, the word is translated as "cause it to be forgotten." I accept *Ustadh* Mahmud's manner of writing this word, because of the fundamental Muslim belief that the text of the Qur'an is secured by God against being forgotten or lost (verse 9 of chapter 15 of the Qur'an). The meaning must, therefore, be "cause to be postponed," not "cause to be forgotten."

Moreover, *Ustadh* Mahmud argued that, if the Mecca period revelation had been abrogated permanently, Muslims would have lost the best part of their religion. Both messages had to be revealed in the Qur'an as the final revelation in Muslim belief, leaving human beings free to communicate with God directly through the Qur'an itself. Through God's word, the Qur'an, God is addressing each and every Muslim, provided that he or she approaches the Qur'an with the appropriate reverence and expectation. Anyone who claims to have acquired fresh insights from the Qur'an may proclaim his or her knowledge and support it by scriptural and rational arguments, leaving it to the other Muslims to accept or reject his or her claim. In this way, argued *Ustadh* Mahmud, Muslims will come to appreciate, and to implement in policy and legislation, that interpretation which is in best accord with *hukm al-waqt*, "the dictates of the time."

An Assessment

In assessing the theoretical validity of *Ustadh* Mahmud's proposal for the "Evolution of Islamic Legislation," we need to note the following. The Qur'an and *sunna* can, in fact, be classified in the way he suggested. Subject to a slight degree of overlap, which he admitted and explained in terms of the continuity of revelation,[36] the texts of Mecca do provide for fundamental principles of justice and equality, while those of Medina permit discrimination on grounds of gender and religion. Moreover, the dichotomy and its consequences can easily be appreciated in terms of historical context, in the sense that inferior status for women and non-Muslims was unavoidable in the concrete circumstances of the seventh century.

It seems reasonable to me to argue that the verses of the Mecca era were merely postponed and not permanently abrogated and that those verses should be enacted into law under the appropriate circumstances. Assuming that there is a Second Message of Islam designed for future implementation, how do we know that the present time is appropriate for its implementation? In response to this question, *Ustadh* Mahmud emphasized modern human achievements in both technology and social sciences. He argued that the

---

[36] See Taha, *Second Message*, p. 125.

prevalence of notions of constitutionalism and human rights make it both morally undesirable and politically impracticable to relegate women and non-Muslims to the status of second-class citizens. He maintained that these notions subject all persons to the rule and protection of the law and deny Muslim men private, direct guardianship over women. He also used the rise of the international human-rights movement and concern for women's and religious minorities' rights as very significant factors in support of the proposition that the twentieth century is the appropriate time for the implementation of the Second Message of Islam.

He turned arguments pointing out human-rights violations and the use of force in national and international relations into arguments in support of his position, by saying that these events and policies in fact emphasize the urgency of peace and the rule of law. He regarded, for example, modern advances in the development of nuclear weapons as, paradoxically, signs of hope. Insofar as they make global war and conflict increasingly unthinkable, these apparently lethal advances force people to seek to maintain and reinforce peace and stability.

Although these arguments may seem convincing to the rational mind, especially one that is already committed to their underlying moral and philosophical underpinnings, it may be argued that the question of timing still remains one of value judgment and subjective belief. We may wish and strive for peace and stability and believe in the need for total respect for constitutionalism and human rights and yet fail in our endeavor. The possibility, however, does not relieve a modern Muslim from the duty of taking a position on what he or she believes to be in accord with the dictates of the time and acting accordingly. Fear of innovation, prejudice, and vested interest may delay the adoption of such a position, but, in the final analysis, he maintained, there be no viable Islamic alternative.

The practical opportunity to propagate the Second Message if Islam would seem to be an integral part of the theory itself as it presupposes the suitability of the present historical context. The execution of *Ustadh* Mahmud for apostasy and political offenses, however, seems to challenge this basic assumption. If the implementation of *shari'a* imposed by former President Numairi is to continue in the Sudan, and if other Muslim countries follow the examples set by the Sudan, Iran, and Pakistan in applying *shari'a*, there may be no future prospects for open propagation of the Second Message of Islam. In this way, the execution of the author of the theory and the founder of the movement may have far-reaching consequences for the practical viability of his approach.

Another dimension of the impact of the execution of *Ustadh* Mahmud is the apparent organizational confusion and leadership crisis currently suffered by his followers, *al-Jumhuriun*, the Republicans, in the Sudan.[37] Since the date of the execution of *Ustadh* Mahmud and the banning of the group's public activities in January, 1985, the Republicans have not resumed their usual activism in propagating the Second Message of Islam. This inaction seems to persist despite the overthrow of Numairi and restoration of democratic liberties since April, 1985. It remains to be seen whether this is due to the initial shock and the magnitude of the loss of the founder and leader of the movement or a permanent phenomenon. In rational and material terms, however, it would seem to be imperative that someone must continue to propagate the theory if it is to reach and be accepted by the masses of Muslims who can bring about its eventual practical implementation.

Another possible, albeit seemingly irrational, scenario has been hinted at in the literature of the group, namely, the possibility of direct divine intervention. In his own metaphysical writing and through various pamphlets which he approved for publication in the name of the group, *Ustadh* Mahmud stated his belief in the imminent coming of the Messiah.[38] In one of his major books, for example, he argued that Resurrection and the Final Day in the Qur'an have a dual meaning.[39] In their first and closer meaning, these cosmic events will materialize in this life, be maintained, through the coming

---

[37] Interview with Sa'id At-Tayyib Shaib, the highest ranking member of the group, published in the Al-Ayyam daily newspaper of January 5, 1986, p. 9.

[38] Kahlid Duran, "The Centrifugal Forces of Religion in Sudanese Politics." *Orient* 26 (December, 1985): 596. Cf. Riffat Hassan, "Messianism and Islam," *Journal of Ecumenical Studies* 22 (Spring, 1985): 261.

[39] *Al-Qur'an wa Mustafa Mahmud wa l-fahm al-asri* (The Qur'an, Mustafa Mahmud, and Modern Understanding) (Omdurman, 1971), especially chapters 9 and 10. Mustafa Mahmud is an Egyptian author who wrote on the subject of a modern understanding of the Qur'an.

of the Messiah. In the second and ultimate sense, he added, Resurrection and the Final Day mean the end of this world and the beginning of the next life. The implication hinted at in this aspect of *Ustadh* Mahmud's writings, but never explicitly stated, is that the Second Message of Islam will be implemented by the Messiah. The present author is not competent to reflect on this matter of metaphysical knowledge and belief. In relation to the issue under discussion, however, it may be noted that, according to the logic of the cosmic event, there will be no need for propagation and gradual acceptance and implementation of the theory of the Second Message. Everything will be achieved in a single stroke in an overwhelming and compelling fashion, leaving no room for disagreement on delay.

The third logical possibility is, of course, the work of *Ustadh* Mahmud may never be implemented through wide acceptance and total application by Muslims, whether gradually or immediately. What would remain to be considered in such a case is whether his work will have some impact short of total implementation. At one level, there will always be the impact that the man and his life's work have already had in his own immediate environment, the way in which he has affected his followers and influenced events in the Sudan. The precise implications of this dimension remain for the participants to assess and appreciate. *Ustadh* Mahmud's influence at this level, however great it may be, would be insignificant, in my view, when compared to the likely impact of the man and his life's work on the future of Islamic thought. His contribution to this field may be appreciated when his writings are discussed, at the scholarly level, by students of Islam throughout the world.

Finally, is it possible that *Ustadh* Mahmud's work will be completely forgotten within a few years, without having any lasting impact? I do not think so. Whatever Muslims may think of the answers, he has no doubt raised fundamental and searching questions. I also believe that his basically rational and scientific approach will provide a good model for other Muslim scholars. More important, I would submit, is his personal example of commitment and courage. To have pursued his goals so selflessly and consistently for forty years, especially through his own personal lifestyle, is an exceptional achievement. The example of the single man's living for and by his convictions, more than dying for them, is truly inspiring not only to Muslims but also to all other people of the world.

Conclusion

Seen in this light, the life and work of *Ustadh* Mahmud are significant to all religion. In concluding this preliminary article, however, we need to emphasize the importance of his contribution to the relations between Muslims and non-Muslims. As clearly shown above, *shari'a* is inconsistent with the fundamental constitutional and human rights of non-Muslim citizens of an Islamic state. Consequently, on the one hand, Islamization through the application of *shari'a* would be disastrous for these citizens. It is largely in rejection of the implications of being non-Muslim citizens under *shari'a* that Sudanese non-Muslims have resorted to armed rebellion since 1983. Yet, there is no way for avoiding the above-noted objectionable aspects of the public law of *shari'a* through traditional law-reform techniques. On the other hand, the alternative position of living under a purely secular constitutional and legal order is also unacceptable to the Muslim majority that believes that it has a religious obligation to organize its public life in accordance with Islam. This does not have to be in accordance with *shari'a* which, as noted above, is the historically traditional, but not necessarily the only valid, interpretation of Islam.

Without an Islamic reform methodology that is capable of reconciling the legitimate demands and expectations of both segments of the population, violent confrontation is clearly unavoidable. The only possible outcome of such a confrontation is to force one segment of the population to abandon its current position, which is unlikely except as a temporary solution. The Islamic reform methodology proposed by *Ustadh* Mahmud would achieve complete reconciliation between the two positions and, thereby, provide a lasting solution. Under his approach, Muslims would be able to live under a constitutional and legal system derived from the permanent and fundamental principles of Islam without violating the constitutional and human rights of non-Muslims.

Needless to say, such reconciliation is relevant and desperately needed by all Muslim countries facing this dilemma today. Moreover,

Ustadh Mahmud's understanding of religion and its role in society is helpful to all societies, Muslim and non-Muslim alike. It would be helpful, I believe, even for countries that have sought to resolve the problems of reconciling religion with the requirements of pluralism through separation of church and state. Within these societies, it seems to me, there is a residue of tension between religion and pluralism that calls for innovative treatment of the issues. The historical model he provided for interpreting Islamic religious law might well be adapted by other religious traditions. However, the most immediate benefit to non-Muslims and their relations with Muslims, flowing from *Ustadh* Mahmud's Islamic solution reconciling full equality between non-Muslims and Muslims and the sources of Islam, is the providing of a solid Islamic religious basis for authentic dialogue to occur between the two, for full dialogue can take place only between equals – "equal with equal," *par cum pari*, as the Roman Catholic Church put it at Vatican II.[40]

The life and death of *Ustadh* Mahmud Muhammad Taha have come to pass but not, I hope, the significant contribution he has made through both his life and his death. As one of his many close associates for several years, I can personally testify to his supreme courage and integrity. I can also testify to his exceptional humanity, humility, and compassion. Can all this come to pass without lasting effect? I believe not and hope not. It is the light and spirit of such persons as *Ustadh* Mahmud, not the power and wealth of the manipulators of people and events, that have, in my view, substantial and lasting impact on the advancement of the human experience.

---

[40] See Leonard Swidler, "The Dialogue Decalogue: Ground Rules for Interreligious, Interideological Dialogue," J.E.S. 20 (Winter, 1983): 3 (rev., September, 1984): "Seventh Commandment: *Dialogue can take place only between equals.*"

MUSLIMS AND NON-MUSLIMS[*]

Khalid Duran[**]

The relations of Muslims with people of other faiths are determined by a variety of cultural, economic, historical and socio-political factors that constitute, at times, an intricate web of interrelated strands. In the present case priority is given to the religious dimension. This makes it necessary to distinguish between what is purely religious, in the sense of theological, and what is cultural or sociopolitical in the sense of historical accretions to – or elaborations of – the original core of tenets.

Theology is the self-understanding of Muslims as a *chosen community*. The term is not usually used by Muslims, who regard it as a Mosaic expression and take it to be indicative of Jewish exclusivism. And yet, in the final analysis, the concept of chosenness is fairly much the same in both religions. Al-Qur'an (the Koran) calls Muslims "the best community ever brought forth by God for the benefit of humanity," (*khaira ummatin ukhrijat li-n-nas*).[1] Muslims are also called the "people of the middle" or "a people in the center."[2] There is a whole literature on the exact or possible meaning of this term, with most commentators taking it to signify "model community," the community of the golden mean and, therefore, the community of

---

[*] Leonard Swidler, Paul Mojzes, eds., *Attitudes of Religious and Ideologies Toward the Outsider* (Lewiston, NY: Edwin Mellen Press, 1990).

[**] Khalid Duran (Muslim), see above, p. 49.

[1] Al-Qur'an II, p. 84.

[2] *Ibid.*, p. 143.

88

salvation, a community to be emulated by the remainder of humankind.[3] Muhammad Iqbal (d. 1938), who is acclaimed as one of the leading thinkers of Islam in this century, spoke of the Muslim community as a "model for the final unification of mankind."[4] This leads to the conviction that there can be no lasting peace in this world until Islam is spread to all the corners of the globe and made to prevail against other beliefs.

Such a missionary view need not cause conflicts, however, because there also are the clear-cut injunctions in Al-Qur'an that there should be no compulsion in religion[5] and emphatic statements such as "to you your religion and to me my religion."[6] And yet, it is self-evident that such a concept of chosenness is bound to collide with the assertion of other identities.

Quasi-theological is the belief that Islam is identical with political supremacy. There is little in Al-Qur'an to warrant such a belief, but the historical development of the community made Muslims see things that way. The Prophet's companions saw their new religion triumph during the lifetime of the founder. Unlike the Christians, they did not have to wait for three hundred years to attain worldly power. Early Islam was not a religion of the catacombs. Muhammad's followers had it the other way round; they experienced three hundred years of political triumph before suffering the first serious setbacks.

This engendered a belief that Islam and political power go together. Almighty God came to be seen as rewarding the believers with supremacy over others. The correctness of the faith came to be equated with a monopoly on government. After the "heathen" Mongols destroyed Bagdad in 1258 – the seat of the Caliphate and the greatest city of the world in those days – Muslims sought to counter such challenges by coining the motto "Islam is religion and state" (al-islam din wa daula). History had accustomed them

[3] Khalid Duran, "In Quest of Muslim Identity," in Charles Fu & Gerhard Spiegler, eds., *Religious Issues and Inter-religious Dialogues* (New York/London: Greenwood Press, 1989).

[4] Muhammad Iqbal, *The Reconstruction of Religious Thought is Islam* (Lahore/London: Muhammad Ashraf, 1930).

[5] Al-Qur'an X, pp. 99-100.

[6] Al-Qur'an CIX, p. 6.

to seeing religious commitment and worldly might go hand in hand. It would hardly be an overstatement to say Muslims had been pampered by the mundane success of their early history. Later on they often behaved like the spoiled children of history, and quite a few continue to do so even today, despite two centuries of European colonialism and its protracted aftermath.

It is an ingrained conviction with many Muslims that the loss of political supremacy is the result of a slackening of the faith. Things can be remedied only if the believers return to the pristine purity of the faith, if they become practicing and committed Muslims again.[7] Whatever lands have been lost can be regained once the believers are motivated by Islam, as in the olden days, instead of allowing themselves to be lured away by "foreign" ideologies. This idea became strong in twelfth-century Spain, prevailed in nineteenth-century India, when Hindus, Sikhs and Britishers took over from the Muslim rulers, and surged up again in the Near East after the disastrous 1967 defeat at the hands of the Israelis, when Jerusalem was lost to Islam once again as it had been lost to the Crusaders in the eleventh century.[8] Iqbal, the aforementioned poet-philosopher, expressed the conviction that Muslims could regain lost glory by a return to the right faith and correct practice in his little volumes of Urdu poetry entitled *Complaint and Answer to the Complaint (Jawab-e Shikwa)*. Many others have done the same, and hardly less eloquently. We might even speak of a genre of literature devoted to such soul-searching: "What caused our downfall? How can we regain for Islam the glory it enjoyed during the days of our ancestors?"

This belief in the relationship between the correctness of the faith and the right to rule is symbolized by the institution of the Caliphate. This institution is not mentioned in Al-Qur'an and is, therefore, strictly speaking not part of Islamic theology (the tenet of the human being as God's Caliph, "vicegerent," on earth is a different matter altogether). However, the Caliphate played such an important role in history that it entered the Muslim

---

[7] Khalid Duran, "The 'Golden Age' Syndrome. Islamist Medina and Other Historical Models of Contemporary Muslim Thought," in *Revue suisse de sociologie*, No. 3, 1983. Republished in *Islam and the Modern Age*, Vol. 15, No. 2, (New Delhi: Islam and the Modern Age Society, May 1984).

[8] Fouad 'Ajami, *The Arab Predicament.*

psyche as an inalienable component of the belief system and came to be regarded as an element of "normative" Islam. No doubt, there have been attempts by Muslim theologians at divesting Islamic principles of this Caliphal legacy by explaining the Caliphate as an historical accident.[9] While such reasoning stands on firm ground as an academic exercise, it has failed to have much impact on the Muslim self-image as a community that regards the loss of political power as a kind of aberration. Outside Shiism few would go so far as Khomeini, who regarded the "Islamic state" as superior to all other categories, with the interest of the "Islamic state" having precedence over the norms of Islamic law and ethics. When he said that there could be "no Islam without tears," he actually meant "no Islam without bloodshed."[10] While this was an excess and obvious deviation from the hallowed norms, it nonetheless strode, albeit in a grossly exaggerated manner, in a direction along which some Muslims in their thought tend to move as a result of the historical development undergone by their community.

Political subjugation of others mostly did not imply forced conversion. The original rationale for the insistence on supremacy was that Muslims had to be protected, understandable enough in view of the persecution suffered during the Prophet's days in Mecca, the wars of the heathens from Mecca against the Muslims in Medina, as well as the threat of Persian and Roman invasions of Arabia. Soon enough, however, the right to rule was taken for granted, with no rationale required, because it was now regarded as a divine compensation and a distinction for God's chosen community.

The link with theology proper is provided by God's favorites if the Muslims did not observe God's commands,[11] a warning reminiscent of that given to the Jews, whose chosenness depends on their being up to the mark – this, at least, is how some orthodox Rabbis interpret it. The distinction of being God's favorites might manifest itself in many ways, political supremacy being certainly one of them, and for many Muslims the

---

[9] Leonard Binder, *Islamic Liberalism* (Chicago/London: The University of Chicago Press, 1988), Chapter 4.

[10] See the Khomeinist journal *Crescent International*, Toronto, Nov. 1, 1983. Reproduced in Khalid Duran: *Islam and politischer Extremismus* (Hamburg: DOI, 1985), p. 105.

[11] Al-Qur'an IX, p. 39, XXXXVII, p. 38.

most plausible manifestation: "Seek ye first the political kingdom and all other things shall be done unto you."[12]

The association of Islam with rule is, therefore, more than quasi-theological. It is semi-theological. Outstanding theologians have come up with reinterpretations allowing for an Islam shorn of political power and yet secure and sovereign, a complete code of life, perhaps more cogently than the Islamists with their disfiguring of Islam as a political ideology. Nonetheless, such intellectualist reinterpretations rarely catch on with the masses. As a community, Muslims are burdened with the triumphalist legacy of an imperial past, making it difficult for them to integrate into a pluralist society where all are equal partners and no single community rules supreme.

I. An Insidious Numbers Game

As a result of this near obsession with political power is the conflictive numbers game witnessed in most states with sizable Muslim populations. In many Third World countries correct statistics are hard to come by. Do Muslims in Nigeria and Tanzania constitute a majority or minority? With regard to both these states Christians claim to be in majority, giving the Muslims no more that 25-35%, with a few conceding to Islam some 45%. Muslims generally insist on being not less than 65% in both states, some Muslims going up to 75% in their estimates. More neutral academics with less religious commitment estimate the Muslim population in both Nigeria and Tanzania to be between 55% and 60%.[13]

Does Kenya have a Muslim population of 25-30%, or merely 15%? The same question is asked about Cameroon, Ghana, Liberia, Mozambique and several other states. Are the Muslims of Sierra Leone more than half of the population or less? What about Bourkina Fasso? Do Muslims constitute two thirds of Sudan's population or more? How about Chad? Everywhere there are claims and counter-claims.

---

[12] This is how the Lord's Prayer was 'misappropriated' by Kwame Nkrumah during Ghana's struggle for independence. That this is but vicarious for a larger phenomenon, especially in the world of Islam, was aptly recognized by Kenneth Cragg. *Counsels in Contemporary Islam* (Edinburgh: Edinburgh University Press, 1965), p. 31.

[13] Emilio Galindo Aguilar, *Encuentro Islamo-Cristiano*, Madrid, Aug. 1988.

Fundamentalist Copts claim that 30% of Egypt's population is Christian, while official estimates speak of only 12%, a figure corroborated by non-Egyptian Catholic academics in Cairo. The government does not want to disclose the correct statistics because if our real numbers become known, hotheads among the Copts argue, Egypt might turn into another Lebanon.[14]

It could be argued that correct statistics might put an end to the deadly numbers game. Just as likely, however, is that a census result would be disputed by everybody, with each party accusing the government of favoring the other side. Even if the census were conducted by an international agency, such as UNESCO, conflicts might fully erupt that have, so far, been only simmering. Muslims of Guinea Bissao, on learning that they stand no chance of forming a majority, might opt to secede. Muslims of Egypt might say: "Now that it has been established without any doubt that the Copts are only 15% and not more, they have to shut up once and for all."

In countries such as Sudan, however, devastated by decades of civil war, such clarity might prove wholesome, if in no other way then by finally bringing about the secession of the non-Muslim South, rather than have all the peoples involved bleed to death. To carry out a census in such a way as to obtain reliable results is, however, a Herculean task in war ravaged countries that never had the necessary infrastructure nor the trained personnel for such an endeavor.

Census information produced by many Muslim states is to be treated with much caution. Afghan government officers in charge of population counts under the *ancient regime* have readily admitted to the manipulations they were asked to carry out by their ministry because it was thought advisable to inflate the numbers in order to obtain larger funds from UN agencies. While the number of Afghans were officially given as being above 16 million, such officers hold the view that in reality the figure was closer to 13 million, possibly as low as 11. As the same time they admit the difficulty of obtaining the correct number of females. While 11 million Afghans were counted, 2 million were added as the approximate number of females they

---

[14] Personal communication during interviews in Egypt in November-December 1981.

had not been able to count because of culturally motivated resistances. To this were added another three million for UN purposes. This is but one instance to illustrate the problem.[15]

II. The Bane of Muslim Separatism

Senegal, with a Muslim majority of almost 90%, was ruled for two decades by a Christian president, Leopold Sedar Senghor. Christian president Julius Nyerere ruled for 24 years over Tanzania with its Muslim majority. Chad was likewise ruled for more than a decade by Christian presidents, although Muslims are probably in the majority. Islamists were unhappy about this state of affairs, and many non-Islamist Muslims too. The rule of Christians over Muslim majorities was often regarded as the effect of colonialism. On the other hand, no objection was raised to the Muslim Amadou Ahidjo ruling over Cameroon despite the fact that Muslims constitute hardly more than one third of the country's population. When Ahidjo ceded the presidency to Paul Biya, a representative of the Christian majority, this was deplored and Muslims rose in revolt, which in turn provoked a backlash by the Christians. Uganda has barely a 10% Muslim population but there were no Muslim objections when dictatorial Idi Amin brought his country into the ICO (Islamic Conference Organization).

In the meantime Leopold Senghor ceded peacefully to his chosen successor, Abdou Diouf, a Muslim. Julius Nyerere did the same with Hasan Mwinvi. Tanzania, thus, has a Muslim president. But Sudan has been ruled by Muslims since independence (1956) and they show no preparedness to hand power over to a non-Muslim, despite the fact that Dr. John Garang, leader of the SPLM ("Sudanese People's Liberation Movement") is admittedly the ablest politician and most qualified administrator.[16]

---

[15] Personal communication by the officers in charge of the census with whom I happened to be associated in resistance activities. Several of them have confirmed, independent of each other, that Afghanistan's population might not have been more than 13 million, possibly as low as 11-12 million.

[16] See my short biography of "Colonel Dr. John Garang de Mabior," in *Orient*, Journal of the German Orient Institute (Opladen, W. Germany: Leske Verlag, Fall 1985).

This shows a basic unpreparedness of many Muslims to accept being ruled by non-Muslims or to enter into a genuine power sharing as the prerequisite to a democratic pluralism.

A further result of this concern with political supremacy is the tendency found in many Muslim communities to secede from those areas of their state that hold a non-Muslim majority. The secession of India's predominantly Muslim areas from the rest of the overwhelmingly Hindu country in 1947 led to the establishment of Pakistan as a separate state for Muslims. This is but the most conspicuous example of a world-wide trend.

To be sure, there is no such thing as a Muslim separatism on purely religious grounds. Invariably, there is more than one factor of a very worldly nature involved. The difference from other types of separatism, such ones not involving any Muslims, is that various economic and political grievances are aggravated by the common Muslim proclivity to hold religious biases as primarily responsible for any discrimination suffered. The widespread and profound Muslim sense of being victimized because of Islam adds a special dimension.[17]

A comparable case might be the conflict between Sinhalese and Tamils in Sri Lanka, which is both ethnic-linguistic and cultural-religious. But even where such parallels exist, the Muslim case is still burdened with the extra weight of its imperial legacy and the semi-theological notion that government over Muslims ought to belong to Muslims. Neither Sinhalese Buddhists nor Tamil Hindus are propelled by such motivations. For them it is a clash between two different nationalities or ethnic groups speaking different languages and professing different religions. They are not conditioned by a sacred law, such as the Islamic *shari'a*, stipulating that their faith cannot be properly lived as long as the rulers follow another faith. Many Muslims believe that Islam is not fully implemented if the government is not in the hands of Muslims, because only they will enforce the *shari'a*. The fact that most Muslim governments do not enforce the *shari'a* either, is a

---

[17] Khalid Duran, "Die Geschichte christlich-islamischer Beziehungen aus muslimischer Sicht," in Jochen Wiezke, ed., *Islam* (Hamburg: Missionswerk der Evang. Kirche, 1986).

different matter. The important thing is that the choice rests with Muslims.[18] Occasionally, though, opinions are voiced that a tolerant non-Muslim government might be preferable to a rule of Muslims who are totally opposed to the *shari'a*. In the sixties and seventies many Turks left home for West Germany because they realized that there they could observe certain *shari'a* injunctions outlawed in Turkey (e.g., the wearing of traditional oriental costumes and headgear, the running of certain types of private religious schools).[19]

Furthermore it goes without saying that the notion of the unicity of religion and state in Islam might be allowed to fall into oblivion when material conditions are particularly favorable and might be jeopardized by an insistence on the *shari'a*. Thus the privileged and prosperous Muslim community of Sri Lanka never entertained any separatist ambitions. The fact that is a small minority of less than 10% played a role too. Incited by Islamist missionaries from abroad, even Sri Lankan Muslims began to demand a partial introduction of the *shari'a* for their community, such as the raising of *zakat* (the traditional Islamic tax for charitable purposes). It is not to be ruled out that a swelling of Sri Lankan Muslim community to 20% or more might have induced them to envision some kind of separatism too. The tendency is universal. While it is usually only a minority within Muslim minorities that nourishes separatist ambitions there is always the likelihood of an increase in times of crisis.

A few examples might serve to further illustrate this phenomenon. Muslim separatistism in Burma and Thailand is essentially ethnic in nature. Burmese Muslims are mostly of Bengali stock, speak Bengali and are concentrated in the area adjacent to Bangladesh. They are a kind of spillover of overpopulated Muslim Bengal into what used to be lesser populated Burma, as in the Indian province of Assam to the north of Bangladesh. The Muslims of Thailand live mostly in the Pattani region bordering on Malaysia. They are Malay by origin, speak Malay and would

---

[18] Khalid Duran, *Re-Islamisierung and Entwicklungspolitik* (Cologne/London: Weltforum Verlag, 1983).

[19] Khalid Duran, "Der Islam in der Diaspora: Europa and Amerika," in W. Ende & U. Steinbach, eds., *Der Islam in der Gegenwart* (Munich: Gerlag C.H. Beck, 1984).

not be citizens of Thailand had not Thai imperial rule expanded southward into Malay areas.

In both cases there is a clash of interests between the ethnic majority, the *Staatsvolk,* and the minority that is linguistically and culturally oppressed, politically outcast, economically exploited and educationally disadvantaged. On top of this, the governments of Burma and Thailand do at times display a kind of Buddhist chauvinism in no way less oppressive then, let us say, the Muslim chauvinism of some Indonesian authorities toward their non-Muslim Chinese citizens.

It is, therefore, difficult to say what factor is more decisive in those minorities' resistance. It seems primarily to be a fight for equal rights in a state dominated by an intolerant ethnic majority. The religious dimension provides a powerful symbolism, often causing the protagonists to believe that it is all about Islam and its survival in a hostile environment. The struggle, then, becomes a *jihad,* a "holy war."

If the Arakan region were to secede from Burma and join Bangladesh or emerge as an independent state, Muslims in other parts of Burma would suffer all the more. They would then be treated as the fifth column of an enemy state. Since there are not many Muslims in other parts of Burma, the problem would not be a huge one. It was, however, an enormous difficulty for Indian Muslims after the establishment of Pakistan. Today, Pakistan has a Muslim population of roughly 100 million. Almost the same number of Muslims continues on the other side of the border as citizens of the Hindu-dominated secular state of India. This is not only the largest Muslim minority anywhere in the world, it is probably the largest of all religious minorities in our age. More than a million Indian Muslims migrated to Pakistan and almost another million died in the bloodshed at the eve of India's partition and the subsequent pogroms.

This migration, one should hold, was an exercise in futility, causing enormous suffering without any gain. Had the Indian Muslims stayed on, the community in India would be stronger and in a better position to maintain its own among the Hindu majority. In Pakistan, the refugees became a burden not only economically, but they also proved to be linguistically and culturally quite different from the "sons of the soil," notwithstanding the uniting bond of the Islamic faith. The Islamic bond had been overestimated. It is, no doubt, strong, but it is not a miracle weapon. Forty years after the establishment of the separate Muslim homeland, those refugees from India, who remained a distinct ethnic group, created their own political party to defend their interests against the indigenous majority population.

The party is called *Muhajir Qaumi Mahaz* ("Refugee National Front"). However, the term *muhajir* has a much deeper meaning than the word refugee. There is a religious connotation to it that provides the clue to understanding the phenomenon of Muslim separatism. A *muhajir* performs a *hijra* (hegira), that is, he migrates from where he lives, and where he cannot practice his religion properly, to another place where he is in a position to live Islam fully. The pattern was provided by the Prophet when he left his beloved Mecca for Medina and set up the first Muslim polity over there. This "flight" or "migration" is called in Arabic *hijra,* and the Prophet and his Companions who migrated in this manner become *muhajrin* – refugees on the path of God, not migrants for worldly gains.

III. A Manichean Partition of the World

The event was taken to be so crucial that it became the Year One of the Islamic calendar, called the *hijri* calendar. Islamic history did not start with the birth of Muhammad, but with his migration for the sake of establishing Islam on sure grounds. Ever since, oppressed Muslims have sought to emulate the "good exemplar" and migrated to safer areas without restrictions on Islamic practice. This concept provided a stimulus for Muslim separatism because it was taken for granted that Muslims left behind in "enemy" territory would come over, being religiously obliged to do so. Many socio-political developments in countries with Muslim populations cannot be properly understood unless these notions are taken cognizance of. They provide the key to the understanding of the Muslim psyche.

For instance, at the beginning of the Afghan war (March 1979 and, more intensely, January 1980) many refugees headed for Pakistan and Iran not just to escape the horrors of war, but because they believed – or were told by their religious leaders – that there was no other way left but to perform *hijra.* Soon resistance leaders realized that such a mass exodus only served abolished by Kemal Ataturk in 1924 only, and ever since there have been several attempts at re-establishing it. Till 1924 most Sunni Muslims used to hold the Friday service in the name of the Ottoman Calpih, even in territories never under Ottoman suzerainty. An exception is Morocco, the king of which holds a position comparable to that of the Ottoman Caliph. In India, too, Muslims used to conduct the Friday service in the name of the Ottoman Caliph. The British aggression against the Ottoman Empire during World War I, therefore, caused a crisis. The "Khilafat Movement" in India was launched with the aim of protecting the Caliphate against the British. Later, Indian Muslims attempted to persuade Kemal Ataturk not to abolish the Caliphate. The abolition of the Caliphate meant that they could no longer conduct their Friday service in the name of the spiritual head of Islam, and therefore, India would no longer be *dar al-islam* and they would then have to perform *hijra.* Many of them, however, have never been fully reconciled to the new circumstances – and this contributed to the creation of Pakistan, even though in Pakistan, too, there is no Caliph in whose name to perform the weekly service.

This *shari'a* legacy engendered a curious phenomenon in some Muslim regions of China where every Friday the weekly service is celebrated, after which the believers perform an ordinary noon prayer as on every other day. They are not sure whether they live in *dar al-islam* or in *dar al-harb.* They do not want to miss the Friday service, which is obligatory. However, since there is no Caliph in whose name to conduct the service, they feel that it might not be valid. To be on the safe side they also perform the daily noon prayer, hoping that at least one of the two will be all right, if not both.

Modern day Muslim laborers in Europe mostly know little or nothing about those ancient concepts of *dar al-islam* and *dar al-harb.* Residual notions, however, persist. Many view their sojourn in a non-Muslim society as a temporary necessity and long to return to sources of purity that become more and more imaginary. Their low social status in the host country prevents them from getting better acquainted with the foreign culture in the midst of which they live. What they get to know are mostly superficialities; large segments of society remain in accessible to them; their knowledge of the people among whom they live remains restricted; they perceive only a few aspects of life in the West. The host country remains largely foreign to them. It is repellent and threatening, because they witness the absorption of their children into this strange world.

The picture looks all too familiar, scarcely different from that of any Chinatown in New York or San Francisco. In the case of Muslims there is always a likelihood of traditionalists reverting to the divisive concepts of old. The community learns from them about *dar al-islam* and *dar al-harb,* age-old terms that acquire a new tangibility. European xenophobia and new racial tensions become all the more explosive once they are made to fit into a religious frame of reference. A laborer from Turkey or Tunisia, on learning that leading West German politicians hold Islam responsible for the resistance to cultural assimilation among those immigrant communities, is prone to discover the meaning of *dar al-harb* afresh, because he actually lives in a world that is not his own, that is hostile to him as a Muslim. He yearns for the *dar al-islam,* an "abode of peace," where he can feel at home. Misery, however, prevents him from returning to his country of origin, unless he is forced to.

Others, more confident of the dependence of affluent societies on immigrant labor, set up islands of *dar al-islam,* self-chosen ghetto communities attempting to be as self-sufficient as possible. They do so by making full use of the legal possibilities offered by Western democracies without subscribing to those democratic norms within the narrow confines of their own communities. This turns their ghettos into virtual bastions of *dar al-islam* within the *dar al-harb.* They now seek to obtain the semi-independence of the Ottoman *millet* system, this time not for non-Muslim communities in an Islamic state but for Muslim communities within a non-Muslim state. Since the host society is not used to Muslim minorities and not prepared for such an eventuality, there is aggressiveness on both sides.

Some such Muslim diaspora communities demand separate schools and the enforcement of their family laws, their law of inheritance etc. Controversies such as the one over the Rushdi affair help to galvanize their

demands.[20]   While the insistence on following their own (*hijri*)
calendar – important because of the holidays – might seem justifiable in a
democratic society, other demands are not. Authoritarian education and the
infringement upon their youngsters' free choice of a professional line or
marriage partner pose serious problems. Most critical are the restrictions on
the freedom of Muslim women, especially the *shari'a* prohibition of girls to
marry non-Muslims.

IV. From Aggressive Proselytizing and Communal Chauvinism To a New sense of Mission

There is no gainsaying the fact that Islam is a missionary religion, with
a sense of mission comparable to that in Christianity. Some Muslims tend to
dispute this, but this is evidently a modern reaction against a concept of
missionary work that has come under fire in a secularized West. It would be
futile to enter into a discussion of minute details such as the question
whether certain missionary practices dear to some Church organizations are
acceptable from an Islamic point of view or not. Over the centuries, Muslim
missionary activities have developed differently in different parts of the
world. Most present-day Muslims are not aware of those rich varieties of
missionary practices within their own tradition. To give just one example,
mention could be made of the Indo-Pakistani type of singing called *qawwali*.
Nowadays it is solely associated with Islamic spiritual values. *Qawwali* are
Sufi songs sung by three or more singers. Only specialists know that this is
based on an old Hindu tradition. Early Muslim missionaries merely changed
the terminology, so that the texts of those songs are now devotionally Islamic
and no longer Hindu.

Qawwali were a potent means whereby large masses of Hindus were
converted to Islam. The instruments to accompany these songs are the tabla
and harmonium – a harmonium adapted to a singer squatting on the ground
rather than standing. This type of harmonium seems indispensable to much
of Indo-Pakistani music. Few people realize that it was introduced only

---

[20] Daniel Pipes, *The Rushdie Affair. The Novel, the Ayatollah, and the West* (New York: Birch Lane, 1990).

around 1800 by Christian missionaries seeking to emulate Muslim missionary practices.

Such observations are stunning to many Muslims who see things only the other way round and believe that Islamic mission has always been blunt and direct, unlike the Christian mission which is considered to be devious and surreptitious. As a result of the colonial experience, many Muslims regard Christian missionary activities as some kind of a subversion, an enticement of people by hook and by crook, camouflage and stealth.

The Islamic sense of mission is expressed in the famous dictum *wa ma 'alaina illa l-balagh* ("our task is only to pass on the message"). In other words, there should be no attempt at brainwashing. The more subtle ways of influencing people in order to prepare them for the message are to be eschewed as unethical. While this is a widely shared belief, there have always been many Muslims who thought differently. To be an effective missionary has been the aim of many who devised all kinds of strategies and tactics indistinguishable from those of their Christian counterparts.

The present-day organizational disadvantage of Muslim missionary work is due primarily to the general backwardness of the societies concerned, but the situation is changing rapidly. Oil-rich states have put enormous sums at the disposal of newly created missionary organizations who are now in a position to recruit well-educated personnel. Seeking to surpass Christian missionaries, they concentrate – just like those – on providing educational and medical facilities.[21] In 1990 Islamic missionary endeavors are still a far cry from their well established Christian counterparts, but it is not to be ruled out that the two might be at par in the not-too-distant future.

The fact that Islamic mission as an organized effort at proselytization at all lags behind Christian missionary activities is due chiefly to the colonial interlude, but not solely so. Another factor is a certain haughtiness and self-conceit that developed during periods of Muslim political supremacy, an attitude to the effect that Muslims felt it below their dignity to win people over. "Truth speaks for itself," was the argument of a ruling community that

---

[21] See such publications as the Saudi daily newspaper *Al-Riyadh,* Nov. 14, 1989: "al-mamlaka takaffalat bi-ta'lim ad-din al-islami..."

regarded it as a privilege to be Muslim. Traces of this attitude can still be found in various parts of the Muslim world, making converts feel ill at ease.[22]

Important in the present context is that both attitudes bear the potential of friction. While the missionary attitude is confrontational, the overbearing posture of the exclusivists is generally discriminatory, not very different from racism or communal antagonisms in places such as Los Angeles or New York. There is manifold divisiveness among Muslims themselves, preventing, e.g., Indian Muslims of East Africa from being one with their native fellows-in-faith, or Arab Muslims in the United States from harmonizing with African-American converts, etc. Given such superiority complexes inherited from an imperial past, it is small wonder that many French people loath Iranian Muslims as self-conceited, or that many Germans complain about the obnoxious self-righteousness of the Turks in their midst.

Hindus ridiculed Muslims for their self-righteousness by saying jestingly "let them set up their Pakistan ('land of the pure')." Muslims responded by actually naming their separate homeland Pakistan – a name necessarily provocative to Indians. Muslims accused Hindus of *Apartheid*, but ended up by responding in kind instead of ridding themselves of the attitudes they originally revolted against.

All the same, Islamic religion – or "normative" Islam – provides ample scope for a concept of mission adjustable to a pluralist society. Expanding the aforementioned dictum that "we have no other obligation but to pass on the message," Muslims would quote such verses from Al-Qur'an as "We sent you but as a conveyor of the glad tidings and as a warner," or "You are not to dictate them."[23]

From there it is not far to the other central theme of Al-Qur'an, namely, humanity's responsibility for this world, its mission as God's vicegerent – humanity as the administrator (Calpih) of the earth. This is a broader sense of mission and a more essential one than that of mere

---

[22] This observation is based on some two dozen interviews with converts from various countries.

[23] Al-Qur'an III, p. 144; VII, pp. 184, 188; XV, p. 89.

proselytizing. Muhammad Iqbal emphasized this central notion in his famous *Reconstruction of Religious Thought in Islam*,[24] and Ali Shari'ati, the intellectual pathfinder of Shi'ite resurgence in Iran, did likewise.[25]

As such, there is no inherent inability in Islam to conceive of mission as something above and beyond proselytizing. The difficulty lies with an onerous historical legacy that has come to be misunderstood as Islam per se. It would be patently wrong to gloss over this formidable obstacle to pluralism. Muslims need to be made aware of disparities between their faith and their practice. This will remain difficult as long as education remains the privilege of a few percent of the population, with the standards of religious education, moreover, on the decline.

V. Secularism Needs a Second Start

Relations between Muslims and non-Muslims might be vastly improved if secularism were to be given a second try. Indonesia, Iraq, Syria and Turkey are the only countries in the world of Islam that are avowedly secularist, apart from the large minority of Muslims in India and the near-majority in Nigeria. In all of these states, secularism has been discredited by a variety of factors.

Indonesia is perhaps the least critical, but also the least typical case. Many Indonesian Muslims are only superficially Islamized. They subscribe to the basic tenets of Islam, but rarely in an exclusivist manner, while their lifestyle is scarcely affected by the Middle Eastern patterns of behavior that accompany the *shari'a*. Indonesian Muslims may be more devout than their coreligionists in various other countries, yet they are generally less cut off from their roots in indigenous traditions. Significantly, a fundamentalist insurrection called itself *dar al-islam*, because Islamists feel that Indonesia has yet to be properly Islamized. Although it is the state with the largest Muslim population in the world, Indonesia has remained, in many ways, a rimland of the realm of Islam – different from India (Pakistan) which

---

[24] Muhammad Iqbal, *The Reconstruction of Religious Thought in Islam* (Lahore/London: Muhammad Ashraf, 1930), Chapter I.

[25] Ali Shari'ati, *On the Sociology of Islam,* translated from Persian by Hamid Algar (Berkeley: Mizan Press, 1979).

the interests of the Russians and began to encourage their compatriots to stay on in Afghanistan as long as humanly possible. The millions that crossed over into the neighboring countries then did so merely for the sake of physical survival without even a chance to dream of spiritual bliss. However, the initial impulse to flee was provided by the age-old pattern of *hijra* and the Afghans in Pakistan are called *muhajirin,* whereas political refugees without a religious motivation are called *panahgir.*

A century earlier Muslims fled in the other direction-from what is now Pakistan (then British India) to Afghanistan, because some of their leaders held the view that India under infidel rule was no longer a place for Muslims to live. Tens of thousands migrated to Afghanistan, with most of them perishing on the way through what was then a desolate wilderness.

The concept of *hijra* cannot be fully understood without reference to the *Manichean* division of the world that developed fairly early in Muslim history and found its way into the *shari'a,* the ancient law of Islam that became sacrosanct to many Muslims. The Manichean partition of the world envisions an "abode of peace" (*salam, islam*) and an "abode of war" (*harb*). A *muhajir* performs the *hijra* from the *dar al-harb* to the *dar al-islam.*

Many a time Muslims were locked in dispute whether to declare a certain territory as *dar al-harb* and make *hijra* incumbent upon the believers or not. A typical example is the above-mentioned case of British India. Only a minority among Muslims decided for *hijra;* the majority came round to the comforting view that since the British did not prevent Muslims from practicing their religion, there was no justification for declaring India to be *dar al-harb* and to migrate to the nearest part of *dar al-islam* (Afghanistan). The same controversy erupted from the establishment of Pakistan when the majority of Indian Muslims was convinced by their leaders, such as the Minister of Education, Abu l-Kalam Azad, that they could live in India as in *dar al-islam.* It was a difficult proposition for those suffering frequent pogroms that made India look like a real *dar al-harb* to them. All the same, it was still the most reasonable option in a situation altogether desperate.

According to the *shari'a,* a major criterion for a territory being either *dar al-islam* or *dar al-harb* is the freedom to hold the weekly service (Friday) in the name of the Caliph as the supreme Muslim leader. The Caliphate was changed from a rimland into a heartland, replacing, in more than one way, the Arab world and Turkey as the core of Muslimhood.

Indonesian secularism, Enshrined in the "Five Principles" (*pancha sila*) of the state's constitution, is special in that it postulates belief in God. It does not postulate adherence to a given religion, but rejects atheism. In principle, this should be acceptable to Muslims, and indeed, it has been hailed by many, because Al-Qur'an calls upon other believers to join Muslims on a common platform, namely, the worship of God. Al-Qur'an appeals to all believers with the words "let us get together on a word between us (dialogue)."[26]

Indonesian secularism, thus, is different from secularism elsewhere, as for instance in India and Turkey, which adopted the Western concept of the state's neutrality with regard to religion. And yet, Indonesian Islamists object to it because they hold that since the overwhelming majority of Indonesians are Muslims, the country should be turned into an "Islamic State," a concept of which there extist at least two dozen different definitions.[27] Many Muslims traditionalists demand that Indonesia should, at least, declare Islam to be the religion of state, as is the case in most Muslim majority countries that are not "Islamic States" in the Islamist sense. This controversy, which has sometimes deteriorated into insurrections on some of the islands, is almost exclusively religiously motivated, though envy against the wealthy Chinese minority plays a role just as much as fear of the disproportionate influence in public affairs of a Christian minority which is ahead in education.

Indonesian Muslim traditionalists and Islamists might gladly have subscribed to the state ideology of *pancha sila* had Muslims been a minority in Indonesia. In any event, the majority of Indonesian Muslims seems to stick to *pancha sila,* and the concept has been generally beneficial to all communities, liberal Muslims just as much as Christians and other minorities.

Turkey is a kind of counter pole in the sense that *laiklik* (laicism) as enshrined in the Turkish constitution goes beyond the secularism of most

---

[26] Al-Qur'an III, p. 64.

[27] Khalid Duran, *Islam und politischer Extremismus* (Hamburg: DOI, 1985).

Western states, because it imposes certain restrictions upon the religious practice of government servants, who are not allowed to attend religious functions while in office or to perform prayers in their office precincts, a common practice in other Muslim countries. Restrictions on religious education have been abandoned, but there are strong resentments among many Turks against *laiklik* because of the severity with which it was originally enforced and maintained by more or less dictatorial military regimes.[28]

The "Socialist Party of Arab Rebirth" (*Baath*) ruling in Iraq and Syria is secularist, aiming at uniting all Arabs regardless of their adherence to Islam or Christianity or other sects and heterodoxies as well as atheist ideologies. Both regimes, however, rose to power through military coups, lack a sufficiently large popular base and have been at times several repressive. This has discredited secularism and allowed Islamists to become the strongest force of opposition.[29]

Opposition to secularism is widespread and not limited to the Islamists. Even liberals and reform theologians tend to reject it as something pertaining exclusively to the intellectual development of Western Christianity. Not even Sudan's radical humanist, Mahmoud Muhammad Taha (d. 1985), was prepared to profess secularism, although from the viewpoint of a political scientist his ideas would have to classified as secularist.[30] Iqbal branded secularism Machiavellism, because he too understood it as the separation of politics from ethics.[31]

The understanding of secularism as unethical politics might have been generated by a school of radical secularists in England, headed by George Holyoake, who were uncompromisingly anti-religious. The crux of the matter, however, seems to be the problematic translation of the term, as well

---

[28] Khalid Duran, "Ataturk's Laicism in the Light of Muslim History", in Sencer Tongue, ed., *The Reforms of Ataturk* (Istanbul: RCD Cultural Institute, 1975).

[29] Khalid Duran, *Islam und politischer Extremismus* (Hamburg: DOI, 1985), documentation pp. 33-38.

[30] Mahmoud Mohamed Taha, *The Second Message if Islam,* translated from Arabic by Abdullahi An-Na'im, (Syracuse University Press, 1987).

[31] Muhammad Iqbal, *Jawab-e Shikwa* (Lahore: Muhammad Ashraf, 1944).

as the fact that it was introduced into the Arab world by Christians with socialist tendencies, such as Salama Musa in Egypt in the 1930s.

In Arabic, "secularist" is sometimes rendered as 'alamani, making it look like "worldly" (from 'alam), or "this worldly" as opposed to "other worldly"–which does indeed come close to the original Latin saeculum (century = age = world). Sometimes "secularist" is translated as 'ilmani, which denotes something like "scientific" or "scientistic," smacking of "materialistic." It has also been translated as la dini ("irreligious"). This is how it appeared in Urdu, a language spoken by some 150 million people. No wonder, then, that secularism was not well received. Secularists such as Abu l-Kalam Azad in India, one of Islam's towering religious thinkers in this century, translated secularism as "neutrality in religious affairs" (madhabi ghair-janibdari). However, while Azad is hailed for his superb translation of Al-Qur'an, Pakistanis declared him a political outcast because he remained faithful to his ideal of an undivided India. New Delhi's espousal of secularism has always been derided by Islamabad as fake.

Pakistan understands itself as an ideological state analogous to Israel because both countries lay claim to a religious scripture as the basis for their statehood. Under the military dictatorship of General Zia ul-Haq (1977-88), the propagation of secularism became a punishable offense. The founding father of the state, Muhammad 'Ali Jinnah (d. 1948), was quite explicit in his profession of secularism. The Islamist dictatorship, therefore, issued a decree prohibiting Pakistanis from "misconstruing" Jinnah's statements as expressions of secularist intent. In Islamist propaganda, "Secularism, Zionism, Communism" became a trinity of evil. There are numerous volumes by Islamist writers solely with the purpose of combating secularism. Few Muslims have dared to refute that kind of propaganda with religious arguments. Nationalist parties ruling in Egypt and Tunisia do in actual fact adhere to a secularist conception of state, and yet the issue is rarely discussed in a direct manner.

The separation of East Pakistan from West Pakistan and the creation of the independent state of Bangladesh in 1971 made matters worse because the Bengalis fought their Pakistani brethern-in-faith under the banner of secularism, translated in Bangla as dharma niropekkhota ("non-interference in religious affairs"). This was to assure the Hindu minority that in an independent Bangladesh the Muslim majority would no longer discriminate against non-Muslim citizens, with the hope that Muslims in the neighboring Indian state of West Bengal would likewise no longer face discrimination by the Hindu majority there.

Secularism was enshrined as a principle of state in the first constitution of independent Bangladesh. The new nation, however, survived only thanks to generous financial aid from Saudi Arabia and Kuwait. The Arab coreligionists saw to it that secularism was soon dropped. It no longer figures as a principle in the revised constitution of Bangladesh, but surfaces whenever the songs of the 1971 *mukti bahini* ("freedom fighters") are played – battle songs which glorify secularism.

Under the constraints of the colonial situation some Muslim leaders did understand the benefits of secularism as a means of achieving the best possible *modus vivendi* with non-Muslims. The leader of the Moroccan nationalist movement, 'Allal Al-Fasi, who also was a scholar of religion and a reformist thinker, analyzed secularism as being in the interest of Muslims, especially in French-ruled Algeria.[32] All the same, he failed to realize the need for secularism as a means of protecting Muslims against themselves, or, more precisely, of protecting some Muslims against some others – not to speak of secularism as a protection of non-Muslims from Muslims. After independence the plight of several non-Muslim minorities became less and less enviable. To be sure, this was due mostly to nationalistic motivations and less to religious bigotry. However, for the people concerned what counts are the practical effects on their lives, not the rationale behind one or the other government decree.

With a Muslim diaspora in Western Europe soon numbering seven million, Islam has become an important factor in Western life. Everywhere Muslim communities are clamoring for equal rights and want to see their religion recognized at a par with the Christian denominations and Judaism. In order to achieve those rights, they make full use of secularist constitutions. The host communities rarely refuse them those constitutional rights. At the

---

[32] 'Allal Al-Fasi, *An-naqd adh-dhati* (Teuan, 1951).

same time, however, the demand for reciprocity is raised more and more vociferously. The increasing inter-penetration of different national societies and religious communities has created new conditions that make such reciprocity incumbent upon communities less and less homogenous. The Muslim argument that secularism is not a homespun device, that the very term as such is foreign to Islamic vocabulary, makes little sense. The term secularism is new to the West too. It is a highly technical term of recent coinage, a concept not understandable unless explained and commented upon. A few Muslim scholars have indeed understood this and endeavored to make it accessible by interpreting it within an Islamic frame of reference.[33] Much depends on a resumption of those seminal efforts, against the heavy odds of bigotry and chauvinism.

---

[33] Sayyid Qudrat-Allah Fatimi, *Pakistan Movement and Kemalist Revolution* (Lahore: Insitutie of Islamic Culture, 1977). Hichem Djait, *La personnalite et le devenir arabo-islamique* (Paris: Editions du Seuil, 1972), Mohammed 'Aziz Lahbabi, *Le personnalisme musulman* (Paris: Presses Universitaires de France, 1967).

POSSIBILITIES AND CONDITIONS FOR A BETTER UNDERSTANDING BETWEEN ISLAM AND THE WEST[*]

·Mohamed Talbi[**]

An Old Antagonism Still Very Much Alive

"To try to analyze the historical relations between Islam and Christianity," wrote Simon Jargy, "in both their religious and sociopolitical components, is to come up immediately against one preliminary fact: although the three great religions of the monotheist faith came from the same roots, they developed separately from each other. They have not supplemented but rather opposed each other in a perpetual conflict."[1]

---

[*] *Journal of Ecumenical Studies*, 25:2, (Spring, 1988).

[**] Mohamed Talbi (Muslim) is Professor Emeritus of the Arts and Sciences Faculty of the University of Tunis in Tunisia, where he served from 1966 to 1970 as Dean, having begun teaching there in 1958. From 1973 to 1977, he directed the History Department at the Centre d'Etudes et de Recherches Economiques et Sociales in Tunis. He has been president of the National Cultural Committee of Tunisia since 1983, and editor of *Cahiers de Tunisie (Revue de Sciences Humaines)* since 1969. He holds a doctorate in history from the Sorbonne (1968), and has received numerous honors; including the Lukas Prize for Outstanding Contribution to Interreligious Amity (Protestant Theological Faculty of the University of Tübingen, 1985), Officier de la Légion d'Honneur (France, 1983), and Officier du mérite Culturel (Tunsia, 1980). He has published a great many articles in journals, books, and encyclopedias, as well as nine books of his own, including *Islam et Dialogue* (Tunis, 1972), *Ibn Khaldun et l'Histoire* (Tunis, 1973), *Manhajjiyat Ibn Khaldun al-Ta' rikhiya* (Beirut, 1981), and *Etudes d'Histoire Ifriqiyenne et de Civilisation Musulmans Médiévale* (Tunis, 1982). He has also participated in many conferences and congresses throughout the world.

[1] Simon Jargy, *Islam et Chrétienté* (Geneva: Labor et Fides, 1981), p. 10.

In this vein, Claire Brière and Oliver Carré have entitled a recent book *Islam, Guerre à l'Occident?* (Islam, War on the West?).[2] The question mark doubtless weakens the threat by placing it within the realm of possibility but without any absolute certainty. The question hangs suspended like a sword of Damocles. This is certainly the picture that will linger in the reader's mind. Concerning Islam, one will only recall the features of Ayyub, a "Muslim Brother" who is a French convert – the wolf already in the fold!-or those of the Egyptian Muhammad 'Abd as-Salam Faraj, the theoretician of murderous violence and Sadat's assassin. The book by Jean-Pierre Péroncel-Hugoz, *Le Radeau de Mahomet* (Muhammad's Raft),[3] is reassuring. A *raft* that is not made fast to "a living civilization, something that Islam now lacks,"[4] is less frightening, even if it is driven by troubled and stormy seas.

Yet, who would have said it? Who would have believed it? "Ten years ago, no one talked about Islam or Khomeini, who was then preaching at Nadjaf in Iraq and was nothing but an old man in exile."[5] Everything was so quiet! Had not the sick man been buried a long time ago? For his part, Khomeini, who has wrongly became a symbol of Islam as a whole, considers the West responsible for all the misfortunes of the Muslims, from the time Islam was founded in Medina down to the colonial era, which, although it has ceased to be a source of military humiliation and the direct cause of economic spoliation, nonetheless continues to exist in more subtle and even more pernicious ways. A decade ago, he wrote:

> From its very beginning, Islam has clashed with Judaism, and the Jews were the first to engage in anti-Islamic propaganda and attacks that, as you can confirm, have never been interrupted down to our days. Subsequently, and for more than three centuries, certain groups, in a sense even more diabolical than the Jews, have infiltrated Muslim countries as colonizers. In the hope of satisfying their colonial ambitions,

---

[2] Claire Brière and Oliver Carré, Islam, Guerre à l'Occident? (Paris: Autrement, 1983).

[3] Jean-Pierre Péroncel-Hugoz, *Le Radeau de Mahomet* (Paris: Lieu Commun, 1983).

[4] *Ibid.*, p. 204.

[5] Brière and Carré, *Islam, Guerre*, p. 9.

they have judged it advisable to prepare the way for the annihilation of Islam.[6]

The question arises whether this misunderstanding between Islam and the West is a congenital vice that is latent, so to speak, in the historical genes of the two societies and the two cultures and, therefore, something wholly inevitable. Has there only been, and is there still only, misunderstanding, or are there some possibilities for a better understanding and, if so, subject to what conditions? This is the problem before us.

Two Models of Society that are Profoundly different from the Very Beginning

If we want to correct misunderstandings objectively, we have to recognize frankly that they are neither without some foundation in fact nor without certain deep-lying roots. The foundations on which the two edifices rest reveal options that have been diametrically opposed from their very beginning – hence, their distinctly divergent social architectures and differences, which have only become more pronounced with time. The historical texture, to be sure, is very complex in both cases. The West, secular today, has not been innocent of theocratic forms of power in the past[7] – based, in particular, on the famous quarrel of the two swords – and in Islam, which has always refused to become secularized,[8] the share of the

---

[6] Ruhollah Khomeini, *Pour un gouvernment islamique,* tr. M. Kotobi and B. Simon, with O. Banisadre (Paris: Fayolee, 1979), p. 10.

[7] See Marcel Pacaut, *La Théocratie, l'eglise et le pouvoir au moyen âge* (Paris: Aubier, 1957). This temptation in the direction of theocracy has not entirely disappeared. As O. Carré rightly observed: "Obviously, it can be said that Islam has something that is peculiar to itself in that, unlike Christianity, it is inseparably a religion and a government. In its original principles, this is undoubtedly true. In history, however, religion and government are always very closely interlaced, in Christianity as well as in the Muslim empire. And, in our own time, the 'Marxist Christianities,' the 'Christians for socialism' in Brazil or in France, and the Polish Catholic Church, for example, also know very well, like the Muslim brothers, how to be *logical* in their faith down to the most committed, and even violent, political actions" (Brière and Carré, *Islam, Guerre,* p. 176).

[8] With the exception of Turkey, 'Ali'Abd al-Raziq (b. 1888), in his treatise *al-Islam wa-usul al-hukm,* published in Cairo in 1925 just after the abolition of the caliphate, tried to justify the separation of Islam and the state. This led to a lively reaction, especially on the part of Rasid Rida, and he was deprived of his chair in the theological university of al-Azhar. His book has been translated into French by Léon Bercher under the title *L. 'Islam et les bases du pouvoir in the Revue des Etudes Islamiques* (Paris) (1933), pp. 353-390, and (1934), pp. 163-222. See Erwin Isak Jakob Rosenthal, *Islam in the Modern National State* (Cambridge, U.K.:

spiritual element in the administration of the state is steadily and remorselessly receding like the famous "skin of sorrow" (*peau de chagrin*). However, through the tangled influences, borrowings, and adjustments dictated by contingencies, the archaeologist of cultures and civilizations can easily discover two models of society that are fundamentally opposed in their basic outlines.

In the Western scheme, from the beginning, the leading idea behind the control of sociopolitical space was based on the separation of two very distinct realms: that of Caesar, and that of God. Under the circumstances, when announcing his Reign, Jesus had hardly any other choice but to take account of the very definite and indelible frontiers of Caesar's empire. In the case of Islam, the ground was initially virgin, so to speak, and did not impose any particular constraint on the architect: hence the option of a strongly integrated sociopolitical structure, without any private sector. Muhammad did not find himself confronted with any Caesar at Medina but was free to do as he liked. The *sahifa*,[9] the charter or constitution of Medina – the first

---

Cambridge University Press, 1965), pp. 85-102 and index; Malcolm H. Kerr, *Islamic Reform* (Berkeley: University of California Press, 1966), pp. 179-180; and Abdallah Laroui, *L'idéologie arabe contemporaine* (Paris: Éd. Francois Maspero, 1967), p. 24. The ideas of 'Ali'Abd al-Raziq are echoed by our contemporary, Muhammad Ahmad Khalaf-Allah in *Al-Qur'an wa-l-Dawla*, 2nd ed. (Beirut, 1981); and in *Al-Quran wa mushkilat hayatina almu'astra* (Beirut, 1982). *See idem, Al-Islam al-Din wa-l-Islam al-Dawla in Al-Turath wa-l-amal al-siyasi*, Actes du Colloque de Rabat (25-27 November 1982) Montreuli, France: Tipe, 1984), pp. 97-103. See also in the review *Al-Wahda*, No. 1 (October, 1984), *Al-Mawdu 'iyya al-diniyya*, pp. 121-126. All these studies emphasize the fact that the form taken by power in Islam is not theocratic, which is true. In particular, the caliphate has no foundation in scripture. It is nonetheless true that Muslim society has to be governed according to the principles of the Revealed Law (*Shar'*), and sometimes very specific provisions are found in it (concerning heritages, marriage, divorce, penal sanctions, etc.). While Islam is not theocratic, it is undoubtedly nomocratic, with imposed limits on secularism. See Mohamed Talbi, "Les structures et les charactéristiques de l'Etat islamique traditionnel," in the Official Documents of the International Symposium on La Vision Morale et Politique de l'Islam, held by UNESCO in Paris, December 7-19, 1982.

[9] Concerning this *sahifa*, consult Muhammad Hamidullah, *Le prophète de l'Islam* (Paris: J. Vrin, 1959), vol. 1, pp. 124-137. See also R. B. Serjeant, "The Sunnah Jami'ah, Pacts with the Yathrib Jews, and the Tahrim of Yathrib: Analysis and Translation of the Documents Comprised in the So-Called 'Constitution of Medina,'" *Bulletin of the School of Oriental and African Studies*, vol. 41, part 1 (1978), pp. 1-42; and U. Rubin, "The 'Constitution of Medina.' Some Notes," *Studia Islamica*, vol. 62 (1985), pp. 5-23. Muhammad Ahmad Khalaf-Allah, who had not thought of the famous saying of Jesus, "Render therefore to Caesar the things that are Caesar's and to God the things that are God's" (Mt. 22:21), has written: "The Qur'an is the

piece of writing of its kind in the annals of history – therefore traced the rough outline of a state in which the respective parts of the temporal and spiritual powers were fairly balanced, without there being any watertight partition between them. There was no dichotomy in human beings or in their sociopolitical extensions. The oneness of the creed was matched by the oneness of the *umma*. "The Community, which is your own, is a single community, and I am your Lord. Worship me!" (Qur'an, XXI, 92).

The *shari'a*, the code of life drawn up by the *faqihs*, modeled the features of traditional Muslim society in great detail and at all levels of the public and private sectors. There was nothing like this in Christianity, where – with the exception of the very restricted field of cannon law, especially concerning the annulment of the marriage ties – legislation has been primarily inspired by natural law. This falls within the realm of Caesar. In Islam, one might judge matters in the light of Revelation. "Those who do not judge in accordance with what God has revealed" are described as *kafirun* (deniers or rejecters) (Qur'an, V, 44), *zalimun* (unjust) (Qur'an, V, 45), and *fasiqun* (perverse) (Qur'an, V, 47).[10] Christianity, which shaped the origins of Western society and to a large extent still serves as its inspiration, has placed its emphasis, outside of its theological and cultural aspects, primarily on ethics. Islam, on the other hand, which is law-oriented, is at the same time a religion, code, ethical system, society, and culture. It is a whole. At all levels, the Muslim lives constantly with God.

The return to the *shari'a*, therefore, is a fundamental demand made by all Islamic movements, no matter what their tendencies. This demand is so strong at the basic level that many countries such as Pakistan, the Sudan, and

---

first Celestial Book, and also the last Celestial Book, which puts an end to the theocratic state and gives rise to the modern state, to the state that is presided over by a president elected by the people and not chosen by Heaven, and this is the state that is described in modern times as a democratic state" (in *Al-Qur'an wa mushkilat,* p. 31). We might recall that democracy has its own antecedents in antiquity, Greek in particular, and that historically it was introduced, in the present day, in the countries of Islam under European influences. The position taken by Khalaf-Allah falls within the framework of an *ijtihad* – which is still not an *ijma'* – which attempts to justify it by a satisfactory interpretation of the sources, the Qur'an in particular. We might add that democracy is not necessarily secularism.

[10] See also the Qur'an, V, 42, 48, and 49, where the Prophet is invited to decide questions justly according to what has been revealed by God; some opponents refused to accept his decision (XXIV, 48).

Mauritania – not to mention Saudi Arabia and Iran – have had to yield to it. Today, the problem of the *shari'a* can no longer be evaded. Under the auspices of the Islamic Conference Organization, an organ[11] has recently been created to discuss the matter. This kind of organ is not likely to arrive at quick and revolutionary solutions until its path has been properly smoothed by many free and independent studies by courageous writers who are indisputably Muslim, so as to ensure their credibility. Between the secular solution of the Turkish type – unthinkable today in countries with a large Muslim majority – and a mere return to the "codes" drawn up during the third century (of the Hijrah = ninth century c.e.), there is a middle way of a true *ijtihad* (applied reasoning), a genuine effort toward adaptation and interpretation which will really make it possible to judge the problems of our time in a modern and realistically progressive spirit, without missing the mark or yielding to recession and in accordance with "what God has revealed." This is a commonplace idea that has been run through the mill repeatedly without ever producing any really practical, tangible results. It seems that whenever Islam is tentatively feeling after its way and the West becomes disturbed, solutions for our troubles are sought in divergent directions, in accordance with the basically contrary schemes that determined the axial configuration of the two societies: secularism on one hand and loyalty to the *shari'a* on the other. However, if dialogue is to have any meaning and if we are really to profit by our differences instead of passively and negatively enduring their consequences, Islam must realize that there is an ineradicable Caesar-side to every person that is indispensable for the creative dynamics of history, while the West must realize that Caesar is also only a human being and that, as such, he is in the final analysis subordinate to God, the true Ruler of everything that exists (*Malik al-mulk*) (Qur'an, III, 26), who is the source of all being and all power.

---

[11] This organ, in the present case an Academy of Fiqh, has its headquarters in Jidda, Saudi Arabia. It is directed by a Tunisian, Habib Belkodja, who assumed office in early October, 1984.

Another feature of the profound difference between Islam and the West is the situation of women[12] in the two societies. From the beginning, Muslim society opted for sexual segregation;[13] Western society, for integration. This is still visible to the naked eye in the urban and rural fabric of both societies, despite modern developments and changes that have blurred their original forms and outlines. What is more, these developments, once thought final and irreversible, are now once more coming into question. Is there any sound reason for sexual segregation? Is wearing the veil a strict religious obligation for a born-free Muslim woman?[14] At the beginning of the twentieth century, the battle was raging between feminists and modernists on one hand and anti-feminists and conservatives on the other. The modernists seemed definitely to have won, which opened a breach in the wall separating the two societies. Now, however, we see the black Iranian *chador* or *himar* once more in favor and becoming more common instead of disappearing quietly. For Muslim women, the return to primeval sources, advocated by Islamists, often takes the form of a voluntary, more-or-less-definite return to the *gynaeceum,* that is, to the original social model. As far as the founding principles, if not always the facts, are concerned, two worlds continue to be in direct opposition to each other in their social options with respect to one major problem, that of women: a *legally* mixed society in

---

[12] The bibliography is only too full. We might mention the following: *La femme,* Recucils de la Société Jean Bodin, vol. 11 (Brussels, 1959), and vol. 12 (Brussels, 1962); Nawal al-Sa'dawi, *al-Mar'a wa-l-jins* (Cairo, 1972); 'Ismat al-Din Karkar, *al-Mar'a min khilal al-ayat al-qur 'aniya* (Tunis, 1979); Eric Fuchs, *Le désir et la tendresse, sources et histoire d'une éthique chrétienne de la sexualité it du mariage* (Paris, 1979; Moulay Rachid Abderrazak, *La condition de la femme au Maroc* (Rabat: Fac. des sciences juridiques, économiques et socials 1981), mimeographed; C. R. in Ibia, no. 153 (Tunis, 1984), pp. 163-168; Souad Charter, *La Femme Tunisienne, citoyenne ou sujet* (Tunis, 1975).

[13] A recent article entitled "al-ikhjilat" (coeducation) points out that "our religion strictly [*qati*] forbids women to mingle with men...and that the male and female sexes should be separated in education, in public places, and everywhere else [*wa fi kulli makan*)..."(*Al-Madina* [a leading newspaper in Saudi Arabia], no 2392 [October 3, 1984], p.7). The *Muslim World* (a Karachi weekly), no. 30 (February 2, 1985), under the headline, "Kuwaiti students demand ban on co-education," stated: "The union urged the government to ban or restrict co-education and mingling of men and women at colleges and the Kuwaiti University."

[14] According to the traditional *fiqh,* women of a servile condition are forbidden to wear the veil, which polarized sexuality in the Middle Ages around the *jariya,* the prime figure of the anti-wife and heroine of erotic poetry.

which women appear in public with uncovered faces, and a society that is, *in principle,* segregationist, in which women, under the traditional code of the *fiqh,* show themselves only when clad in the *himar.* The female form, whether veiled or unveiled, thus becomes the symbol of two irreconcilable ethical systems whose respective champions can only engage in a dialogue of the deaf, whether their words are laudatory or reproving. Only the future can tell which will prevail.

The differences are no less great with respect to the original family model, although modern transformations have greatly altered, on both sides, the original picture in this field as well. Unlike Christianity,[15] Islam[16] has no prejudice against sexuality. Sexual pleasure, within the bounds of lawful unions, is sought for its own sake as a natural and healthy activity for every living being. Nor is there anything in Islam opposed to the dissolution of marriage[17] – which considered a contract between two partners, not a sacrament – although such a dissolution is strongly deprecated as being "among lawful things the most hateful in God's eyes" (*abghadu l-halal ila Allah*). However, in order to safeguard morality and to ensure a certain stability for the family, Islam grants the man a "degree" of primacy (*daraja*) (Qur'an, II, 228) over the women.[18] The *faqihs* justify this primacy by all kinds of socioeconomic conditions, which were very real in traditional

---

[15] For the traditional church, "sexual pleasure is a sinful pain," as the holy pope, Gregory the Great, said (quoted in *Pro Mundi Vita Dossiers* [Brussels], no. 3 [1983], p. 4, n. 4). For the church Fathers, "marriage, which habituates one to sensual pleasures, that 'pus' of the soul, can only represent a downfall" (see Marie-Odile Métral, *Le mariage, les hésitations de l'Occident* [Paris: Aubier Montaigne, 1977], p. 320).

[16] See the thesis by Adelwahab Bouhdiba, *Sexuality in Islam,* tr. Alan Sheridan (London and Boston: Routledge and Kegan Paul, 1985; *La Sexualité en Islam* (Paris: P.U.F., 1975).

[17] See the excellent 35 pp. file prepared by *Pro Mundi Vita* of the problems posed to the Christian conscience by divorce (*Dossiers,* no. 3 [1983]).

[18] The original Christian position is hardly different. Christianity and Islam assert "the equality of men and women before salvation," but this has no social implication. Concerning Christianity, we read in ibid., p. 5, n. 8, that "the principle of equality did not have its present meaning: it was part of a natural hiearchy in which the woman's place was subordinate to the man...there had to be a 'reasonable subordination of the woman to the man' because 'authority' is necessary and the man 'is the one most capable of exercising it.'" As for the *Dictionnaire de droit canonique* (Paris: Letouzey, 1953), under the article "Woman," it defines the legal situation of women in the Roman Catholic Church with two words, "inferiority" and "incapacity." This argument is fully comparable with that of the traditional Islamic *fiqh.*

society, as well as by physiological conditions. This primacy is particularly evident in polygamy – today prohibited in Turkey and Tunisia and subject to more-or-less-severe restrictions in the other Islamic countries – and in the right of unilateral repudiation (also abolished in Tunsia) for the benefit of the husband, provided there is no provision to the contrary in the marriage contract.[19] We might also mention female circumcision, a pre-islamic practice preserved as *makruma* (commendable), which is unknown in the Maghreb (North Africa) but widely practiced in other Islamic countries (for example, on eighty-five percent of all Egyptian women[20]) and intended "to weaken [*taltif*] the female sexual appetite."[21] Nevertheless, Muslim women have always enjoyed much freedom in the management and disposal of all their personal property, without any control by their husbands, contrary to Western women, who did not acquire the same rights until quite recently. The Islamists lay much stress on these advantages.

The social fabric is naturally projected into the urban fabric. As a result, in the traditional Muslim city, "the home, with its various room and buildings, is almost always arranged around an inside courtyard and opens onto this courtyard. In this respect it differs essentially from the cities of Europe."[22] Muslim city-planning, a projection of the social order, is distinguished by the use of enclosed areas that serve as a refuge for domestic life from the "indiscreet glances of intruders. This concern for total intimacy, for confinement so to speak, as a reflection of Muslim organization of the

---

[19] Women were able to include a clause in their marriage contracts granting them the same rights as their husbands in case they were repudiated. See the notarial formulas in the marriage contract preserved for us by Ibn al-'Attar, *Kitab al-watha'iq wa-l-sijillat* (Madrid: P. Chalmeta and F. Corriente, 1983), pp. 7-19.

[20] The percentage was mentioned by Péroncel-Hugoz in *Le Radeau*, pp. 178-179. This high percentage can be explained by the fact that Egypt belonged to the school of al-fiqh al-Shafi'i (150-204/767-820). In Sunnism, in fact, only this school considers circumcision a religious obligation that must be strictly observed (*wajib*). See al-Sharabasi, *Yas'chunaka*, 3rd ed. (Beirut, 1980), vol. 2, pp. 31-32.

[21] Al-Sharabasi, Yas'alunaka, vol. 1, p. 254.

[22] E. Wirth, "Villes Islamiques" in *La Ville Arabe dans l'Islam*, Actes du Colloque de Carthage-Amilcar (March 12-18, 1979), under the direction of Al Bouhdiba and D. Chevallier (Tunis, 1982), p. 196.

family, is evident in both the city block and the individual house."[23] Their quarters thus easily take on the cell-like forms in which blind alleys, practically unknown in the West, along with houses that avoid looking out on each other, constitute the privileged capillaries of a selective circulatory system aimed solely at acting as a screen against passers-by.

So, the misunderstandings between Islam and the West are not the product of mere chance or the result of miscellaneous and transitory facts but are deeply rooted in quite different or frankly contradictory social options. They are reflections of oppositions with respect to dogma, ethics, culture, and civilization, and as such they are to be found on the same level as basic identifications. In spite of infiltration, interference, and the very recent and superstructural Westernization in Islam of wide social strata, they continue to underlie the judgments and discourses on the other, as well as both individual and overall reactions. These misunderstandings help to compose the standard image that each society forms of the other in its own mirror.

Playing with Mirrors

These mirrors are naturally those of the greatest number of the people, that majority that is both flattered and conditioned by the media and the best-selling books – without there necessarily being any *a priori* ill will. This conditioning is, in fact, reciprocal, and cannot be otherwise in a world where the written word is a commodity subject to the structures of the market, that is, to the pressure of the laws of supply and demand. The power to correct the image, which in principle is held by the specialists and elites, is particularly limited by the fact that it is subject to a two-fold difficulty: first, the market structure does not encourage the penetration of a commodity that goes against the stream; second, the specialists themselves, in all sincerity, do not succeed completely in escaping from the impact of the ideas around them. Without going so far as the pessimism of Claire *Brière*, who says "it is useless to speak of dialogue when nobody speaks the truth,"[24] we must honestly admit that bringing about a better understanding is an arduous and,

---

[23] A. Daoulatli, *Tunis sous les Hafsides* (Tunis, 1976), p. 34.

[24] Brière and Carré, *Islam, Guerre*, p. 130.

above all, a long-term task. It calls for asceticism and perseverance in the faith.

Meanwhile, this playing with mirrors reflects painful and unflattering images to us from both sides. In the Western mirror, Islam is, of course, obscurantist and fanatical. Its religion is an artful or crude plagiarism of Judaism and Christianity – in short, a fraudulent version.[25] For a long time Muhammad was considered an imposter; whether a common imposter or one of genius made little difference. In serious and more recent books, he is considered more as a well-meaning crank who became successful – the strength of the myth prevailing over reason – and who believed himself authorized, with the help of success, to "resort to any methods whatsoever and even to carry out acts of vengeance that were hardly the mark of any great nobility of soul."[26]

In addition to the historical and religious motivations behind misunderstanding, there are other psychological, cultural, or socioeconomic factors. The process is well known; it is that of amalgamation and generalization. The words of one neophyte, Ayyub, a French shopkeeper who became a "Muslim Brother" – in other words, one tree in the forest- became, whether "*mezzo voce o allegro forte,*" those of "all Muslims together,"

---

[25] E. g., reference might be made to the words of the Swedish writer, Tor Andrae, translated into French as *Les origines de l'Islam et le Christianisme* (Paris, 1955); C. C. Torrey, *The Jewish foundation of Islam* (New York: Jewish Institute of Religion Press, 1933); David Sidersky, *Les origines des légendes musulmanes dans le Coran et dans les vies des prophètes* (Paris: Librairie Orientaliste Paul Geuthner, 1933); Fr. Gabriel Thery (who wrote as Hanna Zacharias), *De Moïse à Mohammed;* Thery's disciple, Fr. J. Berteul, *L'Islam ses véritables origines,* with a preface by Admiral Auphan; Patricia Crone and Michael Cook, *Haggarism: The Making of the Islamic World* (New York: Cambridge University Press, 1977). The famous Soviet orientalists, S. P. Tolstov and E. A. Belayev, base their books on the same postulates. We do not critize freedom of research, provided it is sincere and serious, since such freedom is indispensable for the advancement of knowledge. Nonetheless, it is true that the books mentioned are not in agreement about understanding between Islam and the West. They fall within the framework of a polemic that has repeated itself for centuries and has already proved its sterility. Writers are free to persist in the same direction, but we should warn their readers that they are faced with an impasse. To be fair, it should be added that the works of many orientalists take a different view and present a picture of Islam, with infallible erudition, that is both more respectful and more objective; e.g., L. Massignon, H. Laoust, K. Cragg, W. M. Watt, L. Gardet, J. M. Anawati, W. C. Smith, J. Berque, etc. Should we include Frs. M. Lelong and R. Caspar, who are working so hard for dialogue among the orientalists?

[26] D. Sourdel, *L'Islam médiéval* (Paris: Presses universitaires de France, 1971), p. 31.

122

"stamped, in various ways, by this language of radicalism."[27] This leads automatically to the conclusion that "any attempt at a 'dialogue,' therefore, seems to be either vain or utopian."[28] In plain words, we are invited to stand by with folded arms, in order not to spoil the game of those who are projecting images at the distorting mirror.

Concerning Muslim behavior, the current press prefers to offer its customers the images for which they are most eager – those aspects that are most time-worn and shocking to the Western mind. From the images offered on the television screen, the average Western particularly remembers those of the Iranian women landing at Rome, early in August, 1983, after an airplane hijacking. Veiled in black and avoiding the camera's eye, they symbolize Islam for the Westerner, who also remembers that they cut off the hands of thieves in Mauritania, the Sudan, and elsewhere and that they stone women taken in adultery. The British television film about an unusual although true event – the stoning of a Saudi princess – was a great success. Thereby, the image of a primitive and barbarous Islam is formed in the mental mirror of the average Westerner. The Western tourist who visits Islamic countries cannot fail to bring back images of dilapidated cities where grievous poverty exists alongside excessive wealth. In political matters, it is enough for one to recall – without comments – that the rates of participation in elections are rarely less than ninety-nine percent, in order to calculate the degree of freedom in Islamic countries. One is told that Islam is tolerant but discovers that the mosques are closed to Westerners, while the West opens its churches to all. As for human rights – let us not even mention that!

To sum up, faced with an over-developed West, Islam, which has barely emerged from the colonial era, now finds itself wholly in the zone of underdevelopment, with all the political, social, economic, and cultural consequences that this involves. V. S. Naipaul, after visiting the Islamic countries in Asia, finally had nothing to report except hunger, violence, and obscurantism. That impression, which is identical to that of the average Westerner, is clearly apparent in the title for the French translation of his

---

[27] Brière and Carré, *Islam, Guerre,* p. 33.

[28] *Ibid.,* p. 34.

book, *Among the Believers: An Islamic Journey,*[29] namely, *Crépuscule sur l'Islam* ("The Twilight of Islam"). In short, the political, cultural, and socioeconomic image of the Muslim is more or less roughly reflected in the Western mirror, which shows either an emir squandering millions on luxury and orgies, a suppliant making bad use of the aid so "generously" granted, or the needy immigrant who does not succeed in becoming a part of the society that has accepted him or her and who, driven to a marginal existence, excites more or less strong feelings of rejection.

For its part, the West has no better an image in Islam's mirror. There, too, when we leave well-informed circles or those that have adopted the Western style of life, we find no lack of distortions – due to omission, selection, generalization, or simplification. "The West is an accident,"[30] the result of a wrong turn taken at the beginning. The Judeo-Christian scriptures have been falsified, or at best altered, or badly interpreted. Christians naturally worship three gods. A typical sermon in Cairo, quoted by J. P. Péroncel-Hugoz, turns around this theme: "The Nazarenes (the followers of Jesus of Nazareth) are cannibals; they eat God's body; they worship a lamb."[31] The Egyptian Shaikh 'Abd al-Hamid Kishk asked in amazement, "How can anyone believe that God came out of a vagina?"[32]

It is not surprising, therefore, that the West has abandoned its faith. Islam looks on it especially as being secularized. It sees in it the idolatry of matter pushed to an extreme, an "animistic alliance" between science and nature. Its power is in the purest materialistic style, and in that respect it carries within itself, sooner or later, the seeds of its inevitable decay. Western civilization corrupts humanity; it is by its very nature either corrupt or corrupting. It is hard to see how the West can reproach Islam for

---

[29] (New York: Alfred A. Knopf, 1981). French: (Paris: Albin Michel, 1981). In February, 1985, Syrian President Hafiz Al-Asad was given another seven-year mandate, with a vote 99.97% in his favor. Out of 6,520,428 votes, only 376 were opposed. See *al-Ra'y* (a Tunisian weekly), February 15, 1985, p. 3. This requires no comment; one need only recall that the Syrian city of Hama was razed by artillery fire under the same regime!

[30] This expressions is from Roger Garudy, *Promisses de l'Islam* (Paris: Seuil, 1981), p. 17.

[31] Péroncel-Hugoz, *Le Radeau,* p. 27.

[32] Quoted in ibid., p. 30.

polygamy when it has millions of child-mothers. In some countries and some churches,[33] marriages between homosexuals are permitted, and adultery is so widespread that it is no longer considered a crime. A Muslim returning from the West retains the memory of sex shops, shows, and cinema halls, many of which specialize in pornography, not to mention the commercial television channels, either clandestine or free and authorized, which disseminate scenes of debauchery. The image of a permissive West is engraved in the Muslim's mind. It matters little that all this is not of fundamental importance in Western civilization: It is a part of everyday life. The West is quickly identified in the film "America Sex O'clock." It preaches virtue and practices vice.

Politically, of course, the West is regarded as aggressive and domineering. It addresses Islam and all the weak countries of the earth in the language of the wolf in the fairy tale. Its arguments are always the best. It has built its prosperity on the spoliation of the goods of three-fourths of the populations of the globe, which yesterday were colonized and today are still being exploited by an unjust economic system that drains off their riches to the West and rigs its own trading terms. It squanders monstrous sums on engines of death, while other peoples are dying of hunger by the thousands. The West is perfectionist in everything, including barbarity. Its barbarity is qualitatively sophisticated and quantitatively horribly devastating. It is no longer in the primitive stage of a few chopped-off hands or a few people hanged at street corners. It has progressed to the advanced stage of the highly developed techniques of crematoriums and nuclear bombs, which are now "clean." We are now protected against the regrettable consequences that stained the heroic feats of Hisoshima and Nagasaki, but are they a thing of the past, washed in the waters of repentance? Who knows, if war should break out between the great powers of civilization?

---

[33] In 1979, Arcadie, the French homosexual movement, included nearly 40,000 members (see *Le Monde*, May 27-28, 1979). The first "union of homosexual friendship" was held in the last two weeks of December, 1979, in Paris, in a Protestant church in the 19th district (see *Le Monde*, December, 1979). This practice has also occurred in some Protestant churches in the U.S.A. and the Netherlands.

This is the picture that Sayyid Qutb, one of the alleged fathers of Islamism, paints of the West, the shock of which he sustained in the country where it is best expressed, the United States:

> We were a minority, those of us who stood up for Islam in America, during the years I spent there. Some persons adopted a defensive attitude to justify their Islam. But I myself did quite the opposite. I took an offensive stand against that modern and Western anti-Islamic ignorance, with its incoherent religious beliefs and its disastrous social, economic, and moral situations. All the descriptions of the "hypostases" of the Trinity, original sin, and redemption are only harmful to reason and conscience! And this capitalism of accumulation, of monopolies, of usurious interests – nothing but greed! And this egotistic individualism that prevents any spontaneous solidarity other than that imposed by law! This materialistic, shabby, sapless view of life! This bestial freedom that has been called "co-education"! This slave market called the "emancipation of women," these subterfuges and anxieties in a system of marriage and divorce so contrary to natural life! This strong and ferocious racial discrimination! And so on. In comparison, what intelligence, what a lofty outlook, what humanity we find in Islam![34]

And the Jews? Do they belong to the East or to the West? Here, and there, they are above all the Other. In any case, each of us always has our own Other, and Other is by definition the inferior. Now, the Jew is the Other, the totally Other *par excellence*. What the Jews are reproached with is simply being themselves. For centuries, they have been bathing in waters that are strange to them, sometimes sweet, sometimes sour. They are still irreducible, insoluble, unassimilable – in a word, indigestible. Why dwell any longer on the subject? Antisemitism is a well-known fact. The last Holocaust – with which the Arabs had nothing to do, but for which they are still paying the bill – is still present in everyone's memory. In a courageous article published in *The Maghreb*,[35] Sherif Ferjani reminds us that our

---

[34] S. Qutb, *Jalons sur le chemin* (in Arabic) (Union Islamique Mondiale, 1964), p. 160. Quoted in Brière and Carré, *Islam, Guerre*, p. 160. Let us draw attention to Cahbbi's thesis, *L'Image de l'Occident chez les intellectuels tunisiens dans la seconde moitié du XIXe siecle* (The Image of the West among the Tunisian Intellectuals during the Second Half of the Nineteenth Century), University of Reims (France), 1983, 2 vols. mimeographed, 586 pp.

[35] *The Maghreb* (a weekly magazine published in Tunis), No. 58 (May 29, 1982), pp. 11-12. Under the subtitle, "Le racisme anti-juif," it read: "While anti-black racism does not often take the form of hatred, anti-Jewish racism, on the contrary, is becoming increasingly virulent and

Muslim societies, even on the level of vocabulary, and despite the cordial relations that very often become knotted, continue to foster an anti-Jewish racism that is more or less unconscious and thoughtless. More recently, a newspaper in Medina[36] entitled an article by the traditionalist, Abu Muhammad 'Abd al-Haqq al-Hashimi, "Reasons for the Humiliation of the Jews" (*Mujibat dhillat al-Yahud*). Holocaust! Humiliation! We understand why the Jews found it necessary to have a state of their own in order to preserve their dignity and to provide a possible refuge in case of danger. Like scalded cats, they are afraid of cold water wherever they may be, for at any moment it may suddenly start to boil, heated by the flames of ineradicable Antisemitism. If, in keeping with the best of our traditions of hospitality and tolerance, we had welcomed our unfortunate and sorely tried cousins, what might have been the situation in the Near East, which today is plunged into a nightmare with no end yet in sight? However, it is useless to speculate; we cannot remake history.

---

hateful. There is, of course, a confusion between the Jew and the Zionist – which is becoming increasingly deliberate, especially with the development of integrism – but the phenomenon lies much deeper than a mere confusion, whether unconscious or deliberate, between Zionism and Judaism. It is quite simply a question of racism with regard to the Jew as such, having its origin in the opposition between the Jewish community and the Muslim community at Medina when Islam first appeared. For this reason, there is no better way to insult somebody than to treat him or her as a Jew. In popular language, the Jew is the same as a dog or a pig (just as the Arab is referred to in racist language in Europe). The Jew is often described as "treacherous," "cowardly," "stinking of offal." Hence, anything that can be done to a Jew is justified. Thus, one who is persecuted will 'innocently' ask, 'Am I a Jew, to be treated like this?' The final argument to confound an opponent is to point out that he is choosing exactly the same attitude as a Jew and then ask, 'Have you understood? Are you a *Jew*?'"

This kind of racism is largely kept alive by the mass media. E.g., I recall a poem aimed at inciting bestial hatred against the Jews, which a girl recited on a television broadcast, to the general approbation of the audience, as described in the pages of *The Maghreb,* by Emna Belhaj Yahia. This is only one example. It is enough to watch the so-called religious (and pseudo-historical) films to realize the part played by television is keeping up this racist hatred by the picture it presents of non-Muslims – especially Jews – as being "deceivers," "traitors," "cowards," and persons against whom one must always be on guard. What do our cinema and television critics do about all this? They are always on watch for any reference to Jews in a film or a stage production so that they can complain about pro-Zionism (sometimes correctly, but often incorrectly, as was the case following the showing of the film, "Norma Rae"). If a Jew, or a person of Jewish origin, protests this racism – as Gilbert Naccache did – he or she is accused of being a Zionist. If someone else takes their part – as Mahmoud Ben Romdhane did – that person is accused of having defended somebody who "after all, is a Jew."

[36] Al-Irbi'a, no. 73 (July 18, 1984) p. 7.

It is a painful fact that Jews, once they have become masters, look upon the Other – in this case, the Arab – with the same scorn from which they have suffered so much themselves. The Israeli regime is openly discriminatory. It is sufficient to read the book by an Israeli university professor, a woman of Egyptian origin, Bat Ye'or, entitled The Dhimmi: *Jews and Christians under Islam*[37] to see how, by deceptively selecting certain facts to the detriment of many others, it is possible to distort history and paint a picture of Islam that arouses dislike and hatred. There can be no doubt that from all sides our respective mirrors reflect pictures of the Other that – to say the least – foster chauvinism and discourage understanding. Most of them prefer to reflect caricatures. That is amusing, flattering, and reassuring – but not, alas, innocently so!

The Persistence of Caricatures

So, we continue to be the unconscious victims of caricatures, whose reign, over both sides, has never been seriously disturbed. Our prejudices, our stereo – types, and our infantile desire to exert ourselves to the utmost in asserting our respective superiorities have become more strongly entrenched from age to age. To tell the truth, the caricaturist is not a forger or falsifier and does not invent. The art is more subtle. It consists of dwelling on certain features, of selecting and accentuating defects, which makes a formidable impact. It is an art that is not new. It comes to us from the depths of our history, our separate histories. Since it is buried in our collective subconsciences, by successive stratifications over the ages, it determines our reactions and calls for a social psychoanalysis. Here is how Saint John of Damascus (d. about 749),[38] who lived in the entourage of the Ummayyad caliphs, turned the Qur'an to scorn with a consummate art of caricature:

> There is also a chapter "on God's she-camel," in which he says
> that there was a she-camel sent by God that drank up the

---

[37] Bat Ye'or, *The Dhimmi: Jews and Christians under Islam,* tr. David Maisel, Paul Fenton, and David Littman (Rutherford, Madison, Teaneck, NJ: Fairleigh Dickinson University Press; London and Toronto: Associated University Presses, 1985). French: *Le Dhimmi: profil de l'opprimé en Orient et en Afrique du Nord* (Paris: Anthropos, 1980).

[38] Concerning St. John of Damascus, see Daniel J. Sahas, *John of Damascus – The Heresy of the Ishmaelites"* (Leiden: E. J. Brill, 1972).

whole river and that could not pass between two mountains because of the lack of room. However, he says, there was a certain people in that region, and one day that people drank the water, while the she-camel drank it on the following day. When it had drunk the water, it fed the people by giving them milk instead of water. But, he says, these men were wicked; they rose up and killed the she-camel. However, that she-camel had given birth to a small she-camel, which, he says, after the death of its mother, cried out to God, who raised it up to himself. Then we ask them: "Where did that she-camel come from?" and they tell us that it came from God. We ask: "Did it have any relations with a male camel?" They tell us, no. "And where did this birth come from?" We ask: "After all, we see that your she-camel has no father, no mother, and no ancestry, then after giving birth herself, she comes to a bad end. But there is no trace of her sire, and as for the little she-camel, she has been elevated to the heavens. So, why did not your prophet, who according to what he says has spoken with God, tell you where that she-camel grazes and who are the men who milk her and drink her milk? Are we to believe that she has been mistreated and died of it, like her mother, or has she entered into Paradise to open its ways for you so well that she will cause this river of milk you talk about to flow for you? For you say that three rivers flow into Paradise, one with water, one with wine, and the third with milk. If your she-camel, your forebear, is outside of Paradise, it obviously must have perished of hunger and thirst, or else other men are having the benefit of its milk. Your prophet, therefore, boasts in vain of having talked to God, for the mystery of the she-camel was not revealed to him. If, on the other hand, the she-camel is in Paradise, it is continuing to drink up the water, and you will be dying of thirst among all the delights of Paradise. If, now, you want to draw some wine from the neighboring river, owing to the lack of water (which has all been drunk by the she-camel), you will have to drink it unmixed, and then there you are – overheated, stumbling about drunk, and soon fast asleep, only to wake up with a hangover that will make you forget the pleasures of Paradise. How is it, then, that your prophet never thought that accidents of this kind might happen to you in this delightful Paradise? He has never taken the trouble to find out where the she-camel is – and you yourselves never asked him the question while he was feeding you endless dreams about the three rivers."[39]

---

[39] Quoted from Alain Ducellier, *Le Miroir de l'Islam,* Col. Archives (Paris: Julliard, 1971), pp. 136-137. Reference to the Qur'an: VII, 73-77; XI, 64; XVII, 59; XXVI, 155; LIV, 21; XCI, 13; and doubtless still more in the sermons of the *qussas,* the popular preachers who spread or invented hundreds of legends for the edification of the people.

'Adb al-Jabbar b. Ahmad al-Hamadani (d. 1024 A.D., year 415 after the Hijrah), for his part, aimed his darts at the remission of sins and the simony in the church to which it led, with the same obvious desire to ridicule those things and excite laughter:

> One of the strongest features of their religion is that a sinner will say to a bishop or priest: "Let me repent: give me absolution, and take my sins on yourself." In return, he offers him a more or less sizable payment, depending on whether he is rich or poor. The bishop then holds out his mantle and takes delivery of the payment. Then he says to the sinner: "Very good! Come on now! Tell me your sins one by one so that I can know what they are and take them on myself." The sinner in question – whether man or woman, king or peasant – starts in and tells what was done, one thing after the other, until he or she finally says: "There ! That's all!" The bishop then says, "Those are certainly great sins! But I take them upon myself and give you absolution. Be happy." He then wraps his payment in the folds of his mantle, throws it over his shoulder, and often adds: "Oh! How heavy they are – the sins lumped together in this mantle!"
>
> A well-known and widespread custom among them is also for a woman to confess her sin to the bishop. She says, "A man had relations with me on such and such a day." The bishop then questions her, "How many times?" She replies with such and such a number. The bishop then goes on: "Tell me now! Was this man a Christian or a Muslim?" Sometimes she may answer, "A Muslim." The bishop then flies into a great rage and demands an additional payment. She either agrees, or else the angry bishop goes away crying out: "A Muslim has fornicated with her, and she wants me to give her absolution! And she has only offered me so much!" She then implores him to come back and she gives him an extra payment, and he is satisfied.
>
> One day one of their bishops is asked, "What has all this to do with true repentance?" He replies: "Why not profit by it? We fool them with the hope of their redemption, for if we did not do it and did not take their money, our churches would soon be in ruins."[40]

---

[40] *Tathbit Dala'il al-Nubuwwa* (Beirut, 1966), pp. 190-121. Quoted from A. Charfi, *Al-fikr al-Islami fi l-radd 'ala al-nasara ila nihayat al-qam al-rabi'* (Tunis: M.T.E., 1986), p. 443. The author is one of the most eminent figures of mu'tazilism.

Traumas and Failures of Communication

The two texts we have just quoted are only samples, many more of which could easily be cited. *There is a tradition of misunderstanding.* Both the past and the present have combined to place obstacles in the way of mutual and respectful understanding. After all, such an understanding was always – and still is – troublesome to all who deny the right to differences of opinion and who try, more or less unconsciously, to impose a hegemony of their own model of society and thought. Caricatures have the advantage of being revealing at two levels: in portraits they emphasize a feature that is considered unusual, disturbing, or reprehensible, while of the portrait painter her or himself they reveal underlying fears, prejudices, and traumas – in short, all the fantasies that are born from the shock of encountering the Other, which we try to dispel by a kind of apologetic and facetious therapy that creates reassuring stereotypes. Both Islam and the West resort to the curative and comforting virtues of caricature because they have both been traumatized; thus, the past flows into the present with, so to speak, an unchanged constancy in modes of reaction, with the collective memory – through a certain teaching of history – playing the role of stabilizer and modulator.

Of course, positive developments do, nevertheless, take place. Otherwise, why write? Human rights, even when violated, and certain thrusts toward international solidarity bear witness to this. However, their movement is constantly impeded at every turn, and they are unceasingly denounced as treason by the self-righteous in both camps – at best as naive, and at worst self-interested – for the benefit of the Other. Among those who work for understanding, who is there who has not met with misunderstanding in her or his own circle?

The appearance of Islam was an initial shock for the West. Its awakening is felt as a new trauma. Apparently, no one had foreseen this phenomenon or seriously expected it to happen. Further, we find that Islam is no longer confused. It is giving proof of a new dynamism. It is not surprising that it should win followers in Africa, but that a religion that is considered primitive, obscurantist, and fanatical should become established in America and Europe and make progress there among the natives – and sometimes among persons of importance – is something that really baffles all understanding. There are estimated to be nearly 2,000,000 Muslims in France alone, including 400,000 of French nationality (including *harkis* – North African native soldiers who served formerly in the French Colonial Army) and 35,000 converts,[41] including Maurice Bejart, Michel Chodkiewicz (the director of *Seuil*), Roger Garaudy, and Vincent Monteil. The West no longer feels safe, even within its own traditional borders. It fears the militancy of the Islamists. It sees them everywhere and overestimates their numbers and influence, as often happens when people give way to panic. "A specter is haunting Europe," wrote Claire Brière, "Islamic fanaticism."[42] To observe the five ritual *salats* (prayers) is to be an Islamist. To fast during the month of Ramadan is even worse. To insist on a mosque? When will we seen the *chador?* To avoid provoking an already touchy public opinion still further, the authorities "wisely" refuse![43]

It is a fact that most Muslim immigrants do not become integrated in the West, and their rate of demographic growth, which in the long run can upset certain balances, gives reason for fear. They bring their own way of life with them to their host countries, and, after encouraging the economic boom, they are the very ones who are considered responsible for unemployment. Moreover, the West needs the natural resources of the Muslim countries and harbors serious fears on this subject. The rise of Islamist regimes of the Iranian type can threaten its interests. The oil shock was decisive in causing the West to view Islam as a factor that might have a destabilizing effect on a certain world order, one that is preponderantly Western. It is to be feared that these and similar speculations do not encourage understanding. When vital interests are at stake, everyone counts pennies and tries, first of all, to keep what he or she has.

---

[41] See Brière and Carré, *Islam, Guerre,* p. 11.

[42] *Ibid.,* p. 10.

[43] E.g., we might mention that two building permits were rejected early in September, 1983, on at Lyon and the other at Sevran, for fear that the Islamic centers might "become a center of support for fundamentalist terrorism or a target for extremists" (see *L'Action* [Tunis], September 11, 1983). We can also mention cases where the church and the local authorities contributed to the success of such projects. In Belgium and Holland, especially, the atmosphere is rather liberal.

Of course, Islam also has its own grievances. The shock for it has been even more severe. For a long period of time, it was simply outside the general course of history. Islam no longer amounted to anything, and it was thought that it would never amount to anything again. Today, its place is entirely in the ranks of the Third World. It is still lacking in technological know-how, which represents real power. It imports everything, both material and cultural goods, and runs a serious risk of losing its soul by doing so. The shock caused to Islam today by its collision with an excessively powerful West is wholly out of proportion with its first encounter with the Persian and Byzantine civilizations, which were then relatively decadent. It had been in a position of strength and is now in a position of weakness. For the last several decades, in order to meet the challenges directed at it,[44] Islam has held three conflicting ideas about society: Islamist, reformist, and modernist. Contrary to what the Western media would lead us to believe, it is not Islamism – despite its spectacular success in Iran – that is at present the leading force in most Muslim countries.

After all, although Roger Garaudy prophesies that Islam will be a leading power in the future of the West – a future that most Westerners believe and hope will be largely imaginary – the West, for its part, is already a leading power in Islam today, to the point of practically submerging it. In all Islamic countries there are large social classes that are completely Westernized, even in their eating habits. In the cities you will see T-shirts setting off attractive bosoms, which – even if they are of local manufacture – tell you in English or "Keep cool" or offer you the "fruit of the loom." "Our very identity is in danger," warn Islamists, who, in order to dissociate themselves from these Western fashions, let their beards grow and emphasize the immaculate whiteness of their tunics in contrast to the close-fitting jeans that they regard as a symbol of permissiveness among the young moderns.[45]

---

[44] There have been countless symposia on the topic of "Islam and the Challenges of Our Time"; e.g., one was held November 12-16, 1984, by the Centre d'Etude et de Recherche Economique et Sociale (CERES) in Tunis.

[45] See A. Bouhdiba, "La société maghrébine face à la question sexuelle," in *Cahiers Internationaux de Sociologie*, vol. 76 (1984), pp. 91-110, who sums up his article: "The

Traumatized by the sudden and massive invasion of Western culture, it is the marginal elements of Islam that react – because the governments in power generally deny Islam the safety valves of a free press and the judgment of fair elections. These elements react with a destabilizing and destructive violence that may even go so far as to engage in and justify criminal activities,[46] These are the convulsions of a civilization suffocating under a mass of strange foreign influences that it has not had enough time to "Islamize," that is, to adapt and integrate, as was formerly the case. This is something that is immediately apparent and explains the pessimistic observation of J. P. Péroncel-Hugoz, after his lengthy stay in Algiers and Cairo, that "Arab-Islamic civilization today is no longer alive; it is dead."[47]

Such is the Islamic civilization, something that, once more, has been buried a bit too quickly. However, it is impossible to hold a dialogue with the dead. On both sides, the discussion is frozen by traumas both old and new.

Reviving Discussion and Conditions for Understanding

First of all, we have to admit that Islamic civilization, while traumatized, is certainly not dead. By its dynamism, Islam is proving every day that it is not "the very model of a frozen society,"[48] nor is it condemned to extinction. Any revival of discussion must be based on the elimination of such illusions.

It is said repeatedly that no real dialogue can take place until "each one has accepted the Other as he is."[49] This is a correct principle in itself and a condition *sine qua non* for any exchange between equals, but, in fact,

---

traditional model of sexuality in the Maghreb, based on the hierarchy of the sexes, the seclusion of women, the sense of modesty and honor, the demarcation between what is public and what is private, is today faced with the competition of another conception, one relying on medical science, permissive, and of a secularizing nature."

[46] Abd as-Salam Faraj is certainly the most thorough theoretician of political crime as justified for religious reasons. See his short treatise, *L'Obligation manquante*, partially translated into French in Brière and Carré, *Islam, Guerre*, pp. 199-204.

[47] Péroncel-Hugoz, *Le Radeau*, p. 204.

[48] *Ibid.*, p. 215.

[49] *Ibid.*, p. 21.

this principle becomes such a worn-out commonplace and convinces so little that those who claim to uphold it are no longer even aware that it has nothing to do with their line of argument. The difficulty is real. After all, is it possible to understand the Other as he or she really is? "The Other," in fact, is always perceived through the distorting eyes of the individual "I" or the social "we," or even more often through both lenses at the same time. We are – all of us – prisoners of our own egos and our own group mentality, and it is practically impossible for us to free ourselves *completely* from our prison bars. We perceive the outer world only through a frame of reference in which the categories of resemblance and dissimilarity and of contiguity and opposition give a distorted reflection of our perceptions, help to arrange them in order, and shape them into images. "The Other" is always "shaped" or "constructed." "The Other" is the image that is projected on the screen of my individual "I" through the filtering lens of my social "we." This constraint is inherent in our individual being, which is the bearer of endogenous cultural values. It constitutes a natural blockage, a kind of immunizing code that preserves our identity.

We are then presented with three ways out. I can keep my distance from and exclude the Other from my own sphere of being. I then begin to speak of the Other in a language of exclusion, of an openly racist and downgrading type, which is based on anathema and excommunication when the religious element enters into the picture. With more or less veiled condescension, I can also experience a desire to approach the Other more closely and to include him or her in my own sphere of being. As a kind of phagocyte I then begin to talk a language of inclusion, which is gladly all-embracing, civilizing, and paternalistic. This language, with its underlying connotations of implicit superiority, is always ambiguous. The language of the anthropologist or orientalist often wavers between these two poles. The third way out is the one that goes through the narrow gate. It consists of estimating the difficulties and recognizing them fairly and clearly. However, this recognition does not remove the difficulties. Nevertheless, *to a large extent*, it makes it possible to overcome them and to get beyond them. This naturally presupposes a willingness to listen to the Other and therefore a certain openness, respect, and humility. Without yielding one iota of my identity, that is, of my options and convictions, I can *respect* the identity of the Other, with her or his own options and convictions, and build my relations with her or him on a basis of *complete equality*. My own freedom is hers or his, and *vice versa*.

Let me make it quite clear that it is not a question of tolerance but of respect. Tolerance is associated with the medieval mentality; at that time it represented a certain degree of progress. Robert's dictionary defines it as the fact of "not forbidding or requiring *although it would be possible to do so*." Tolerance, therefore, is not a right. It is an act of pure indulgence by someone in a dominating position. It implies inferiority and condemnation. We tolerate error, although we are entitled to prohibit it in the name of Truth. What is tolerated is perceived as an evil that cannot be extirpated except at the price of a greater evil. To tolerate this evil is to put up with it temporarily and unwillingly, as an act of pure charity and with a certain condescension dictated by a benevolent superiority. Respect, instead, is a right and presupposes the complete and absolute equality of the partners. Only respect can guarantee the dignity of all. In respect there is neither inferior nor superior. In tolerance there is the one who tolerates, at a higher level, and the one who is tolerated, at a lower level, while this disparity is eliminated in respect.

The most sacred form of respect is that which is owed to truth and to the free exercise of thought. The first thing necessary in order to unclamp discussion is to restore its primary function, which is to conduct a calm and mutual search for the truth; in other words, it is necessary to speak fairly and without passion. Now, on both sides, many still continue to conceive of communication only in terms of apology or contempt. This kind of discussion, conducted like jousts in closed lists, is still what we hear only too often in symposia on the topic of Islam and the West. Accusations and defense pleas follow one after the other. *Destructio destructionis*, it was said, when Latin was still spoken. This game of mutual assassination still goes on. The alternate whitewashing and blackening of characters does not encourage communication. As soon as one's dignity is attacked or words are hidden behind a mask, there is an end to discussion. Neither one, on either side, is a dupe or a lackey. As long as the respective preachers of Islam and the West do not make use of the spoken or the written word except to utter hymns of glory or to denounce their neighbors, the electric current of communication can no longer pass between them but can only produce angry sparks.

As far as Islam is concerned, it is particularly distressing to see certain apologists persist in denying facts that are well known to all. There is no lack of specialists on Islam in the West. Rather, the contrary is true, and this emphasizes even more the childishness of a certain kind of apologetics that are based on omission and the rejection of evidence. Islam, however, has no need to veil its face in shame. It can only be helped by self-criticism, which would rid it of its more negative qualities – since all civilizations have their own dead branches – in order to bring out its positive qualities, by liberating "Islamic reason," as Mohammed Arkoun would say,[50] and by making its spokespersons into effective thinkers, at their community level, and lucid and believable speakers in their communication with the West. That narcissism that still lives in the past – al-turathiyya at all costs – is nothing but a debilitating subterfuge and an evasion. The past has no meaning unless it acts as a driving force for the present and a healthy vision of the future.

As far as the West is concerned, it must accept the idea that Islam is no longer suffering from an inferiority complex. It is already something to be reckoned with, and with its enormous potentialities it will have to be reckoned with increasingly. It would be a good thing for writers on both sides to stop dipping their pens in rosewater, but neither should they dip them in vinegar. Claire Brière, who is so quick to accept unfavorable reports, or even mere gossip, is very reticent about the positive side. J. P. Péroncel-Hugoz tries to discredit Garaudy[51] by veiled hints and litotes. He deprecates such reputable scholars and men of integrity as Professor J. Berque or Father Michel Lelong,[52] who, with objectivity and devotion, are trying to build a solid bridge between Islam and the West by pointing out the true values of culture, faith, and civilization that can and should encourage genuine

---

[50] See Mohammed Arkoun, *Pour une critique de la raison islamique* (Paris: Maisonneuve et Larose, 1984).

[51] Péroncel-Hugoz, *Le Radeau*, p. 18.

[52] *Ibid.*, p. 20.

communication in depth. Instead of that, there is a preference for idle reports that find a ready public. In fact, if the obsolete writings of "yesterday's orientalists who were primarily concerned with justifying colonialism"[53] have been rejected, they have finally been replaced by less dusty literature that is better able to satisfy the tastes of a certain contemporary Western public that is content to contemplate *Mahomet's Raft* floating away from the heights of their own self-assured superiority. The ghost, who when awake is frightening, is in the way exorcised.

Péroncel-Hugoz is certainly not impelled by any preconceived ill will. On the contrary, he asserts his sympathy for Islam,[54] and there is no reason to question it. This is precisely what makes his book very interesting as a symptom. It is much more a testimony about the West than about Islam, about the observer rather than the one observed, about the mirror that reflects the image rather than the object reflected. On both sides, there is a temptation in the name of realism – to which we can subscribe, provided it is not made the sole and privileged dimension of behavior for a more-or-less-deliberate purpose of depreciation – to cover up the ideal cultural models, that is, the great ethical and intellectual values that constitute the true greatness of civilizations and explain their creativity, their permanence, and their power to stimulate and mobilize thought.

To belong to Islam or to the West is first of all to adhere to a frame of higher references, even if these references are only imperfectly assumed in the gray neutrality of everyday behavior. Every individual, depending on one's degree of maturity, preserves some degree of awareness of these references, which constitute a value for building up one's identity and an element of pride. Therefore, to ignore ideals – and rely only on a certain realism – is simply to deny the existence of a culture while retaining only its most negative leavings and refuse, and so to supply the distorting mirrors – which it is unnecessary to mention again – with images that are especially pernicious because they are fallaciously clothed in a pseudoscientific objectivity. Overcoming this reductive and depreciative

---

[53] *Ibid.*, p. 15.
[54] *Ibid.*, pp. 13, 48.

vision is a primordial condition for removing the obstacles to discussion and freeing the circuits of communication. For example, while the writings of Kamil Hasain and Michel Lelong–which emphasize the deep-lying convergences between Islam and the West–bring those civilizations closer together, the writings of Sayyid Qutb and Claire Brière–which are based primarily on false observations–tend only to separate them. After all, there can be no exchange when there is no reciprocal esteem.

However, nobody can be forced to change their ink to break their pen. Even the most unfair and most outrageous criticisms are almost never based on deliberate illwill but, rather, on opposite beliefs, options, and styles. The fundamentalists–whether Msgr. Marcel Lefebvre, the Rev. Jerry Falwell, and Tim Lallaye,[55] or Hasan al-Banna, Sayyid Qutb, and 'Abd as-Salam Faraj–as well as the unbelievers, who are sometimes inspired by a scientism and chauvinism that are equally outrageous and extreme, are, nevertheless, our partners; while I have a sacred right to differ and to express my thoughts

---

[55] Is it necessary to point out that fundamentalism is not peculiar to Islam? In his presidential campaign on November 6, 1984, Ronald Regan benefited by the active, if not perhaps overloud, support of the Rev. Jerry Falwell, leader of the fundamentalist "Moral Majority" (see *L'Action* [Tunis], September 6, 1984, p. 12, under the heading "Présidentielles Americanes," according to a dispatch from l'Agence France Presse). This organization is the incarnation of the American Right; its determinist theorlogy, of a post-millenary type, exalts the role of Israel and the United States–the country of free enterprise–for the salvation of the world. Concerning this subject, consult the brief but very well-documented analysis of Robert G. Clouse, "The New Christian Right, America, and the Kingdom of God." *Liberty* 79 (July-August, 1984): 8-10: "The dispensationalist theology that the New Christian Right desires to follow teaches that God's purpose is not centered in America but in Israel" (p. 9). In fact, Falwell wrote: "I firmly believe God has blessed America because America has blessed the Jew. If this nation wants her fields to remain white with grain, her scientific achievements to remain notable, and her freedom to remain intact, America must continue to stand with Israel" (p. 9, in refernce to Falwell's *Listen America!* [Garden City, NY: Doubleday, 1980], p. 98). Moreover, while the Muslim integrists stress the return to the Qur'an and the *shari'a* for the political, economic, and social organization of the state and denounce moral depravity, the American fundamentalists demand a return to the Bible and to a stricter morality. Tim Lallaye wrote: "Two thirds of the world today is enslaved in communism and socialism. America is the human hope of the world, and Jesus Christ is the hope of America. Our present weakness, confusions, bureaucracy, immorality, and other natural evils cannot be traced to the Bible or to Christians but to the subversive erosion of basic Christian principles that have made this the greatest nation under God that the world has ever known. Unless we return to the Bible principles that provided our nation's greatness, we will pass like others before us" (p. 9, in reference to Lallaye's *The Bible's Influence on American History* [San Diego: Master Books, 1976], p 59).

freely, their right to do so is equally sacred. There is one condition, however: they must not resort to violence or to intellectual terrorism. All violence is plainly answerable to justice and carries in itself its own condemnation. However willing we may be to listen to the other side, beyond a certain point we have to make up our own minds and let the fires of extremism burn themselves out. Even better, we can also reverse the current to our own advantage. For my part, I would advise all the responsible authorities on our theological faculties to reserve a wide space on their library shelves for those books that are most critical of Islam, because to be forewarned is to be forearmed. After all, one of the best ways to remove the obstacles to discussion is to listen to the Other, even under the least favorable conditions.

We have sufficiently stressed the right to the free expression of thought so that we can now assert that, in our opinion, resorting to polemics only leads to an impasse. After centuries of sterile experiences some people may continue to engage in polemics, which is certainly distressing. Polemics are always and inevitably in opposition to understanding. They do not allow any victory in the opposite camp and they serve only to harden positions by unceasingly encouraging and stimulating chauvinism. They are both sterile and dangerous: sterile, because at the present point it is practically impossible to discover or invent the slightest new argument since everything has already been said over and over again, and there is already an antidote to the most subtle arguments on both sides; dangerous, because, among the masses and in the media in particular, they have repercussions that serve to keep misunderstandings alive and aggravate them still further. If we are to open the door to dialogue, our only choice is to close the door to polemics.

We must prefer crossroads to blind alleys. Instead of making confrontational occasions of our references to history and religion and to our problems of today and yesterday, it would be better and more profitable for all to take both our past and our present for granted and make a joint effort to reap the benefit of our convergences. Westerners, for example, would do well to correct their ideas about the *Jihad,* which is wrongly equated with holy war and violence. We Muslims would so well to remember that, if we were colonized, it was first of all our own fault: we were "colonizable," and that was not at all to our credit. History gives nothing for nothing. In order to conduct a dialogue, both of us must first stop our whining, grumbling attitudes. Islam, in particular, must set to work and make itself respected by the seriousness of its thought and its achievements. To be respected one must simply be *worthy* of respect.

Among all our present problems, one in particular poisons the relations between Islam and the West: that of Palestine. Nothing can be expected from the diehards of the Israeli regime – with the United States government leading them – who refuse to acknowledge the very existence of the Other, that they are beings having their own dignity and are entitled to self-determination. Nor can there be any solution unless the partners succeed in burying their grievances, then embark on a path of reconciliation between Jews and Arabs by forgetting their mutual wrongs and building a better future for all. All those who, either on Islamic soil or in the West, believe in the need to rebuild the broken bridges must make a united effort to bring about heart-to-heart reconciliation. No political tactic, however indispensable and useful it may be, can permanently replace such genuine reconciliation. If this reconciliation is to be more than a weak and superficial shell, it is first necessary for us to restore, in a deep and meaningful way, the image of the Other: Jew, Christian, and Muslim, whether believer or non-believer. The golden rule means that we must always receive a mirror image of the Other in which the latter can recognize herself or himself. Without brushing over faults, we can do this, *provided* that we do not ignore the good qualities of others and that we ascribe to them in the hierarchy of values, the intensity to which they are rightfully entitled. We can then strengthen our mutual esteem, since there can be no communication without esteem.

However, esteem is not enough. Knowledge is also called for. Today, orientalism is under fire. It has a bad press – and certainly not without reason. However, many of those who oppose it forget that they were trained in its school and owe to it their own critical spirit. With all its positive and negative aspects, orientalism has made it possible to accumulate an enormous mass of knowledge. To it we owe the publication and translation of many masterpieces of Islamic thought and literature; above all, it possesses a solid tradition: the first Chair of Arabic in Paris, at the College de France, dates from 1539, and at Cambridge from 1633, not to mention the

Studia Arabica,[56] which originated in the thirteenth century. In view of this phenomenon, how is it possible not to wonder at the extraordinary lack of curiosity which as been shown by Islam?[57] We must think seriously about this backwardness and try hard to make up for it; we must, for our own part, train specialists in all fields of Western knowledge. In order to communicate, it is first necessary to know *what* to communicate. While knowledge is a power that has often been used for the worst purposes, it can also be directed toward better ones.

Mutual Acculturation and Confluence

All cultures are both synchronic and diachronic. In *synchrony* there is the idea of homogeneous elements that constitute a system in a given space-time structure and fit together, each in harmony with (*syn*) the other, while in *diachrony* the emphasis is on what separates (*dia*) and distinguishes during a process of development. Every culture oscillates between the *syn* and the *dia*, and the *dia* – once perfectly absorbed – is constantly absorbed by the *syn*. It is a case of rupture and equilibrium. Any living and "evolving" culture is therefore conflictual by its very nature and is especially conflictual because of the abundance of *dia* elements within it. After a certain point, it feels itself attacked and develops a mechanism of control, that is, rejection.

However, when the *syn* elements are in the majority in a given culture, it has a tendency to develop a myth about its originality to such a point that it will deny ever having borrowed anything.[58] It also tends to adopt a "stabilized" position and to proclaim its own purity. There is, however, no such thing as cultural virginity. *Reinkultur* is a myth that was staged by a voluntarist political act. Every culture that vibrates in harmony at a given point in the present time is the resultant of a diachrony, that is, of a chronological evolution in the acculturative process. In short, we are all

---

[56] Concerning the *Studium Arabicum* of the Dominicans, which "was flourishing in 1250" in Tunis, consult Charles Emmanuel Dufoureq, *L'Espagne catalane et le Maghrib* (Paris: Presses universitaires de France, 1966), pp. 104-110.

[57] See Bernard Lewis, *The Muslim Discovery of Europe* (New York: W. W. Norton, 1982).

[58] E.g., we might recall the long theological-linguistic discussion about the purity of the Arabic language, especially as expressed in the Qur'an.

acculturated. Those who deny or depreciate this evidence, generally for ideological reasons of a narrowly nationalist type, mythify the synchrony to the detriment of its diachronic complement. They either place themselves outside of history or give it a prearranged interpretation that tends to command attention as "constructed" and definitive "representation," together with – as its more-or-less-deliberate purpose – the obstruction of sociocultural exchanges. It is a perfectly obvious and well-known fact that Islam and the West have a long history of symbiosis and exchange.[59] Nevertheless, if there is some confusion in our present-day criteria, it is because all healthy acculturation presupposes the conscious acceptance of responsibility for the past – an acceptance that necessarily leads to esteem – as well as reciprocity. As soon as acculturation is seen as a massive, dominating, and one-sided invasion – that is, as soon as the conditions of the exchange are too seriously unbalanced and human dignity is slighted – civilizations develop protective mechanisms within themselves that generally take on forms hostile to foreign values, with a view to restricting their importation or stopping it altogether. Just now, however, the true situation happens to be concealed under a cloak of carelessness and a lack of balance.

Apart from some important exceptions, which have no real influence on the masses, the West has placed too much trust in the superiority of its own model and, by the very extent of its successes and achievements (which have literally transformed our life on earth), has found itself doomed to engage in an anthropological, socioeconomic, and ethnocentrist religious-philosophical discussion, which, thanks to an almost systematic blackout, has gone so far as to deny or ignore the fact that, at a decisive turning-point in its history, Western culture and civilization were able to profit by knowledge and values borrowed from Islam. Quantitatively, its secondary-school history textbooks grant a ridiculously limited amount of space to Islam, while "qualitatively" they give more space to the appearance, that is, especially the expansion, of Islam, which is described as violent and aggressive (*jihad*), while breathing hardly a word about its enormous legacy to civilization. In

---

[59] E.g., counsult Joseph Schacht and C. E. Bosworth, eds., *The Legacy of Islam*, 2nd ed. (Oxford: Clarendon Press, 1974).

this way, Western civilization is ritually described as Judeo-Christian, which is not incorrect, of course, considering its dominant characteristics. However, we forget that it is not solely Judeo-Christian, and Garaudy is certainly not wrong in writing – even if in an occasionally over-strained tone – that by denying its "third heritage," which it owes to Islam, this civilization has "cut itself off from dimensions of primordial importance."[60] As a result of this mutilation, the Westerner has some sympathy for Athens and Rome but none whatever for Baghdad or Cordova. Under these conditions, how can they understand one another or reach any understanding whatsoever?

Western protectionism has been matched by an Islamic protectionism, especially during the last decade or so[61] – ever since Islam, freed of its complexes, has regained confidence in its message and its own values. The products of the West have invaded the Islamic market to the point of smothering it, both physically and culturally. Islam does not reject everything out of hand, but from now on it intends to make a free and intelligent choice insofar as it can, even if its efforts seem to be rather unsystematic. It proposes to turn the page of the forced cultural crossbreeding imposed by the relationship of rulers to ruled. The main protectionist filter that we are trying to install everywhere, with various therapeutic specificities and indications, bears the name of *shari'a*. A return to *shari'a* is being demanded by a great majority everywhere in Islamic countries, but the whole point is to know which *shari'a* it should be.[62] Is it the code roughly drawn up during the third century (ninth century, C.E.), revived more or less whenever necessary, as the Islamists would like it to be, or is it a radically new draft based on foundations (*usul*) to meet the needs of a century whose main characteristic is one of constant change, with steadily increasing acceleration? Better

---

[60] Garaudy, *Promesses de l'Islam*, p. 17.

[61] See the official documents of the first symposium on *La crise de l'evolution civilisationnelle dans la patrie arabe* (*Azmat al-tatawwur dl-hadari fi l-watan al-arabi*), Kuwait, April 6-12, 1974; also see the official documents of the symposium held at Rabat, Novemter 25-27, 1982, on *Legs et action politique (Al-turath wa-l-'amal al-siyasi)* (Paris, 1984).

[62] An Academy of Islamic Legislation (*al-majma' al-fiqhi al-islami*) has been established under the auspices of the Organization of Islamic Conferences, headquartered in Jidda. See note 11, above.

understanding must necessarily depend on a clear awareness of this new requirement, which appears to us to be totally irreversible.

Islam and the West find themselves equally in the same crisis. Islam is seeking its own way. This is the etymological meaning of *shari'a* ("the way," as it is also of the talmudic Hebrew *halakhah* and the New Testament *hodos*). The West, for its part, confronted with its ethical contradictions and disturbances, has lost its illusions, not to mention its sense of triumph. Moreover, our universe is shrinking. We have no choice except to agree to good neighborliness in the interest of all, insofar as possible. I have written elsewhere that, in this era of satellites, computers, and increasingly sophisticated audiovisual techniques, our planet is "already too small for our ambitions and our dreams."[63] Henceforth, whether willingly or not, every person is the neighbor of every other person. Cultural protectionism of any kind is no longer anything but a completely illusory rearguard action. It is also quite illusory, however, to think that a single civilization – in this case the Western one – can impose its categories on the universe to the exclusion of all the others. Some consoled themselves with that hope in the nineteenth century. Today, nobody any longer believes it seriously.

In the order of creation, and for believers in accordance with the Creator's Plan (*sunnat Allah*), we are undoubtedly passing through a decisive mutation. We must now combine the particular with the universal, preserve our identities without going into seclusion, and both give and receive in a free exchange of sharing and fruition, not one of monopoly and domination. Is the West quite sure that there is nothing it can borrow from the Islamic model? Garaudy – a thinker whose successive searches for a new social order for what will soon be six billion human beings have been unfairly described as the sign of a biased instability – doubts this with a clairvoyance that deserves consideration. There are *promises* in Islam[64] for the West, and, in the West, there are *ways open* for Islam.

---

[63] Muhamed Talbi, "Une communauté de communautés: Le droit à la différence et les voies de l'harmonie," *Islamochristiana*, vol. 4 (1978). p. 11.

[64] Title of R. Garaudy's book, *Promesses de l'Islam*.

We have deliberately emphasized the fundamental oppositions between the two model societies, but are they doomed to remain completely separated from each other? Do they contain only positive factors on one side and only negative ones on the other? The West has favored immanence, while Islam is, above all, the religion of transcendence. However, any excess, in either direction, involves risks. The West has deified matter, and Islam has suffered from enormous technological backwardness. Perhaps the West should realize that the realm of Caesar, no matter how specific it may be, is also, after all, the realm of God. Consequently, property is not the "right to use and abuse" (*jus usendi et abusendi*) inherited from the Romans a conception that for human beings is alienating, desacralizing, and enslaving since, in the final analysis, "The Realm of Heaven and Earth belong to God and God is the final goal of all."[65] The motto of the 1789 French Revolution was "Liberty, Equality, Fraternity [in inclusive terms, "Solidarity"]." After many struggles, this revolution succeeded in implanting political liberty among the principles of morality. The Russian Revolution of October, 1917, stressed equality, which it is still trying to establish at the cost of liberty. Since then, we have been constantly torn between two temptations: that of individualism, which inspired the Declaration of Human Rights of 1948, and that of collectivism, which attracts the poor, that is, the Third World. Meanwhile, we have lost the sense of "solidarity." However, Islam is precisely the religion of "solidarity." Will its role consist of reintroducing "solidarity" in the universal equation, with a view to elaborating the civilization of the space age – a civilization with a renewed humanism, an unbounded humanism in which ethical values will act as a counterweight to an overwhelming material power? Let us at least dream of it, both for our own well-being and for better understanding.

In order to play this part – if only in a dream – Islam first has to restore its full health. Meanwhile, it is important for us to reflect on the efficiency of the West, which has succeeded, even at the cost of many injustices, in making God's earth more fruitful to the point where it supplies us with a large

---

[65] Qur'an, Surat al-Nur XXIV, 42. This principle of the absolute royalty of God, the only real owner of everything in heaven and earth, is asserted in no fewer than twenty-seven verses. See index to the Qur'an under *mulk*.

percentage of our daily bread, a percentage that – alas! – may go on increasing with time.[66] Instead of creating a mentality of grumbling and mutinous charity cases, we will do better to revise our models, to engage in self-criticism, and to assert our dignity by our ability to solve our difficulties and our problems – first of all by our own resources, which are tangible and real. Know-how, in particular, is not served up on a silver platter but must be earned.[67]

For Islam, the recovery of economic health, the key to everything else, is a pressing and vital necessity. The West, for its part, is familiar with problems of overproduction, overdevelopment, and unemployment. This situation can lead to bankruptcies and narrow and disastrous rivalries, but it can also lead to an intelligent joining of interests. It is up to us to choose what path we will follow. It is not in the interest of the rich – whether individuals or nations – to be too rich or for the poor to be too poor.[68] In order to continue to produce, to continue to become rich, it is necessary to be able to sell, but it is impossible to sell except to those who can pay – that is, in

---

[66] M. Zalzala, an Assistant General secretary of the Arab League, warned of "the impending aggravation threatening the Arab world's food situation" ("Alarming food situation in Arab world," in *Le Temps* [Tunisian daily], December 12, 1984, p. 16). "The Arab world imports $25,000,000,000 worth of food, which constitutes thirty-six percent of the entire world's food exports."

[67] At the initiative of the Organization of Islamic Conferences, an Islamic Foundation for Science, Technology, and development was established on May 10, 1983. Let us hope it will fulfill its promises.

[68] This shift on the plane of material civilization and life standard is a comparatively recent phenomenon. Of special interest in this regard is a book by Gabriel Marc, *Le développement en quête d'acteurs* (Paris: Centurion, 1984). Making use of Fernand Braudel's classic, *Civilisation matérielle, économie et capitalism du XVe au XVIIIe siècle* (Paris: A Colin, 1967-; tr. Miriam Kochan as *Capitalism and Material Life, 1400-1800* [New York: Harper & Row, 1973]), Marc confronts us with figures that force us to pause and reflect: "In 1700, on the basis of the 1960 exchange rate of the dollar, the gross national product per inhabitant ranged from 150 to 190 in England and from 250 to 290 in the British colonies in America (the future U.S.A.). In 1750, it was 170 to 200 in France, 160 to 210 in India (140-180 by 1900!), and 228 in China (but 170 by 1950!). Globally speaking, by about 1800, the GNP per person in Western Europe was about $213; in North America, $266; in what is now the Third World, about $200. In 1976, however, on the basis of the same 1960 exchange rate, the Western European GNP had reached $2,325, but the Third World's only $355" (p. 92). In short, less than two centuries ago, that is, "before the Industrial Revolution, the life standard was almost the same everywhere in the world, approximately $200 a year on the basis of the 1960 exchange rate, with a slight advantage in favor of the ancient Asiatic civilizations" (p. 93).

accordance with the purchasing power of the consumers, who are being sought everywhere more and more. Poverty is ruinous for the rich, not only *intra-muros* but also *extra-muros*. It is no longer possible for any effective and permanent development strategy to be other than universal and directed toward the long term. Any excessive imbalance, especially on a worldwide scale, involves all kinds of risks of earth-shaking disaster. It is in the interest of Islam and the West, along with all other cultures, to mobilize their moral and material resources to avert these dangers.

Humankind being what it is, however, it is naive to hope that wisdom can prevail without some struggle. There is no example in history of those poor, whether individuals or nations, who have been able to improve their lot without struggling to bring about an increasingly just distribution of wealth. To write is to fight. It is the duty of the best writers of the West and of Islam to gird themselves for the battle to create a confluence of interests.

It is not only economic challenges that face us, however. As our frontiers are opened up, irreversibly and more and more widely, to people and ideas, another major problem of our time can no longer be treated in isolation: that of women's liberation. Jean-Pierre Cot and Dominique Taddei recently wrote as follows in *Le Monde*: "The demand for equality of the sexes is probably the most revolutionary change of our time, because, by its very principle, it denies the most ancestral division of labor, and thus the most widespread forms of domination."[69] This phenomenon, with its various intensities and accelerations, is irreversible and universal. It is illusory to think that Islam will escape indefinitely the feminist revolution and preserve for all time its model of the separation of the sexes, even if Islam wins resounding victories here and there for a short time. Wearing the veil in town and the strict separation of the sexes in school – from the primary through the higher grades – and at work are still the rule in certain Islamic countries, but for how long? In most of the countries of Islam, Muslim women are joining feminist movements and are complaining and demanding more every day. They are expressing themselves in print, as, for example, has the Egyptian physician, Nawal al-Sa'dawi.

---

[69] September 13, 1984, p. 19.

The traditional Islamic model is breaking down on all sides. Today, all Muslims think that the Qur'an, taking full account of the time of its revelation, was a gigantic revolution for the benefit of women. More and more people add that its original impulse has been broken on the rocks of conservatism and that it is in urgent need of liberation. Islam's future is linked to the future women. In all this way, in both a low and a high register, "the demand for equality between the sexes" is to be heard in the West as well as an Islam. This results in a certain laxity of morals, which explains the reactions of the Islamists who describe "woman's liberation" (*tahrir al-mar'a*) as "women's shamelessness" (*istihtar al-mar'a*).[70] Every form of evolution has its own risks, What is certain is that laxity, in the space age and the age of video-cassettes, can no longer be contained by regional frontiers. Morality is no longer only an affair of the family or even of the nation but involves all of us. Therefore, instead of fulminating against scandals–which, of course, are committed only by our neighbors–we would do better to pool the contributions of all our cultures, and in the case of believers all the resources and all the strength of their faith, in order to work out a code of ethics that is able to cope with a challenge that affects all of us on a universal scale.

At the level of faith, in a world that is becoming everywhere more pluralistic as well as secularized,[71] Jews, Christians, and Muslims–whether in Islamic or in Western countries–no longer have any alternative but to explore in common their various points of agreement. All of us, in Muslim

---

[70] The problem of the equality of the sexes and women's liberation has been passionately discussed in two Islamic symposia in Tunis. The first, financed by the Konrad Adenauer Foundation within the framework of the Centre d'Etudes et de Recherches Economiques et Sociales (CERES), on the topic "L'Islam aujourd'hui face aux défis de notre temps" (Waqi' al-Islam wa tahaddiyat al-'asr), was held November 12-16, 1984; the other, at the initiative of the United Nations University, which entrusted its organization to Mustapha Filalik was held on the topic "Le réveil religieux islamique" (al-sahwa al-diniyya al-islamiyya), on October 29-30, 1984. See the statements made by Filali to *al-Ra'y* (an opposition weekly in Tunis), November 16, 1984, p. 9, demanding "the return to Islamic values," noting that "women's liberation is only women's shamelessness, born of a blind imitation of everything that is most abominable in Western civilization."

[71] Concerning disislamization, see Mohammed Talbi, "Islam et Occident," *Islamochristiana*, vol. 7 (1981), pp. 62-71. According to a survey by B. Hermassi, five percent of all Tunisians openly proclaim themselves to be atheists (see *15.21* [a Tunis review], no. 8 [1984], pp. 44-46). According to a sample survey carried out by SOFRES, seventy-nine percent of the French proclaim themselves Roman Catholic (see *Le Figaro*, October 28, 1981, p. 12).

terminology, are *ahl al-kitab* ("people of the book"), hearkening to the revealed word of God. All our ethical systems, which have in common the fact of being scales of values that rely on and lead to God, meet together. It is unnecessary to repeat here what has been very well said by Father Maurice Borrmans in an article discussing whether Christians and Muslims have something to say and do together in the contemporary world.[72] Today's world, which is more easily than ever penetrated by good as well as evil, can no longer be saved except as a whole, by an intelligent, deeprooted study of the best of the cultures of all peoples.

To be sure, there are still – and will always be – aggressive and anachronistic proselytisms[73] that are tuned toward the outside while the edifices within are crumbling. This does not, however, prevent bridges from being progressively built. Jews, Christians, and Muslims – often with their minds wide open to the other great religions – are learning to listen to each other and to work together. These efforts, which are still too much limited to groups of initiates and not very well – or even badly – understood by outsiders, are all promises for the future. Let us mention, among many others, the Association of French-Language Believing Writers (L'Association des Ecrivains Croyants d'Expression Francaise), which holds a Judeo-Islamic-Christian symposium every year in Chantilly (a suburb of Paris); the Fraternité d'Abraham, which for many years has been bringing all the spiritual children of the "father" of monotheism closer together in a permanent dialogue; the Islamic-Christian Research Group (Groupe de Recherche Islamo-Chretien), which is relatively new and has a branch at Tunis presided over by Professor Saad Ghrab; the International Religious

---

[72] "Chretiens et Musulmans ont-lis quelque chose à dire ou à faire ensemble dans le monde k'aujourd'hui?" *Islamochristiana,* vol 4 (1978), pp. 27-46.

[73] We should note, e.g., that al-Bayan (a Tunis weekly) published a report in its issue of November 29, 1984, p. 16, that American missionaries, at a recent congress on "The Gospel and Islam," had announced the collection of $1,000,000,000 to launch a campaign to convert the Muslims to Christianity, since "the harvest is ripe." Michael Nazir-Ali, in his book, *Islam: A Christian Perspective* (Exeter: Paternoster Press; Philadelphia: Westminister Press, 1983), says, "The modern missionary movement won, as we have seen, millions of converts from Islam to Christianity" (p. 156). The West, for its part, denounces the pressure exerted on the Christians in the southern part of Sudan to convert to Islam – not to mention the Philippines, Indonesia, and the various rivalries in Africa.

Liberty Association, with headquarters in New York; the World Conference on Religion and Peace, whose fourth session at Nairobi (August 23-31, 1984) was attended by 600 delegates (including forty-two Muslims), who represented sixty-two countries; and, of course, the Islam and the West International (Islam et Occident International).

The World Council of Churches has included the Christian-Muslim dialogue in its program, and, besides the many meetings it had already organized, it invited representatives of all major religions to its General Assembly (July 24-August 11, 1983) in Vancouver. Since Vatican II (1962-65), the Roman Catholic Church has published a review specializing in the dialogue with Islam, with the collaboration of both Christians and Muslims: *Islamochristiana.* In the first volume of *Initiation à la pratique de la théologie*,[74] several chapters were written by non-Christians, including one Muslim. In this way, as far as faith is concerned, bridges are slowly being built between Islam and the West. Perhaps one day their thoughts may converge. We are gradually getting away from the unilateral and patronizing talk about the Other – the orientalist form of which caused particular indignation to E. Sa'id – in favor of a dialogue of equality with the Other.

This makes the official attitude of Islam all the more regrettable, since, when confronted with a dialogue, it adopts a reserved and distrustful attitude as if it suspected some snake-in-the-grass. In Islam's favor, we can only mention certain private initiatives, such as those due in particular to A. Bouhdiba, Director of the Centre d'Etudes et de Recherches Economiques et Sociales (CERES, in Tunis), or occasional ones, such as the meeting of a political nature at Tripoli (February 1-6, 1976). To this day, no internationally recognized and representative Muslim organization has officially included a dialogue with the West or Christianity in its program. The Organization of Islamic conferences (Jidda), which is an association of member-states, is open to dialogue, thanks especially to the personal beliefs of its Secretary-General, H. Chatty, and it gives financial support to Islam et Occident International, but it neither possesses an adequate permanent

---

[74] Bernard Lauret and Francois Refoulé, eds., *Imitiation à la pratique de la théologie,* vol. 1, *Introduction* (Paris: Cerf. 1982).

structure nor publishes any specialized periodical in this field. Nor has the World Muslim Congress (Karachi)–whose Secretary General, Inamullah Khan (a man open to new ideas) was elected president of the Bureau of the World Conference in Religion and Peace at Nairobi, in 1984–included dialogue in its official activities. The Muslim World League (Mecca) is even more reserved, in spite of a few hesitant and short-lived attempts or contacts.

In contrast to this absence of adequate Muslim structures specializing in other faiths, the Vatican has a "Secretariat for Non-Christian Religions," and the World Council of Churches has a department that specializes in "Dialogue with People of Living Faiths." There is no equivalent structure in Islam. There is, of course, an explanation for this deficiency. However, if it persists too long, it will no longer be excusable, and, above all, it will be very prejudicial to ourselves. It would be tragic if the situation that prevailed in the Middle Ages–at a time when *Studia Arabica* were flourishing in the West, without any counterpart in Islam–should be repeated! Once again, Islam could only stand to gain by training occidentalists and specialists in non-Islamic religions, by creating within itself structures that are open to dialogue, and, in a word, by becoming more "competitive," more credible, more translucid, and more lucid. The Konrad Adenauer Foundation financed an Islamic symposium in Tunis in 1984.[75] When will a Muslim foundation finance a Christian symposium? On such a day, there would be a prodigious leap forward in understanding.

Better Understanding

It is in our very nature not to be perfect and yet constantly perfectible, neither angels nor beasts, simply human beings–in the image of God for Jews and Christians, and inspired with the breath of the Lord for Muslims–who, because of this fact, have an innate sense of the Absolute and aspire to it. At no matter what level, from the simplest to the most complex, from the level of the family to that of peoples and states, complete understanding is an ideal–or a myth?–toward which the curves of our

---

[75] See note 70, above.

impulses and our infirmities aspire asymptotically. Thus, we die without ever having truly understood or been understood.

Misunderstanding is a break in equilibrium, which – when confined within the reasonable limits of our right to be different – is perhaps just as necessary for our psychic and intellectual progress and the dynamism of history as a certain imbalance is indispensable for our physical growth. We advance by falling, while remaining providentially upright. Complete understanding – assuming it were possible – means, at its fullest, immobility. Pushed to the extreme, it is neither possible nor even desirable. A certain mixture of misunderstanding, that is, of irreducible identity and irrepressible specificity in apprehension and appreciation, is necessary for an exchange, for creativity, and for mutual enrichment, just as a difference in concentration is indispensable for osmosis. Better understanding, therefore, does not consist merely of sharing our convergences but also in clearly allowing for our divergences – not in a chauvinist spirit of opposition or aggression, but in a spirit of complementarity in mutual esteem and respect. It is not healthy that a culture should be forced to lose or, worse, to sell its own soul.

To sum up, Islam needs the West and the West needs Islam, and all of us together, with our vocations, or our universal pretensions, need the other culture, all the cultures, vigorous and very much alive, that is, not emptied of their own soul and their own genius. This idea, which, when taken abstractly, is simple and obvious, has been so obscured and clouded over in our actual behavior by our pretty interests and deep-rooted prejudices that we end up banishing it from our thoughts altogether.

Although we are not sure we have escaped a threefold peril – the danger of indulging in commonplace, systemizing, and irritating the reader – we have tried to clear a few paths that might lead to a better understanding. In short, we have agreed "to dream of a dialogue" because, in spite of disagreements, we do not think with Brière,[76] that, after all is said and done, "nobody is right." In any case, we refuse to side with those who exaggerate the point. In spite of that, however, we are not incurably and

---

[76] Brière and Carré, *Islam, Guerre*, p. 130.

excessively optimistic, at least about the immediate future; what the distant future will be, we simply do not know. One thing, however, is certain: if we simply fold our arms or if we fan the flames of controversy, that future will be a very ugly thing. If, instead, we take up the challenge, there is some chance that, if we bet on the better side, we might still win. In the end, it is a question of faith.

ISLAM AND SOCIOECONOMIC DEVELOPMENT: REFLECTIONS INSPIRED BY MOHAMED TALBI[*]

· Khalid Duran[**]

I. The Scope for Defense and Offense
How to Tackle the Topic

Is Islam compatible with present-day notions of development? This question has been raised repeatedly, answered differently by Muslims of diverse sects, tendencies, and schools of thought. Liberals tend to downplay the *shari'a*, the traditional law of Islam, which they mostly know only superficially, and base their optimism on a selective reading of the sources, picking out what seems to suit their developmental expectations. Islamists ("fundamentalists") are even more optimistic, because they believe that Islam offers its own plans for economic salvation, just as much as it is the only means to spiritual bliss. Holding Islam to be radically different and, of course, superior to human-created systems, they project the *shari'a* as an "Islamic system of economics" (also of education, government, transport, etc.), as a "complete-code-of-life," as the panacea to all our woes – be it taxation or recreation, tribulation or vacation.

The recent spate of literature on Islam and development rarely broaches the issues worrying the experts in the field, in the sense that practical matters disappear behind a mass of theoretical propositions

---

[*] *Journal of Ecumenical Studies*, 25:4, (Fall, 1988).

[**] Khalid Duran (Muslim), (See above, p. 49).

unrelated to reality. Nor is there much genuine theology involved. The link to the primary sources of Islam is mostly construed. A brand new voluminous literature on an "Islamic system of economics" is surely interesting insofar as it is the produce of an impressive elite in an important part of the Third World. However, it fails to make the point as far as Islam is concerned. This Islamist thought does not clarify what is specifically Islamic about it or, where there seems to be a truly specific element, how far this is defendable as normative Islam rather than as a fairly unrelated concept developed by someone who happened to be a Muslim, among other things. It invariably boils down to the questions of "Why Islamic?" and "Islamic how?"

Had those writings been presented as "Egyptian economic theories," "Iranian development concepts," "a Turkish economic system," "Arab development strategies," or even "debates on development in the Muslim world," there would be less controversy and frustration. Those specifically interested in matters Islamic would still scrutinize all those writings in the hope of uncovering some genuinely Islamic components that make a difference. However, they might no longer feel as much at a loss as after studying dozens of volumes on "Islamic economics."

The Islamist claim to (re)present something truly and uniquely Islamic has not been fulfilled and, therefore, causes disappointment. Authoritative standard works on "Islamic economics" do not exist. There are only a few tentative books on questions of socioeconomic development by outstanding Muslim thinkers with a religious bent of mind and a training in theology. Not all of those rare books are readily available, and none is being promoted, so the question of a best-seller on Islam and economics does not arise. Instead, we are swamped with the stray reflections of gifted journalists, such as the Egyptian Sayyid Qutb (d.1965) and the Pakistani S. A. A. Maududi (d. 1979), thinkers are not scholars, imaginative laypersons but not well-grounded theologians or economists, skillful agitators but not responsible administrators. They have filled libraries with Islamist propaganda, just as we have libraries replete with the works of orthodox scholars who are not thinkers. The books produced by both groups are enjoyable to read for the one thing they all share: polemics.

A discussion of "Islam and economic development" is, therefore, forced into the politically tight corner of withstanding the Islamist onslaught. Unmasking Islamism for its shallowness and alienation from the divine message is surely a worthwhile exercise, though not actually constructive. For a positive contribution one has to dig out the rare examples of well-reasoned, intellectually honest, and religiously motivated attempts at delineating Islamic specificity without absurdities and self-distortions. There is, then, little choice but to follow the method of treasure-hunting, with the concomitant danger of blowing a discovery out of proportion, of over-estimating a thought experiment because of its rare originality and cogency, of wrongly assessing as mainstream Islamic what might be condemned to a future in a sectarian hide-out. Since both methods are not frequently met and since there is comparatively little Muslim critique of Islamism (critique from a religious perspective) and even less Muslim highlighting of the exceptions to the rule (such treasure-hunting is commonly left to non-Muslims), an attempt in this direction is being made here, stimulated by Muhamad Talbi's refreshing reflections – of one who is both scholar and thinker.

II. Confusing an Ethical Impetus with Government Regulations

As an adolescent, spending some weeks in Sarajevo, the capital of Yugoslavia's Muslim region, I was impressed by the force of Islam chiefly through its institution of *auqaf,* the voluntary bequeathing of property for charity. Those pious foundations used to be of paramount importance in many Muslim countries. In Algeria, prior to the French occupation in 1830, most of the cultivated land was *auqaf* property, and the entire educational system was run on that basis. People were fairly prosperous and educated then. *Auqaf* bore some resemblance to an American-style "network," with the maximum number of people connected to it. The disadvantage of this "state capitalism" was that the colonial administration found it easy to handle. Simply by taking over all *auqaf* holdings, they got enough of what they needed for a thorough exploitation, without having to resort to brutal measures of expropriating individually. In Sarajevo there was scarcely any major edifice that did not belong to the *auqaf*, and, in 1955, some of those buildings were still strikingly modern, having been built just before World War II with what was, then, the most advanced technology and architecture. *Auqaf* represented anything but Ottoman stagnation. There was no question of petrification in medieval patterns. It was a compatible institution in tune with the trends of the time.

In those days there were no "Islamic banks' and no institutions of an "Islamic system of economics." Whenever we discussed the economic or sociopolitical aspects of Islam, we used the word "*auqaf*" to denote all that. Under it we subsumed most economic activity of the Muslim community: mosques, schools, hospitals, hostels, and hotels were all *auqaf* property. Whether Islamists or not, *auqaf* filled most of us young Muslims with pride, for it showed us the successful transformation of Islam's moral impulse into economic power and social welfare.

In 1955, *auqaf* had been grabbed by Yugoslavia's communist government, so only a few mosques continued with limited funds from *auqaf*. The edifices, however, stood tall, bearing impressive testimony to Muslim social commitment. As such, they were a galling challenge to the totalitarian state with its fierce repression of religion, Islam in particular. Many Muslim leaders were still in jail, and there was a tight control on all Islamic activities. Yet we felt exhilarated. It was a great thing to belong to such an "efficient" community with so many imposing structures devoted to the common weal. It looked to us as if we had no difficulties in beating the other side with its own yardstick of material progress. We were convinced that, given a chance, we would be ahead of them, due to our superior institution of *auqaf*.

No doubt, pious foundations exist in many cultures. A Protestant pastor in Denmark might be housed in a Christian *auqaf*, that is, the church might provide accommodation in a building set up as a pious foundation, bequeathed by some member of the parish. Still, the way *auqaf* developed as a Muslim institution seems fairly unmatched. The Hispanic institution of *monte de piedad* probably comes closest to that of *auqaf*, as, in all likelihood, it was partly stimulated by the Muslim example in Spain. *Auqaf* is a concrete and viable expression given to Muslim ethics. It is a "homespun" – not a foreign – device, based on genuine religious motivation. As such, it contrasts sharply with the Islamists' chimeric "Islamic economic system," which is "reactionary" in the true sense of the word, because it is a reaction to "foreign" systems experienced as superior. Aside from this, it has been more propaganda than reality, until now.

What has happened to *auqaf* since then? Significantly, the Islamist literature on our "complete-code-of-life" hardly ever mentions it. It does not seem to be a characteristic of their version of Islam. The key concepts of their ideology are the "profit-and-loss-sharing" of the "Islamic banks," *zakat,* and their unfathomable paper-tiger called *bait al-mal* (originally an Arabic equivalent of "finance ministry"). It would be patently futile to counter their tall claims and similarly exaggerated glorifications. *Auqaf* is no wonder weapon. As a matter of fact, it is scarcely an economic measure at all. An economist would have to classify *auqaf* in a rubric to be shared with other items. The decisive point is that here Islamic ethics had been given a practical expression that has captivated the imagination of many generations and engendered mechanisms whereby communal welfare was effectively promoted. In the final analysis, the continuation or revival of this success story depends on the strength of faith. It is a moral issue. The administration of *auqaf* property would still be subject to political decisions of either a more capitalist or a more socialist outlook. Here, however, the abundance of historical precedents provides some guidance.

The question of *zakat* is basically not very different. It used to be levied as a tax in the earliest days of the Caliphate, but even a "fundamentalist" thirteenth-century theologian of the stature of the Ibn Taimiya reasoned that a Muslim government had the right—and was obliged—to raise any tax deemed necessary for the community and that the totality of taxes could, or should, go by the name of "*zakat.*" The introduction of *zakat* as an additional tax for Muslims in Pakistan, analogous to the church tax in some European countries, has had results not very different from what we observe in the Christian environment. Large numbers of Pakistani Muslims resort to tax evasion. *Zakat* has not had the desired result, partly because for decades it used to be projected as a miraculous tax that would mean less taxation and more welfare. Since those expectations were impossible to meet, disappointment was great and eroded the Islamic commitment of many believers. If Ibn Taimiya's arguments are not heeded, the only other viable resuscitation of *zakat* seems to be that of Mahmud M. Taha in Sudan (d. 1985), who put the moral principle above the historical model. *Zakat*, then, would be superseded by *'afu*, which implies a much larger sharing of property, but one based on free decisions. Like *auqaf, zakat* would be what it originally signified, a moral "purification" not tied to any particular percentage of one's property. The historical model comes closest to what we now call a property tax. In the Qur'an, *zakat* is mostly mentioned in one breath with prayer (*salat wa zakat*) and evokes the notion of repentance, a cleansing of sins.

Interest-free banking is not a monopoly of Muslim economic thought, but it is certainly an important notion in Islamic law. The Professor Fadl ar-Rahman, one of the greatest scholars of Islam in our times, argued convincingly that the *riba* ("usury") prohibited in the Qur'an was something very different from the interest we pay on bank loans today. *Riba* in the time of the Prophet was primarily an exorbitant interest on consumer loans, ranging from 100 to 200 percent. Throughout history, however, many Muslim scholars have understood *riba* to mean every type of interest, no matter how small the percentage. Thus, there exists a weighty psychological obstacle to legalizing any interest rates at all, even if only from eight-and-a-half to sixteen percent.

Muslim history, however, has also witnessed the sad spectacle of "circumvention," or the devious art of practicing whatever was found profitable, provided it was properly camouflaged. The science of subterfuge was highly developed and found expression in many a *kitab al-hiyal* ("book of ruses"). For more than a century now, reformers have labored hard to rid Muslim societies of this mentality of circumvention, trying to stop people from taking recourse to *hila* ("subterfuge"). Incidentally, in this respect the Jewish defenders of *halakha* and the Muslim advocates of *ash-shari'a* act like twins. "Islamic banking" is seen by many critics as little more than a reemergence of that age-old art of honoring the *shari'a* by devising skillful means of circumventing it. For reformists this is precisely the major argument against the Islamist economic network.

III. An Islamist Reenactment of Potemkin

Numberless international institutions and organizations dealing with "Islamic economics" or various development issues are branching out—and not only all over the Muslim world. In fact, one can easily notice a peculiar preference for Western countries. Luxembourg, for instance, has become the matrix for "Islamic banking," as have Frankfort and Geneva. In the Muslim world Sudan is the country with the largest number and richest variety of "Islamic banks." This appears particularly odd in view of the fact that this country has been in the throes of death ever since 1983. It is apparent that there is something weird about this mushrooming of "Islamic" development institutions in the most unlikely places. One does not have to probe deeply into these matters in order to realize that there is something fishy about them.

In reality, most of those institutions serve the interests of Islamist parties and do not represent the community at large. They tend to be establishments or front organizations of political parties such as the "Muslim Brotherhood" in several Arab states, the NIF ("National Islamic Front") in Sudan, the *Jama 'at-e Islami* in Pakistan and India, or their offshoots. In a few cases the initiative rests, with somewhat independent individuals, but those are very individualistic enterprises, indeed. Moreover, if they are not in any way allied with the Islamists, they are definitely not opposed to them either. So far there is no Muslim alternative to the "Islamic banks" and other Islamist development institutions.

An almost uninterrupted chain of international conferences on questions of "Islam and development" is being sponsored by the above-mentioned institutions in order to endow them with credibility. Curiously enough, those conferences and seminars, too, take place more in Western countries than at home, through in the Muslim world there is no dearth of them. Monitoring such meetings and analyzing their discernible trends has turned into a university discipline and helped some Western scholars on to well-earned fame—a lucrative fame, moreover.

Outsiders scarcely realize how one-sided and artificial this activity is and how unconnected it is to Muslim community life. In the few instances where something like a grassroots level was attained, the enterprise soon flopped, accompanied by enormous controversy, if not scandal. In such cases, however, it is being treated as an isolated phenomenon and is not seen as a manifestation of the international network behind it all. Such was the case in Egypt in 1988, when the "Islamic banks" succeeded in attracting large numbers of Egyptian expatriates (working in the Gulf countries) as their customers. The Egyptian government, anticipating fraud of unmanageable proportions, took action against those banks without, however, reporting on the international ramifications of the scandal and without naming related Islamist bodies in other countries. The cosmopolitan personalities advocating and representing this type of "Islamic development" in international organizations and academe remained untarnished. Attention focused on the Egyptian businessman Ar-Rayah and the narrow confines of his local finance speculations. His compatriot, Gamal 'Attiya in Luxembourg, was never mentioned, nor was the Pakistani politician and professor of "Islamic economics," Khurshid Ahmad, one of the top figures of this pan-Islamist syndrome.

Turkish Islamists are led by Necmettin Erbakan, a professor of economics who received his university education and professional training in West Germany. Twice he shared government responsibilities as a junior coalition partner. Erbakan exploited those opportunities beyond measure and influenced government policy out of proportion to the size of his small "National Salvation Party." There can be no doubt as to the specificity of his program which differed starkly from that if his social democratic coalition partners (Prime Minister Ecevit's *Halk* Party), whose efforts he so adroitly sabotaged. The specificity of Erbakan's program lay in his emulating the policies of West Germany's most conservative leaders, such as former foreign minister Franz Josef Strauss and the late Professor Ludwig Erhard, who was an economist himself. Otherwise, there was nothing in the writings of dealings of Erbakan's part that stood out for being distinctly Islamic, except for ostentatious mosque construction. It might well have all been sane and sound, and it would make perfect sense to call this a "Muslim democracy" analogous to the "*Christiana Democrazia*" in Italy or Germany. However, it is not plausible why all that had to be declared as an incomparable "Islamic system," as something divine rather than human. This self-inflationary attitude of the Islamists not only discredits them politically, but it also has obscured the issues academically.

The late military dictator of Pakistan, Zia al-Haqq, took his revenge on the "Islamic Social democrats" of executed Prime Minister Bhutto. Workers whose lot had been improved in the name of "Islamic Social Democracy" were now humiliated in the name of "Islamic fundamentalism." Zia al-Haqq reversed Bhutto's populist policies and favored the entrepeneurial class. While Bhutto's government had purposely favored the rural population over urban dwellers, the military regime did the opposite. This is all well and good, but what, then, are we to believe about Islam?

In Iran "Islamic development" is as controversial now as it was in 1979, when the present regime came to power. Ten years of theocratic rule have not been enough to settle the question of nationalization. Does Islam stand for a larger government sector or a larger private sector? What are the proportions of each sector in a mixed economy, one *Islamically* mixed? Opinions among the ruling clergy are bitterly divided on these issues. The longer the controversy rages, the clearer it becomes that each party uses Islam as a shield for its very personal ends. This scarcely needs to be corroborated. Just in case some believers have difficulties ridding themselves of illusions, the Shi'ite divines keep the controversy alive, though it has long since degenerated into a monstrous absurdity. According to his followers, Khomeini issued some 22,000 *fatawa* (statements of expert opinion on questions of theology and religious law). They want this legacy to be the major (if not exclusive) source of guidance for Muslims for all time to come. In terms of economics this has not brought us any further. Even if we refrain from judging Shi'ism in light of Iran's abysmal realities, this copious output of Islamist theory is anything but an outpouring of the Holy Spirit. The existence of those many tomes is about the clearest proof that nothing cogent can be expected from Iran. Or, should we wait for another 22,000 *fatawa* before concluding what the "economic system" of Islam is and what it is not?

The truth is that normative Islam – the Qur'an and the Hadith – does not supply us with clear-cut formulas to answer these questions. There is not even much material or Medinese precedent on which to pin any interpretations connected with these issues. The Qur'anic revelation is concerned with other matters. It aims at refining the moral conscience of believers. This is to aid them in their deliberations on questions of politics and economics. The Qur'an was written by neither Adam Smith nor Karl Marx, by neither Lord Keynes nor Milton Friedman. Islamist claims that it competes with all of those are misleading.

IV. A Thought Experiment to Extricate Ourselves from the Impasse

As opposed to the Islamo-Facism of Khomeini's theocracy, we find, at the other end of the spectrum, an "Islamic Left" that believes in a modern trinity of "Islam-democracy-socialism," or "Islamic social-democracy." A former president of Iran, the deposed Abu l-Hasan Banisadr, personified the romantic Third World revolutionary who loves to read his academic research back into the Holy Scripture, or vice versa, however clumsily and arbitrarily. Finally, there are the many Muslim skeptics who are convinced that there can be no emulation of Japanese or Brazilian development success until and unless Muslims are subjected to a thorough secularization.

While Bhutto's "Social-Democracy" was disestablished by the Islamist military, Islamist President Banisadr introduced a copy of Bhutto's development concepts in Iran – in the name of Islam, of course. It is small wonder, then, that many Muslims feel confused. Some give up, having reached the conclusion that the answers lie elsewhere. Islam and economics, they aver, should be treated separately. Seventy years ago a similar situation drove Turkey into Kemalist secularism. The adherents of the revolutionary preacher 'Abd al-Hamid Khan Bhashani in Bangladesh were mostly destitute peasants. His views on development bore a certain resemblance to Maoist tenets. The saintly Mahmud M. Taha in Sudan was a wealthy engineer who gave away all his belongings and lived Gandhi-like. His ideas on Islamic development bore the mark of romantic socialists such as Owen. Utopian socialism continues to keep many Muslim reformists spellbound. Such leaders as Bhutto and Banisadr, with their teams of indigenous experts, made full use of the research by development specialists at Western universities, with whom they had rubbed shoulders during their student days and later.

Their attempts at finding Islamic legitimization by a rather far-fetched linking up with Qur'anic verses might not have been swaying, but their Islamist successors have been even less cogent, as well as less coherent.

The problem with both tendencies has been that they relied less on the moral injunctions of the Qur'an. The first half of the revelation, those parts of the Qur'an revealed in Mecca, yield a forceful stimulus, but the common tendency has been to look for technical instructions. Those, however, are scarce even in the Medinese second portion of the revelation. Banisadr's *iqtisad-e tauhid* ("economics of divine unity") makes pathetic reading, underlined by an unmistakably good intention. sincerity, and religious eagerness. Following an entirely different track, the moralist Mahmud M. Taha's argumentation is compelling, but he neither passed on to concrete economic thought nor propounded development concepts.

An attractive picture could be put together if Mahmud Taha's theological groundwork were complemented with Banisadr's concrete economic schemes. One could still argue, then, that the ethical preamble is universally religious and not specifically Islamic, while the development concepts are the common property of a global vanguard. Nonetheless, such a testimony would be at least as authentically Islamic as any analogous Vatican document is genuinely Catholic. Total originality seems neither feasible nor absolutely necessary. What Muslims require and long for is a morally appealing sobriety consistent with the sources and shorn of fallacies and facile constructions. For the vast majority, a pragmatic approach does not run counter to Islam unless religious susceptibilities are unnecessarily offended. The Islamist manipulation of those susceptibilities has generally been counterproductive. In countries having experienced Islamist development under dictatorships – such as Iran, Pakistan, and Sudan – this has produced more nihilism than optimism. The question is no longer what Islam provides with regard to economic development, but the demand now is for an Islamic formula to overcome the cynicism created by the broken promises of the Islamists.

V. Oil on the Flames of the Hottest Issues

Development is not a phenomenon restricted to banking and the acquisitions of technology. The social factor is equally, if not more, decisive. The Islamist attitude toward labor unions is alarming, to say the least. In times of opposition to an "infidel" government, they set up rival unions or subvert existing ones. Once in power they tend to outlaw their rivals, while their own unions turn into "Yellow unions," analogous to what we witness in the Soviet bloc. There is, however, little use in discussing such details since they can all be subsumed under the heading of "democracy." Islamism, as long as it does not change its negative attitude toward democracy, amounts to little more than the form of fascism specific to the Muslim world, comparable to fascism in Spain under Franco (which differed from fascism in Germany).

The highly centralized totalitarian state cannot maintain the loyalty of a sufficient number of people in Middle Eastern countries that are mostly multinational, ethnically and linguistically diverse, and religiously divided. The Persian-Shi'ite theocracy of Khomeini is at odds with the ethnic minorities of Arabs, Baluchs, Kurds, and Turkmens; with the linguistic minority of the Azeris; and with the religious minorities of Sunnis, Baha'is, Jews, Zoroastrians, and Armenians and other Christians. The Islamism of the Muhajirin and a few Panjabs in Pakistan is an even more tenuous case, while the multifaceted Sudanese civil war is perhaps the worst instance. In all those states democracy is the precondition for industrial nations.

As if there were not already enough divisive factors, Islamist rule in Pakistan endeavored to disenfranchise women and the illiterate peasant population. With more than ninety percent of the population excluded from the political process, development efforts are condemned to failure. Reliance on international relief aid for refugees and the export of mercenaries (a major source of income for Pakistan under Zia al-Haqq) is not only too temporary and fragile a basis for development, but it is also patently un-Islamic. One does not have to be a Muslim to understand that the neglect of agriculture under the Shah was both uneconomic and immoral. Nor does one have to be a pious believer to be appalled by the vulgar luxuries of a small ruling class while the dependence on food imports increases. (It was abusive under the Shah and became unbearable under Khomeini). Likewise, one does not need to be steeped in traditional morals to feel aggrieved by the separation of tens of millions of families because the men have to migrate in order to keep their dependents alive, back in Pakistan, Turkey, Egypt, Sudan, Tunisia, Algeria, Morocco, Mali, Senegal, etc.

The first victim of economic misery in the Muslim world is the family, because an ever-increasing number of families have to live separated from one another, often not seeing each other for several years. As this gives rise to promiscuity and prostitution, there is a desperate longing for the protection of the most essential human ties. To this the Islamists react with the worst type of self-deception. The answer to this extremely grave problem is not the reinforced seclusion of women, as the Islamists would like to have it. As long as no work can be provided to allow families to stay together, all efforts should concentrate on providing better housing so as to ensure a modicum of privacy. The little extra privacy desired by most Muslims would be a second step. The Islamist talk about Islamic architecture is frivolous as long as it presupposes a living standard out of the reach of the average person.

In Iran the revolutionaries were realistic enough to demand the barest necessities of life for the "damned of the earth" (*mustaz'afin*). The Islamist leadership, however, soon set other priorities. The demotion of women to the position of second-class citizens in Iran and Pakistan only aggravates the anomalous situation created by massive migration of the men. Women in many Muslim countries have to fend for themselves in a way Europe experienced during and immediately after World War II, when millions of men either died or were prisoners of war far from home. Europe rose from the ashes rapidly because women were in a position to contribute their share. Islamists behave suicidally by further incapaciting women. Anachrist elements at the fringes of the Islamist movement resort to different and radical measures, especially in Egypt. Those might be dubious and devious but they highlight the utter failure of mainstream Islamism with its abstract approach to social problems.

CHRISTIAN-MUSLIM DIALOGUE:
CHRISTIAN PERSPECTIVES

EDITORIAL

CHRISTIAN DIALOGUE WITH NON-CHRISTIANS[*]

Leonard Swidler[**]

From the first year of its existence the *Journal,* at least to a limited extent, dealt with religious dialogue beyond the circle of Christians. Quite appropriately the non-Christians first turned toward were the Jews. Efforts have expanded in that area and will continue even more so in the future. With Number 1 of Volume 5 JES moves still further into the dialogue between Christians and non-Christians. Several authors wrestle with problems inherent in the confrontation between the world religions.

Until recently there really did not seem to be any problem for the Christian when he faced the non-Christian religions. There was no problem because the vast majority of Christians almost never encountered a non-Christian religion – except Judaism, and it was usually pigeon-holed by conversion, ghettoizing and oppression. The only other contact the average Christian had with non-Christian religions was either through some exotic stories or promotion of Christian foreign missions. But this relative isolation is growing dramatically less possible for the average Christian because of a variety of reasons, prominent among which is the explosion of mass communications and mass travel. As a consequence Christians are now

---

[*] *Journal of Ecumenical Studies,* 5:1 (Winter, 1968).

[**] Leonard Swidler (Catholic) see above (first page of Introduction).

becoming aware that they do have a problem in the confrontation with non-Christians.

It used to be quite clear that the Christian attitude toward non-Christian religions should be that of one having the truth over against error; the consequent actions for the Christian was to promote conversion wherever possible. Perhaps most Christians felt (and many still do) that non-Christians were so hopelessly mired in error that if they were not converted to Christianity they would be eternally lost. However, as Christian theologians began to know more and more about non-Christian religions, many similarities with Christianity were perceived. Complete rejection of other religions as totally erroneous became rather difficult under those circumstances.

One theological response to this new situation was to set up a comparative scale, with Christianity as the standard against which other religions were to be measured – much as the Roman Catholic Church did with itself vis-a-vis other Christian Churches (cf. *Constitution on the Church*), or Orthodox theologians do. Whatever was found in Islam, Hinduism, etc. that was the same as in Christianity was true and good, and to the degree the particular non-Christian religion approximated Christianity (read: Catholicism, Orthodoxy, *vel alii*), to that degree it was good and true – but, of course, why be satisfied with half or even three-quarter measures?

Today, however, this rather imperialistic and self-centered attitude is felt by many Christians to be no longer (if it ever was) appropriate. It is felt that Christians must be much less self-confident in the face of God's Providence. They must come to the other religions, which have been on earth for hundreds and even thousands of years, with a humility that seeks to learn what roles they play in God's Providence, in what ways they manifest God to man, how they lead man toward salvation. As the Second Vatican Council has so dramatically restated, the Spirit is not confined within the Roman Catholic Church – nor within Christianity! Christians are *obliged* to seek Him wherever He can be found.

But if Christians are to come to the other religions in humility to learn something more of God and His will for man and the world, they must meet them with openness and in dialogue. If Christians are going to be receptive to the truth they must shut off no possible avenue of its approach; they must be open to truth (God) everywhere, and follow it when it is found, even when it means a modifying or abandoning of earlier presumedly unchangeable positions (e.g., the complete reversal of the Papacy on religious freedom, from Gregory XVI in 1832 to John XXIII in 1963).

If Christians are going to be involved in dialogue they must listen to the other person. But if they are really listening to the other person, they must be open to the possibility of being persuaded by him. If they are not, they are not really listening, but are just preparing to answer. And if the Spirit is in some way speaking through the other person, they will not hear Him—of what greater sin can a Christian be convicted than refusing to hearken to the Spirit?

But if the stance of the Christian toward non-Christian religions is to be that of openness and dialogue, what of conversion? what of the whole missionary enterprise? This is a very complex and agonized problem that cannot be analyzed, let alone solved, in an editorial. In fact, it will not be solved by any one person, but will yield only to much thought and experimentation—and error—by many deeply concerned Christians and non-Christians all over the world and in all stations of life.

What does seem clear is that Christians are called upon to witness to Christ before the whole world, and that an essential element of this witness is serving the world. Thus it is clear that the Christian is following the Gospel if, for example, when living among Muslims he serves their needs, as through teaching, medical work, etc. If a Muslim, because of this witness, becomes a Christian, "God be praised." If he should not decide to become a Christian, "God be praised." But the Christian does not serve the needs of the Muslim neighbor in order to entice him into Christianity, but rather because he loves him as his neighbor.

It also seems clear that Christians ought not approach and attempt to convert, say, Hindus who are informed and committed, but must come to them in openness and dialogue. But what of those who are largely ignorant and indifferent or, at most, superstitious (perhaps like many millions of nominal Catholics among the poor of Latin America)? They must be helped to be able to make a free commitment. But how can they make a *free* commitment if they are in ignorance? Obviously they must have knowledge to act freely, but can a person born into a Buddhist culture be said to make a free religious commitment if he is taught only the best about Christianity and is left in ignorance of the religion of his culture? I believe not. But is it the task of the Christian in a Muslim land to help ignorant Muslims to become better Muslims? I believe *yes,* in the following sense.

Perhaps the Christian, without in any way denying or hiding his Christian commitment, could, when directly dealing with religious matters, describe the Muslim teaching on the matter as well as he could (perhaps with the help and presence of a Muslim teacher?); he could also describe the Christian teaching, stressing the similarities, without obscuring the differences. Should the man eventually choose to remain Muslim, he would be a much better Muslim than before. Is such a procedure used by any Christian missionaries at present? I do not know. Is such a procedure even practicable? I do not know. But by Gospel command Christians must seek to be present in all lands to witness to Christ. They could not, and should not, avoid having direct confrontation on religious matters. But when it comes it must be open, seeking the truth wherever it may be, and dialogic, listening and speaking to all persons.

EDITORIAL
ON CHRISTIANS AND JEWS...AND MOSLEMS[*]

George H. Tavard[**]

Even before the contemporary Age of Dialogue, Christians have, at their best moments, looked to Jews to learn more about God's design for mankind. One could draw a long list of important links in the Christian theological tradition which resulted from intellectual and spiritual confrontation with Jews – not least in the field of Old Testament exegesis and meditation. One can show that the very structure and nature of the Christian liturgy derives from the experience of the early Christians, who prayed within the traditions and with the forms of Jewish prayer. One can also evaluate the indirect contribution of Jews to the great theological syntheses: in the 13th century, for instance, Thomas Aquinas quoted a number of Jewish scholars with respect and approval. In any case, we could conclude that the Christian tradition would be very different from what it is, if Jews had not contributed to it.

There has also been another, less acknowledged, partner in the up-building of Christian thought: Islam. I would venture to say that at no time after the Hegira do we find an enriching of Christianity by Judaism without a parallel enriching by Islam. This is obviously demonstrable in the case of the

---

Journal of Ecumenical Studies, 8:2 (Spring, 1971).

[**] George H. Tavard (Catholic) was a *peritus* at Vatican II and a member of the Vatican Secretariat of Christian Unity. He is a world-known ecumenist, author of numerous books and articles and an Associate Editor of the *Journal of Ecumenical Studies*.

"entrance of Aristotle" into Europe by way of Spain and Sicily, in the interest of the early Franciscans and Dominicans in Islam, in the theologies of Raymund Lull and Nicholas of Cusa, in the Christian Cabbalists of the Renaissance. In our own time, Vatican Council II found it impossible to publish a decree on the Christian attitude toward Jews that would not also speak to the problem of Christianity's relationship with Islam. We may think that this was simply due to the art of public relations (one had to take account of public opinion in Egypt, Syria, Jordan, Iraq, Lebanon, etc.) and ecclesiastical politics (one had to placate both the American bishops, inclined to friendliness with Jews, and the bishops of predominantly Moslem countries, inclined, naturally and often culturally, to friendship with Moslems). Yet the opportunism displayed in this instance may betray a deep-seated requirement of the wider Ecumenism.

Insofar as Judaism presents a challenge to Christian theology, this arises from the claim of both Jews and Christians to be heirs of Abraham and to have inherited the Covenant in its successive forms, Noachic, Abrahamic, Mosaic. But exactly the same claim is made by Islam. The Koran lists Noah, Abraham and Moses among the prophets; Mary and Jesus belong also to the historical sequences of the special friends of God. Thus, the basic theological question with which Christianity is confronted by the continued existence of Judaism as also a People of the Covenant, is also raised by Islam. Besides this, the semitic roots of Islam relate it especially to the Old Testament and to the spiritual patrimony of Jesus' ancestry in a way which (in the context of contemporary folklore) appears more obvious than in the case of modern Judaism. Furthermore, the fact that the career of Mohammed is relatively recent sharpens the edge of the Christian-Moslem question. For the Moslem claim stands to the Christian like the Christian to the Jewish: both rest on the assumption that the more ancient religion is fulfilled and abolished by the newer.

During the preparatory phase of Vatican II, in the yet unwritten prehistory of the Council's *Declaration on the Church's Relations with Non-Christian Religions,* a small team of *periti* tried to write a text that would have been much more theological than the *Declaration* eventually became. Specifically, the "mystery of Judaism" was examined; and an attempt was made to incorporate the doctrine of Paul's *Letter to the Romans*, ch. 11, into the conciliar declaration. It was soon discovered, however, that no such exploration of doctrine was possible. The team found that the other consultants and members of the Secretariat for Christian Unity were not in agreement on the meaning of the Pauline passage and on its relevance to current relations between Christians and Jews; the insertion of an interpretation of *Romans 11* in the *Declaration* had to be abandoned. Attention was then given all but exclusively to more immediately concrete questions: the remains of anti-semitism among Catholics, and the expression, "deicide." Whatever reasons militated against giving such a theological dimension to the *Declaration*, the text finally promulgated by the Council remains unfinished at the very point where Christian theology needs to arrive at a clear position. For if one cannot determine the exact place of Judaism in the Christian pattern of salvation, the place of the Christian community itself would seem to remain uncertain. The self-identity of the Church hangs in the balance as long as we have no firm conception of the religious identification of Judaism in relations to Jesus and to his disciples.

Patently, the interpretation of Paul's *Letter to the Romans* cannot involve Islam directly, since this faith developed six centuries later as a separate religion with a claim to a new prophet. As a Jew, Paul would not be tempted to include among the People of the Covenant those whom the Bible identifies as the descendants of Abraham through Ishmael. Yet, as a recent convert to the Christian faith, Paul, according to *Galations* 1:17, travelled to Arabia: "Immediately, without seeking human advisors or even going to Jerusalem to see those who were Apostles before me, I went off to Arabia." One cannot tell whether Paul went to the Jewish diaspora in Arabia or to the Arabs themselves and to the other tribes which bordered on the land of Israel. Yet the children of Agar, not unlike the Samaritans of old, are not Gentiles; they also belong to the family of Abraham and they are sons of the Promise. The suggestion may then be entertained that Paul's thought in *Romans 11* remains obscure because a third term was missing in his treatment of the subject: Israel after Jesus should be seen in its relation to the other children of Abraham. This could not be done adequately as long as this third biblical group had not defined and unified its relationship to the

Covenant. This was achieved by Mohammed in the Koranic Revelation and the religion of Surrender to the One God. Before Islam, we had a relationship between three variables of which only two were known. The advent of Islam was therefore a necessity for Christian (and, perhaps, also for Jewish) self-definition in relation to Abraham and to the God who revealed himself to Abraham. As I have written elsewhere, "The religions of the Book are one, and Mohammed is one of their prophets."[1]

This leads me to the paradoxical and – at this time – dangerous proposition that there can be no fruitful dialogue between Christians and Jews unless Moslems are included. It may even turn out that the key to the Jewish-Christian dialogue will come from the witness and contribution of the religion of Islam, and that, as long as Moslems are not partners in the dialogue, Christians and Jews will simply exchange platitudes. For, apart from Islam, there is no third party to judge their fidelity to the One God, and no point of comparison to gauge the value of their biblical monotheism.

Unfortunately, recent history makes a dialogue between Jews and Moslems unthinkable. Too many political, economic and merely human problems need to be solved before such a dialogue becomes a less than remote possibility. I would even think that, with rare exceptions, a genuine dialogue between Christians and Moslems cannot be initiated until a lasting peace is restored in the lands of the Bible, which are holy to the three religions concerned. If this is indeed so the dialogue between Jews and Christians may have to be postponed indefinitely. For the three religions of the Book cannot meet together until Moslems are invited to sit with us, and until they can accept the invitation with integrity.

The day this editorial arrived at the JES editorial office, the first meeting of the Jewish-Christian-Muslim dialogue took place at Temple University – Leonard Swidler.

---

[1] *La Religion a l'epreuve des Ides Modernes* (Paris, 1970), p. 110.

TOWARD THEOLOGICAL UNDERSTANDING OF ISLAM[*]

R. H. Drummond[**]

Understanding Islam has always been exceedingly difficult for Christians. From the earliest stages of its expansion until the Western political dominance of the Muslim world which began with the end of the eighteenth century, Islam was in a special way, partly because of geographical contiguity, the chief religious, cultural and military competitor of the European Christian world. Rivals are generally unable to acknowledge the good points of each other; Christians and Muslims have been no exception[1]. Both Christianity and Judaism were on the scene beforehand and possessed criteria to interpret and evaluate the new movement. Unfortunately, they generally did not give to the matter the same serious theological attention that Muhammad gave to the relationship of his own prophetic role to the great monotheistic faiths that preceded him.

A key figure in the founding of what has been called the "deformed image of Islam" long held by Christians was the church father John of

---

[*] *Journal of Ecumenical Studies,* 9:4 (Fall, 1972).

[**] Richard Henry Drummond (Presbyterian) received a B.D. from Gettysburg Theological Seminary and a Ph.D. from the University of Wisconsin. He was a missionary in Japan for a number of years and more recently has been Professor of Ecumenical Mission and History of Religions at Dubuque Theological Seminary. Besides numerous articles, Dr. Drummond is the author of *A History of Christianity in Japan* (Grand Rapids, Michigan: Wm. B. Eerdmans, 1971).

[1] Hendrik Kraemer used the term "fraternal enemies" to describe their relationship, *World Cultures and World Religions* (London: Lutterworth Press, 1960), p. 30.

Damascus (d. ca. 752).[2] John was born about fifty years after the *Hijrah* (the Migration of the fledgling Muslim community in 622 from Mecca to Medina, the event marking the beginning of the Muslim calendar) and before entering upon monastic life had, following his father, held high office under the caliph of Damascus. His knowledge of Muslim faith was considerable, his tone generally calm and fair, but as a part of his methodology of theological controversy he resorted to ridicule and began the long tradition of accusing Muhammad of pretending to receive revelations in order to justify his sexual license.[3] Nicetas of Byzantium in the ninth century went beyond this position to conclude after much subtle argumentation that the God worshiped by Muhammad was in fact the devil who had opposed God from the beginning.[4]

In general Greek speaking polemicists considered Islam to be a composite religion made up of borrowed elements, its law deriving from the law of Moses.[5] But almost all Christian writers took offense at what they considered the sensual aspects of Paradise as depicted in the Qur'an. Not a few were angered over the Quranic affirmations of God as the "cause" of evil. Many held that Islam served the goddess Venus and a few asserted that Islam in fact worshiped her.

Both Greek and Arabic materials began to be made available to the Latin West by was of Spain. One of the most important of the Arabic materials translated into Latin in Spain was the pseudonymous *Risalah,* or *Apology,* which dates from before the eleventh century and came to be widely disseminated and influential in Western Europe during the Middle Ages. This work devoted much of its attention to discussions of Scripture and the Trinity, but it stressed in detail those events in the life of Muhammad which

---

[2] Norman Daniel, *Islam and the West, the Making of an Image* (Edinburgh: The University Press, 1962), pp. 3-8, passim. *Cf.* J. Windrow Sweetman, *Islam and Christian Theology* (London: Lutterworth Press, 1945), pt. 1, vol. 1, pp. 1-83.

[3] J. P. Migne, *Patrologia Graeca,* vol. 94, cols. 761-780; 1585-1597; *ibid.,* vol. 96, cols. 1335-1348.

[4] Anatrope XXVIII (99-101), *ibid.,* vol. 105, cols. 797-800.

[5] Theodore Khoury, *Manuel II Paleologue, Entretiens avec un Musulman* (Paris: Les Editions du Cerf. 1966), pp. 114, 142.

it held to reveal him as sexually indulgent and a murderer. In addition to criticism of the general religious practices of Islam, it was largely negative in its evaluation of the teaching of the Qur'an as a whole, focusing its attack upon the concept of the holy war (jihad).[6]

In general the view of Western scholastics was that the Islamic emphasis upon the unity of God was correct, but deficient of course in its lack of the doctrine of the Trinity and the Incarnation. They saw the Qur'an as valuable only in so far as it seemed to corroborate the Christian Scriptures; as a whole it was considered an irrational book. Medieval scholastics regarded the prophethood of Muhammad as unauthentic: untruthful, morally evil, unverified by miracles. The lack of authentication by miracles was held to be a particularly glaring fault by the scholastics. Criticism of the person of Muhammad focused on his alleged sexual immorality and use of military force to achieve religious ends. The assertion was that the quality of his character made it impossible to accept his claim to be a true channel of divine revelation. The ethics of the Qur'an were determinist and, in so far as they could be approved, only copies of Christian originals. Both the prophet and the book were, in short, offensive to medieval European standards of rationality and sexuality.[7]

John of Damascus, as most later scholastics, considered Islam a Christian heresy, but neither in his case nor in that of later interpreters for a long period was there any serious attempt to understand and evaluate Islam as having significance in the history of salvation as this concept was understood in medieval Christendom. We may cite, however, certain steps in the lengthy process by which the Western image of Islam has gradually come to be altered.

Admittedly, the bitter theological contests of Hellenistic and later Western Christianity hardly contributed to the creation of a temper of mind favorable to calm and impartial evaluations of a religious tradition rising organizationally and geographically apart from historic Christendom. But political and cultural factors were perhaps equally important elements in the

---

[6] Daniel, op. cit., pp. 6-7.

[7] Ibid., pp. 271-275.

development of the Western image of Islam. Almost from the first generation after the death of Muhammad Christians in the Middle East, including the Byzantine Empire, came to be in a defensive position militarily. We may recall that until the rise of Venice in the eleventh and twelfth centuries the Mediterranean Sea was largely a "Muslim lake"; Christians could sail and trade thereon only by Muslim sufferance. In spite of important contributions from Christians to it, Islamic civilization, especially in its foci in Medina, Damascus, Baghdad, Basra, Cairo and Cordova, came to surpass anything that Europe, with the one exception of Byzantium, could offer. Christians therefore resented not only Muslim military power but also the general superiority of Islamic culture.

The Crusades constitute the first massive Western "counter-attack" to the centuries-long Muslim dominance. They were essentially failures from the standpoint of either military or religious expansion,[8] but they initiated a stream of cultural contacts which the West was then relatively more prepared to receive and which never entirely ceased thereafter. Even more important than the Crusades, however, were the cultural communications made possible through Muslim Spain and Sicily. As is well known, the Latin translations not only of Arabic versions of Aristotle and Neoplatonic philosophers but also of Arab philosophers themselves greatly disturbed and stimulated the European universities of the 13th century. The works of Albertus Magnus, Thomas Aquinas and other giants of the day owed much for their primary motivation to the presence of this challenge. Of great significance in the development of European religious life and thought was the influence of Sufi Muslim mystical writers on some of the great Spanish Catholic mystics. The high level of cultural achievement and social

---

[8] One is encouraged to note that at least a few European Christians of the time were sensitive to the essentially un-Christian nature of the Crusades. Among these were Ramon Lull and Francis Bacon. *Cf.* Ramon Sugranyes de Franch, "The Springtime of Missions in the Thirteenth Century," *History's Lessons for Tomorrow's Mission* (Geneva: W.S.C.F., 1960), p. 80.

refinement seen in Muslim Spain and Sicily attracted many Westerners who were eager to learn the *artes Arabum.*[9]

It is significant that Spain was the home of Sufi scholars who wrote most appreciatively of Christian faith. In Spain, particularly in Cordova and in Toledo, were to be found the "Mozarabs," Christians under Muslim rule whose primary language was Arabic and who lived largely in Arab style, to the extent of keeping harems and practicing circumcision. These men studied deeply Arab literature and the sciences and were exceedingly active as cultural transmitters of Islamic civilization. In Sicily under the Norman dynasty a similar cultural symbiosis took place, and the Hohenstaufen Emperor Frederick II (1215-1250) apparently drew the more modern conclusion of developing a religious relativism. Subsequent Muslim cultural influence upon the European Middle Ages was due also in no small part to their common participation in the Neoplatonic religious tradition, in which process of course the Sufis played an important role.[10]

A particularly interesting example of this religio-cultural development is seen in the person and thought of Nicholas of Cusa (1401-1464), who became a cardinal of the Roman Catholic Church. Nicholas, though of German origin, was an outstanding figure in the cultural as well as religious activities of the Italian Renaissance. As an expression of his humanist studies, he returned from a trip to Constantinople in 1437 with the vision of reconciling Christianity with Islam. We may recall that this was almost on the eve of the Council of Ferrara and Florence (1438-39), which explicitly declared that "all pagans, Jews, heretics and schismatics have forfeited eternal life and are destined to everlasting fire."[11] In his book *De Pace Fidei* Nicholas anticipated the position of the Enlightenment of the eighteenth century by stating that there is in fact only one religion, the cult of those who

---

[9] A distinguished Spanish scholar, Eladio Aranda Heredia, has shared with me personally his conviction that Spanish culture has been more deeply influenced by the Arabs than by the Roman Empire.

[10] Hendrik Kraemer, *op, cit.,* pp. 41-42, 46-47. A major point of Kraemer's study is that Islam is culturally primarily the mediator of the heritage of Hellenistic civilization.

[11] *Cf.* Karl Adam, *The Spirit of Catholicism* (Garden City, New York: Doubleday & Co., 1962), pp. 172-175.

live according to the principles of wisdom. The worship, he affirmed, even of the gods of pagan polytheism witnesses to the one God, and the divine Logos affirms the essential concord and unity of the great religions.[12]

Other humanists, such as Pico della Mirandola, Erasmus and Francisco de Vitoria, as a result of their studies of the great writers of classical antiquity came to appreciate in a new way particularly their ethical concerns. Early Renaissance humanists had a strong moral purpose and found much in Homer and Plato, Cicero, Virgil, Seneca and Plutarch that accorded with their own sense of Christian morality. But views of Islam like those of Nicholas of Cusa were rare. The prevailing practice was rather to furnish what a German Islamic scholar has termed *Schauermärchen and Greulpropaganda* regarding Muhammad and his religion.[13] In the Reformation period the position of Luther may be considered as in one sense representative of Protestant thought. He generally refrained from the scurrilous language of the previous period, but he considered the faith of Jews, Turks and Papists to be all of one type. While he had some kind things to say about both Jews and Turks – and some not so kind – his position is at least in part revealed by his reason for urging the town council of Basel in 1542 to change their decision and to permit the publication of Theodore Bibliander's Latin translation of the Qur'an because he wanted Christians to know what an "accursed, shameful and desperate book it is."[14]

Luther saw Islam as a demonic power of eschatological dimension and as God's chastisement (*Zuchtrute*) for the sins of Christendom. He also regarded rationalism as a primary characteristic of the Muslim faith, but before all the decisive criticism of Luther was that Islam rejects Jesus Christ as the God-man and Savior and sets in place of Christ a human prophet, not as mediator, but as the decisive communicator of revelation (*Offenbarungsträger*). Luther at least technically rejected the position of the Crusades with their notion of a holy war, but he considered it the divine duty

---

[12] *De Pace Fidei* 10-12, 16-18, 68; *Nikolaus von Kues Werke,* Paul Wilpert, ed. (Berlin: Walter de Gruyter & Co., 1967), vol. I, pp. 341, 342, 344, 366, *Cf.* Daniel, *op. cit.*, pp. 276-278.

[13] Emanuel Kellerhals, *Der Islam* (Basel: Basler Missionbuchhandlung, 1945), p. 316.

[14] *Ibid.*, p. 319. "Wie gar ein verflucht, schändlich, verzweifelt Buch es sei."

of the Holy Roman emperor to wage war against the Turks, not as *homo Christianus* but as *Kaiser Carolus*.[15] This conclusion is perhaps logical in the light of Luther's concept of the "two kingdoms," but the question may be seriously asked whether this mode of thought represents any distinct theological advance beyond Muhammad's concept of *jihad*.

The Enlightenment (*Aufklärung*) of the eighteenth century, in spite of its fondness for reason and the "natural religion" of man, found much in Islam that was congenial to its spirit. The horrors of the wars of religion following the Reformation had evidently impelled many of the more thoughtful and sensitive among the educated classes to take the further step, for which the Reformation had itself prepared the way, of rejecting the theological as well as ecclesiastical claims of the Christian Churches in their complete structural integrity. Men came increasingly to feel that they did not have to take any theological or confessional position "whole cloth."

At this time as the *Lettres curieuses ét edifiantes* of the Roman Catholic missionaries sent back from China created an enthusiasm for things Chinese in Western Europe, a veritable *goût Chinois,* to the extent that Voltaire expressly set off China in favorable contrast to "Christian" Europe, an appreciation for Islam developed in the heartland of Europe that was unprecedented. The Dutch scholar Hadranus Relandus (1676-1718), who was professor of Oriental Languages at the University of Utrecht, published in 1705 a two volume work entitled *De religione Mohammedanica libri duo,* which can be designated as the first scientifically objective representation of Islam to appear in Europe.

The spirit of the Enlightenment can be seen in Gotthold Lessing's *Nathan der Weise,* which represents the three religions of Christianity, Islam and Judaism in the parable of three brothers. Lessing does not say which of the three religions is the true one that makes men acceptable before God and man (*vor Gott und Menschen angenehm*), but the implication is of at least relative equality in salvific value. The Enlightenment saw a deep kinship to its own spirit in the rigorous monotheism of Islam, its strong moral emphasis, its decisive break with the dogma of the atoning sacrifice of a God-man, its

---

[15] *Ibid.*, pp. 313-319.

184

spiritual worship without use of images, and the loving devotion of its mystics.

My reason for dwelling somewhat on the Enlightenment is that while its influence upon Christian theology was but partial and varied, it constituted the beginning of a specific tradition in the wider intellectual community of the Western world which has continued unbroken and with perhaps increasing force to the present day. The presence of this tradition as an important element of contemporary Western civilization constitutes a significant challenge to Christian theology as it attempts to grapple with the problem of the meaning of the religions of the world in salvation history. The tradition is at its best neither irreligious nor necessarily theologically naive.

Concerning the theological interpretation of Islam, however, the influence of the Enlightenment on Christian orthodoxy in the narrower sense was small, on Pietism close to nil. In the English speaking world Thomas Carlyle broke new ground with an appreciative evaluation of Muhammad in his *Heroes and Hero Worship*. Carlyle approved of the "sincerity" of the Qur'an and rejected the traditional European view of Muhammad as a "common voluptuary." He saw the "soul of Islam" as aspiring toward cooperation with the good and just divine "Law of the World" in a manner essentially no different from Christianity at its best.[16] His work, however, was by no means representative of the official Christian community or of Christian theologians. Increasingly, to be sure, men took a different tone, and the vituperative language of the ages of *odium thologicum* came less to be heard among theologians of stature.

In the twentieth century we see the emergence of more perceptive and balanced understandings. Already in 1910 the Anglican missionary Temple Gairdner of Cairo was writing of the need for Christians to recognize the light of Christ, however "broken," to be found among the non-Christian

---

[16] The American writer Washington Irving in his *The Life of Mahomet* (New York: A. L. Burt Col, n.d.) wrote largely without rancor. He rejected views that Muhammad was an imposter or personally inclined to the use of force, but his conclusion was that, in spite of "the pure and elevated and benignant precepts as are contained in the Koran," as a prophet Muhammad had been deluded by mental hallucinations (pp. 328-332).

religions. The Report of the Jerusalem Conference of the International Missionary Council held in 1928 revealed new understanding and appreciation of the other religious traditions of mankind. In particular the Report affirmed that "We recognize as part of the one Truth that sense of the Majesty of God and the consequent reverence in worship, which are conspicuous in Islam."[17]   A fresh modesty with regard to the Christian responsibility in relationships with Muslims was manifested by James Thayer Addison in 1942.[18]   In more recent years some of the finest theological writing of our generation has come from the pen of Kenneth Cragg, who writes of Islam with a depth of sympathetic understanding and affection hardly to be equalled previously.[19]

One of the most important recent contributions to the problem, however, is that made by the Dutch scholar Arend Th. van Leeuwen. Some of the most eminent contemporary Islamic specialists writing in English, French and German are Christians who approach Islam as a kindred religion, but van Leeuwen brought to the problem unusually wide missiological as well as theological acumen.[20]   He sees both Christianity and Islam as the missionary arms of Judaism, Judaism making its entry into the nations through them.[21]   He regards Muhammad therefore as the counterpart of Paul: both directly confronted the Jews in polemical stance but both were apostles of the Hebraic faith in a new form, one to the Greeks, the other to the Arabs.[22]   Islam is in effect Judaism stepping outside itself into the Arabic

---

[17] *Ends and Odds*, Study Papers from the Anglican Archbishopic in Jerusalem, no. 1 (April, 1971), p.2; The Jerusalem meeting of the International Missionary Council, *The Christian Life and Message in Relation to Non-Christian Systems of Thought and Life*, New York City: I.M.C., 1928, vol. I, p. 410.

[18] James Thayer Addison, *The Christian Approach to the Moslem*, New York: Columbia University Press, 1942, pp. 11-40.

[19] To cite only a few of his many books, Kenneth Cragg, *The Call of the Minaret*, New York: Oxford University Press 1956; *The House of Islam*, Belmont, California: Dickenson Publishing Co., 1969; *Alive to God*, London: Oxford University Press, 1970.

[20] Cf. Geoffrey Parrinder, *Jesus in the Qur'an*, New York: Barnes & Noble, 1965, p. 10.

[21] Arend Th. van Leeuwen, *Christianity in World History*, London: Edinburgh House Press, 1965, p. 251.

[22] *Ibid.*, pp. 220, 250.

world as Christianity is Judaism stepping outside itself into the Greek (Hellenistic) world. Van Leeuwen also sees Islam as discharging the missionary role which Jewish Christianity failed to perform, a role which he believes only a Semitic community could perform. In this context note should be take of the importance of circumcision in Muslim practice, although it is nowhere mentioned in the Qur'an. The practice corresponded to ancient Arab custom and greatly facilitated the acceptance of Islam by all the tribes of the peninsula. Muhammad, according to Leeuwen, thus assumed the historic role, the missionary responsibility, of the Jewish people toward the whole of the Semitic world.[23]

Both Muhammad and Paul start from the premise that Abraham was no Jew. Both appeal to the religion (or faith) of Abraham as older than the Torah; both proclaim that those who *follow* Abraham, not those who merely name him, are his nearest of kin (or sons). But Muhammad, according to van Leeuwen, neither envisaged nor intended a radical break with Judaism.[24] The movement decisively detached itself from Judaism but without the theological significance which Paul saw in the separation of the Church from the Synagogue.[25] Muhammad apparently regarded the military victory of the Muslims at Badr as of comparable divine significance with the deliverance of the Israelites at the Red Sea.[26]

Van Leeuwen makes much of the significance of the Semitic image of Islam in the rise and expansion of its empire. Islam took full advantage of the anti-Hellenistic reaction of the Syriac world to Byzantine rule, and it must not be forgotten that the position of Jews under Islam especially in Spain, was relatively more favorable than under Christians.[27]

---

[23] *Ibid.*, pp. 221-226.

[24] *Ibid.*, pp. 230-231.

[25] *Ibid.*, pp. 239, 249. Van Leeuwen speaks also of a two-fold Muslim break with paganism and Judaism (and Christianity), but the latter break was by no means of comparable theological significance, in Muslim thought, i.e., not comparable with Paul's understanding of the Christian separation from Judaism.

[26] *Ibid.*, p. 240.

[27] *Ibid.*, pp. 256, 248-249.

Van Leeuwen in the effect assigns to Muhammad and the Muslim faith a specific and significant role in the history of salvation. He makes Muhammad an authentic prophet of the God of Abraham and regards his faith and the movement derived from it as essentially one with biblical faith and the biblical people of God. Van Leeuwen does not draw these conclusions in the terms which I use at this point, but I believe that they are legitimate inferences from the line of his argument. For him Islam, together with Judaism and Christianity, are to be sharply differentiated from the "ontocratic" nature religions of the world. Islam is therefore an instrument in the hands of the living God unto the salvation of the nations.

Van Leeuwen briefly touches on the important problem of the nature of the criterion to be used in a Christian evaluation of Islam. The mere use of the name Christian, he asserts, does not in every case guarantee similar content of either faith or moral life; he notes that the Christianity of some of the tribes of Ethiopia of the seventh century, as adapted to their ancient customs, differed much more drastically in many respects from what we understand by Christianity than did Islam.[28] Tor Andrae has said of one form of the Christianity that penetrated into the Arabian peninsula prior to Muhammad: "There is scarcely any other form of Christianity in which the evangelical thought of the forgiveness of sins and our sonship with God is so completely quenched as in this Syrian monastic religion. The pious man has to earn his forgiveness of his own power by life-long penitence and self-torment."[29]

Recent Roman Catholic thought on this subject has developed in directions largely similar to those of Protestants. In-depth, non-polemical scholarly studies of Islam have appeared early in this century. We may note, for instance, Louis Massignon, French orientalist and historian, who late in life became a Catholic priest of the Byzantine rite. His deep love for the Islamic world apparently developed in considerable part as a result of studies

---

[28] *Ibid.*, p. 218.

[29] Tor Andrae, *Der Ursprung des Islams und das Christentum*, p. 282, quoted in Lawrence E. Brown. "The Failure of Christianity under Muslim Rule," *History's Lessons for Tomorrow's Mission, op. cit.*, p. 65. Browne writes also of the lack of the sense of the saving grace of Christ or of spiritual power in the Eastern churches of the period, p. 67.

in Muslim mystics. His doctoral thesis (*la Passion d' Al-Halladj, martyr mystique de l'islam*) was published in 1922, and this focus of interest remained central to his thought and studies until his death in 1962. Other Catholic scholars were also to find at least in part the origin of their empathy and consequent theological understanding of Islam in the Muslim mystical tradition.

Through his studies of mysticism among non-Christians, Louis Gardet came to apply an emerging Catholic theological consensus specifically to his efforts to find possible theological meaning in the faith and life of Muslim mystics. He saw Catholic theology as now teaching that explicit faith in the one, just God – who can manifest himself authentically even in "deficient" expressions – somehow includes (*entraine*) implicit faith in all the revealed (Christian) mysteries. "If it is true that God does not cease to offer his actual grace to every soul in this world, it is evident that a righteous person (*ame droite*), regardless of the religious tradition to which he belongs, can be in a state of grace." Furthermore, if the mystical life is indeed the normal (even if not common) development of the life of grace, it is clear that one who participates therein can be, even unbeknownst to himself, the witness of this mysterious grace of Christ acting, as it were "at a distance" to penetrate the heart and bring it into conformity with divine love.[30]

At about this same time the most careful kind of scholarly work was being done by a member of the Pontifical Institute of Oriental Studies in Rome, Thomas O'Shaughnessy, S.J. In his *The Koranic Concept of the Word of God* (Rome, 1948) and *The Development of the Meaning of the Spirit in the Koran* (Rome, 1953) O'Shaughnessy showed himself to be in the forefront of technical specialists in Islamic studies. He had, however, apparently no openness whatever to the kind of empathy or theological understanding evinced by Gardet. The documents of Vatican II, on the other hand, were to show that Gardet was by far the truer representative of contemporary developments in Roman Catholic thought.

---

[30] Louis Gardet, *Experiences Mystiques en Terres Non-Chretiennes,* Paris: Alsatia, 1953, pp. 174-175.

Another scholar contributing to the background work which led to Vatican II was the English convert to Catholicism, Robert Charles Zaehlner. In his book *At Sundry Times* (London, 1958), which appeared in the United States under the title of *The Comparison of Religions,* Zaehner forthrightly affirmed Muhammad to be a prophet sent by God, precisely in the sense that Christians understand these terms.[31] In the long appendix written for the American edition of his book, Zaehner analyzed with considerable linguistic detail Quranic passages on Jesus and tried to show how "very much nearer" the Christology of the Qur'an is to orthodox Christianity than to the christology of the orthodox Muslim tradition. While one can hardly avoid the conclusion that with reference to certain points his argument is somewhat forced, he makes a convincing case for the larger conclusion that Muhammad himself had a distinctly higher theological view of "Jesus son of Mary, the Word of Truth, the Word of God" than almost all subsequent Muslims, except for certain Sufi mystics, have been willing to acknowledge. Zaehner concludes that for Muhammad Jesus was very much more than a prophet, that he was a special creation into which God's spirit was breathed and that the Qur'an seems to associate original creation, the birth of Christ and the universal resurrection at the end of history in a kind of redemptive scheme. He therefore feels that any fruitful approach to Muslims on the part of Christians must be made through the Qur'an itself.[32]

Among the documents of the Second Vatican Council, "The Declaration on the Relationship of the Church to Non-Christian Religions" effects of course the work of more persons than professional Islamcists or other specialists in history of religions. The work done on logmatic aspects of the problem by men such as Karl Rahner, Hans Küng, Heinz Robert Schlette and others was of comparable importance. But in the context of the long, unhappy history of Christian-Muslim relationships the words of this document with reference to Islam may surely be regarded as of momentous historical as well as heological significance. "Upon the Moslems, too, the

---

[31] R. C. Zaehner, *The Comparison of Religions,* Boston: Beacon Press, 1962, p. 197.

[32] *Ibid.,* pp. 195-217. Among other Catholic Islamic scholars at work in this period may be mentioned J.M. 'Abd al-Jalil, G. C. Anawati and Roger Arnaldez.

Church looks with esteem. They adore one God, living and enduring, merciful and all-powerful, Maker of heaven and earth and Speaker to men. They strive to submit wholeheartedly even to his inscrutable decrees, just as did Abraham, with whom the Islamic faith is pleased to associate itself. Though they do not acknowledge Jesus as God, they revere him as a prophet. They also honor Mary, His virgin mother; at times they call on her, too, with devotion. In addition they await the day of judgment when God will give each man his due after raising him up. Consequently, they prize the moral life, and give worship to God especially through prayer, almsgiving, and fasting."[33] In this necessarily limited and arbitrarily selective account of Roman Catholic developments we may perhaps properly conclude with reference to a post-Vatican II work of Louis Gardet. At the end of his massive volume *L'Islam, religion et communauté* Gardet comes to the conclusion that a Muslim *qua* Muslim may have the explicit faith necessary to salvation. If a Muslim sincerely tries to be faithful to the moral demands of Islam, if his intentions are right, if he repents of his wrongs and responds to the overtures of his Lord, can we not assume, Gardet suggests, that he is then in favor with God, that he belongs invisibly to the visible Church, even though he himself might not so understand his situation, and that he belongs already *"d' une certain façon"* to the people of God. Such a man would therefore be saved not in spite of belonging to Islam but precisely in committing himself to believe and live by those truths which the Muslim tradition, in so far as it is their source, insistently transmits and which, given a man's sincerity of heart, divine grace is able to illumine and exalt to his eternal benefit.

Gardet believes that the great non-Christian religions participate in a mysterious way in the march of mankind toward the Good News (*la Bonne Nouvelle*) and that the infinite mercy of God will cause to be saved the many who make it their refuge.[34]

---

[33] Walter M. Abbott, S.J., ed., *The Documents of Vatican II,* New York: The America Press, 1966, p. 663. *Cf. ibid.* (Lumen Gentium II, 16), p. 35.

[34] Louis Gardet, *L'Islam, religion et communauté,* Paris, Desclee de Brouwer, 1967, pp. 417-418, 419-429.

The question may now legitimately be asked: by what standard may Christians properly evaluate Muhammad and the Islamic movement? We can hardly use "Christianity" as our standard, for we shall be asked: what form of Christianity? It is Christianity as understood by Paul or by John? Is it the Christianity of the great christological controversies? If so, what side of a particular controversy is the norm? Is the Christianity of the creeds the norm, none of which says that God is good or that Jesus "went about doing good?" Or should we take the Christianity of Gregory the Great as our criterion, the medieval scholastics, Meister Eckhart, the Reformers, Torquemada, Francis Xavier, or Zinzendorf? Are we to think in terms of older or new Roman Catholic teaching, of Protestant orthodoxy or liberalism of Eastern Orthodoxy or of Monophysitism? The variety of manifestations, not to say extremes, in this arbitrary list suggests the difficulty in deriving significant value judgments from formal or nominal classifications. The difficulties encountered in a confrontation of "Islam" with "Christianity" – for both reveal comparable ambiguities – are among the reasons compelling me to focus the last part of this paper primarily on the Qur'an.[35]

My intent here, however, is not the comparative study of religions; it is theological interpretation from the perspective of Christian faith. I make this interpretation on the basis of criteria which I hold to be representative of authentic Christian faith: the Scriptures of the Old and New testaments, particularly as they witness to the supreme norm, Jesus the Christ, and as they are interpreted in the context of the guidance of the Holy Spirit and of the fellowship of the community of faith.[36] These criteria serve to evaluate and criticize empirical Christianity as much as any other community of faith. It we use them to interpret Islam, no confessional or institutional interests need be served. On this basis, then, my intent is to interpret theologically the phenomena of Muhammad the Prophet of God and the Qur'an, of which he claimed to be the channel of revelation.

---

[35] On the problem of the question of the definition of "Islam," see Kenneth Cragg, *The Call of the Minaret, op. cit.*, p. 29.

[36] *Cf.* Richard H. Drummond, "Authority in the Church: An Ecumenical Inquiry," *The Journal of Bible and Religion*, vol. XXXIV, no. 4 (October, 1966), pp. 339-341.

The faith of Muhammad was an uncompromising monotheism, and the primary issue in his prophetic ministry was that between worship of one God and idolatry, which he generally understood in terms of polytheism and the worship of images as they were found in the pagan Arabia of his time. There are those interpreters who say at this point that the Allah of the Qur'an is not "the God and Father of our Lord Jesus Christ," that profound and irreconcilable differences exist between these two understandings of the nature of the Godhead. Statements of this kind, however, would seem to depend upon definitions of God which would, if applied with the same rigor, equally put into the category of the radically different (from leading New Testament concepts) the concept of God of many, if not most, of the prophets of the Old Testament and possibly of some of the writings of the New. There are differences in the understanding of the nature and work of God as held by Amos and Hosea, by Paul and James, by Second Isiah and the writer of the book of Revelation. Yet we are not accustomed to regard these men as referring to a different God in their proclamation of his word. Even Kenneth Cragg, who affirms that the differences between the Muslim and Christian understanding of God are far-reaching, insists that the Christian and Muslim faith in the one supreme sovereign Creator-God refers to the same Being.[37]

The New Testament seems to suggest in its understanding of the significance of the suffering of Jesus the Messiah, seen as the Son of the Living God, that in some way God the Father also suffers.[38] Donald Baillie speaks of "the widespread modern tendency to modify the impassibility doctrine,"[39] and in comparison therewith the Qur'an has no concept whatsoever of the atoning suffering of God. For Muhammad the entire

---

[37] Cragg, The Call of the Minaret, op. cit., p. 36.

[38] Cf. Jn. 1:14; 2 Cor. 5:18; 1 Pet. 2:24 Cf. The Hebrew of Jer. 31:20; 48:36. Luther understood this mystery so as to say "da steydet Gott mit Gott." Cf. Kazo Kitamori, Kami no Itami no Shingaku, Tokyo: Shinkyo Shuppansha, 1958, pp. 17-27; English edition, The Theology of the Pain of God, Richmond, Virginia: John Knox Press, 1965, pp. 20-25.

[39] Kenneth J. Woollcombe notes that in spite of this "widespread modern tendency" major theologians have given the problem relatively little attention in depth. His own article is learned and helpful. "The Pain of God," Scottish Journal of Theology, vol. 20, no. 2 (June 1967), pp. 129-148.

matter of how it is cosmically possible for God to forgive lay hidden in the mystery of his sovereign will. Yet the main thrust of early Greek theology affirmed the impassibility (non-suffering) of the Father, and Cyprian coined the derogatory nickname of Patripassians for the Modalistic Monarchians whose theological position seemed to suggest the "absurdity" of the suffering of God the Father.

We have to do here with theological differences of perhaps considerable importance, but these differences were not considered in the history of the Church of such significance as to warrant classification of those differing as not deserving the name of Christian. The differences, also of some importance, between the understanding of the nature and work of God in Old Testament and New have not, in the main stream of Christian thought, been considered such as to warrant denial to either witnessing community of the right to belong to the people of God. Similarly, my contention is that the differences which obtain between the New Testament and the Qur'an and which are of considerable significance are yet the differences of those belonging to the same stream of religious apprehension; they are differences within the family, not between those who are within and those who are without. Just as we consider the prophets of the Old Testament as authentic prophets of God in spite of certain differences from the witness of the New, so, I believe, should we regard Muhammad – and his message – as an authentic, although not infallible, prophetic servant of the same God.

There is no doubt that by the historic standards of Christian orthodoxy Muhammad and the Qur'an would be classed as heretical even though familial. Specifically, his view of Jesus combines elements of Arian, Nestorian and Docetic teachings. One might reply that wider variations have appeared in the stream of Christian history, sometimes without formal classification as heretical, but the point at issue is whether Muhammad and the movement to which he gave birth have some significance in the history of salvation, whether, on the basis of the central message of the Christian Scriptures, they have been instruments of the God of Abraham to the furtherance of his salvific purposes toward mankind. Muhammad was utterly convinced that this was so, and in spite of the long tradition of Christian interpretation to the contrary I am in essential agreement with this aspect of the understanding of his prophethood. Let us briefly consider in order the reasons for this conclusion.

Firstly, in contrast with the natural religions of blood and soil, the God of Muslim faith is one, transcendent, sovereign and free, the Creator of the heavens and earth. His will is sovereignly free of his creation and, in particular, of the structures of human society. The ethics which derives from his will is therefore sociologically free, not beholden to the interests of king or priest. Even though Islam in Medina and afterwards was in principle a theocracy and after Muhammad the role of prophetic criticism of the state was rarely given its due, Muhammad himself was primarily prophet and only instrumentally political ruler. He was not *imprimis* concerned with state-directed ethics even though at Medina this area necessarily occupied much of his attention. He was first of all a prophet of God concerned with the preparation of men to meet their Maker, and the whole apparatus of state was for him but an instrument in the service of this central purpose. The ethics of the Qur'an is rooted in the will of God, who is good and other than man.

Similarly to the prophets of biblical tradition. Muhammad saw God as the Lord of history, as revealing his will and purpose to men, as working within them and in their midst. The Qur'an apparently has no concept of "secular history" with independent significance of its own. Apart from the will of God human life for Muhammad was naught but meaningless folly and disaster, and the truly important was the Hereafter. But the life of this world had a real though secondary and derivative significance; it was the place where God speaks and acts and where men are called to free faith and responsible action.

The Qur'an is not merely a book which reveals law; it also reveals God, whose hands are spread wide in bounty.[40] Islam, at its best, is not a bargaining religion; it creates free and responsible men who love God and

---

[40] *Qur'an* 5:64. For the numbering of the verses of the Qur'an I use the translation of M. M. Pickthall, *The Meaning of the Glorious Koran*, New York: The New American Library, 1961.

want to do his will. The ethics of the Qur'an is at bottom an ethics of the heart.

Muhammad was a religious leader remarkably free from fanaticism or institutionalism. His profound respect for the monotheistic faiths which had preceded him, his long held and obviously sincere desire to have constructive and co-operative relations with their respective adherents, show a man essentially above self-service and merely partisan loyalties.

In the history of the Christian Church one of the touchstones of Christian faith has been the answer to the question: what do you think of Jesus, the Christ? On the basis of the Qur'an we may judge the answer of Muhammad to be as in the following paraphrase: I believe that Jesus the son of Mary is the Messiah, the prophet and messenger of God, the Word of God. Special is he among the prophets, and to him God gave clear signs and God strengthened him with the Holy Spirit. He was born of a virgin pure and preferred above all the women of creation. He was taught of God and healed the sick, gave sight in the blind and raised the dead by the permission of God. He is illustrious in this world and in the Hereafter, one of those brought near to God, one of the righteous. He was sent as a messenger of God to the Children of Israel and came confirming that which was before him of the Torah and yet making lawful some of that which had been forbidden before. In the midst of widespread unbelief he called out men to be his helpers in the cause of God, men who could help because they had surrendered to the purpose of the Lord of the worlds. God caused him to follow in the footsteps of the prophets who had gone before him, gave him the Gospel and placed compassion and mercy in the hearts of those who followed him. He was a pattern of conduct for the Children of Israel, God made him (and Mary) a sign for all peoples; he is God's revelation for mankind and a mercy from him.[41] In the Gospel given him is guidance and a light. Generally no distinction is made among the prophets of God, but God

---

[41] The citations in the Qur'an upon which the above affirmations are based are (in order) as follows: 2:87 (cf. 4:64); 3:42; 5:75; 66:12; 3:47; 19:20 (cf. 4:156); 5:110; 3:49 (cf. 4:157); 3:45-46; 3:48-49; 3:50; 3:52; 5:111; 57:27; 43:59; 21:91; 19:21.

exalted some above others. Of those who are thus exalted I (Muhammad) instance particularly Jesus, son of Mary.[42]

There are certain reservations that Muhammad made with regard to classical Christian confessions of faith. He rejected the notion that the Messiah is the "son" of God; he avoided even the term "Father" as designative of God because of its suggestion of physical paternity and pagan deities who mate.[43] For Muhammad, Jesus, son of Mary, however exalted was only a messenger, a slave of Allah, a part of the creation, and yet a special part of creation, one before whom, like Adam, the angels should fall down in obeisance. Muhammad apparently rejected the historical fact of the crucifixion and therefore its atoning significance. Rather than the resurrection he stressed the ascension of Jesus. But those who follow Jesus he believed to be set by God above those who disbelieve, and the spread of the Christian faith to be veritably the result of the work of God.[44]

As a biblically oriented Christian I am not able to share this (Quranic) confession in toto. But I am profoundly grateful for it. Above all, I can not bring myself to be hostile to a religious teacher who has such an exalted conception of Jesus the Christ. I feel myself impelled even further to express that "genuine word of love for Muhammad from the followers of Christ" which the Christian scholar Daud Rahbar has recently asked for.[45] I believe I owe him that element of sympathy which a Muslim writer has called "a fourth dimension."[46] I see him as an authentic Prophet of God, even though, like other prophets both before and after the time of our Lord, neither morally perfect nor doctinally infallible. And the movement which is called Islam I regard as an instrument of God in the history of salvation with at

---

[42] Qur'an 5:45-57, 68; 2:253. Cf. 2:136, 285; 3:33, 84. In Q 3:33 we note that Allah also "preferred" Adam and Noah and the family of Abraham.

[43] Cf. Parrinder, op. cit., p. 131.

[44] Q 4:171-172; 43:59; 5:75; 5:116; 5:72-73; 5:17;4:157-158 (cf. 5:110); 3:55; 61:14. R. C. Zaehner has tried to show that these passages in fact do not constitute a rejection of the crucifixion and resurrection of Jesus. Op. cit., pp. 210-214.

[45] Daud Rahbar, "Muslims and the Finality of Jesus Christ in the Age of Universal History," The Ecumenical Review, vol. 17, no. 4 (October 1965), p. 364.

[46] Mohamed Talbi, quoted in R. Marston Speight, "Some Bases for a Christian Apologetic to Islam," The International Review of Missions, vol. 54, no 214 (April 1965), p. 193.

least some of the thankful affirmation and cautious qualifications that I make of the movement that is called Christianity. I believe therefore that as Christians we are obliged under God to incorporate this evaluative understanding into our faith-concepts both of the nature of the Church of Jesus Christ and of the Missiological imperatives which are an integral part of its life and work.[47]

The wider meaning of the evaluative understanding of Muhammad and of Islam which I have suggested above is specifically related to the Christian doctrine of God. The primary affirmation of Christian faith is of God the Father Almighty, Maker of heaven and earth. In the context of this faith the Church fathers of the first three or four centuries of our era emphasized the biblical affirmations of the unviersal grace and providence as well as universal creative activity of God. In a number of noteworthy cases, such as Justin Martyr, Clement of Alexandria, Minucius Felix, Origen, Theophilus of Antioch, etc., the wider saving as well as revelatory activity of God in his creation was affirmed. The breakdown of the Roman Empire in western Europe, however, was a primary factor, I believe, in the emergence of theological concepts which tended to overlook and in effect to deny the wider scope of earlier Christian understanding.

The second major Christian affirmation of faith, "Jesus Christ His only Son our Lord," whom God has sent, came to be understood in much of medieval Europe as unrelated to the wider geographical as well as cosmic range of the thought of older Christian, especially Greek, theologians. Western Europeans, their ties with the rest of mankind largely severed, the more so after the Muslim conquests, tended to forget that Jesus Christ could properly be considered only as representative of the Creator Spirit who has been at work in all ages "at the heart of all being and in every human soul."[48] Jesus of Nazareth is the supreme and normative manifestation not only of the person and will of the Father but also the primary focus of his work to redeem, restore and fulfill the entire cosmos, specifically the whole of

---

[47] Cf. Richard H. Drummond, "Toward Theological Understanding of Buddhism," *Journal of Ecumenical Studies*, vol. 7 no. 1 (Winter 1970), pp. 19-22.

[48] John V. Taylor, *C.M.S. News-Letter*, London: no. 303 (April 1967), p. 2.

mankind. To accept Jesus of Nazareth as the sole authoritative or normative revelation of God, however, does not mean that he is the totality of God's revelation, or that the temporal "point" of the Christ event constitutes the whole of God's redemptive work in the world.

The third major Christian affirmation of faith is of the Holy Ghost, the universal Spirit of the living God, who is to glorify the Christ and lead men into all the truth (Jn. 16:13-14). This is to say that while we recognize and affirm the particular clarity of the evidences of divine working in the great events and prophetic personages of the people of Israel, and supremely in Jesus the Christ, we do not see the activity of God as confined to only one cultural tradition in the history of mankind. If God is Lord of history, he is Lord of all of it and certainly cannot be considered as having excluded himself from what has been quantitatively or numerically its larger portion. Christian faith, then, if it is faithful to biblical perspectives, must affirm that God through his Son and in his Spirit has been and is at work in the whole of human history and that "wherever he has acted he has acted as in Christ," that is, in a manner of which Jesus the Christ is the prime exemplar.[49] Contemporary theology asserts a necessary connection as obtaining between the orders of diving creation and redemption; this means that the revelatory and saving work of God cannot be excluded from any time or place of human history. It means that the biblical record of divine activity can be seen as representative and normative but not as exclusive. The Bible reveals the primary "who" and "how" of God's work in the world but not its totality.

The practical consequences of this understanding are enormous. It means that we are free to look for the signs of God's work in every man and culture, traces (*Spuren*) of grace which, as Karl Rahner has said, we have heretofore looked for too ineptly and with too little love to recognize.[50] Concretely, we are free to perceive with van Leewen or Zaehner God's work in the person and prophethood of Muhammad, with Massignon or Gardet his

---

[49] V. E. Devadutt, *The Bible and the Faiths of Men,* New York: Friendship Press, 1967, pp. 41-48.

[50] Karl Rahner, "Das Christentum and die nichtchristlichen Religionen," *Schriften zur Theologie,* Einsiedeln: Benziger Verlag, 1964, vol. 5 p. 153.

presence among Sufi mystics, with Gardet his salvific work within every sincere and ethically aspiring Muslim.

In this context of faith we see the Church of Jesus Christ as that portion of the people of God chosen (not for privilege but for service) to manifest and witness to the saving love, presence and work of God unto the restoration of his cosmos. The Church is a sign to the nations, therefore, of the work of God for their salvation, a sign of his universal lordship and universal salvific intent. The Church is a sign of God's grace and in an authentic, albeit non-exclusive way also his instrument to reveal his grace and truth to all men. Through that Church, as Eugene Hillman has written, Christ is "sacramentally present" among the nations.[51] By its witness of word and life it gives visible though imperfect demonstration of the reality of its Lord, who, however, may be authentically known also through other means or instruments. This is all to say that while the Church knows "by name" the Lord and Savior of all men and, when true to itself, recognizes and heeds his voice, it can find no eschatological ultimacy in its own institutional forms and properly sees these forms to be but one of perhaps several "converging" foci of divine presence and activity in human history.

As I have written elsewhere, a major problem of contemporary Christian theology is to understand the historic non-Christian religions in such a way as to be faithful to the biblical doctrines of the universal creativity, providence and grace of the triune God and also to a biblically derived understanding of the Church and its mission. The missiological problem is to recognize the cosmic scope of this divine presence and work, and, within the context of such perception, to recognize, through the criterion of the Christ event, truth and value in the other religious traditions of mankind without falling into disobedience to the divine commission to proclaim the Gospel to the whole creation and to plant the Church as the eschatological community which points to the consummation of history in the Lord Christ.[52] The Church must obey this commission because it has been

---

[51] Eugene Hillman, *The Church as Mission*, New York: Herder and Herder, 1965, pp. 38, 51.

[52] Richard H. Drummond, *op. cit.*, pp. 20-21.

"told" to do so (not only in Matthew 28:16-20); not to obey is to be unfaithful to its very nature as well as to its "externally" assigned commission.

Paul Tillich held that authentic dialogue among men of different religious traditions obviates conversion in the sense of change of formal religious affiliation;[53] I do not. Not to allow the possibility of such change as a viable option for men is radically to limit human freedom, to support, at least in theory, the older way of thinking of Christendom or Islam as self-contained cultural block-units wherein change of formal religious affiliation was practically a cultural impossibility. We are not yet liberated entirely from the shackles of these older ways – it would seem that men are even less free in this respect in Islam than in lands of primarily Christian heritage – but the movement of history seems definitely to be in the direction of human freedom. And the freedom of man demands that we allow the winds of the Spirit to blow freely.

So long as we do not make institutional aggrandizement or the religio-cultural domination of men our aim, when we remember that the true Church will be known perfectly only in the *Eschaton*, we have the right under God, I believe, to invite men to be disciples of Jesus Christ within the fellowship of the institutional Church. If, as the Muslim scholar Isma'il R. al Faruqi has written, it is our obligation as men of religion to go into the world and teach our knowledge of the truth, men ought properly to be free to respond to that witness with outer as well as inner signs of acceptance.[54] This is not spiritual or institutional imperialism but the right of man to change. Many people are now rightly sensitive to the human suffering which not infrequently has been occasioned by change of institutional religious affiliation and subsequent personal and sociological dislocations. No man of

[53] Paul Tillich, *Christianity and the Encounter of the World Religions,* New York: Columbia University Press, 1963, p. 95. Tillich elsewhere strongly emphasized that "conversion" is an ontological necessity. This, however, he understood in "an opening of the eyes, a revelatory experience." It did not mean for him change from one religious affiliation to another. *Cf. Biblical Religion and the Search for Ultimate Reality,* Chicago: University of Chicago Press, 1964, p. 65.

[54] Isma'il R. al Faruqi, "Prospects for Dialogue," *The Sacred Heart Messenger,* vol. 102, no. 9 (September 1967), p. 30.

conscience dare take these consequences lightly, certainly not in the case of conversions from Islam to Christianity. Yet to deny them to men would be to rob human history of one of its greatest sources of creative dynamism. Dare we forbid our fellow men the sublime contributions to the enrichment of human life made, albeit through much physical as well as mental suffering, by the outer as well as inner conversion of men like Paul and Augustine, Toyohiko Kagawa, and Sundar Singh? Freed from motivations of fear or self-interest, this kind of conversion becomes one of the highest expressions of human dedication and creative living. Mission that invites others to fellowship and sharing at the deepest levels of human experience is therefore the highest compliment that one man can pay another. To withhold this invitation when it can be "fittingly" made is in the final analysis disrespectful of others' humanity. Mission is properly expressive of respect as well as love; it looks toward the healing of wounds and the crossing of boundaries. Properly understood and motivated, mission is the most divine of human tasks.

ISLAMIC-CHRISTIAN DIALOGUE:
APPROACHES TO THE OBSTACLES[*]

P. Jacques Lanfry[**]

Introduction

Why limit to Christians and Muslims the research that justifies this article? To be more precise, why not also take into account Jewish believers? As is known, their faith is chronologically located at the source of the religious current from which issue the three great religions that recognize Abraham as Father. Let me explain.

Even if the Qur'an acknowledges as divinely inspired the Torah of Moses, the Psalms of David, and the Gospels, these books do not appear to be known directly in the Qur'an, nor are they even cited textually, as, for example, when the Gospels quote Isaiah or the Psalms; rather, they are simply named and that is all. The Qur'an retains a certain number of Judeo-Christian traditions, biblical and non-biblical, which comprise some noteworthy and shared values in the three religions. These religious traditions derive from Jewish or Christian spheres contemporary with the

[*] *Journal of Ecumenical Studies,* 14:3 (Summer, 1977). Revised from the author's Report presented to the Seminar on Islamic-Christian Dialogue at Tripoli, Libya, February 1-5, 1976.

[**] Jacques Lanfry (Catholic) studied theology at the Seminary of St. Sulpice, Paris, and Arabic literature at both the Institute des Belles-Lettres Arabes in Tunis and the Faculté des Lettres in Algiers. He was ordained a priest as a member of the Society of the White Fathers, serving as assistant general from 1957 to 1967. He is a consultor on the Secretariat for Relations with Non-Christians in Rome. His books include *Ghadames, étude linguistique et ethnographique* (Algiers, 1968), and *Ghadames, Glossaire (parler des Ayt Waziten)* (Algiers, 1973).

beginnings of Islam. Their primary source is not always the Bible. Certain episodes about the Patriarchs recorded by the Qur'an are not of direct biblical origin; one Qur'anic tradition on Jesus is found only in an apocryphal gospel (see Qur'an 3:49). Hence we can see what kind of information the Qur'an conveys to the Muslims about the Jewish and Christian faiths. Strictly speaking, no common scriptural basis exists between Muslims and Jews or between Muslims and Christians. The Qur'an is separate, apart.

Moreover, a widespread conviction among Muslims, based on this or that verse of the Qur'an (and not without underscoring its objective importance), affirms that the very text of our Bible, with its two great divisions, does not conform to the authentic text – a text that has undergone certain manipulations (*tahif*) at the hands of Jews and Christians alike, or by Jews and Christians of false faith or of no faith. Muslims do not read the Bible (not, in fact, unlike Christians, who are similarly ignorant of the Qur'an). Thus, Holy Scripture cannot serve as a common point of reference, a serious obstacle on the path of understanding. Christians and Jews of course possess the Old Testament in common, and it constitutes a privileged basis with mutual appeal – an interesting but useless fact in the Muslim dialogue as long as this deep-rooted prejudice remains.

The Qur'an retains traces of the serious difficulties raised by Arabic Jews opposed to nascent Islam. It is very hard on the Jews. The Qur'an acknowledges Jesus as God's chosen prophet-"messenger." It manifests, at least in certain verses, confidence and consideration for Christians, such as in this verse: "Of all men thou wilt certainly find the Jews, and those who join other Gods, to be the most intense in hatred of those who believe, and thou shalt certainly find those to be nearest in affection to them who say, 'we are Christians.'" (5:85). There is nothing like this regarding the Jews. but in spite of such positive attitudes toward Christians, the Qur'an opposes certain essential articles of the Christian faith. It overwhelms some Christians with reproach for their unfaithfulness to divine Revelation and, above all, for their infidelity to monotheism, as revealed by God to Abraham and to those who followed the Father of the Believers.

The history of Islamic-Jewish relations is quite different from that of Christian-Islamic relations. We should think not only of the current struggle of the Arabs against the Israeli state, but let us recall also from the past the long period of coexistence in Spain, for example, when Jewish communities were in contact with the Muslim towns of Andalusia. Between Christians and Muslims, however, there were the struggles of the Christians against the conquests by Caliphate powers on the one hand, and the other, conquest and domination of Muslim countries by Western powers (usually considered Christian by the Muslims) – all this complex past is at the root of the deep wounds, grievances, and prejudices. They have only compounded the difficulties at the doctrinal level and the disagreements over scriptural traditions.

One is doubtless inclined to hope that the time will come when Christians, Jews, and Muslims will be able to study together, objectively and in tranquility, the obstacles to mutual understanding. But the experience of problems and delays encountered in ecumenical efforts among separated Christians invites our caution in these delicate, diverse, and heterogenous areas which are only now becoming accessible. It seems much more prudent at present to define the interlocutors, with the firm hope of uniting them one day. Moving too rapidly or aimlessly risks burking or bungling the real issues.

The following text draws essentially from a report to the Seminar on Islamic-Christian Dialogue in Tripoli, Libya, in February, 1976. The Seminar's organizer, Colonel Kaddafi, extended invitations to Christians and even to the Vatican itself in order to initiate this dialogue with Muslims. He himself expressed the sincere hope of one day seeing a tripartite meeting of Jews, Christians and Muslims on the religious questions, but, in fact, Tripoli was only a two-party meeting.

The author of this report is informed on Islamic-Christian problems, but much less so on Jewish problems. This is why that subject is absent, for these remarks are limited to a communication presented at Tripoli as part of a contribution to the development of relations between Muslim and Christian believers.

Can the thirteen centuries of history which Christians and Muslims have in common serve as a lesson for today's believers? The two groups have inherited a sum of prejudices and an ensemble of behavior patterns which have left their mark on the level of conscience and in the inner recesses of the mind. A Lebanese Muslim recently said: "Christianity and Islam are two sister religions. Both are monotheistic. Rarely have two religions had such close relations down through the centuries as have Christianity and Islam. Yet these relations have been those of hostility rather than friendship. Their belief in God has separated them far more than it has united them. Why is it that hostility rather than friendship has governed these relations? What are its causes? Are they essential or accidental causes? Can we rediscover the authentic sources common to the two religions, and from them draw new understanding that will contribute to the moral regeneration of people today? Now, more than ever, Christianity and Islam must subordinate their relations to their spirit of charity and mercy rather than to any other consideration."[1]   In order to suppress the prejudices and reduce the misunderstandings which today are still the cause of so much havoc, especially where Christian or Muslim communities happen to be a small minority (in the Middle East, Sudan, the Philippines, or Ethiopia, for instance), believers – and, it would seem, Christians first of all – are invited to contemplate and to repent of past faults, to weigh and evaluate actual prejudices and misunderstandings, to examine and make known the already prodigious efforts that have been made to reduce and suppress them, and to give expression to hopes and regrets in the interest of keeping one another better informed.

I. Admitting Past Errors and Injuries

"Muslim-Christian relations are as old as Islam. They have appeared in the most contradictory forms. There were hard and painful periods on both sides," admits a former Christian member of the Vatican Secretariat for relations with Non-Christians,[2] periods of Muslim conquests and of crusades, recent periods of colonization and, still more recently, those of

---

[1] Resume of an article entitled "Relations between Christianity and Islam," by Hassan Saab, published in Arabic in *Travaux et Jours,* Beirut, no. 14-15 (32 pp.).

[2] In "For an Islamo-Christian Dialogue," by Joseph Cuoq, in *Bulletin* of the Secretariat for Non-Christians, English ed., no. 1 (May, 1966), pp. 23-27.

struggles for independence. A semi-official document frankly states that "...Past events as well as those of recent years have left a deep feeling of bitterness towards the West in certain regions of the world. In the course of history there have been short but happy periods of collaboration, at Damascus, Baghdad, and Toledo. But such items on the credit side of the balance go little way towards correcting in the minds of the Muslims the firm impression that Christians have always blocked the development of their civilization. According to their reading of history, the Crusades first of all helped to bring to an end the most brilliant period of their existence. Then they complain that colonialism rendered less fruitful than had been hoped the renaissance (*nahda*) which began in the 19th century."[3]

This bitterness, the same document goes on to admit, "has suddenly flared up again in recent years in connection with their struggle for liberty. Every one of their reviews and newspapers, all their political and...religious leaders, have stressed the link between the distant past and what is happening as the present moment, and they have all found this comparison to be one of the most effective arguments to sway the emotions of the East against the peoples of the West. Even the political and economic maneuvering of the West, carried out by men who are well-known as being without faith in any religion, is seen and explained to their own people as a continuation of the Crusades in but another way,"[4] or of colonialism. Imperialism today is very quickly accused of being Christian-inspired, even if Christians themselves deny any such collusion or confusion. And the responsibilities of traditionally Christian countries in the dramatic difficulties

---

[3] *Guidelines for a Dialogue between Muslims and Christians* (Rome: Edizioni Ancora, 1969), p. 83-hereafter cited as *Guidelines*. The text continues: "In point of fact the reality was a great deal more complex than one might gather from these reactions, but we have no desire here to indulge in detailed historical analyses. What we are trying to do is to understand how our partner in dialogue feels about these things." Father Robert Caspar provides a keen appreciation of this "Islamo-Christian encounter...begun in misunderstanding...carried on over the centuries with open hostility, the clash of arms, and apologetical controversies...armed conflicts giving rise to a body of ideological literature aimed at providing them with a doctrinal foundation and fanning the ardor of the combatants....On both sides, detraction and apologetical rhetoric flourished" ("La Religion Musulmane," in *Les relations de l'Eglise avec les religions non chrétiennes* [Paris: LeCerf, 1966], pp. 201-236).

[4] *Guidelines*, pp. 83-84.

surrounding the Palestinian affair have only added to the misunderstandings of history.[5] If Christians today are earnestly invited to renounce the political methods of the Crusades, and of colonial and imperialist enterprises, they must also examine themselves with regard to other errors and injustices if their dialogue with Islam is to be an honest one.

In fact, beyond political and economic confrontations, a vast cultural and religious misunderstanding between Christians and Jews has developed in the course of history. Each has dramatically ignored the other and each has disregarded the proper value of the other.

In the Middle Ages, the scientific and philosophical contribution of the Arabs (Muslims) was clearly paramount, a fact recognized in the West only by a well-informed elite. With a few notable exceptions (Ramon Lull and Thomas Aquinas), it was rare for Christian theologians to ponder the religious abundance of Islam. Professor Norman Daniel has recently outlined for us the essentials in the false representation of Islam by Western Christians.[6] This is what made Prof. Abd al-Rahman Badaoui respond: "What monstrous slanders and what frightful lies have been heaped upon our Prophet and upon Islam! I myself have seen the disastrous effects, still rooted in the opinions of both simple people and the educated alike.... All sorts of circumstances have contributed to the formation and growth of this misunderstanding: circumstances in the religious, political and even economic sectors...with its origins dating as far back as St. John Damascus."[7]

However, let us not accept too readily Christian ignorance and misjudgment about Islam as normally deliberate or intentional. We must not forget that for centuries the Christian Greco-Latin West was wrapped in deep ignorance of Muslim reality because of a lack of knowledge of the language and of Arabic culture. Eastern Christians, aware from birth of this

---

[5] Ibid., p. 84, where the document adds: "...Whatever judgment we express should be based on charity, justice, and honor...[and] at least we should show our sympathy for those who suffer most..." This is not the place to give a full review of the attitude of the Holy See on the one hand and of Christians on the other regarding a just solution of the Palestinian question. An objective investigation of their positions will suffice to exonerate them of all accusation.

[6] See his two books, Islam and the West (Edinburgh, 1950), and Islam, Europe and Empire (Edinburgh, 1965).

[7] Interview in the Cairo review, Images, March 13, 1965.

very culture, have not been quite so terribly locked into their prejudices as the Christians of the West. And the Eastern churches of Antioch, Damascus, and Baghdad have been attentive to Muslim reality, so to promote, under present social and political conditions, mutual understanding.

One cannot therefore overemphasize the work of linguists and of Western orientalists who have granted Westerners an understanding of Islam and also some access, through Eastern culture, to knowledge of the truths and religious values conveyed in the Qur'an and Muslim traditions.

Christians could no doubt complain as well of having been misunderstood by their Muslim brothers and sisters, even though the exigencies of the Muslim-Christian controversy during the Middle Ages led quite a number of Muslim scholars to take a close interest in Christian dogma. The fact is that all too often the other's religion has been judged on the basis of the "practice" and everyday behavior of its followers, and not according to the ideal proposed or to the precepts revealed. Each one knows that there is a fundamental injustice here, even as it is unjust to appraise the other's religion solely on the basis of personal criteria. If, indeed, sincere efforts were made in the West at various times to comprehend the Muslim religious experience "from the inside," they enjoyed but a fleeting existence and hardly disturbed the accumulated mass of prejudices. It is of these prejudices, therefore, that the Christian of today is asked to become aware. The Second Vatican Ecumenical Council was pleased to repeat that "although in the course of the centuries many quarrels and hostilities have arisen between Christians and Muslims, this most sacred Synod urges all to forget the past and to strive sincerely for mutual understanding."[8] To forget the past does not mean that one ought to ignore the present consequences of it – on the contrary; pardon for past errors cannot be exchanged between Christians and Muslims unless they are of a firm mind to "convert" their mentalities and attitudes. As Professor Abd al-Rahman Badaoui has said: "We must do our best to see to it that every false concept and all the lies attributed to the one or the other religion disappear. By this joint effort at

---

[8] Declaration on the Relationship of the Church to Non-Christian Religions, *Nostra aetate* (October 28, 1965), no. 3. English translations of Council texts are taken from Walter M. Abbott, SJ. ed., *The Documents of Vatican II* (New York: Guild Press, 1966).

profound and sincere understanding, we could dispel all misunderstanding growing out of religious differences."[9]

There is an issue that disturbs the Muslims more than any other in their approach to Christians: it is the silence and reserve of Christians regarding Mohammed. He is, for Muslims, of course, the last and the greatest of the Prophets. Our reticence on this subject surprises and scandalizes them. They do not understand why we refuse to grant Mohammed the respect they themselves grant to the person of Jesus.

The question is difficult and deserves to be treated by competent and discerning experts who know the exigencies of both the Christian and the Muslim faiths – experts who know as well the dimensions of heartfelt respect (and not just out of courtesy or politeness) that we owe to each other. The fact is that for many years among us Christians there has been a tradition or an ingrained tendency to disparage and judge severely Islam's Prophet. We Christians ought to become fully aware of what we have said and written in the past (and even recently) about Mohammed. There has been inexcusable subjectivity in our harsh judgments, not to mention the written errors regarding Mohammed, the respected Prophet of Islam. As we are well-informed about these unfortunate attitudes, let us express at the opening of a dialogue with Muslims our sincere and deep regret for these erroneous judgments and abusive expressions, such fruitless and inappropriate utterances for a Christian. This small step is a prerequisite to any endeavor toward friendly and confident relations with the Muslim believer.

II. Weighing the Importance of the Prejudices to be Combatted

In an interview given to the Lebanese daily, *L'Orient,* Father Joseph Cuoq said: "The past was the past. Let us file it away in the archives and together, now, write a new history in which brotherhood will replace opposition, and mutual love, indifference. Come and see: we have rebuilt our house."[10] Though, it must be added, the great mass of Christians have yet to learn from those responsible what is this renovated outlook with

---

[9] Interview, March 13, 1965 (see above, note 7).

[10] Reprinted in *Informations Catholiques Internationales* (I.C.I.), November 15, 1965.

regard to the Muslims which the Second Vatican Council bids them develop in the spirit of the Gospel. Owing to historical analyses and to the efforts of conversion realized in recent years, the Christian authorities are quite aware for the future of the various prejudices to be combatted. Thus the *Guidelines* of the Secretariat for Non-Christians acknowledges that "we have to make a thorough re-evaluation of our way of looking at things. We are referring in particular to certain 'ready-made' judgements often proferred to the detriment of Islam. A fundamental point would seem to be to avoid harboring in our innermost hearts hasty or rash judgements which would appear ludicrous to any sincere Muslim." It would not be a waste of time, therefore, to list some of these "ready-made" ideas on Islam "so that we may have the matter straight in our own minds before engaging in dialogue."[11]

The same directory applies itself to a rapid enumeration of those prejudices which, on the level of language, behavior, and written judgments, are constant in the way they present themselves. Its interest in doing this is not merely to denounce them, but to provide immediate proof that they do not correspond in reality and truth to authentic Islam, even though they have been encouraged at times by certain failings or decadent aspects which Muslims are the first to denounce in their own history. It is a fact that many Christians with little education too often imagine Islam to be the religion of fatalism, legalism, and fear, of laxism, fanaticism, and opposition to progress. These are false accusations which continue to be directed toward Islam by numerous Christians.

But people of knowledge and experience know very well that "if Muslims believe in the Divine Decree and accept without questioning the inscrutable Will of God," developing in its regard perfect obedience and admirable patience, the individual is aware too of the need to make a personal effort of reflection (*ijtihad*) since one also creates or invents one's own acts and is denied all passive resignation and fruitless abandonment by the present Reformists. Likewise, if Muslims love the Law, the perfect expression of the will of God, they know that "actions are only worth the intentions behind them," and that "piety" is also reverential fear and

---

[11] *Guidelines*, pp. 86-87.

confident expectation before the mystery of divine mercy. One cannot therefore accuse them of legalism, just as it would be unjust to assert that Islam is the religion of fear. "There is no question of a 'religion of fear'; it is a matter of obeying God because one trusts in his Mercy and one loves his Commandments." Furthermore, "in 1965 one of the principle daily papers of Cairo published an article by the *shaykh* of al-Azhar, entitled *al-Islam, din almahabba* (Islam, religion of love). It was mainly a question of the love of one's neighbor, but based on faith in God."[12]

To correct more decidedly the "false notions" prevailing with regard to laxism in Islam, the same directory stresses that "there is a moral code in Islam based on the Qur'anic *akhlaq* (customs) and it is very strict....It would be quite wrong to say that there is no family morality in Islam. It does exist and it has many fine points....[And] an act of disobedience...deserves punishment...." It goes on to explain that it is Muslim zeal which have led many to see there a fanaticism too easily sustained by fairy tales and ridiculous formulas. As for opposition to progress, this is a social defect which some Christian societies have also suffered; it is to confuse particular historic situations with the religious message which attempts to give them life and meaning. "It is really very difficult to see anything in Islam itself that is opposed to the findings of modern science...[though] it is quite true that there are communities in certain parts of the Islamic world whose social structures, dating from the Middle Ages, give the impression of being completely static....The Christian must be on the alert to discover the sincere efforts at renewal being made in contemporary Islamic thought."[13]

Other prejudices are still expressed or implied in certain socio-political attitudes. Too often, Christians have the idea, rightly or wrongly, that the distinction between religion and the state does not exist in Islamic countries. Basing themselves on particular situations or dramatic events in which religious factors alone are taken into consideration, they conclude that there is no room in Islamic society for anyone who is not a Muslim, just as it is impossible to guarantee freedom of religious choice or to maintain there

---

[12] *Ibid.*, pp. 91, 92.

[13] *Ibid.*, pp. 92-100.

the free exercise of their religious worship. Certain competitive methods of presenting the religious challenge to non-believers, in Asia and Africa, sometimes encourage such prejudices, as does the rejection by some predominantly Muslim countries of a certain cultural or religious pluralism. The Secretariat for Non-Christians gives particular attention then to this question, showing that Islam also recognizes a distinction between religion and the state, though the two sides may approach it from different angles,[14] and that many modern states now have a different understanding of it.

There is yet another domain in which incomprehension is almost total, though it involves the highest forms of charity and of mutual aid. Christians and Muslims throughout the world are far from respecting one another when they dedicate themselves to the aid of disinherited populations; work to educate new generations in the schools, colleges, and universities; or serve the sick and dying in hospitals and dispensaries. Very quickly, the most violent accusations of treacherous proselytism are exchanged and amplified instead of concentrating on healthy religious "competition" in the realm of respect of persons and societies. The duty of the apostolate as conceived by one or the other religion is often expressed by strife and the expending of energy in which the glory of God is no longer assured.[15]

---

[14] In this it bases itself on theoretico-historical studies, such as that of Shaykh Ali Adb ar-Raziq. *L'Islam et les bases du pouvoir* (Cairo, 1925; French translation in *Revue des Etudes Islamiques,* 1933, III, pp. 353-391, and 1934, II, pp. 163-222), as much as on socio-political positions of religious leaders such as Shaykh al-Bashir al-Ibrahim of Algeria, in his editorials in *al-Basa'ir* (reprinted in his book, *'Uyun al-Basa'ir: Fasl ad-din 'an ad-dawla*).

[15] Another misunderstanding arises constantly and unconsciously from that deep-seated conviction that the West (Europe and America) represents the "perfect model" of human culture, parliamentary democracy, economic development, and the successful balance between faith and reason. The rest of the world, and thus the other religions, are then automatically judged on the basis of such criteria, which make one form the historical realization of Christianity (successful or not, from the point of view of faith, God only knows!) the necessary model for all modern evolution! From there it is but a short step to the exclusion of others from the benefits of culture, if not of salvation. There was a time when the principle, "Outside the church there is not salvation," was applied literally, producing in its wake a certain scorn, or at least profound indifference, toward all other forms of religious experience.

III. Efforts Made by the Christians

What is important for the subject here treated is not the more or less exhaustive enumeration of the prejudices and misunderstandings that still exist, but rather the presentation of the efforts made by both sides to suppress and diminish them. In what concerns Christians, they can here affirm that their efforts in the last quarter century have been sincere as well as immense and varied. It is not possible to give a full account of what has been done, though the highlights will be recalled, since such a survey necessarily encompasses the areas of thought and action, at the level of both persons and societies, in secular as well as religious domains. And it should be stressed here that if the texts of the Second Vatican Council represent the happy outcome of the courageous research of a few brave pioneers, since 1962-1965 they constitute for Christians the essential charter for renewal of relations with Muslims.[16]

Encouraged by the Council, the various local churches inaugurated a new mode of behavior; for this they attempted to secure the collaboration of some special "secretaries." At the Vatican level, Paul VI established, on Pentecost of 1964, the Secretariat for Non-Christians, which had as successive presidents and animators Cardinals Marella and Pignedoli. On March 1, 1965, an Under-secretariat for Islam was added to it, with the essential task of promoting a Muslim-Christian dialogue in all its dimensions, directly, while working at the same time to bring about a change in the mentalities of the Christian populations. A diligent reading of the *Bulletin* of the Secretariat[17] gives one an idea of its undertakings and initiatives, just as the introduction to its *Guidelines* provides some notion of the spirit of its

---

[16] The first text, very brief, is to be found in the Dogmatic Constitution on the Church, *Lumen gentium*, no. 16. The second constitutes all of no. 3 of the Declaration on the Relationship of the Church to Non-Christian Religions, *Nostra aetate* (*cf.* the second of the four conferences of this seminar: "The doctrinal bases common to the two religions, and different areas of convergence").

[17] The *Bulletin* began to appear in May, 1966, with editions in English and French, at the rate of four issues a year, with supplementary "booklets" and other publications included from time to time. Since 1974 (with issue no. 25), this has been reduced to a single bilingual edition. For a survey of the Secretariat's activities, see Michael L. Fitzgerald, "The Secretariat for Non-Christians Is Ten Years Old," in *Islamochristiana,* review of the Pontifical Institute of Arabic Studies (I.P.E.A.) of Rome, no. 1 (1975), pp. 87-96.

interventions. "The aim of such dialogue is not to 'convert' the other party, nor to make them doubt their own faith. It should quite simply stimulate those taking part not to remain inert in the positions they have adopted, but to help all concerned to find a way to become better people in themselves and to improve their relations with one another, so as to make the world as a whole a better place in which to live."[18]

Numerous have been the Christian theologians, historians, exegetes, and legal scholars who have tried in the last half century to update the knowledge of the Christians world with regard to Muslim religious experience. There has been no lack of books and reviews on the subject, in which such men as Massignon, Montgomery Watt, Asin y Palacios, Gardet, Anawati, Jomier, Hayek, Moubarac, and many others have placed their learning and skill at the service of better dialogue. Is it not first necessary, after all, to provide Christians with a scientifically exact and religiously sympathetic acquaintance with Islam and Muslims? Several Catholic theological faculties, especially in Rome at the present, include instruction at university level on "the religious reality" throughout the world, with a more or less important place given to Islam. The professors strive to present the Islamic religion to Christians in a way recognizable to Muslims by having recourse to the Qur'an and to the classical works of the Muslims themselves.[19] [At Temple University, Philadelphia, Christians, Jews, Muslims, and others are instructed in Islam by Muslim professors – who are also engaged in dialogue by their Christian, Jewish, and other professorial colleagues. J.E.S. editor]

---

[18] *Guidelines*, pp. 9-10.

[19] Space is lacking here to provide an exhaustive bibliography in all the principal languages. We shall simply cite, as a model of its genre, Louis Gardet, *L'Islam, religion et communauté* (Paris: Desclee de Brouwer, 1970), which sets forth the "first principle" of all true dialogue: "Each one must be concerned to get to know the other as he is and *as he wishes to be*" (p. 420). This principle was the first of the main themes of the Islamo-Christian encounter at Cordoba in September, 1974 (see the report on this meeting, Maurice Bormans, "Le Congrès islamo-chrétien de Cordoue – 9-15 september 1974," in the *Bulletin* of the Secretariat for Non-Christians, Rome, 1975/X-1, no. 28-29, pp. 199-205). Let it suffice to mention that for the city of Rome alone, courses in Islamology are offered by the Gregorian, Lateran, Urban, Antonian, and Regina Mundi Universities, while a more specialized training is given at the Pontifical Institute of Arabic Studies.

If scientific publications have multiplied in number, studies more specifically consecrated to Muslim-Christian dialogue have also appeared on the scene to attack head-on the prejudices mentioned earlier and to propose new ways of acting. Thus *The Guidelines for a Dialogue between Christians and Muslims* has gone into successive editions in many languages.[20] It is a small booklet in which the authors do not try "to fix definite formulae for such a dialogue, but rather to define the spirit in which it should take place. We should be animated," the authors go on to say, "by a deep respect and a disinterested love for those who are taking part in this dialogue with us. This does not mean that we must agree with our partners all along the line, but what it does exclude is merely expressing disapproval or indulging in polemics" (p. 9).

The diffusion of documents such as this has made possible an increase in the number of new initiatives to remedy former attitudes; for instance, the revision of certain cathechetical manuals and textbooks for young Christians in which the faith of their Muslim friends is presented with respect and understanding,[21] regional meetings between those in charge of local churches – Catholics and Protestants – to put into practice the "new spirit," share experiences of dialogue, and resolve problems and conflicts in which the religious factor appears basic; where local situations permit, Muslim-Christian conferences or seminars,[22] temporary loan or permanent transfer of places of worship from one community to the other,[23] participation in the formal opening of new mosques and churches (whether in the Middle East or

---

[20] The *Guidelines* are in their 2nd English edition (Rome: Edizioni Ancora, 1971); *Les Orientations pour un dialogue entre chrétiens et musulmans*, 3rd French edition (Rome; Ancora, 1970); *Christiani e Musulmani: Orientamenti per il dialogo fra cristiani e musulmani*, 1st Italian edition (Rome; Ancors, 1971); *Musulmanes y Cristianos: Orientaciones para un dialogo entre Cristianos y Musulmanes*, 1st Spanish edition (Madrid, 1971).

[21] For instance, by the Catechetical Center of Paris, and *Recherches fraternelles* in Mali.

[22] See Michael L. Fitzgerald, "The Secretariat for Non-Christians Is Ten Years Old," *Islamo-christiana* (I.P.E.A., Roma, no. 1,1975), pp. 87-96; John B. Taylor, "The Involvement of the World Council of Churches in International and Regional Christian-Muslim Dialogues," pp. 103-114; Abdelmajid Charfi, "Quelques reflexions sur la rencontre islamo-chretienne de Tunis (11-17 novembre 1974)." Also see the rubric "Dialogue in the World," a regular feature of the *Bulletin* of the Secretariat for Non-Christians.

[23] At Cologne, and later at Lille.

in Africa);[24] exchange of messages on the occasion of special celebrations, in particular at the end of the month of Ramadan;[25] and reciprocal visits of delegations from Cairo or Riyad and the Vatican for the purpose of improving mutual understanding.

It was the desire of Pope Paul VI that there be in Rome itself an institute staffed by specialists in Islamics where the Arab language could be studied and scientific research could be carried out into Islam and the culture arising from it. This investigation is pursued with the regular collaboration of Muslim scholars, and on the basis of texts and books which Muslim religious tradition has developed from early centuries down to our own times.

[24] Muslims were present at Kampala, Uganda, in 1969, when Pope Paul VI blessed the cornerstone of the Basilica of the Martyrs of Uganda. And President Gamal 'Abd an-Nasir participated in 1965 at the blessing of the cornerstone of the new Coptic-Orthodox cathedral of Cairo (Abbassiyeh). In Kampala, the Pope told the leaders of the Muslim communities: "How can we express our deep satisfaction in meeting you, and our gratitude to you for granting our lively desire to greet, in your persons, the great Muslim communities spread throughout Africa? You thus enable us to manifest here our high respect for the faith you profess, and our hope that what we hold in common may serve to unite Christians and Muslims ever more closely, in true brotherhood....In our prayers we always remember the peoples of Africa, for the common belief in the Almighty professed by millions of them must call down upon this continent the graces of His Providence and Love, most of all, peace and unity among all its sons. We feel sure that, as representatives of Islam, you join in our prayer to the Almighty, that He grant all African believers that desire for pardon and reconciliation so often commended in the Gospel and in the Qur'an." And he added: "May the shining sun of peace and brotherly love rise over this land, bathed with the blood of generous sons of the Catholic, Christian, and Muslim communities of Uganda, to illuminate all of Africa! And may our meeting with you, respected representatives of Islam, be the symbol of, and the first step toward, the unity for which God calls us all to strive for His greater glory, for the happiness of this blessed continent!" (*Bulletin* of the Secretariat, English ed., no. 12 [December, 1969], 4th year/3, pp. 156-157).

[25] See "Christians and the Fast of Ramadan" (*Bulletin* of the Secretariat, English ed., no. 7 [March, 1968], 3rd year/1, pp. 41-44), in which are given the texts of two radio messages composed by Father Joseph Cuoq, then under-secretary of the Secretariat for Non-Christians, and read by him over Vatican Radio on the occasion of the close of the fast of Ramadan, 1967. In the first, entitled "Introducing the Fast of Ramadan to the Christians," Father Cuoq said: "The spirit of drawing close to God and of submission to His Will, expressed by the fast of Ramadan, is a genuine religious value. Christians can only rejoice to find it expressed by others....So let us rejoice at seeing God so honored by millions of men and women, adults and adolescents, sometimes at very great sacrifice....Therefore we invite you who are Christians and have tried to understand Islam from inside rather than outside to show your Muslim neighbors your appreciation of this religious act...."The second message, "To the Moslem Communities: Greetings for Ramadan, 1967 (30 December 1967)," began a practice which has been continued ever since, and to which the late King Faysal once refereed in the course of a speech welcoming delegations of pilgrims to Mecca (January, 1968).

Meanwhile, a renewed Christian theology of non-Christian religions, already given expression in the texts of the Council, enabled each of them, and Islam in particular, to be more clearly situated in the history of salvation. The "religious value of the Muslim faith" no longer needs to be proved; it "bears...on great religious truths – strict monotheism, God's Word spoken to men by the prophets, the origin and end of the world, the resurrection and the Judgment...." Even though "*on the level of doctrine*, the two faiths [Christian and Muslim] are formally different, despite many common elements....*on the level of religious attitudes* determined by the motive of faith, the essential characteristics of the Muslim faith give it a high religious value in itself and can even open it up to the economy of salvation which God has willed" because it is "a theocentric, personal, supernatural faith."[26] One may better understand, then, the declaration of the Second Vatican Council in its Dogmatic Constitution on the Church: "The plan of salvation also includes those who acknowledge the Creator. In the first place among these there are the Muslims, who, professing to hold the faith of Abraham, along with us adore the one and merciful God, who on the last day will judge mankind."[27]

Always in the same spirit of clarification sought by Pope John XXIII, the Second Vatican Council wished to affirm at the same time the requisites of religious freedom and to condemn all forms of religious proselytism. And we know that very strict instructions on this matter were conveyed everywhere. Thus, with regard to the missionary activity of the Catholic Church it is stated that "Christian charity truly extends to all, without distinction of race, social condition, or religion. It looks for neither gain nor gratitude. For as God has loved us with a spontaneous love, so also the faithful should in their charity care for the human person himself...[by] taking part in the strivings of those peoples who are waging war on famine, ignorance, and disease, and thereby struggling to better their way of life and

---

[26] R. Casper, "The Religious Value of the Moslem Faith," in *Bulletin* of the Secretariat, English ed., no. 13 (March, 1970), 5th year/1, pp. 25-37.

[27] *Lumen Gentium*, no. 16. Professor Louis Gardet gives a good resume of the various positions of Christian theology with regard to non-Christian religions in a chapter of his book, *L'Islam, religion et communauté* (Chap. II, additum on "L'Islam du point de vue chretien," pp. 407-418, especially p. 417). Father J. Moubarac delineates very well the new perspectives of this Christian theology in Book 3 of his *Pentalogie Islamo-chrétienne*, especially pp. 93-130.

to secure peace in the world."[28] And as the Vatican Council "declares that the human person has a right to religious freedom," it also asserts that "religious bodies have the right not to be hindered in their public teaching and witness to their faith, whether by the spoken or by the written word. However, in spreading religious faith and in introducing religious practices, everyone ought *at all times* to refrain from *any* manner of action which might seem to carry a hint of coercion or of a kind of persuasion that would be dishonorable or unworthy, especially when dealing with poor or uneducated people."[29] Absolute condemnation of all proselytism and a reminder of the duty of the apostolate, that is "to present one's faith," such are the two pillars of an exacting "religious freedom."

It is clearer than ever before, to the whole world, that Christianity should not be confused solely with the fate of the traditionally Christian countries of the West. In every corner of the world, Christians consider themselves full-fledged citizens of the city in which they live and of the country the love, without any discrimination, adopting as their own the words of Gamal 'Abd an-Nasir (then President of the Arab Republic of Egypt), spoken at the saying of the cornerstone for the new Coptic-Orthodox cathedral in Cairo: "The equality of opportunities is one of the first principles proclaimed by revealed religions, because by brotherhood, and equality between citizens and their opportunities, we can build the type of healthy community that religions aim at....Over the centuries, Christians and Muslims have always been brothers....God has never called us to fanaticism but to love...[so] no distinction is made between citizens [though] we may encounter difficulties....We must invite the fanatics to wisdom, whether they

---

[28] Decree on the Missionary Activity of the Church, *Ad gentes,* no. 12.

[29] Declaration on Religious Freedom, *Dignitatis humanae,* nos. 2 and 4, which goes on to add: "Such a manner of action would have to be considered an abuse of one's own right and a violation of the right of others." In this same vein, the "Hong Kong Memorandum" (1975) stated: "Of special concern for our religious communities in some situations is the matter of proselytism. We are moved to call upon all religious bodies and individuals to refrain from proselytism, which we define as the compulsive, conscious, deliberate, and tactical effort to draw people from one community of faith to another" (in John B. Taylor, "The Involvement of the World Council of Churches in International and Regional Christian-Muslim Dialogues," in *Islamochristiana,* no. 1 [1975], p. 101).

be Muslims or Christians....This is a problem that concerns the whole nation,"[30]

IV. Hopes and Regrets

Let me confide to the reader certain mute sufferings. Both sides want so much to be recognized for what they are and above all for what they wish to become in the fullness of their faith. Christians experience deep suffering whenever their friends cast doubt on their belief in the One God. On this point, did not Professor Mahmud Abu Rayah himself have to fight his co-religionists who regard Christians as unbelievers, having no God and "Associationists" – in brief, creatures automatically condemned to the fires of hell?[31] Christians run the risk at times of being deeply offended by this doubt hurled at their monotheistic belief, a monotheism which is just as unbending as that of their uslim brothers and sisters. The Christian mysteries do not run counter to the unity and uniqueness of the divine *nature*. This will have to be demonstrated to them continually in the manner of Cardinal Koenig when he presented his theological conference on March 31, 1965, at the University of al-Azhar on the subject of Christian monotheism and the Christian struggle against every form of atheism, ancient and modern.[32]

We are just as sensitive, if not more so, to the constant refutation of our Sacred Scriptures. The wish is often expressed that we Christians might produce an "authentic Gospel" (*injul sahih*), which, we are perfectly well aware, signifies that the Gospel we are presently using is unauthentic (*ghayr*

---

[30] The President went on to say: "Where there are Muslim fanatics altogether to extreme, Christians must show moderation; where there are extreme Christian fanatics, let Muslims in their turn show proof of moderation. [For] the country does not know nor does it recognize any sectaranism" (discourse of July 24, 1965, in *Proche-Orient Chrétien*, tome 15 [1965], pp. 384-387).

[31] See his book, *Din Allah wahid* (The Religion of God is One) (Cairo: 'Alam al-Kutub, 1970), 2nd ed., in which he refutes his co-religionists by means of Qur'anic texts, and proves that Christians are and remain "People of the Book."

[32] "In Cairo we were told of the happy surprise of many listeners, professors and students of the Great Mosque when they heard the Cardinal of Vienna proclaim, without reservation, absolute faith in the One God" (Louis Gardet, *L'Islam*, p. 424). For the integral text of the Cardinal's conference, in its French version, see *Mélanges de l'I.D.E.O.* of Cairo (Dominicans), no. 8.

sahih). An assertion of this sort does not so much offend our intelligence, which is inclined to be humble before historical science and the requirements of textual criticism (which is highly developed and carefully defined); rather, it is in our hearts as believers that such a repetition of unsubstantiated legends, injurious to our faith, leaves its wound.

Furthermore, Christians too often hear talk of a Holy Alliance against the growing forces of materialism or of communism, and they fear then – are they right or wrong in this? – that Muslim-Christian collaboration has only negative aims. Cardinal Duval of Algiers has said that "one must not seek in this dialogue a closing of the ranks aimed at uniting Christians and Muslims against a common enemy. The basis of dialogue between Christians and Muslims is the action of God in the lives of both. It is not for me to say whether Muslims can profit from the example of Christians; but many Christians – and this involves a requirement of their faith – are aware of having received help from sincere Muslims to affirm, in all areas of their life, the transcendence of God, by prayer, the sense of his presence, and the thought of his judgements, and a human conception of the duties of almsgiving and hospitality."[33] A dialogue of action, composed of a convergence of interests of values, would not satisfy the Christian who expects a fraternal sharing of religious experiences in which each may speak of God to others. It is faith in God that must reunite us and urge us to serve our brothers and sisters. It is because we believe in the living God, who is just, who gives love freely and is merciful, that our "common commitment" to the service of humankind has as its aim to promote and defend life, justice, freedom, and mutual love.

For this reason, Christians would like to be better understood in their current efforts. Let us make a distinction between their efforts and witness, and the deeds of the nations – lay-States, and sometimes atheist – whose free citizens they are. Faith in God is first and foremost an intimate and personal reality. It is submission to God alone and to no one else. This is the basis of its strength to resist all the modern new idols and its weakness as well since it

---

[33] Interview accorded by Cardinal Leon Duval to *Révolution Africaine* (December 25, 1965), weekly of the F.L.N.

refuses to use the means of "Human force." Today's Christians have rediscovered the significance of prophetic behavior through a conversion whose dimensions are ill-appreciated by their friends.   They are often accused of collusion or political intent when what they are really trying to do is to hold to the level of a strictly religious affirmation, in pure faith and without relying on any material support.   Was this not the case, in fact, with the conciliar declaration on Judaism?   Hassan Saab, a Lebanese Muslim, could write: "It is regrettable that fear of zionist exploitation of the Declaration has prevented the Arabs from closely examining it in its totality. The Catholic Church, focused on its own truth, turns for the first time to look at the reflections of truth in other religions.   Islam is presented as a sister religion.   The Christian is exhorted to cease all discrimination, not only against Jews but against all non-Christians.   In this new attitude, the Church deserves to be imitated rather than criticized."[34]

Thus, has the time not come for both sides, whenever they have a choice between various theological schools on a point of doctrine or practice, to prefer that school which more clearly favors encounter with the other party and mutual existence in peace and friendship?   Though Christians and Muslims envisage differently the difficult distinction between "religion" and "state," is it so hard to imagine them opting for doctrines which protect pluralism   and   reject   every   sort   of   privilege   hidden   behind denominationalism, feudalism, and provincialism?   In the modern world there are many countries whose citizens belong to different religions.   Over and above simple peaceful co-existence, must not believers seek together criteria for work and culture based exclusively on the personal worth of individuals, without any privilege being attached to their confessional

---

[34] In the Lebanese daily, *L'Orient* (December 6, 1964). Mr. Saab added: "The Church comes very close to the Qur'anic concept of the unity of the family of God, as well as the Qur'anic idea of the unity of the people of the Book, this people comprising Jews, Christians, and Muslims who adore God, the Father of Abraham, the Father of all monotheists. Christianity and Islam cannot but agree on the Declaration and rejoice at its spirit. This agreement is hampered by their differences of zionism, and not by Judaism."

adherence? This would solve many conflicts and would help to avoid others in many African and Asian countries.[35]

Conclusion

It is difficult, of course, after centuries of polemical combat or in the horror of certain present-day dramas, to trust in the complete disinterestedness of the interlocutor. Christians are well aware of this difficulty, and, yet, they would like to hope that their friends will believe them more after this conference in which they have presented the sum of their efforts, endeavoring to do so in truth and humility. The mistakes of the past and of the present have been and are at once acknowledged and denounced in what remains of them today: prejudices and misunderstandings which can only be suppressed little by little through a long effort of clarification, conversion, and sensitization. The hope of Christians is their certitude that some of their Muslim brothers and sisters are bent on doing as much from their side to make themselves better known in the fullness of their faith and the totality of their tradition, including their Sacred Books. The discussion to follow should throw further light on our common

---

[35] Should not the experiment of Lebanon--"a common homeland of religious communities united by the same faith in God, the same attachment to the primacy of the spiritual, and the same will to live in peace and brotherhood," as Lebanese President Helou said in his address to Pope Paul VI on the occasion of the latter's visit of Beirut in 1964--be carried through, by means of process of laicization, carefully understood, and free of all religious discrimination? (For the text of the President's speech, see *La Croix,* French Catholic daily, December 4, 1964; also in *Docmentation Catholique,* January 3, 1965; English text in *L'Osservatore Romano,* December 4, 1964.) It was in the same country of Lebanon, in the setting of the "Cenacle Libanais," that Christians and Muslims were able to join together (May-June 1964) in saying: "[The speakers affirm] the meeting point of the two religions in their faith in the one God, and in their desire to unite in fostering spiritual values and common moral principles which safeguard the dignity of man, proclaim his right to the highest kind of human life, and lift up the world in a breath of charity, peace, and concord. They are convinced that Lebanon is the chosen land for such a Muslim-Christian dialogue, and that on the day it becomes more vitally aware of the content of these two messages, it will have contributed to the renewal and the safeguard of the spiritual energy of man." The manifesto continues: "They commit themselves before God to bring about a permanent fraternal encounter which permits all to draw upon the intimate riches of the two universal religions, each of the partners acting in full conformity with the teachings of his religion, while seeking to understand what the other religion contains of lessons, exhortations, and norms aimed at bringing man closer to his fellowmen and brothers" (see *Ephémérides islamo-chrétiennes,* bulletin no. 2 (September 1, 1064-April 30, [1965], pp. 143-144).

road, uncover yet a thousand more obstacles along the way, and give us the courage to help one another as brothers and sisters to overcome them one by one. For their part, Christians know they must persevere by means of protracted patience, comforted by these words of Pope Paul VI: "May your work make the light of God's glory...shine ever more brightly in the world. And may Christians learn in their turn to know and properly esteem 'what treasures a bountiful God has distributed among the nations of the earth' (*Ad Gentes*, 11). Thus do you lend your personal collaboration to the plan of God in history. conscientiously and humbly, even though you do not yet see its fruits or success here below. We must give witness of patience, faith, and detachment...."[36]

---

[36] Allocution delivered during an audience for members of the Secretariat for Non-Christians, September 25, 1968. See *Bulletin* of the Secretariat, English ed., no. 9 (December, 1968), 3rd year/3, pp. 115/116.

THE DOCTRINAL BASIS COMMON TO CHRISTIANS AND MUSLIMS AND DIFFERENT AREAS OF CONVERGENCE IN ACTION[*]

Maurice Borrmans[**]

Christians and Muslims have had, fundamentally and from the very beginning, a common spiritual heritage. For they all, with one voice, say; God exists and God is one. By this they bear witness that matter, life, and

[*] *Journal of Ecumenical Studies*, 14:1 (Winter, 1977). This lecture was written first for the Muslims who were attending the Congress of Tripoli, Libya, February, 1976, and, second, for the Christians who were present there. For the Muslims, it was meant to show the insights we already have in common concerning the Mystery of God. For the Christians, it attempted to explain how the Christian vision of the One God can try to meet the unyielding monotheism of Islam. It was an opportunity to meditate together on what is common to both sides, and to reflect on the religious motives which impel believers of both religions to serve their fellow humans in this present time.

One will not find here an essay in comparative theology; it should have included a mention of the basic differences in doctrine which keep Muslims and Christians apart, i.e., God's revelation in Jesus Christ, the Word incarnate, and the historical expression of God's great love through the Cross and the Resurrection. The present lecture thus had a very precise aim, and its limitations come from the concrete requirements of the Congress of Tripoli. It could not deal with all the possible attitudes a Christian can take, but could be only "the view-point of a Catholic concerned with unity," unity among Christians and unity among all who seek God.

[**] Maurice Borrmans (Roman Catholic) was ordained into the priesthood in 1949. He received his Docteur es lettres from the Sorbonne in 1971, specializing in research on the Fiqh, Hadith, and Muslim spirituality. He has taught for more than twenty years at the Pontifical Institute of Arabic Studies in Rome, and is editor of *Islamochristiana*, which was founded in 1975 to give a scientific approach to Christian-Muslim dialogue. He has also published numerous articles in several French and Italian journals.

spirit do not owe their origin to necessity or pure chance, but to the Creator
who is spirit and life.

I. A Common Heritage

A. The Ways of Knowing God

They knew, by experience, that this world is not self-made and that
humanity has not fashioned its history on its own. They recognize that the
wonders and greatness of the cosmos and of history, as well as the gigantic
progress made by modern science, imply, and indeed postulate, a "master
builder." They affirm that the human mind is capable – and this is already a
gift from God – of knowing that God exists and that God is endowed with all
the attributes of perfection.

Christian and Muslim theologians have established, in ways which
differ but are analogous, proofs for the existence of God, in the same way
that the sacred scriptures of each of the two religions invite meditation upon
the "signs" of God and the "pointers" to God in the worlds which are open to
human investigation: that which has its beginning in time requires the
existence of an "eternal" being. Contingent being supposes a necessary being.
The harmony in the universe supposes someone who directs this harmony.
Human nature itself makes people desire to discover the One who made
them, who guides them and who awaits them. So it is that for Christians the
First Vatican Council wished to recall once more this fundamental dignity of
human intelligence, made in such a way that it can arrive at a knowledge of
the Creator by means of the manifold created signs with which it has been
provided.[1]

---

[1] "The same holy Mother Church holds and teaches that God, the origin and end of all things,
can be known with certainty by the natural light of human reason from the things of creation:
'for since the creation of the world his invisible attributes are clearly seen, being understood
through the things that are made' (Rom. 1:20); and she teaches that it was nevertheless the
good pleasure of His wisdom and goodness to reveal Himself and the eternal decrees of His
will to the human race in another and supernatural way, as the Apostle says: 'God, who at
sundry times and in divers manners spoke in times past to the fathers by the prophets, last of
all in these days has spoken to us by His Son' (Heb. 1:1-2)" (*Const. de fide catholica*, cap. 2;
TCT 58).

Muslims and Christians know by experience that humanity is, in fact, not able to carry out this magnificent program. Throughout history we see that it has often preferred, and still prefers today, falsehood to truth, injustice to justice, death to life. It refuses to acknowledge truth; it murders and enslaves; and it fashions for itself idols to its own likeness! That Christians should call this "original sin" and Muslims see in it the action of the "soul which incites to evil" does not change the basic fact which can be stated as follows: humanity cannot alone achieve perfection. It bears a deep wound which leads it to turn in on itself and to refuse God's signs and commands. This is the sin which is seen by believers to be an act of disobedience and a betrayal, and the principal source of depravity, both social and personal.

Christians often meditate on a text of St. Paul: "For what can be known about God is perfectly plain to humans since God has made it plain. Ever since the creation of the world God's everlasting power and deity – however invisible – have been there for the mind to see in the things God has made. This is why such people are without excuse; they knew God and yet refused to honour God or to thank God; instead, they made nonsense out of logic and their empty minds were darkened....They have given up divine truth for a lie and have worshipped and served creatures instead of the creator, who is blessed for ever" (Rom. 1:19-25).

Christian thought down the centuries has always affirmed that there are two sources of knowledge; creation on the one hand and revelation on the other. The First Vatican Council restated this in very clear terms: "The Catholic Church...holds that there are two orders of knowledge, distinct not only in origin but also in object. They are distinct in origin, because in one we know by means of natural reason; in the other, by means of divine faith. And they are distinct in object, because in addition to what natural reason can attain, we have proposed to us as objects of belief mysteries that are

---

The original texts of the decrees and canons of the Councils have recently been republished by the Institute of Religious Sciences in Bologna, Italy. The volume is entitled: *Conciliorum Oecumenicorum Decreta* (Bologna: Instituto per le Scienze religiose, 1973). An English translation of the most important documents is to be found in *The Church Teaches* (St. Louis; Herder, 1955), abbreviated TCT.

hidden in God, and which, unless divinely revealed, can never be known."[2] This is why Christians and Muslims are at one and the same time people of reason and people of faith. They are believers and it is quite legitimate for them to think that they have a doctrinal basis in common.

B. *The Heritage Common to Christians and Muslims*

What are the aspects of this common doctrinal basis which make it possible for Christians and Muslims to consider themselves as sharing in one and the same religious heritage? Both are united by faith in God, in God's angels, and in eternal destiny which is to follow death and resurrection. They both have the certitude also that God has sent prophets and has communicated the divinely-revealed word in sacred books, though they may differ in regard to the identity of the former and the character of the latter. This is why they are both equally believers, and it is in the mystery of these beliefs that they find the ultimate reasons for their manner of behaving here on earth and for their commitment as human beings. Of course, there is divergence between the beliefs of Muslims and Christians on many substantial points, but there is convergence also with regard to essential realities.

Let them, in a spirit of fellowship, give consideration to the divine realities which unite them, even if the terms they use are different and the way they designate them arises from an outlook and a religious sentiment which sometimes diverge more than they converge.[3] We quote here the text which rallied the unanimous agreement of Christians during the Second Vatican Council 1962-1965, found in the *Declaration on the Relationship of the Church to Non-Christian Religions.* The members of the Council declared, in the introduction, that: "All peoples comprise a single community, and

---

[2] *Const. de fide catholica,* cap. 4; TCT 75. The same Constitution, in chapter 3, declares: "Because man depends entirely on God as his creator and lord and because created reason is wholly subordinate to uncreated Truth, we are obliged to render by faith a full submission of intellect and will to God when He makes a revelation" (TCT 63).

[3] These difficult problems of Christian-Muslim dialogue have been considered by Professors Ali Merad and Roger Arnaldez in the journal *Islamochristiana* (Rome; Pontificio Istituto di Studi Arabi) 1 (1975). Many passages of these articles, "Language commun et dialogue" (pp. 1-10), "Dialogue islamochretien et sensibilites religieuses" (pp. 11-24), would be relevant here.

have a single origin, since God made the whole human race to dwell over the entire face of the earth. One also is their final goal: God. His providence, His manifestations of goodness, and His saving designs extend to all people against the day when the elect will be united in that Holy City ablaze with the splendour of God, where the nations will walk in His light" (par. 1).[4]

In the same way it is recognized that: "People look to the various religions for answers to those profound mysteries of the human condition which, today even as in olden times, deeply stir the human heart: What is a human being? What is the meaning and the purpose of our life? What is goodness and what is sin? What gives rise to our sorrows and to what intent? Where lies the path to true happiness? What is the truth about death, judgment, and retribution beyond the grave? What, finally, is that ultimate and unutterable mystery which engulfs our being, and whence we take our rise, and whither our journey leads us?" (par. 1). Now to these questions Islam gives replies which are very similar to those of Christianity. This makes it possible for the *Declaration* to affirm: "Upon the Muslims, too, the Church looks with esteem. They adore one God, living and enduring, merciful and all-powerful, Maker of heaven and earth and Speaker to humanity"
(par. 3).

C. *God – One, Living, and Subsisting*

Christians, and those who have preceded them, have always believed in God, living and subsisting. Their books, on every page, bear witness to God's oneness. The Jew loves to repeat: "Listen Israel: Yahweh our God is the one Yahweh" (Deut. 6:4), and the Christian affirms: "I believe in one

---

[4] The *original Latin text* of the Constitutions, Decrees, and Declarations of the Second Vatican Council can be found in the volume *Conciliorum Oecumenicorum Decreta* (see note 1). There is a handy English translation, with notes and comments: Walter M. Abbott, ed., *The Documents of Vatican II* (London: Geoffrey Chapman, 1966). For a French translation, with the Latin original side by side, see du Centurion, ed., *Concile oecuménique Vatican II (constitutions, décrets, déclarations, messages)* (Paris, 1967). An Arabic translation has been published by Dar 'al-alam al-'arabi, Cairo, separate fascicles, n.d. Numerous studies have appeared on Vatican II, for example in the French series *Unam Sanctam*. Of particular interest is the volume in this series edited by A. M. Henry and entitled *Relations de l'Église avec les religions non chrétiennes* (Paris: Cerf. 1966).

God, the Father almighty, creator of heaven and earth, of all things visible and invisible," because of Jesus' reminder that the first and greatest of the commandments is: "You must love the Lord your God with all your heart, with all your soul, with all your strength, and with all your mind" (Lk. 10:27; Deut. 6:5). St. Paul also makes this explicit: "There is one Lord, one faith, one baptism, and one God who is Father of all, over all, through all and within all" (Eph. 4:5-6). So when they say, with the Psalmist, "Who else is God but Yahweh, who else is a rock save our God?" (Ps. 17:32), Christians are bound to Muslims who also proclaim that "there is no divinity except God."

Throughout the centuries each Council has recalled with insistence that there is only one God. Definitive expression to this was given in the First Vatican Council: "The Church believes and professes that there is one true and living God, the creator and lord of heaven and earth. He is all-powerful, eternal, immeasurable, incomprehensible, and limitless in intellect and will and in every perfection. Since He is one unique spiritual substance, entirely simple and unchangeable, He must be declared really and essentially distinct from the world, perfectly happy in Himself and by His very nature, and inexpressibly exalted over all things that exist or can be conceived other than Himself."[5]

For Christians and Muslims "Yahweh is God indeed; there is no other" (Deut. 4:35); "We for our part acknowledge no other God than Him" (Judith 8:20). God is the only God: "He is God, one, God alone" (Qur'an 112:1-2) says the Qur'an, as also the Psalms (Ps. 17:32). Questions and statements are parallel: "Who is like Yahweh our God?" (Ps. 112:5); "Like

---

[5] *Const. de fide catholica*, cap. 1; TCT 355. *The Apostles' Creed* states: "I believe in God the Father almighty, creator of heaven and earth" (TCT 1); *The Nicene Creed* (325); "We believe in one God, the Father almighty, creator of all things both visible and invisible" (TCT 2); the *First Council of Constantinople* (381): "We believe in one God, the Father almighty, creator of heaven and earth, of all things both visible and invisible" (TCT 3); the *Council of Florence* (1442): "The Church firmly believes, professes and preaches that the one true God, Father, Son and Holy Spirit, is the creator of all things visible and invisible. When God willed, in His goodness He created all creatures both spiritual and corporeal. These creatures are good because they were made by the Supreme Good, but they are changeable because they were made from nothing. The Church asserts that there is no such thing as a nature of evil, because every nature insofar as it is a nature is good: (TCT 94).

Him there is none" (Qur'an 112:4). God is "the first and the last" (Is. 41:4), the One "who does not change" (Mal. 3:6), because God is the one who subsists for ever, the Ever-Sure, who "does not grow tired or weary" (Is. 40:28), the Eternal One (Is. 40:28) whose face abides, true being, the All-sufficient. "Yahweh lives" (Jer. 4:2; cf. Qur'an 2:255). God lives "for ever and ever" (Ap. 1:18), the "Living God, the Undying" as the Qur'an says (Qur'an 25:60). Therefore God remains the sole inheritor of all things since with the Psalmist we can say: "Before the mountains were born, before the earth or the world came to birth, you were God from all eternity and forever" (Ps. 89:2).

D. *God – Creator of the Heavens and the Earth*

God, the Living One, is made manifest to us as the Creator who "in the beginning created the heavens and the earth" (Gen. 1:1), the "Creator of the heavens and the earth" (Qur'an 1:117). God is the All-Creator, the fairest of creators, the Maker, the Shaper. God does what God wills without being subject to any necessity.[6] "Yahweh, my maker, my preserver" (Ps. 118:73), exclaims the Psalmist, and adds: "All creatures depend on you to feed them throughout the years....You turn your face away, they suffer, you stop their breath, they die....You give breath, fresh life begins, you keep renewing the face of the world" (Ps. 103:27-30). God is the Guardian, the All-benign, the Giver and the All-provider. God is not "Heedless of creation" (Qur'an 23:17) and "it is in Him that we live, and move, and exist" (Acts 17:28). Christians and Muslims are at one in saying this.

The believer will never finish admiring the works and deeds of God in creation and in history. Does not the Psalmist say: "I look up to your heavens made by your fingers, at the moon and the stars you set in place – ah, what is man that you should spare a thought for him, the son of man that you

---

[6] This was also stated by the First Vatican Council in the following terms: "In order to manifest His perfection through the benefits which He bestows on creatures – not to intensify His happiness nor to acquire any perfection – this one and only true God, by His goodness and almighty power and by a completely free decision, from the very beginning of time has created both orders of creatures in the same way out of nothing, the spiritual or angelic world and the corporeal or visible universe. And afterwords He formed the creature, who in a way belongs to both orders, being composed of spirit and body" (*Const. de fide catholica*, cap 1; TCT 256).

should care for him? Yet you have made him little less than a god, you have crowned him with glory and splendour, made him lord over the work of your hands, set all things under his feet....Yahweh, our Lord, how great your name throughout the earth" (Ps. 8:4-7, 10)? It is with reason that, faced with the wonders of creation and the wonder of wonders which is humanity, the Psalmist should exclaim again: "How many wonders you have done for us; you have no equal. I want to proclaim them again and again, but they are more than I can count" (Ps. 39:6). "It is good to give thanks to Yahweh, to play in honour of your name, Most High, to proclaim your love at daybreak and your faithfulness all through the night" (Ps. 91:2-3). This is why true believers are ever ready to give thanks.

E. *God Who Loves Humankind*

God is the All-knowing, the All-wise. God knows the whole of creation, as the Psalmist recognizes: "Yahweh, you examine me and know me, you know if I am standing or sitting, you read my thoughts from far away, whether I walk or lie down you are watching, you know every detail of my conduct. The word is not even on my tongue, Yahweh, before you know all about it; close behind and close in front you fence me round, shielding me with your hand" (Ps. 138: 1-5). God is indeed the most Generous, the Benevolent, the one who has knowledge of everything, the All-preserver, the Lord. "He sees the whole human race; from where He sits He watches all who live on the earth, He who moulds every heart and takes note of all people do" (Ps. 32:13-15). This is why Christians, together with Muslims, call God the "All-seeing," the one who is "watchful over everything" (Qur'an 4:86) and who has "numbered everything in numbers" (Qur'an 72:28).

Humankind, therefore, must confess that its destiny is dependent on God's decree. God is the Arbiter and Judge whose justice and equity Muslims proclaim and of whom the Psalmist affirms: "He loves virtue and justice" (Ps. 32:5). Believers then have nothing to fear from their Creator. St. Paul reminds them: "We know that by turning everything to their good God co-operates with all those who love Him....With God on our side who can be against us?" (Rom. 8:28-31). So the believer accepts the fact that

God grasps and outspreads, for God puts in our way what can profit us and what is harmful to us, and brings forward or postpones the appointed times. The Christian is pleased to meditate on the following text: "Yahweh gives death and life, brings down to Sheol and draws up: Yahweh makes poor and rich, He humbles and also exalts. He raises the poor from the dust, He lifts the needy from the dunghill...He safeguards the steps of His faithful but the wicked vanish in darkness" (1 Sam. 2:6-9). Thus the Psalmist can proclaim: "I will celebrate your love forever, Yahweh, age after age my words shall proclaim your faithfulness" (Ps. 89:2).

F. *God Who Pardons and is Merciful*

For all believers God is vengeful, but is above all witness over everything. "God of revenge, appear," says the Psalmist, "Rise; judge the world; give the proud their deserts; how much longer are the wicked to triumph? Yahweh knows exactly how people think, how their thoughts are a puff of wind" (Ps. 93:1-3, 11). God will never disappoint the creature. God suffices as guardian, as guide, as helper. Truly God gives security for God, as the Muslims say, is "the Merciful, the Compassionate," "the most merciful of all." God, as Christians and those who have preceded them have learned, is "a God of tenderness and compassion, slow to anger, rich in kindness and faithfulness; for thousands He maintains his kindness, forgives faults, transgression, sin; yet He lets nothing go unchecked" (Ex. 34:6-7).

This is why believers are not afraid to acknowledge their sin, exclaiming with the Psalmist: "From the depths I call you, Yahweh, Lord, listen to my cry for help! If you never overlooked our sins, Yahweh, Lord, would anyone survive?" (Ps. 129:1-3). "Have mercy on me, O God, in your goodness, in your great tenderness wipe away my faults; wash me clean of my guilt, purify me from my sin....Against none other than you have I sinned, having done what you regard as wrong...Create a clean heart in me, put into me a new and constant spirit, do not deprive me of your holy spirit" (Ps. 50:3-6, 12-13). Muslims know that "humanity has been created fretful" (Qur'an 70:19), "sinful, unthankful" (Qur'an 14:34), and even "very foolish" (Qur'an 33:72). But all believers are equally aware that they can say to God: "Turn to me and pity me" (Ps. 85:16), for God is the first to turn to people in order to pardon their sins, since God is very patient. All-clement, All-compassionate, All-loving. Does the Qur'an not say: "Ask forgiveness of your Lord, then repent to Him: surely my Lord is all-compassionate, all-loving" (Qur'an 11:90)? For God has claimed to be merciful (Qur'an 6:12) and a hadith echoes this: "My mercy precedes my anger.

G. God – Worthy to be Praised and Glorified

Who, then, is this generous Creator and merciful Judge who is "the light of the heavens and earth...light upon light" (Qur'an 24:35)? As the Psalmist says: "Yahweh is king, robed in majesty, Yahweh is robed in power, He wears it like a belt....Yahweh reigns transcendent in the heights. Your decrees will never alter: holiness will distinguish your house, Yahweh, for ever and ever" (Ps. 92:1-5). Majesty and generosity are God's, whose "will is sovereign" (Ps. 113:11). Christians and Muslims call God the Holy One, the Most High and Inaccessible, the Great and All-embracing, with whom are "the keys of the Unseen; none knows them but He" (Qur'an 6:59), as the Qur'an says. God is transcendent, the one who is to be praised and glorified. How could God the All-high, the All-great, powerful over everything, possibly be unworthy of these Beautiful Names? God is "the King, the All-holy, the All-peaceable, the All-faithful, the All-preserver, the All-mighty, the All-compellor, the All-sublime...the All-mighty, the All-wise" (Qur'an 59:23-24). God it is who "gives the victory."

This can only lead humans to a better knowledge of this Being who is both near and distant and whom Christians call "the one who comes." They can easily adopt the Muslims' prayer which closes the litany of the Beautiful Names of God, asking God to be able to approach the Mystery "by every Name of yours which You have called Yourself or which You have revealed in Your book or which You have taught to one of your creatures or whose use You have reserved according to the knowledge that You have of your own Mystery." For the Messiah, Jesus, son of Mary, has said: "Eternal life is this: to know you, the only true God" (Jn. 17:3) and they believe, as

Christians, that they have learned from the very Messiah some of these names which "until then had been hidden" (Col. 1:25).

H. *God Who Sends Prophets*

Such is the substance of the religious heritage which Christians and Muslims have in common. Flowing from this there are many other things than can be considered common or analogous. Muslims and Christians believe that God has spoken in history "at various times in the past and in various different ways, through the prophets" (Heb. 1:1), "by revelation or from behind a veil, or by sending a messenger to reveal whatsoever He will, by his leave" (Qur'an 42:50-51). Both Muslims and Christians call Abraham "God's friend," and Moses "God's interlocutor," and we find in their lives models of faith and obedience. The Second Vatican Council has twice recognized this fact. The first time is in its meditation on the history of salvation which "includes those who acknowledge the Creator. In the first place among these are the Muslims who, professing to hold the faith of Abraham, along with us adore the one and merciful God, who on the last day will judge humankind" (*Lumen Gentium* par. 16). Secondly there is the passage of the *Declaration on the Relationship of the Church to Non-Christian Religions* which recognizes that Muslims "strive to submit wholeheartedly even to God's inscrutable decrees, just as did Abraham, with whom the Islamic faith is pleased to associate itself" (*Nostra Aetate,* par. 3).

It is true that Christians and Muslims differ with regard to the criteria for recognizing that prophecy which is definitive, Christians consider the "fulness of prophecy" has been realized in Jesus, but they recognize that the spirit of prophecy continues to be made manifest from generation to generation. Muslims, on the other hand, see in Muhammad "the seal of the prophets," recognizing at the same time that there is a "mystery of Jesus" of exceptional dimensions. Authentic dialogue requires that each side should respect totally the viewpoint of the other and show extreme patience, leaving it to God to purify this viewpoint, illuminate it, and perfect it. In the same way that the Christian must not ask a Muslim to recognize in the Messiah all the qualities which Christianity attributes to the Messiah, so also Muslims are invited not to require that a Christian should recognize as belonging to Muhammad all the qualities which Islam attributes to Muhammad. The same thing can be said with regard to sacred books, bearing in mind nevertheless that both Christians and Muslims recognize that the divine words entrusted to the prophets have been recorded in books which they must read, meditate upon and comment upon in order to understand their "apparent and hidden" meaning.[7]

I. *God Who Raises the Dead to Life and Fulfills Human Desires*

There are still more things common to all believers. All know that there are other beings, angels and demons, whose missions have been assigned to them by God and who are, as it were, witnesses of human history. All are aware especially that the world will come to an end in time just as it began in time. The face of the Creator alone will abide. All things will return to God by means of a recapitulation spoken of, with an abundance of imagery, in all the sacred books. Thus the Psalmist can ask: "Tell me, Yahweh, when my end will be, how many days are allowed me, show me how frail I am. Look, you have given me an inch or two of life, my life-span is nothing to you" (Ps. 38:5-6).

---

[7] True dialogue is, in fact, based on complete respect for the beliefs and behavior of the partner in dialogue. It aims at improving mutual awareness and understanding, while seeking to penetrate God's inscrutable decrees. It flourishes in an atmosphere of friendship, frankness, gentleness, mutual confidence, and patience in the face of the various stages that have to be covered.

For some general information on Christian attitudes toward dialogue see the directives given by Pope Paul VI in his encyclical letter *Ecclesiam suam* [August, 1964; Latin and Italian texts in the *Osservatore Romano*, 10-11.8.1964; English translation: *The Church in Modern World* (London: Catholic Truth Society, 1965); French translation in the *Documentation catholique*, Paris, 6.9.1964, pp. 1058-1093]. See also *Guidelines for a Dialogue between Muslims and Christians* (Rome, Ancora: Secretariat for Non-Christians, 1971), 2nd impression, with editions also in Frence, Italian and Spanish.

A first preliminary survey of efforts dedicated to Christian-Muslim dialogue has been published in *Islamochristiana* 1 (1975), including: Michael Fitzgerald, "The Secretariat for Non-Christians Is Ten Years Old," pp. 87-96; John B. Taylor, "The Involvement of the World Council of Churches (W.C.C.) in International and Regional Christian-Muslim Dialogue," pp. 97-102; Emilio Galindo Aguilar, "Cordove, capitale califale du Dialogue islam-chrétien, pp. 103-114; and Abdelmajid Charfi, "Quelques réflexions sur la recontre islamo-chrétien de Tunis," pp. 115-124.

The Second Vatican Council recognizes the fact that Muslims, like Christians, "await the day of judgment when God will give all their due after raising them up" (*Nostra Aetate*, par. 3). The hour will come. Its precise moment remains hidden, but some of its signs are known, particularly Jesus' second coming. Christians, in their creed, affirm that: "He will come again in glory to judge the living and the dead," and a hadith even states that "there is no other mahdi except Jesus." This day will be the Resurrection Day, the Last Day, the Day of Retribution, the Day of Judgment, though Christians and Muslims base themselves on different proofs in affirming the resurrection. It will be the Day of Muster when "all the nations will be assembled before God" (Mt. 25:32). "Upon that day people will issue in scatterings to see their works and who so has done an atom's weight of evil shall see it" (Qur'an 99:6-7). "All the truth about us will be brought out in the law court of Christ, and each of us will get what is deserved for the things done in the body, good or bad" (2 Cor. 5:10), in the hope of hearing God's words: "Well done, good and faithful servant; you have shown you can be faithful in small things, I will trust you with greater; come and join in your master's happiness" (Mt. 25:21).

Christians and Muslims affirm that there exists and Abode of Reward, Paradise, and an Abode of Punishment, Hell, though they differ widely in the description they give of these places and in their understanding of what constitutes their essential elements. Does not Jesus announce in the Gospel that "those who did good will rise again to life; and those who did evil to condemnation" (Jn. 5:28-29)? Whereas Islamic tradition recognizes the existence of "pleasures of the mind and the senses," often interpreted metaphorically, and would seem to confine the "vision of God" to a few rare moments and to the "nearest amongst the elect," since "the eyes attain Him not" (Qur'an 6:103), yet "upon that day faces shall be radiant, gazing upon their Lord" (Qur'an 75:22-23), Christian tradition has always affirmed that "when it is revealed we shall be like him because we shall see him as he really is" (Jn. 3:2). The First Vatican Council restated this in the following terms: "God, in His infinite goodness, has destined the human being to a supernatural end, namely to share in divine realities which completely transcend human understanding" (*De fide*, cap. 2). In any case, Muslims and

Christians are united in affirming that at this moment each soul will be "at peace," "well pleased, well pleasing" (Qur'an 89:28) and that the "Mystery of God" awaits us—as would seem to be indicated by a hadith which echoes Isaiah and St. Paul—a mystery "which no eye has seen, no ear heard, no heart imagined" (Ghazali, *Ihya', k.al-mahabba*). Thus history has its finale and creation its fulfillment: to meet the Lord of All-Being.[8]

J. *Humankind and Worship*

It is out of fidelity to this idea of God, humankind, and history, that Christians and Muslims alike, yet in their own ways, seek to submit to the mysterious will of God. They thus accomplish true *"islam"* as did Abraham and his son, Moses and al-Khidr, Mary, and her son and his Apostles, all of whom were among "those who submitted." Christians say, and here they are in agreement with a Muslim view which is completely justified, that is by faith that a person is saved. They repeat the words of the author of the Epistle to the Hebrews: "Anyone who comes to God must believe that He exists and rewards those who try to find Him" (Heb. 6:11). Hence the whole of human conduct must consist in obedience to God. Christians and Muslims can echo the Psalmist: "Here I am! I am coming. In the scroll of the book am I not commanded to obey your will? My God, I have always loved your law from the depths of my being" (Ps. 39:8-9). Is not the ideal of the perfect believer to be acting always in conformity with God's law? "Expound to me the way

---

[8] It would be interesting, within the framework of dialogue on religious experience, to study together what God's "good pleasure" means for Muslims and Christians. For Catholic Christians it is considered to be a process of justification which transforms the creature's very being. Thus the Council of Trent (1545-1563) states: "Justification is not only the remission of sins, but sanctification and renovation of the interior man through the voluntary reception of grace and gifts, whereby a man becomes just instead of unjust and a friend instead of an enemy, that he may be an heir in the hope of life everlasting....The only formal cause is the justice of God, not the justice by which He is Himself just, but the justice by which He makes us just, namely, the justice which we have as a gift from Him and by which we are renewed in the spirit of our mind" (*Decretum de iustificatione,* cap. 7; TCT 563). But the same council declared that one cooperates freely and efficaciously: "If anyone says that the free will of man, moved and awakened by God, in no way co-operates with the awakening call of God by an assent by which man disposes and prepares himself to get the grace of justification; and that man cannot dissent, if he wishes, but, like an object without life, he does nothing at all and is merely passive: let him be anathema" (*Canones de iustificatione,* can. 4; TCT 578).

of your statutes. Yahweh, and I will always respect them. Explain to me how to respect your law and how to observe it wholeheartedly" (Ps. 118:33-34); such is the prayer the Psalmist suggests.[9]

The Second Vatican Council states that Muslims "prize the moral life, and give worship to God, especially through prayer, almsgiving and fasting" (*Nostra Aetate*, par. 3). Though the rites and forms of prayer, fasting, and almsgiving may be different, the reality remains the same: we are all trying to adore God in truth, "confessing with your tongues, attesting to the truth in our hearts and showing our sincerity by our acts." For we refuse any kind of hypocrisy, since Jesus told Christians: "And when you pray, do not imitate the hypocrites" (Mt. 6:5), and the Qur'an states: "The hypocrites seek to trick God, but God is tricking them" (Qur'an 4:141). Prayer, invocation, litanies, meditation, intercession, and retreat are all old customs which are common to Christians and Muslims. In these, and in these alone, can they find the continuous renewal of their spiritual energy and their moral resolution. Numerous are the expression of worship and faith which Christians and Muslims hold analogically in common. On the basis of a fundamentally religious personalism we hold that each person is responsible before God alone for his or her personal development and faith. Yet at the same time we require that each should belong to a particular community, the *Umma* for Muslims, the Church for Christians, providing a living milieu which teaches the content of the faith and keeps a check on its authenticity, while at the same time it brings about an appreciation for religious and moral values in rites and in human relations. Does not each community have its own rites for incorporating new members, its special places of worship (mosques and churches), a body of religious leaders (the "men of religion" in Islam; priests, ministers, and religious in Christianity)?

---

[9] The whole of Psalm 118 could be quoted here. It presents a meditation on "love of the Law," a religious attitude common to all believers, whether Christians or Muslims. All seek true wisdom and could adopt the prayer of the Sage: "God of our ancestors. Lord of mercy, who by your word have made all things, and in your wisdom have fitted man to rule the creatures that have come from you, to govern the world in holiness and justice and in honesty of soul to wield authority, grant me Wisdom, consort of your throne, and do not reject me from the number of your children" (Wisdom 9:1-4).

K. *Humankind and Recognition of the Rights of God*

Since Christians and Muslims desire in this way to recognize the rights of God and to submit God's commands, they try to follow a pattern of human behavior which corresponds to what God has ordained for human happiness. The "commandments" which were handed down to Moses also form a moral and religious heritage common to us. "Honor your father and your mother....You shall not kill. You shall not commit adultery. You shall not steal. You shall not bear false witness against your neighbor. You shall not covet your neighbor's house. You shall not covet your neighbor's wife, or servant, man or woman, or ox, or donkey, or anything that is your neighbor's" (Ex. 20:12-17). Respect for persons and for their freedom which puts us under an obligation to state together that "there can be no constraint in adhering to a religion,"[10] the fundamental equality of men and women (having due regard for the diversity of their functions and missions), the glorification of almsgiving, hospitality, fidelity to one's promises, concern for the common good at the price of subordinating private interests to it – all this has for a long time been the habit of believers in both Islam and Christianity.

They have learned, as is to be found repeated in certain hadiths which may extend to cover the whole of humanity, that "believers are but brothers" and that "no one is a true believer until he loves for his brother that which he loves for himself" (Ghazali, *Ihya, k.al-mahabba*). The Gospel is constantly reminding us that the second commandment is like the first: "You must love your neighbor as yourself," and that it is on the works of faith that we shall be judged on the last day. Happy those who will then hear said to them: "I was hungry and you gave me food; I was thirsty and you gave me drink; I was a

---

[10] The Second Vatican Council judged it useful and necessary to dedicate a complete document to this important question. *The Declaration on Religious Freedom* states among other things: "This Vatican Synod declares that the human person has a right to religious freedom....In matters religious no one is to be forced to act in a manner contrary to his own beliefs. Nor is anyone to be restrained from acting in accordance with his own beliefs, whether privately or publicly, whether alone or in association with others, within due limits. The Synod further declares that the right to religious freedom has its foundation in the very dignity of the human person, as this dignity is known through the revealed word of God and by reason itself. The right of the human person to religious freedom is to be recognized in the constitutional law whereby society is governed. Thus it is to become a civil right...provided with an effective constitutional guarantee" (*Diginitatis Humane*, par. 2, par, 15).

stranger and you made me welcome; naked and you clothed me, sick and you visited me, in prison and you came to see me...[for] in so far as you did this to one of the least of these my brothers or sisters, you did it to me" (Mt. 25:35-40). Is it not said in a hadith that "whoever gives relief to a believer for one of the afflictions of this world, will be relieved by God from one of the afflictions of the Day of Resurrection"?[11]

II. *Areas of Convergence*

A. *The Challenge of the Modern World*

Such are the aspects of the doctrinal basis common to the two religions. These provide meeting-points for reflection and research. But can believers be content to enumerate their points of convergence and to respect the points of divergence while their contemporaries look on, silent and cynical spectators of theoretical and academic dialogues? The modern world presents thousands of challenges to faith in God, with regard to the manner in which it is to be justified, as well as the ways in which it is expressed and influences daily life. Should not Christians and Muslims renew their methods and exchange experiences so that together they may face up to the challenges of modern thought and give positive answers to the questions set by an atheistic culture? Believers have not finished exploring the dimensions of faith, particularly those corresponding to the expectations of the scientific culture of our age. Is there not here a first area of convergence for our religious investigations today?

If one states with Jesus the Messiah that "no servant can be the slave of two masters" (Lk. 16:13), one is bound to acknowledge that paganism is forever springing up again and that the new idols are more powerful than

[11] The hadith continues: "Whoever makes life easier for someone who is in difficulties, God will make everything easier for him in this world and in the next. Whoever 'covers' a Muslim, God will 'cover' him in this world and in the next. God comes to the help of each of His servants as long as each comes to the help of his brothers" (Ghazali, *Ihya'*, *k.al-mahabba*). These hadiths are to be found in Ghazali's work as an introduction to a section on "the exchange of attributes."

ever, these idols which oppress God's creatures in the name of the state, of sex, or of money, in the name of technical achievements, productivity, or the consumer society, or in the name of empty fame, false freedom, and illusory happiness. People today are waiting for a new freedom which will allow them to recognize their God and, by this very fact, to recognize their own essential natures. Cannot this struggle to free their brothers and sisters from all forms of oppression unite Christians and Muslims, in accordance with the invitation issued by the Second Vatican Council in its *Declaration on the Relationship of the Church to Non-Christian Religions?*" Although in the course of centuries many quarrels and hostilities have arisen between Christians and Muslims, this most sacred Synod urges all to forget the past and to strive sincerely for mutual understanding. On behalf of all humankind let them make common cause of safeguarding and fostering social justice, moral values, peace and freedom" (*Nostra Aetate,* par. 3). Will the Psalmist's vision be fulfilled, thanks to the efforts of all? "Love and Loyalty now meet. Righteousness and Peace now embrace; Loyalty reaches up from the earth and Righteousness leans down from heaven" (Ps. 84:11-12).

B. *The Believers' Commitment*

Faith in God is the very basis of such a commitment to the service of our sisters and brothers, for there lies in each of them that person which "God has created to his image," as is stated in both the Bible (Gen. 1:26) and the hadith.[12] Jesus told Christians: "Love your enemies and pray for those who persecute you; in this way you will be the children of your Father in

---

[12] Of course, many experts interpret his hadith in the following way: God created Adam to "his" image, that is in conformity with the image which God had of Adam, an image existing from pre-eternity in the mind of God. It would seem that Ghazali interprets the hadith rather differently, given the context in which he uses it. He declares in fact: "The special proximity pertaining to man is alluded to by God's word: 'They will question thee concerning the Spirit. Say: The Spirit is of the bidding of my Lord,' for God explains that it is something divine, beyond the range of created intelligences. Even clearer is His word 'When I have formed (Adam) harmoniously, and breathed into him of My Spirit;' that is why God made the angels bow down before Adam. This is what is shown also by his word: 'We have made you a viceroy on the earth,' for Adam merited to be God's viceroy only by reason of this resemblance. This is referred to by the Prophet's saying: 'God created Adam to His image', to the point that certain narrow-minded people have come to believe that the only image is an external image, that which is perceived by the senses..." (Ghazali, *Ihya', k.al-mahabba*).

heaven, for he causes his sun to rise on bad as well as good, and his rain to fall on honest and dishonest alike....You must therefore be perfect just as your heavenly Father is perfect" (Mt. 5:44-48). Muslims know that, according to Ghazali, believers of old said: "Put on the habits of God....Perfection for the believer consists in approaching the Lord by following the way of His attributes which are most praise-worthy: knowledge, justice, goodness, kindness, bounty, mercy, good counsel, encouragement to do good and preservation from harm."[13] Is it not this way, leading to an "exchange of attributes," that is referred to in this other hadith *qudsi* quoted by Ghazali: "The closer my servant comes to me through superogatory practices the more I love him, says God; and when I love him I am the ear by which he hears, the eye by which he sees and the tongue by which he speaks"?

It is because one believes in the living God who loves life and wishes to see it produce all its fruit that one strives to protect life wherever it is threatened – helping the sick and the dying in hospitals, developing medical research and methods of medical treatment in laboratories, condemning abortion and euthanasia in permissive societies, disapproving methods of birth control which are over-simple, refusing war and homicidal experiments on a planetary scale. It is because life is a gift from God that humankind cannot dispose of it as it wills. Councils and popes have never ceased reminding Christians of this fact, whatever might be the difficulties of the present time.[14]

It is because one believes in a just God who created the good things of this world for all its inhabitants that one fights against all forms of discrimination, whether their motivation be sexual, racial, cultural, religious, or national. One combats the selfish accumulation of wealth in different

---

[13] Ghazali, *Ihya', k.al'mahabba.* It would be fitting here to consider the entire "fifth cause of love (of God)" as expounded by Ghazzali: "resemblance and likeness, for like is attracted to like, and a form has a greater inclination to a (similar) form."

[14] Reference could be made, among other documents, to the encyclical letter of Pope Paul VI, *Humanae vitae,* 25.7.1968, on "birth control" and responsible parenthood and complete respect for the nature and ends of the conjugal act and in fidelity to God's purpose with regard to the "transmission of life." See the Italian text in the *Osservatore Romano,* 1.8.1968; English translation, *On the Regulation of Birth* (Tipografia poliglotta vaticana, 1968); French translation in the *Documentation catholique* (Paris, 1.9.1968), pp. 1442-1458.

forms of capitalism, whether these are practiced by individuals or by governments, in the East or in the West. One struggles against the unjust division of natural resources and the selfishness of some rich countries that forget to give assistance to poorer countries through the channel of international organizations. This, at least, is what the best Christians are trying to do untiringly, taking part wherever they can in the fight against underdevelopment and for the progress of nations "without expecting any reward other than that of doing God's will," with complete respect for persons, cultures, and civilizations. Their work and suffering is offered in the service of life and of humanity, in a spirit of equality with all, and with respect for all forms of freedom.[15]

It is because one believes in a God who is free to create and to initiate things that one defends everywhere freedom values: freedom of movement and freedom of expression, freedom of thought and freedom of religion. For freedom alone allows the flowering of the human spirit in each person and each community; freedom alone gives humanity the opportunity to be responsible for its own acts and to achieve integrated personalities; freedom alone gives the believer the joy of adoring God without constraint and of offering a service worthy of God. "Human dignity demands that one act according to a knowing and free choice. Such a choice is personally

---

[15] Is it necessary to recall here that Christian charity is shown to all, without distinction of race or creed, without proselytism and without any type of pressure being exerted? This is the constant attitude of Catholics, shared by many Protestants. See the Hong Kong Memorandum of 1975, quoted in John B. Taylor, "The Involvement of the World Council of Churches (W.C.C.) in International and Regional Christian-Muslim Dialogue," *Islamochristiana* I (1975): 97-102.

On social matters and questions concerning "development" reference can be made to recent papal documents, such as *Mater et magistra* of Pope John XXIII, of 15.5.1961, on "recent developments concerning the social question in the light of Christian doctrine" [Italian text in *Osservatore Romano*, 15.7.1961; French text in the *Documentation catholique*, Paris, 6.8.1961, pp. 946-990; English translation: *New Light on Social Problems* (London: Catholic Truth Society, 1961)], and the letter of Pope Paul VI, *Populorum progressio*, of 26.3.1967, on the complete and harmonious "development of peoples" [Italian text in the *Osservatore Romano*, 28-29.3.1967; English translation: *The Great Social Problem* (London: Catholic Truth Society, 1967); French translation in the *Documentation catholique*, Paris, 16.4.1967, pp. 674-704; Arabic translation, privately edited by the Secretariat for Non-Christians, *Risala jami'a liQadasat al-Baba Bulus al-sadis fi Taqaddam al-shu'ub wa-rtiqa'i-ha* (Jounieh, Lebanon: Paulist Publishers)].

motivated and promoted from within. It does not result from blind internal impulse" (*Gaudium et spes,* par. 17), declared the Second Vatican Council.

Finally it is because one believes in God who is Peace and who gathers that one strives to create a human family on an international scale, while at the same time respecting national cultures. This too is why one encourages dialogue as the sole means for resolving conflicts and why one combats all forms of nationalism that are closed and inward-looking. It is because one believes in a God of mercy and pardon that one rejects the spirit of vengeance and any justice that might in fact be unjust. For pardon alone can revive in the prisoner, the condemned person, or the sinner, that strength of soul which enables the start of a new life, and only human mercy can bear witness here below to the limitless and endless mercy of God.

C. *Believers and Our World of Today*

Life for all, justice for all, freedom for all, the unity of the human family – these are the human values which, since they are at one and the same time values of faith, undoubtedly constitute possible common ground for the commitment of believers amidst the contemporary problems of civilization. Despite some fundamental divergences in matters of doctrine, particularly with respect to the approach to the divine mystery and to the role of prophets in history, all have a common doctrinal basis sufficient to justify, in the name of faith itself, their commitment on behalf of humanity, through a "dialogue of values" where we ourselves must be ready to pay the price. These various areas of convergence have been brought to the consideration of Christians by the Second Vatican Council in a long document entitled *The Church in the Modern World.* This document aims at defending the absolute dignity of humankind which lives under the eye of God and in submission to divine laws, fully respecting life, justice, equality, and freedom which are among the fundamental contemporary rights.

This document first reminds believers of the "human conditions" today: its hopes and fears, the psychological, moral, and religious transformations that are taking place; new imbalances; more universal aspirations; a deeper questioning. Three broad areas are given priority:

human dignity, the unity of the human community, and the promotion of human action in the universe. Believers, conscious of *human dignity* but also of the manifold contradictions within people, have the duty of reminding all of the dignity of the mind destined for truth and wisdom, of the dignity of conscience destined for freedom and uprightness, yet accepting at the same time dialogue with all representatives of contemporary atheism. Believers concerned for the *human community* have the duty of insisting on the community aspect of the human vocation: the interdependence of person and society, the primacy of the common good, respect for persons, respect and love for adversaries, the essential equality of all people, the need to go beyond a purely individualistic ethic. Believers, convinced of the *value of human action,* have the duty of respecting the autonomy of earthly realities while at the same time helping to bring about the fulfillment according to God's plan for creation. Are they not awaiting "a new heaven and a new earth" (Apoc. 21:1)?

D. *The Dignity of Earthly Values*

Some urgent problems are then put forward for the attention of Christians. These can constitute further common ground for the commitment of believers. The first of these is the *dignity of marriage and of the family:* the holiness of marriage and the family, the fundamental value of conjugal love, the fruitfulness of marriage, respect for human life from birth and even before birth, the eminent dignity of woman and the promotion of her interests. The second area of concern is that of *cultural development:* the relationship between faith and culture, the harmony of different values within cultures, the recognition that all have a right to culture, efforts to achieve an integral human culture. A third series of questions concerns the *socio-economic order:* economic development for human benefit, removal of socio-economic inequalities, social justice in industrial disputes, participation in management and in the running of the economy, private property and concern for the common good, the use of the world's resources for the benefit of the whole of humankind. In fourth place is *politics:* the cooperation of all citizens in the life of the nation through democratic systems which respect the liberties referred to above. Finally, there are the *maintenance of peace and the building up of a community of nations:* proscription of war, or at least its "humanization" when sin forces us to tolerate it; the struggle for a growing and general disarmament; work for international cooperation in all fields (economic, social, cultural); and the development of international bodies.[16]

III. *Conclusion*

It is perhaps through such action on behalf of life, justice, freedom, and fellowship that believers can today prove the human effectiveness and the real credibility of their faith in God. They cannot invoke God as Creator and Saviour of all if they refuse to believe in a familial spirit toward all. Christians say: "Anyone who says, 'I love God,' and hates her or his brother, is a liar, since whoever does not love a brother that is seen cannot love God, who is not seen" (1 Jn. 4:20); "our love is not to be just words or mere talk, but something real and active" (1 Jn. 3:18). Muslims are well aware that they are required to act in conformity with their faith: "Work, and God will surely see your work, and his Messenger, and the believers" (Qur'an 9:105). Christians and Muslims seem, therefore, to have a certain common ground, as regards both belief and commitment. For this reason it is important to define to what extend religion constitutes, for each side, an "ideology for life," and to what extend faith in God encourages believers to dedicate themselves wholly to the achievement of social justice. In the very fight against prejudices and in attempting to lessen misunderstandings they will discover

---

[16] To make efforts and declarations for the establishment of peace has been the constant concern of leaders of the Catholic Church. Reference would be made here to the encyclical letter of Pope John XXIII, *Pacem in terris,* of 11.4.1963, on "peace between nations founded on truth, justice, charity, and freedom" [Italian text in the *Osservatore Romano,* 11.4.1963; English translation: *Peace on Earth* (London: Catholic Truth Society, 1963); French translation in the *Documentation catholique,* Paris, 21.4.1964,pp. 513-546]; to Pope Paul's speech to the General Assembly of the United Nations in New York, on 4.10.1965 [French text in the *Osservatore Romano,* 6.10.1965; and in the *Documentation catholique,* Paris, 17.10.1965, pp. 1729-1738: English translation: *The Pope's Appeal for Peace* (London: Catholic Truth Society, 1965); and to the institution, by Pope Paul VI, of a Day of Peace to be celebrated annually on January 1st. "No more war, no more war," he had said to the delegates assembled at the United Nations, " it is peace, peace, which must direct the destiny of peoples and the whole of humanity."

how much unites them already. For this to come about it is desirable that believers should listen to the inspirations God gives them today, and that they should extend their activity on behalf of their fellow humans for the glory of God and the joy of humankind. Then they will hear the Psalmist saying to them: "Happy those who find their strength in you, Lord; they will set out on the road" (Ps. 83:6).

CHRISTIANITY AND WORLD RELIGIONS: DIALOGUE WITH ISLAM*

· Hans Küng**

I am happy to see again leading figures in interreligious dialogue who – long before I entered this field – have done so much pioneering work: John Cobb in Christian-Buddhist dialogue; Raimundo Panikkar in Christian-Hindu dialogue; and the "elder statesman," whom I was especially eager to meet, Wilfred Cantwell Smith. Professor Smith has done more than anyone else to promote what this conference calls "a universal theology of religion," an encounter of different religions, especially from a Christian perspective.

This year is also the one hundredth anniversary of Temple University. This symposium, I believe, is probably the most suitable way to celebrate such a centennial. I recall another centennial of another university where a conference like this was also held. It was the centennial of the American University in Beirut, almost twenty years ago, to which I was invited, along with Cardinal Willebrands, head of the Roman Secretariat for Christian Unity, and Dr. Visser't Hooft, then secretary general and now honorary president of the World Council of Churches.

* In Leonard Swidler, ed., *Toward a Universal Theology of Religion* (Maryknoll, NY: Orbis Books, 1987), pp. 192-209.

** Hans Küng (Catholic) studied at the Gregorian University in Rome and at the Sorbonne and Institut Catholique in Paris, where he received his Ph.D. He was Professor of Dogmatics on the Catholic Theology Faculty of the University of Tübingen 1960-80, and of Ecumenical Theology since 1964, and is an Associate Editor of the *Journal of Ecumenical Studies*. His bibliography covers 50 pages.

There were, however, significant differences between the two conferences. At Beirut we Christian theologians met one week, and Muslim theologians – invited from all over the world – met another week. I asked the president of the conference (who was the former president of the United Nations General Assembly), Charles Malik, foreign secretary of Lebanon at that time, whether it would not be possible to meet with the Muslim scholars; in the end, however, it was so arranged that we did not meet. Today I am convinced that if a serious dialogue between Christians and Muslims would have been started twenty years ago, Muslims (who were already *then* practically the majority in Lebanon) would have long since received the rights that are still being fought over after thousands and thousands of victims. I think Lebanon could have remained what it was then called – "the Switzerland of the Near East" – a beautiful, happy country, whereas today many sections of the capital are destroyed, hostility is rife, and much of the land is occupied by Syrians, Palestinians, and Israelis – a real *catastrophe.*

Thus, when we speak about interreligious dialogue, it is not just a matter of a few theologians debating some abstract questions. I am convinced that the Vietnam war was, behind the scenes, also heavily grounded in religious antagonism, in that case between Buddhists – Buddhist monks especially – and the Catholic regime of Diem and his princes, together with the colonial powers. And I am also convinced that the antagonism between India and Pakistan, the war between Iraq and Iran, and the whole situation in the Middle East are largely grounded in religious antagonism. I am, of course, well aware that these conflicts are not just a matter of religion; there are also political, military, economic, and social aspects. Yet battles and wars become fanatical when they have a religious base. We in Europe have enough experience of what it means to conduct "religious wars."

I am convinced it would be possible to avoid this kind of war. I am not an illusionary; I have seen it happen in Europe. After having had several hundred years of wars between Germany and France, Germany and Poland, but especially Germany and France – the origin of World War I and World War II – religiously committed persons after World War II said, "Enough!" (In this case, they were Christians, but I am sure that persons like Gandhi and others from other faiths would have said the same thing.) I am convinced that it could have been done because at that time we had not only technocrats in European governmental agencies (as we have them now in Brussels), but also the likes of Konrad Adenauer, Robert Schuman, Charles DeGaulle, Alcide DeGasperi, and others who, because of ethical and religious convictions, thought that we must put an end to warfare. One of the greatest achievements of this century, I believe, was to bring together nations that had considered themselves hereditary enemies.

So why should it not be possible – of course with adequate preparation – to do this also in the Near East? Somebody must make the effort. We must urge what I proposed to Muslims in Lebanon, to Christians in Lebanon, and to Israelis in their Foreign Ministry: They must begin something like a "trilateral" conversation, a "trialogue," as it is called. Of course, it will demand sacrifices; persons are needed who will commit themselves even when it is very dangerous.

I remember the story the former chancellor of the Federal Republic of Germany, Helmut Schmidt, told me of his trip down the Nile with Anwar Sadat. Sadat, then president of Egypt, said that he was convinced that there would never be peace in the Near East without having peace among the religions, and that was why he wanted to establish a common sanctuary for Jews, Christians, and Muslims.

Hence, I would very willingly subscribe to what Wilfred Cantwell Smith has said at this conference about the religious dimensions of all history. It is our intellectual error not to see those dimensions, and I think that this error has been committed especially by politicians. This error has also been committed by many development experts – all those Western advisors, Europeans and Americans, who, for instance, advised the Shah of Iran not to bother with the religious dimension, because they themselves did not think it important. They thought only about technocratic problems – and we have seen what has resulted.

My thesis, therefore, is: No world peace without peace among religions, no peace among religions without dialogue between the religions, and no dialogue between the religions without accurate knowledge of one another. This is one reason why we are assembled here. We can no longer regard the world religions simply as existing side by side; rather we must view them together – in interdependence and in interaction. Today, no religion can live in splendid isolation.

I am well aware of the fact that there will always be persons (in certain religions more than in others) who will ask, "Why should we talk to each other?" I asked a European specialist of the Arab world why should we talk to each other, and what, in his opinion, the solution is for Jerusalem. He was quite candid when he said, "War." I believe that this is the alternative to religious dialogue: war. I told him that we had already had a number of wars – without resolving anything. I am convinced that interreligious dialogue is of the greatest importance not just for politicians concerned with conflicts in the Near East, but for all human beings involved in the ordinary business of life.

Another element that should concern us in this issue is the fact that out of every six persons in the world, one is Muslim and two are Christian. This is one of the reasons why I have chosen the encounter between Christianity and Islam as a model for interreligious dialogue. I could also talk about the encounter between Christianity and Hinduism, or Christianity and Buddhism, though of course the approach would have to be different, because these religions are so different. These dialogues are especially important for us Americans and Europeans, partly because Hinduism and Buddhism still are for us largely unknown universes. We have not had direct conflict with these Eastern religions, whereas the history of Europe, since the seventh century, has also been a history of conflict with Muslims. This must be borne in mind today in a period of re-Islamization as a fundamental reason for the pressing need of dialogue with Muslims.

Dialogue with Muslims? Who is ready in Islam to have dialogue? Perhaps Khomeini? I have met Muslims all over the world who find recent developments in Iran catastrophic; such developments, they feel, are blocking mutual understanding and are propagating prejudice against Islam. I believe, however, that it is precisely at *this* time that we need to talk about our relationship to Islam, and not simply to think about the terrible things that have happened in Iran. Such events should not deter us. I am convinced – without going into detail here – that the present situation in Iran is ultimately an episode (as was the "reign of terror" within the French revolution), after which a process of normalization will begin. But it is important that we now actively prepare for that process and not just wait for it to happen.

I now want to speak as a theologian. I am not speaking as a politician, nor as a specialist in comparative religion. I have studied many religions, talked to many of their adherents, and visited many of their countries. However, as a theologian, I have to answer a particular question: How can Christians today come to terms with the claims made by the Muslim faith? I shall take up questions that will help us to thoroughly examine our altered ecumenical stance toward other world religions in general, with a view to greater broadmindedness and openness; and I shall try to focus the questions so that they will help us to reread our own history of theological thought and faith against the background of Islam. I do this as a Christian theologian; from my Christian basis, I want to take other religions seriously.

To a great extent Christians still regard Islam as a rigid entity, a closed religious system, rather than a living religion, a religious movement that has been continually changing through the centuries, developing great inner variety, all the time shared by real persons with a wide spectrum of attitudes and feelings. I think no one has done more than Wilfred Cantwell Smith to make it clear that Islam is not just a system of the past or a collection of theories we have to study, but a reality today; Professor Smith has urged us to make an attempt to understand *from the inside* why Muslims see God and the world, service to God and to their fellows, politics, law, and art with different eyes, why they experience these things with different feelings from those of Christians. Keeping Iran in mind, we must first grasp the fact that even today the Islamic religion is not just another strand in the life of a Muslim, what secularized persons like to refer to as the "religious factor" or "sector" alongside other "cultural factors" or "sectors." No, life and religion, religion and culture, are dynamically interwoven. Islam strives to be an all-embracing view, an all-encompassing perspective on life, an all-determining way of life – and so in the midst of this life a way to eternal life. Islam is referred to as paradise, salvation, liberation, redemption, but it is not just a way in this life, with the focus on only the here and now. This leads to one of the eight questions I should like to raise – and they are all very delicate questions.

1. Islam – A Way of Salvation? of Eternal Salvation?

I pose the following question (not least because of the ambivalent attitude of the World Council of Churches, which, due to the conflicting standpoints of its member churches, chose not to answer it even in its 1979 "Guidelines for Dialogue with People of Different Religions and Ideologies"): Can there be salvation outside the Christian churches, outside Christianity? This is a question of great urgency today, because if we think Muslims are going to hell anyway, it is not really worthwhile to engage in a dialogue with them. Thus I do not understand why the WCC does not speak out on this matter.

The *traditional Catholic* position, as forged in the first centuries of the Christian church by Origen, Cyprian, and Augustine, is generally well known: *extra ecclesiam nulla salus*. No salvation outside the church. Thus for the future as well: *extra ecclesiam nullus propheta*. No prophet outside the church. The Ecumenical Council of Florence in 1442 defined this very clearly:

> The Holy Church of Rome...believes firmly, confesses and proclaims, that no one outside the Catholic Church, neither heathen nor Jew nor unbeliever, nor one who is separated from the Church, will share in eternal life, but will perish in the eternal fire prepared for the devil and his angels, if this person fails to join it [the Catholic Church] before death [Denz. 714].

Does that not settle the claim of Islam, at least for Catholics? It seems to have done so for more than five hundred years.

Today, at any rate, the *traditional* Catholic position is no longer the *official* Catholic position. We cannot change the words, because the conciliar statement was, indeed, an infallible definition, but we are allowed to say the contrary! The Second Vatican Council declared unmistakably in its "Constitution on the Church" that "those who, through no fault of their own, do not know the Gospel of Christ or his Church, but who nevertheless seek God with a sincere heart and, moved by grace, try in their actions to do his will as they know it through the dictates of their conscience – they too may achieve eternal salvation" (Art. 16). This is valid even for atheists of good will.

Particular mention is given by Vatican II to those who, due to their background, have the most in common with Jews and Christians through their faith in the one God and in doing God's will: Muslims. "But the plan of salvation also includes those who acknowledge the Creator, in the first place among whom are the Muslims: they profess to hold the faith of Abraham, and together with us they adore the one, merciful God, the judge of humanity on the last day" (*ibid.*). Thus, according to Vatican II, even Muslims need not "perish in that eternal fire prepared for the devil and his angels" – they can "achieve eternal salvation." That means that Islam, too, can be a way of salvation.

The next problem is, what about prophets? The "Constitution on the Church" and the "Declaration on Non-Christian Religions" mention Islam but do not mention Muhammad. So I turn to my second question.

2. Muhammad – A Prophet?

Of course many religions do not have prophets in the strictest sense. Hindus have their gurus and sadhus, the Chinese their sages, Buddhists their masters – but they do not have prophets, as do Jews, Christians, and Muslims. There is no doubt that if anyone in the whole of religious history is termed *the* prophet, because he claimed to be *just that*, but in no way *more* than that, it was Muhammad. But may a Christian assert that Muhammad was a prophet? Christians, if they pause to survey the situation, must admit the following (especially in light of the Hebrew Bible):

• Like the prophets of Israel, Muhammad did not function by reason of an office assigned to him by the community (or its authorities), but by reason of a special personal relationship with God.

• Like the prophets of Israel, Muhammad was a person of strong will who felt himself fully imbued with a godly calling, fully consumed, exclusively appointed to his task.

• Like the prophets of Israel, Muhammad spoke to the heart of a religious and social crisis, and with his passionate piety and revolutionary proclamation he opposed the wealthy ruling class and the tradition it was trying to preserve.

• Like the prophets of Israel, Muhammad, who mostly called himself the "Warner," sought to be nothing but the verbal instrument of God and to proclaim not his own, but God's word.

• Like the prophets of Israel, Muhammad untiringly proclaimed the one God who tolerates no other gods and who is at the same time the good Creator and merciful Judge.

• Like the prophets of Israel, Muhammad required, as a response to this one God, unconditional obedience, devotion, submission, which is the literal meaning of word *Islam*: everything that includes gratitude to God and generosity toward fellow human beings.

• Like the prophets of Israel, Muhammad combined monotheism with humanism or human values, belief in the one God and God's judgment with a call to social justice, and a threat to the unjust, who go to hell, with promises to the just, who are gathered into God's paradise.

Whoever reads the Bible – at least the Hebrew Bible – together with the Qur'an will be led to ponder whether the three Semitic *religions of revelation* – Judaism, Christianity, and Islam – and especially the Hebrew Bible and the Qur'an, could have *the same foundation.* Is it not one and the same God who speaks so clearly in both? Does not the "Thus says the Lord" of the Hebrew Bible correspond to the "Speak" of the Qur'an, and the "Go and proclaim" of the Hebrew Bible to the "Stand up and warn" of the Qur'an? In truth, even the millions of Arab-speaking Christians have no other word for God than "Allāh."

Might it not therefore be purely dogmatic prejudice that recognizes Amos and Hosea, Isaiah and Jeremiah, as prophets, but not Muhammad? Whatever one may have against Muhammad from the standpoint of Western Christian morality (armed violence, polygamy, a sensual lifestyle for males), the following facts are indisputable:

• Today there are almost eight hundred million persons in the huge area between Morocco to the west and Bangladesh to the east, between the steppes of central Asia to the North and the Island world of Indonesia to the south, who are stamped with the compelling power of a faith that, like virtually no other faith, has molded into a universal type those who confess it.

• All those persons are linked by a simple confession of faith (There is no God but God, and Muhammad is his prophet), linked by five basic obligations, and linked by thorough submission to the will of God, whose unchangeable decision, even when it brings suffering, is to be accepted.

• Among all the Islamic peoples there has remained a sense of fundamental equality before God of an international solidarity that is basically capable of overcoming race (Arabs and non-Arabs) and even the castes of India.

I am convinced that, despite all the renewed fears of Islam, there is a growing conviction among Christians that, in the light of Muhammad's place in world history, we must correct our attitude toward Islam. The "scourge of exclusiveness," arising from Christian dogmatic impatience and intolerance, condemned by the British historian Arnold Toynbee, must be abandoned. Regarding the figure of the prophet, I believe the following must be admitted:

• Arabians in the seventh century rightly listened to and followed the voice of Muhammad.

• In comparison to the very worldly polytheism of the old Arabian tribal religions before Muhammad, the religion of the people was raised to a completely new level, that of a purified monotheism.

• The first Muslims received from Muhammad – or, better still, from the Qur'an – endless inspiration, courage, and strength for a new religious start: a start toward greater truth and deeper understanding, toward a breakthrough in the revitalizing and renewal of traditional religion.

In truth, Muhammad was and is for persons in the Arabian world, and for many others, *the* religious reformer, lawgiver, and leader; *the* prophet per se. Basically Muhammad, who never claimed to be anything more than a human being, is more to those who follow him than a prophet is to us: he is a model for the mode of life that Islam strives to be. If the Catholic Church, according to the Vatican II "Declaration on Non-Christian Religions," "regards with esteem the Muslims," then the same church must also respect the one whose name is embarrassingly absent from the same declaration, although he and he alone led the Muslims to pray to this one God, for through him this God "has spoken to humanity": Muhammad the prophet.

But does not such an acknowledgment have very grave consequences, especially for the message he proclaimed, the teachings set down in the Qur'an?

I think for the peoples of Arabia Muhammad's prophecy led to tremendous progress. Whatever we Christians do with this fact, we must affirm that he acted as a prophet and that he was a prophet. I do not see how we can avoid the conclusion that on their way of salvation, Muslims follow a prophet who is decisive for them. This leads us to an even more difficult question. If he is the prophet, what, then, about the Qur'an?

3. The Qur'an – Word of God?

The Qur'an is more than an oral tradition, which can be easily altered. It is a *written* record, set down once for all time; it cannot be altered. In this respect it is similar to the Bible. Because of its written form, the Qur'an has retained a remarkable constancy from century to century, from generation to generation, from person to person, despite the changes and variety in Islamic history. What is written is written. Despite all the different interpretations and commentaries, despite all the forms taken by Islamic law (the *shari'ah*), the Qur'an remains the common denominator, something like the "green thread" of the prophet in all Islamic forms, rituals, and institutions. One who wishes to know not only historical Islam, but also *normative* Islam, must, still today, return to the Qur'an of the seventh century.

Although the Qur'an in no way predetermined the development of Islam, it most certainly inspired it. Commentators came and went, but the Qur'an remained a source of inspiration. Commentators came and went, but the Qur'an remained intact. It is the one great constant in Islam amid all the countless variables. It provided Islam with moral obligation, external dynamism, and religious depth, as well as with specific enduring doctrines and moral principles: the responsibility of the individual before God, social justice, and Muslim solidarity. The Qur'an is *the* holy book of Islam; it is understood to be, in its written form, not the word of a human, but the word of *God*. For Muslims, God's word became a book. Our question is: Is this book really the word of God?

Here we can turn to Wilfred Cantwell Smith who was one of the first to focus this question concerning the authorship of the Qur'an. For centuries this question was never posed as a serious issue. It would have threatened with excommunication Muslims as well as Christians – the former if they had doubted it, the latter if they had affirmed it. And who can deny that this question has caused deep political divisions among the peoples of the world, from the first Islamic conquests in the seventh century to the Crusades and the capture of Constantinople, to the siege of Vienna in modern times and the Iranian revolution under Khomeini. Just as naturally as Muslims from West Africa to central Asia and Indonesia have answered this question affirmatively and have oriented their lives according to the Qur'an, so believing Christians all over the world have said no. This negation was later restated by secular Western scholars of comparative religion who took it for granted that the Qur'an was not at all the word of God, but wholly that of Muhammad.

In 1962 Wilfred Cantwell Smith posed this question in clear terms, threatening though it was for both sides. I cannot but agree with his assertion that the two possible answers, both of which were supported by intelligent, critical, and thoroughly honest persons, in fact relied upon an unquestioned, insistent *preconviction*. On both sides, the opposite viewpoint was seen as either superstitious or lacking in faith.

It is true then, as Smith's Canadian colleague and my friend Willard Oxtoby claims, that a rule of thumb in the study of religions is that "you get out what you put in"? In other words, is it true that those who regard the Qur'an as the word of God from the start will repeatedly see their conviction confirmed in reading it, and vice versa?

Can we allow this contradiction between Muslims and Christians to perdure, unsatisfactory as it is from an intellectual standpoint? Are there not increasing numbers of Christians and Muslims who have become better informed about the faith of others and about their own position, and who are, therefore, posing self-critical questions? Let me outline the situation from both points of view.

a)   *Self-critical questioning of an exclusively Christian understanding of revelation.* This, of course, is a very delicate question for us. Many

Christians are not ready to face this question, but are content to let the great majority of humanity be consigned to hell. It must be recalled, however, that Adam was not the first Jew, but the first human being. And the first covenant was not with the people of Israel, but with the whole of humanity. In contemporary religious literature, besides talk of erroneousness, benightedness, and guilt, there is a wealth of positive statements about the world outside Israel, in the distant past, and outside Christianity, since then. The thinking behind these positive statements is that originally God bestowed self-revelation upon the whole of humanity. Indeed, both the Hebrew Bible and the New Testament teach that non-Jews and non-Christians can also know the true God (I cannot go into details here). These texts explain this possibility in terms of the revelation of God in creation.

Considering this biblical background, and reading it now to see what we could learn for our time, we cannot exclude the possibility that countless persons in the past and in the present have experienced, and are experiencing, the mystery of God on the basis of the revelation of God in creation, and that such experience involves the grace of God and true religious faith. And we cannot exclude the possibility that in this context certain individuals have also, within the bounds of their religion, been endowed with special insight, entrusted with a special task, a special charism.

Many Christians do not realize that the Catholic Church has excluded as an error the claim that outside the church there is no salvation, no grace. By implication, there *is* grace outside the church. There can be special charisms outside the church. How, then, can we deny that outside the church there also are persons who have such charisms, including prophetic gifts? *Extra ecclesiam gratia!* If we recognize Muhammad as a prophet, to be consistent we must also admit that the message of Muhammad was not of his own making; the Qur'an is not simply the word of Muhammad, but the *Word of God*. And the Qur'an is much more important for Muslims than is the prophet!

b)   *Self-critical questioning of the Islamic interpretation of the Qur'an.* I come now to the hardest point in discussion with Muslims. It is a question that applies, uncomfortably, to both sides, but it must be faced. The question concerns the Qur'an (or the Bible) as the word of God. That the Qur'an is the word of God I do not contest. However, there is the further question: *How* is the Qur'an (or the Bible) the word of God? Does revelation directly fall from heaven, so to speak? Is it, as some maintain, dictated word for word by God? Is there nothing human in this word of God? It must be remembered that not only Muslims believe this; fundamentalist Christians look upon the Bible in the same way. The fundamentalist Christian says: All this is dictated by God, from the first phrase to the last. There is nothing that changes, nothing to interpret. Everything is clear.

Today it is important that the Qur'an as the word of God be seen in its historical context. Many Muslims would tell me that it is blasphemy to think that this word of God could also at the same time be the word of a human being. I would answer only in a provisional way. When the first Jew asked this about the Hebrew Bible, he was excommunicated; this was Spinoza, the seventeenth-century Jewish philosopher in Amsterdam, who started critical exegesis of the Bible. The first Catholic to raise this question was a disciple of rabbis in Paris at the time of Bossuet, also in the seventeenth century. He was exiled and had to publish his books in Amsterdam. That was Richard Simon. Thus the Catholic Church missed the chance to formulate a critical approach to the Bible as early as the seventeenth century. Reimarus, the first Protestant to propose a critical approach to scripture, also had the greatest of troubles, in Germany, and as a matter of fact did not even dare to publish his work. The great poet Lessing published it after Reimarus's death, claiming that, although it was not his own view, it was worthy of discussion. Later on, Lessing admitted that he shared Reimarus's views, and he was told not to speak of it further.

So who would be surprised if today in Islam there are similar reactions? It is dangerous to take up this matter publicly. But I know that Muslim students say in private what they will not say in public. I am accustomed to such a situation in the Catholic Church, having raised the same questions for Christians that I am proposing for my Muslim friends.

This is, then, not only a question for Muslims. It is really contrary to the word of God if we say that this word is at the same time the word of a human being and that it has been influenced by a human medium? There are a few Muslims, like the Pakistani Fazlur Rahman at the University of

Chicago, who entertain such thoughts and provide supporting evidence from Islamic tradition. Such scholars are often attacked by orthodox Muslims, as was Rahman, who was even forced to flee his own country. This question, however, cannot be suppressed. If even the Catholic Church, with all its organization and power, was unable to suppress the issue, neither will Islam be able to do so, for Islam does not even have a magisterium or a Holy Office. (In Islam it is mainly the masses of the believers who can prove to be threatening and dangerous.)

Is it not possible to understand and experience the Qur'an as a great witness to the all-merciful God, as Muslims do, without viewing it as *dictated* by God? Such an understanding would also be a help in dealing with the question of capital punishment and other issues that *have* to be changed, and not only by reinterpretation but by admitting that certain practices that were necessary or meaningful in a past historical context are no longer fitting for our present context.

4. What Are the Main Common Elements Among Muslims, Jews, and Christians?

a)   The basic common area among Muslims, Jews, and Christians is found in their faith in *one and only one God*, who gives meaning and life to all.

b)   Jews, Christians, and Muslims are also of one mind in their belief in the *God of history* – the God who is not *above*, but *in*, history, intervening, calling in a hidden way.

c)   Jews, Christians, and Muslims agree in their belief that the one God is an approachable partner. God can be addressed.

d)   Finally, this God is a *merciful and gracious God*. The Arabic *al-Rahmān*, the "merciful one," is etymologically linked to the Hebraic *rahamim*, which, together with *hen* and *hesed*, represents the semantic field for the New Testament *charis*, the Vulgate *gratia*, and the English "grace." This shared belief has a political relevance. I have been told that for the Camp David Agreement it was not unimportant that a believing Christian, a believing Jew, and a believing Muslim came together and saw that they finally had to do something for world peace.

These shared beliefs clear the way for more difficult questions.

5. Is the Qur'an Portrayal of Jesus Accurate?

It is well known that the Qur'an speaks of Jesus of Nazareth, and always in a positive manner. This is astonishing when one considers the very different attitude of Jewish sources and also the centuries-old history of hatred and vilification between Christianity and Islam. How can we assess these passages theologically? A close examination of the texts of the Qur'an relevant to Christianity reveals that all the material concerning Jesus found in the Qur'an is integrated *in a fully coherent manner into the whole theological conception of the Qur'an.* From whatever tradition this testimony to Jesus may stem – and I shall go into this more closely – the whole is conspicuously permeated with the spirit of Islam, with Muhammad's intense prophetic experience of the one God. On the basis of this experience, Muhammad had no cause whatsoever to contradict Jesus (in fact he *does not* contradict him): the preaching of Jesus he makes his own, and both the virgin birth and miracles are acknowledged without envy by the prophet. There is but one disclaimer: Jesus may not be made into a god; he may not be put alongside the one God as a second deity. For Islam, that would be the ultimate abomination.

The position of Jesus in the Qur'an is unambiguous. Dialogue is therefore not aided by contemporary well-meaning Christians who read more into the Qur'an than it contains, claiming that in the Qur'an Jesus is called the "Word" of God. For the Qur'an, however, he is not the Word of God in the sense of the prologue of John's Gospel, in which the preexistent divine *logos* became flesh. If the Qur'an acknowledges the virgin birth of Jesus, it is a sign of God's omnipotence, but emphatically not a sign of the deity of Jesus.

In other words, for the Qur'an Jesus is a prophet, a greater prophet than Abraham, Noah, and Moses – but certainly not more than a prophet. Further, just as in the New Testament John the Baptist is the forerunner of Jesus, so in the Qur'an Jesus is the forerunner of, and undoubtedly the encouraging example for, Muhammad. According to the Qur'an, Jesus was created directly by God as a second Adam (this is the meaning of the virgin birth), unlike the Prophet.

For this reason, Christians should avoid wanting to make "anonymous Christians" of Muhammad and Muslims, as some theologians (among them my friend Karl Rahner) have attempted; such attempts run counter to the Muslims' understanding of themselves. We must never give others names they cannot apply to themselves. If we call them "anonymous Christians," then we also should be willing to be called "anonymous Muslims." Then of course there arises the question, whether Muslims would not like to make Jesus an anonymous Muslim.

If we who represent Christianity concern ourselves with a revaluation of Muhammad on the basis of Islamic sources, especially the Qur'an, we hope that Muslims might eventually do what Jews have begun to do: Jewish scholars have started to study Jesus, to do research on him. Our hope is that in time Muslim scholars also will consider the historical sources and will come to a revaluation of Jesus of Nazareth on the basis of those sources – that is, the Gospels themselves.

The portrait of Jesus in the Qur'an, I would say, is too one-sided, too monotone, for the most part lacking in content; in the Qur'an Jesus simply proclaims monotheism, calls to repentance, and performs miracles. This is a weak, one-dimensional picture in comparison, for example, with the Jesus of the Sermon on the Mount. Precisely because legalism is a central problem in both Judaism and Islam, it is important to examine Jesus' position concerning the law and legalism; he was, after all, executed because of his stand against legalism. According to Islam, Jesus did not really die; he simply was assumed into heaven. It is, however, important to recognize that according to the original sources of the first century he really did die. We must, I believe, rely on these sources. I am aware that it is said, "But Muhammad received his revelation directly from God." Here again we have a historical problem.

6. What is the Central Theological Difference?

The focal concern of Jesus himself was to overcome legalism by fulfilling the will of God in love, in view of the coming reign of God. For the

Christian church, however – and here we come to the decisive difficulty – the focal concern slowly shifted from the reign of God to the person of Jesus and his relationship with God. The debate between Christianity and Islam remains focused on this question. Up to now, the decisive Christian objection to Islam has been that Islam disputes the two related central doctrines of Christianity: The *Trinity* and the *incarnation*. Indeed, the Qur'an addresses Christians:

> People of the Book, do not transgress the bounds of your religion. Speak nothing but the truth about Allāh. The Messiah, Jesus, the son of Mary, was no more than Allāh's apostle and his Word, which he cast into Mary: a spirit from him. So believe in Allāh and his apostles and do not say [of Allāh, that he is] "three." Allāh is but one God. Allāh forbid that He should have a son! [sura 4:171]

Furthermore, there is no truth in the assertion of Christian apologists and many scholars of religion that Muslim theologians have always misinterpreted the Christian doctrine of the Trinity (three in one) as a doctrine of tritheism (three gods). There is a certain misunderstanding of the Trinity in the Qur'an, I believe, but that is not so important. As early as the medieval controversies there were many Muslim theologians who understood the Christian doctrine quite well. But they were simply not able to understand what the Jews as well could not grasp: that when there is one godhead, one divine nature, the recognition of three persons in one God does not automatically lead to the relinquishing of that faith in one God that Abraham stood for, and Moses, and Jesus, and finally Muhammad also.

Why distinguish at all between nature and person in God? It is obvious that the *distinctions* between one and three made by the Christian doctrine of the Trinity do not satisfy Muslims. All these concepts of Syrian, Greek, and Latin origin are more confusing to them than enlightening, a game of words and concepts. How can the one and only God, asks the Muslim, be a conglomeration of hypostases, persons, processions, and relations? Why all the dialectical tricks? Is not God simply God, "combined" neither in this way nor that?

According to the Qur'an, "Unbelievers are those who say, 'God is one of three [or 'three-faced'].'" This viewpoint, which was completely unacceptable to Muhammad, is flatly rejected by the statement, "There is but one God" (sura 5:73). This brings me to my seventh question.

7. How Are We to Assess the Central Theological Difference?

That which applies to the doctrine of the Trinity applies also to christology. I think that today if Christians and Muslims (and Jews as well) wish to come to a better mutual understanding, they must *return to the sources* and then look critically at all subsequent developments.

I know this is a difficult point, especially to our Orthodox Christian brethren, who do not want to go back behind the councils of the fourth and fifth centuries to the New Testament. It is not merely for archeological reasons that we should want to go back; all the churches, including the Orthodox churches, are founded – as all the fathers of the church say – "on the New Testament." When the term *homoousios* was objected to, because it was not in the Bible, Athanasius said, "Read the Bible and then you will understand it correctly." Read the Bible, read the New Testament, and the relationship between Father, Son, and Spirit will be more understandable – and it will become clear that the dogmas of the fourth and fifth and seventh centuries are not a little different from what was said about Father, Son, and Spirit in the New Testament. It can also be shown that what was said about Jesus in the beginning was somewhat different and may be easier to understand that what was said in Greek in the fourth and fifth centuries.

I acknowledge the intentions of those councils and their decisive content, but I also understand that for persons not educated in this tradition, who do not understand *hypostasis, physis, homoousios, homoiousios, homoousios kata panta,* this language can be not just mysterious but meaningless. So it makes sense to ask how the first disciples, who were Jews, understood Jesus. Such a question opens many complex but fruitful issues. In the beginning our church was a church of Jews. Then it became a church of Jews and gentiles, but what remained finally was a church of gentiles. Where are the Jewish Christians today? I met one recently at Harvard. He came to me after my lecture and said, "I am so grateful that you spoke about Jewish Christians" – he had become one.

It is unfortunate that after the destruction of Jerusalem under the Emperor Hadrian in the year 132 and the flight of all Jewish Christians to the East, the growing church was almost completely uprooted from its Jewish soil. The gentile, Hellenistic Christians did not really care. I do not want to blame them; we probably would have done the same thing. The whole Roman empire despised Jews, and gentile Christians despised Jewish Christians. It was rather sickening; but they "knew not what they were doing." Though difficult and delicate, the question of the early Jewish Christians must today be reexamined.

I have found that some scholarly research has been done, but it had been completely silenced, especially in dogmatics, both in Eastern Orthodox churches as well as in Catholic and Protestant churches. In fact, the picture of Jesus in the Qur'an may well have had something to do with the Jewish Christians. Muslims, of course, traditionally say that the quranic depiction of Jesus had nothing to do with human factors; it was all dictated by God. I have respect for this – a conviction of faith – but from a historical approach to the Qur'an, further questions arise. The picture of Jesus in the Qur'an, because it is a sympathetic picture, cannot come from orthodox Christianity, for the Qur'an continually protests against orthodox christology. So where does the picture come from? There is an evident, though surprising, answer. The picture of Jesus in the Qur'an is very analogous to the picture of Jesus in Judeo-Christianity.

It is difficult to prove historico-genetic links between the two pictures, for we do not know much about the Arabian peninsula before Muhammad. I would, however, like to quote a famous – and conservative – Protestant exegete, Adolph Schlatter of Tübingen, who as early as 1926 had traced connections between gentile Christianity, Jewish Christianity, and Islam:

> The Jewish-Christian church died out in Palestine only *west* of the Jordan ["West Bank" we say today]. Christian communities with Jewish practice continued to exist in the *eastern* regions, in the Decapolis, in the Batanaea, among the Nabataeans, at the edge of the Syrian desert and into Arabia, completely cut off from the rest of Christendom and without fellowship with it....For the Christian of this time, the Jew was simply an

enemy, and the Greek attitude, which overlooked the murders by the generals Trajan and Hadrian, as if they were the well-earned fate of the evil and contemptuous Jews, was accepted by the church as well. Even leading figures, such as Origen and Eusebius, remained astonishingly ignorant about the end of Jerusalem and of the church there. In the same way, the information they give us concerning the Jewish [i.e., Judeo-Christian] church in its continued existence is scanty. The Jewish Christians were heretics because they would not submit to the law that applied to the rest of Christendom and were therefore cut off from that body. None of the leaders of the imperial church guessed that this Jewish Christendom, which they held in contempt, would someday shake the world and cause a large part of the dominion of the church to break away. [Here Schlatter plays the prophet:] That day came when Muhammad took over many of the beliefs preserved by Jewish Christians – their awareness of God, their eschatology with its proclamation of the Day of Judgment, their customs and legends – and launched a new mission as "the one sent from God."[1]

Is Muhammad then, according to Schlatter, a "Judeo-Christian apostle" in Arabian dress? That is an astonishing claim, which Schlatter, incidentally, had substantiated as early as 1918 in an essay on the development of Jewish Christianity into Islam.[2] Forty years earlier, Adolf von Harnack had perceived the wider influence of Jewish Christianity on Islam, or more precisely of gnostic Jewish Christianity, and in particular of the Elkesites, who stood for strict monotheism and rejected the ecclesiastical teaching concerning *hypostasis* and "Son of God."[3]

Considering the present state of research, any direct dependence of Islam on Jewish Christianity will continue to be disputed. Yet the similarities are amazing. Muhammad rejected the orthodox (and Monophysitic) Son-of-God christology, yet accepted Jesus as the great "messenger" (*rasul*) of God, indeed as the "messiah" (*masih*) who brought the gospel. The Jewish scholar Hans-Joachim Schoeps (probably the foremost Jewish scholar on Judeo-Christianity) states:

---

[1] Adolf Schlatter, *Die Geschichte der ersten Christenheit* (Tübingen, 1926), pp. 367f.

[2] Adolf Schlatter, "Die Entwicklung des jüdischen Christentums zum Islam," *Evangelisches Missionsmagazin* (1918), pp. 251-64.

[3] This is documented in Adolph Harnack, *Lehrbuch der Dogmengeschichte* (Tübingen, 4th ed., 1909), vol. 1, p. 537.

Even though it is not possible to clearly establish the precise connection, there can be no doubt about Muhammad's indirect dependence on sectarian Judeo-Christianity. It remains one of the truly great paradoxes of world history that Jewish Christianity, cut off from the Christian church, has been preserved in Islam and so has been able, to this day, to continue its influence.[4]

Strangely enough, these pieces of historical knowledge have hardly been known in Christian theology up to now, let alone been taken seriously. There is still much to be investigated, such as the history of Muhammad's cousin-by-marriage, Waraqa, who was a Christian (probably speaking Hebrew, certainly not a Hellenistic Christian) and who according to the sources early drew Muhammad's attention to the relationship between his revelation experiences and those of Moses. Be that as it may, what we have here are previously unimagined possibilities for trilateral dialogue between Jews, Christians, and Muslims. Discussion of such matters will perhaps be uncomfortable in the beginning, but will eventually be of advantage to all concerned – for we need not be afraid of the truth.

In this context we must bear in mind that in his struggle against ancient Arabic polytheism, according to which Allāh had daughters and maybe also sons, Muhammad had no choice but to reject the heathen-sounding term "Son of God." This was polytheism. And yet Muhammad took up the story of Jesus as it was being circulated in Arabia at the time and gave it his own meaning. What had happened so often in the Bible now happened in the Qur'an: an old tradition was not simply handed down; it was interpreted so as to make it relevant to contemporaneous experience. The same thing happened in the New Testament: just as Christians referred many elements ("prophecies") of the Hebrew Bible to Jesus, even though these passages originally meant something quite different, so Muhammad used much of what he had heard (probably not *read*) about Jesus to refer to his own time. For Muhammad, Jesus' greatness consisted in the fact that, in him and through him as the servant of God, God had been at work. Thus Muhammad's "christology" (if you wish) was not far removed from that of the

---

[4] Hans-Joachim Schoeps, *Theologie und Geschichte des Judenchristentums* (Tübingen, 1949), p. 342.

Judeo-Christian church. What will be the ultimate consequences of all these new findings?

8. What Should Muslims and Christians Do?

We are faced with a problem of extraordinary moment, the consequences of which are not yet visible. If the exegetical and historical data outlined above are accurate and open to further clarification, then both sides in the Muslim-Christian encounter are faced with the challenge to stop thinking in terms of alternatives – Jesus *or* Muhammad – and to begin thinking instead, despite all the limitations and differences, in terms of synthesis – Jesus *and* Muhammad. This does not mean that everything has to be put on the same level. We have to recognize that Muhammad himself wanted to be a witness to Jesus – not to a Jesus of the Hellenistic gentile Christians, but, rather, to a Jesus as seen by his first disciples, who were Jews like Jesus himself.

As I already have pointed out, I have no intention of rejecting the early councils; rather, what needs to be done, in our contemporary ecumenical context, is to rethink what it means to call Jesus the Son of God or the Word of God. Inasmuch as today we have come to a new, and we think, clearer understanding of the concept "Son of God," perhaps we can better explain this belief to contemporary Jews and Muslims. So, with all due reservations and in the hope that others will join the discussion, let me try to comment, very briefly, on these two pivotal questions: How might a Muslim today view Jesus? How might a Christian understand Muhammad?

a)   In what way might *Muslims* view *Jesus*?

According to the Qur'an, Muslims already see Jesus as the great prophet and messenger of the one God, designated by God to be the "Servant of God" from his birth to his exaltation, as one who, along with the message he proclaimed, was of lasting importance to Muhammad.

Certainly, for Muslims, Muhammad and the Qur'an remain the decisive guideline for faith and conduct, life and death. I do not expect Muslims to simply accept the Bible.

However, if in the Qur'an Jesus is called the "Word" of God and bringer of the "gospel," should not Muslims try to gain a broader understanding of this gospel and take it seriously? Understood in the light of the message and conduct of Jesus, Islamic law, which is often characterized even by Muslims as oppressive, would perhaps receive a less stringent interpretation – commandments being given for persons, not persons for commandments. Also, in the light of Jesus' person and message, the Qur'an could be interpreted in a way that would make for greater personal freedom – not from the law but from legalism, as was the case with Jewish Christians.

Furthermore, the picture of both the life and death of Jesus – and according to our earliest sources his death is undeniable – and of his new life with God and in God might enable Muslims to come to a deeper understanding of a God who lives and suffers with human beings. The death of Jesus, endured in the name of this very God, might provide meaning for suffering and failure, not only for success. Islam has been a religion of success; failure, however, is also a reality of human life.

b) How might *Christians* view *Muhammad?*

Many Christians already look on him as a prophet of importance for many peoples of this earth, who was blessed with great success in his lifetime and throughout these subsequent centuries.

Certainly, for Christians, Jesus Christ and the good news he proclaimed are the decisive criteria for faith and conduct, life and death: the definitive Word of God (Heb. 1:1ff.). Thus Christ is and remains the *definitive regulating factor* for us Christians, for the sake of God and humanity.

However, insofar as Christians, following the New Testament, acknowledge the existence and value of prophets even after Christ, should they not take Muhammad and his message more seriously – especially because Muhammad understood himself to be part of the Judeo-Christian tradition?

Christians need to take Muhammad more seriously in order that the one, true, incomparable God might always occupy the center of their faith. I think my friend John Cobb would agree that Christocentrism without theocentrism is valueless, for Jesus is the Word and, as Cobb has stressed, the Wisdom of God. Christians also need to hear Muhammad's warning against the dangerous idolatry of listening to other gods, as well as his admonition that faith and life, orthodoxy and orthopraxis, belong together, even in politics. Thus, Muhammad could provide for us Christians, not the decisive, guiding norm that Jesus gives us, but a *prophetic corrective* in the name of the one and same God: "I am nothing but a distinctive warner" (sura 46:9).

The questions and issues we have looked at can present difficult challenges for everyone involved: Eastern Christians, Western Christians, Hellenistic Christians, Judeo-Christians, and of course for our Muslim brothers and sisters. The observation of a Pakistani friend of mine, a Muslim scholar, Riffat Hassan, is appropriate:

> Every religion has its problematic point, a crucial point that seems to be indisputable, not negotiable, and which is the main difficulty for the others. For Christians, this point is christology, that Jesus is the Son of God. For Jews, it is the promise that Israel, with its land, is the People of God. For Muslims, it is the Qur'an as the Word of God – Son of God, People of God, Word of God.

I think, as she does, that we should discuss these issues with reverence, with great esteem for all those who hold one of them as their professed faith, knowing that this matter is very delicate.

But I come back to my beginning: we stand before the alternatives of war and peace. I am certain we can have peace among nations only if there is peace among the religions, and especially among Judaism, Christianity, and Islam. And that will happen only if we are able to speak together as brothers and sisters.

HANS KÜNG'S THEOLOGICAL RUBICON[*]

Paul F. Knitter[**]

In Hans Küng's address to this conference he has once again proven himself a pioneer of interreligious dialogue. What he has been doing throughout most of his theological career, he was doing again – exploring new territory, raising new questions in the encounter of Christianity with other religions. Although Küng has made his greatest contribution in the inner-Christian, ecclesial arena, he has always realized – and increasingly so in more recent years – that Christian theology must be done in view of, and in dialogue with, other religions. As he has said, Christians must show an increasingly "greater broadmindedness and openness" to other faiths and learn to "reread their own history of theological thought and faith" in view of other traditions. As a long-time reader of Küng's writings, and as a participant with him in a Buddhist-Christian conference in Hawaii, January 1984, I have witnessed how much his own broad-mindedness and openness to other religions has grown. He has been changed in the dialogue.

Yet I suspect – and this is the point I want to pursue in this response – that in his exploration of other faiths Küng the pioneer has recently broken into unsuspected territory and stands before new paths. He

---

[*] In Leonard Swidler, ed., *Toward a Universal Theology of Religion* (Maryknoll, NY: Orbis Books, 1987), pp. 224-230.

[**] Paul F. Knitter (Catholic) received a Th.D. from the Protestant Theology faculty of the University of Marburg, Germany. His many publications include *By No Other Name?* He is Editor of the book series "Faith Meet Faith" with Orbis Books. He is Professor of Theology at Xavier University, Cincinnati.

has been led where he did not intend to go. I think Küng, in his dialogue with other religions, now finds himself before a theological Rubicon – a Rubicon he has not crossed, one that he perhaps does not feel he can cross. I am not sure. That is what I want to ask him.

In Küng's previous efforts at a Christian theology of religions, he inveighs against the Christian exclusivism that denies any value to other religions; he rejects an ecclesiocentrism that confines all contact with the Divine to the church's backyard. Yet despite this call to greater openness, it seems to some that Küng hangs on to a subtle, camouflaged narrowness. Even though he proposes that we replace ecclesiocentrism with theocentrism, he still adheres to a Christocentrism that insists on Jesus Christ as "normative" (*massgebend*) – that is, as "ultimately decisive, definitive, archetypal for humanity's relations with God."[1] Because Christ is normative for all other religions, Küng ends up by replacing Christian exclusivism with a Christian inclusivism that recognizes the value of other religions but insists that this value must be fulfilled, "critically catalyzed," and find "full realization in Christianity." "That God may not remain for them [non-Christians] the unknown God, there is needed the Christian proclamation and mission announcing Jesus."[2] Jesus and Christianity remain for all other religions the final norm, the only real fulfillment.

This is what Küng proposed in *On Being a Christian*. From recent conversations and from his conference paper, I think that he is now not so sure about these earlier christocentric, inclusivist claims that insist on Jesus as the final norm for all. I suspect that, like many Christians today, he stands before a theological Rubicon. To cross it means to recognize clearly, unambiguously, the possibility that other religions exercise a role in salvation history that is not only valuable and salvific but perhaps equal to that of Christianity; it is to affirm that there may be other saviors and revealers besides Jesus Christ and equal to Jesus Christ. It is to admit that if other religions must be fulfilled in Christianity, Christianity must, just as well, find fulfillment in them.

---

[1] Hans Küng, *On Being a Christian* (New York: Doubleday, 1976), pp. 123f.

[2] *Ibid.*, pp. 113, 447.

From my reading of his paper, I see Küng standing at this Rubicon, at river's edge, but hesitating to cross. Let me try to explain.

Muhammad, More Than a Prophet?

In his efforts to urge Christians to recognize Muhammad as an authentic prophet, Küng can only be applauded. Most Christian theologians in dialogue with Muslims hesitate to dare such an admission.[3] But in recognizing Muhammad as a prophet, Küng, it seems to me, is *implicitly* affirming Muhammad as "more than a prophet" – that is, as a religious figure who carries out a role analogous to that of Jesus Christ.

Küng admits that as a prophet Muhammad is "more to those who follow him...than a prophet is to us." He is a "model," an archetype, for all Muslims – he through whom God "has spoken to humankind." Such an understanding of Muhammad, however, is essentially the same as that of the early Jewish christology that was lost and that Küng seeks to retrieve. This early christology, this picture of Jesus "as viewed by his first disciples" – which, as much as we can tell, most likely reflects Jesus' own view of himself – saw Jesus as a prophet, as the eschatological prophet, as he who was so close to God that he could speak for God, represent God, mediate God. But this is basically the same description of Muhammad's role. Therefore, in its origins, the Christian view of Jesus was essentially the same as the Muslim view of Muhammad: they were both unique revealers, spokespersons for God, prophets.

Küng's own christology enables Christians to go even further in affirming analogous roles for Muhammad and Jesus. Küng recognizes the truth and validity of the Chalcedon Hellenistic christology, with its stress on two natures, one person, pre-existence. Yet in his own christology as presented in *On Being a Christian*, in his own efforts to interpret what it means to call Jesus Son of God and savior, Küng uses what is much more of an early Jewish-Christian, rather than a Hellenistic, model.

---

[3] See David Kerr, "The Prophet Muhammad in Christian Theological Perspective," *International Bulletin of Missionary Research*, 8 (1984), p. 114.

To proclaim Jesus as divine, as the incarnate Son of God, means, Küng tells us, that for Christians Jesus is God's "representative," "the real revelation of the one true God," God's "advocate...deputy...delegate... plenipotentiary."[4] But, again, this is basically the same role that Muhammad fulfills for his followers. Therefore, from a Christian perspective, Muslims in speaking about Muhammad as "the seal of the prophets" and Christians in speaking about Jesus as "son of God" are trying to make essentially the same claim about both figures. I think, therefore, that Küng could agree with Kenneth Cragg's argument that the Islamic notion of prophethood and the Christian notion of incarnation, from very different perspectives and with very different images, are saying the same thing: that their founders were closely "associated" with God and were "sent" by God, and are utterly reliable revelations of God.[5]

So I think that Küng might go a further, logical step in what he can say about Muhammad. He points out that if Jesus is understood according to the model of early Jewish Christianity as God's messenger and revelation, Muslims would be more able to grasp and accept this Jesus. I am suggesting that if Jesus is so understood, then Christians would be more able to accept Muhammad and recognize that in God's plan of salvation, he carries out a role analogous to that of Jesus. If, following Küng's keen insights and suggestions, Muslims might be able to recognize Jesus as a genuine prophet. Christians might be able to recognize Muhammad as truly a "son of God." (And if the title "son of God" is understood, as Küng recommends, not so much as God's "ontological" son but as God's reliable representative and revelation, perhaps Muslims would be more comfortable in using this title for Muhammad.)

But for Christians, for Prof. Küng, to make this move, to recognize the parity of Jesus and Muhammad's missions, would be to step across a theological Rubicon (as it would be for Muslims as well!). I'm not sure if

---

[4] Küng, *On Being a Christian*, pp. 390f., 440, 444, 449.

[5] Kenneth Cragg, "Islam and Incarnation," in John Hick, ed., *Truth and Dialogue in World Religions: Conflicting Truth-claims* (Philadelphia: Westminster, 1974), pp. 126-139.

Küng feels willing or able to make this step. I think I can put my finger on the chief reason for his hesitation.

How Is Jesus Unique?

The chief stumbling block in Christian dialogue with Islam is not, as Küng suggests, "the person of Jesus and his relationship with God." In his paper Küng has convinced me that Jesus' person and relationship with God can be so understood as to allow for the person of Muhammad to share in this same relationship – in Muslim terminology, both are prophets; in Christian terms, both are sons of God. The problem comes not from the way Küng understands Jesus' relationship to God, but from the exclusivist *adjectives* he feels must qualify that relationship: Jesus is not only a prophet but the *final*, normative prophet; he is not only son of God but the *only*, the unsurpassable son of God. (Muslims, with their insistence that Muhammad is the seal of the prophets, reflect this same problem. Here I am addressing my fellow Christians.)

This, I suggest, is the pivotal, the most difficult, question in the Christian-Muslim (as well as the Christian Buddhist/Hindu dialogue): Is Jesus the one and only savior? (For Muslims: Is Muhammad the final prophet?) Is Jesus God's final, normative unsurpassable revelation, which must be the norm and fulfillment for all other revelations, religions, and religious figures?

As I suggested before, Küng, in his earlier publications, would answer all these questions with a firm yes. Although all religious figures can be said to be unique, for Küng Jesus' uniqueness is in a different category; Jesus is God's normative, ultimate criterion for judging the validity and value of all other revelations. Küng expressly warns against placing Jesus among the "archetypal persons" that Karl Jaspers has identified throughout history; Jesus is ultimately archetypal.[6] It is this insistence on Jesus' absolute, normative uniqueness that keeps Küng from going further in his recognition of the value of other religions. Muhammad may be a prophet; but he cannot be "more than a prophet," as was Jesus. If other religions are valid,

---

[6] Küng, *On Being a Christian*, p. 124.

Christianity possesses "absolute validity."[7] If other religions are ways of salvation, they are so "only in a relative sense, not simply as a whole and in every sense."[8]

If one presses Küng or most Christian theologians for the central, the foundational, reason why they maintain this absolute, normative uniqueness for Jesus, I think the only real reason they can give is an appeal, perhaps indirect and uncritical, to the *authority* of tradition or the Bible. This is what scripture affirms of Jesus; this is what tradition has always taught – there is "no other name" by which persons can be saved (Acts 4:12). There is "one Mediator between God and humanity, the man Christ Jesus" (1 Tim. 2:5). Jesus is the "only-begotten Son of God" (John 1:4). True, Küng, in *On Being a Christian*, attempts to give some empirical verification of this traditional assertion of the superiority of Christ's revelation. As I have attempted to show elsewhere, however, serious objections can be raised to his claims that without Christ the other religions cannot really adapt their spiritualities to "modernity," to the demands of our world-affirming technological age. I am not at all certain, as Küng suggests, that without the gospel the other religions are caught in "unhistoricity, circular thinking, fatalism, unworldliness, pessimism, passivity, caste spirit, social disinterestedness."[9] So the chief reason, it seems, for claiming the finality and normativity of Christ over all other religious figures remains the inner-Christian, traditional one: this is what the Bible and tradition have always maintained.

I believe that Küng, along with many other Christians, however, is feeling the inadequacy of these traditional claims. I think he is on the brink of suggesting that such claims for the universal finality and normativity of Christ may not be an essential element in the Christian witness to all peoples. Yet, from his conference paper, I am not sure. For instance, when he tells us that "For Christians, Jesus Christ and the Good news he proclaimed are the decisive criteria for faith and conduct, life and death: the definitive Word of

---

[7] *Ibid.*, p. 114.

[8] *Ibid.*, p. 104.

[9] *Ibid.*, p. 110; see also pp. 106-119; and Paul F. Knitter, "World Religions and the Finality of Christ: A Critique of Hans Küng's *On Being a Christian*," *Horizons*, 5 (1978), pp. 157, 159.

God (Heb. 1:1ff.)" and that Christ is "the definitive regulating factor for Christians, for the sake of God and humanity," is he using the phrase "for Christians" as a restrictive qualifier? *Only* for Christians? Would he be ready to recognize that for Muslims, Muhammad is "the definitive Word of God"? For Buddhists, Buddha is "the definitive regulating factor"? In such a view, Christians and Muslims and Buddhists would still have to witness to each other. Jesus, Muhammad, and Buddha would all have universal relevance for all peoples. But there would be no one, final, normative revelation for all other revelations. If Küng is saying this, he is saying something different from what he has said in earlier publications. He has crossed a theological Rubicon. But has he?

Crossing the Rubicon from Inclusivism to Pluralism

I am asking Küng–as well as other theologians (e.g., John B. Cobb)–for greater clarity on this "Rubicon question" concerning the uniqueness and finality of Christ. Such clarity is needed by both fellow Christians and non-Christian partners in dialogue. Although Küng, echoing Arnold Toynbee, does well to excoriate "the scourge of exclusivism," is he perhaps unconsciously advocating a more dangerous, because more subtle, scourge of inclusivism? As Leonard Swidler has pointed out, authentic, real "dialogue can take place only between equals...*par cum pari*."[10] But no matter how much truth and good one recognizes in another religion, if one enters the dialogue convinced that by God's will the final, normative, unsurpassable truth for all religions resides in one's own religion, that is *not* a dialogue between equals. It is, as Henri Maurier attests from years of experience in African interreligious dialogue, a conversation between "the cat and the mouse."[11]

It seems to me that an inclusive christology, which views Christ and Christianity as having to include, fulfill, perfect other religions, is really only

---

[10] Leonard Swidler, "The Dialogue Decalogue," *Journal of Ecumenical Studies*, 20/1 (1983), p. 10.

[11] Henri Maurier, "The Christian Theology of the Non-Christian Religions," *Lumen Vitae*, 21 (1976), p. 70.

a shade away from the theory of "anonymous Christianity" so stoutly criticized by Küng. The theory of "inclusive Christianity" may not assert that other believers are already Christians without knowing it; but it does affirm that these believers must become Christians in order to share in the fullness of revelation and salvation. Küng has called persons of other religions "Christians *in spe*" (in hope) who must be made "Christians *in re*" (in fact).[12] It seems to me that Küng's evaluation of Radhakrishnan's Hindu tolerance might apply to his own understanding of Christian tolerance: It is "conquest as it were by embrace in so far as it seeks not to exclude but to include all other religions."[13]

Does Küng still hold to such an inclusive christology and theology of religions? Does he realize its possible harmful effects on dialogue in the way it implicitly but assuredly subordinates all other religions to Christianity?

My question takes on a sharper focus in Küng's concluding exhortation that we stop thinking "in terms of alternatives – Jesus *or* Muhammad" – and start thinking "in terms of synthesis – Jesus *and* Muhammad, in the sense that Muhammad himself acts as a witness to Jesus." I am not sure just how Küng does or can understand that "and." Is it the "and" of equality (like "Son and Spirit") or the "and" of subordination (like "law and gospel")? Previously, Küng would have had to come down, I believe, on the side of final subordination insofar as he has insisted that Christ is God's final norm for all persons of all times. But I am not sure what he would say today.

My final question is more of a personal request. In asking for more clarity, I am really asking Hans Küng to step across the Rubicon. I believe that his own christology, as well as his own doctrine of God, implicitly allows him to do that. I suspect that the press of interreligious dialogue has also made the possibility of crossing more urgent.

Might I also point out that in making the crossing, he would be in good company. Other Christian thinkers have moved from an earlier

---

[12] Hans Küng, "The World Religions in God's Plan of Salvation," in Joseph Neuner, ed., *Christian Revelation and World Religions* (London: Burnes and Oates, 1967), pp. 65f.

[13] Hans Küng, *Does God Exist? An Answer for Today* (New York: Doubleday, 1980), p. 608.

inclusivist position of viewing Christianity as the necessary fulfillment and norm for all religions, to a more pluralist model that affirms the possibility that other religions may be just as valid and relevant as Christianity. They have admitted that other religious figures, such as Muhammad, may be carrying out, in very different ways, revelatory, salvific roles analogous to that of Jesus Christ. Among such thinkers are not only Ernst Troeltsch and Arnold Toynbee, but also a number of Christian theologians who have more recently shifted from an inclusivist Christocentrism (Christ at the center) to a pluralist theocentrism (God/the Ultimate in the center): Raimundo Panikkar, Stanley Samartha, John Hick, Rosemary Ruether, Tom Driver, Aloysius Pieris.[14]

Granted Prof. Küng's respectability and his influence, and given the caution and thoroughness with which he makes all his theological moves, I feel that if he were to cross the Rubicon to a more pluralist theology of religions that does not need to insist on Christ or Christianity as the norm and fulfillment of other religions, he would be, once again, a pioneer leading other Christians to a more open, authentic, and liberative understanding and practice of their faith.

But I ask you, Hans Küng, do you think such a new direction in Christian attitudes toward other religions, such a crossing of the Rubicon, is possible? And would it be productive of greater Christian faith and dialogue?

---

[14] Raimundo Panikkar, *The Unknown Christ of Hinduism* (Maryknoll, N.Y.: Orbis, revised edition, 1981); Stanley J. Samartha, *Courage for Dialogue: Ecumenical Issues in Inter-religious Relationships* (Maryknoll, N.Y.: Orbis, 1982); John Hick, *God Has Many Names* (London: Macmillan, 1980); Rosemary Ruether, *To Change the World: Christology and Cultural Criticism* (New York: Crossroad, 1981); Tom Driver, *Christ in a Changing World: Toward an Ethical Christology* (New York: Crossroad, 1981); Aloysius Pieris, "The Place of Non-Christian Religions and Cultures in the Evolution of Third-World Theology," in Virginia Fabella and Sergio Torres, eds., *Irruption of the Third World: Challenge to Theology* (Maryknoll, N.Y.: Orbis, 1983). See also Paul Knitter, *No Other Name?* (Maryknoll, N.Y.: Orbis, 1984).

CHRISTIAN-MUSLIM DIALOGUE: A REVIEW OF SIX POST-VATICAN II, CHURCH-RELATED DOCUMENTS*

John Renard**

I. Introduction

Twenty years ago, during the period between the second and third sessions of the Second Vatican Council, two panels of experts were given the task of drafting texts on Islam to be included in the evolving documents on the church and on ecumenism. The material, discussed early in the third session, was incorporated into a new "Declaration on the Relation of the Church to Non-Christian Religions," which was essentially completed in November, 1964, and definitively approved in October, 1965. *Nostra aetate's* remarks about Islam seem quite reserved and polite in retrospect, but, given the prior history of Roman Catholic attitudes toward – or simple inattentiveness to – Islam, the texts on Islam were quite remarkable and even revolutionary.

---

* *Journal of Ecumenical Studies,* 23:1, (Winter 1986).

** John Renard, S.J. (Catholic), is Associate Professor of Theological Studies at St. Louis University, where he has taught since 1978. He holds a B.A. (philosophy and classical languages) and an M.A. (biblical studies) from St. Louis University, and a Ph.D. in Islamic Studies from the Dept. of Near Eastern Languages and Civilizations, Harvard University (1978). An ordained Jesuit priest, he served as a Visiting Research Fellow at the Institute of Asian Cultures, Sophia University, Tokyo, during the Summer of 1983 and the Winter of 1985. In early 1986, Paulist Press published his translation from Arabic, with notes and introduction, of the *Letters on the Sufi Path by Ibn 'Abbad of Ronda* in its Classics of Western Spirituality series.

A great deal of action and reflection on relations between Christians and Muslims has occurred during these two decades, especially among Christians at the ecclesiastical level or with church sponsorship of one sort or another. In May, 1964, Pope Paul VI established the Vatican Secretariat for Non-Christians, with a special department on Islam. Two years after sponsoring landmark meetings between Muslims and Christians in Cartigny, Switzerland (1969), the World Council of Churches established its "Sub-unit for Dialogue with People of Living Faiths and Ideologies." In 1977 the National Council of the Churches of Christ in the U.S.A. formed a Task Force on Christian-Muslim Relations, with headquarters at the Hartford (CT) Seminary.

Christian interest in the possibilities of and need for dialogue between Christians and Muslims has grown steadily since Vatican II, and a number of important church-related documents have appeared since 1969. An overview of six such works is presented here in the hope of bringing to light some of their major themes and emphases. Because the writings I have selected vary in many ways, they are not simply comparable. It is possible, nevertheless, to discern in them thinking about Islam that various church groups have been engaged in lately.

The documents I have chosen are listed here chronologically, in order of publication: The Vatican Secretariat's *Guidelines for a Dialogue between Muslims and Christians*[1] (hereafter VS 1); *A New Threshold: Guidelines for the Churches in their Relations* with Muslim Communities,[2] from the British Council of Churches (hereafter, BCC); the World Council of Churches' *Christians Meeting Muslims: "WCC Papers on Ten Years of Christian-Muslim Dialogue*[3] (hereafter, WCC); *The Muslim-Christian Dialogue of the Last Ten Years*[4], published by Pro Mundi Vita, "an international information and research center under Catholic auspices" (hereafter, PMV); *Orientations pour*

---

[1] By Joseph Cuoq and Louis Gardet (Rome: Edizioni Ancora, 1969).

[2] By David Brown (Oxford: Bocardo and Church Army Press, 1976).

[3] No editor named (Genega: World Council of Churches, 1977).

[4] By Maurice Borrmans (Brussels: Pro Mundi Vita Bulletin, no. 74 [September-October, 1978]).

un dialogue entre Chretiens et Musulmans,[5] from the Vatican Secretariat (hereafter, VS 2); and *Christian-Muslim Relations: An Introduction for Christians in the United States of America,*[6] sponsored by the N.C.C.C.U.S.A. Task Force (hereafter NCC).

What follows is a summary of the documents, based on a consideration of four facets of the material: (1) the shape of the documents – their purpose, scope, and method; (2) background information on the participants in the dialogue (especially Muslim), from the point of view of amount and importance, type, level, and organization of information; (3) various approaches to dialogue itself – its history, theoretical foundations or presuppositions, actual practice, and prospects or suggestions for the future; and (4) a somewhat lengthier recapitulation of the principal religious and moral/social themes in dialogue.

II. The Shape of the Documents: Purpose, Scope, Method

Beginning with the most specific and the narrowest in scope and proceeding to the more general and broader treatments, one discovers considerable variety among the documents. WCC offers an anthology of fourteen relatively brief "reflections, statements, memoranda of ten years of Christian-Muslim dialogue," plus an introduction. The collection is intended to help the reader "pause for a moment and look back at the problems faced and the results achieved,"[7] Nine of the items (if one includes the introduction, "Present and Future Patterns of Christian-Muslim Dialogue") deal specifically with Christian-Muslim interaction; four others contain reflections and suggestions from a solely Christian perspective regarding the concept and conduct of dialogue itself; and two report on meetings attended by members of traditions other than Christianity and Islam, as well as by Christians and Muslims. Of the nine pieces in the first category, six report on actual Christian-Muslim conversations, and three are unilateral Christian reflections about the nature of Christian-Muslim dialogue, its

---

[5] By Maurice Borrmans (Paris: Les Editions du Cerf, 1981).

[6] By R. Marston Speight (Hartford: N.C.C.C.U.S.A. Task Force on Christian-Muslim Relations, 1983).

[7] WCC, p. vi.

presuppositions, implications, etc. In general, WCC's material is highly positive in tone. The book offers no serious overall evaluation of the reports and is not intended to be a critical analysis of the discussions.

PMV's *Muslim-Christian Dialogue of the Last Ten Years*, written by Maurice Borrmans, covers a time span equal to that of WCC, but PMV begins and ends slightly later. The middle twelve pages (of fifty-two) summarize the proceedings of some fifteen Muslim-Christian meetings held between 1969 and 1978. Though its scope is comparable to that of WCC, PMV's purpose and method are very different. Borrmans begins with a short identification of "Muslims today", and a sketch of the histories of Islam and of Christian-Muslim relations through the centuries. He then establishes a clearly Roman Catholic context and perspective, referring to Vatican II as containing the "new charter of Muslim-Christian dialogue," and suggesting that the Vatican Secretariat's 1969 *Guidelines* is a fuller articulation of that charter. More importantly, PMV attempts a critical analysis, a "rough balance-sheet of this decade of encounters and colloquia, in order to evaluate successes and failures, strengths and weaknesses."[8] The largest single segment of PMV is given over to posing some hard questions and making some suggestions as to which specific issues need further attention. Borrmans sounds hopeful but is quite frank in his criticisms. Some of the PMV material reappears (evidently verbatim in some cases, insofar as that can be ascertained by comparing the English of PMV with the French of VS 2) in Borrmans' 1981 writing of the newer Vatican *Guidelines* to be discussed below.

Two documents move beyond a consideration of the more "official" of formally organized type of interaction. BCC and NCC present their materials in response to the actual and growing need for Muslims and Christians living side by side to understand each other.

BCC was inspired by the increasing number of people in Ireland and Great Britain from non-Christian traditions. "The largest group of these are Muslims, and their strongly expressed resolve to affirm their separate religious and cultural identity poses questions both to Christians and to those

---

[8] PMV, p. 52.

institutions in our society which have grown out of our Christian heritage."[9] BCC's forty pages are devoted to three main areas of concern: information about Muslims, theological issues (the most important single section), and practical problems and suggestions.

NCC attempts to do, on a larger scale, for Americans what BCC seeks to do for British churches. NCC's author, R. Marston Speight, acknowledges that "the image projected by Islam upon the imagination of the average American is one of an intolerant, legalistic and fatalistic religion practiced by backward, ferocious and scheming people." As a growing but as yet not fully recognized religious minority, "Muslims have become the neighbors and fellow citizens of Christians in the United States." Hoping to "provide background for Christian-Muslim rapprochement" and to suggest ways of avoiding the growth of bigotry – but without judging Islam in terms of Christian beliefs – the author refers to himself as a "sympathetic observer who tries to understand that religion as Muslims do, that is, insofar as it is possible for a non-Muslim to grasp it."[10] Nearly half of NCC is given to reducing prejudices and stereotypes by providing three chapters of background on the origin and history, religious practices, and present shape of Islam as a global phenomenon. Another thirty-two of its eighty-five pages discuss the history of Muslim-Christian relations and key theological issues especially related to the intersection of the two traditions. The remainder of NCC contains practical suggestions and information.

The Vatican Secretariat has sponsored two relatively lengthy documents, VS 1 in 1969, and VS 2 in 1981, the latter a substantial – almost total – rewriting of its forerunner. These are the broadest in scope of all six documents. Their stated purpose is more general, and their method is more theoretical than practical. Evident facts of cultural, ideological, and religious pluralism, in the face of which simple tolerance and mere coexistence are no longer sufficient to maintain peace in the world, form the point of departure of both Vatican writings. They affirm the absolute necessity of dialogue, but caution that their goal is not to "fix definite formulae for such a dialogue, but

---

[9] BCC, p. v.

[10] NCC, pp. 1-2.

rather define the spirit in which it should take place."[11]   In general, the purpose of any dialogue is to "stimulate those taking part not to remain inert in the positions they have adopted, but to help all concerned to find a way to become better people in themselves and to improve their relations with one another...."[12] In the words of VS 2, "true dialogue involves the bold venture of individuals who wish to be enriched by their differences, to share their common values, and to respond as individuals to the calls the Lord addresses to each one most intimately."[13]

VS 1 and VS 2 take the need for specifically Muslim-Christian dialogue to be virtually self-evident; it must be seen as an essential dimension of life wherever believers of both traditions "live, work, love, suffer, and die" together.[14]   Given that need, however, both documents emphasize the further need to focus on Islam as a religious faith, as a "progress towards God and final realization of" human potentialities. Muslim-Christian dialogue must be kept from deserting the spiritual level in favor of the temporal, for "One will never really get to know any Muslim...until one has discovered" in that person the religious values for which he or she lives.[15]

Both VS 1 and VS 2 are constructed in six chapters. Borrmans has kept many of VS 1's topic-headings, especially in the last three chapters. There he has retained both the order of chapters and, on the whole, the order of topics within them, but he has transformed VS 2 into a genuinely new approach by changing the overall emphasis and tone, rearranging the order of the first three chapters adding a good deal of totally new material, and especially by addressing each topic from a slightly different angle and filling out the discussion with new illustrations and more extensive documentation from Vatican II and from both Muslim and Christian Scriptures. All things considered, VS 2 is a significant improvement on its

---

[11] VS 1, p. 9.

[12] *Ibid.*, pp. 9-10.

[13] *Ibid.*, p. 9.

[14] VS 2, p. 167.

[15] VS 1, p. 162.

predecessor, even though the former is in some ways more academic and seems to presuppose more background information about Islam. A slightly more detailed comparison of the two documents will emerge in subsequent sections of this article. For now, one example will suggest their difference: Whereas VS 1 begins with "The Attitude of a Christian Taking Part in Dialogue," followed by two chapters containing background on Islam as a religion and as a contemporary global phenomenon, VS 2 begins by introducing *both* parties to the dialogue as one finds them now, then describes attitudes required of both sides, and finally sets forth the Islamic religious values with which Christians need to be better acquainted.

III. The Use of Background Information

A second set of evaluative criteria can be found in the various ways the six documents use, or even omit, "factual" information about the participants in the dialogue – particularly about Muslims. Information usage follows directly, of course, from a given document's purpose, scope, and method. Here I have tried to take into consideration the amount and type of information (for example, historical, religious/devotional, explicitly theological, social/ethnic); organization (for example, use of Muslim or Christian categories in speaking of religious matters; use of geographical, political, moral frames of reference, etc.); and level of complexity or sophistication (for example, previous knowledge taken for granted, use of skeletal outline format, more analytical treatment, and interpretation geared to highlighting concepts and attitudes rather than simple statement of "beliefs and practices").

WCC is the least "informative" of the documents, understandably, for its purpose is to report on discussions among Muslims and Christians presumed to possess ahead of time the requisite familiarity with the crucial issues on their meeting agenda. Paradoxically, a Muslim would learn far more about Christianity from the collected papers than a Christian would about Islam. The reports summarize directly more explicitly Christian than Islamic matters. On the whole, one can get some sense of attitudes of both Muslim and Christian participants toward dialogue, world community, religious freedom, the need to face shared social problems, and so forth. The single most discussed, religious issue is that of mission; some key features of that discussion will appear in the fifth section of this article.

PMV's background survey provides some more-or-less predictable fundamentals about Islam. Data about Christianity includes only information about the history of its encounters with Islam, beginning with the seventh century. The focus is on the need to appreciate Islam's "twofold design for temporal civilization and spiritual adventure" in contrast to the way the "Church has given up its dreams of Christendom in order to be at the exclusive service of the Gospel,"[16] and on problems arising from the resultant differences in attitudes toward religious minorities (depending on which is the dominant tradition in a given place).

BCC gives a very sketchy summary of Islamic religious tenets, of Islam's geographical spread and ethnic diversity, and of the principal subgroups within the larger community of Muslims. Following that is a similarly skeletal outline of Christian-Muslim interaction century by century, with a short inventory of "the main factors which must be considered in any assessment of relationships between the two religious in this modern age."[17] Further information occurs under the heading of theological issues related to the eventual development of a "theology of religions."

Of all the documents, it is NCC that gives the most extensive treatment of historical, religious/devotional, and ethnogeographical background on Muslims. It includes, as do PMV and BCC, a historical survey of Muslim-Christian relations, but it has a somewhat heavier emphasis on attitudinal and moral issues immediately pertinent to its discussion of dialogue itself. NCC's informational chapters are excellent. The first of them summarizes historical origins and developments under the headings of "A People: The Arabs," "A Man: The Prophet Muhammad," and "A Book: The Qur'an," with some important correctives to still-prevalent stereotypes about the early spread of Islam. Religious and devotional practice is treated under the two classic Islamic categories of duties of worship and duties of human relationships. The author has succeeded in making the expected

---

[16] PMV, pp. 51-52.

[17] BCC, p. 5.

mention of "The Five Pillars" come to life even for the jaded professional Islamicist. A chapter on contemporary Islam gives a very helpful four-page segment on "Islamic resurgence in the modern world." This situates the need for Christians to understand Islam in a context that is immediate and concrete, and it short-circuits the all too common tendency to regard Muslims as oil merchants who must be humored if the "Western" driver wants to stay on the road.

VS 1 and VS 2 both contain similar kinds of background information, but as suggested above, VS 2's rearrangement of the opening chapters gives it a significantly different overall tone and approach. Both of the Vatican documents differ "pedagogically" from PMV, WCC, and NCC in type and level of information as well as in organization. First, whereas PMV and NCC begin with historical data about Islam and then move to more specifically religious topics (with which BCC begins) and finally go on to identify who and where Muslims are today, VS 1 and VS 2 present historical data only incidentally or by way of illustration. Second, neither VS 1 nor VS 2 is as concerned as any of the other documents with the particulars of Christian-Muslim interaction through the centuries. Third, information about Islamic religious values occurs in VS 1 especially, and to a slightly lesser extent in VS 2, from the perspective of the Christian's encounter with those values. For example, VS 1 addresses briefly the questions of how a Christian ought to speak about and read the Qur'an.

Fourth, both Vatican documents eventually get around to providing a picture of Islamic religious values that takes into account the major topics contained in NCC, but the perspective is different, particularly in VS 2. For example, NCC's second chapter and, to some degree, VS 1's second chapter present information under headings that tend to "objectify" and focus on what Muslims believe and do. VS 2's third chapter has succeeded in capturing an authentic sense of attitudes, aspirations, and ideals, rather than listing the contents of a creedal statement. Where NCC talks of "Belief in Prophets," and VS 1 of "The Message of the Prophets," VS 2 explores the Muslim desire for "Imitation of a Prophetic Model." Fifth, treatment of who and where Muslims are now varies considerably. In BCC, NCC and VS 1, surveys of Muslim unity and diversity appear *after* sections on religious themes, while

VS 2 and PMV (both written by Borrmans) begin by presenting the people of Islam as one finds them today. VS 2 identifies Muslims as "interlocutors" in the dialogue and prefaces its description of the contemporary Muslim community with a brief acknowledgement of the other interlocutors, the Christian churches. This is the only mention of specific details from the history of Christian-Muslim interaction to be found in either VS 1 or VS 2, and it is largely a summary of PMV.[18]

Finally, I find NCC the most successful in presenting an overall objective summary of Islam as a historical religious tradition that has now achieved truly international and global stature, while VS 2 succeeds most admirably in focusing the reader's attention on the essential humanity and ideals of Muslims.

IV. Approaches to Dialogue

Several of the documents make a special point of attempting to draw material for reflection from the history of Muslim interaction – alternately described as encounter, hostile or friendly, or as a deliberate attempt at true dialogue. According to NCC, one "overall feature that has marked the encounter of Islam and Christianity through the centuries has been that of alternating ascendency and descendency,"[19] that is, the dominance of one or the other as a civilizing force especially in the Mediterranean area. Speight spotlights several key controversies of long standing, and points to a new and growing spirit of conciliation that is itself, however, not without its own historic precedents. History reveals two areas of religious concern, the doctrinal and the moral, that contain potential for both unity and division. NCC outlines briefly a "new approach" in which doctrinal difficulties "should be met frankly and then bypassed." Two steps are needed: careful listening, and a willingness to cease insisting that the "other become like ourselves."[20] Moral issues need to be subjected to the "right kind of mutual moral critique," in such a way that one's moral choices can be "tested by the ethical

---

[18] PMV, pp. 7-11.

[19] NCC, p. 37.

[20] Ibid., pp. 47-48.

insights of the other." Unifying factors are likewise related to "common elements in our beliefs" and to "our common situation in the modern world."[21] Once the areas of disagreement have been met frankly and bypassed, dialogue can begin to "capitalize on our similarities." NCC then suggests an analysis of common themes in Christian and Muslim prayer as one example of accentuating the positive.

PMV, VS 1, and VS 2 all take their cue from a key text in *Nostra aetate*: "Over the centuries many quarrels and dissensions have arisen between Christians and Muslims. This Sacred Council now pleads with all to forget the past, and urges that a sincere effort be made to achieve mutual understanding, for the benefit of all..."[22] PMV adds to that text a comment that very well sums up the tenor of the three Catholic documents in this regard. Once it had acknowledged past enmities, the Council chose not to go into a detailed "pronouncement as to their cause, expressions, or consequences." What was sought was a mutual understanding that leads to a change of mind and heart that brings freedom from prejudices and, above all, "joint action to safeguard and foster social and global values which are closely allied to faith and religion: justice, peace, and freedom."[23]

All three Catholic writing allude liberally to the Qur'anic injunction to believers to "vie with one another in good deeds." In its further elaboration of what is needed for the spirit of dialogue, PMV describes three virtues that are quite similar to those recommended in NCC: "knowing how to keep silent, how to listen, how to be moderate." The first involves putting aside preconceived ideas, allowing the others to be what they are and what they want to be. The second means the capacity to wait for a "moment of grace," when the other unveils his or her secret "dreams of sanctity." Moderation demands that one put aside the arrogance of "striking declarations, blunt assertions, and long-winded conclusions," ever mindful that "people live in the current of history, amid what is provisional, and in sin."[24] Given the

---

[21] *Ibid.*, pp. 48, 52.

[22] E.g., PMV, p. 13.

[23] *Ibid.*

[24] *Ibid.*, p. 50.

historical record, this will take "one or two generations of persistent effort on either side to get rid of prejudices, renew attitudes, and deepen spiritualities."[25]

VS 1 and VS 2 both devote two full chapters to picking up where Vatican II leaves off. VS 1 entitles its first chapter "The Attitude of a Christian Taking Part in Dialogue" and its fourth, "How to Prepare for Dialogue." VS 2's parallel chapters, two and four, are entitled, "The Occasions and Paths of Dialogue" and "Bearing in Mind Present Obstacles." Chapter one of VS 1 and chap. 2 of VS 2 overlap to some extent in choice of topics discussed, but VS 1 is slanted almost exclusively toward what is encumbent on the Christian partner in dialogue. The latter begins with two "general conditions" of dialogue: dialogue involves relationships among persons, not comparison of systems, and is therefore concerned more with today's problems than with those of the past; second, Christians must be willing to "belong psychologically" to the world of Muslims – that is, have some genuine cultural appreciation for it. VS 1 then discusses four "attitudes to be adopted in practice" in relationships at any level of interaction: authentic friendship, accepting the Muslim as he/she wishes to be known, serious preparatory study, and willingness to learn from one another. The third section of the chapter describes four attitudes associated explicitly with religious interaction: frank statement of one's Christian position, making clear that one is a Christian, renewing knowledge of one's own faith, and a new understanding of what Muslims consider true and holy. VS 1 then moves into a fuller coverage of these last Islamic values in chap. 2.

VS 2's expanded and thoroughly refashioned approach to "Occasions and Paths" (chap. 2) contains four sections, after a short introduction that reiterates the conviction that dialogue is "constitutive of the person." "Places and Times" points out some of the primary sociocultural contexts in which Christians and Muslims can expect to meet each other – work, schools, etc. A second section suggests four "Ways and Means," which are the more "general attitudes" of VS 1 but refocused so it is clear that both Christians and Muslims need to adopt them. They include: welcoming one another,

---

[25] *Ibid.*, p. 44.

understanding one another, living and sharing with one another, and the willingness to dare and risk. A short section on Christian attitudes on the faith of others advises, "It is in this spirit of welcoming, understanding and sharing that the Christian is called by the Church to consider and ponder the mystery of the religious search as it is expressed and embodied in the great historical religions." It is a thoroughly positive approach based on a belief in the "unfathomable mystery of the religious choices of individuals."[26] Believers in Dialogue," finally, must cultivate four essential attitudes: dialoguing in the presence of God and under God's impulse, becoming demanding witnesses for one another, attempting the impossible, and settling for the provisional and incomplete.

The topics explored in "How to Prepare for Dialogue" (VS 1) and "Bearing in Mind Present Obstacles" (VS 2) are almost exactly parallel, but VS 2 has rearranged some of the topics in the second section, made the issues in the third section more specific, and added a fourth section, "Not Forgetting the Obstacles that Remain." Both chapters begin with the need to acknowledge and move beyond past injustices. The two central sections of each recall the most common Christian stereotypes of the Islamic faith as well as prevalent Muslim views about Christianity. Among the former are suspicions that Islam is fatalistic, legalistic, laking in moral standards, fanatical, static, and obscurantist, and a religion of fear. Widespread Muslim beliefs about Christianity include, for example, that Christians have altered their Scriptures so as not to have to face the more demanding truth of the authentic word of God; that the doctrines of Jesus' divinity, the redemption, and the Trinity are either simply unacceptable or redundant; that Christian monotheism is not of the purest; that the church is nothing but a temporal power; and that Christians have not been faithful to the message of Jesus.

These are some of the very difficulties NCC suggests we must meet frankly and bypass. VS 2 agrees altogether; however, while it is on the subject of divisive elements, it is at pains to recall that some obstacles cannot be made to vanish or be forgotten except at the price of a "false irenicism." Practical difficulties are, for example, directly tied to such matters as the

---

[26] VS 2, pp. 45, 49.

prohibition of certain foods for Muslims, the feasibility of mixed marriages, inappropriate proselytism, and the treatment of religious minorities. In its conclusion VS 2 envisions four levels of dialogue: of the heart, where partners share as brothers and sisters; of daily life, where they together promote human values with God as the guarantor; of speech that is at once about God and humanity; and of silence, so that God can speak directly to the heart of each person.[27]

It is more difficult to characterize WCC's stance since the document is a collection and is not representative of a clearly unified position. WCC is in some ways at the opposite end of the spectrum from VS 1 and VS 2, to the extent that WCC is given wholly to summarizing actual meetings, while the Vatican papers are almost entirely theoretical. Nevertheless, WCC does make some important statements on the past, present, and future of dialogue. Dialogue between Christians and Muslims is necessary because of the common historical roots of the two religions, the attitude of "self-criticism" they share, and the increasing intermingling of Muslim and Christian populations.[28] Through dialogue both parties can "honour together our conscious dependence upon God in a world that often seems to deny" God. In other words, one may speak of a motive beyond that of a sense of interdependence. Dialogue holds the hope of "some convergence" short of having to settle for the least common denominator, and must be conducted according to three principles: frank witness, mutual respect, and religious freedom.[29] Lest it be reduced to an exercise in comparative religion, dialogue must maintain a highly personal dimension. From the perspective of authentic dialogue, conversion takes on a new meaning as "a growing mutual awareness of the presence of God in an encounter in which each becomes responsible for the other and where both seek openness in witness before God."[30] And there are further theological foundations for this dialogue. Both parties have received an ethical mandate from a loving and

---

[27] *Ibid.*, p. 170.

[28] WCC, pp. 67-70.

[29] *Ibid.*, pp. 89-91.

[30] *Ibid.*, p. 115.

loved All-Merciful God. Both have been given creation and the power that it entails as a trust. Acknowledging their shared spiritual affinity with Abraham, Muslims and Christians can own their divergences as well, for both traditions agree that there can be no compulsion in religion.[31]

An apt conclusion to this section is a statement produced at a 1976 meeting held in Tripoli. Although it does not appear in WCC, PMV quotes it as the "charter for Muslim-Christian dialogue today":

-to learn the lessons taught by history in order to retain the fruitful experiences and to avoid the errors of the past;

-to see to it that each side comes to know the other as it wants to be known: revision of textbooks, utilization of the mass media, increase in the number of professorships in Islam and Christianity, and cooperation between them.

-to be fair enough, on either side, to guarantee to all religious minorities all the rights and obligations the majority enjoys;

-to recognize each religion's "duty of apostolate" and the authentic witness each must give, while respecting human liberty – which involves condemnation of any kind of proselytism;

-to define more clearly the exact scope and methods of dialogue.[32]

Several of our documents also go into some detail on the most practical ways of providing and/or recognizing concrete circumstances suitable for ongoing dialogue, such as seminars, socials, and joint neighborhood projects, to name only a few. Interested readers are directed especially to NCC's and BCC's last chapters.

V. Themes in Dialogue

As the foregoing section has made clear, the nature of dialogue itself is one of the predominant themes in dialogue. In addition, all six documents eventually come around to dealing with what VS 2 calls the "triple perspective of all authentic dialogue," namely, issues relating to the wonders of the universe, human dignity, and the grandeur of God.[33] The differences

---

[31] *Ibid.*, pp. 120-121.

[32] PMV, p. 41.

[33] VS 2, p. 34.

among the documents have to do largely with emphasis, points of departure, and organization.

Taken together, they present a broad spectrum of approaches, ranging from simply reporting actual themes taken up in past organized dialogue sessions (WCC), through a restatement of those themes along with critical analysis and commentary and sketchy suggestions as to topics that need to be addressed in the future (PMV), a selective and more in-depth look at several central themes (NCC), and the more sweeping and theoretical treatment of virtually all the major themes listed in PMC and WCC (VS 1 and VS 2), to a small-scale attempt to situate the central issues in a still broader systematic context – not less than a proposal for a "theology of religions" (BCC).

In its summary of deliberations of past colloquia, PMV suggests that their themes "fall easily into two categories – specifically religious topics or action programmes realizable more or less immediately."[34] The former include agreements on belief in one, subsistent Creator who has spoken through prophets and who will bring history to its fulfillment, and disagreements on such central tenets as the meaning and mission of Muhammad and Jesus and the respective roles of *da'wah* and mission in Islam and Christianity. The latter have to do with possible collaboration in articulating how faith relates to science and technology, to cultural and economic problems, and with the clear need to come to terms with the "different designs Islam and Christianity have for organizing and inspiring society."[35] As for the future of dialogue on specifically religious topics, PMV recommends an emphasis on convergence of attitude about the mystery of God (to be taken up, perhaps, in colloquia devoted to the "Names of God," connections between faith and reason, and the "vision of God" in the two traditions). Human dignity could be studied with a focus on its scriptural sources, its exemplification in heroes and saints such as Abraham, and the concept of sanctity itself. Talk about Muhammad and Jesus, the Qur'an, and the various Christian "mysteries" mentioned earlier will remain very touchy for some time to come. Meanwhile, concerted action "in the service of life,

---

[34] PMV, p. 36.

[35] *Ibid.*, pp. 37-38.

justice, freedom, peace, brotherhood" will have to face such issues as contraception and abortion; suffering death and euthanasia; war, racism, and materialism – to mention only the most obvious.[36]

WCC is likewise helpful in providing an inventory of important topics. Since its papers are all brief, none treats a single issue in great detail (with one exception; see following paragraph). Some of the reports seem a bit more confident than PMV about the potential for fruitful discussion around major theological differences,[37] but most of WCC proposes questions that need to be addressed. One of the reports suggests further study of four issues, in the belief that "theological and spiritual renewal can prepare us for social renewal." First, achievement of a wider vision of world community as interracial, intercultural, and international, for example, would involve Muslims and Christians together in seeking justice for the Palestinians. Second, reconsideration of notions of revelation "may help us to be more faithful to our own tradition as well as being more appreciative and coherent with our neighbour." Third, a variety of political and cultural contexts must be seen as viable possibilities for interaction – that is, not merely either a secular state or a religious state. Fourth, since dialogue is listening to God as well as to one another, the "spiritual basis and eschaltological dimension of worship and prayer" must be seen as essential to dialogue. In other words, Muslims and Christians need to talk about how they relate their spiritual lives to demands for "justice, brotherhood, and human dignity."[38]

WCC's report on a 1976 "Planning Meeting for Next Steps in Christian-Muslim Dialogue" constitutes the most detailed single scheme of its kind to be found in any of the six documents. A section on preparation for dialogue outlines several goals and several types of behavior to be avoided, such as the preceding section of this article brought up. Three further sections speak of: "living in dialogue," including education, family life, worship, and prayer; sociopolitical issues – especially faith and politics in both traditions, social justice, and development – all with specific application to

---

[36] *Ibid.*, p. 49.

[37] WCC, pp. 60-61.

[38] *Ibid.*, pp. 91-92.

trouble areas in the Middle East, developing nations, and situations where Muslims and Christians find themselves in political tension; and theology and dialogue, with a focus on four areas: revelation; interreligious attitudes; faith, science, technology, and the future of humanity; and Christian mission and Islamic *da'wah*.[39] This last item is a recurrent theme in WCC. Perhaps more than any other issue, it renders dialogue absolutely critical even as it makes it more sensitive.

Much hard feeling remains among both traditions as a result of past practice of mission and *da'wah*; debate over what positions ought to be adopted in the present is quite heated; and there is strong consensus that this topic cannot be sidestepped in the future. One of WCC's papers discusses only this question and explains why misunderstandings and barriers to communication have developed around it. At least from the Muslim point of view, negative effects of the "arrival of the Christian missionaries in the company of European colonizers" are still very much in evidence. WCC contains a report on a 1976 "Consultation of Christians and Muslims Concerning Christian Mission and Islamic *Da'wah*," to which it has prefixed the editorial remarks published in a collection of all the papers from the Consultation. The Muslim co-editor makes four important points: First, Islam was misrepresented and portrayed in such a way as to discredit it and its adherents. Second, Christian missionaries often took advantage of the sick, the poor, and the immature by offering education, financial help, and medical treatment, often acting "as an organic part of colonialism and cultural imperialism." Third, Islam was often subverted in favor of "nationalism, secularism, modernism, socialism, even communism." Fourth, Christians have often considered Muslims political rivals, and the former sometimes appear more zealous for the de-Islamization of the Islamic world than they are troubled by the de-Christianization of the Christian world.[40] This Muslim's Christian counterpart presented neither a rebuttal nor a similar critique of Islam. The Consultation's joint "official" statement

---

[39] *Ibid.*, pp. 143-151.

[40] *Ibid.*, pp. 131-132.

acknowledges that there may in some instances be good reason for continued Muslim suspicion of Christian intentions.[41]

In its chapter on "Theological Perspectives in Christian-Muslim Relations," NCC examines in greater detail some of the questions only hinted at in PMV and WCC. Speight has selected six tightly interconnected themes (in addition to the theme of dialogue itself, to which he turns briefly at the conclusion of the chapter): Islam's view of other religions, Christianity's view of other religions, absolute truth as a guiding concept, mission and conversion viewed from both perspectives, religious liberty, and the nature of the Christian mission. After calling attention to several of the positions mentioned in VS 1 and VS 2's sections on Muslim beliefs about Christianity (see the sixth paragraph of section IV, above), NCC offers an excellent summary of the Qur'an's view of religious pluralism: God wants people to "outdo one another in good deeds," and the Scripture seems to assume that all religious communities are ultimately oriented toward God. Speight's commentary on the Qur'anic text is intriguing.

> He [God] saw that for the sake of humankind's clear grasp of duty and capacity to judge between truth and error, a diversity of religions would serve better than uniformity. However, there is no need in the diversity for theological rivalry among the religions, since the question of ultimate truth is not at stake...[it is] a contest out of which all will emerge winners.[42]

Controversy has, nontheless, developed and is an undeniable feature of Muslim-Christian relations.

However, Christianity, NCC notes, has no satisfactory explanation for religious pluralism. It suggests that we move beyond the three commonly expressed approaches to the question – that other religions are merely human and therefore enemies (does not allow for dialogue at all), or are alternate paths to God (a view that surrenders too much and denies uniqueness), or are true and good but incomplete (too imperious in seeking to subordinate all to Christianity). Recognizing that no rational solution is readily available, the Christian must fall back on his or her Christian identity by confessing that "God has met us in Jesus Christ." Christians must admit to having no

[41] *Ibid.*, pp. 138-141.
[42] NCC, p. 56.

monopoly on truth and must seek to "discern in Islam that which reflects sympathetically what we know of God's revelation to humankind," while bearing in patience the fact of divergences.[43] This naturally raises the issue of relativism. Speight advises that Muslims and Christians stay with their respective "points of contact with Truth," in the awareness that these are not Truth itself, and that "the Truth to which they expose themselves is greater than their grasp of it."[44]

On mission and conversion NCC points out that Islam's apparent flexibility toward Christianity is, however, more theoretical than practiced. (Islam considers Christianity a divinely revealed religion, whereas the converse is not the case.) In practice, both traditions are highly exclusivist. Speight proposes as a solution a new understanding of the concept of conversion as essentially a change in one's relationship to God, without explicit reference to confessional allegiance. For the Christian, to insist that there is no possibility of a relationship to God apart from Christianity is to take a presumptuous step beyond affirming the revelation Christians have received. "We cannot," says Speight, "be certain of the existence of other ways to God, nor can we deny the existence of such ways. We can hope for such; we can infer from the character of God that they exist; but finally, Christian faith is founded on only one certainty: Jesus Christ is the way to God."[45] NCC finds "ample scope for interfaith cooperation: in an understanding of conversion as above all a turning to God that results in, "among other things a commitment to maintain and enhance the well-being of the human family."[46]

NCC suggests that American Christians keep in mind three things about the key matter of religious liberty. First, Christians may seem to be more tolerant than Muslims toward members who depart from their ranks, but what appears to be tolerance may actually be indifference resulting from the "disintegration of the Christian communal life during the last two

---

[43] *Ibid.*, p. 58.

[44] *Ibid.*, p. 59.

[45] *Ibid.*, p. 61.

[46] *Ibid.*, p. 62.

centuries or more." Second, the idea of complete freedom of religion is a nonbiblical concept. It is the result of an extreme form of individualism that sets the individual in potential conflict with the community. Third, individualism is not as common elsewhere as it is in the U.S.A.; where Islam is a majority presence, religious liberty means protecting the community against divisive forces such as unbelief or erosive ideologies. That said, the problem of how religious minorities are treated remains serious. "How can the full dignity of minorities be assured without encroaching upon the freedom of the majority to be itself full?"[47]

Finally, NCC makes three points about how a deeper understanding of Islam can clarify the Christian's idea of mission. First, mission involves all Christians in a loving approach toward others in the name of Christ. Second, mission is not for the purpose of planting an ideology, but "to explore...the scope of similarity and to bear the burden of separation from others, in the hope that, by the power of God, the separation might be overcome."[48] Third, the mission to "all nations" is to make disciples not of the church, but of Jesus Christ; the living Christ must not be confused with cultural baggage or with social, political, economic, and theological values. The key is to personalize the interreligious encounter by "manifesting the power of a transforming friendship with the Living Christ."[49]

Moral and religious themes occupy two chapters each in VS 1 and VS 2. Each document's fifth chapter treats shared human projects. In its "Perspectives for Muslim-Christian Dialogue," VS 1 discusses two major developmental issues, those relating to the human personality of the individual and those relating to a more brotherly-sisterly society. Pressures of modern society on the individual, models of the family in Christianity and Islam, and the interaction for cultures viewed as expressions of the "social personality" of nations are the main topics. In a short reflection on how dialogue can lead to truly sister-brotherly attention to the world's most pressing problems, VS 1 focuses on economic and social development and

---

[47] *Ibid.*, pp. 63-64.

[48] *Ibid.*, p. 65.

[49] *Ibid.*, p. 66.

the interaction of diverse peoples. The document cautions that these matters are to be addressed always within an explicitly religious context and with reference to an Absolute.[50]

Once again, VS 2 takes a fresh look at the material, referring more frequently than VS 1 to both the Qur'an and Vatican II (especially *Gaudium et spes*). A chapter on "Requisite Human Collaboration" speaks of the need for people of good will to respond together, united in message and action, to the most blatant inequities many suffer. The chapter's four sections recall explicitly the "triple perspective of dialogue." The first section describes the "fulfillment of the world" as a call for a new creation through discovery of new relationships between humanity and nature. The second and third sections, the lengthiest of the four, analyze needs for "The Service of Humanity" and "Stewardship in the (Earthly) City."

The former of the two examines the two traditions' views on the source of human dignity, inquiring how the two might respond to the dignity of life (all that has to do with embodiment), of the spirit (seeing all education, culture, and science as an intervention of the Spirit of God), of conscience (objective norms of morality), and of freedom (with adequate education and guarantees). That section concludes the Beatitudes call Christians to collaborate with Muslims in serving the marginal, oppressed, aged, infirm, poor, strangers, and all who are deprived of rights. The third section attempts to propose ways of laboring together in pluralistic societies. Five urgent challenges present themselves: preservation of the dignity of marriage and family, maintaining progress in the arts and culture in forming a world that is at once humane and technological, insuring economic and social balance that avoids the excesses of both collectivism and capitalism, guaranteeing human rights through harmony of political communities, and establishment of community of nations and international peace by repudiating all forms of violence.

VS 2 places all these themes in a solidly religious context in its final section on "The Human Imitation of Divine Action." For Christians this is a question of embodying the ideal of Jesus Christ; for Muslims, of living out

---

[50] VS 1, pp. 119-133.

the divine qualities of knowledge, justice, and mercy. In both instances there must be a kind of "exchange of attributes."[51]

More properly theological themes appear in the final chapter of VS 1 and VS 2. What the earlier document calls "The Spirituality of a Christian Taking Part in Dialogue" the later entitles "Possible Religious Convergences." For both Vatican documents, the key concept is that of an "open spirituality" that allows one to marvel at the work of the Spirit in other religious traditions. An "Ecumenism of the People of the Book" (VS 1) is made possible only if one is converted from a static spirituality, in which one is a prisoner of extrinsic certitudes and values, to a dynamic spirituality which recasts those same values and certitudes into a passionate search for the traces of God's word among human beings.

Both documents then elaborate on their chosen themes so as to highlight aspects of convergence between Islam and Christianity. The wording of subheadings is strongly suggestive of differences in tone and emphasis in the two works, with those of VS 1 hinting at parallel concepts and those of VS 2 at more direct convergence; for example, "The Great God and the God of Love" (VS 1) and "The Mystery of God" (VS 2), "The Book and the Word of God" and "The Gift of the Word," "Prophets and the Prophetic Mission" and "The Role of Prophets," "Community and Church" and "The Presence of Communities," a sixth "station along the mystical journey of meeting and sharing," entitled "The Paths of Holiness." In all but the section on prayer, VS 2 makes considerably greater use of Qur'anic and Biblical texts.[52]

Perhaps the most theologically ambitious of the documents, especially given its brevity and the size of its intended readership, is BCC. Its opening statement gives only a tiny clue as to what will follow:

> The blunt fact is that the Churches in Britain are ill-prepared to discuss the theological questions raised by the existence of other faiths, simply because they have hitherto paid little attention to them. Christian theology has been written by and large, and even within the universities, as if other faiths had

---

[51] VS 2, pp. 129-146.

[52] VS 1, pp. 135-158; VS 2, pp. 147-165.

nothing to teach them about the relationship of God with his world. It will take some years for the theologians and governing bodies of our Churches to adjust to the realities and perspectives of the pluralist society which Britain, in common with the rest of the world, is rapidly becoming.[53]

Author David Brown's observations are clearly applicable to churches all over the globe, which is all the more reason for him to make his rather bold proposal for a "theology of religions."

BCC's approach consists of five main elements: First, an authentic response to the "unique act of God in Christ" makes Christians responsible for witnessing to that mystery, in full awareness that their affirmation of it "is different, in its essential inner meaning, from Muslim statements about God."[54] The second has to do with Christians' responses to other religions and to Islam in particular. Authentic responses to the presence and action of God can be discerned across the whole spectrum of religious belief and practice. Christians must strive to interpret the Islamic experience in light of that. They can find a model for such an interpretation in their own recognition of the Hebrew Bible; here is a precedent for Christian relationship with a religious tradition that does not accept Christian faith as a whole. At the very least, the Christian can in no way presume to limit the action of the Holy Spirit. To sum up the second point: "It is possible, while using Christian categories, to accept that there is, and always has been, a living relationship between God and the peoples of Islam, which has been grounded in part, though not fully, in what they have learnt of him as they practiced their our religion."[55] Third, it is important to take account of factors that unite Muslims and Christians (common humanity, citizenship, religious heritage – many of the items discussed in VS 1 and VS 2, for example) as well as those that divide (social problems and theological differences).

In the fourth element, Brown stresses the need to develop a "theology of religions" on the basis of two principles of interpretation. The first principle is an "inclusivist" interpretation of God's revelation in Christ that

---

[53] BCC, p. 8.

[54] *Ibid.*, pp. 8-9.

[55] *Ibid.*, p. 12.

underscores its "relevance to everything else in the universe." Human unity under divine kingship, the universality of Jesus' ministry, the patterns of early Christian encounters with "the nations," and the New Jerusalem's openness to receive all people are but a few Biblical incitements to an inclusive view. The second principle, a variation on the first, is an inclusivist or universalist view of Christ. Whereas the idea of Christ as Savior tends to be exclusive, "Christ the Word" and "Christ the Second Adam" are inclusivist interpretations of Jesus' divinity and humanity, respectively.[56]

Fifth, Christians live in "the modern Antioch," and their task is, finally, to cross a new threshold, as the early Christians did more than once, toward an "understanding of other faiths in relation to the purposes of God." Three new insights will emerge: (1) that "God is to the universe as our Lord was to his contemporaries in Palestine," which will lead to the "writing of new 'theologies of religions,' to stand between the present expositions of natural and of revealed theology, and the revision also of biblical theology in inclusive rather than exclusive terms"; (2) that Christians will regard with greater humility the human dimensions of ecclesiastical institutions and customs; and (3) that what is unique of Christianity will emerge with new clarity.[57]

VI. Conclusions

Since the documents described here are so varied, it is difficult to make an across-the-board evaluation of them. One might, however, suggest as a touchstone the deceptively simple question, "To what extent does a particular document truly advance the cause of Christian-Muslim dialogue?" I propose five specific ways of assessing the degree to which the six documents contribute to that cause.

First is the question of effectiveness in persuading readers that Christians and Muslims *must* dialogue. Judged by this standard, none of the works sounds so urgent an alarm as to rouse more than a few who are not already convinced of the need. All in some way presuppose an awareness of

---

[56] *Ibid.*, pp. 12-22.

[57] *Ibid.*, pp. 23-24.

the necessity of dialogue and depend for their efficacy on the conviction of the already-convinced. None of the six is quite a match for the almost diametrically opposed approach of a work such as L. Sumrall's *Where Was God When Pagan Religions Began?* with its chapter on "Islam: Worshipping the Wrong God."[58] What is lacking in all the documents is a way of "reaching the unecumenized" and of persuading even those amenable in principle to Christian ecumenism that Christian-Muslim dialogue is critical to the broader ecumenical engagement of Christians with non-Christians. A focus on the issue of secularization and the ways in which Christians and Muslims respond could provide a starting point.[59]

Several of the documents can, nevertheless, be quite useful as tools in the hands of those who are already conscious of a pressing need. Judged by the second standard, educative value, NCC will prove the most helpful. Soon to be more readily available and specifically written for an American public, NCC is highly recommended for schools, adult education, and church study groups. Used with some imagination by a sensitive leader or teacher, the book will go a long way toward raising American awareness.

Potential for stimulating in-depth reflection, the third touchstone will be found preeminently in VS 2. Even when its translation into English (now in progress, I am told) becomes available, VS 2 will pose no little challenge to its reader. It is a highly sensitive and beautifully conceived work which is rather "heady" in some ways, but on the whole it is well anchored in genuine human concerns. The kind of reflections VS 2 can facilitate will require and presuppose the educative potential of a book such as NCC. Finally, VS 2 is actually a product of over a dozen years' work, refining and polishing as it does the initial offerings of VS 1.

Fourth, stimulus to action is an important criterion. Here again it is NCC that is most successful and practical. Its careful suggestions cover a

---

[58] Lester Sumrall, *Where Was God When Pagan Religions Began?* (Nashville: Thomas Nelson Publishers, 1980).

[59] See, e.g., Horst Burkle, "Secularization – A Theme in Christianity's Dialogue with Non-Christian Religions," in Annemarie Schimmel and Abdoljavad Falaturi, eds., *We believe in One God: The Experience of God in Christianity and Islam* (New York: Seabury Press, 1979), pp. 113-135.

wide range of activities that can bring Christians and Muslims together, as well as a variety of situations in which Christian tact and considerations toward the needs of Muslims will produce far more immediate results than any organized "official" dialogue can hope for.

Finally comes the matter of hard-headed realism about the possibilities of Muslim-Christian dialogue. Only PMV begins to address this issue directly enough, and its caveat is worth quoting here at length:

> There is too much ready talk about wider ecumenism with the People of the Book, in the mistaken idea that Muslims and Christians are intent on unity and common truths after the manner of Catholic-Protestant-Orthodox ecumenism. This only does harm, because the aims and methods of Muslims and Christians are thus confused with the brotherly and evangelical exchange between various Christian communities. While dialogue should be marked by the same ecumenical spirit, based on respect, understanding and reconciliation in prayer, the difference between [interreligious] dialogue and ecumenism needs pointing out. Muslims and Christians together will never envisage any kind of reunion or unification. Though together able to honour God and proclaim the dignity of man, they know that, for all, Jesus Christ remains the "sign of contradiction" and therefore of absolute difference. The Muslim-Christian dialogue can never be equated with ecumenism. The very word "dialogue" is ambiguous: some people prefer to use the word "encounter." It would seem, however, that over the last ten years Muslims and Christians have got used to "dialogue" in a vague sense, a sense which they can make richer as progress is made in their exchanges within the framework of "holy rivalry" proposed by the Koran to the People of the Book.[60]

Closely connected with the need for Christian realism is another matter hinted at in PMV but otherwise not approached in the six documents. It is the evident fact that there are surely as many Muslims as there are Christians who have given no thought to, much less actively desire, dialogue. Muslim-Christian dialogue is simply not "popular" in any sense of the word. As mentioned earlier, NCC and VS 2 are especially good on a general sense of Muslim views of Christianity. However, in the final analysis, realism in dialogue requires that one acknowledge, without losing enthusiasm for

---

[60] PMV, p. 46.

dialogue, that not everyone is willing to listen. With that we have returned full-circle to the first criterion.

MUSLIM DIALOGUE WITH JEWS AND CHRISTIANS

BASES AND BOUNDARIES OF JEWISH, CHRISTIAN, AND MOSLEM DIALOGUE[*]

Zalman M. Schachter[**]

I am deeply aware that the unprecedented dialogue a-trois in this conference is fraught with new problems which increase the complexity of our meeting. There are places where Christians and Jews will be able to ally themselves against Moslems, and Moslems and Christians against Jews. There are positions of three-way mutual agreement as well as situations of mutual disagreement. I cannot take for granted that the Moslem and I will share what the Christian and I do, and so on, round and round. What is tacit in one relationship is necessarily explicit in another. When I make explicit what is tacit, I may create problems.

---

[*] *Journal of Ecumenical Studies*, 14:3 (Summer, 1977).

[**] Zalman Schacter (Jewish) was born in Poland; attended schools in Vienna, Belgium, and France; and graduated and was ordained in 1947 by Central Yeshiva Tomchei T'mimim Lubavitch in Brooklyn. He holds a M.A. from Boston Univ. and a D.H.L. from Hebrew Union College (1968). He served as rabbi and Hebrew school principal for two Massachusetts congregations, then taught at the Univ. of Manitoba, 1956-75 (Dept. of Judaic Studies – professor, chairperson). He has also taught at Brandeis, Univ. of Calif. at Santa Cruz, Naropa Institute, and Pacific School of Religion; served as facilitator at several growth and clergy-training centers; and served on the editorial boards of *Judaism and Sh'ma*. Since 1975, he has been Professor of Religion in Jewish Mysticism at Temple University. He has six drama credits for production research and assistance, and translated and narrated a two-album recording. "The Seven Beggars of Reb Nahman & the Torah of the Void." He has published eight monographs, most recently, *Fragments of a Future Scroll* (1975); over a dozen contributions to books; and nearly fifty articles and translations.

Moreover, I am convinced of the need to conduct our dialogue with other members also, not physically present, who are committed to other ways, Bibles, and dogmas which express emphases concerning God and the Cosmos that are different from ours. All of this makes our dialogue exceedingly delicate. We cannot retreat from the challenge, though the dynamics are very complex, and we will need to keep all of this in mind while we are trying to evolve the right manners for this new phase of dialogue. May God grant that we stay conscious of this.

Our Dialogue Takes Place in Exile

How does one live with exile? Exile is one of the ways in which traditional Jews experience life differently than do their Moslem and Christian counterparts. We are in *Galuth*. We participate in dialogue against the background of exile. With the exception of a few exalted souls, Christians lost the sense of exile in the year 321 when Emperor Constantine converted to Christianity. The religion of oppressed ghetto dwellers now sat in the drivers' seat of the *saeculum* and controlled political events. From that time on, salvation for Christians became a private matter between the soul and its God. The messianism of Christians no longer needed this world to come into its own. Triumphalism claimed its fulfillment here on earth under the rule of the triple-crowned vicar of Christ. All that now mattered was the spread of the Holy Roman Empire. Only oppressed nations after the resurgence of nationalisms had messianic dreams of temporal significance. If a Christian felt alienated and marginal it was interpreted as his or her personal problem. Until Vatican II the church did not see itself as the *ecclesia* in waiting for the end of the exile, but as the church arrived.

In Islam, to my knowledge, although there too an expected Mahdi is part of the eschatology, there is no sense of exile. Once the Jahaliyin and idolators were removed from Mecca, a new world order began.

Except on the Sabbath when we Jews share a few moments of exilelessness, we stay aware of exile. I ask my partners in this dialogue to remain aware of exile, which I believe we all share, as the basic condition of an unredeemed world.

Dialogue Is Not Arbitration or Disputation

There is a myth, begotten by marketplace and parliament, that the individuals involved in dialogue will have power given to them to change the thinking of the faithful of their own community. The Jewish community has given me no such power. If I go too far out, I will be repudiated by my own community. The dialoguer who goes too far afield is discredited and with this the effectiveness of dialogue as a changer of consciousness is undermined. Dialogue is not even part of seminary curricula. With the notable exception of the Hebrew Union College of Cincinnati, there are no chairs in Christianity and Islam in Jewish seminaries. I suspect that the same is true of Christian and Moslem seminaries vis-a-vis other religions. In the past we have studiously ignored one another, and still there is tension between us. But in conferences such as this one we become the instrument of the Power that wants us to connect, the Power which I believe is at the core of the urge for dialogue.

Thank God we are not in a disputation. We may look to a discussion in which all partners are equal, open to each other and caring for the truth, each responding from the position of a loyal adherent to his or her own religion, standing in the presence of the God who witnesses the sharing. As Malachi 3:16 has it, "then did those who respect God speak, each to his fellow, and the Lord heard and listened and wrote it all into his book entitled 'The dialogues of those who fear the Lord and honor his Name.'"

Our Poor Acts of Faith

To us Jews, and in some measure to Christians and Moslems, the revelation of Sinai is crucial. But what if we could construct a working time machine which could take us to participate in the receiving of the Torah at Mt. Sinai? As we teach this event in the tradition of Scripture and Midrash, there were present the souls of the born and yet unborn receiving the Law in seventy languages. All the earth trembled when the entire Torah, up to the last insight yet to occur to a diligent student, was given to Moses and the vast multitudes, of whom the 600,000 men from twenty to sixty years old were only the nucleus, surrounded by elders, women, children, slaves, and the mixed multitudes. Echoes of that event are still in the air and can be heard by those with holy ears.

Would this, in fact, be what we would find at the other end of a trip in time? When I am in a mood for historic facts, in touch with what I know of the nature of Hebrew—with the documents of covenants of the ancient Near East—I think there were fewer people there. All the eisegetics of the Midrash that came in subsequent times managed to help people accept the momentousness of the revelation, but were they warranted by the factic reality, or were they a pious strategy intended to exhort the faithful?

The Midrash, even if unfactual, was not untrue. I am in need of the Midrash where I am a viscerotonic celebrator of the holy feasts and mysteries, a devotee. On that level and in only that universe of discourse do I accept the Midrash as reality. The Midrash is true in the same way that God is love, or Brahman is Atman, and the Lord is King. (The word "is" is a convenience for the English ear. In Hebrew it is lacking, as in "Adonai Melekh.") Rabbi Yishmael stated that "the Torah speaks in the language of men." I understand this to mean that the symbolic language of the Torah motivates our hearts and behavior more powerfully than would a factual record of events.

I so not base my values and my life as much on facts as on faith. So, despite the facts, I make an act of faith which places me at the foot of Sinai, and I accept the Law and the revelation. If this is so with regard to the Sinai revelation, how much is it true of an event less public and in the view of only the one person who reports it? Were not all the revelations of the prophets like that reported in Daniel? "And I Daniel alone saw the vision and the people with me did not see, though a great quaking fell upon them and they fled" (Dan. 10:7). Had we been present, all that we could have reported would have been that this holy man claimed to have experienced a vision. But what about the truth in that vision? This I allege by an act of faith, distinguishing it from a common hallucination. I base my life on such acts of faith, and I will try to persuade my children to make similar acts of faith. I will do so in emulation of Father Abraham of whom the Bible states, "For I know him that he will command his children and his household after him and they shall keep the way of the Lord" (Gen. 18:19), but this is an act of faith and love. I have been talking about my own faith and the problems associated with it. If my own faith is on such shaky ground, then what about the claims of other religions, especially the ones with which I am in dialogue today?

Granted even the most generous reading of their positions, what facts do I have? A carpenter's son from Galilee spouts holy sayings culled from the popular piety of his day, heals some folks in the same way as did Elijah and Elisha, makes grandiose claims, and dies without fulfilling them. Then I have the testimony of his bereaved disciples, which is about on the same level of credibility as that of the disciples of Rabbi Judah the Prince who, it is claimed, came back after his demise to recite the sabbath sanctification and, when this became part of local gossip, ceased to come (Kethuboth 103). I also have the testimony of a zealot persecutor of Jesus' followers, who on the road to Damascus fell victim to a seizure and reported afterward that he saw an apparition reproving him, "Why dost thou persecute me?"

What of the claim that an unlettered man rode a miracle horse to heaven to get the true and latest version of the revelation which any form critic can see as a bowdlerized version of Jewish Midrash served up in new ethnic clothes and at the service of the children of Ishmael instead of those of Isaac?

Deflating Inflated Faith Claims

I am aware that I am treading on pious toes. But please watch; I also stepped on my own. What I am saying is not that the world faiths to which we belong have no factual basis at all. What I *am* saying is that we are *all* on shaky ground, and that we need to deal not so much with the external facts but with our own *acts of faith*. These we need to take seriously because we stake our lives on them and invest them with supreme value. These acts of faith are not the result of facts. On the contrary, facts in this world are more often the result of acts of faith on which we base our actions. Our acts of faith create realities for us and others. So that we do not become arrogant in the process of inflating our truth claims which are based on our own acts of faith and put down those of others, I must make these statements so that in a sober and humble fashion we may talk about our traditions without undue triumphalism.

The major impediment to communication among our three religions is the dogmatic stance which we assume for the sake of the propagation of faith. We quote authorities who knew no more truly than we know but whose energetic assertions "snow" us. Their energy is the result of worldviews so dominated by their inner scene that they did not permit any of the doubts that are brought on by reality maps that did not match their dogma. Against the refrain, "it ain't necessarily so," we bluff others who are not of our faith, and we bluff our own people – not deliberately as con artists, but out of desperation at the lack of hard evidence, and we bluff ourselves as a strategy against our own fickleness, our "crooked heart" as Jer. 5:23 calls it. Then again, acts of faith are not made on an empty heart. We have within it our soul, the most reliable teacher. As we watch the process in which the soul becomes thought or speech, we notice that many a time we ease ourselves into convenient cliches that have little of the new insight in them. Once more we are trapped by habits which are the dunghill upon which the creeds feed. It takes vigilance and humble courage to make acts of faith. After all, where faith is weak, there is an abundance of beliefs. With this in mind we may be more humble about our tradition and our sureness, yet also a bit more proud of the holy process in our inner being which keeps teaching and guiding us.

The Aquarian Challenge

Besides the challenge of past history we also face the challenge of the present New Age. The Aquarian age is empirical, experiential, humanistic, multioptional, fluid, mystical; it is existential, integative, ecumenical, aware of non-verbal dimensions, with a view of God that is radically immanent, while at the same time utterly transcendental, non-anthropomorphic, and apopathic. Instead of being particularistic in regard to salvation and the conditions that make for it, it is universalistic and non-institutional, heuristic and empirical. This view takes most seriously "by their fruits ye shall know them," and the fruits are manifest in the realm of better human living and interaction. It demands to see the fruits in better and more harmonious relationships, and to see a consciousness that is higher, more integrated and with the physical, multi-dimensional, centered, and ecologically aware. The new humanism wedded to transpersonal psychology has challenged all of us by presenting a viable and deeply religious option to the Bible religions.

Here, too, we make some acts of faith. I believe that there is something in Judaism that is in some sense closer to the divine intent than even the best that Aquarian psychology can produce. At the same time I maintain that Judaism without holistic Aquarian psychology will be farther from the divine intent than Aquarian psychology alone. We three can meet the challenge of Aquarian psychology most significantly in the field of spiritual direction, Tarika, Maussar, and Kabbalah. About these things we must talk with one another from real live experience, not only from books.

The Dialogue of Devoutness

Once we realize the shakiness of the factual fundaments of our acts of faith and come to a tentative agreement that the Biblical and Qur'anic notions of holiness are not too far apart, then we realize that the holier we become, the stronger the impression our acts of faith make on the universe. But where do we learn how to fulfill the command, "holy ye shall be for holy am I the Lord your God"? We search the sources of our traditions and find an entire literature devoted to spiritual direction. We read about holy souls and the paths they took on their way to holiness, the anecdotes in which their lives and conversations taught more than what one can learn in the academy, the counsels they gave to seekers, and their day-to-day, breath-by-breath witness.

There are few conversations in this universe as deeply satisfying to the heart as the dialogue of the devout. Unfortunately, such dialogue took place mostly among the people of each religion separately. If this profound sharing were to take place between zaddik, saint, and dervish, monk, murid, and hasid, we would have a model of what one of the highest forms of conversation could be. One of the prime topics of that discourse would be counsel that would help the spirit gain the service of the flesh for the sake of the divine. The dialogue is a sharing of how best to surrender and conform to the divine will, how to receive divine wisdom for our guidance, how to read Scripture for the sake of the spirit, how to emulate – imitate – divine attributes. The counsel gained in such dialogue helps the worshipper to worship, the mediator to mediate, the adorer to adore, and the virtuous one who wished to become a devotee to become a virtuoso of devoutness, a saint.

Neighbors on the Shelf of the Head Bookshop

In the past such exchanges were rare occurrences. Most of the instances found in the literature were motivated by a competitive spirit that might be expressed as follows: "If this goy-kaffir-pagan serves God with such zeal and devotion, how much more need I who have the true religion serve God with zeal and devotion?" Nowadays these exchanges are becoming the more common. The conversation is motivated by the consideration that one's own tradition may lack a certain way, approach, attitude, or advice that another tradition has deeply fostered. The popularity of bookshops specializing in how-to-become-enlightened literature is an index of New Age spirituality. Their shelves are packed with Yoga, Vedanta, Zen, Tibetan and Teravada Buddhism, Tantra, Sufism, Kabbalah, Hassidism, Tarot, I-Ching, and Christianity in its mystical form.

In the literature, in retreats and workshops, and by attendance at worship with others, Christians and Jews can learn about Zikr; Moslems and Jews can learn from the stately rising and abating rhythm of the Mass; and both Christians and Moslems can learn much from shabbat and davvenen for their own holy resting and praying.

Shankara, AlGhazzali, Luria, and Eckhart meet in the mind and discuss how the infinite becomes finite. Reb Nahman, Ramakrishna, Shams al Tabriz, and St. Francis prod one to adoration among the trees. Rob Moshe Kobriner, St. Jean-Vianney, Junaid, and Hakuin keep urging us to the simple, humble essentials of steady, everyday holiness. This dialogue of devoutness produces such hybrids as Christian Yoga and Catholic Zen, and it once produced a Raimond Lully, a Kabir, a Bahya ibn Paquda, and an Abraham, the son of Maimondes.

The dialogue of devoutness is the dialogue of devotional empiricism. It does not seek to improve on what is divine in the spiritual life, but on what our human response is to the divine challenge. What used to be secret teaching from master to initiate has now come out of the closet.

The Eso/Exo-teric Switch

Andre Guenon and Friedtjoff Schuon found in Houston Smith their American spokesperson. His point is that the greatest sharing between religions takes place in the realm of the esoteric, not the exoteric. Behind all religions there stands the *philosophia perennis*. This view accounts for the difference between religions as mere accidents of time and clime, space and race. Though I find this view not quite convincing, for reasons I hope to detail elsewhere, it is nevertheless pervasive in our culture. There is much agreement today that what all religions share is more important than are the their differences.

The hallmark of the Aquarian Age is that the esoteric has taken the place of the exoteric, and there is more agreement concerning the esoteric teachings and their empirical value than concerning the exoteric aspects. Many of the exoteric observances are being discarded, often out of ignorance and carelessness, or lack of proper instruction in doing them so that they work in one's life. Pragmatic rationalists among members of the hierarchies give their consent to this because the practices seem to divert a person from the essentials, toward minutiae that in superstitious minds have taken on a magic heaven-coercing quality. Thus the Catholic Church is discarding Latin, novenas, holy water, incense, and the concern for extreme unction; "tantric" means formerly at the disposal of the faithful. This is on the official level, while such practices as exorcism, use of incense, and anointing have moved to the counterculture.

Among Jews there is less observance of the midnight lament, the ablutions of the miqveh, the kapparot with live rooster or hen, and the holy days of Succoth and the New Moon. As I hear it from Moslems, Ramadan has for some become less a period for fasting during the day than for feasting at night. This switch is akin to the one that occurred in the use of our sacred and vernacular languages, Hebrew, once referred to as the holy tongue and reserved for prayer and sabbath conversation, has become the language of the marketplace and the election campaign, while Yiddish, the once secular vernacular, is now used for the study of Torah and colloquy with God.

The esoteric aspect has become the public face of religions. As mentioned before, head bookshops are stocked well with St. John of the Cross and St. Theresa of Avila, but one will be hard pressed to find a catechism or a Kyriale. The Kabbalah is much better represented than volumes dealing with home life and daily prayer. On the Moslem side, one will find only rarely a book of Hadiths or Salaat, but Sufism is overflowing the shelves.

All this causes the guardians of religion great anxiety and concern. Does it mean that what once was considered essential is no longer valid? Was the synagogue/church/mosque wrong in maintaining our differences all along? Is the effort to get us to dialogue together nothing but another ploy to homogenize all cop out from real commitment? These anxieties cannot be averted by reverting to a strict fundamentalist position. Whenever tradition is challenged to renew itself, it must meet these crises. Whenever a religion refuses to renew itself, it finds itself without adherents. How do we steer the course between removing all the surface tensions between religions, thus losing what is special in each, and the building of concrete walls between us? Perhaps we need to explore this again and, after exploring, reformulate our teachings on the differences of our religions. Let us each look at the teachings concerning the status of the adherents of our sisterfaiths.

The Theology of Goy

In the age preceding this Aquarian era, known as the Piscean Age, we worked with words rather than with functions. Words were very powerful. "Abra Kadabra" (Aramaic for "it is created as it is spoken") and "Hocus Pocus" (a vulgarization for "Hoc est enim Corpus meum") were words for religious magic. The proper formulae for prayer were vital requirements for receiving an answer. Theology has to be in precise legalese and a clause such as "filioque" could split a church. The difference between one synagogue and another was in the use of "w'yatzmah purqaney," and Sunna and Shia split similarly over such either/ors.

It is easier to teach in flat blacks and whites than in shades of gray. The higher the contrast between right and wrong, saved and damned, the easier it is to run the magisterium and the institutions. For us Jews it was simply the choice between Jew and Goy. Even Jews who were not well educated or did not abide by the expected norms were called "Goy". Originally the word did not have pejorative connotations. We are called "Goy" too. "'Amkha' Yisrael Goy Ehad Ba'aretz" ('Thy people Israel one nation on Earth"; from the Sabbath afternoon liturgy). I am sure the word became laden with pejorative meaning by all the pain inflicted upon us by Centurion, Crusader, and Cossack, to the point that when one referred to a *Nazi* by that word it had lost all human connotation and became synonymous with inhuman villain.

Today I am in dialogue with "Goyim." Who are you to me in that category? Jews are agitated by the question "Mihu Yehudi?" (who is a Jew?), and the agitation extends to "Mihu Goy?" which is the other end of this polarity.

In many aspects of Jewish thought and Law I have discovered, instead of a binary yes-versus-no relationship, one that is graduated in the middle range and this is what I wish to share at this time. In Halakhah there is a descending order of persons. The highest rank is occupied by the High Priest. He is the only one to enter the most holy sanctuary, and this only on Yom Kippur. Below him is the average priest. Below the Kohen Hediot stands the Levite, and below him the first born in the family. All other Israelites come next, and they are followed by the Gerey Zedeq, the righteous proselytes who have embraced Judaism as their own religion. Below them stand the ones forbidden to marry Israelites, the Mamzer, child of adultery and incest, and Goyim. But even among Goyim there is a scale in which the Hasidey Umoth Ha'olam (the devout of all nations) rate highest; they are followed by the Ger Toshav, the sojourner (to whom we will return), and any other son of Noah (that is to say, any non-Jew of general ancestry). Below him is one who worships stars and constellations (idolators); below these are the seven nations of Canaan, and below them the Amalekites.

There are occasional aggadic statements to the effect that a learned Mamzer is higher than an unlettered High Priest or that regardless of one's status each person is rewarded according to one's deeds. There are also distinctions regarding freemen, bondsmen, and slaves.

We are concerned here with the categories of Son of Noah and Ger Toshav. According to rabbinic tradition, based on the convenant made with Noah and his children, God prohibited to them idolatry, bloodshed, sexual depravity, theft, and the living limb (to eat part of an animal that is still alive), and ordained that they establish courts of Law. Anyone who accepts these commandments and lives by them is to be accorded all the courtesy with which the Torah charges us concerning the stranger in our midst. Such a person is to have the same rights before the Law and is invited to worship with Jews, though still forbidden to intermarry with them.

Whenever I have talked with Christians about this I found that the category of Ger Tashav, although satisfying to some,[1] is not satisfying to others, and it does not satisfy me. Under this category an Advaitin Vedanitist, a Jnani Yogin, and a Zen Buddhist would enjoy the same status as a Christian and a Moslem. Somehow I feel that the Islamic model of the "peoples of the book" challenges our present thought on this matter. We must clearly separate two issues here. What happens if a Jew becomes a Christian or a Moslem? The Law holds that even if Jews renounce their religion, they still remain Jews; nevertheless, they incur severe ostracism in the community for embracing Christianity or Islam. The other issue deals with non-Jews who by their act of choice become Christians and Moslems. They are better than Henotheists (an option open for the children of Noah). They hold beliefs which Albo in his *Iqqarim* claims are essential, i.e., there is a supreme God whose will is revealed to humankind, and who rewards those

---

[1] During the last century, Aime Palliere became a Ger Toshav. He sought to become a Roman Catholic priest. During his seminary years he became a member of the Salvation Army. His search led him to Judaism to which he sought to convert. He corresponded with Rabbi Elia Benamozegh of Livorno, went to visit him, and later continued his correspondence with him. Instead of leading him to full conversion as a Ger Zedeq, an option that would have required that Palliere renounce his allegiance to Christianity. Benamozegh suggested the category of Ger Toshav, an option that had fallen into disuse since the destruction of the second temple. By assuming the status of Ger Toshav, Palliere could participate in Jewish worship, though he could not lead as officiant, nor did this entitle him to marry a Jew. Palliere accepted this suggestion, and there grew around him a circle of Gerey Toshav in Paris.

who keep to this revealed way and punishes transgressors. Here Christians and Moslems definitely are closer to us than are Zen Buddhists.

Alas, we Jews do not have a forum such as a Sanhedrin in session these days, and opinions are private until someone publishes a responsum and this responsum is accepted by the majority. I know of no such work concerning the status of Christians and Moslems today. It is clear that the Ger Toshav category is inadequate to deal with members of the other Bible religions, who in my opinion deserve a special status ranking above Ger Toshav and below Ger Zedeq. This category will allow us hopefully not only to tolerate one another but also to learn from one another.

The Dialogue of Good News

I am deeply intrigued to hear the good news others proclaim. It is in the nature of each religion to emphasize one or another aspect. Our daily prayer in the grace after meals asks God to send to us soon Elijah-Al Khidr with the good news of redemption and consolation. Elijah wears many garbs and disguises. When a Christian proclaims what he knows as good news, I want to hear it. I cannot hear it though if it addresses itself only to those who belong to the visible church. None of us here reject the truth stubbornly out of truculent recalcitrance to God; hence we can in some sense connect with salvation in what is called the invisible church. We Jews dealt with the category of the children of Noah. The Moslems accept non-Moslems who believe in One God as Muumin. So what is our message? All three of us share the good news of turning to God. Tshuvah, Metanoia, Tawba. All three of us share the good news of the ultimate kingdom of God right here in this planet. Can we not share in the dissemination of that message? We all believe in the consequentiality of human life. We all share the sense of "in illo tempore" time which allows us to keep in touch with the seasons of hope and revelation, and the advent of redemption. We all share in the belief that some of God's blessed will and wisdom are manifested to humankind. We all share in the belief and hope in the ultimate transcedance of the limitations of the flesh and society.

In the areas where we do not share, we still need to be able to hear what good news the other proclaims, without getting "up tight." Each one of us has some aspects that are well developed in the faith and others that are either over-developed so that they have become top-heavy or underdeveloped because we have heard only through a wall and seen through a veil. We need each other as mirrors. How do I look to you? I must tell you how you look to me so that we have accurate reflections of whether we manifest what we proclaim.

The Dialogue of Indebtedness

James Parkes once gave a sermon which has often been reprinted under the title "Christianity's Debt to Judaism." I think that there are some issues on which we all need to declare out debt to each other. Islam has given us the first thrust in the direction of scholasticism. Maimonides and Aquinas came on the heels of Ibn Sina and Ibn Rushd. It was Islamic thought and scholarship that made us enter into dialogue with philosophy. It was so fruitful in its own day that I cannot believe that there is at present hardly any of this dialogue going on.

It is clear to me that Mohammed, in his hadiths and in the formulations of the Qur'an which depended on his vocabulary and the state of his awareness, did what he conceived as bringing the shariya of Judaism and Christianity into line with the condition of his day and age. Even during Mohammed's life, Islamic law changed to fit the changing conditions. There must have been developments in the shariya to deal with the industrial revolution. I would like to learn more about this. I would like us to be able to enter into a dialogue on ecology, holy places, medical ethics, food technology, etc. We all owe Islam a debt for keeping an untarnished Tawhid – unity of God – before our eyes in the past. We now need to dialogue on Tawhid in cosmic terms.

The issue of abrogation also needs detailed and caring exposition so that we know clearly what Islam teaches on the abrogation of the other Bible faiths and prophecies. It will be delicate and difficult, but necessary to do, since there were many developments in Judaism and Christianity after the Qur'an. It is a situation similar to that of Vatican II when it dealt with rabbinic Judaism after Christianity.

which is authorized for Moslems. I do know that Sufis have a four-level
hermeneutic close to that of our Kabbalists, but I have as yet no sense of
hermeneutical dialogue with Islam

We Agree to Disagree
What is it that we will not be able to agree on? What is it that we will
have to learn to live with in each other?

It seems to me that a Jew will have to learn to live with the following
aspects of Christianity. The person of Jesus of Nazareth is bound to stay
central and in the position of the Christ, the Messiah of the first coming.
Both Jew and Christian will have to wait for the Shalom order to be
instituted by the one who will complete history and fulfill the Messianic
expectations dealing with turning swords into plowshares and having lions
living with lambs. The teachings of Paul concerning the Law will remain a
shibboleth between us until the day comes when we all no longer see by
looking through the glass darkly, and the Tree of Knowledge will have been
supplanted by the Tree of Life.

With Moslems we will have to negotiate matters of the shariya and
the issue of abrogation. On the matter of the Razulship of Mohammed, we
may find accommodation. I pray that we learn to agree first on matters
dealing with more practical issues and find a way for the children of Issac and
Ishmael to live in peace.

I am convinced that learning Torah together is an important prelude
to the kind of dialogue we will hold with each other when our eschatological
expectations will have been fulfilled. I trust we each will find that we were
right, though not quite in the way we thought we would be. Only by holding
on to our shape and color do we form the mosaic in which we are God's tiles.

BASES AND BOUNDARIES FOR INTERFAITH DIALOGUE: A CHRISTIAN VIEWPOINT*

Monika Konrad Hellwig**

This paper is written directly from experience. It is not a survey of previously-published scholarly and official church statements. While in itself useful and necessary, such a survey scarcely seems to serve the purpose of the present dialogue.[1] A statement from experience, on the other hand, is useful

* *Journal of Ecumenical Studies,* 14:3 (Summer, 1977).

** Monika Konrad Hellwig (Roman Catholic) holds an M. A. and a Ph.D. (1968) from Catholic University of America, and completed other graduate studies at the Universities of Notre Dame, Oklahoma, and Pennsylvania. From 1962-64, she was a ghost-writer/research assistant at the Vatican, then handled the English Language Desk at Pius XII International Center in Rome. She taught at Catholic University and at De Paul, then became a lecturer at the Theology Dept. at Georgetown University, where she is now a full professor. She has frequently lectured and conducted workshops for diocesan and parish groups, clergy, etc., in the U.S. Venezuela, Ghana, Uganda, and Kenya. She has written numerous articles and several books, most recently *The Eucharist and the Hunger of the World;* she is also contributing to an interfaith collection of Passover Haggadah (ed. Leon Klenicki) and to Alan T. Davies' forthcoming Paulist Press book, *Anti-Semitism and the Foundations of Christianity.* She is an Associate Editor of J. E. S.

[1] Such surveys are available, though none cover the whole area of the three-way dialogue. Besides the documents listed specifically in note 2 below, current official or semi-official instances of dialogue are recorded in the periodicals, SIDIC, *Oigins, The Bridge* (all reporting mainly those encounters with Catholic participation), and in the various publications of the World Council of Churches (reporting mainly Protestant initiatives organized on an international scale). On the history of Jewish-Christian relations, there exists a huge literature. A very comprehensive bibliography is available in Roy A. Eckardt, *Elder and Younger Brothers* (New York: Scribner's, 1967), pp. 179-184. The history of Christian-Islamic and Jewish-Islamic relations is not as readily or extensively accessible to English-speaking

only in proportion to its fidelity to what is actually taking place within the community as a whole. The task of this paper, therefore, is understood as one of discerning within the Christian communities at present the possibilities for a deeper engagement in dialogue with the Jewish and Muslim communities, and discerning likewise the factors that may restrain the Christian communities from such deeper engagement.[2] What may be the possibilities and restraints operating with the Jewish and Muslim communities is understood here to be the task of the complementary papers.

It must be acknowledged clearly at the outset that Christianity is not a univocal tradition, and that Christian communities and denominations today will not all agree to particular proposals concerning dialogue. In order that there may be a clear and sharp focus, this paper is presented primarily from the point of view of the Roman Catholic tradition, with an acknowledgement of major differences with other groups where appropriate. The task is further complicated by wide doctrinal variation even within particular

---

readers. An excellent "Introductory Bibliography" is offered in James Kritzeck, *Sons of Abraham* (Baltimore: Helicon, 1965), pp. 117-126.

[2] For the Roman Catholic community, the Documents of Vatican II have been taken as setting out an Official Church consensus. They are available in Walter M. Abbott ed., *The Documents of Vatican II* (New York: America Press, 1966). Of particular interest are *Lumen Gentium* (the Dogmatic Constitution on the Church), pp. 14-96; *Nostra Aetate* (the Declaration on the Relationship of the Church to Non-Christian Religions), pp. 660-668. This last is further developed in relation to the Jewish community by the *Guidelines for Jewish-Christian Relations,* issued December 1, 1974, by the Vatican Commission for Relations with the Jews (*Origins,* January 9, 1975, pp. 463-464); by a statement on *Pastoral Orientations with Regard to the Attitude of Christians towards Judaism (La Croix,* April 18, 1973); and by a pastoral message of the U. S. Bishops, *The Church and the Synagogue,* issued November 20, 1975 (*Origins,* December 4, 1975, pp. 384-386).

In relation to Islam, the Declaration, *Nostra Aetate,* is further developed in *Guidelines for a Dialogue between Muslims and Christians* (Rome: Edizone Ancora, 1969), promulgated by Paul Cardinal Marella on behalf of the Vatican Secretariat for Non-Christians. The Tripoli statement "Moslum-Christian Dialogue" of February 6, 1976 (made jointly by Vatican delegates and Muslim representatives), *Origins,* March 18, 1976, was not endorsed by the Vatican Secretariat.

Outside the Roman Catholic Church, the principal documents available are from the World Council of Churches, but represent papers read by individual participants at W.C.C. conferences rather than statements of the Council as such. They include *Dialogue between Men of Living Faiths* (New York: World Council of Churches, 9173); *Christian-Muslim Dialogue* (New York: World Council of Churches, 1972); *Jewish-Christian Dialogue: Six Years of Christian-Jewish Consultations* (New York: World Council of Churches, 1975); and *Toward World Community* (New York, World Council of Churches, 1975).

churches and denominations, especially the range of positions from a strictly fundamentalist to a radically critical interpretation of documents and doctrines.[3]

It might at first sight appear that it is our common convictions that propel us to dialogue and our unique convictions that set the limits to that dialogue. A more complex pattern is here proposed: it is the very nature of the Christian's commitment to proclaim the experience of Jesus of Nazareth as Savior and Word of God that propels the Christian community to dialogue with respect for the freedom and the truth of the others.[4] More particularly it propels Christians to a dialogue with other communities claiming a message of universal salvation. Among these the dialogue becomes more immediately urgent with those whose proclamation of universal salvation stems from the same biblical roots but branches out into quite different interpretations of history.[5]

This will certainly appear as a highly contrary thesis. Yet it is evident that if Christians could regard Jesus as savior of a statically defined Christian sector of the human race, there would be little urgency or theological need for dialogue. Christians could then live side by side with those of other persuasions, quietly minding their own business, inquiring perhaps into the folkways and beliefs of other communities for diplomatic or purely academic reasons. Such dialogue would remain forever peripheral to Christian theology and Christian identity. It is precisely because they proclaim a universal salvation, and proclaim the centrality of Jesus of Nazareth as a saving power in the history of the whole human race, that Christians are driven to dialogue by a systematic and practical exigence that arises out of the very center of the Christian understanding and commitment. The

---

[3] By "strictly fundamentalist" is here meant that understanding which insists on the literal sense of the words as self-evident to the contemporary believer. By "radically critical" is meant that style of interpretation which is willing to submit the words to investigation by any and all available scholarly criteria from any discipline.

[4] The assertion is made in conscious contradiction of the positions usually taken in dialogue situations, e.g., in almost all the documents listed in note 2 above.

[5] This theme has been noted frequently and probably should be attributed originally to Judah Halevi, *The Kuzari*. See translation by Hartwig Hirschfeld (New York: Schocken, 1964), p. 227.

Christian understanding and commitment can not be authentically maintained within the Christian community if it is not in fact engaged in the continuous dynamic of serious dialogue with outsiders.

The subject matter of such dialogue obviously is not a debate over the conflicting truth claims of different traditions. Sober reflections on the nature of religious language and religious experience and on the cultural and epistemological bases of religious claims have long since convinced thinking persons of all traditions that there is no "unbiased" procedure by which to judge among the conflicting truth claims of different traditions. The subject matter of such dialogue from the Christian viewpoint must be concerned with the nature of salvation. Because Christians are committed to proclaiming salvation in Jesus the Christ, they are required by their own commitment to seek an understanding to what that salvation is, why it is linked to the person of Jesus, and how it can be universally meaningful. Christians are bound to tell their story and to listen in order to learn what others hear in it. Likewise they are bound to listen to stories of the other traditions, to try to find out what their understanding of salvation is; why it is linked to particular persons, events, and teachings; and how it can be meaningful in terms of their own experience. They are bound to this simply by the demands for inner coherence of their own stance.

Thus far the need for dialogue would direct Christians equally toward Hindus, Buddhists, and even Marxists. But the demands become very much more urgent in relation to Jews and Muslims, though the pattern is not quite symmetrical in these two relationships. The Christian community looks toward the Jews with the claim that the Christian community, though still looking forward to a final fulfillment, has already experienced through the person of Jesus the definitive realization of the promises and hopes of Israel. For its own self-understanding, therefore, the Christian community is required to search not only for the sense in which those hopes and promises were understood by Israel before the time of Jesus, but also for the way they are understood now by those who expect salvation in the Jewish tradition and not through the person of Jesus of Nazareth. In other words, without intent to proselytize but rather for their own understanding of their own position,

Christians are driven to ask Jews what it is that they expect and do not see in the person and the followers of Jesus of Nazareth.[6]

When Christians turn in the direction of the Muslims, their question and their quest are somewhat different. In effect they must ask themselves, and therefore they must ask the Muslims, why the message of salvation in Jesus the Christ with its universal claim has in the course of history been complemented by a vast people, gathered from many nations, coming likewise to worship the God of Israel, but in a distinctively different tradition that denies the universality of the Christian claim. For their own self-understanding, Christians must ask themselves what the experience of being called to salvation is for those who are brought into submission to the one God as followers of the Prophet. They must ask wherein lies the difference between Christians and Muslims in the interpretation of the ancient hopes and promises passed on to them from Israel.

Of course, these questions to Jews and Muslims could be asked simply in the context of ethnology and of social and political and cultural history, and within these contexts they could be answered. But if these answers were to be taken as complete, they could lead only to a sense of the cultural relativity of all convictions and a certain cynical indifference to the truth claims of one's own tradition. The questions must be asked seriously in a theological context, expecting further insight into the various ways that the need for salvation is experienced and understood, and into the various ways that persons, events, and teachings promising salvation have been experienced and understood.

The dialogue concerning the meaning of salvation can not and does not take place in a vacuum, however. It assumes the meaning of some common terms and understandings and the need to explain some unique terms. What follows is an attempt to set out the more important points in each of these categories from the Christian perspective.

---

[6] This thesis is consonant with the potentially significant but actually little noticed dialogic ecclesiology set out by Pope Paul VI in his inaugural encyclical letter, *Ecclesiam suam,* August 6, 1964, A.A.S., Vol. 56 (1964), pp. 609-659, available in English translation, *His Church* (Huntingdon, IN: Our Sunday Visitor Inc., 1964).

Judaism, in its concern for the practical and the mystical, owes much to Christianity for systematic theology. The current rabbinate as a clerical and pastoral, instead of a judicial, vocation came to us as a result of the influence of Christianity. One cannot listen to synagogue music without sensing the influence of sacred music from the church. Modern seminary education is clearly modeled after the Christian paradigm.

At times I wish that the dialogue had developed before we copied from Christians and Christians from us. We might have voiced our caveats to the total vernacularization of the Christian liturgy. Our experience with Reform Judaism might have helped the church. Conversely, we needed to learn some of the caveats for candidacy to seminaries without a sense of vocation. Heinrich Heine said, "Wie es Christelt sich, so Juedelts sich." I only wish that would have been the result of critical scrutiny, not merely external emulation.

The Dialogue of Hermeneutics

In this dialogue we need to share information. How does a Jew read the Bible? What are the canons of legitimate interpretation? How does the Christian come to an interpretation of the text? In recent years teams of scholars have worked together in new and very helpful translations of the Hebrew Bible. Some Jews have made fine contributions to the understanding of the New Testament, bringing to bear parallel sources from the Talmud and the Midrashim. Other Jews have worked on the Qur'an and made worthy contributions quoted by Moslem scholars.

For all that books can offer us, the vital contact comes from studying texts together, with getting to see with the eyes of the other. In this way I have come to a fair understanding of Roman Catholic and Neo-Orthodox Protestant hermeneutics. I have met a number of Christian Old Testament scholars who knew our hermeneutic of Tanakh, though I have yet to meet a Christian scholar of Talmud Rabbinics.

Unfortunately I have no sense of Moslem hermeneutics of the Kitab al Muqqadas, the Bible. It seems to me that the way in which the Qur'an views the Bible is more a reworking of oral midrashic material than of the texts themselves. I am not even aware of an Arabic translation of the Bible

Chief among the common points of departure is certainly our understanding of the One God, transcendent, benign, provident, all-powerful, intervening in history to judge and redeem, self-revealing to those who seek, forever mysterious but offering the possibility of personal relationship in prayer and the direction of one's life.[7] To know that others claim self-revelations from the same God that we ourselves worship is an invitation to discover the content of the revelation as perceived by the others. To know that others worship the same God that we worship is to know also that somewhere in our experience there lie possibilities for common prayer, though it may only be a prayer of wordless quiet. To hold that this God intervenes in history to judge and to redeem implies a willing ear for testimonies expressing perceptions from other traditions of the judgements and the redemption.

The basis for assuming that the three traditions are in a sense on common ground here is that for all three God is an ultimately inscrutable mystery, and the self-revelation that is received is never exhaustive of the reality. Nor is that self-revelation ever apprehended in strictly appropriate concepts or in univocal images; religious language can only be the language of poetry, of analogy, of subtle hints of the inexpressible. From a fundamentalist position in which this is not admitted, there can be but little meaning to dialogue with a tradition other than one's own. If the assumption is made that not only the revelation, but all the language in which it is apprehended and expressed, is divinely guaranteed as timeless, changeless, beyond critical examination, having intrinsic and exclusive validity quite independent of historical and cultural conditioning, then there can not be a common ground from which dialogue between traditions can take place.

A second common point of departure is the (often unspoken) assumption that history has a goal, that time is not only cyclic (which it assuredly is) but also linear, that salvation is not only a salvation of the human spirit from the world but is quite comprehensively salvation of the world. The god of the biblical religions is not seen as other than Master of

---

[7] Almost all joint statements resulting from interfaith dialogue begin at this point; a clear example is in the Tripoli statement, *Origins*, March 18, 1976, p. 617.

the universe, Lord of history, Lord of all being, and Ruler of the day of reckoning. All history is under God's judgement, and all peoples are God's people summoned to find their own fulfillment in doing God's will. That will is recognized constantly as justice – justice on a grand social scale, not only a certain relative justice in one-to-one relationships.[8]

This common base seems to offer very clear grounds for dialogue among the three traditions on matters of social justice and the relief of large-scale human suffering and deprivation. At least in theory, it offers a basis for meaningful dialogue in matters as thorny and urgent as colonial oppression, racial oppression, remnants of slave trading, the State of Israel, the plight of the Palestinians, various liberation struggles, societal role restrictions on women, deprivation of civil rights of certain groups, and so forth. These obviously are not points at which dialogue might be expected to begin, but neither may they be categorically ruled out as possible areas of dialogue. The self-interest and mutual distrust of power groups may pose almost insurmountable obstacles, but the religious bases for dialogue on these issues exist in the teachings concerning a goal for all history, the ultimate unity of the whole human race before God, and the divine demand for social justice that does not exclude the poor and powerless.

Again, it must be noted that such a common base does not appear so clearly from positions more or less approximating the fundamentalist one. When it is understood that the law of God and the plan of God have been set forth once and for all, explicitly and in every detail, there can be little room for moral questions about new situations that arise in the course of time, and obedience to the divine will is readily reduced to private lives of individual persons and to certain archaic patterns of association in groups within the tradition. For dialogue among traditions there can be even less room. Yet it must also be noted that such a common base seems to be equally absent in certain liberal positions which see almost all elements of the tradition as culturally relative and expendable, simply because such positions adapt very readily to fit the national or partisan interests of their own group, and they read the situation from that vantage point.

---

[8] *Cf., ibid.*, resolutions 3-9, p. 618.

A third common base or point of departure is closely linked to the second, but does appear to be a different point. This is the election or vocation of each person and the election or vocation of the community. It is a calling to a way of life that is a communion with God and a call to community or peoplehood with prescribed patterns of relationship and duties toward others. The three traditions make reference to the same basic vocation stories concerning Noah, Abraham, and Moses, which are models of individual election but also of the elections of the people. Each tradition interprets history rather differently in the light of these stories, in applying the election or calling to itself. Yet this appears as a common point of departure and as a conviction that rather peremptorily impels the traditions to dialogue with one another (as has indeed happened, peacefully or otherwise, since early times).[9]

A community which claims to have been chosen in some special way as God's instrument of redemption of the world is compelled to ask itself how it stands in relation to other communities that claim a similar election from the same God, if only because of the need to define its own claim for its own members. Yet each community can really only come to an authentic answer to its own question in the process of open dialogue that solicits testimony from the other communities as to how they interpret their traditions and their election in the changing contexts of the present. There is no other way to distinguish oneself or one's position from others than that which begins with an attentive inquiry into the nature and the characteristics of the others.

It may seem paradoxical, yet it seems that it is the very universality and apparent mutual exclusivity of our claims that provides the necessary basis for a fruitful and substantive dialogue. Any position that attempts to reduce or obscure the claim to a unique election related to the universal plan of God would seem to reduce rather than enhance the foundations for dialogue. So, of course, will any position that sees the doctrine of election as simple, fully explicit, and univocal, and as having attained a timeless formula capable of direct and universal application. Any position between these two

---

[9] This theme is set out rather clearly by Kritzeck, *Sons of Abraham*.

moves naturally into dialogue in its quest for a more comprehensive and coherent understanding in the contemporary context.

A fourth common base has been quietly assumed in the presentation of the preceding three. This is the common heritage of biblical lore and spiritual ancestors. There is an available common language of symbols (found in persons and events), and an available common pool of models and points of reference. The biblical stories that form the common lore seem also to be precisely those that offer the most basic and universal insights and understandings, the most archetypal images and visions. Moreover, these biblical stories with their symbolism have remained both foundational and explicit in all three traditions. They carry assumptions and attitudes that may not be underestimated, as to creation, the providence of God in history, the nature of the faith response, or submission and obedience. It is, for instance, quite clear to 'Christians that when Jews and Muslims speak to each other about Isaac and Ishmael, each may not like what the other is saying, but they both understand very well what it is that they are discussing. Likewise, when Christians invoke the Pauline understanding of Isaac as the child of the promise, and claim thereby to be the true children of Abraham, Jews may object to the exegesis, but they object because they understand it. All of this offers a not insubstantial base for effective dialogue on important issues for three traditions concerned.[10]

Having given brief consideration to these four points of common basis, one is left with the task of considering those unique convictions or positions of Christianity which are bound to affect the possibilities of dialogue with the other two traditions. First and most obvious among these is the Christian preception of revelation and redemption as focused in the person of Jesus of Nazareth. At first sight this seems to be primarily a hindrance to dialogue, something for which the Christian community should apologize, explaining that it can do no other than to hold and proclaim this, but that it nevertheless wishes to enter into dialogue with its biblical neighbors.

---

[10] *Ibid.*

As pointed out in the beginning of this paper, however, such an admission and apology would seem to be premature. If the aim in dialogue is a fuller understanding of the position of the other, in order the better to grasp the inner logic of one's own position and in order to achieve some clarity and authenticity in relations with the other tradition, then the central and constitutive claim on which one's own tradition rests must be placed centrally in the dialogue also. As such, it offers a rather solid platform for an exchange of perceptions and perspectives. In confrontation with Jews and Muslims, Christians must either be silent or must give an account of what the revelation and redemption are that they have experienced in the person of Jesus of Nazareth, and they must attempt this account in language other than the technical "churchy" language which already assumes the experience. They must attempt to account for their experience and conviction in language that is experientially meaningful to those who are outsiders to the Christian tradition.[11] Such attempts can not but be sources of thoroughgoing renewal within the Christian community itself, although they will be regarded as dangers to "the Faith" by those holding more fundamentalist positions in which the technical "churchy" language stands in its own right as divinely guaranteed. Likewise, such dialogue can not but be a source of more coherent relationships with the outsiders to the tradition, although certain more liberal elements within the Christian tradition will see a danger to the ecumenical or dialogic endeavor whenever the unique claims and teachings are put forth as subject matter for interfaith conversation.

At this point, some crucial limits or restricting boundaries to the dialogue may be noted. They are not doctrinal but practical. Christians can not speak very clearly about revelation and redemption experienced in Jesus of Nazareth in the presence of Jews because centuries of anti-semitism and oppression obscure the testimony. Likewise, Christians have considerable difficulty inquiring of Jews concerning the Jewish understanding of revelation and redemption, because Jews tend to suspect a proselytizing drive and are

---

[11] Contemporary Christian theology is already well stocked with efforts to do this in relation to the existentialist perceptions (e.g., the writings of Bultmann, Tillich, Rahner), in relation to the Marxist experience (e.g., the works of Moltmann, J.B. Metz, G. Gutierrez, and J. L. Segundo), and in relation to many other currents of thought and experience.

conscious of being a minority for whom the possibility of discrimination, contempt, and outright persecution is never remote. Even in Israel today, the situation can not be said to be substantially more favorable; Jews readily interpret such inquiry as judgmental on the conduct of the State of Israel and its relations with the Palestinians, while Christians are embarrassed by being unable in conscience to give the unconditional approval to everything Israel does, which is often demanded as a prelude to serious dialogue.[12]

When Christians address themselves to Muslims in dialogue concerning revelation and redemption experienced in Jesus the Christ, and revelation and redemption as experienced according to the teachings of the Prophet Mohammed, there are again obstacles which are not doctrinal or theological, but rather practical and historical. Christian voices are heard by Muslims in the context of the Crusades and of colonialism under Christian auspices, so that any message of peace, humility, reconciliation, and forgiveness sounds quite hollow. Moreover, the Christian gospel advocacy of simplicity of life and the blessedness of the poor is seen as ludicrous in the context of the colossal economic imperialism of the "Christian" West against which all Third World nations must contend. At the same time, the situation is not much better in the other direction, because Christians are likely to hear anything the Muslims say in the context of a fear of Holy Wars, internal violence in Muslim countries, terrorism, despotic governments, oppression of women, and harsh persecution of non-Muslims. Much as this may be a caricature, it does in practice tend to cloud and obscure testimonies concerning the true nature of Islam.

These practical considerations may not be underestimated. The possibility for any genuine dialogue at all certainly depends on the willingness of some scholars and religious representatives to achieve a physiological distance from these historical and practical stumblingblocks, by willingness to consider not the achievements of the other parties but the aims and desires intrinsic in the religious position of each. More habitually each group evaluates its own position by its ideals and the position of the others by

---

[12] This observation is based on the author's own experience in Jerusalem among academics well disposed toward and well prepared for interfaith dialogue, during the academic year 1975-76.

their performance. From this nothing but further prejudice and failure of understanding can arise.

Yet even when these problems have been somewhat overcome by persons and groups particularly dedicated to dialogue, there remains at all times the question as to the extent to which they represent their respective communities. It is a frequent experience that groups with a mandate from their communities to engage in dialog draw up a coherent and far-reaching statement that represents real progress in mutual understanding among the partners to the dialogue, only to find at the end of their labors that the respective mandating authorities in their own communities will not approve the statement. Such statements are then frequently reduced to rather unsatisfactory evasions and compromises that were already in vogue before the dialogue was set up.[13] What seems to be at stake is the question whether dialogue with the other traditions can be delegated to specialized groups or whether it must be conducted at the heart of the religious and theological enterprise of each community.[14]

Having noted the negative aspects that restrict dialogue concerning the central issue for Christians, one must note two further unique convictions from the Christian viewpoint which play an important role in dialogue. One of these is the role of the church or, more accurately, of the many Christian churches which exist today in a state of considerable ambivalence toward one another. Though the churches do act jointly on some issues, and although there have been great ecumenical advances in the contemporary experience, it must frankly be admitted that the Christian churches, claiming to live by the same gospel of Jesus the Christ, are in a condition of rather extensive dissociation from one another. There is a double disadvantage for interfaith dialogue in this condition of dissociation. Not only does the dialogue tend to represent and speak for some churches and not others, but the very concept of church and the understanding of the role of the church in the society at

---

[13] This can certainly be said for the Jewish-Christian statement that was drawn up before Vatican II, in relation to what appeared in the approved texts, and again for the repeated efforts of the Vatican's post-conciliar commission.

[14] The author is indebted to Juan Luis Segundo for this insight, which is a recurring theme in the latter's writings.

large and in the redemption do in fact vary widely from church to church. The primary referent in this essay is the self-understanding of the Roman Catholic Church.

The role of the church is bound to present problems to Jewish and Muslim partners in dialogue inasmuch as it is not coextensive with a people racially, ethnically, culturally, or politically. In fact, theologically, the church can only be understood as that community of witnesses that mediates between Jesus the Christ and the final realization of the Reign of God among all human persons and peoples which Jesus proclaimed and promised. The church may be understood as an assembling or a movement of such witnesses in history, although it most obviously appears as an institution and usually as a rather powerful hierachic structure.[15] As many reflective Christians view it today and have viewed it in the course of history, the church is necessarily a counterculture force, a critique of any established regime and social structure, a radicalizing force that judges every situation in relation to the vision of the promised Reign of God.[16] Clearly this is by no means the way the church (or the larger churches taken as a group) has in fact conducted itself in most matters throughout the history of Christianity. Therefore, although it may puzzle and antagonize the outsider to the Christian tradition, Christian partners in the dialogue may say without any sense of hypocrisy or inconsistency that "the church does not condone" actions and situations which the outsider sees being done by Christians and perhaps even by those who appear as church representatives.

The church claims to be the gathering of those who have been "reborn" in the experience that Jesus who was crucified and died has burst forth again in irrepressible and unquenchable vitality that permeates the whole human race and all history with new and undreamed-of possibilities of fulfillment, reconciliation, and community. In Christian theology such persons become a witness community in a double sense: they have witnessed in the rebirth in their own lives the coming of the Reign of God,

---

[15] These conflicting modes are expressed very clearly in *Lumen gentium.*

[16] *Cf.* Hans Küng, *Structures of the Church* (Notre Dame, IN: University of Notre Dame Press, 1964) and *The Church* (New York: Sheed & Ward, 1967). Also, J. B. Metz, ed., *The Church and the World of Politics* (New York: Paulist Press, 1967).

and they bear witness to others by their community life, their hope, their service, and their transforming impact. They do this, ideally, "from within," that is, in community with similarly "reborn" persons – all willingly and creatively changing their relationships with one another to express what they have experienced.[17]

In this ideal picture, the "elect among the nations" who are called to this witness function are not thereby cut off from their diverse cultural and political affiliations, though these all become relativized in the light of an over-riding interest in the community of all the human race – an interest which is most particularly concerned with the poor, the outcast, and the suffering, as perennially represented by the Crucified.[18] The issue is of course immensely complicated by the fact that through the centuries, sometimes by conquest, sometimes by princely "conversion" of whole peoples, there came about the identification of Christianity with the whole of Western culture and with the political structure of Europe, which we named Christendom, which was in due time extended also to the whole of the North and South American continents. It is quite common to speak of these as "Christian nations" and indeed governments often invoke Christian beliefs in their support, as in the power struggles of the West with the Communist countries, but from the point of view of most Christian ecclesiologies (which strongly favor separation of church and state) the term is almost meaningless.[19] Most Christian spokespersons, whether church officials or theologians, will not accept the actions of their governments as attributable to the Christian community as such.

The clarification of this position is obviously rather important to interfaith dialogue, because both Jews and Muslims envisage as the ideal an integrated peoplehood in which the religious convictions are expressed in

---

[17] For an analysis of the various models and perceptions of the church, see Avery Dulles, *Models of the Church* (Garden City: Doubleday, 1974). And *cf.* Pier Cesare Bori, *Koinonia* (Brescia: Paideia Editrice, 1972).

[18] *Cf.* J. B. Metz, "The Future in the Memory of Suffering," in J. B. Metz, ed., *New Questions on God* (New York: Herder, 1972), pp. 9-25.

[19] This has not always been so and not universally so now. For example, Spanish and Portuguese colonialism were officially sanctioned by the Catholic Church, while the Church of England is nationally established in a bond of mutual support with the government.

political, legal, economic, and cultural as well as religious ritual forms. This
sets some limits or boundaries to the dialogue, which again involves practical,
historical, as well as theoretical, problems. It may be very puzzling and
irritating to Jews that Christian nations and even Christian churches have
stood so aloof in the Lebanese civil strife, instead of leaping to the defense of
their "Christian brothers and sisters" against the Muslims of that country.
Israeli Jews may find it hard to understand that the so-called Christian
nations do not experience any particular bond with the Christians of
Lebanon, while all Jews may be horrified that the churches have generally
been more concerned to disentangle the questions of social justice involved
in the conflict than to support "their own".[20]

A parallel problem arises in dialogue with Muslims, who frequently
ask why Christian nations and Christian churches express support for the
State of Israel when they should be supporting and defending their Arab
Christian brothers and sisters from aggression, land expropriation, exile,
deprivation of political rights, and harsh oppression.[21] Thus Jews and
Muslims use the same argument as an obstacle to dialogue, though for
diametrically opposed practical purposes. The strong and fairly monolithic
alignments of interest in the case both of both Jews and Muslims on a
worldwide basis render it urgent, but also difficult, for Christians to represent
their own total allegiance to the gospel as taking priority over their qualified
allegiance to any particular group. It may well be that it is only in the context
of a three-way interfaith dialogue that this particular element of dialogue can
be put in its proper perspective.

The last and most crucial point to be made concerning the unique
claims and teachings in the Christian tradition is of course that of the
Trinitarian conception of God and the claim of divinity made on behalf of
Jesus of Nazareth. It may seem at first sight that the very admission of these
two doctrines simply vitiates all that has gone before. It seems so because
the history of previous encounters over the centuries may suggest that

---

[20] The author has heard both positions expressed rather frequently.

[21] Expressed vigorously to the author by Muslim Arabs both in the U.S. and during a stay on
the West Bank.

interfaith dialogue comes to an impasse at that point. But previous encounters were conducted with a frame of reference much closer to simplistic fundamentalist positions, and much less aware of the cultural relativity and analogous nature of all religious language. It would seem to be supremely worthwhile to re-engage in dialogue precisely on these points, remembering again that the point of the dialogue is not proselytizing but the clarification of one's perception of the position of the others, in order thereby to clarify one's perception of one's own position and engage in more realistic and authentic relationships.

It should be no secret to Jews and Muslims that the doctrines of the Trinitarian Godhead and of the divinity of Jesus have been and are the subjects of searching inquiry, reflection, and renewed attempts at appropriate formulation by Christian scholars within their own circles, quite apart from the demands of interfaith dialogue.[22] At the risk of over-simplification within this limited space, it may be said very briefly what the minimal formulations of these ancient doctrines are.[23] As to the Trinitarian "image" or conception of God, one may say with Josef Ratzinger that Christian faith is at pains to preserve at all costs a paradox it is not able logically to resolve – a paradox that reflects as faithfully as it can – certain irreducible elements of the Christian experience. Christians worship the transcendent God of Israel, yet they know that in Jesus they had a self-validating experience of what it is to be in the presence of God uttered or expressed within history and within the human community, and at the same time they know that their experience of the presence and the power of God was not only in the person of Jesus long ago in history, but is in the Spirit that is alive and active now within the community of believers. Moreover, Christian faith is committed to the confident conviction that these diving self-revelations may be trusted, that God is in inner reality truthfully as God is revealed to us

---

[22] E.g., in Paul Tillich, *Systematic Theology* (Chicago: University of Chicago Press, 1951); in Karl Rahner, *Theological Investigations*, especially Vol. 13 (New York: Seabury, 1975); in Jürgen Moltmann, *The Crucified God* (New York: Harper, 1974); in the various Christologies of the "process theologians"; etc.

[23] There is no possibility for present unanimity among Christians on this point; therefore, particular and generally accepted authors are followed here.

in history, though the reality clearly transcends what human knowing and imagining can grasp.[24] Jesus is experienced as the fullest possible, and therefore the definitive, self-expression of God in history and within the human community. Yet it must be said quickly that Jesus is not seen dissociated from the rest of the human race, but rather as "heading" or incorporating the human race within his own person and experience – a process that is seen as being yet unfinished.[25]

The scandal of the particularity of the claims made for Jesus certainly stands at the heart of Christian faith, and raises the question as to the possibility of dialogue. Inasmuch as the religious language of the divinity claim – Son, Word, Image, light from light, one in being with the Creator, and so forth – is capable of the most varied and nuanced interpretations, much careful exploration of the meaning would seem to be appropriate in interfaith dialogue. However, the appropriate pathway into this exploration is by way of that which can be judged by outsiders by reference to their own experience. With reference to Christology that approach is through the experiential analysis of what is meant by salvation and why Christians claim a foretaste of salvation in their association with Jesus as the Christ.

It would seem to be suitable to conclude this essay with the question whether there is a language or a model that might serve in such interfaith dialogue as has been envisaged here. A language and model that would seem to be appropriate from the point of view of all three traditions is the biblical notion of the covenant or alliance of God with the people. As presented in the Hebrew scriptures, there appears to be only one covenant, expressed in various modes of participation – the covenant of creation realized in the Noachic covenant, very precisely focused and explicitly expressed in the intimate participation of the Abrahamic and Mosaic covenant. Jews have been willing to grant that Christians and Muslims claim rather a complementary participation in the Abrahamic covenant, and each claims in its own way to bring that covenant to its consummation. Inasmuch as all three traditions own and understand this language of covenant, it seems

---

[24] Josef Ratzinger, *Introduction to Christianity* (New York: Herder, 1970), Part I, Chap. 5.

[25] *Cf. ibid.*, especially Part II, and Piet Schoonenberg, *The Christ* (New York: Herder, 1971).

to provide an appropriate arena for an exchange of the alternative interpretations of the history of salvation (and the salvation of history).[26]

There is a further image that seems to offer a very viable context for dialogue, and that is the image of the seed and the tree with the two great branches, proposed by Yehuda Halevi.[27] Israel sees itself as a witness people for God and as situated at the heart of the redemptive process, yet does not generally reach out in proselytizing efforts. Christianity and Islam see themselves as rooted in the revelation and promised redemption inherited from Israel, but as sent out to embrace all the nations. This much has not changed since the time of Yehuda Halevi, and the image appears to be as generative now as it was then.

---

[26] *Cf.* Kritzeck, *Sons of Abraham.*

[27] *Ibid.,* p. 227.

NEW PERSPECTIVES FOR A JEWISH-CHRISTIAN-MUSLIM DIALOGUE*

Mohammed Arkoun**

I have been involved in interreligious dialogue, especially Muslim-Christian dialogue, for more than twenty years. During this time I have attended many meetings, conferences, and seminars; given several lectures and courses; and written books and articles dealing more or less with the cultural and scientific conditions of a modern, critical view of the religious legacies of these three monotheistic communities.

The ongoing political struggle between several Muslim societies and Western societies, the tragic ongoing conflict between "Jews" and "Arabs" (actually Israelis and Palestinians), the presence in European societies of important Muslim minorities – all generate more and more obstacles, misunderstandings, and misrepresentations that feed the social "imagination" of every nation or community against the "Others." Instead of seeing new possibilities opening up for learning, integrating, and revising old prejudices, we too often witness violent mass-media campaigns against "Islamic radicalism," "Islamic fundamentalism," and "Islamic violence and terrorism." Almost no newspaper or journalist speaks of liberal Islam, although there are liberal Muslim intellectuals in each of their countries who write, teach, and

* *Journal of Ecumenical Studies*, 26.3, (Summer, 1989).

** Mohammed Arkoun (Muslim) was born in Algeria, educated there and in Paris. He is the author of numerous articles and books. He is Professor of Islamics at the Sorbonne in Paris and has been visiting Professor at Temple University.

participate in the heated debates on current issues. Leonard Binder seems to be about the only scholar who has published a book with such a title as *Islamic Liberalism* (Chicago: University of Chicago Press, 1988).

This situation is not favorable to a fruitful dialogue among the three monotheistic religions. The fact is that most competent theologians themselves are not intellectually prepared to engage in and to follow up an inquiry on common theological issues on a new scientific basis. On the contrary, from my own experience I can point to the frequent open opposition of official Christian theologians who consider my attempt to initiate a critical evaluation of Islamic reasons as a dangerous threat to Christian theological reason. The use of the human and social-scientific methodologies is rejected as irrelevant to a "spiritual" perspective that is central in the "study" of religions; it "reduces" the "faith" to an ordinary object of knowledge.

This kind of debate is well known as has been recurrent since the Middle Ages when philosophers and theologians struggled over "truth" by opposing "faith" and "reason." It is vital that we not fall again into this wrong-headed scholastic debate. Even though in fact many theologians, and also social scientists, are still prisoners of the old repeated categories, themes, or concepts, we must, nevertheless, get beyond their dogmatic statements and contradictions. This can only be done by training in the new scholarship in the context of the new intellectual-spiritual framework of thinking, writing, evaluating, and knowing – approaching the ultimate question of *meaning*.

Nevertheless, I must again stress the *psychological* obstacle that dominates most participants in the current religious dialogue. Members of each community feel obliged to stand up against the others – not to enter into the other' perspectives, but to protect, proclaim, and ascertain the specific "values" or unsurpassable "authenticity" or their own religion. Theological references are then used as *cultural systems for mutual exclusion*, never as tools to cross the traditional boundaries and to practice *new* religious thinking.

The most despairing fact is that scholarship – even in the departments of religion, history, anthropology, or sociology in secular (public or private) universities – most frequently does not help us to move toward this new religious thinking. Religions are still taught separately with very few, weak interdisciplinary exchanges. More than that, Islam is not present as a case study in the majority of the departments mentioned. When and where Islam *is* taught, it is most often relegated to departments of "Near Eastern Studies," or to a "Middle Eastern Center" if it is taught in a department of religion. There is no opportunity to develop a common approach and a significant program for the three "revealed religions," or "religions of the book." Again, each religion is taught apart from the others. No one is exposed to the questions – eventually the criticisms – of the two others. Even my experience at the Religion Department of Temple University for two years (1988-1990) confirms this situation totally, although my colleagues, as individuals, are totally open to the comparative perspectives I am mentioning.

Scholars involved in the study of any religion can test, and confirm, my assertion through their experience. There are only two kinds of institutions where religion is taken as an object of study: First are theological seminaries or institutes (such as Princeton Theological Seminary or the Institute Catholicque in Paris), where all religions are considered from the viewpoint of *Religio vera* (with mutual exclusion). Second are departments in secular universities with the usual divisions or distinctions among,

(a)   primal, archaic societies, with primal religions studies by "ethnographers";

(b)   premodern, traditional societies with conservative, rigid, fundamentalist religions (mostly Muslim societies);

(c)   modern, developed societies where Christianity is the dominant religion, strongly committed to the trend of modernization. The Euro-American model of learning, thinking, and production of culture and civilization is equated to Christianity (especially the Protestant churches promoted by Max Weber to the historical role in the generation of capitalism, liberal philosophy, and the underlying political and economic system of the "West"). These divisions and categories have a powerful impact on teaching and scholarship. This points up the hierarchical relationship between *political* reason and so-called *scientific* reason, as far as the study of religions is concerned. (I leave out of this oveview the case of technological and scientific reason in the hard sciences.)

During the colonial period, from 1800 to 1960, Christianity shared the supremacy of capitalist knowledge and power in undertaking a conversion of primitive people chained to "wrong" religions. In the present period of "decolonization" or liberation, Christianity still has the historical privilege of being the religion of highly developed societies. It has participated in secularizing thought and situations to such an extent that Christians accept being, sociologically, a minority among atheists and secularized religious citizens. The status of religion is strongly questioned in societies such as France and even Italy; the debate between Christianity and "modernity" or secularism does not include other religions, especially Islam and Judaism, that are present everywhere in European societies. This shows how societies that are deeply concerned with scientific knowledge and technology can remain closed, even hostile, to "values" and "cultures" considered alien, disturbing, primitive, or uncivilized. It is amazing how these "modern," "free," "egalitarian" societies are reluctant to consider their prejudices, intellectual conservatism, xenophobia, and cultural narrowness – combined with an arrogant claim of superiority, true knowledge, and progress (certainly true in material civilization, which is not necessarily supported by a commonly shared intellectual modernity).

In this context where struggling ideologies are at work, it seems totally romantic, irrelevant, and useless to engage in debates between religions about traditional faiths, values, or dogmas. Positive and efficient initiatives should be taken in the field of education – primary and secondary schools, universities, the mass media, nongovernmental organizations, and other private and public institutions – so as to promote a new teaching of history, *comparative* cultures, *comparative* religions, *comparative* philosophies and theologies, *comparative* literature and law.

History is still taught for *nationalist* purposes; it is a glorification of the nation or the community, not a critical analysis of all the historical forces at work in a large area disputed by several nations for their own interest. This approach would lead to a better understanding of the ideological role of all religion in the genesis of "nations" and nationalism. We know how this issue was central in the nineteenth century and still is today in Muslim and all third-world countries. It is not acceptable to teach religious "values" on one side and to let political leaders manipulate these "values" for imperialist purposes on the other. Although this situation is known at present, nothing is undertaken by the states or by the religious institutions to elucidate the relationships between "values" and political strategies; the programs of education are still largely desperately deficient concerning this huge, ongoing, and universal issue.

Comparative methodology is still largely absent in current teaching and scholarship. Here I would mention only one example to show how far we are from what I call new religious thinking. While *revelation* is claimed to be the common supreme reference for Judaism, Christianity, and Islam, each community speaks for its own (and "true") conception of revelation, without any kind of distinction among the three levels of the concept:

(a)   Revelation as the word of God, transcendent, infinite, unknown to us as a whole, only fragments of it having been revealed through prophets like Jesus; this level is well expressed in the Qur'an by such expressions as "the well preserved Table" (*al-lawh al-mahfuz)* or "the Archtype Book" (*Umm al-Kitab).*

(b)   The historical manifestations of the work of God (level 1) through the Israelite prophets (in Hebrew), Jesus of Nazareth (in Aramaic), and Mohammed (in Arabic). Originally, this level was *oral*; it was memorized and transmitted orally during a long period before it was written down. In the case of the Qur'an the revelation lasted twenty years and was written down another twenty years after the death of the prophet. In the case of Jesus, it is interesting to note that the wording was in Aramaic, a Semitic language sharing all the cultural connotations of Semitic culture in the Middle East, while the Evangelists reported the teachings of Jesus in Greek, a fact that led to the decisive shift from a Semitic to a Greek-Mediterranean culture. Likewise, the later translation of the Hebrew Bible and the Gospels into Latin and other languages had immeasurable consequences on the emergence of new cultural *codes*, or new semiological systems – not effectively considered up to now by theologians or historians.

(c)   The third level is the most influential in the history of the Book/book. Here, we raise new problems and open up a new space of intelligibility for the three religions; it is no longer a question of an *encounter* between the religions but, rather, a program for a common endeavor to reinterpret the totality of our religious and theological traditions. The third level means the revelation written down and preserved in what I call the *official closed canons*. This concept is extremely important; it refers to many *historical* facts depending on social and political agents, not on God. Let us elaborate it more clearly.

A *linguistic corpus* or canon is a body of texts collected in one or several volumes; in the case of the "holy" texts, we have a sacralized copy called *Byblos* (the Book) or *Mushaf* (the pages arranged together in a single copy) for the Qur'an. In Arabic, "Qur'an" refers at the same time to all three levels. (The Mu'tazilit school endeavored to distinguish the third level [*Mushaf*] from the first and even the second. They asserted the theory of God's created speech, unfortunately rejected by "orthodoxy," which has been the prevailing conception since the eleventh century C.E.)

Who decided about the texts to be collected, the way to transcribe it when the alphabet in Hebrew or Arabic was still uncertain, especially for the vowels? Who decided that text A belonged to revelation and text B or C or D did not? Who fixed the number to texts to be included in the canon and then closed the canon so that no text could be added or suppressed and no word changed or read in a way different from the "original" form given when the canon was closed?

The Rabbis, the church Fathers, and the *'Ulama* (the Companions and the followers—*Sahaba and Tabi'un* for the Qur'an) made all these decisions; they are the official "authority" recognized in each "tradition." Tradition, then, means a lengthy process with successive agents leading to a final result that for the three communities is commonly labeled the "Holy Scriptures" or the "Holy Book." The lengthy process that led to the constitution of the official closed cannons has been studied by philologists from the *historicist* perspective since the nineteenth century. The German school is particularly known in this trend of "modern" scholarship: even the Qur'an was studied for the first time with this philological approach by German scholars—among whom Th. Noldeke has a prominent place.

This is not the place to mention the positive and negative aspects of the philological study of religious texts in general. More important and enlightening for the dialogue are two points that I wish to stress. First, modern linguistics and semiotics have developed a theory of *texts*. What are the roles of the "author" and the "reader", and what is their interacting impact on the text? While these are the main questions raised in literary criticism, they have not yet been fully applied to sacred religious texts.

Second, the official closed canons are the common, large linguistic and cultural space in which revelation is approached, interpreted, and used in the three revealed religions. The theological status of revelation in each tradition does not and cannot affect the canon as a collection of texts insofar as these texts are read as *linguistic* theological commandments. Linguistic evidence should precede any theological speculation on revelation, not the other way around as we have done for so many centuries.

Since the witnesses of revelation have all disappeared, there is no possibility for later generations to have access to the "word of God" except through *texts* collected in the official closed canons. There is no point, then, to objecting to a linguistic, semiotic reading of the texts from the perspective of the differences among Christian, Jewish, and Islamic *theological* definitions of revelation. These definitions are legitimate in maintaining the living tradition of each community, but they cannot be used to justify the rejection of the linguistic evidence that may differ from, correct, or deny the dogmatic definitions generated by later mental projections of various beliefs on the original texts.

I have shown all this with the example of the Qur'an (cf. my *Lectures du Coran*[1] and *Critique de la Raison islamique*[2]). The methodology and the problematic, however, should be generalized to the other official closed canons to provide a common epistemological basis for the study of the societies of the Book/book – "*B*" referring to levels (1) and (2): "*b*" to level (3), including all the juridical and theological literature derived from the official closed canons through the special methods and postulates of medieval exegesis or philological procedures, or even the well-known technique of *Formgeschichte*.

The linguistic and semiotic reading of the official closed canons is enriched and enlarged by all the recent developments of political, cultural, and social anthropology. The new definitions of myth, rationality, and reason

---

[1] (Paris: Maisonneuve et Larose, 1982).

[2] (Paris: Maisonneuve et Larose, 1984).

related to the concept of the "imagination" provided an open scientific framework that will deliver us from the reductionist interpretations of the sacred as it triumphed with the demythologization approach. Unfortunately, however, as I pointed out above, present scholarship – let alone the "managers of the sacred" – is frequently not acquainted with the new trends in anthropology represented by Clifford Gertz, Claude Leve-Strauss, J. Goody, E. Gellner, P. Bourdieu, James Boom, etc. The *ethos* of academic scholarship is still dominated by postulates proper to the Age of Enlightenment reason viewing religion as a negative influence on human societies and doomed to vanish with the triumph of science. A strong trend in secularism is linked to this view. New anthropology, on the contrary, reinterprets all rationalities produced throughout history without any attempt to declare one of them superior to the others. This has been done and still prevails with theological reason on one side and, on the other side, its most explicit enemy: positivist, historicist, scientistic reason. Both, however, are criticized by a critical reason that uses several methods and is flexible enough to submit its own findings to the same critical tools and strategy.

This is, in very short, allusive terms, my proposal as a Muslim scholar – not to contribute, I repeat, to an encounter that would mean that we think and work within the framework of *I and we vs. you and them* but to the creation of new space of intelligibility and freedom. We need to be emancipated from inherited traditions not yet studied and interpreted with controlled methods and cognitive principles.

Muslims are currently accused of being closed-minded, integrists, fundamentalists, prisoners of dogmatic beliefs. Here is a liberal, modern, humanist, Muslim proposal. I await the response of Jews, Christians, and secularists to my invitation to engage our thoughts, our endeavors, and our history in the cause of peace, progress, emancipation, justice through knowledge, and shared spiritual values.

JESUS IN JEWISH-CHRISTIAN-MUSLIM DIALOGUE*

Fathi Osman, Zalman Schachter, Gerard S. Sloyan, and
Dermot A. Lane**

* *Journal of Ecumenical Studies*, 14:3 (Summer, 1977).

** Zalman Schachter (Jewish) has been Professor of Religion in Jewish Mysticism at Temple University since 1975. Previous teaching experience includes the University of Winnipeg, Brandeis University, the Univ. of Calif. at Santa Cruz, Naropa Institute, and the Pacific School of Religion. He has service as facilitator at several growth institutes and clergy training centers. He holds a D.H.L. from Hebrew Union College (1968). Rabbi Schachter has written widely in the fields of Hebrew literature, Jewish Mysticism, and human relations.

Gerard S. Sloyan (Roman Catholic) is a professor of religion and past department chairperson at Temple University, where he has taught since 1967. From 1950-1967, he taught at Catholic University of America (instructor to professor), after three years serving as curate in two New Jersey parishes. His many books include *Is Christ the End of the Law?* (Westminister, 1978), *Commentary on the New Lectionary* (Paulist Press, 1975), and *Jesus on Trial* (Fortress, 1973), and he has published dozens of articles in liturgical and biblical fields. He is an Associate Editor of J.E.S.

Mohamed Fathi Osman (Muslim) holds degrees from Cairo and Alexandria Universities, and Princeton University (Ph.D., 1976). He lectured at Oran University (Algeria), Riyadh University (Saudi Arabia), and Princeton, before coming to Temple University as an assistant professor of religion in 1975 (on leave 1976-77). He has also served as a translator, and as a governmental advisor in Egypt and Algeria. *Arabic Quarterly* has published two of his articles, and *An Introduction to Islamic History and Historiography* is in its second edition.

Dermot A. Lane (Roman Catholic) holds a B.A. from University College, Dublin, and studied theology at Holy Cross College, being ordained in 1967 in Dublin. He completed doctoral studies in theology in 1970 at the Angelicum in Rome. He is a Professor of Systematic Theology in Holy Cross College and Mater Dei Institute of Education in Dublin, chairs the Irish Theological Association (1977), and is Ecclesiastical Assistant to the World Union of Catholic Women's Organizations. He taught at the Summer Institute at St. Michael's College, Winooski, VT, 1976 and 1977. Author of several articles and *The Reality of Jesus*, he is editing a forthcoming book on liberation theology.

INTRODUCTION

The following is a Jewish-Christian Muslim dialogue on Jesus in the form of three brief review articles on a book and a response by the book's author. The book is by a Christian, and the reviews are by a Jew, another Christian, and a Muslim. The book at the basis of this dialogue is Dermot A. Lane's *The Reality of Jesus* (Dublin: Veritas Press, 1975), 180 pp., fl.80, paper; American edition: (New York: Paulist Press, 1977), 180 pp., $3.95, paper.

There are many important potential topics of dialogue among Jews, Christians, and Muslims, but one of the most key is the significance of Jesus of Nazareth. Jesus is central to Christianity, and is both the central bridge and barrier between Christianity and Judaism, and Christianity and Islam. Obviously the three-way dialogue on Jesus here is only the most modest of beginnings. However, the longest of journeys must start with a first step.

Leonard Swidler

Fathi Osman

The current renewal taking place in theology could be summed up in terms of a return to the origins of Christianity. This going back to the beginnings brings us into direct contact with the person of Jesus Christ....[T]he full mystery of Jesus Christ can be broken down into two parts....(a) the Christ-Event, and (b) the universal significance of that event for understanding life itself....The historical side of the Christ-Event consists in the given fact that a man called Jesus of Nazareth appeared two thousand years ago within the history of Judaism. The theological significance of this fact is to be found in the confession that this Jesus of Nazareth is the definitive visitation of God to mankind in history....The Jesus part of [the simple formula "Jesus Christ"] refers to the historical side of the Christ-Event, whereas the Christ part embraces the theological significance of this given fact. Unfortunately popular usage has tended to employ the word "Christ" as a proper name for Jesus of Nazareth whereas in primitive Christianity the word "Christ" was a title designating a specific function within the socio-religious traditions of Judaism. A more accurate way therefore of using this formula would be to talk to Jesus who is called the Christ...[1]

This introduction by Dr. Dermot A. Lane to his book *The Reality of Jesus* is so attractive to a Muslim reader. According to the Muslim faith, the Muslim accepts the historical fact of Jesus, and so can meet with such a Christian analysis about Jesus Christ half way. A matter of "significance" can naturally tolerate different points of views, and thus Muslims would not feel so far from Christians if the gap between them has been simply identified as a difference in understanding the theological significance of a certain fact which is admitted by both, however serious this difference of understanding may be. This approach to the "mystery of Jesus" is fruitful in addressing non-Christian readers of this interesting book, especially Muslims.

The author does not like to introduce "Christology from above," a way which "tends to take for granted the divinity of Jesus Christ."[2] He points out that another choice would be "to begin Christology from the other end, concentrating on the man Jesus giving rise to what is called a 'low Christology' which starts 'from below'."[3] However, Dr. Lane makes it clear that one can adopt such a low Christology as a starting point "and then proceed to allow this starting point to be drawn in whatever direction one's study of the Christian sources dictates."[4] A third possibility "would seem to present itself here that would steer a middle course between the two extremes of a closed low Christology and a rigidly high Christology."[5] An Instruction from Rome in 1964 points out that there are "'three stages of tradition' behind the gospels as we know them today. These are first of all the original words and deeds of the historical Jesus which were delivered according to 'the methods of reasoning and exposition which were in common use at the time'. The second layer...is made up of the oral

---

[1] Dermot A. Lane, *The Reality of Jesus* (Dublin/New York: Veritas Press/Paulist Press, 1975/1977), pp. 9-1.

[2] *Ibid.*, p. 16.

[3] *Ibid.*, p. 17.

[4] *Ibid.*, pp. 17-18.

[5] *Ibid.*, p. 18.

356

proclamation by the apostles of the life, death and resurrection of Jesus"[6] and their fuller understanding "of the words and deeds of the historical Jesus in the light of the Resurrection and Pentecostal experiences."[7] At last the compilation of this apostolic preaching into the written form of the gospels as known today comes as a third layer. The Instruction indicated "the importance of taking into consideration the origin and composition of the gospels as well as making due use of 'the legitimate findings of recent research'"[8] so as to ensure a full understanding of the texts.

In this way, a Muslim can see that the differences between the Muslim faith in Jesus and the Christian faith may be put as a problem of understanding and interpreting "the words and deeds of a historical Jesus," a layer which came after the historical facts. At most, it would be a problem of misunderstanding on the side of any of the two parts, more than a problem of an intentional forging or deluding. The Qur'an refers clearly to a special place of Jesus in his relation to God, which is different from the place of any other prophet, even if the Qur'an rejects the notion that Jesus may be called "Son of God": "The Messiah, Jesus son of Mary, was only the Messenger of God, and His Word that he committed to Mary, and a Spirit from Him. So believe in God and His Messengers, and say not 'three'...God is only one God. Glory be to Him – that He should have a son" (4/171). According to the Qur'anic terminology "a Messenger of God" may not be an ordinary man: "Praise belongs to God...who appointed the angels to be Messengers" (35/1). A special relation between Jesus and the "Holy Spirit" – the "Spirit of the Holiness" as expressed in the Qur'an – is also mentioned: "And we gave Jesus son of Mary the clear signs, and confirmed him with the Holy Spirit" (2/253): "When God said, 'Jesus son of Mary, remember my blessing upon thee and upon thy mother, when I confirmed thee with the Holy Spirit, to speak to men in the cradle and of age; and when I taught thee the Book, the Wisdom, the Torah, the Gospel; and when thou created out of clay by my leave as the likeness of a bird and thou breathest into it and it is a bird by My leave, and

---

[6] *Ibid.*, p. 25.

[7] *Ibid.*

[8] *Ibid.*

thou healest the blind and the leper by My leave, and thou bringest the dead forth by My leave...'" (5/110). A Muslim scholar from India – probably a Shi'i as his name shows, Dr. Hasan Askari – has referred to such significant verses in an interesting article in this *Journal* before.[9]

In regard to the end of Jesus' life, the Qur'an states: "When God said, 'Jesus, I will bring thee to death, and I will raise thee to Me, and I will purify thee of those who believe not. I will set thy followers above the unbelievers till the Resurrection Day'" (3/55). The other Qur'anic statement about the event may not be seen as really contradictory, if it is not interpreted literally as dealing with the historical event or the physiological death: "...and for their – the Jews' – saying, 'We slew the Messiah, Jesus son of Mary, the Messenger of God – yet they did not slay him, neither crucified him, only a likeness of that was shown to them...and they slew him not of a certainty – no indeed; God raised him up to Him" (4/157-8).

On the other hand, through dealing with "a historical minimum in the life of Jesus,"[10] Dr. Lane states that "Jesus appears first and foremost as a man among men...He experienced fatigue, hunger, disappointment, loneliness and the usual limitations in knowledge that belong to the human condition...Jesus is seen as a Rabbi...Jesus is understood as a prophet within the long line of prophets that had gone before him."[11] In his introduction, the author mentions that "a low-ascending Christology reinstates the mystery of Jesus Christ in its original biblical context where it properly belongs. Within this original context biblical research would seem to suggest that the New Testament Christology itself began with the man Jesus."[12] In this light, a Christian may see the Muslim's faith in Jesus as preliminary, but not false or intentionally depreciating. It is true that the author mentions also that "Jesus emerges as one speaking with great authority...In particular his claim to forgive sins highlights this authority...Most of all Jesus appears as one who

---

[9] J.E.S., 9 (1972): 477-488.

[10] Lane, *Reality*, p. 32.

[11] *Ibid.*, pp. 32-33.

[12] *Ibid.*, p. 18.

dares to assume a unique personal closeness to...God...This allows him to address Yahweh as Abba – Father."[13]

However, Dr. Lane indicates that the details of the arrest, the trial, and the execution "are extremely difficult to disentangle from a critical point of view."[14] The interpretation of these events was also difficult, even for the disciples of Jesus themselves who understood the death of Jesus on the cross as a failure, and so "The cross was indeed both a stumbling block and a sheer scandal."[15] The author reminds us more than once that "...the mystery of Jesus Christ is a reality that took hundreds of years to fully unfold itself into a clearly defined framework."[16]

He points out that "the formulation of [the] relationship between Jesus and the monotheistic God of Judaism took place in various stages...He is identified as the Son of Man, the Suffering Servant, the Son of God, the Lord, the Son of David, and eventually as the Word. These titles initially at least were functional...Gradually these titles, through the experience of prayer and worship, took on a confessional dimension...Eventually with the expansion of Christianity into the Hellenistic world the ontological implications of both function and confession were spelled out."[17] Dr. Lane gives a significant clarification of the difficulties which surround the interpretation of the Christ-Event as a result of the historical environment. He says, "Because the earliest formulation of the Christ-Event in the Palestinian community was centered around Jesus as the Christ who is to come in the Parousia, it would seem that the particular question of the precise relationship between Jesus and God did not arise explicitly at this early stage."[18] "Jesus is never called God in the Synoptics or in the early preaching of the *Acts of the Apostles*. Instead most of the evidence...is concentrated in the latter half of the first century....[The destruction of the

---

[13] *Ibid.*, pp. 36-37.

[14] *Ibid.*, p. 42.

[15] *Ibid.*, p. 43.

[16] *Ibid.*, p. 10; see also p. 12.

[17] *Ibid.*, p. 72.

[18] *Ibid.*, p. 84.

temple necessitated a clear break for Christianity away from the confines of Judaism with its strict Monotheism."[19]   Whenever these historical circumstances are admitted, the climate for an inter-religious dialogue becomes so convenient for all the concerned parts. As Dr. Lane puts it, "The initial foundations in the New Testament of the universal significance of the Christ-Event that we have been exposing...were to become the object of theological reflection and heated debate in subsequent centuries. Within the cross-fire of ideas it was to take another four hundred years to iron out clearly the full universal significance of the Christ-Event."[20]

Dr. Lane's deep treatise of *The Reality of Jesus* allots three chapters after the introduction – 46 pages – to the historical part of "the Christ-Event," while the approximately 100 remaining pages are devoted to the theological interpretation.   The reader – especially the non-Christian – will perhaps be eager to delve further into the historical research than does the author in this book, but the Irish publisher reminds us on the cover that the book, "integrates the findings of biblical research with the developments of dogmatic theology. It brings together the 'old' and the 'new' into a fresh synthesis. In particular the book has been written for preachers, teachers, and students of the good news of Jesus Christ." These particular readers of course will be more interested in the theological interpretation. However, it is very promising for inter-religious dialogue that a Catholic theologian provides such historical and critical background of the "Christ-Event" for the present and coming generations of Christian theologians. Dr. Lane explains precisely how different interpretations of the Christ-Event can rise: "Obviously the mode of existence belonging to the risen Christ of faith is radically different and therefore discontinuous with the mode of historical existence which attached to the earthly life of Jesus. It is in this sense that there is a distinct dimension of discontinuity, a discontinuity which is specifically historical. The reality of the risen Christ of faith is unhistorical or

---

[19] *Ibid.*, p. 90.

[20] *Ibid.*, p. 93; see also pp. 132-133.

better, trans-historical, and is therefore to that extent discontinuous with the Jesus of history."[21]

A Muslim reader would appreciate such statements of the Irish Catholic theologian about the relation of Jesus Christ to God as the following:

> It is important to distinguish here between the revelation of a reality and the reality itself. The expression of a reality especially through the historical revelation of that reality is not equivalent to the reality itself. If this were not so there would be no expression or revelation but rather pure naked reality. The mystery of Jesus Christ is the expression or revelation of God to man in historical form The mystery of God however is not exhausted in Jesus. There can never be a total expression of God on the level of creation. The finite can never contain the totality of the infinite. The mystery of Jesus Christ is the key to the mystery of God. It must not, however, take away the mystery of God. In the light of these observations it is much more desirable to talk therefore about Jesus as the image of the invisible God than to talk simply about Jesus as God.[22]

> The Incarnation...is not an isolated exception but rather the definitive culmination of a process already set in motion through the gift of creation. To this extent creation is the basis of Incarnation and Incarnation is the fullness of creation. In a certain sense creation is itself a form of "incarnation" in that it mediates however obscurely traces of the divine power and presence which become formalized in the Christ-Event.[23]

> [The] suggestion that the Incarnation is a mystery continually taking place around us in the light of the mystery of Jesus Christ is acknowledged by the Second Vatican Council when it points out that "by his Incarnation the Son of God has united himself in some fashion with every man." Here the Council clearly recognizes the equality, the dignity, and the sacredness of each and every individual as the vehicle of God's incarnate grace.[24]

> [This] reintroduces the mystery of Jesus Christ into the mystery of God. For too long Christology has been divorced from theology...Indeed at times Christology tended to become an

---

[21] *Ibid.*, p. 157.

[22] *Ibid.*, pp. 125-126.

[23] *Ibid.*, p. 135.

[24] *Ibid.*, p. 141.

end in itself. This can be seen in certain forms of myopic christocentricism which can be misleading.[25]

More recently another Catholic theologian, the German Hans Küng, in his latest work, *On Being a Christian*, "doubts that Christ pre-existed in the Godhead before his human birth and believes the early church's definitions of the diety of Christ to be Hellenistic. To him the point is simply that God was present in Jesus revealing himself and making known his claims on man and his offer of forgiveness. The test of being a Christian 'is not to this or that dogma...but the acceptance of faith in Christ and imitation of Christ'" (*Time*, January 3, 1977). In regard to "salvation," the author of *The Reality of Jesus* emphasizes "the Catholic tradition which acknowledges the necessary role that man must plan in the coming to be of faith...[and which] is summarized in the doctrine of 'justification by faith and good works'."[26] This doctrine implies without prejudice to the priority of God's invitation that man must cooperate actively in the reception of the diving gift of faith."[27]

The writer of this review, being a Muslim, finds in such a statement a solid ground for a fruitful dialogue between Muslims and Christians, and hopes that more parallel efforts would be made by Muslim theologians in understanding and expressing a Qur'an Christology.

Zalman M. Schachter

Treat this discussion as an exercise in hope. I would for this moment only suspend past pains and disappointments and suspend also my conviction that where we are now as Jews and Christians is better than any other place-better because it is our reality. Further, I also believe that the separate voices of our official religions will ultimately contribute more in the unanimous peace in praise of G-d than a plain chant in which all blend...

There is little that a Jew can say upon reading Lane. This book puzzles me. Here is a man who documents how all of present-day Christology hangs on a hair. The farther he returns to the past the more traces of the unique, special, the second person of the Trinity vanish and

---

[25] *Ibid.*, p. 142.

[26] *Ibid.*, p. 161.

[27] *Ibid.*

what remains is a teacher of Aggadic Pharisaism who differed from the other teachers of Halakhic Pharisaism.

Lane's method is a sort of last-ditch stand when a person encounters the conflicting claims of historic material and of creedal dogma. The two are not compatible and the means of the low-ascending theology are just not able to sway the historian while the believer is threatened by the historic stuff which makes his or her lush creedal significance to his or her Christ who pales into one of the many teachers in the *Sitz im Legen* which the historian gives, then why bother believing? I cannot believe that just another rabbi teaching Aggadah to fisher-folk would excite the regular Christian to participate in a Mass done in Jesus' memory. So who is Christ?

Call him by his Hebrew term, the *Mashiah*, annointed one, and claim his descent from David in order that there will be fulfilled that "a sprout come forth from Jesse..." and you run into the trouble of: (a) The job description given to that messiah has not been fulfilled by him. The irenic order of universal Shalom has not yet arrived. As we are told of R. Menahem Mendel of Vitebsk who, when he lived in Jerusalem, once heard a madman blow the ram's horn on the holy Temple mount. When people came to him and said "The Messiah has arrived; he blew the ram's horn." R. Mendel opened the window, looked out, and said, "No. He has not come. Everything is still as it was before." The state of exile continues unrelieved and for us Jews aggravated by inquisitions, expulsions, pogroms, and extermination camps. One might cry out: "If it is as you say that *you* are saved – how come you make *us* suffer so much?" No, the seat of the Davidic Messiah has not yet been occupied by his rightful descendant, and that is that. And (b) What sense is there in the genealogy which traces Joseph's descent from David if Joseph had nothing to do with the biological event of Jesus' birth? So, even if the Shalom order had arrived, Jesus could not be billed as the Davidic Prince of Peace. Both on the fact of exile and on the theory of Davidic descent, we have no Messiah as yet. To some extent I feel ashamed to raise those old disputed issues, but somehow the Christologist is not ashamed to lay the heavy claims on Jesus and there is after all this tradition which we Jews experience in countless ways as leaning on us and urging us to accept this Christ as the Messiah we expect, and we can only push back by retorting: We will accept a biological descendant of David as the Messiah when through him the Shalom order is established.

But wait, is there only one messiah spot for Jesus to occupy? Ever since the break between Judah and Joseph, the Kingdom of Israel from the Kingdom of Judah, there has been a claim for the coming of a Messiah, son of Joseph. This Messiah comes not to redeem sinners – this belongs to the Davidic Messiah – but to redeem the righteous and to teach them that they too need to come to Teshuvah (turning – *metanoia*). Being a descendant of Joseph the Zaddik he, as the Midrash (Vayosha 24) has it, will, after having served as a leader of the Jewish troops, be killed by a warrior from the West named Armilus (Romulus). He is, as the Jewish tradition places him, the righteous suffering servant of Isaiah 53 who is to be martyred. Let's put this together. An Ephraimite, a descendant of *Joseph* who comes from Galilee (no need for the census story at all), who lives an exemplary holy life (perhaps there is an underplaying of other companions he may have had in favor of fisherfolk, publicans, and sinners which may have helped in making converts among the Gentiles of the Roman empire, but not in Jerusalem where Nicodemus and Joseph of Arimathea become more important), and is martyred by "Romulus" could very well have become the Mashiah ben *Joseph* for Jews. If Christians would have so spoken of Jesus then the chances are that Jews would have been able to join Christians in the Good Friday lament and count Jesus as one of the ten Martyrs of the State and included his death with that of Rabbi Aqiba in the dirges of the Yom Kippur martyrology. Jews could have even added the extra bite of bread at the conclusion of the meal as a memorial and have had a cup of thanksgiving – Eucharist – for the same intention and prayed in the daily liturgy for the resurrection of the Josephite Messiah that he might lead us to meet the Messiah ben David. But...the Gospel writers were prisoners of hope. Too impatient to postpone their hopes for the salvation of *this* world, they pushed it up to heaven, and as soon as the temporal order was in their hands Christians became triumphalists in an unredeemed world. Not content to assign the dignity of Messiah Ben Joseph to Jesus, claims were made for the New Adam that the world's condition refused to substantiate and all the transubstantiations subsequently did not change the accidents of wine, bread, death, and martyrdom.

But why identify the second person of the Trinity with the Messiah and come with inflated claims when we can, instead of turning to the synoptics, turn to John? His formulation of Jesus as the *Memra,* the *Logos,* the Word that was G-d, was with G-d, was made flesh creates the more significant Christology. Of the three tasks so well described by Rosenzweig in his *Star of Redemption,* Creation, Revelation, and Redemption, the real claim was made that Jesus is the *Revelation.* That equates Jesus with Torah, not with Mashiah. If there be a being who so lives as the Creator in Heaven wishes the being to live that he or she becomes a living Torah, at least Jews of a mystical, aggadic, Kabbalistic-Hassidic persuasion seem to have a stronger theological warrant for dialogue. The Zaddik is G-d's possibility for humanity in a physical body. The Zaddik is Torah, who decrees and G-d agrees; for the Zaddik's sake the all was created. "G-d does not need a world," the Maggid of Mezericth teaches, but since Zaddikim like to lead worlds, he creates worlds for them. Zaddikim can heal and help, but most of those who see them utter the blessing. "Blessed art Thou L-rd our G-d King of the Universe who has apportioned of thy wisdom to them who fear thee." The Zaddik, at once an archetypal model for behavior, is also an accessible model and anyone who will follow the Zaddik – in the older sense of *imitatio* – can also become a zaddik. There are tractates of all other commandments in the Talmud, but for Love, Faith, Awe, and devotion only a living Zaddik can serve a generation as the tractate of the duties of the heart.

The Zaddik is the Sinai event for all those who stand in a positive relationship to the Zaddik. The Zaddik serves the souls of the disciples and devotees as a general soul which is for the disciple the interface to G-d's grace, light, and love on this plane. Now all those teachings are more compatible to the soteric claim of Christianity. The Paraclete, the mediator, the WAY to the Creator, all these are what the Zaddik is for mystical Jews and the Torah is for all Jews in general. The Christian can say that, fulfilling the Torah, Jesus became the Torah now immanent in his heart and soul without making at the same time the extravagant claim for Jesus to be the fulfillment of the redemption. For, although the Torah was given at Sinai, no Jew expected that this would so transform the whole world that it would usher in the irenic realm of G-d's kingdom. It is on the contrary a revelation – a survival guide and handbook of how to manage in a world that is not yet redeemed.

Having stated the above from a Jewish position, is this not also close to the Christian one? The final redemption still awaits another COMING. In the meantime, there is the word made flesh, the paradigm of the fullest G-d in the fullest human, the *sotor*, reconciler, connector to the Creator. On the Jewish side such an open and clear statement gives possibility to the notion that Jesus is for Christians who follow in his footsteps, pray in his name to the Creator, love one another as he had loved his disciples, and await the redemption with the light of the world having poured itself – *kenosis* – into the souls of his followers. He is the word that the Christian hears spoken of the Creator in the tongue of the man, the rebbe from Nazareth. His followers once named Nazarenes can now be seen by Jews as Nazarener Hassidim in the same way as Jews who follow the Satmarer Rebbe as Satmarer Hassidim and those who follow the Belzer are Belzer Hassidim.

There is yet a deeper aspect of Christology worth considering from the principle of dialogue. There is the experience of the Christ (I do not mean the Messiah aspect, but the Son of G-d aspect) which is the confidant, the compassionate, the Holy, the one who is all sacred heart, who is the love of G-d which is also the G-d is love and he who abides in love abides in G-d and G-d in him. True, this aspect is far from the ken of the exoteric Jew but close to the esoteric one who is a hassid or follows the kabbalah. I remember a conversation I once had visiting the late Thomas Merton at Gethsemani. Merton responded to my question what the Trinity meant to him by quoting the Greek fathers who said that G-d is awesome might and creative power is the Father, G-d as loving and compassionate and working to bring all souls to their reconciliation and salvation in the Son. G-d as this love is revealed to the human mind and gives human being the revelation of G-d's will and wisdom is the Holy Spirit. I responded to this that I believe that G-d creates, and, if this dimension of an infinite number of dimensions is talked about under the name "Father," this has not only enough biblical and theological warrant for Jews but is no point of quarrel. That God loves and in this capacity is called the Son also makes a certain amount of sense to a kabbalist. For in the Zohar the Tetragrammaton is interpreted to mean YHVH as follows: Y is the Father – Hokhmah, wisdom. H is the Mother – Binah, understanding. V is the Son – Ziyr Anpin, the heart and the compassion, the one really pointed to in the YHVH; and H at the end is the Daughter – the Shekhinnah, the sabbath, the divine presence and, yes, the Ruah Haqodesh – the Holy Spirit. As long as we do not exclude the other manifestations by declaring that there are only three, we have further room for dialogue and understanding. Now it is also true that the Kingdom of the YHVH has not yet begun on this earth and, as Zechariah foretold, that will happen on "THAT DAY on which YHVH will be one and His name ONE."

What this calls for is a willingness to admit that all our formulations about G-d are nothing but tentative stammerings of blind and exiled children of Eve responding to the light deeply hidden in the recesses of their nostalgic longing for the untainted origin in which one needed not to look through the glass darkly but could see. This can even make us proud of our traditions and heritage as the storehouse of those stammerings of the souls that were filled by G-d with the grace of that holy moment that defied definition and that was forced by ecclesiastical lawyers to be encapsulated in a stateable wording. The mistake that was made was to take the ecstatic exclamations of the overwhelmed souls and to make them numbered *articles* of creeds instead of *acts* of faith made in fear and trembling.

It is this move which, for all the balance in Lane's book, he did not make. It is indeed difficult to say that the magisterium of the church – that the Torah and all its commentaries – are *deo gratis* what we do have and treasure, but only as the human snapshots of moments of G-d's nearness; that, although we cannot improve on the divine which flows into our vessels, we can and must take responsibility for keeping these vessels clean and transparent and not at all as essential as the light they contain. Perhaps we are as dogmatists, small souls of small faith who do not dare trust that G-d will be with us as G-d was with our forbears and that G-d will not abandon us nor forsake us.

It then behoves the poor of the spirit of all creeds and denominations to support each other in the desperate acts of faith which we make in the face of the exile and the holocausts and enter into a dialogue among fellow servants and children of *one* Creator.

Gerard S. Sloyan

It is not often that a scholar interested in the reality of Jesus masters modern critical study of his message and by indirection his person, as well as what Christian tradition has made of him doctrinally as the Christ of God, in the interests of a modern synthesis of the two. Protestant scholarship tends to take a giant step from modern criticism, either historically skeptical in a Bultmann-to-Conzelmann line or admitting more historical validity to the gospels over a Käsemann-to-Jeremias spectrum, to a presentation of Jesus Christ as the object of the church's faith. Even those such as Pannenberg and Moule or J. A. T. Robinson who try to keep a foot in the other camp, biblical in the first case and systematic in the other two, are not greatly troubled by the inhibitions imposed by the christological councils on the results of critical-historical method. Roman Catholic expositors of the mystery of Jesus Christ, for their part, tend to be at ease in systematic categories (e.g., Rahner, Kasper) of biblical (e.g., Vawter, Brown), but not to take on the complex task of viewing Christ through second-,fifth-, and twentieth-century eyes.

The Irish Catholic scholar whose work is here under review reports creditably on work in progress in the several disciplines. What emerges is a Jesus Christ in whom the learned and those acquainted with the problems which the learned face can believe. Missing from the treatment is any attempt to cope with faith in Christ on mythical terms apart from the historical, such as characterizes numerous contributors to John Hick's recent symposium, *The Myth of God Incarnate.* Dermot Lane means to be historically grounded throughout. A problem that necessarily arises from this choice is his insufficient attention to religious myth in the period of the formation of the gospels and, on new terms, of the Church Fathers and the early councils. The determined attempts of the latter at clear speech about the ineffable, which included some philosophical language, do not eliminate the mythic component from the formulas arrived at. The terms of myth (even "Father," "Son," and "Spirit") are poetic and dramatic, and no attempts to speak of its historical or ontological correlate can dispel the questions it raises.

The overall report submitted by Dr. Lane on the present state of biblical, historical, and systematic scholarship in Christology is so well done that to cavil at certain small matters could seem ungenerous. A resume of his achievement should therefore precede attention to a few points of criticism. He holds throughout for the continuity between the creation, defined as God's continued support of finite being, and the work of human salvation achieved through the Incarnation. The manifestation of God "perfectly" through the man Jesus is the high point of God's self-disclosure through creatures. The latter can be called an incarnation of God with a lower-case "i." Consequently, the enfleshing or en-manning of God's *Logos* is not to be thought of as a sharp break with all that went before, least of all as the correction of an initial blunder on God's part or failure to create humanity in grace. The Christology of this book is Scotist in its contention that God was fittingly revealed in a man at a certain point in history, apart from the need to redeem humanity from sin. Dr. Lane draws on Teilhard's exposition of the cosmic Christ, which in turn derives from the hymnic developments found in Col. 1 and Eph. 1. His modern theological mentor is Karl Rahner, whose evolutionary Chritology holds that the universal human capacity for self-transcendence, to which God's reaching out to every human being corresponds, achieves its peak in Jesus of Nazareth. That Incarnation is unique because of both God's unique choice of Jesus and the latter's unique obedience. The matter is put this way: "Jesus different in kind in his relationship with God but not to the extent that he becomes isolated from the rest of mankind with whom he has [is?] fully identified. This difference in kind is based on his difference in degree from the rest of mankind."[28] As is frequently the case in *The Reality of Jesus,* this statement does not receive the metaphysical justification it requires. Rather, reference is provided to two other authors who make the same affirmation. This is not said in criticism so much as in illustration of the limits of a sketch as brief as the present one. Rahner's extended treatment, found in several dense essays,

---

[28] *Ibid.,* p. 132.

goes on to hold that the personal union of God's *Logos* with each risen saint
will constitute no less than a multitude of personal Incarnations, that of the
one Mediator Jesus preserving its unique character from his earthly days.
The Lane thesis does not explore his hypothetical question.

It is essential to the author's argument that the historical character of
the Incarnation claimed for Jesus (a dogma which gradually unfolded itself
upon the infant church, as the divinity of Jesus became clear[29]) be
maintained. He is convinced that the "only mode of access we have to the
divine Sonship of Jesus is in and through his humanity."[30] Elsewhere, he
states that the "perfection of humanity mediates divinity so that by being true
Man Jesus is true God...[He] realizes in the fullest possible way the graced
capacities of man and thereby incarnates a real (hypostatic) unity between
God and man.[31] Since the pre- and post-ressurection continuity of the man
Jesus is essential to belief in a historical and not merely a mythical
figure – though faith in him as risen to life in the final age necessarily
mythicizes him – the gospels must record a discernible historical figure, or
they provide no basis for the kind of faith the church professes. "As a general
rule we can say that the 'higher' Christology tends to become [viz,
maintaining the descent of the *Logos* into humanity], the greater the need to
return to the historical Jesus as a source and check."[32] Historical research
into the gospels must be seen as a permanent and necessary feature of
contemporary Christology, safeguarding our understanding of the full
mystery of Jesus Christ.

In Chapter 3, "Rediscovering the Historical Jesus," Dr. Lane explores
the first layer of gospel material which discloses him as an "eschatological
prophet" whose "words and deeds...brought him into direct conflict with the
official leaders of Judaism."[33] This chapter is perhaps the least rigorous of
all for, while giving evidence of the complexity of the problem of discovering

---

[29] *Ibid.*, p. 133.

[30] *Ibid.*, p. 120.

[31] *Ibid.*, pp. 138-139.

[32] *Ibid.*, p. 149.

[33] *Ibid.*, p. 40.

Jesus' authentic sayings, it largely sets the problem aside and posits a quite arguable authentic core. The statement in a later chapter is more guarded, which holds for the "eschatological suggestiveness of the words and deeds of Jesus such as the announcement of the Kingdom of God, the critical call to repentance, the setting up of a new table fellowship, and the promise of salvation."[34] There is a very subtle distinction to be made here which the Irish scholar fails to make, namely between the traditional materials, already theologically developed, which are the first stratum of the gospels, and undeveloped historical reminiscences of which the present gospels provide no examples. In failing to make the distinction he gives the impression that the words and deeds of Jesus, leading to the teaching which he lists above, are fairly readily available as history. This is simply not true. It is compounded by the attribution to Jesus of various phrases that are clearly examples of Matthean or Johannine thought. This practice is strange in its omission of a caution which the author could easily have issued. In brief, the important claim for the historicity of Jesus of Nazareth is weakened by being insufficiently minimal and even by the false insinuations, through inadvertence, of its wider extent. Throughout, there is a mild insensitivity to the Jews when gospel statements about them are paraphrased.

An observation needs to be made about Dr. Lane's suggestion that, "What was formerly called person now approximates to what we call nature and what was known as nature in the past is understood today as person."[35] Three modern authors are cited in support of this contention which, if it were widely thought to be true, would cut several Gordian knots. In fact, however, Nestorius in proposing his "person of the union" in the spirit of Dr. Lane's suggestion could not convince his contemporaries at Ephesus that he did not have in mind a second principle of unity in Christ. Moreover, reference to "the impression given by Apollinarius and continued by Cyril to some extent that the human nature had no hypostasis thus implying that it was an impersonal *an-hypostatic* human nature," is not only a considerable understatement, but also the very reason why neither Cyril nor III

---

[34] *Ibid.*, p. 155.

[35] *Ibid.*, p. 113.

Constantinople (A.D. 680-681)—which specified the *Logos* as the one *hypostasis* in Christ—would let the Lane position stand.

If he is right about the exact reverse understanding of person and nature then and now, he must be referring to the situation before and possibly at Nicaea (325) which successively faded through the period of Ephesus (431), Chalcedon (451), and II Constantinople (553). In any case, forgetting his own counsel, he writes: "This union of God and man in Jesus is an absolute and complete union so that we can say Jesus is the Word Incarnate and mean by this that Jesus is the divine *person (hypostasis)* of the *Logos*, who is the perfect self-expression of God, made flesh."[36] That is perfectly good Cyrillian doctrine, whereas consistency on the author's part would have required the statement that Jesus possesses the divine *nature (hypostasis)* of the *Logos*, which is the perfect expression of God, and in him is made flesh. That consistency might have made the ecclesiastical censor read the sentence twice. It would also have drawn a Cyrillian thunderbolt. The present reviewer happens to think it a better expression of the mystery.

These observations are minor in light of the overall excellence of the author's achievement. He has provided a Christology well suited to those determined to hold fast to the historical character of the gospels and the traditions of the church. If at times his irenic spirit has led him to reconcile opposites out of the Christian past, correction can be made in future editions.

Dermot A. Lane

Much progress has been made over the last ten years in the area of interfaith discussions among the major religions of the world. The emergence of the "global village" through easy travel facilities and instant tele-communications has opened up fundamental questions about religious differences. More explicitly, from the Catholic side, the Second Vatican council, especially through its *Declaration on the Relationship of the Church to Non-Christian Religions (Nostra Aetate)*, 1965, created a new climate of openness toward and dialogue with the major religions of the world. Within this situation the Catholic Church singled out the unique position of the

---

[36] *Ibid.*, p. 132.

Judaic and Muslim religions (N.A.a.4; N.A. a.3; L.G. a.5). In 1974, the Holy See set up two new commissions; one for Islam, and the other for Judaism. In January, 1975, "Guidelines and Suggestions for Implementing the Conciliar Declaration *Nostra Aetate*" were issued. These initiatives by the Catholic Church have done a lot to break down prejudices and misunderstandings on all sides.

One of the problems of interfaith dialogue and dialogue at the international level is that it tends to become bogged down by questions of procedure, protocol, and diplomacy. In addition when dialogue does take place it often addresses issues which by-pass fundamental questions. For instance discussions about the relationship between the church and Israel or the Bible and the Qur'an must sooner or later return to the fundamental questions of Jesus. To this extent the editor of the *Journal of Ecumenical Studies* is to be commended for initiating an interfaith discussion around the foundational reality of Jesus.

Though *The Reality of Jesus* was primarily written with a view to working out the significance of Jesus within a Christian perspective, it is all the more interesting to have an inspection of one's work from the outside by a Jew and a Muslim as well as by a fellow Christian. I, therefore, welcome and value the observations of all three participants in this discussion.

In the short space allotted to me I can only briefly comment on the more significant suggestions of my reviewers and then go on to indicate some of the key areas of development in Christology that might be of interest to a Jewish-Christian-Muslim-trialogue.

Fathi Osman's reading *The Reality of Jesus* as a Muslim is most interesting and encouraging. He has clearly grasped the general thesis of the book. He keenly appreciates the value of a low-ascending-Christology from a Muslim point of view. His acknowledgement of the fact that as a Muslim he can go along "half way" with the christological analysis outlined in *The Reality of Jesus* is a clear indication of the progress taking place in the Muslim-Christian encounter as well as an invitation to future dialogue. Osman's response is a vindication of the importance of the historical approach in theology when dealing with interfaith questions.

I must confess to finding the reaction of Zalman Schachter puzzling. He begins by adopting a highly literalistic critique of *The Reality of Jesus* and of Christianity in general. He objects that he will only "accept a biological descendant of David as the Messiah when through him the Shalom order is established." He then proceeds to outline from a Kabbalistic point of view a series of most interesting and suggestive ideas about Jesus that might be explored in dialogue. These include Jesus as "the word made flesh, paradigm of the fullest G-d in the fullest human, the *soter*, reconciler, connector to the Creator...the compassionate, the Holy, the one who is all sacred heart, who is the love of G-d..." In fact, Prof. Schachter will find on pp. 117-146 of *The Reality of Jesus* bases other than mystical for a discussion of these very suggestive points.

From a Christian point of view, Gerard Sloyan has many helpful and constructive observations to make. He put his finger on a christological nerve-center when he asks about the use of the terms "person" and "nature." There is the patristic period whose usage is the least clearly defined in spite of conciliar statements; then there is the later received interpretation of these terms through Aristotelian-Thomistic ontology; and finally there is the twentieth-century psychological understanding of the terms. When I claim there has been a reversal in the meaning of these terms, I am referring to the second and third phases. It might be argued, as Walter Kasper does, that these two are complementary and that taken together they reflect what the first phase was about. This is an attractive solution, but it raises serious questions as to the meaning of pre-twentieth-century traditional Christology. Does it necessarily follow that several Gordian knots would have to be cut if one holds that "person" and "nature" have come to mean something quite different today from what they meant, say in the last two centuries? Surely our contact with the living tradition of Christianity does not depend simply on verbal continuity.

If progress is to be made in the Jewish-Christian encounter, then it is essential that we take a more extensive look at the relationship that exists between Jesus and Judaism. For too long it has been said that Jesus makes sense only "over and against" Judaism. This simplistic point of view has been a source of much Antisemitism in Christian circles. However, critical studies in recent times by Jews and Christians clearly bring out the Jewishness of Jesus and his teaching (G. Vermes, D. Flusser, R. Aron, B. Z. Bokser). Not only that, but it can be argued convincingly that Christianity grew out of an "intra-Jewish critique of Israel and that the early Christian interpretation is truly a Jewish interpretation of Jesus" (E. Schillebeeckx, *Jesuz Het Verhaal van een Levende* [Bloemendaal: Nelisson, 1974], p. 25). In other words Christianity is an extension of a particular form of Judaism. One of the central issues in Palestine during the time of Jesus was the question about what constituted the Torah. It is within this context that Jesus criticizes what he regarded as the human-made elements of the Law which get in the way of the close relationship between God and the individual that is intended by the Torah. In order to bring about a return to the Torah, Jesus preached repentence and *metanoia*. This in turn would prepare the people for the coming Reign of God. For Jesus the really important thing in life was adherence to the Torah which consisted in doing God's will. Thus, far from diminishing the center-piece of Judaism, Jesus is the champion of the Torah as a particular way of life that unites the individual with God. This dimension of the Jewishness of Jesus and his teaching must surely figure prominently in the Jewish-Christian dialogue. The Jewishness of early Christianity and Christianness of first-century Judaism has much to contribute to the understanding of both traditions.

Another important consideration that should affect interfaith dialogue, especially at the level of Christian-Muslim discussion, is the current widening of christological horizons. At present there is a definite shift taking place from an exclusive Christology to an inclusivist Christology. Once the religious value of the other major world religions is recognized, as do the documents of the Second Vatican Council, then one is moved implicitly to an inclusivist Christology. This means, in effect, that the starting point of future Christology must be an acceptance of God's universal activity in and through other religious peoples and communities. It is against this background that Christology will work out its unique understanding of God as active in the life, death, and resurrection of Jesus. This inclusivist Christology will then show how Jesus personifies and crystalizes the universal presence of God in other world religions. From there this Christology will move on to indicate how something radically new took place in the life of Jesus and how this something new is normative for the Christian understanding of God in the world.

In conclusion it should be remembered that all religious peoples are united in their common search for God. The Jew, the Christian, and the Muslim are all concerned to promote a personal appreciation of the mystery of God. There are many ways to the one true God. This diversity should not be divisive, but rather enriching. The Christian way is one that is centered around Jesus Christ as the personal embodiment and expression of God's presence in the world. For the Christian, Jesus' cause is God's cause. To say this, however, is by no means to remove or destroy the mystery of God. Instead, it is to deepen our awareness of the one basic, incomprehensible mystery that encircles and envelopes our lives. If *The Reality of Jesus* helps in any way to open up that mystery, then it will have achieved its primary purpose.

THE QUR'AN AND THE CONTEMPORARY MIDDLE EAST*

Kenneth Cragg**

It is reported that on the first Friday after the June War of 1967, the sermon at congregational prayer in the Great Mosque in Mecca was based on the Quranic verse (47.35) which reads: "Do not weaken and call for peace; you will overcome." The words are repeated almost *verbatim* in 3.139: "Do not weaken, nor grieve; you will overcome, if believers you be." The formula for fortitude, implicit in these words and requiring the characteristic Quranic quality of *sabr*, or endurance under adversity, is perhaps the most dramatic and symbolic example of active commentary from the Islamic Scripture upon the current scene.

Not all the relevance of the Book of Islam to present politics is so explicit. But that forcible example, to which we will return in conclusion, seems to warrant reflection on the more general, if often only implicit, bearing of the Qur'an upon contemporary Arab Muslim thinking about historical experience in the recent past and, in particular, about the confrontation with Zionism. Such reflection may point to compelling issues

* *Journal of Ecumenical Studies,* 11:1, (Winter 1974).

** Bishop Kenneth Cragg (Anglican) received his B.A., M.A., and D. Phil. from Jesus College, Oxford University. He has taught in Connecticut and at Union Theological Seminary in New York, at the University of London, and at the University of Ibadan, Nigeria. Now based at the University of Sussex in Brighton, England, Dr. Cragg is editor of *The Muslim World Quarterly,* is a contributor to the *Journal of World History* and the *Encyclopedia Britannica,* and translated Arabic works into English. Ecclesiastical posts have included being Assistant Bishop in the Archbishopric in Jerusalem and, most recently, Bishop of Egypt, in Cairo. His last books include *The Event of the Qur'an* (London, 1971) and *The Mind of the Qur'an* (London 1973).

of inter-religious concern, in being itself a study of religious existence under stress. The paragraphs that follow are offered in that double sense.

Our first duty, clearly, is to recognize the difficulty of bringing into related focus the contents of the Qur'an and the context of contemporary history. The subject is at once both elusive and pervasive. Mosque preaching and political leadership are deeply preoccupied with the dilemmas of war and peace, of justice and territory, of suffering and victory. The mosque sermon proceeds from and with the Qur'an while political speeches are often studded with quotation. In this way the time and the text are brought insistently together. Yet, for that very reason, the mutual relation is not easy to determine, still less to define. The external observer will do well always to keep his conclusions open. The habit of citation is one thing, the sense of its authority another. There is always the question whether the text is governing the will that quotes it, or merely serving its turn, and there is the further question whether the quoting and the meaning are at one. Does the use of the Qur'an realise its potential? Is the potential of the Scripture truly active within the selecting pressures through which it is invoked? Insofar as the latter are an immediate Middle Eastern form of deep and common human themes of distress and bitterness, how far do they take us into feasible religious converse proceeding from the Scripture?

There is no need to elaborate here the theme of current history in the Middle East as a deep, active tension, in which fundamental realities – justice, fear, suffering, resentment, force, pride, humiliation, hope – are at issue, behind the sanction of those perennial denominators of human life: territory, land, tradition, culture, power, and politics. One of the greatest experiments of modern history, namely Jewish re-enlandisement and Zionist statehood, has inevitably collided with Arab nationalism. Israeli success has entailed in Arab experience a bitter trauma of frustration, deprivation, and injustice. Early irenic dreams of a feasible compatibility of Jewish statehood and Arab dignity have evidently been disproved and have long ago receded from Israeli thinking, which is now explicitly and confidently self-sufficient and self-secured. One of its paradoxes, and they are many, is that it requires of Palestinians just that acceptance of *diaspora* existence in statelessness which the whole logic of Zionism declares to be finally intolerable. It has cruelly evoked a depth of Palestinian devotion to the same territory, which no honest Israeli can sensibly deny. For every three Israelis, there are two Arab refugees. The fact that this cost in suffering has been tangled and compounded by Arab miscalculation and misreading of destiny only sharpens the bitterness and enlarges the tragedy.[1]

But tragedy is precisely that dimension of history which Quranic Islam is least minded to measure or to face. (One has to say here Quranic Islam, since the whole development of Shi'ah experience lies outside the definitive Scripture and must itself be regarded as a minority verdict within the Muslim household.)[2] The underlying conviction of the Qur'an about history is that it ought to come right, to side unmistakeably with justice and truth, and to vindicate the faithful. Delay, as noted in the initial quotation, must not be interpreted as denial. Nor must it be thought to argue compromise and accommodation. Rather it invites to unswerving assurance and a stance of unyielding awaiting of the right.

The Quranic view of history, as siding with justice, and of faith, as enjoying vindication, lies intrinsically at the core of the Scripture, more vitally than any single quotation will show. The Hijrah, or emigration of the Prophet Muhammad from Mecca to Medina, is the pivotal event of his career. It is also the great watershed of the Book itself, the hinge before and after which all else is reckoned. The emigration from a focal point of religious preaching to a potential center of political authority came after thirteen years of unremitting loyalty to a wholly verbal mission, to what the Qur'an calls al-balagh, "the communication." This is frequently said, in that period, to be his only responsibility (5.99; 16.35; 24.54; 29.18; 36.17; 42.48;

---

[1] This paragraph deserves, of course, the kind of elaboration and documentation for which space here allows no opportunity. Two of the most perceptive presentations, in a situation in which history itself often becomes partisan, are: Christopher Sykes, *Crossroads to Israel: From Balfour to Bevin*, London; and *Search for Peace in the Middle East, A Quaker Study*, London, 1970.

[2] The Shi'ah are a divergence within Islam, dating from the third decade after Muhammad and involving, among other factors, the experience of unremitting adversity and the perplexing suffering which gave the rise to a faith about "the passion of Husain" which, embodied the Shi'ah ritual, has remained a powerful symbol of "redemption" in Islam. But that experience lay outside Quranic history and, like much else in general Islam, postdates revelatory status in the pure sense.

64.12, etc.) But steadily there grew upon him the conviction that, if the word alone did not suffice to win and hold allegiance and obedience, then loyalty to the word required that its herald and mouthpiece go beyond the vocal sphere and become its active "establisher," its forceful vindicator, in the name of God. This is the Hijrah. This was the significance of Medina as the Prophet's city, the means and the base for the reduction to submission of the Meccan rejectors whose obduracy inspired the emigration. The Battle of Badr, as the first event after the Hijrah on the road to that success, is known in the Qur'an as *Yaum al-Furqan*, "the day of criterion" (8.41), meaning that the signal victory of the few over the many had discriminated forever the true from the false, the right from the wrong. That victory stands, in a sense, as the Exodus of Islam, the decisive, almost traumatic, event which fixed forever the *mores* of the soul, the assumptions of the faith.

These are that right triumphs and that due force are its proper instrument and means. The Qur'an itself has *Al-Furqan* as one of its own titles (2.53; 2.185; 3.4; 25.1) and the association is very close between the Book which is definitive in the spirit and the power which is definitive in the world. Throughout, in Muhammad's later career, and in the subsequent "mind" of Islam, there is this ready identification between the essential and the external, between the faith in the heart and the prospering of its way in the world. "Obey God and obey the Apostle," is its frequent refrain (3.32; 3.132; 8.20; 58.13, etc.), joining in a single, uncomplicated simplicity the historical order of Muhammand's rule and the theological sovereignty with which it shares identity, as far as the believer's guidance is concerned – and the believer's duty.

"God sent no prophet," declares 4.63: "except that he should be obeyed, by God's ordering." This "obedience" has been traditionally understood as not simply a mental credence or a spiritual cognizance, but a political allegiance. The great Ibn Khaldun (d.1406 A.D.) in his monumental study of history interprets it as meaning the necessity of group-loyalty and state-form to any and all prophetic status and heavenly apostolate. So it is that war is better than *fitnah*. Sedition and conspiracy against truth are a greater evil than the power which defends faith and crushes unbelief (cf.

2.191; 2.217; and 8.39: "Make war until there be no more *fitnah*," i.e., no more active resistance, no more contumely, no more unbelief).

This Philosophy of the necessarily powerful sinews of religion is, of course, implicit in the very term *islam* which houses, and in measure conceals, the ambiguity that must be present here. The verb *aslama* (of which *islam* in the common, verbal noun) means both to submit, and to become a Muslim The faith dimension interpenetrates with the state dimension. So it was in the expansion of Islam. What people accepted was not merely a "message," spread by an "evangelism," but also a sovereignty bringing and enforcing a polity and rule. So complete is the identity between power in the service of religion and faith in the behest of force, as Islam and the Qur'an characteristically and confidently combine them.

This is not to say the the Qur'an is oblivious of the menace in this ambiguity, of the possibility that when power is successful submission may be merely prudential and the faith within it, therefore, mere semblance and so, finally, irreligious. There is an intriguing passage in 49.13 where certain desert Arabs came and said: "We have believed (*amanna*)," and Muhammad was directed to reply to them: "You have not believed. You should say: 'We have submitted' (*aslamma*). For faith has not yet entered your hearts." This significant distinction plainly involves the fact that *islam* politically could and did happen without *islam* religiously, and that the disparity (or contradiction) should be detected and repaired.

The same awareness underlies the frequent Quranic theme of *nifaq*, or hypocrisy, which becomes prominent, naturally, once success is achieved. Then hangers-on become numerous. The Book calls them *munafiqun*, "hypocrites." Their dissimulation has to be exposed though that very exercise may drive them to a subtler form of pretence, whence follows a descending spiral of suspicion and countering falsehood which, in its nadir, means a forfeiture of true religion.

That danger is understood as the necessary price of the indispensable reliance on power. For there are even greater dangers – the likely extinction of the faith itself (than which there can be no greater evil) unless this risk is run. Power may have its complications. But to shoulder them is realism and, in Islamic terms, is religious consistency and religious loyalty. A faith that has only Gethsemanes to offer in response to its enemies is manifestly unsuited to this world, just as a state which renounced power would be seen as chronically sick.

The Quranic treatment of Jesus, however we derive or explain it historically, fits into this scheme. It was not given to Jesus (the 'Isa of the Qur'an) to lead a successful prophetic mission in those manifest external terms that house the achievement of Muhammad. But, by the same token, his non-political status, his innocence of state-success, are not Islamically seen as a deep theme of travail by which suffering is illuminated and redeemed. Jesus, as the honoured messenger who is not called to an effective rulership, is not left naked to his foes. He is rescued by divine intervention (see Surah 4.158 f.) and raptured to heaven, to security, and to "vindication." It cannot be that he should be left to mere victimization at the hands of Jewish detractors. The God who "established" Muhummad in the signal victory of efficient religious statehood "establishes" Jesus in the different currency of heavenly exaltation, rewarding his faithful word, but foreclosing and precluding his redemptive "establishing" of grace by its paradigm in the Cross.

The theme of the Quranic Jesus, which in a different context would deserve far more detailed study,[3] is here simply taken as a further confirmation of the essential role of vindication as a historical necessity. History cannot be allowed to be tragic. The Quranic sense of power for justice and of justice *via* power is too strong to let itself be finally perplexed or halted by the tangle of sorrow, the entail of suffering, the mystery of vicariousness, which, for other perceptions, are written so deeply across the human story. Islam, characteristically does not relish issues of theodicy, nor stay to question the divine sovereignty which it so strongly and uncomplicatedly enthrones in heaven.

It is, therefore, only another of the paradoxes of the East that this highly expectant world of Arab Islam, this instinctively oriented soul of

---

[3] The topic has been explored, in part, in the fascinating Muslim study, *City of Wrong, a Friday in Jerusalem*, by Muhammad Kamil Husain, Cairo, 1954; paperback English translation, New York: Seabury Press, 1964. Se also the present writer's *The Call of the Minaret*, New York, 1956, pp. 294-304.

insistence about historical justice, should be the arena of the Zionist penetration which, with equal insistence, requires its neighbors to "suffer" it. The very ambiguity of that verb is eloquent. For Israel, in asking to be "tolerated" behind secure borders is, in all the given circumstances, asking to be "suffered" in a much deeper sense, to be "suffered for," in that her being there, her viability on her own terms, exact this grim price of tragedy of those who, in territory, rights, and person, pay the grievous historical cost of what Israel demands to be. The form and fabric of successful Zionism as we know it can only have peace in its chosen context of time and place by dint of a Palestinian reading of what history entails in terms that run counter to all the instinctive assumptions, the habits of mind, of the Quranic world.[4]

The practicalities of Middle East peace, if and when it comes, will doubtless turn on factors more immediate, more material, than those of theology and the Islamic soul. Yet, if such peace is ever to be a spiritual liberation of energies, as distinct from a calculation of necessity, it will need to embrace a positive quality of compassion, of anger transmuted, of evil transcended, of suffering redeemed. What hints are there in the Qur'an of these dimensions? Could there be a ministry of inter-religious relationship in the service of these ends?

It will be clear from the argument thus far that it would be false to the Islamic understanding of Divine sovereignty in history to expect a logic of non-violence to develop from Quranic premises. While there have been concepts of passivity in expectation of God in some forms of Islamic Sufism, these have an esoteric and unrepresentative quality. Nevertheless, if there is the will to recognize them, there are certain powerful indications in Quranic sources that might serve to undergird the sort of reaction to events which looked beyond tragedy to "some new thing."

---

[4] It is remarkable how much Palestinian Resistance poetry indirectly recognizes this situation in its frequent likening of the tragedy of Palestine to the crucifixion of Jesus. This occurs, remarkably, in Muslim poets, for example in the *Divan* of Mahmud Darwish, who dogmatically do not believe that the Cross happened. Yet they draw a close parallel between a suffering country (as they see it) and a victimized Christ. This stance has a deep danger in it ("See the same people doing the same things," it seems to say). But, at the same time, it may point beyond "victimization" to the question of what the victim does with his or her sorrow. If we say, as one Arab Christian priest lately wrote: "Every refugee camp is a Gethsemane," it is only true *qua* distress; it is not true (not yet true) *qua* the transmuting of the evil.

One might be argued from the concept of *itmi'nan*, or inner peace of soul, a quality which subdues the restless claims and appetites of human beings, in an inward tranquillity which is the prerequisite of peaceableness in the outer world. This inner peace means at least a readiness to be at peace with the world, in that a compulsive belligerence is surmounted in the centre of the will. This in no way implies some relinquishment of the demands of justice but, rather, the kind of dimension which, in the New Testament phrase, "leaves room for the judgment of God."

One Cairo scholar and writer, Dr. Muhammad Kamil Husain, who has strongly stressed this Quranic "will to peace within the heart," has also developed the fundamental Quranic concept of *Shirk*, in a way that disqualifies all absolutes, even those that seem to have justice with them. *Shirk*, of course, is the most reprehensible of all *zulm*, or evil. It means whatever violates the rights of God. Violators, in the original days of Islam's genesis, were the false idols of the pagan pluralism vainly worshipped. Today they are the tyrannies of nation, class, or system, which people all too readily exalt to ultimate status. To relativize all that would otherwise usurp what belongs to God alone is the active intention of *Tauhid*, or unity. That sole Godness of God is denied when race, or state, or class, or dogma or cause establish an authority over the mind that, in effect, dominates where only God should rule. The other side of that rule is a submission of all things, not least those that have just claims, lest they become all-compelling. *Tauhid* and *Shirk*, in their fullest significance, require us to distinguish resolutely between invoking God for a cause and submitting a cause to God. The distinction, and the active sense of it, are surely part of the deep relevance of the great Islamic call to worship: *Allahu akbar,* "greater is God."

Further to this context, there is the basic principle of Divine mercy in the Qur'an. "God has prescribed for Himself mercy." says Surah 6.54. It is oftentimes through one's mercy to others that the Divine mercy operates in history. God fulfills His mercifulness through the action of those who believe in Him. Or, conversely, as Kamil Husain puts it, the practice of mercy is the core and meaning of the belief. Such a conviction points away from hardness of heart in the adversities of history and forward to perspectives of hope.

It may be right to find this corroborated in the distinctive Quranic call to *Istighfar*. For this is one of its richest and deepest terms.[5] It means the "seeking of forgiveness" from God, as the constant duty of believers. The sense of evil done – whether by oneself against others or by others against oneself – requires this posture of spirit by which, in the one case, repentance is practised and, in the other, forgiveness is sought. It seems clear that people cannot pursue the will towards forgiveness (whether for themselves as doers or for others who have wronged them) without being active partners either way with the mercy of God. There is about Quranic *Istighfar* a protective aspect, both as to evil in retrospect and to evil in prospect. It seeks to be rid of its menace both within and without. This, in turn, suggests an alertness to the human tragedy as a whole, an awareness of solidarity in evil as history knows it, a recognition of the tangled complexities of sin as being a complicity of many factors, none of them to be lightly exonerated and all of them in need of mercy. It points – if there is the will to let it do so – in the direction of an inclusive *catharsis* in which evil is not, finally, a theme of neutralism, nor of vengeance, but of forgiveness sought and found. No one can deny that such an inclusive *Istighfar* would fit the current Middle Eastern scene.

Of course, it will and must be said that this is not the feasible thinking of bodies politic or states, based as they are on power. Nor must the outsider *will* such an inclusive interpretation upon the Arab Muslim, even though he may aspire to help him will it. States, it must be acknowledged, have to deal in realism and in the terms of power, or else, as Machiavelli observed long ago, we would have to conclude that they are sick.

But, even on this realist ground of the state, it needs to be remembered that the political in Islamic theory is always at the behest of the Divine. If the state was always understood as indispensable to religion's authority, it was also understood to be instrumental to the Divine will. The principle works both ways. If there was, about the Islamic marriage of faith and power, an almost frightening authority to require, there was also the

---

[5] This rich term is the theme of study, at better length, in my *The Mind of the Qur'an*, London, 1973, Chapter 7.

deep obligation to serve, the ends of God. In the very claim of the state on the Divine favor there resides, for those with wills to see, the claim of the Divine mind upon the state's assumptions. That being the case, the last analysis is never properly *political*, but spiritual, not national rights but human concerns, not the past recovered for justice, but the present retrieved for compassion. By such a calculus, the state has no final right to make human dignity subservient to politics, nor hostage to arguments of power if these over-ride the claims of people, of persons in their human need. For it is only in terms of the latter that sovereignty is truly "under God."[6]

It may be that the reader is impatiently protesting that such prescripts of compassion, such pleas of obligation for the peaceful retrieval of human tragedy, are addressed to the wrong quarter. They are, it must be justly said, the obligations of Zionism and of Israel. It is the intruder who must respond to compassion, who must reverse the power-stance, and undo his forcible dispossession of others. Indeed he must. The conscience of Israel, if we may use the term, is the largest question mark of present history, in the light of both of Israeli memory of diaspora and holocaust and of Arab tragedy. There can be no right finality about a state for every three of whose citizens there are two refugees. Hardness of heart begets its like: peace kindles at the sight of its own features.

The conscience of Israel, however, is not Quranically determined, as that of Islam is. Further, the Arab mind is rightly aware that the European, Hitlerite, Stalinist, historical "necessity" for the new homeland and for its state-form, is not at all at the door of Arab history. On the contrary, minorities of Jews, prior to Israel, had security in Arab lands and would continue to do so apart from Israel. It was the provocation of the new state, which, in the form in which it chose to constitute its haven, deranged indigenous Middle Eastern Jewry into needing it. Why should Arab history and Arab people take the cost of the reparation to European shame?

In relating its innocence of European crimes to its suffering from their entail in Palestine, the Arab mind insistently distinguishes between hostility

---

[6] As the phrase goes: *Al-Mulk li-llah*, "the ownership, the Lordship, the property rights in all things, are God's."

to Israel and enmity to Jewishness. This stance is a genuine discrimination which needs greater recognition in the West than it frequently receives. Yet it is one which, in all the circumstances, it is difficult humanly to sustain. For aside from the frailty of all ideals, there is also the degree to which Israeli self-justification in political and spiritual terms coincides with that persistent sense of having God in possession which the Qur'an so steadily reproaches in its remonstrances with the self-serving people of "the covenant."

So, while the Qur'an enjoins and enforces the historic continuity of the monotheisms, beginning with Abraham, through Moses and beyond, it also has repeated occasions of necessary reproach to Jewry for obstinacy and pride. It can, therefore, be consciously or unconsciously liable to invocation by Arab Muslims against any sort of apprehension of the logic by which Israel vindicates itself. In that sense it must be admitted that the Qur'an does not predispose the Muslim mind to the sort of magnanimity about renascent Zion, its vision, and its compromise, which Israel is ultimately going to need from the Arab soul, if ever its securities and aspirations are to be more than power-based and ruthlessly wrought. Rather the picture of Jewry in the Qur'an can serve a reader's temptation to see the now three-quarter-century confrontation as a further, bitter installment of the arrogance from which Muhammad himself once suffered. If there is to be reconciliation, history has set for it the toughest of scenes.

But that is no ground for renouncing hope. We return where we began, to the concept of *sabr*. Is history under God the handmaid of justice for which we wait, with endurance against adversity, until right vindicates our steadfastness? "Do not weaken and sue for peace –*fa antum al-a laun* – you are (future sense) the upper ones," and the verse we quoted. Such *sabr*, so understood, has much to commend it – fortitude, tenacity, unyieldingness, an admirable persistence which does not bow to fate. Is it not well to refuse the kind of peace which connives against honor, the peace of the pusillanimous? "God is with the patient," says the Qur'an. "Let them hold out" (8.46). Such patience is the virtue that persists until it is rewarded with restitution. It is the keeping open of the option of retaliation. It is the expectation of the feasibility of the *status quo ante*. It is the refusal to admit that history may be irrecoverably tragic: in that very circumstance we may still be in truth and deed "the upper ones." Or is there, beyond such refusal, another pattern of recoverability?

Here lies the deepest reach of the issue of peace in the Middle East, as implicitly studied in the potential of Quranic thought. Here, therefore, is one of the largest themes of inter-religious openness, the one to the other, in heart and conversation. However unworthily the church has served it, however remotely even understood it, there lies at the heart of the New Testament an understanding of suffering, not as an episode calling for tenacity on the way to requital, but as an achievement of acceptance on the way to reconciliation. It was not, as the Gospel believes it, by escape, or retaliation, or holding out for justice, that Jesus redeemed the world. It was by bearing, and so bearing away,[7] the evil men did to Him, that Jesus, in the drama of the Cross, set men free for a peace which stood in the power of sacrifice, a peace which incorporated its enemies, and from which faith learned to apprehend the mind of the eternal God. Out of events in which we can fully identify what is tragic about us all, we see the path of the wisdom and the power of God, reconciling the world to Himself.

Is it not there that we can say: *Allahu akbar,* "great is God," and in that measure of His greatness set our measure of what history requires of us?

---

[7] Echoing the actual double meaning of the Greek participle in John 1.29. The Cross affirms that it is only in "taking" the wrong that we can "take it away."

THE LACK OF JEWISH-ARAB DIALOGUE IN ISRAEL AND THE SPIRIT OF JUDAISM: A TESTIMONY*

Haim Gordon**

The simple idea which I shall put forth in this article is that the spirit of Judaism is suffering an eclipse in Israel. One reason for this eclipse is the lack of Jewish-Arab and Jewish-Muslim dialogue. Here these developments will not concern me, for two reasons. First, I shall be addressing the existential responsibility of each Jew for the spirit of Judaism. The responsibility may be influenced by economic or social or historical developments, but, if it becomes the sole effect of such developments, it is no longer a personal responsibility. Second, dialogue, as Buber described it, can

---

* *Journal of Ecumenical Studies*, 23.2, (Spring, 1986).

** Haim Gordon (Jewish) is Senior Lecturer in the Department of Education at Ben Gurion University, Beer Sheva, Israel, where he has taught since 1975. He has taught at the University of South Alabama (1983-84) and at the Frei Universität Berlin (6 mo.). A recipient of foundation grants for a peace-education project in accord with Martin Buber's philosophy for development of a peace curriculum in Israeli schools, he has worked for seven years on education for peace and dialogue between Arabs and Jews throughout the Mideast. He holds a B.A. and an M.A. from Tel Aviv University and Ph.D. (1975) from George Peabody College for Teachers (Vanderbilt University). His books include *Martin Buber: A Centenary Volume* (co-edited with Jochanan Bloch: KTAV, 1984), *Dance, Dialogue, and Despair: Existentialist Philosophy and Education for Peace in Israel* (University of Alabama Press, 1986), and "Educating for Peace: Testimonies of Spirit" (Orbis, forthcoming). His nearly twenty articles have appeared in numerous educational, religious, and philosophical journals, most recently including "Dialectical Reason and Education: Sartre's Fused Group," *Education Theory* (Winter, 1985); and Sartre's Struggle against the Holy," *International Journal for Philosophy of Religion* (in press).

break through the influences dominating the "It" world and create a new ontology. Such can be done by each person, by each "Thou."

Yet, two questions arise even before I present this idea. What do I mean by the spirit of Judaism? And, who am I to judge that the spirit of Judaism is suffering an eclipse? Since I am not a rabbi or a spiritual leader or a theologian or a politician, who gave me the right to make such a forceful judgment? Let me address the latter question first.

My answer has three responses. First, I am merely an educator with some philosophical background. Yet, when a house is on fire, even the youngest and least talented child can sound the alarm. Second is the well-known Jewish legend about the Hasidic congregation who prayed one Yom Kippur, fervently and devoutly, but the rabbi and the entire congregation felt that their prayers were heavy and could not rise to heaven to open the gates of redemption. The rabbi cried and beseeched, but the gates remained closed. Suddenly, a young boy sitting in the last benches, a shepherd who had no learning or knowledge of the holy script, let out a loud and screeching whistle. The congregation was astounded and wanted to admonish the boy—how dare he thrust profanity into the holiness of Yom Kippur! But the rabbi turned to the congregation and falteringly said: "Let him be, he whistled with true *kavana*, with true intent to reach God. Now the gates of redemption have finally opened." My third response is the simplest. I have spent the past five years working intensively on promoting Buberian dialogue between Jews and Arabs.[1] I have succeeded partially and failed greatly. I have also sensed where and how such a lack of dialogue is diminishing the power of spirit in Judaism. I will not be able to articulate all that I have sensed, but I can at least raise the alarm—and perhaps whistle screechingly.

---

[1] Here are some of my writings on this work: "Buberian Learning Groups. A Response to the Challenge of Education for Peace in the Mideast," *Teachers College Record* 82 (Winter 1980): 291-310; "Buberian Learning Groups: The Quest for Responsibility in Education for Peace" (co-authored with Jan Demarest), *ibid.* 84 (Fall, 1982): 210-225; "Existentialist Writings and the Enhancing of Trust: A Method Developed in Buberian Learning Groups," *Israel Social Science Research*, vol. 1, no. 1 (1983), pp. 65-78; *"Buberian Learning Groups: Existentialist Philosophy as an Ariadne Thread in Education for Peace,"* *Teachers College Record* 84 (Fall, 1983): 73-87. Also see my "Ecumenical Events" report in *J.E.S.* 21 (Summer, 1984): 628-629.

To return to the first question: I have no definition of the spirit of Judaism. I doubt whether any such definition would satisfy myself or others. I can point out that the spirit of Judaism may emerge in Jews' daily deeds – if they attempt to perform those deeds in a manner that will help them relate to God. However, one must immediately add that those deeds include relating to the Other as a person, as worthy of being related to justly. The Jew cannot kill, steal, or be a false witness in a manner that will help him or her relate to God. Such is a contradiction in the Jew's essential being – not only because these deeds defy the Decalogue. Defying the Decalogue is a grave sin, but sins may be forgiven; God is not only the God of justice but also the God of mercy. Such deeds are a contradiction in the Jew's being, because the Jew must learn from daily human encounter and from striving for a just and meaningful encounter between people how to understand the divine encounter between the patriarch and God, or Israel and God in the Bible. Without such daily learning, one's relation to the Bible and to God becomes insipid or fanatic; no longer is it vital and humane. None of this is new, and it is couched in general terms, but it suffices to allow me to point out where and how the lack of Jewish-Arab dialogue in Israel eclipses the spirit of Judaism.

II

Undoubtedly, the opportunity for dialogue exists. Israel is an open society: Jews and Arabs meet in the streets, at work, in offices, at Israeli universities, in the market, at the seashore. Furthermore, the Western Wall, Judaism's most holy shrine, is physically attached to El Aktza, one of Islam's most holy mosques. The call to prayer from El Aktza's minarets is often heard by the Jews praying at the wall, yet no meaningful dialogue has occurred or is occurring. Here and there one may find breaches in the barrier of existential mistrust[2] that divides Jews and Arabs – I personally

---

[2] One can characterize the relations between may Jews and Arabs living today in Israel as being based on existential mistrust, which may be defined as a relationship that arises between two persons (or two nations) when one of the persons (or nations) believes that the other denies one's right to exist and to realize one's potential in that portion of the world to which one is attached. The relationship is expressed by the attitude: If I want to exist, I must not trust you.

initiated one such breach – but the barrier stands firm, alienating Jews from Arabs, allowing no dialogical encounter to occur.

The barrier is very much an outcome of political exigencies. I have no doubt that the political aggressiveness and, at times, the religious fanaticism of Arab leaders – from the Mufti of Jerusalem in the 1930's and 1940's to Kadaffi or Abu Iyad today – has been a prime contributor to this sad situation. I also know that some Jewish leaders have diminished the possibility of dialogue. Furthermore, I am quite sure that the spirit of Islam is also suffering from its lack of dialogue with the Judeo-Christian heritage and from the fact that Muslims are rarely willing to engage in Buberian dialogue with Christians or Jews. However, for the purposes of this article, the manner in which the spirit of Judaism suffers due to a lack of such dialogue is what concerns me here. I believe that the spirit of Judaism is being eclipsed in two realms in which it needs to be expressed; the realms often intermingle.

The first realm is that of the *daily deed*. In Israel and on the West Bank and the Gaza Strip there live almost 2,000,000 Arabs, about 650,000 of whom live in Israel and are Israeli citizens. About 1,250,000 live in the West Bank and Gaza Strip under Israeli military rule. All these Arabs, but especially those who are not Israeli citizens, are subject to prejudice, to hatred, and often to exploitation and oppression by Jews. Thus, the Jew lives in a mileu characterized by two standards of justice: There is one standard of justice for relations between Jews and another for relations between Jews and Arabs. The fact that Jews accept the legitimization of this situation-band by their daily deeds support it – is a compliance with the kind of oppression that Jews hated when they were oppressed in a Christian or Muslim society. It is also a rejection of their personal responsibility to pursue justice. Put more bluntly, when a rabbi calls a press conference in Israel in order to announce that the Jewish soldier who shot and killed an unarmed Arab teenage girl in her home, in front of her family, because he identified her as one of those who threw rocks at a Jewish car – when a rabbi announces that this Jewish soldier was acting in accordance with Jewish justice – this rabbi is not only lying and inciting to murder but also eclipsing the spirit of Judaism. Worse, the rabbi is defiling that spirit.

I suspect that many Jews fear to enter into dialogue with Arabs because it would demand changing their basic attitudes toward Arabs and toward the dual standard of justice which they support. Their way of life rejects the daily deed by which one pursues justice. In Judaism the deed is to be done not only because it is a commandment of God but also because we learn through attempting to perform the deed where we have been mistaken in our former perceptions, attitudes, and behavior. Hence, the attempt to enter into dialogue with Arabs is a way for Jews to perfect themselves and to learn about their relation to other people, to their heritage, and to God. In short, the entering into dialogue is there, waiting to be done, and Jews do not attempt to do it.

Many Jews in Israel cite two reasons for their refusal to engage in dialogue with Arabs. The prevalent reason is that they need to muster their spiritual strength primarily in order to ensure Jewish existence in the face of Arab aggression. The second reason is that, in this period of alienation, Jews must direct their spiritual efforts primarily in conveying the traditional Jewish heritage, especially as expressed in Jewish *halakah* and other sources. Each reason is based on an important truth, but this truth has been stretched beyond its legitimate area of validity. In its current form, it has become a lie.

Since the Holocaust there is no need to emphasize the importance of ensuring Jewish existence. We Jews dare not disregard the rhetoric of Arab and Muslim religious fanatics, such as Kadaffi and Khomeini, who openly say that they wish to exterminate us. One terrible mistake of the Jews in Europe was that they viewed Hitler's warnings and speeches as mere rhetoric – but his rhetoric led to the gas chambers of Auschwitz, much as Khomeini's rhetoric has sent many untrained Iranian teenagers to become cannon fodder to Iraqi guns. Yet, in Israel the large majority of Jews believe that ensuring Jewish existence means primarily the strengthening of the Israel Defense Force. Thus has an important truth acquired its most superficial interpretation. It is superficial because ensuring Jewish existence is a spiritual challenge no less than a military challenge. Now, as in biblical times, without the strengthening of the Jewish spirit military might will not ensure a Jewish existence.

For a Jew, relating to an Arab living in Israel as a Thou entails a risk, but by engaging in such risks the Jew expresses and learns about his or her own otherness. It is a responsibility which Jews can evade, but by assuming such a responsibility our Jewish life retains its vitality. Dialogue with an Arab may often end in failure, but if we do not attempt we will never know the ways through which other persons open up to us, as Jews. However, these points are mere explanations which conceal the fact that Jewish-Arab dialogue is a way of strengthening the spirit of Judaism because it is the right thing that needs to be done today, despite the risk, and because of the responsibility, despite the possibility of failure. In deciding to do the right thing, the Jew has no better teachers than the Hebraic prophets, who took the risks, assumed responsibility, and persistently met with failure.

Those Jews who advocate that we must direct our spiritual efforts primarily to conveying the traditional Jewish heritage, especially as expressed in the halakah and in other sources, have expressed a half truth. I agree, as most Jews would that we must direct our spiritual efforts primarily to conveying this heritage. The problem is the interpretation given to these words. Is the Jewish heritage merely a tradition of learning and *pilpul*, of keeping kosher and wearing a skullcap? Does that tradition not also include Abraham bargaining with God so as to save Sodom and Gomorrah? Does it not also include the Hasidic rabbi who said, "There is no room for God in one who is full of oneself"?

I believe – and many traditional Jewish sources support this belief – that the attitude of Abraham and the Hasidic rabbi are more central to the spirit of Judaism than is learning *halakah*, primarily because the spirit of Judaism emerges when a person acts as a free person, when one assumes responsibility for that section of the world in which one finds oneself, when in one's daily life one strives to learn from God to seek both justice and mercy. As it is written in the Sayings of the Fathers: "One who learns in order to do will be given the opportunity to learn and to teach, to guard and to do" (IV, 6). More bluntly, whether the advocates of Jewish *halakah* like it or not, the State of Israel as a secular state is a historical fact; within this history the Jew must act and must learn in order to do. Learning cannot – must not – come instead of the deed; emphasizing learning alone is a rigidification of Judaism which weakens its spirit. And one of the deeds that needs to be done is to dialogue with our Arab neighbors.

Why do I concentrate on the importance of Jewish-Arab dialogue for the spirit of Judaism? Are there not other realms in which the spirit of Judaism is being eclipsed? The metaphorical answer is that a chain is as strong as its weakest link. Similarly, a person's attempts to act in accordance with what needs to be done are impeded by his or her greatest weakness. That weakness hinders one's becoming whole and directing one's powers in a way that will enhance one's spirit. Dialogue with Arabs is our weakest link. The ontological answer was developed by Buber, Marcel, and Berdyaev, among others, in a manner analogous to Hegel's master-slave dialectic. When a person relates to other persons merely as objects to be manipulated and mistrusted, the manipulator becomes an object that is manipulated and mistrusted. Such persons cannot relate spiritually because they perceive themselves, and exist, as objects. They have forfeited their freedom and creativity, their ability to love and to have faith. One may be able to restore such a person's subjective freedom and ability to relate spiritually by encouraging him or her to take the risk of being a person, by helping him or her to engage in dialogue with those other persons formerly perceived as objects to be manipulated and mistrusted.

III

The second realm in which the spirit of Judaism is being eclipsed by the lack of Jewish-Arab dialogue is the *relationship among the Jewish nation, the land of Israel, and God*. The reader of the Bible will discern that the land of Canaan was promised to Abraham and to his progeny under certain conditions. The main condition was that Abraham's descendants and heirs relate wholly to God. In this context "wholly" means both to worship as whole beings and to worship God alone. Worshiping the gods of the land, the Baalim, was strictly forbidden, as was the worshiping of other idols. The Bible also reveals that this promised Land was always inhabited by other peoples. The relating wholly to God and the worshiping of God alone were to be done in those historical conditions with their specific historical exigencies, which may have included war against one's non-Israelite neighbors or living side-by-side with them. Generally, if we exclude the demand to destroy idols or to respond forcefully to attacks of cruelty, God did not allow the Israelites to relate viciously or unjustly to their neighbors. Why?

Before I answer this, I need to point out that I am referring to biblical times not only because the Bible is the source of the spirit of Judaism but mainly because that period is somewhat analogous to ours. During the long diaspora, when works of religious genius such as the Talmud, the Kaballah, and the Hasidic legend were created, the Jew never lived as a member of a sovereign nation. The spirit of Judaism was expressed in historical conditions which did not include living in one's own land, surrounded by some neighbors who are enemies and others who seek peace. Hence, the political and social exigencies which arise when a nation lives on its own land do not appear in any of the post-biblical Jewish writings. We must look to the Bible so as to learn about the relationship of the Jew to the land and to the neighbors living there.

I contend that the reason that the Israelites were not permitted to act viciously and unjustly toward their neighbors has to do primarily with the ontology of faith. (Here I reject as superficial the attempts both of Hermann Cohen to introduce Kantian imperatives into Judaism and of Emil Fackenheim to explain Judaism in terms acceptable to the American Liberal.) Learning from Kierkegaard, Bonhoffer, Buber, and others, I would hold that one cannot relate wholly to God if one is cruel and unjust. The ontology of relations which the cruel or unjust person creates locks him or her into an existence characterized by the division of one's being which Kierkegaard described at length in his discussions of despair and of dread, which he believed Macbeth exemplified. Only a wholehearted turning to God and to other human beings will enable vicious, unjust persons to emerge from the realm of ruinous relations which they have created – and which are slowly eroding their personalities and their very being. But few, very few, are capable of such a wholehearted turning. Kind David's admission of his guilt to the prophet Nathan is one salutary example, and remember that David was guilty of killing Uriah the Hittite, a non-Israelite living in the land of Israel.

Two interwoven trends which have emerged in contemporary Israel and are in opposition to God's treaty with Abraham are the worshiping of the land and the exploiting and oppressing of those non-Jews who inhabit it. The worshipers of the land, such as the Gush Emunim Movement and the Tchiyah Party, hold that the land of Israel is holy, because it was given by God to the Jews. Hence the Jew must do everything, including acts of violence and aggression, to evict the Arab inhabitants from the land and to resettle the Jews there. They base their reasoning on those sections of the book of Joshua outside the context of the entire Bible. The period of conquest of the land of Israel can not and must not be the sole way the Jew learns from the Bible how to live as a Jew. In such learning the Jew is replacing the part for the whole and thus distorting his or her relationship to the spirit of the entire Bible, which is a description of an encounter of the chosen people with God. Further, on need only read the publications of the Gush Emunim Movement and the Tchiyah Party to discern that those Jews who condone and participate in the violent eviction of Arabs from their land have begun to worship the land of Israel. Instead of worshiping the God of Abraham and Moses, they worship a new Baal–the land that Joshua conquered.

Having already indicated how the oppression of Arabs ruins the Jew as a spiritual being, I can only add that this oppression creates a division in the being of the oppressors which will not allow them to relate wholly either to the land or Israel or to God. There is only one way for the Jew to live as a whole being. Again and again one reads in the Bible that the Jew must pursue justice and mercy on the land which was promised to the Jews by the God of justice and mercy; otherwise, the Jew is not worthy of inhabiting that land.

IV

I have described how the lack of Jewish-Arab dialogue eclipses the spirit of Judaism. How could such dialogue–once it came into being–enhance the spirit of Judaism? I have three partial answers. First, historically, many works of Jewish spirit developed in an atmosphere of dialogue with the neighbors of Israel. Second, dialogue creates an onotogical situation in which one can much better express the spirit of Judaism. Third, it is hoped that Jewish-Muslim dialogue will create a new realm of interaction from which both sides will benefit. Each answer deserves further elaboration.

Abraham, Moses, Amos, and Job are just a few of the biblical figures who expressed the spirit of Judaism while attempting to engage in dialogue with non-Jews. In the Middle Ages dialogue between Jews and non-Jews was prominent: Judah Halevi's *Cuzari* is a dialogue between a rabbi and a nonbeliever on the merits of the Jewish faith; many of Maimonides' works were written to guide Jews who were in dialogue with Muslim thinkers and philosophers. In the twentieth century, Martin Buber and Franz Rosenzweig wrote as Jews in dialogue with members of other faiths. (I even discern such a quest for dialogue in the black humor of Philip Roth and the search for truth that characterizes some of Saul Bellow's Jewish characters – but I may be reading my own views into their works). The thrust of this abbreviated survey is that one can hardly imagine Jews grappling to express the spirit of Judaism without the constant dialogue that arises with the non-Jews encountered.

It is important to recall that dialogue, as Martin Buber described it, is not an identifying with the Other but rather a recognizing of and relating to the otherness of the specific person who confronts me, as well as demanding that he or she recognize and relate to my own otherness. During our long, difficult history, when the Jews related dialogically to the otherness of their neighbors, they were also expressing their own otherness. In a few instances this expressing crystallized into works which captured and revealed the spirit of Judaism. In the twentieth century, the Jews' return to the land of Israel has meant encountering the Arabs living there. Relating to these Arabs dialogically, as persons whose otherness we must recognize and confront, can open a new phase in the expression of the Jews' otherness, of our Jewish being.

Martin Buber, especially, and such other theologians and philosophers as Gabriel Marcel and Nicolas Berdyaev also, have pointed out that dialogue creates a new ontology of relations. Freedom, trust, and personal responsibility accompany and arise together with the dialogue relationship.

Hence, the ontological milieu within which exists the person who related dialogically is conducive to acts and deeds which can express the spirit. Buber repeatedly pointed out that the demand from the Jew to create such a milieu was the most important message he read in the Bible. He also noted that it was extremely difficult to create such a milieu. Therefore, one must seek to relate dialogically while performing the everyday deed – and with persons whom one daily encounters.

Living in an ontological milieu of trust, dialogue, and personal responsibility is not only much more relaxing than living as a mistrustful person, but it also allows one to direct one's energies to the deed that needs to be done, which the exigencies of the specific moment demand. It allows one to collect and unify one's being and to direct it to a spiritual goal which transcends the realm of everyday objectivity. Then, perhaps, in a certain few moments that cannot be planned, the person will be able to perform deeds which express the spirit of his or her heritage.

Perhaps one of the most promising revelations in the sad and exciting century for world Jewry is the awareness that we Jews have much to learn from dialogue with other faiths. Here, once again, Buber was a trailblazer, even though his deeds and thoughts were often scorned by other Jews. However, Buber primarily addressed the Christian world and, at times, a thinker from the Far East (Gandhi). He never addressed Muslims, even though he resided in Israel from 1938 until 1965 and heard the muezzins crying daily from the minarets of Jerusalem, but he has left us a legacy of dialogue and pointed out the way we can follow. Furthermore, Buber has shown us that through dialogue with the Christian world certain aspects of Judaism which were concealed for centuries can be discerned and discussed. For instance, the Jewishness of Jesus is now a respectable topic which can be discussed among Jews, and the New Testament can be referred to as a book of revelation with ties to the Hebrew Bible; it is taught in Israeli schools and universities. We have learned much from this development. I believe that a similar learning will arise once we establish dialogue with Muslims, but, as Buber intimated, where that dialogue will lead us is a mystery.

V

I have purposely not addressed one significant question: Are there Arabs and Muslims who are willing to engage in dialogue with us? The answer, of course, is both Yes and No. We are living in a situation which is not amenable to dialogue. Many Arabs and Muslims respond fanatically and destructively to the existence of the Jewish state and to the Jews who reside in the land of Israel; nevertheless, during my five years of work in educating for peace I have encountered a few Arabs who sincerely believe that dialogue is the only way to emerge from our years of strife. They point out that Mohammed believed in a living relationship with all faiths. I now believe that many persons in the Arab world harbor a wish for dialogue which is often concealed by the rhetoric that Arabs love and admire. The following incident lends additional support to my belief.

Some months after President Anwar Sadat was assassinated by religious fanatics, Egyptian television held a series of discussions on whether Islam sanctions the killing of nonbelievers. During such a discussion one sheikh presented a long tirade denouncing nonbelievers and holding that Islam sanctions killing them. A young bearded imam responded:

> As I read the Qur'an, killing is not only despicable, but totally anti-religious. Dialogue is the only way to relate to nonbelievers. But let me tell you a story which appears in the commentary to the Qur'an.
>
> As you know your patriarch Abraham, who was also the father of the other two monotheistic faiths, was always happy when he had a guest for his noonday meal. One day he was sitting in his tent; suddenly, he discerned a wayfarer approaching him. He ran to him and invited him to dine. The old man readily accepted the invitation.
>
> While they were washing their feet, Abraham said: "But there is one condition to our eating together. After the meal we will pray together to the one God and thank him for his bounty." The man answered: "I cannot do that. I have been praying to idols for sixty years. Just for one meal I cannot give up my faith." Abraham grew angry, but the man remained stubborn, and after a short argument he got up and left.

Suddenly the angel Gabriel appeared and said: "Abraham, Abraham, you truly have sinned." "Why? asked the patriarch. "Because God has been feeding that pagan for sixty years, and He has patience with him and with his lack of faith. And you cannot feed him one meal without demanding that he convert."

Abraham immediately arose and ran after the pagan and, after many entreats, convinced him to return to his tent and to dine. He promised to make no conditions as to the prayer after the meal. When they finished dining the pagan asked Abraham why he had changed his mind. Abraham told him about Gabriel's admonition. The pagan replied: "If your God has waited patiently for me sixty years, he must be the true God. Let us pray to him together."

Even if the door to dialogue with our Arab neighbors is only partially open, we Jews must courageously enter this new realm of existence. It is an exciting realm in which, through our daily deeds, we may be able to contribute to the rejuvenation of the spirit of Judaism.

MUSLIM DIALOGUE WITH HINDUS

THE BASIS FOR A HINDU-MUSLIM DIALOGUE AND STEPS IN THAT DIRECTION FROM A MUSLIM PERSPECTIVE[*]

Riffat Hassan[**]

Hindus and Muslims have lived together in the subcontinent of India, Pakistan, and Bangladesh for over 1,000 years. During this time many kinds of conflict – for example, historical/political, socioeconomic, cultural, theological, philosophical, psychological, and personal – have existed between these two religious communities. There have also been periods of violence when members of one community (generally the majority community) have perpetrated acts of aggression upon members of the other (generally the minority community). Sometimes these acts of aggression have been brutal to the extent of being barbarous, and sometimes their magnitude is shocking,

[*] In Leonard Swidler, *Religious Liberty and Human Rights in Nations and in Religions* (Philadelphia/New York: Ecumenical Press/Hippocrene Books, 1986), pp. 125-141.

[**] Riffat Hassan (Muslim) is Associate Professor of Religious Studies at the University of Louisville (KY), where she has taught since 1976. She has also taught at the Louisville Presbyterian Theological Seminary; the University of Punjab in Lahore, Pakistan (her birthplace); Villanova (PA) University; the University of Pennsylvania; and Oklahoma State University, Stillwater, OK. She holds a B.A. in English literature and philosophy and a Ph.D. in philosophy (1968) from St. Mary's College, University of Durham (England). She has been involved in the Kennedy Institute (Georgetown University) Jewish-Christian-Muslim Trialogue since 1979, and with several local, national, and international groups dealing with women of faith, peace concerns, and interreligious dialogue on both scholarly and popular levels. She has published widely in Pakistan and the U.S., especially on the life and work of Iqbal, including *The Sword and the Sceptre* (Iqbal Academy, 1978) and *An Iqbal Primer* (Aziz Publishers, 1979). Her articles in the *Journal of Ecumenical Studies* have concerned Islam and human rights, and Islam and Messianism. She is at present writing a major book on women in Islam and in the Qur'an.

as was the case when – in the bitter aftermath of the partition of the subcontinent into India and Pakistan in August, 1947 – a bloodbath took place in which tens of thousands of human beings (Hindus, Muslims, Sikhs, Christians, and others) were massacred. The nature and number of communal (particularly Hindu-Muslim) riots[1] which have taken place in post-partition India are undoubtedly causes of serious concern to those who would like to see the peoples of this ancient land live together in peace. The troubled history of Hindu-Muslim relations in this area is, thus, clearly recognized at the outset of this essay. I do not attempt to negate or mitigate the fact that, in a number of ways, Hindus and Muslims are, and have always been, antagonistic to each other's realities as well as aspirations – and that this leads at times to all kinds of negative consequences, including physical violence.

The perspective from which this essay is written, however, while acknowledging the problems of Hindu-Muslim relations in Pakistan, Bangladesh, and (chiefly) India, focuses on the possibilities of Hindu-Muslim dialogue in this region. This perspective is grounded in my belief that, despite all the problems that Hindus and Muslims have had vis-à-vis one another through the centuries, they have been able in their millennium of coexistence in one geographical area to develop and maintain a pluralistic society which is as genuine as may be found anywhere in the world.

Since human beings are imperfect, any human society they create is imperfect. No pluralistic society in the world is free from a sense of dis-ease or tension, but this state of dis-ease or tension is not necessarily an evil. In fact, very often it is a blessing since it militates against a society's becoming stagnant and apathetic. Pluralism is good precisely because it embodies points of view which are not identical or even harmonious and thus cannot lead to a totalitarianism in which human differences are not tolerated and all human beings are subjected to the supreme oppression of having to conform to uniformity imposed from without. It is the effort to evolve a pattern of

---

[1] An interesting sociological analysis of communal rioting in India is contained in R. A. Schermerhon's monograph, *Communal Violence in India – A Case Study*, ed. Syed Z. Abedin (Kalamazoo, MI: Consultative Committee of Indian Muslims, 1976).

"the good life" within the framework of differing perspectives and values which makes pluralistic societies creative and dynamic.

As most Americans have heard, "There is no such thing as a free lunch." There is a price to be paid for pluralism, just as there is a price to be paid for democracy. Hindus and Muslims in the subcontinent have paid, and are paying (especially Muslims in India[2]), the price for pluralism, but – given the state of the world in which we all live – I believe that their experience of coexistence represents a significant achievement. The spirit of this experience is reflected in what may be called "a dialogue of life," which has been going on for centuries between Hindus and Muslims of the subcontinent. Such a dialogue was, and is, unavoidable and inevitable, given the fact that Hindus and Muslims have inhabited the same physical and cultural world since the tenth century.

The dialogue of life which emerges out of the processes of life is not a contrived matter. It arises "naturally" as it were from the interaction, positive and negative, obvious and subtle, verbal and nonverbal, between various peoples or persons. This dialogue is not the sort of dialogue we talk about in academic meetings because this dialogue proceeds not in accordance with rationally debated, mutually agreed-upon criteria or guidelines for dialogue but in accordance with the existential needs of those who generate this dialogue. However, to ignore either the reality or the importance of this dialogue of life in any discussion of Hindu-Muslim dialogue in the

---

[2] The situation of Muslims in India is eloquently described by K. L. Gauba, who converted to Islam from Hinduism but rejected the two-nation theory (according to which Hindus and Muslims were two separate nations and chose to live in "secular" India rather than in "Islamic" Pakistan), in *Passive Voices: A Penetrating Study of Muslims in India* (Lahore: Pakistan Foundation, 1975). The following passage summarizes the author's feelings and the intent of the book: "It is with some sorrow and regret that the work was undertaken as the writer was no believer of the two-nation theory, and strongly opposed the partition of the country into two dominions of India and Pakistan. But after over twenty years in India as an Indian citizen, it must with sorrow be declared that its much proclaimed secularism is hollow, and much as the American Negro, though American, cannot rid himself of his color the Indian Muslim, though Indian, is nevertheless by and large unable to survive the inferiority of being a Muslim. It is said he keeps aloof from the 'mainstream.' After reading the book the reader will be able to decide for himself whether the Indian Muslim does not join the mainstream or is successfully kept away from it" (p. x). Also of interest to those who want to understand the psychology of Muslims in India is chap. 6 of W. C. Smith, *Islam in Modern History* (Princeton: Princeton University Press, 1977).

subcontinent is to cheat oneself of what is perhaps the most valuable resource available to those of us who are committed to bringing about better understanding and relations between the two major religious communities of this ancient and vast civilization. In today's world many theologians realize the need for making "theology from above" coalesce with "theology from below." Likewise, there is a great need today to make "dialogue from above" coalesce with "dialogue from below." While it is true that the reflections and discussions of scholars produce ideas and schemata which play an important, perhaps even a crucial, role in molding the ideas and attitudes of the common people, it is even more true that grass-roots dialogue is what has the greatest impact on pragmatic reality.

While we must never permit ourselves to forget the violations of human rights which occur in and between India, Pakistan, and Bangladesh and seek constantly to strive for justice on behalf of all those who are discriminated against by the political and cultural systems prevailing in these countries, we must also seek to remember that for a millennium Hindus and Muslims have not only been neighbors in one physical region but have also had to face the same kinds of problems: the curse of massive illiteracy, poverty, and superstition; the burden of an ever-increasing population pressure in an area where tremendous inequities exist in terms of distribution of power and wealth; the difficulties of survival in societies run by incredibly corrupt persons – to mention just a few of the many problems which confront the common Hindu and Muslim living in the subcontinent. Facing common problems creates a strong bond between human beings regardless of caste, creed, or color. Anyone who has lived in the subcontinent understands what is meant by the first whole truth of Buddhism – that life is *dukkha* (suffering) – and this truth which is learned experientially by the teeming masses of Indians, Pakistanis, and Bangladeshis militates against self-centered isolationism or selfish indifferences toward the plight of others. Suffering may not always lead to wisdom or compassion, but wisdom and compassion are seldom found in those who have not suffered. It is my belief that the people of my subcontinent – Hindus, Muslims, and others – possess much wisdom and compassion and that this is born of their suffering.

It is perhaps an irony or a paradox that those who are able to suffer deeply are also able to rejoice deeply. In few places in the world have I experienced the deep sense of joy I have felt in the homes of the people of my subcontinent. It is hard to describe to those who do not belong to this world what human relations mean to people of this world – Hindus, Muslims, and others. In this world, human relations are cherished far above material things, and the joy which a person feels in having or in being a mother, father, brother, sister, spouse, child, relative, or friend to another radiates through all the vicissitudes of fortune. In their attitude to family and friends, Hindus, Muslims, Sikhs, Christians, and other peoples living in the subcontinent are amazingly similar. They are also very similar in believing that people should meet and greet each other with courtesy and respect, especially when they address someone older in age, and in considering hospitality to others a very important value and virtue.

Aside from these similarities which provide the basis for a dialogue of life between Hindus and Muslims (and others) in the subcontinent, there are also other cultural bonds. One of the most important of these is the bond of common language. Hindus, Muslims, and Sikhs who speak Punjabi, for instance, gravitate toward each other. I have met Hindus and Sikhs living in the Western world who become tearful when they hear that I come from Lahore, a city loved by all the Punjabis, even as Delhi is loved by all those who speak Urdu. How important language is to a people is illustrated dramatically in the case of the alienation of the people of what was formerly East Pakistan from the state of Pakistan. This process of alienation began in the early 1950's. Bengali was not given the status of Urdu, which was declared to be the one national language even though the Bengalis constituted the majority of the people of Pakistan. The insensitivity shown by the federal government of Pakistan to the East Pakistanis' sentiment regarding Bengali did not diminish with time and continued to exacerbate the problems existing between the two wings of the country.

Here it would not be inappropriate to refer to the supreme irony embodied in the secession of East Pakistan from Pakistan, a country which had been created so that Muslims could live together according to the Islamic Shari'a. Critics of the creation of Pakistan had always upheld that religion could not be made the basis of statehood. For instance, Maulana Abu'l Kalam Azad, an outstanding Muslim who became a disciple of Mahatma Gandhi, said in his autobiography:

> It is one of the greatest frauds on the people to suggest that religious affinity can unite areas which are geographically, economically, linguistically, and culturally different. It is true that Islam sought to establish a society which transcends racial, linguistic, economic, and political frontiers. History has, however, proved that after the first few decades, or at most after the first century, Islam was not able to unite all Muslim countries into one state on the basis of Islam alone.[3]

Having watched the course of events preceding the 1971 civil war from which East Pakistan emerged as Bangladesh from very close quarters as a senior officer in the Federal Ministry of Information in Pakistan, I am convinced both that East Pakistan would not have seceded from Pakistan if a political instead of a military solution had been attempted, and that the loss of East Pakistan represents not so much an inability on the part of Islam to hold together two physically noncontiguous and culturally diverse regions as it does the failure of the Pakistan government to uphold Islamic principles of justice in the country as a whole.

The creation of Bangladesh did not represent a rejection of Islam as a way of life, as the majority of the people of Bangladesh continue to be devoutly Muslim, nor did it represent a well-considered rejection of Pakistan as a state as is shown by the tragic fact that today there are tens of thousands of Bengalis from Bangladesh who are working in Pakistan, having acquired forged papers making them citizens of Pakistan. At the same time, it must be pointed out that cultural bonds can and do at times transcend religious convictions. During the pre-war period, for instance, the East Pakistanis revolted violently when the government of Pakistan prevented Radio Pakistan, Dacca, from broadcasting the writings of Rabindranath Tagore since he was a Hindu. It is sad but not surprising that the culturally illiterate government of Pakistan should have failed to appreciate the universalism of Tagore since it is unable, to this day, to appreciate the universalism of Iqbal

---

[3] *India Wins Freedom: An Autobiographical Narrative* (Bombay: Asia Publishing House, 1959), p. 227.

and insists jingoistically on making him exclusively the poet-philosopher of Pakistan.

Moving beyond the Hindu-Muslim dialogue of life, which is rooted in a common culture, I would like to refer to another extremely important realm of life in which the Hindu-Muslim dialogue has existed since the advent of the first Sufis into India: this is the realm of spirituality. All students of this area know how deep the spiritual quest of the children of this soil has been since the worldliness of the Vedic Aryans was superseded by the otherworldliness of the Upanishadic way of life and vision as well as the teachings of Buddhism, Jainism, and other ascetic sects. The Muslim mystics who came to India found the ground prepared for their work. Their passionate proclaiming of the existence of a loving, forgiving, saving God with whom a personal relationship could be established through single-minded devotion touched many hearts. It was Muslim Sufis, not Muslim soldiers, who converted masses of Hindus to Islam. Such conversions ought to have pleased the custodians of the Islamic Shari'a and Muslim rulers in India, but they did not. To holders of both secular and religious power in Islam, the Sufis have, since the early centuries of Islam, appeared as a great threat since they acknowledge the authority and sovereignty of no one but God and also because their devotion to God does not always exhibit itself in prescribed ways. For instance, knowing how important music was to the worshipful people of India, many Sufis adopted music in their worship – a practice frowned upon by the so-called "Shari'a-minded" Muslims. Regardless, however, of the attitudes of the Islamic establishment toward them, the mystics of Islam developed a spiritual bond with masses of Hindus, both those who converted to Islam and those who did not. The influence of Islamic mysticism on the Hindu bhakti movement and of Hindu mysticism on Muslim spirituality is well known, and it is noteworthy to mention here that Iqbal was very proud of being "a Brahmin's son" who represented a synthesis of Hindu and Muslim spiritual insight.[4]

---

[4] In this context, reference may be made, for instance, to the following verses:

Mir and Mirza have staked their heart and faith on politics,
it is just this son of a Brahman who knows the secrets (of reality)
(S. A. Vahid, ed., *Baqiyat-e-Iqbal* [Lahore, 1966], p. 225)

Many messianic ideas are also common to Hindus, Muslims, and the other peoples of the subcontinent, and veneration is shown generally to all "saints" irrespective of their religious origin. Muslim scholars such as Fazlur Rahman deplore the appearance of messianism in Islam and attribute it to foreign influences, but I believe that there were also substantial reasons and forces within the Islamic tradition which contributed to it and that, although the Qur'an does not provide explicit support for it, it nevertheless has important spiritual, psychological, and emotional value for the masses of Muslims and constitutes a bond with other people who share their messianic hopes and ideas across the barriers of differing religious ideologies.[5] I have heard of Hindus visiting Muslim shrines, and I used to know Bengali Muslims who kept icons of the goddess Kali in their homes as protection against the evil eye. These Muslims were not idolatrous, since they did not deify Kali but regarded her as a savior – or intercessor – figure to whom they could address their fears and aspirations in much the same way that they would to Sufi saints.

Besides the dialogue of life and dialogue at the level of spirituality and the interchange of ideas and practices related to messianic beliefs, Hindus and Muslims in the subcontinent have also had a continuing dialogue on the basis of their common intellectual-aesthetic heritage. Literature, music, and philosophy are but a few areas in which Hindus and Muslims have much in common. There are many Hindus who love Iqbal, just as there are many Muslims who love Tagore. I remember how deeply touched I was several years ago when as a doctoral student working on Iqbal's philosophy I asked Mulk Raj Anand, a noted Indian novelist and scholar, about his feelings toward Iqbal, and he told me that one of his life's deepest desires was to visit Lahore and pay homage at the tomb of Iqbal, who had been his mentor at one time and whom he loved deeply despite the alienation brought about between Hindus and Muslims by the Muslim separatist movement in India. A year later, Mulk Raj Anand wrote to me telling me that he was

---

Look at me for in Hindustan you will not see
another son of a Brahman familiar with the secrets of Rum and Tabriz

(*Zabur-e-'Ajam* [Lahore, 1948], p. 17)

[5] See my "Messianism and Islam," *Journal of Ecumenical Studies* 22 (Spring, 1985): 261-291.

happy in that he had indeed been able to fulfill his desire and pay his respects at Iqbal's mausoleum.

Having mentioned the areas in which I believe a dialogue already exists between Hindus and Muslims in the subcontinent, let me refer now to two areas in which there is either no, or minimal, dialogue between Hindus and Muslims living in India, Pakistan, and Bangladesh. The first is that of dialogue relating to historical/political issues; the second, dialogue relating to theological issues.

The first area is exceedingly difficult for a number of reasons, including the basic one that dialogue presupposes that a peer relationship or a relationship of equality exists between the dialogue partners. Dialogue of certain kinds cannot take place between obviously unequal people. That is why dialogue seldom takes place between masters and slaves and between men and women. In India, Muslims are not equal to Hindus; in Pakistan and Bangladesh, Hindus are not equal to Muslims in many ways. In the matter of writing history, particularly of the last 1,000 years, the historians of the subcontinent encounter serious difficulties. There is great pressure on Hindu historians to write history from the Hindu and the Indian nationalist point of view and on Muslim historians to write history from the Muslim and the Pakistani and Bangladeshi nationalist points of view.[6] Both viewpoints are obviously limited and biased. There is imperative need for writing a history which is comprehensive and just, which shows the mirror to Hindus and Muslims alike. Confronting our mutual history can sometimes be as painful as confronting our personal history if this history is a checkered one, but it is necessary to do so in order to be free of the shadows of the past. Knowing what we did or did not do does not alter the history of the past, but this knowledge – if accepted with courage and honesty – can lead to a different kind of future. It is one of the prime tasks of those interested in promoting Hindu-Muslim dialogue in the area of historical-political discussion to

---

[6] It is to be noted that the nationalist point of view also changes with every new government, particularly in Pakistan and Bangladesh. Each successive (mostly military) regime orders the rewriting of history to "expose" the evils of the previous regime. In any case, Muslim children living in Pakistan are taught that their history began with the first advent of the Muslims into India; they have no sense of identification with the earlier history (including that of the Indus Valley Civilization whose major excavated remains are in Pakistan) of the subcontinent.

emphasize the need for an accurate chronicling of all the facts which led to the alienation of Hindus and Muslims in the pre- and post-partition periods and leads, every now and then, to violence and the violation of the rights of weaker people.

Included in this "objective" history must be the role played in Hindu-Muslim relations by the British imperialists who left India in great haste once they accepted the fact that the golden days of the British Raj were over. So many problems – political, geographical, economic, cultural, and psychological – were the legacy of this Raj to the people of India: Hindus, Muslims, Sikhs, and others. Although almost four decades have gone by since the departure of the British from their most prized imperial possession, people of the subcontinent are still discovering how variegated, widespread, and vicious the results of the British colonial policy of "Divide and Rule" have been. One very important part of any endeavor to establish better relations among the peoples of the subcontinent must be a thorough review of the British role in India, so that the responsibility for the atrocities which were committed against the various victims under the different phases of this rule – particularly the momentous upheaval of the pre- and post-partition period – can be correctly allocated.

As a Muslim and a person committed to dialogue, I do not believe in carrying the baggage of recrimination and bitterness from one life-period to another, but I do believe very strongly that peace is predicated upon justice, and a just evaluation of the past is necessary for establishing peace in the present and the future. Criticism of the British conduct in India does not, of course, mean that the British should be made scapegoats for all the problems which arose among the major religious communities in India. There are undoubtedly a number of problems which preexisted the coming of the British and are related to fundamental differences among these communities.

Without honest and deep self-probing and self-criticism, authentic dialogue with oneself or another is impossible. Hence it is necessary for all the peoples of the subcontinent to look into their own traditions and into their own hearts and minds and souls to discover the sources of these negative feelings and thoughts toward the "other" that periodically erupt in destructive modes of conduct. As stated by a philosopher, those who do not know their history are condemned to repeat it. We who come from a civilization which is not only one of the oldest in the world but also one of the most complex and reflective must understand our history if our future is to be better than our past, but this understanding of history must be comprehensive, not selective. We have to look not only at those periods or events in history which prove our particular bias but also at all the good and the bad together, and to take responsibility, both as individuals and as communities, for our own contribution to the difficulties which exist in our part of the world. However, we must not acknowledge guilt for that for which we are not responsible. The world, it is said, consists of givers and takers. It also appears to consist of persons who acknowledge guilt for everything and those who acknowledge guilt for nothing. Neither attitude is correct from the perspective of Islam, for neither conforms to the idea of justice. A just evaluation of our past requires that the specifics of history be examined closely and that responsibility be allocated for significant events, negative or positive, after proper consideration of all available evidence. And even that is not enough. It is not enough to hold any group – Hindus, Muslims, British, or any other – responsible for any particular event without specifying also which person or persons within the group were involved and what other circumstances (such as the time period) surrounded the event. We distort history by simplifying it. An extremely good example of this is provided by the way in which American television gives world news, particularly in situations (for example, the U.S. hostage crisis in post-revolutionary Iran) in which Americans are involved, directly or indirectly.

Authentic dialogue is not based on abbreviations, even as it is not based on hairsplitting elaborations of known facts. It is based on a clear and careful understanding of what we call "facts" seen in their historical context. Once we are able to identify the sources of a conflict correctly, it becomes possible to transcend the conflict – to forget and forgive, as it were – but as long as we continue to evade a just evaluation, we are trapped in a process of scapegoating either ourselves or others. This, in Qur'anic terminology, is "Zulm," and God tells us not to be "zalimin."

While speaking of history, perhaps a few words are in order about the way in which Muslims and Hindus view it philosophically. According to

414

Kana Mitra, for Muslims, "the universal ideal needs to be concretized in society and in history," whereas, for Hindus, "the concrete is a stepping stone to the universal ideal but the universal can never be fully concretized in history."[7] While her first statement is correct, Muslims would have no difficulty in also affirming her second statement. Like Hindus, Muslims also do not believe that the universal or the transcendent can ever be fully embodied in a material entity. If they believed otherwise, they would be guilty of deifying history as the Marxists are. Here, the following quotation from W. C. Smith's *Islam in Modern History* is relevant:

> Not that Islam...even in its most legalist form, ever became fully idolatrous. Attention was never *confined* to the this-worldly manifestation of value. For the Muslims, involvement in history, though absorbing, is at the most only the obverse of their coin, the reverse of which, polished, brilliant, and pure gold, is in the other world. Islam begins with God, and to Him it well knows we shall return. Its endeavor to redeem history, though total, is derived; it is an endeavor to integrate temporal righteousness in this world with a timeless salvation in the next.[8]

Finally, we come to the area of theological dialogue between Hindus and Muslims in the subcontinent. This is, in a way, the most difficult or problematic of all the areas discussed so far. In view of the fact that I have virtually no personal experience of participating in a Hindu-Muslim theological dialogue, I am hesitant to theorize regarding the methodology to be employed in such dialogue. What I can offer are some reflections and suggestions which might be useful to those who believe, as I do, that theological dialogue between Hindus and Muslims is urgently required in order to eliminate the gross ignorance regarding the "other" which leads to unjust behavior in times of peace and to gross brutality in times of stress.

Any Hindu-Muslim dialogue on theological issues must be carried out against the backdrop of the fact that Muslims entered the subcontinent as conquerors and that it was natural for Hindus to identify the religion of the conquering people as an embodiment of imperialism and militaristic power. The scope of this essay excludes the possibility of exploring the conduct of

---

[7] See p. 428f. below.

[8] *Islam in Modern History*, p. 4.

various Muslim rulers in India in general to determine if and to what degree Hindu allegations regarding Muslim aggression toward non-Muslims in this area are warranted by history. Such questions, of course, need to be asked and must be answered in the context of the political/historical dialogue mentioned earlier. However, in the context of theological dialogue it is more pertinent to look at questions or issues which effect the way in which Hindus and Muslims perceive each other's religious traditions and the impact which such perceptions have on their daily lives.

There is no question at all that the overwhelming majority of the Muslims in the world, if they have heard of Hinduism at all, think of Hindus as idol-worshippers. In a religious tradition as strictly monotheistic as Islam, where even in the realm of art no human representation is permitted, the making and revering of icons is bound to be regarded as "*shirk*" or association of anything with the One and Only God of humanity and all creation. Not only do most Muslims see Hindus as "*mushrikin*," but they also see them as "*kuffar*" or disbelievers in the one creator God of Jews, Christians, and Muslims. In view of this belief, most Muslims consider interreligious dialogue with Hindus to be an exercise not only in futility but also in sinfulness, since believers ought not to take unbelievers for friends, and dialogue is a friendly encounter which should take place only between or among believers.

At this point it is pertinent to mention that, historically, Muslims have had little or no interest in interrreligious dialogue even with other believers in God, including the "*Ahl-al kitab*" ("People of the Book"–Jews and Christians) with whom they have strong theological and historical links. A partial explanation of this attitude may also be found in A. Toynbee's statement[9] that all three religions of revelation which sprang from a common historical root–Judaism, Christianity, and Islam–have a tendency not only toward exclusivism and intolerance but also tend to ascribe to themselves an ultimate validity. Muslims, who consider themselves the recipients of the final revelation, have, in general, taken the truth of Islam to be self-evident and have not expressed any great interest in having an open-ended

---

[9] *An Historian's Approach to Religion* (Oxford: Oxford University Press, 1956), p. 296.

philosophical and theological dialogue with people of other faiths, except perhaps in places where they have formed a minority component in a pluralistic environment. Also, the fact that until colonial times it was relatively easy for Muslims to assume the superiority of Islam to all other religions is, at least in part, responsible for their unwillingness to probe deeply into the question of the nature and implications of their Islamic identity.

One means of persuading at least some Muslims to participate in a theological dialogue with Hindus is to point out to them that such dialogue is called for by the spirit of many statements in the Qur'an.[10] For instance, the Qur'an refers to the fact that God not only created and honored the humanity of all human beings (Surah 17: *Bani Isra'il*: 70) but also intended Muslims to communicate the message of Islam to all. That the Qur'an is addressed to all is stated many times in the Qur'an; for example:

> Blessed is He Who
> Sent down the Criterion (Qur'an)
> To His Servant, that it
> May be an admonition
> *To all creatures*   (Surah 25: *Al-Furqan*: 1)

> This is no less than
> A Message and a Qur'an
> Making things clear:
> That it may give admonition
> *To any (who are) alive,*
> And that the charge
> May be proved against those
> Who reject (Truth).   (Surah 36: *Ya-Sin*: 69-70)

> This is no less than
> A Message *to (all)*
> *The Worlds.*   (Surah 38: *Sad*: 87)

> Verily this is no less
> Than a Message
> *To (all) the Worlds*:

---

[10] All translations from the Qur'an cited in this essay are taken from *The Holy Qur'an*, tr. A. Yusuf Ali. (All texts of this translation are identical.)

(With profit) *to whoever*
Among you wills
To go straight.   (Surah 81: *At-Takwir*: 27-28)

The universal mission of the Prophet of Islam is also affirmed by the Qur'an; for example:

We have not sent thee
But as a universal (Messenger)
To men, giving them
Glad tidings, and warning them
(Against sin), but most men
Understand not.   (Surah 34: *Saba'*: 28)

There are a number of verses in the Qur'an which refer to God's mercy and justice toward all creatures; for example:

And God careth for *all*
And He knoweth all things.   (Surah 2: *Al-Baqarah*: 268)

Unto *all* (in Faith)
Hath God promised good.   (Surah 4: *An-Nisa'*: 95)

That plurality of religions is sanctioned by God and is, in fact, a part of God's design for humanity is attested by the Qur'an; for example:

To each is a goal
To which God turns him;
Then strive together (as in a race)
Towards all that is good
Wheresoever ye are,
God will bring you
Together. For God
Hath power over all things.   (Surah 2: *Al-Baqarah*: 148)

If it had been God's Plan
They would not have taken
False gods: but We
Made thee not one
To watch over their doings,
Nor art thou set
Over them to dispose
Of their affairs.   (Surah 6: *Al-An'am*: 107)

If it had been thy Lord's will
They would have all believed,

All who are on earth!
Will thou then compel mankind,
Against their will, to believe!   (Surah 10: *Yunus*: 99)

That there is to be no coercion in religion and that the Prophet's mission is simply to communicate the message of Islam is stressed by the Qur'an in many ways; for example:

> Let there be no compulsion
> In religion.
>
> (Surah 2: *Al-Baqarah*: 256)

> But if they turn away,
> Thy duty is only to preach
> The clear message.
>
> (Surah 16: *An-Nahl*: 82)

> The Truth is
> From your Lord:
> Let him who will
> Believe, and let him
> Who will, reject (it).
>
> (Surah 18: *Al-Kahf*: 29)

> If then they turn away,
> We have not sent thee
> As a guard over them.
> Their duty is but to convey
> (The Message).
>
> (Surah 42: *Ash-Shura*: 48)

That the Qur'an advocates gracious conduct and religious tolerance as a life-attitude is clearly seen from the following verses:

> When a (courteous) greeting
> Is offered you, meet it
> With greeting still more
> Courteous, or (at least)
> Of equal courtesy,
> God takes careful account
> Of all things.
>
> (Surah 5: *Al-Ma'idah*: 86)

> Revile not ye
> Those whom they call upon
> Besides God, lest
> They out of spite
> Revile God
> In their ignorance.
> Thus have We made
> Alluring to each people
> Its own doings.
> In the end will they
> Return to their Lord,
> And We shall then
> Tell them the truth
> Of all that they did.
>
> (Surah 6: *Al-An'am*: 108)

> ...If the enemy
> Incline towards peace,
> Do thou (also) incline

Towards peace, and trust
In God: for He is the One
That heareth and knoweth
(All things).   (Surah 8: *Al-Anfal*: 61)

If one amongst the Pagans
Ask thee for asylum,
Grant it to him,
So that he may hear the word
Of God; and then exort him
To where he can be secure.   (Surah 9: *At-Taubah*: 6)

That God's message has been intended, from the beginning, for the guidance of all humanity is shown by the verse:

The first House (of worship)
Appointed for men
Was that at Bakka:
Full of blessing
And of guidance
For all kinds of being. (alamin)   (Surah 3: *Al-'Imran*: 96)

And, further, the Qur'an holds the promise:

One day we shall raise
From all peoples a witness...   (Surah 16: *An-Nahl*: 89)

The first problem to be confronted by anyone interested in bringing about a Hindu-Muslim theological dialogue would be to motivate both sides to enter into such dialogue with openness and seriousness. To have such a dialogue in a Western setting where dialogues are in fashion nowadays is one thing; to have it in India, Pakistan, or Bangladesh is quite another, and to bring it about would require much talent and commitment. If Hindus and Muslims could be persuaded in the interest of truth-seeking or peace-making to engage in a theological dialogue, the major task would be to determine what should be the beginning point of this dialogue.

My experience of Muslim-Christian-Jewish dialogue has convinced me that it is disastrous to begin any dialogue with a discussion on the concept of God, which many theologians assume to be the natural starting point of any theological dialogue in the framework of monotheistic religious tradition. I have never seen any dialogue which begins with a discussion of the Jewish, Christian, or Muslim concepts of God get past the point of hair-splitting definitions and disagreements, leaving the dialogue partners flabbergasted and wondering whether they are indeed talking about the believers in the same God. Any theological dialogue between Hindus and Muslims which begins with a discussion of the concept of God is even more likely to be doomed to disaster. I do not see any way in which the great majority of Muslims can be persuaded to appreciate the 330,000,000 gods of Hinduism, even if they are told that these gods are not ends-in-themselves but merely symbols of ultimate reality. Iqbal is certainly an exceptional Muslim in that he has the courage to say:

> The "kafir" with a wakeful heart praying to an idol is better than a "believer" asleep in a sanctuary.[11]

Such is the absoluteness and starkness of Islamic monotheism that any reference to images of God or incarnations of God turns Muslims off so deeply that most of them feel compelled, theologically as well as personally, to abandon the dialogue. Most of the theological problems which Muslims have had with Christians have also revolved around the issue of Jesus' being the incarnation of God. However, the case of Christianity is different from that of Hinduism in that it preserves the Creator-God of Genesis and thus, from the Islamic point of view, does not lapse into total idolatry.

In my view, in order to eliminate the Muslims' stereotype of Hindus as idol-worshippers, it is better to begin by looking not at Hindu concepts of God but at Hindu experiences of God, particularly at those experiences which Muslims can empathize with. It would, for instance, be very difficult for a God-loving Muslim not to be deeply touched by Tagore's *Gitanjali: Gift Offering of Songs of God*. Some Muslims may feel a little uneasy at the human imagery used by the Hindu poet to depict the divine, but, then, Islamic mystic literature also abounds with such imagery, and the Qur'an itself uses anthropomorphic images for God ("I made a human being with both my hands" [Surah 36: *Sad*: 72]).

Some people – theologians and others – think that theological dialogue does, or should, lead to theological agreement. This, in my judgment, is an erroneous point of view. For instance, no amount of theological dialogue between Hindus and Muslims can lead to the reduction of the monistic

---

[11] *Javid Namah* (Lahore, 1947), p. 40.

principle upheld by many Hindus to the monotheistic belief held by all Muslims, and vice versa. But why should the achieving of theological agreement be so necessary? Why should it not be sufficient for Hindus and Muslims to understand correctly what the religious experience of each is without trying to merge them together? Like many other Muslims, I also believe that there are some Hindus who, in fact, do identify idols with Brahman and, thus, are idolators. But I also believe that there are some Muslims who identify the Word or Law of God with God and, thus, are idolatrous. Whatever be the religious experience of some Hindus or some Muslims, and whether we approve of it or not, I think that it is important to remember in the context of Hindu-Muslim theological dialogue that the two religious worldviews have some extremely important things in common.

To begin with: both Hinduism and Islam conceive of ultimate reality as spiritual, thus making the believer aware of that which is beyond the here-and-now, the eternal and transcendent, which gives human life a purposefulness it would not have if reality were confined to the material. Both Hinduism and Islam insist that all aspects of life are related and must be integrated in order to achieve wholeness, which is the goal of Hindu *yoga* and Muslim *salat*. Neither Hinduism nor Islam permits the bifurcation of life into mutually exclusive domains: the secular and the sacred, the public and the private, the inner and the outer. Again, both Hinduism and Islam hold that knowledge of external and internal reality is to be obtained not only through reason but through all other human faculties as well, with particular emphasis on "the heart," which the mystics regard as the seat of "intuition." People of the Western world – founded as it is upon the Graeco-Roman civilization which upheld reason as the highest human faculty through which alone one could obtain knowledge of ultimate reality – rarely understand what "the heart" or "intuitive faculty" is, but it is due primarily to this faculty that Hindus and Muslims have evolved what are perhaps the two greatest mystic traditions in the history of civilization.

Finally, both Hinduism and Islam have put unequivocal emphasis on the idea that human beings are accountable for their actions and that ethical action is the goal of religious striving. In both there is great emphasis on duty-fulfillment and on the idea that duty to God is inseparable from duty to fellow human beings.

Having pointed out some of the common perspectives on which a Hindu-Muslim theological dialogue can be based, I consider it necessary to point out also that, as a matter of fact, much assimilation of religious/cultural ideas and attitudes has occurred in the Hindu-Muslim world. Both Hindus and Muslims might wish to stress their distinct identities and insist that Hinduism and Islam are utterly different ways of life, but the plain historical reality is that Indian Islam bears the clear imprint of Hinduism, and Hinduism has absorbed much that is clearly Islamic in origin. For instance, while many Hindus have been deeply affected by Islamic monotheism,[12] many Muslims follow a caste system as strictly as the Hindus and take great pride in being "high-caste" (which generally means being descended from the Prophet Muhammad or his blood relatives), even if they are so only by virtue of their descent from high-caste Hindus!

Before I conclude my comments on the various kinds of Hindu-Muslim dialogue which exist, or ought to exist, in the subcontinent, I would like to mention something very close to my heart: the need for a dialogue between Hindu and Muslim women. As a Muslim feminist, I have been deeply concerned for a long time about some negative ideas/attitudes/customs relating to women which are found widely among Muslims of the subcontinent. Some of these practices (for example, demanding the dowry or bride-price for girls at marriage) and concepts (for example, the husband is the wife's "*majazi khuda*" or god in earthly form) are clearly un-Islamic. In fact, the "deification" of the husband is tantamount to *shirk* (association with God) and, thus, an unforgivable sin. However, they have become so deeply rooted in Muslim culture that their association with, or derivation from, Hindu culture has long been forgotten, and they are regarded by many Muslims to be part of the Islamic "Shari'a." While there are woman-affirming resources within both Islam and Hinduism, these have not been used for the liberation of women from the

---

[12] Reference may be made here to Kana Mitra's statement on p. 427, below: "Rammohan Roy, Rabindranath Tagore, Gandhi – all were appreciative of Islamic monotheism."

misogynistic/androcentric and rigid patriarchalism of these two religious traditions. In this era of women's freedom from age-old shackles, Hindu and Muslim women continue to be among the most oppressed "minorities" in the world. They need to dialogue with each other not only to understand their common bondage and servitude and to give each other emotional and psychological support, but also to strive together to evolve academic and sociopolitical ways and means or methods and strategies to change the religiocultural world in which they live and die unsung. In this context, my plea to Hindu and Muslim (as well as all other "disinherited" women of the world) is (with due apologies to Marx): "Women of the world unite; you have nothing to lose but your chains!"

In conclusion, I want simply to say that, as a person belonging to what the Qur'an describes as "a nation in the middle,"[13] I feel that I stand midway between my religious world which is Judaeo-Christian-Islamic (West) and my cultural world which is Hindu-Islamic (East). I have spent more than half my life in the West, which has molded my mind, but where my body and soul are still ill-at-ease. All too often I feel a deep longing to return to the soil of the ancient mystic land where I was born and to the people who speak my language and share my grass-roots values. To be divided – as I am – is to be in a state of perpetual exile. To be in exile is not a happy state, but it enables one to experience more than one kind of reality.[14] It is tragic that the world in which we live today is full of exiles. However, these exiles have a glorious opportunity for dialogue and can do much to create, out of the deep sense of their own fragmented and lonely lives, the vision of a world which is integrated and whole, in which all human beings can find peace.

---

[13] Surah 2: *Al-Baqarah*: 143.

[14] The Qur'an regards "*Hijrah*" (going into exile) to be a part of "*Jihad fo Sabil Allah*" (striving in the cause of God) and considers it to be a state blessed by God.

EXPLORING THE POSSIBILITY OF HINDU-MUSLIM DIALOGUE[*]

Kana Mitra[**]

Islam and Hinduism have been present in the Indian sub-continent for over 1,000 years. During this time there has been a great deal of violence; even today it is not infrequent. There have also been periods of peace. However, whether in war or in peace, Muslims and Hindus have not reacted in a way that indicates mutual understanding and appreciation of each other. In their day-to-day encounter, there is at most a superficial civility during peace; during confrontation they look upon each other as sub-humans. During the 1945-46 riots, I was present in Dacca (Bangladesh). As a Hindu child I was frightened and angered by the war cry of the Muslim rioters, "Allah O Akbar." I did not know that it meant, "God is great!" Similarly, I

[*] In Leonard Swidler, ed. *Religious Liberty and Human Rights in Nations and in Religions* (Philadelphia/New York: Ecumenical Press/Hippocrene Books, 1986), pp. 109-123.

[**] Kana Mitra (Hindu) teaches at both LaSalle University, Philadelphia, and Villanova (PA) University in their Religious Studies Depts., especially in the areas of Eastern and world religions, religious experience, mysticism, and Catholicism. She holds a B.A. and a M.A. from Calcutta University, and a Ph.D. (1980) in religion from Temple University. She has also taught at Temple and Calcutta Universities and at Swarthmore (PA) College. Her dissertation was on "Catholicism and Hinduism: A Vedantic Investigation of R. Panikkar's Attempt at Bridge-Building." An Associate Editor of the *Journal of Ecumenical Studies*, she has contributed abstracts and book reviews and three articles (on human rights in Hinduism, on women in Hinduism, and a Hindu reflection on consensus in theology) to that journal. Four of her articles appear in the *Encyclopedic Dictionary of Religions* (Corpus Publications, 1979), and an article on "Cultic Acts in Hinduism" in *Revelation as Redemptive Experience in Christianity, Hinduism, and Buddhism* (Herder, 1982). She participates frequently in interreligious dialogues and seminars on women in religion.

imagine, the war cry of Hindu rioters, "Bande Mataram" (hail to the mother), did not suggest maternal mercy to Muslim children. The brutal, inhuman behavior of both peoples during confrontation is all too well known.

Of course, there are a few rare cases of genuine friendship between individual Hindus and Muslims. There are even some cases of intermarriage. However, by and large, Muslims and Hindus have stereotyped understandings of each other. Muslims, in general, consider Hindus idolators and polytheists, and educated Muslims are contemptuous of the inequality of the Hindu caste system. Likewise, in general, the Hindu stereotype of Muslims is that they are meat-eating brutes who marry their sisters (cousins), and educated Hindus are contemptuous of Islamic intolerance and *jihad*.

This mutual contempt and isolation of Muslims and Hindus in India seems even more amazing in view of the fact that a large number of Muslims in the Indian sub-continent are of Hindu ancestry. Some recent anthropological studies even indicate the presence of remnants of Hindu attitudes among some Muslims of the sub-continent. For example, Adrian Mayer refers to the presence of caste among Muslims;[1] some Muslims indicate a preference for a vegetarian diet, as it is considered more pure, while Hindus venerate Muslim "pirs" as saints. However, overall, there is an attitude of competitiveness and mutual intolerance between Muslims and Hindus. Is dialogue between them even a possibility?

In order to explore what Muslims and Hindus think about each other's religion, I searched for writings of Muslims of the sub-continent on Hinduism and vice versa. So far, I have found no Muslim author writing exclusively on Hinduism. In Muslim writing, Hinduism is referred to in the context of showing its inferiority to Islam. Even a liberal Muslim such as Amir Ali in his *The Spirit of Islam*[2] has nothing but derogatory remarks about Hinduism and Buddhism. Aziz Ahmed, in *Studies in Islamic Culture in the Indian*

---

[1] Adrian Mayer is an anthropologist of the London School of Oriental and African Studies. His research on Islam in India is referred to by Agehananda Bharati in *Hindu Views and Ways and the Hindu-Muslim Interface: An Anthropological Assessment* (New Delhi: Munshiram Manoharlal, 1981).

[2] 1st ed. (Karachi: Pakistan Publishing House, 1961). The 1982 ed. was used for this essay.

Environment,[3] displays no insight into Hinduism when he admires Schimmel's description of the contrast between Hinduism and Islam: "Hindu genius flowers in the concrete and the iconographic; the Muslim mind is on the whole atomistic, abstract, geometrical, and iconoclastic."[4] Likewise, I found no book by a Hindu author which was written exclusively on Islam. Rammohan Roy, Rabindranath Tagore, Gandhi–all were appreciative of Islamic monotheism. However, they wrote no works on Islam. A contemporary Hindu scholar such as Anil Chandra Banerjee refers to the Islamic Shari'a to demonstrate the intolerance of Islam, in his *Two Nations: The Philosophy of Muslim Nationalism*.[5] It is quite evident that even the scholars among the Muslims and Hindus have not made any serious effort to understand each other's tradition.

Causes for Apathy and Indifference

There are complex historic, anthropological, psychological, sociological, economic, and political reasons for Muslim-Hindu conflict and apathy, some of which are very obvious. The first Muslims who came to India came as conquerors, and the vanquished were the Hindus. There is competitiveness between Hinduism and Christianity, but the first Christians who came to India were missionaries, not political conquerors. That is one of the reasons for lesser hatred and animosity between Hindus and Christians in the sub-continent. Buddhist missionary activity started under the patronage of King Asoka, but it did not lead to empire-building. That is one of the reasons for lesser hostility toward Buddhists by people of other faiths. The historical situation of the encounter between Islam and Hinduism is an important reason for the hostility between the two.

The Arabic culture in which Islam originated and the Indian environment in which Hinduism is nurtured are quite different. Patterns of behavior, standards of civility, attire, food, language–all are different. Meetings of alien cultures naturally produce distrust and misunderstanding.

---

[3] (Oxford: Clarendon Press, 1969).

[4] Quoted in Bharati, *Hindu Views*, p. 74.

[5] (New Delhi: Concept Publishing Co., 1981).

Human beings' ethnocentricity makes them distrust and ridicule the unfamiliar. Moreover, the Indian sub-continent, politically, was never one country. First, Muslim rulers, and later British, made it into one political unit. The nationalistic feeling of belonging to one political unit was a later development among the people of the sub-continent. When nationalistic feelings started to emerge, they were often colored with religious feelings, and controversy over one or two nations for the sub-continent became almost inevitable. Religion has often been used for political purposes in the sub-continent. Sometimes it was used for Hindu-Muslim cooperation against the British, as in the case of the Sepoy Mutiny of 1875, or against each other during pre-partition, mostly by the British, and even after partition, by various political parties. Methodical research into these factors which are causes of the conflict between Muslims and Hindus is vital to the promotion of understanding between them.

Religious Causes

The characteristics of Islam and Hinduism as religions also contribute to the isolationism of these two traditions. Their worldviews seem to be quite different. In Islam, unity of one God and uniformity in ways of belief and patterns of worship are fundamental. Islam advocates one God, one scripture, one seal of prophecy. In other words, singularity or unity is characteristic of Islam as a religious tradition. Hinduism is, instead, characterized by plurality. A Hindu can be a Hindu worshipping many gods or one God or no God. The focal point of Hinduism is not one God but to be worshipful, which is usually referred to by such a Hindu philosopher as Radhakrishnan as respect for truth – *Sraddha*. So, it is said there are 330,000,000 gods in Hinduism, and there may be as many ways of worshipping God. Hinduism, therefore, does not refer to one God, one scripture, or one prophet. Just as unity is characteristic of Islam as a religious tradition, plurality is characteristic of Hinduism as a religious tradition.

Islam and Hinduism are distinctive in other respects also. Islam advocates a kind of theocracy – religious law needs to be political law. The universal ideal needs to be concretized in society and in history. Human beings are vicegerents of God.[6] The Hindu attitude is that the concrete is a stepping stone to the universal ideal but the universal can never be fully concretized in history. That is why, by and large, the Hindu ideal is a-historical or a-political. Islam believes in a final day of judgment; Hindus believe in the cycle of creation and dissolution, the cycle of birth and death. Islam is a missionary religion. F. S. C. Northrup wrote, "For an orthodox Mohammedan, missionary zeal, military power, and political control go together."[7] For Hinduism, the ideal is spiritual freedom, which may not be related to political freedom. This is expressed even in the leadership of the movement for independence in India. Gandhi worked for political freedom more as a spiritual leader; therefore, he never accepted any governmental post. Sri Aurobindo changed from a fight for political freedom to a fight for spiritual freedom. The majority of Hindu monastic orders do not become directly involved in political movements.

Allen H. Merriam, in *Gandhi vs Jinnah: The Debate over the Partition of India*, presented a descriptive and nonvaluational contrast between Islam and Hinduism:

> It may be helpful to view Hinduism as an essentially feminine doctrine and Islam as being far more masculine in character. The Hindu worships the cow as the symbol of motherhood and fertility; many Hindu deities are female, and Hindu art is full of voluptuous female figures....Muslims, on the other hand, worship a very masculine Allah; only men are allowed inside a mosque, and in most Islamic societies women are veiled when in public. It would be quite unusual to have a woman prime minister in an Islamic nation.[8]

He also described very clearly the contrasting concepts of social organization of Hindus and Muslims. The dominant force of Hindu society is the caste system, which is based on the conviction that different humans have different potentialities, determined by one's action in the previous incarnation. Castes

[6] Seyyed Hossein Nasr, *Islam and the Plight of Modern Man* (London and New York: Longman, 1975), p. 18.

[7] From F. S. C. Northrup, *The Meeting of East and West* (New York: Macmillan, 1946), p. 414. Quoted in Allen Hayes Merriam, *Gandhi vs. Jinnah: The Debate over the Partition of India* (Columbia, MO: South Asia Books [in association with Minerva Associates, Calcutta], 1980), p. 9.

[8] Merriam, *Gandhi vs. Jinnah*, p. 9.

and sub-castes produced a decentralized social structure which safeguarded against penetration of any outside force; thus, Hindu society could continue relatively unchanged during the years of Muslim rule. The rigid regulation of caste prohibited the intermixture of castes and of Hindus and non-Hindus, but, paradoxically, it bred an attitude whereby plurality is considered a social norm. Merriam noted that this acceptance of diversity prompted Hajime Nakamura to state, "Toleration is the most conspicuous characteristic of Indian culture."[9] Islam, on the contrary, considers all humans equal by birth. Merriam noted, "All people are called to unite and conform to one community of believers."[10] Islam's emphasis on dogma and a democratic social order has meant the development of a strong sense of community – particularly in India, since it is a minority there.

It is evident that the theological and social assumptions of Muslims and Hindus are different. The differences of convictions generated contempt or, at best, indifference toward each other. Muslims and Hindus feel no need to learn about or from each other. Islam proclaims that it is the only true way – the straight path. The Qur'an and the tradition make some concessions to the "People of the Book," of course. For example, they can gain protection by paying *jizya* (IX:29); and, after the battle of Badr, Muhammad formulated a treaty in which the Jews were included within the commonwealth of Medina.[11] In the eleventh century, Mawardi prescribed that the *Imam* (caliph) had the duty "to wage holy war (*jihad*) against those who, after having been invited to accept Islam, persist in rejecting it, until they either become Muslims or enter the Pact (*zimma*) so that God's truth may prevail over every religion."[12] The conditions of the pact suggest that subordination of the *zimmis* was tolerated, but at least their lives were spared. However, the Qur'an and tradition are vehemently opposed to idolatry. Muhammad's war was against the idolatry in the Arabia of his time. He did not meet any

---

[9] From Hajime Nakamura, *Ways of Thinking of Eastern Peoples: India-China-Tibet-Japan*, ed. Philip P. Wiener (Honolulu: East-West Center Press, 1964), p. 172. Quoted in Merriam, *Gandhi vs. Jinnah*, p. 10.

[10] Merriam, *Gandhi vs. Jinnah*, p. 10.

[11] Ali, *Spirit of Islam*, pp. 56-59.

[12] Banerjee, *Two Nations*, p. 3.

Hindus or witness any image-worship of the Hindus, but the Muslims who came to India considered Hindus idolators because of the image-worship. Therefore, many of them did not want to grant the Hindus the status of *zimmis*. Only some rulers following the Hanafi School of Shari'a assigned *zimmi* status to the Hindus. Hindu image-worhip is one of the most important reasons for Muslim contempt of Hinduism. Image-worship, from the Islamic perspective, is a compromise with the transcendence of God – it is *shirk*. That is why Amir Ali could see nothing noble or sublime in the forms of Hindu worship:

> The sacrifice could be performed only by the priest according to rigid and unalterable formulae; whilst he recited the *mantras* and went through rites in a mechanical spirit, without religious spirit or enthusiasm, the worshipper stood by, a passive spectator of the worship which was performed on his behalf. The smallest mistake undid the efficacy of the observances.[13]

Hinduism proclaims in many ways. From the Hindu perspective, not only can there not be just one way to truth, but also no way can be the perfect and faultless way to truth. Agehananda Bharati has often ridiculed Hindu tolerance. He has identified some modern Hindus as "essential unity" preachers who are no less competitive and polemical than are Christians and Muslims: In his article "Radhakrishnan and Other Vedanta,"[14] he pointed out that Vedantists of the Vivekananda and Radhakrishnan type believe in the superiority of monism. In his chapter "Sohi Allah Wahi Ram? The Anthropology of the Hindu-Muslim Interface," he wrote:

> Urban "essential Unity" Hinduism which includes the sermon of the English speaking Swamis in India and abroad – states that all religions are equal, but implies that since Hinduism is "scientific" and tolerant, it incorporates what all other religions teach, and is hence at least a primus inter pares.[15]

From the perspective of Hinduism, any claim by any tradition to be exclusively true is arrogant, although the contrary Hindu claim seems equally arrogant to others. Hindus consider ultimate truth to be beyond words and

---

[13] Ali, *Spirit of Islam*, p. 160.

[14] In Paul Arthur Schilpp, *The Philosophy of Sarvepalli Radhakrishnan* (New York: Tudor Publishing Co., 1952), pp. 459-479.

[15] In Bharati, *Hindu Views*, p. 72.

letters; hence, the Muslim claim that the Qur'an is the literal word of God is, from the Hindu perspective, a compromise with the transcendence of truth. Since all Hindus – not only the "essential unity" preachers – have been historically surrounded with plurality, they cannot comprehend or sympathize with any doctrine of "One Way." They are contemptuous of such arrogance, or at least indifferent to it. If all ways are ways of truth, even though none is perfect, one can stick to one's own, and there is no need to learn about or from each other.

Inclusivism often generates indifference, whereas exclusivism often generates intolerance and violence. Hindus are critical of the intolerance and violence of Islam. Hinduism as a tradition believes in the transformative quality of religion. Transformation, according to Hinduism, implies a change of personality from fear to courage, from anger to love, from violence to nonviolence. Although an individual or a group of Hindus may not be less violent than an individual or a group of Muslims – as the history of their encounter indicates – nevertheless, in Hinduism nonviolence is considered a cardinal virtue. Hence, Islamic *jihad* is looked upon with contempt by Hindus. Hindus, even the college educated, look upon Islam as an essentially militaristic tradition. One educated Hindu, although not an official "scholar," described Muslim *salat*, in which the group prays by synchronic postures and movements, as military training in preparation for war.

It is evident that Muslims and Hindus neither understand one another nor make any serious attempt to do so. They do not try to go beyond the surface and penetrate that which may not be so apparent to the outside observer. Not only the average Muslim or Hindu but even theologians and philosophers indicate no interest in or understanding of each other. Islamic *kalam* developed primarily outside the sub-continent. Any immanentist tendency in Islam can be explained in terms of interaction with Hellenism. Sufism might have been congenial to the Vedantic point of view, but it need not be explained in terms of its influence. It seems that Muslim theologians, being repelled by Hindu image-worship, made no attempt to find out what lay underneath. In the same way, the post-Islamic Bhakti movement in Hinduism was perhaps stimulated by Islamic monotheism and devotionalism, but it need not be explained in terms of that influence. The nineteenth- and twentieth-century Hindu elites who studied and appreciated the Qur'an found nothing in it which they considered to be genuinely new or not present in Hinduism. No Hindu thinker made any attempt to penetrate Islamic exclusivism or militarism to find out what lay underneath. Muslims and Hindus have confronted each other, but they have generally felt no real challenge from one another to appreciate or learn from or about each other.

Encounter with the West

Muslim and Hindu encounter with the West is a different matter. Both felt a challenge and threat from Western civilization. Both simultaneously admired and condemned Western civilization and values. Muslims and Hindus recognize the value of the advanced scientific knowledge in the West. Apologists of both traditions try to demonstrate that scientific knowledge is part of their heritage as well, and both refer to their respective contributions in mathematics, astronomy, and medicine. Muslims and Hindus recognize and appreciate the value of democracy, individual dignity, and humanism. They do not think that these are recognized values of the West alone. Rather, in polemics, they try to show how these values have been jeopardized in the West. There is ambivalence about technology, industrialization, and material prosperity among Muslims and Hindus, but in general there is appreciation of the bountifulness, health, and hygiene of the West. Modernity, which is equivalent to "Westernity" to many people, has stimulated both Muslims and Hindus to question and reflect on their own traditions – although not about each other's.

The Western attitude toward the sub-continent can be classified as either contemptuous and patronizing or romantic. Modernists of the West tend to highlight the superstition, backwardness, poverty, and dehumanization present in the sub-continent. Romanticists who are concerned about the negative effects of modernism – secularization, manipulation, dehumanization – display an attitude of appreciation for the spiritual and philosophical contributions of the sub-continent. Max Müller in the nineteenth century and Aldous Huxley in the twentieth may be cited as examples of the latter. Both Muslim and Hindu thinkers reacted to the negative criticism of the West with polemics and apologetics, although some self-criticism and social-reform movements were also generated. Muslim and Hindu thinkers reacted to the romantic attitude of the West with a feeling of self-congratulation and complacence. Both Muslim and Hindu writers like to quote the Western scholars who praise their traditions! Muslims and Hindus did not react jointly in their depreciation of some of the Western attitudes, nor did they appreciate each other as a result of their appreciation by the West.

What Can Be Done?

Hindus and Muslims have lived in physical closeness for years, and yet they do not dialogue with each other and show no inclination toward it. I have attempted to analyze some of the causes of this situation. The nature of the respective traditions as such is not conducive to any dialogue, yet the dehumanizing and inhuman relationship between Hindus and Muslims makes it quite evident that dialogue between us is a practical necessity. How can we dialogue? I can see a clue for it in our relationship and reaction toward the West.

In the last half of the twentieth century it is becoming increasingly fashionable to criticize Western values. Awareness of the dangers inherent in modernity is a necessity. There are many good works on this subject.[16] However, when the anti-establishment becomes the establishment, there is the opposite danger.[17] Uncritical condemnation of modernity may lead to uncritical acceptance of all types of superstition. It may lead to complacence, self-congratulation, and passivity. With our awareness of the dangers of modernity, let us not be blind to its stimulating and liberating effects. The history of any religious tradition would indicate how modernity revitalized it by eliminating some of the stagnation. In his lectures to the Western people, Vivekananda–who is considered instrumental in making Hinduism a missionary religion–seemed to be one of its greatest apologists, yet in his lectures to Hindus he seemed to be a vehement critic of their religion.[18]

---

[16] E.g., Ernst F. Schumacher, *Small Is Beautiful* (New York: Harper & Row, 1973).

[17] Paul Tillich, *The Courage to Be* (New Haven: Yale University Press, 1952), ch. 4-5.

[18] Vivekananda, *Complete Works of Swami Vivekananda*, vol. 3, Mayavati memorial ed. (Calcutta: Advaita Ashrama, 1973), pp. 166-167.

After his tour of America and Europe, he indicated his appreciation and admiration of these people for their recognition of the dignity of the individual, hygiene, health, vitality, etc. Modernity generates self-reflection and can be an antidote to the dogmatic adherence to the beliefs of the forebears and mechanical repetition of what they did. Uncritical adherence to traditions can stagnate any religion, as is evident in our two religions of the sub-continent.

The question of human rights is asked and pursued in the Western context. What the rights of human beings as human are is often described in terms of Western categories. This runs the danger of ideological neo-colonialism. Raimundo Panikkar is concerned about this *de facto* neo-colonialism. He points out that at the present time there are three sociologically dominant cultures: technological civilization, the pan-economic systems, and what is popularly called the "Western way of life." He notes that most of the African, Asian, and Latin American cultures, for economic survival, are taking the categories of these dominant cultures for granted, but the indiscriminate adoption of methods that are alien to the local cultures is not producing the desired effects.[19] There is a need to investigate the meaning of human rights, of growth and progress, not simply from the perspective of the dominant cultures – but from the perspective of others as well.

Not only contemplation but also action is needed. Living cannot stop while we are finding out the meaning of life. Indeed, the meaning of living may emerge from living itself, as such existentialists as Camus indicate. Herein lies the contribution of such activists in the field of interreligious and interideological dialogue as Leonard Swidler. Very much aware of the strong points of Western civilization, Swidler indicates "one of the strengths of modern Western civilization has been its stress on effective human action, both individual and corporate." So, he thinks: "The world cannot be 'saved' simply by trying to 'save' the individual persons; the social structure within

---

[19] Raimundo Panikkar, "Alternatives to Modern Culture," *Inter-Culture* 15 (October-December, 1982): 2-4.

which the individual persons live must also be 'saved.'"[20] The content of "saving" is not self-evident and would need ongoing contemplation, but the situation of the relationship between Muslims and Hindus definitely calls for action. One such activity is dialogue, but we are not so inclined. The enterprise of dialogue by Western activists such as Swidler is helpful in this respect, because through such enterprise Hindus and Muslims are getting involved in dialogue.

However, Muslims and Hindus are often suspicious of the Christian initiative in dialogue, which is feared as a covert way of converting. Whatever it is, Muslims and Hindus can appreciate the greater, if not total, understanding about their traditions, understanding by more people from the West. Hans Küng may be cited as an example. His attitude toward Hinduism in *On Being a Christian*[21] – and more recently as expressed in his response to Heinrich von Stietencron in his attempts to dialogue with different world religions[22] – is a clear indication of better understanding. In the first case he finds more superstition and degradation in the Hindu tradition; in the second, more appreciation of its mystical bent. This example itself illustrates the potential of dialogue for the development of mutual understanding. Thus, if we Hindus and Muslims begin to engage in dialogue, there is the possibility of better mutual understanding even if we start to do so reluctantly or half-heartedly by means of Western initiative.

The modern method of the critical approach to history and the different social and psychological sciences can also be helpful in generating an atmosphere of dialogue between Muslims and Hindus. A conventional way of writing Indian history by both Western and Indian historians is in terms of the religious traditions of its rulers. Romila Thapar, in *Communalism and the Writing of Indian History*,[23] traces this tendency back

---

[20] Leonard Swidler, "Interreligious Dialogue: The Matrix for All Systematic Reflection Today," paper for the conference, "Toward a Universal Theology of Religion" (held at Temple University, Philadelphia, October 17-19, 1984), p. 22.

[21] (New York: Doubleday & Co., 1976), ch. 3.

[22] Hans Küng *et al., Christentum und Weltreligionen* (Munich: Piper Verlag, 1984); from typescript of English translation by Leonard Swidler of Küng's response to Heinrich von Steitencron on Hinduism.

[23] (New Delhi: Peoples Publishing House, 1969), p. 4.

to James Mill's *History of British India* (early nineteenth century). She indicates that Mill developed the thesis of dividing Indian History into the three periods which he called Hindu Civilization, Muslim Civilization, and British Civilization – but not Christian. Such characterization of history can and did generate misunderstanding and even hostility among the different religions. For example, Turkish, Persian, and Arab conquerors of India were Muslim, and they themselves often identified their conquest as Islamic. However, the plunder and destruction of Hindu temples by Ghazni (eleventh century C.E.) need not necessarily be interpreted as the intolerance of Islam. Thapar points out that the Hindu King Harsha even appointed an officer, *devot-patananayaka* (uprooter of gods), to plunder the wealth of Hindu temples, but this is not seen as the intolerance of Hinduism.[24]

The fourteenth-century Muslim historian, Zia-ud-din-Barani, in his *Fatawa-i-Jahandari*, condemned the Delhi Sultans for not being zealots in their fight with the infidels and idolators:

> If the desire for the overthrow of infidels and abasing of idolators and polytheists does not fill the hearts of the Muslim Kings; if, on the other hand, out of the thought that infidels and polytheists are payers of tribute and protected persons, they make the infidels eminent, distinguished, honoured, and favoured...how then may the banners of Islam be raised?[25]

Barani showed his admiration of eleventh-century Ghazni by saying that if he could come back again he "would have brought under his sword all Brahmans of Hind...cut off the heads of two hundred or three hundred thousand Hindu chiefs (and)...would not have returned his 'Hindu-slaughtering sword' to its scabbard until the whole of Hind had accepted Islam."[26] Barani definitely seems to have been an intolerant person, but his writings may well not prove intolerance in Islam. Indeed, his indignation about the Delhi Sultans also indicates that not all Muslim rulers were Hindu inquisitors. An analytical, critical approach to the presentation and interpretation of the events of history in India is very important to generate an atmosphere of dialogue. All-India Radio sponsored a 1968 seminar on "The Role of the Broadcaster

---

[24] *Ibid.*, pp. 15-16.

[25] Banerjee, *Two Nations*, p. 10.

[26] *Ibid.*

in the Present Communal Situation," in which Romila Thapar, Harbans Mukhia, and Bipin Chandra presented their critical analyses to suggest the dangers of stereotyped communal understandings of history. Thapar noted that antagonistic projection of a popular group, sect, or religion in history is very harmful, but even "more harmful is the kind of historical writing which is based on communal or near communal assumptions, but such assumptions in a generally uncritical framework are no longer questioned or challenged."[27] This type of self-critical scholarship and its sharing via the mass media needs to be encouraged.

In this context, I would like to refer to a misrepresenting stereotype, even in this conference which intends to generate mutual understanding and harmony between nations and between peoples. The constant conflict between Pakistan and India is referred to as between "Muslim Pakistan" and "Hindu India." This is a historical, political, and ideological misunderstanding of India. India never was and even now is not only Hindu. India does not recognize nationality on the basis of religion.

It is evident that critical historical research where the insights of psychology, sociology, and anthropology are taken into consideration is helpful for dialogue between Muslims and Hindus. Good history cannot be a one-sided narration and analysis of selected events. For example, A. C. Banerjee (in *Two Nations*) gave extensive documentation to suggest that Islamic Shari'a is at the root of Islamic nationalism, but in this work he referred extensively only to the Shari'as which indicate an intolerance in Islam, but not one which shows its tolerance. Thus, one-sidedness may characterize even apparently good, well-documented scholarship. The tendency toward one-sidedness is present among many scholars. Moreover, in the understanding of another's tradition it is necessary to understand it as much as possible as the other does. Adolph L. Wismar disputed T. W. Arnold's[28] view that missionary work is not an afterthought in Islam. Arnold thought that Muhammad himself, and the subsequent missionaries following

[27] Thapar, *Communalism*, p. 10.

[28] Adolph L. Wismar, *A Study in Tolerance as Practiced by Muhammad and His Immediate Successors* (New York: Columbia University Press, 1927), ch 1. He refers to T. W. Arnold, *The Preaching of Islam*, 2nd ed. (London: Constable & Co., 1913).

his example, showed patience and forbearance in their attempt to convert the unbelievers. Arnold quoted from the Qur'an to prove his case. Wismar's refutation is based on the assumption that the Qur'an is Muhammad's word, not God's, as the Muslims believe. He assigned many questionable motives to Muhammad and indicated that Islam is intolerant. Whatever evidence was to the contrary he considered nothing but trickery.

The sociological and psychological study of the phenomenon of religion can help Muslim-Hindu dialogue. James Fowler's study, *Stages of Faith*,[29] describes how faith is dynamic and relational. In *Life Maps*[30] he points out the correlation between stages of faith-development and the capacity of the individual to take on the perspective of another and to widen the circle of those with whom one identifies oneself. Intensity of faith also leads to broadening of faith. This is clearly evident among both Muslim and Hindu mystics. Even in the field of clinical psychology, Muslim and Hindu psychiatrists have tried to apply their respective religious teachings to therapy. Elzibair Beshir Taha of the University of Khartoum, Sudan, in a paper prepared for discussion at the Parliament of Religion held at McAfee, New Jersey, November 15-21, 1985, noted that Qur'anic teachings could be utilized as a technique of cognitive behavior therapy for Muslim patients. At that conference, a Philadelphia psychiatrist mentioned his use of the Bhagavad Gita to help his patients. It is evident that Western ideology and training have stimulated many Muslim and Hindu scholars and thinkers. These people may start dialogues with each other, following the Western example, as many of them do feel the need for mutual understanding between Muslims and Hindus.

However, Muslims and Hindus need to be aware of the dangers of Western civilization as well, and a large number of Western-educated and -trained Muslims and Hindus are critics of Western civilization. They are acutely aware of secularization and its consequences which result from the so-called "scientific," "critical" perspective of the West. Seyyed Hossein Nasr

---

[29] James W. Fowler, *Stages of Faith* (New York: Harper & Row, 1981).

[30] Jim Fowler and Sam Keen, *Life Maps: Conversations on the Journey of Faith* (Waco, TX: Word, Inc., 1978).

discussed this point in *Islam and the Plight of Modern Man*, pointing out succinctly how the Western scientific point of view reduces reality to only one layer, and the symbolic concept of nature is debased by calling it "totemistic" or "animistic," terms loaded with pejorative connotations. Nasr wrote that Muslims trained in modernity are "made to believe that the transformation from seeing the phenomena of nature as the portents or signs (ayat) of God to viewing these phenomena as brute facts is a major act of progress which, however, only prepares nature for that ferocious rape and plunder for which modern man is now beginning to pay so dearly."[31]

Swami Yatiswarananda, a monk of the Rama-Krishna order, met Carl Jung in Switzerland. While he appreciated Jung's understanding of human spiritual need, he was critical of Jung's secular perspective. Jung suggested that the superconscious of the Hindu was included in the unconscious. The Swami felt that we need to reverse our secular perspective of thinking that the body is the outermost layer, and mind and spirit are within it.[32]

Western scientism often leads to secularization, and scholarship of religion ends in reductionistic tendencies. Many Western scholars of religion are also critical of this tendency, such as W. C. Smith. We Muslims and Hindus who are engaging in dialogue by means of Western stimulation need to be aware of this danger; however, critical scholarship can be very helpful in eliminating some of the barriers which now prevent Muslim-Hindu understanding.

Dialogue on the Theological Level

A secular approach to fostering unity between Muslims and Hindus is neither practical nor desirable. Jawaharlal Nehru, the first prime minister of India, had a secular view of progress and advocated unity between Muslims and Hindus on the basis of modern Western civilization. Syed Abdul Latif, who belonged to the liberal Aligarh School of pre-independence India, clearly pointed out Nehru's mistake. He noted that the peculiar philosophy of life is what provides vitality to the people and cannot and should not be

---

[31] P. 19.

[32] Swami Yatiswarananda, *Meditation and Spiritual Life* (Bangalore: Sri Ramakrishna Ashrama, 1979), pp. 20-21.

overcome by the unity fostered by the steamroller of industrialization.[33] M. N. Roy found the resolution of Hindu-Muslim conflict in Communism; only that mighty economic force would have the capacity of cementing the diverse sects and religious creeds of India: "This is the only agency of Hindu-Muslim unity."[34] This position forgets that Muslim and Hindu believers are rooted in the transforming and life-sustaining characteristics of their traditions and that not many would want to trade spirituality for modern amenities. Herein lies the true basis of Muslim-Hindu dialogue: Both have faith in more than a secular understanding of human nature, which is expressed in Qur'anic *al-fitrah* and Hindu *sraddha*. Both trust that it is the sacred – the spiritual – which enables the human to be truly human.

The recognized distinctiveness of the two traditions need not necessarily discourage dialogue. Raimundo Panikkar and W. C. Smith[35] distinguish between *faith* and *belief*. They are of the opinion that contradictory beliefs may be rooted in common faith. Panikkar notes that even such contradictory statements of two persons as "I believe God exists" and "I belief God does not exist" can be rooted in faith in truth. In one instance the faith in truth expresses itself in the belief that "God exists," whereas in the other it is expressed in the contrary belief that "God does not exist."[36] Muslims and Hindus believe in the eternity or perenniality of truth. This is one reason for the Islamic insistence that the Qur'an is the literal word of God and for Hindus' description of their religion as *Sanatana Dharma*. This common trust in truth can enable Muslims and Hindus to undertake what John Dunne describes as "passing over" and "coming back."[37] We Muslims and Hindus need not define and understand our identity over against one another; that produces psychological and sociological barriers and often even spiritual atrophy.

[33] Syed Abdul Latif, *Islamic Cultural Studies* (Lahore: Shaikh Muhammad Ashraf; 1st ed., 1947; 3rd ed., 1960), pp. 27-36.

[34] M. N. Roy, *Documents of History of the C.P.I.* (Delhi: Ed. G. Adhikari, 1970), p. 354.

[35] Wilfred Cantwell Smith, *Faith and Belief* (Princeton: Princeton University Press, 1979).

[36] Raimundo Panikkar, *The Intra-Religious Dialogue* (New York: Paulist Press, 1978), p. 8.

[37] John S. Dunne, *The Way of All the Earth: Experiments in Truth and Religion* (New York: Macmillan, 1972).

Dialogue between Muslims and Hindus, which is a necessity, is not impossible. To begin, we Muslim and Hindu scholars may explore and investigate the parallels that exist between our two traditions, despite their differences and distinctiveness. The well-known Islamic scholar, S. H. Nasr, has written that "...the rich intellectual structures of Hinduism and Buddhism naturally present many resemblances to Islamic intellectuality, since all of them possess a traditional character."[38] This suggests that the parallels can be brought out effectively by a proper method of comparing common, historically initiated, congenial systems. Nasr suggests that Hindu *darsanas* can be compared with appropriate and corresponding Islamic schools with profitable results. Finding parallels and similarities, however, is not enough. The Middle Eastern situation indicates that two people belonging to two traditions which are doctrinally so close does not alone necessarily promote congeniality between them. All the reasons for conflict need to be explored. From the perspective of theology, the distinctiveness of traditions which causes confrontation needs to be recognized, together with the finding of parallels, and the possibility of accepting and appreciating the confronting ideal from within one's own tradition needs to be explored.

One important theological reason for Islam's antagonism toward Hinduism is its image-worship. Muslims may explore whether it would be possible to penetrate beneath Hindu image-worship so as not to consider it idolatry – without compromising the Islamic conviction of the transcendence of God. This is only a suggestion. How and in what way Muslims can recognize and appreciate Hinduism is a matter to be explored by them. My task is to suggest ways by which Hindus can accept and appreciate Islam.

Interreligious dialogue is also intrareligious dialogue. My suggestion that Hindus need to recognize and appreciate Islam leads to the usual Hindu response, "We do that; we recognize and appreciate all religions." Anthropological studies, such as those done by Bharati, indicate different levels of tolerance toward Muslims and Islam among Hindus. He points out that there is some tolerance among grass-roots village Hindus and primarily

---

[38] Nasr, *Islam and the Plight*, p. 42.

among "pamphlet" urban Hindus, while there is hardly any tolerance among the Sanskritists.[39] Even when there is tolerance toward Muslims, it is expressed neither socially in recognizing the Muslim as equal to the Hindu nor ideologically in accepting the exclusivism of Islam as equal to Hindu inclusivism. Socially or ideologically, Muslims and Islam are not considered to be on a par with Hindus and Hinduism. Hindus consider Muslims unclean. The fourteenth-century Arab traveler, Ibn Battuta, recalled the Hindu practice of breaking or giving away their utensils if they were used by a Muslim.[40] This was not done only in Battuta's time; even today many Hindus act similarly. An Afghan Muslim told about his childhood experience of interaction with Hindus. If he were to visit the store of a Brahmin – whom his own father had helped to establish the store – he knew that everything in the store would be washed after he left. This behavior is inhuman and dehumanizing – not tolerant. The Muslim animosity toward Hindus is not without provocation.

In the same way, the Hindu doctrinal tolerance of all religions is not enough, as it is often expressed as an intolerance of exclusivism. Hindu theologians need to explore how they can accept and tolerate exclusivism without compromising their conviction of the transcendence of truth. A clue can be found in the Hindu attitude toward *Ista Debata*. A Hindu who is totally dedicated and loyal to the *Ista* would not even recognize other manifestations of the same deity. This is *Ista Nistha*. The gopis of Vrndavan are examples. They were dedicated to cowhand Krsna of Vrndavan, so they would not even look at King Krsna of Dwaraka. Thus, it should be possible for a Hindu to appreciate the Qur'anic *nistha* of the Muslim.

A major stumbling block to the appreciation of Islam for non-Muslims is *jihad*. In our dialogue, a Hindu could ask the Muslim partner precisely what it means. Does it indicate that all non-Muslims should be killed, as

---

[39] Bharati, *Hindu Views*, pp. 71-94.

[40] Merriam, *Gandhi vs. Jinnah*, p. 6.

Beruni suggested? Is there any room for the recognition of plurality in Islam? What is the ideal Islamic way to deal with the *de facto* plurality that exists in the world? Christianity, like Islam, has an exclusivistic tradition, yet it is very active theologically about the issue of plurality. Is anything similar possible in Islam?

In Conclusion

Muslim-Hindu dialogue *is* a possibility. The Western initiative for dialogue – its scientific, critical spirit – influences Muslims and Hindus to reflect critically about their own traditions. Through that route we Muslims and Hindus can start a dialogue with each other; it is a practical necessity for the Indian sub-continent. We can utilize the modern findings of the social sciences to generate that insight which would break the barriers that exist between us. We can cooperate in sharing our spiritual insights with the West in order to counteract the dangers of secularization, which leads to dehumanization. We can communicate in the depth of our spirituality –which has happened among the mystics of our two traditions. On the scholarly level we can seek parallels. On the theological level we can explore the ways by which we can accept and appreciate each other without compromising our own convictions. We can honestly ask questions about those factors about the other which we find difficult to understand or accept. Interreligious dialogue cannot solve all the problems, but it is a worthwhile effort.

MUSLIM DIALOGUE ON HUMAN RIGHTS

ON HUMAN RIGHTS AND THE QUR'ANIC PERSPECTIVE[*]

Riffat Hassan[**]

It has been very fashionable for some time to use the term "human rights" rather glibly and to assume that everyone knows what human rights are and from whence they came. It is also commonly assumed that human beings do, in fact, posses human rights. There are two objections to this supposition: one practical, the other philosophical. If most human beings living on this earth today possessed what we call "human rights," we would not be having tens of thousands of persons in virtually every place in the world struggling, either openly or surreptitiously, to secure their "human rights." On the philosophical plane on might argue that "human rights" do exist, even though they are not being exercised by all or even most human beings.

This argument may lead to the question: If human rights exist even though they are not being exercised by all or most human beings (many of whom would be truly astonished to know that they had any such rights), then in what sense do these human rights "exist"? It is a historical fact that human rights have never been, nor are they now, the universal possession of humankind, although it is thirty-three years since the United Nations adopted the International Bill of Human Rights containing the Universal Declaration of Human Rights. It may also be argued that, even though all or most human beings do not exercise their human rights, these human rights remain intact

[*] *Journal of Ecumenical Studies*, 19,3 (Summer, 1982).

[**] Riffat Hassan (Muslim), above, p. 403.

since human beings always can exercise these human rights if and when they choose to do so, because these human rights are universally recognized and enforceable by courts of law. In answer to this argument (having remembered how costly it is to go to a court of law and how right Shakespeare was to bemoan the delays of justice), I cite the words of an eminent Muslim jurist:

> It would be pointless to detail the progressive erosion of human rights in so many contemporary constitutions around the world. Against the rising tide of governmental interference and despotism, they are proving like dykes of straw. Under the guise of creating a "welfare state" or "an egalitarian society", most rights have been deprived of all meaning or significance. In some parts of the world they are directly suspendable and often remain suspended. In states that claim socialist objectives, many of these rights are deprived of enforceability through independent courts; in some constitutions they have been made subject to so many constitutionally c inroads as to become devoid of all reality. Even in some countries where they do not suffer from any of the above limitations, judicial interpretation has, in deference to the idea of State activism and the welfare of the people, severely limited their scope. Perhaps never before has man enjoyed so great a capacity for good and for bad as today; yet never before has an individual felt, as now, so helpless in confrontation with the power and weight of faceless governmental agencies. Power like wealth accrues in the hands of those who wield it. The constitutional limitations of the free world appear to provide little safeguard or guarantee against the continuation of this trend.[1]

When Muslims speak of human rights, they generally speak of a multitude of rights, some of which are derived from a reading of the Qur'an, the Hadith, and the Sunnah, and the rest largely from a study of Islamic history and Islamic law. Most Muslims who speak of human rights also assume that these rights do, in fact, exist and are enforceable by courts of law. A survey of the present-day Muslim world (where each day more and more "human rights" are being eliminated as chastisement for "crimes against God") would hardly provide much evidence to support this assumption. All a Muslim can say today, with any measure of honesty, is that *if* an ideal Islamic

---

[1] K. M. Ishaque, "Islamic Law-Its Ideals and Principles," A. Gauher, ed., *The Challenge of Islam* (London: The Islamic Council of Europe, 1980), p. 157.

society existed, *then* the human rights of those who were part of that society would be recognized and would be enforceable by law.

In an article on "Islam and Human Rights," A. K. Brohi, another eminent jurist and a Federal Minister in the Pakistan government, made an observation (also made in slightly varying terms by several other Muslim writers writing about Islam and the Western world) which contained a serious allegation and a serious claim. He wrote:

> There is a fundamental difference in the perspectives from which Islam and the West each view the matter of human rights. The Western perspective may by and large be called anthropocentric in the sense that man is regarded as constituting the measure of everything since he is the starting point of all thinking and action. The perspective of Islam on the other hand is theocentric – God-conscious. Here the Absolute is paramount and man exists only to serve his Maker, the Supreme Power and Presence which alone sustains his moral, mental and spiritual make-up, secures the realization of his aspirations and makes possible his transcendence..... [In the West] the rights of man are seen in a setting which has no reference to his relationship to God, but are posited as his inalienable birthright. The student of growth of Western civilization and culture notices throughout that the emphasis is on human rights within an "anthropocentric" perspective of human destiny. Each time the assertion of human rights is made it is done only to secure the recognition from some secular authority such as the state itself or its ruling power. In marked contrast to this approach the strategy of Islam is to emphasize the supreme importance of our respect for human rights and fundamental freedom as an aspect of the quality of religious consciousness that it claims to foster in the heart, mind and soul of its followers. The perspective is "theocentric" through and through... It seems at first sight, therefore, that there are no human rights or freedoms admissible to man in the sense in which modern man's thought, belief and practice understand them; in essence, the believer has only obligations or duties to God since he is called upon to obey the Divine Law, and such human rights as he is made to acknowledge stem from his primary duty to obey God. Yet paradoxically, in these duties lie all the rights and freedoms. Man acknowledges the rights of his fellow men because this is a duty imposed on him by the religious law to obey God and the Prophet and those who are constituted as authority to conduct the affairs of state. In every thing that a believer does his primary nexus is with His Maker, and it is through Him that he acknowledges his relationship with the rest of his fellowmen as even with the

rest of the creation. In the words of the Qur'an, "Man has been created only to serve God!"[2]

It is very characteristic of Muslim apologetics to make statements such as the above. For that reason alone, it is important to point out certain fallacies in what Brohi is saying. First, what he represented as "Western" and described as an "anthropocentric" perspective on human rights is only the perspective of those who either deny the existence of God or regard it as unrelated to human affairs. No one who is properly described as a "Jew" or a "Christian" shares this "anthropocentric" perspective, and – since Jews and Christians form a significant segment of the Western world – it is unwarranted to make such sweeping generalizations regarding the Western perspective. Second, even though many charters of human rights originating in the Western world do not make a direct reference to God, it does not necessarily follow that God-centered or God-related concepts and laws are excluded from them. Reference to God does not necessarily make sacred, nor does nonreference to God necessarily make profane, any human document. To me it seems truly remarkable that an organization such as the United Nations, where every word of every declaration is fought over in an attempt by each country and bloc to protect its vested interest, could arrive at a document such as the Universal Declaration of Human Rights which, though "secular" in terminology, seems to me to be more "religious" in essence than many "*fatwas*" given by Muslim and other religious authorities and agencies. Third, I am not at all sure that the Islamic perspective may correctly be described as "theocentric" in the way in which Brohi appears to be using this term. Certainly, modern Islam's most outstanding thinker, Muhammad Iqbal, who spent his whole life teaching Muslims how to develop their selfhood and who believed that "art, religion and ethics must be judged from the standpoint of personality,"[3] would have great hesitation in accepting that the highest human morality consisted either in obedience to a law which was externally imposed or in doing one's duty to one's fellow human beings only from a sense of religious constraint. In Iqbal's own words, "There are

---

[2] A. K. Brohi, "Islam and Human Rights," in Gauhar, *Challenge*, pp. 179-181.

[3] M. Iqbal, quoted by R. A. Nicholson in the Introduction to *The Secrets of the Self*, translation of *Asgar-e-Khudi* (Farsi) (Lahore: Shaikh Muhammad Ashraf, 1964), p. xxii.

many who love god and wander in the wilderness,/I will follow the one who loves the persons made by God."[4]

For hundreds of years now, Muslims have been taught that they were created to serve God by obeying those in authority over them and by enduring with patience whatever God willed for them. For hundreds of years, Muslim masses have patiently endured the grinding poverty and oppression imposed on them by those in authority. Not to be enslaved by foreign invaders whose every attempt to subjugate them was met with resistance, Muslim masses were enslaved by Muslims in the name of God and the Prophet, made to believe that they had no rights, only responsibilities; that God was the God of Retribution, not of Love; that Islam was an ethic of suffering, not of joyous living; that they were determined by "*Qismat,*" not masters of their own fate. The heroic spirit of Muslim thinkers such as Syed Ahmad Khan and Iqbal, who were born in India in the last century – products not only of a pluralistic society but also of an East-West synthesis – brought about a Renaissance in the Muslim world and liberated Muslims from political bondage. Their work, however, was not completed, since the traditionalism which has eaten away the heart of Islam continues to hold sway over most of the Muslim world. What we are witnessing today in the Muslim world is of extreme interest and importance, for we are living in an age of both revolutions and involutions, of both great light and great darkness. It is imperative that Muslims rethink their position on all vital issues, since we can no longer afford the luxury of consoling ourselves for our present miseries and misfortunes by an uncritical adulation of a romanticized past. History has brought us to a point where rhetoric will not rescue us from reality and where the discrepancies between Islamic theory and Muslim practice will have to be accounted for.

Although in fact human rights are not universally recognized, universally exercised, or universally enforceable, they are, nonetheless, supremely important; even though many human beings do not understand or enforce them, these are rights which all human beings *ought* to have. These rights are so deeply rooted in our humanness that their denial or violation is

---

[4] M. Iqbal, *Bang-e-Dara* (Urdu) (Lahore: Shaidh Ghulam Ali and Sons, 1962), p. 151.

tantamount to a negation or degradation of that which makes us human. These rights came into existence essentially when we did; they were created, as we were, by God in order that our human potential could be actualized. These rights not only provide us with an opportunity to develop all our inner resources, but they also hold before us a vision of what God would like us to be: what God wants us to strive for and live for and die for. Rights given to us by God are rights which ought to be exercised, since everything that God does is for "a just purpose" (Sura 15:85; 16:3; 44:39; 45:22; 46:3), and renunciation of a God-given right is as virtuous a deed as nonutilization of a God-given talent. Others may or may not recognize our human rights and may or may not facilitate our exercise of these rights, but, as human beings who have a covenantal relationship with God, we must strive under all circumstances to secure and to guard those rights which we believe have been given to us by God and which, therefore, no one else has the right to take away.

Not regarding human rights as a human invention, I do not look for their origin or essence in books of law or history but in those books of scripture which contain God's eternal message and guidance to humankind. By stating, "Towards God is thy limit" (Sura 53:43),[5] the Qur'an – which to me as to other Muslims is the repository par excellence of divine wisdom – gives its readers an infinite worldview embracing every aspect of life. Consequently, it contains references to more "rights" than can be enumerated here. I will, therefore, exercise the preogative of being selective and mention only those rights which, in my judgement, figure importantly in the Qur'an.

---

[5] Translated by M. Iqbal, *The Reconstruction of Religious Thought in Islam* (Lahore: Shaikh Muhammad Ashraf, 1971), p. 57.

I. General Rights

A. Right to Life

The sanctity and absolute value of human life is upheld by the Qur'an which states: "Take not life, which God/Hath made sacred, except/By way of justice and law" (Sura 6:151).[6] In Sura 5:35, the Qur'an points out graphically that in essence the life of each individual is comparable to that of an entire community and therefore, should be treated with great care: "We ordained/For the Children of Israel/That if any one slew/A person – unless it be/For murder or for spreading/Mischief in the land – /It would be as if/He slew the whole people:/And if any one saved a life,/It would be as if he saved/ The life of the whole people."

B. Right to Respect

In Sura 17:70, the Qur'an says, "Verily, We have honored every human being." Human beings are deemed worthy of esteem because they are human. Being human means, according to the Qur'anic perspective, that human beings alone of all creation chose to accept the "trust" of freedom of the will (Sura 33:72). Human beings can exercise freedom of the will because they possess the rational faculty, which is what distinguishes them from all other creatures (Sura 2:30-34). Because human beings are made "in the best of moulds," though they can abase themselves to be "the lowest of the low" (Sura 95:4-6), and can think and can have knowledge of right and wrong, and are able to strive to do the good and avoid the evil, they have the potential to be God's vicegerents on earth. On account of the promise that is contained in being human, the humanness of all human beings is to be respected and regarded – to use a Kantian expression – as an end in itself.

C. Right to Justice

In the Qur'an, tremendous emphasis is put on the right to seek justice and the duty to do justice: "O ye who believe! Be steadfast witnesses for

---

[6] Unless otherwise noted , passages from the Qur'an cited here in verse form are taken from A. Y Ali, *The Holy Qur'an* (Smithtown, NY: McGregor and Werner, Inc., 1946). Those in prose are taken from G. A. Parwez, *Islam: A Challenge to Religion* (Lahore: Idara-e-Tulu'-'e-Islam, 1968).

Allah in equity; and not let enmity of any people seduce you that ye deal not justly. Deal justly, that is nearer to your duty. Observe your duty to Allah" (Sura 5:9). Likewise, "O ye who believe! Be ye staunch in justice; witnesses for Allah, even though it be against your own selves, or your parents, or your kindred, whether (the case be of) a rich man or a poor man, for Allah is nearer unto both (than ye are). So follow not passion lest ye lapse (from truth), nor ye distort truth or turn aside; verily God is well informed of what ye do" (Sura 4:135).

In the context of justice, the Qur'an uses two concepts: "'*adl*'" and "*ihsan.*" Both are enjoined (Sura 16:91), and both are related to the idea of "balance," but they are not identical in meaning. A. A. A. Fyzee, a well-known scholar of Islamic law, defined "'*adl*'" as "to be equal, neither more nor less," and wrote, "in a Court of Justice the claims of the two parties must be considered evenly, without undue stress being laid upon one side or the other. Justice introduces the balance in the form of scales that are evenly balanced."[7] Abu'l Kalam Azad, a famous translator of the Qur'an and a noted writer, described "'*adl*'" in similar terms: "What is justice but the avoiding of excess. There should be neither too much nor too little; hence the use of scales as the emblems of justice."[8] Lest anyone try to do too much or too little, the Qur'an states that no human being can carry another's burden (Sura 53:38) or have anything without striving for it (Sura 53:39).

It is important to note here that, according to the Qur'anic perspective, justice is not to be interpreted as absolute equality of treatment, since human beings are not equal as far as their human potential or their human situation is concerned. Thus, while upholding the principle that the humanness of all human beings is to be respected, the Qur'an maintains that the recognition of individual "merit" is also a fundamental human right. The Qur'an teaches that merit is not determined by lineage or sex or wealth or worldly success or religion—but by "righteousness." Righteousness consists not only of "just belief" ("*iman*") but also of "just action" ("'*amal*'") as pointed out with clarity in Sura 2: 177: "It is not righteousness/That ye turn your

---

[7] A. A. A. Fyzee, *A Modern Approach to Islam* (Lahore: Universal Books, 1978k), p. 17.

[8] *Ibid.*

faces/Towards East or West;/But it is righteousness – /To believe in God/And the Last Day,/And the Angels,/And the Book,/And the Messengers;/To spend of your substance,/Out of love for Him,/For your kin,/For orphans,/For the needy,/For the wayfarer,/For those who ask,/And for the ransoms of slaves;/To be steadfast in prayer,/And practice regular charity;/To fulfill the contracts/Which ye have made;/And to be firm and patient,/In pain (or suffering)/And adversity,/And throughout/All periods of panic./Such are the people/Of truth, the Godfearing." Sura 49:13 tells us that "the most honored of you in the sight of God is the most righteous of you," and Sura 4:95 says: "Not equal are those/Believers who sit (at home)/ And receive no hurt,/ And those who strive/And fight in the cause/Of God and their goods/And their persons./God has granted/A grade higher to those/Who strive and fight/With their goods and persons/Than to those who sit (at home). /Unto all (in Faith)/Hath God promised good: /But those who strive and fight/Hath He distinguished/Above those who sit (at home)/By a special reward."

Just as it is in the spirit of "*'adl*" that special merit be considered in the matter of rewards, so also special circumstances must be considered in the matter of punishments. In the case of punishment for crimes of "unchastity," for instance, the Qur'an, being non-sexist, prescribes identical punishments for a man or a woman who is proved guilty (Sura 2:2), but it differentiates between different classes of women; for the same crime, a slave woman would receive half, and the Prophet's consort double, the punishment given to a "free" Muslim woman (Sura 4:25; 33:30). Making such a distinction shows compassion for the morally "disadvantaged," while upholding high moral standards for others, particularly those whose actions have a normative significance.

While constantly enjoining "*'adl*," the Qur'an goes beyond this concept to "*ihsan,*" literally "restoring the balance by making up a loss or deficiency."[9] In order to understand this concept, it is necessary to understand the nature of the ideal community or society (*ummah*") envisaged by the Qur'an. The

---

[9] G. A. Parwez, *Tabweeb-ul-Qur'an* (Urdu) (Lahore: Idara-e-Tulu'-e-Islam, 1977), vol. 1, p. 78.

454

word "*ummah*" comes from the root "*umm,* or "mother." The symbols of a mother and motherly love and compassion are also linked with the two attributes most characteristic of God, namely "*Rahman*" and "*Rahim,*" both of which are derived from the root "*rahm,*" meaning "womb." The ideal "*ummah*" cares about all of its members as an ideal mother cares about all of her children, knowing that all are not equal and that each has different needs. While encouraging any one of her children to be parasitical would be injurious and unjust, not only to her other children but also to the one who betrays its human promise and lives – in Iqbal's terminology – by "begging," she feels that she has the right to make up the deficiency of a child who, despite its best efforts, still cannot meet the requirements of life. "*Ihsan*" is that which secures what even "*adl*" cannot; it shows the Qur'an's sympathy for the downtrodden, oppressed, or weak classes of human beings (such as women, slaves, orphans, the poor and infirm, and minorities).

D. Right to Freedom

There is much in the Qur'an to suggest that it would support Jean Jacques Rousseau's famous statement, "Man is born free, and everywhere he is in chains." A large part of the Qur'an's concern is to free human beings from the chains which bind them: traditionalism, authoritarianism (religious, political, economic), tribalism, racism, sexism, and slavery.

It is obvious that God alone is completely free and not subject to any constraint. The human condition necessitates that limits be set to what human beings may or may not do so that liberty does not degenerate into license. Recognizing the human propensity toward dictatorship and despotism, the Qur'an says with startling clarity and emphasis: "It is not right for man that God should give him the Book of Law, power to judge and (even) Prophethood, and he should say to his fellow-beings to obey his orders rather than those of God. He should rather say: Be ye faithful servants of God by virtue of your constant teaching of the Book and your constant study of it" (Sura 3:79).

The institution of human slavery is, of course, extremely important in the context of human freedom. Slavery was widely prevalent in Arabia at the time of the advent of Islam, and the Arab economy was based on it. The insistence in the Qur'an that slaves be treated in a just and humane way[10] (e.g., Sura 4:36) is generally recognized, as is the effort made by the Qur'an toward the emancipation of slaves (Sura 24:33; 4:92; 5:89, 9:60; 58:3; 2:177). But a number of writers, including well-known Muslim writers such as Abu'l Ala Maududi[11] and Muhammad Qutb,[12] are of the opinion that, though early Islam did much to alleviate the suffering and uplift the status of slaves, slavery was not abolished by the Qur'an. G. A. Parwez, who has spent over fifty years in Qur'anic scholarship, does not agree with this opinion (which unfortunately, would appear to be the majority opinion) and says:

> In every conceivable way, the Qur'an discouraged slavery and improved the lot of the slaves. The Muslims were urged to be kind and considerate to their slaves. They were told that to emancipate a slave was a meritorious act. They could atone for some of their offences by setting a slave free. Thus the number of slaves was gradually reduced and society was made less dependent on slave labor. The words, "whom your right hand possessed" occurring in the Qur'an are in the past tense and refer to those who had already been enslaved. When they were emancipated through a gradual process, slavery died a natural death. The main source of slaves–men and women–was prisoners in war. The Qur'an laid down that they should be set free either for a ransom or as a favor (Sura 47:4). The door for future slavery was thus closed by the Qur'an forever. Whatever happened in subsequent history was the responsibility of the Muslims and not of the Qur'an.[13]

Keeping in mind the great emphasis which the Qur'an places on human dignity and human freedom, it seems to me inconceivable that any other reading of Sura 47:4 is possible. That so few Muslims have accepted the idea that slavery was, indeed, abolished by the Qur'an indicated how reluctant the others have been to let go of the worst possible kind of power-obsession: to seek to own another human being made by God. It is interesting to reflect on the method and morality of how the majority of Muslims have understood the spirit of Qur'anic ethics. On the basis of two

---

[10] R. Roberts, *The Social Laws of the Qur'an* (Lahore: Sang-e-Meel Publications, 1978), p. 56.

[11] See, e.g., A. A. Maududi, *Human Rights in Islam* (Lahore: Islamic Publications, 1977), pp. 18-19.

[12] See e.g., M. Qutb, *Islam: The Misunderstood Religion* (Lahore: Islamic Publications, 1972), pp. 24-52.

[13] Parwez, *Islam*, p. 346.

statements related to the drinking of alcohol – "They ask thee/Concerning wine and gambling. Say: "In them is great sin,/And some profit, for men;/But the sin is greater/Than the profit'" (Sura 2:219); and "O ye who believe!/Intoxicants and gambling,/(Dedication of) stones,/And (divination by) arrows,/Are an abomination – /Eschew such (abomination),/That ye may prosper" – the Muslims have universally concluded that the drinking of alcohol is absolutely prohibited by the Qur'an. On the basis of a much larger and no less emphatic statement reflecting a deep concern with the problem of slavery, Muslims have not similarly concluded that slavery was prohibited by the Qur'an. Because the Qur'an does not state explicitly that slavery is abolished, it does not follow that it is to be continued, particularly in view of the numerous ways in which the Qur'an seeks to eliminate this absolute evil. A Book which does not give a king or a prophet the right to command absolute obedience from another human being could not possibly sanction slavery in any sense of the word, but this argument does not appeal to those Muslims who hypocritically follow the letter and not the spirit of the law of God.

The greatest guarantee of personal freedom for a Muslim lies in the Qur'anic decree that no one other than God can limit human freedom (Sura 42:21) and in the statement that "Judgement is only Allah's" (Sura 12:40).[14] As pointed out by K. M. Ishaque,

> The Qur'an gives to responsible dissent the status of a fundamental right. In exercise of their powers, therefore, neither the legislature nor the executive can demand unquestioning obedience....The Prophet, even though he was the recipient of Divine revelation, was required to consult the Muslims in public affairs. Allah addressing the Prophet says: "...and consult with them upon the conduct of affairs. And...when thou art resolved, then put thy trust in Allah" (Sura 3:159).[15]

Since the principle of mutual consultation ("shura") is mandatory (Sura 42:38), it is a Muslim's fundamental right to participate in as many aspects of the community's life as possible.

---

[14] Translated by K. A. Hakim, *Fundamental Human Rights* (Lahore: Institute of Islamic Culture, 1975), p. 15.

[15] Ishaque, "Islamic Law," pp. 167-169.

Muslims generally agree that the Qur'anic proclamation in Sura 2:256 ("Let there be no compulsion/In religion: Truth stands out/Clear from Error: whoever/Rejects Evil and believes/In God hath grasped/The most trustworthy/Hand-hold, that never breaks") means the non-Muslims are not to be coerced into professing Islam and that it is the human right of non-Muslims living in territories governed by Muslims that they should have the freedom to follow their own faith-traditions without fear or harassment. But the impulse to proselytize has always been strong in Muslims – as in Christians – even though a number of Qur'an passages state quite clearly that the mission of the Prophet (and the Muslims) to non-Muslims consists only of a faithful transmission of the message of God and that the Prophet (and the Muslims) ought not to feel responsible for the religious or moral choices made by other Muslims or by non-Muslims after they have received the message of God. For instance, "If it had been God's Plan/They would not have taken/False gods: but We/Made thee not one/To watch over their doings,/Nor art thou set/Over them to dispose/Of their affairs: (Sura 6:107).[16] The Qur'an, regarding its own truth as clear and self-evident, does not require the zeal of Muslims to prove it.

It is interesting and important to observe that professing Islam does not, in and by itself, give a Muslim any kind of advantage over any other believer: "Those who believe (in the Qur'an),/Any who believe in God/And the Last Day,/ And work righteousness,/Shall have their reward/With their Lord" (Sura 2:62). On the basis of this verse, all who believe in God and the hereafter and work righteousness can claim not only religious freedom but also religious equality. However, many Muslims – disregarding this and similar verses and the Qur'anic statement that God is *"rabb-a-'alamin,"* God of all peoples whose mercy extends to all creatures (Sura 7:156) – would vigorously dispute the right of non-Muslims to claim religious equality with them. Iqbal was an exceptional Muslim, in that he could go so far as to say: "The infidel with a wakeful heart praying to an idol is better than a Muslim who is sleeping in the mosque."[17]

---

[16] See also Sura 10:99; 16:82; 18:29; 42:48.

[17] M. Iqbal, *Javid Nama* (Farsi) (Lahore: Shaikh Mubarak Ali, 1947), p. 40.

The Qur'an recognizes the human right of religious freedom, not only in the case of other believers in God, but also in the case of pagans (if they are not aggressing upon the Muslims). For instance: "If one amongst the Pagans/Ask thee for asylum/Grant it to him,/So that he may hear the word/Of God; and then escort him/To where he can be secure" (Sura 9:6); and "Revile not ye/Those whom they call upon/Besides God, lest/They out of spite/Revile God/In their ignorance./ Thus have We made/Alluring to each people/Its own doings./ In the end will they/Return to their Lord,/And We shall then/Tell them the truth/Of all that they did" (Sura 6:108).

In the context of the human right to religious freedom, it is necessary to mention that, according to traditional Islam, the punishment for apostasy is death. In other words, a person who is born a Muslim or who becomes a Muslim is to be put to death if he or she later chooses to renounce Islam. There is nothing in the Qur'an which suggests any punishment at all, let alone the punishment of death, for a Muslim who renounces Islam. There is absolutely no reason to assume that the Qur'anic dictum, "Let there be no compulsion in religion" (Sura 2:256), which modern Muslims apply with such magnanimity to non-Muslims, does not or should not apply to Muslims also. (I believe that the death penalty was not meant to be a punishment for apostasy alone but for apostasy accompanied by "acts of war" against the Muslims. Muslim legists, however, obliterated the distinction between the exercise of a human right and the violation of others' human rights in order to terrify the "wavering" Muslims into remaining in the fold of Islam).

The right to freedom includes the right to be free to tell the truth, without which a just society cannot be established. The Qur'anic term for truth is "*Haqq,*" also one of God's most important attributes. Standing up for the truth is a right and a responsibility which a Muslim may not disclaim even in the face of the greatest danger or difficulty (Sura 4:135). While the Qur'an commands believers to testify to the truth, it also instructs the society not to harm the person so testifying (Sura 2:282).[18]

---

[18] G. A. Parwez, "Bunyadi Haquq-e-Insaniqat (Fundamental Human Rights)" (Urdu), *Tulu'-e-Islam* (Lahore), November, 1981, pp. 34-35.

E. Right to Privacy

The Qur'an recognizes the need for privacy as a human right and lays down rules for how the individual's life in the home may be protected from undue intrusion from within or without (Sura 24:27-28; 33:53; 24:58; 49:12).

F. Right to Protection from Slander, Backbiting, and Ridicule

The Qur'an acknowledges the right of human beings to be protected from defamation, sarcasm, offensive nicknames, and backbiting (Sura 49:11-12). It also points out that no person is to be maligned on grounds of assumed guilt and that those who engage in malicious scandal-mongering will be grievously punished in both this world and the next (Sura 24:16-19). The Qur'an also protects the right of a human being to be treated with sensitivity and compassion. It states with solemn simplicity: "God loves not that evil/Should be noised abroad/In public speech, except/Where injustice hath been/Done: for God/Is He who heareth/And knoweth all things./ Whether ye publish/A good deed or conceal it/Or cover evil with pardon,/Verily God doth blot out/(Sins) and hath power/(In the judgment of values)" (Sura 4:148-149).

G. Right to "The Good Life"

The Qur'an upholds the right of the human being not only to life but to "the good life." This good life, made up of many elements, becomes possible when a human being is living in a just environment. According to Qur'anic teaching, justice is a prerequisite for peace, and peace is a prerequisite for human development. In a just society the human rights mentioned earlier may be exercised without difficulty.

H. Other Rights

In addition to those rights, there are several others which are important and should be mentioned in passing: (1) the right to a secure place of residence (Sura 2:85); (2) the right to a means of living (Sura 11:6; 6:156); (3) the right to protection of one's personal possessions (Sura 2:29); (4) the right to seek knowledge (which is emphasized perhaps more than any other right by the Qur'an); (5) the right to develop one's aesthetic sensibilities and enjoy the bounties created by God (Sura 7:32); (6) the right to protection of one's covenants (Sura 17:34; 5:1; 3:177); (7) the right to move freely (Sura 67:15); (8) the right to seek asylum if one is living under oppression (Sura 4:97-100); (9) the right to social and judicial autonomy for minorities (Sura 5:42-48); and (10) the right to protection of one's holy places (Sura 9:17) and the right to return to one's "spiritual center." (According to the Qur'anic teaching – Sura 3:96; 5:97; 22:25 – the *Ka'ba* is the spiritual center of all humankind. However, the government of Saudi Arabia does not permit any non-Muslim to enter Mecca or to perform the pilgrimage which was proclaimed to all humankind by Abraham, as pointed out by Sura 3:96; 22:26; 2:125).

II. Rights of Man, Woman and Child

According to the Qur'an, God created man and woman from a single life-cell or spirit (Sura 4:1; 7:189; 16:72; 30:21). Both man and woman have male and female components (Sura 49:13), and both – together – constitute the human species. It is a clear teaching of the Qur'an that man and woman are equal in the sight of God (Sura 3:195; 4:124; 9:71-72; 16:97; 33:35; 40:40). Being equal before God who is the ultimate source of life and the ultimate standard of value, man and woman cannot become unequal to each other in essence. In fact, however, they are extremely unequal in almost all Muslim societies, where the superiority of man over woman is taken to be self-evident. Having spent seven years in study of the Qur'anic passages relating to women, I am convinced that the Qur'an is not biased against women and does not discriminate against them. On the contrary, because of its protective attitude toward all downtrodden and oppressed classes, it appears to be weighted in many ways in favor of women. But the interpretations of the Qur'an by men (women to this day have never had the right to interpret the Qur'an) have distorted the truth almost beyond recognition and have made the Qur'an a means of keeping women in bondage, physically and spiritually. Many Muslims, when they speak of human rights, either do not speak of women's rights at all[19] or are mainly concerned with the question of how a woman's chastity may be protected.[20] (They are apparently not very worried about men's "chastity.") The most gross violation of human rights in Muslim societies is that of the rights of women, who for centuries have been deprived of the right to be fully human. Muslims say with great pride that Islam abolished female infanticide; true, but it must also be mentioned that one of the most common crimes in many Muslim countries (e.g., Pakistan) is the murder of a woman by her husband. These so-called "honor-killings" are actually extremely dishonorable and are frequently used to camouflage other kinds of crimes.

Female children are discriminated against from the moment of birth, for it is customary in Muslim societies to celebrate the birth of a son and to bemoan the birth of a daughter. Many, if not most, girls are married when they are still minors, even though marriage in Islam is a contract and presupposes that the contracting parties are both consenting adults. Even though so much Qur'anic legislation is aimed at protecting the rights of women in the context of marriage (e.g., Sura 4:19; 24:33; 2:187; 9:71; 7:189; 30:21; 4:4), women can never claim equality with their husbands. The husband, in fact, is regarded as his wife's gateway to heaven or hell and the arbiter of her final destiny. That such an idea can exist within the framework of Islam – which totally rejects the idea of redemption, of any intermediary between a believer and the Creator – represents both a profound irony and a great tragedy.

Although the Qur'an presents the idea of what we today call a "no-fault divorce" and does not make any adverse judgements about divorce (e.g., Sura 2:231; 2:241), Muslim societies have made divorce for women extremely difficult, both legally and through social penalties. Although the Qur'an states clearly that the divorced parents of a minor child must decide by mutual consultation how the child is to be raised and that they must not use the child to hurt or exploit each other (Sura 2:233), in most Muslim societies

---

[19] E.g., R. A. Jullundrhi, "Human Rights in Islam," in A. D. Falconer, ed., *Understanding Human Rights* (Dublin: Irish School of Ecumenics, 1980).

[20] E.g., Maududi, *Human Rights*.

women are deprived of both their sons (generally at age seven) and their daughters (generally at age twelve), thus being subjected to unutterable cruelty. Although polygamy was intended by the Qur'an to be for the protection of orphans and widows (Sura 4:2-3), in practice Muslims have made it a dreadful and dehumanizing instrument for the brutalizing of women's sensibilities. Although the Qur'an made it possible for women to receive not only an inheritance upon the death of a close relative but also other bequests or gifts during the lifetime of a benevolent caretaker, Muslim societies have disapproved greatly of the idea of giving wealth to a woman in preference to a man, even when her need or circumstances warrant it. Although the purpose of the Qur'anic legislation dealing with women's dress and conduct (Sura 24:30-31; 33:59) was to make it safe for women to go about their daily business (since they have the right to earn money, as witnessed by Sura 4:32) without fear of sexual harassment, Muslim societies have put many of them behind veils and locked doors on the pretext of protecting their chastity, forgetting that according to the Qur'an (Sura 4:15) confinement to their homes was not the normal way of life for chaste women but a punishment for "unchastity."

A few words need to be said about the human rights of (minor) children according to Qur'anic teaching. Children have a right to life (Sura 81:8-9; 16:57-59; 17:31); a right to proper nurture and education (Sura 17:31; 2:233); a right to be maintained financially by the father or his heir(s) (Sura 24:61), but to be brought up according to the wishes of both parents (Sura 2:233); and a right to have their interests protected by the Islamic society in which they live, should they become orphaned (Sura 4:2-3 and numerous other references). Anyone reading the Qur'an is deeply touched by its concern for the welfare of orphans and particularly by its reminder to the Prophet, "And He found thee/In need, and made/Thee independent/Therefore treat not/The orphan with harshness,/Nor repulse the petitioner(Unheard);/But the Bounty/Of they Lord – /Rehearse and proclaim" (Sura 93:8-11).

III. In the End

In my judgment, the Qur'an is a very liberating document which holds before us a sublime vision of our human potential, our destiny, and our relationship with God and God's creatures. If Muslims were to exercise all the human rights granted to humankind by God, they would create a Paradise on earth and have no need to spend their time and energy dreaming about the *"hur"* promised in the afterlife. Unfortunately, at this time the spectrum before us appears very bleak, as more and more human rights disappear under the pressure of mounting fanaticism and traditionalism in many areas of the Muslim world. I am particularly concerned about serious violations of human rights pertaining to the rights of women, the rights of minorities, the right of the accused to due process of law, and the right of the Muslim masses to be free of dictatorships. In the end we have what seems to be an irreconcilable gulf between Qur'anic ideals and the realities of Muslim living. Can this gulf be bridged? To me, the answer is immaterial, because those of us who believe that human rights cannot be abandoned, even when they are being denied and aborted, will continue to strive and hope and pray for the securing of these rights – regardless of the chances of success or failure.

RELIGIOUS LIBERTY: A MUSLIM PERSPECTIVE*

Mohamed Talbi**

I. From Old Relations to a New Context

At the outset we have to remember that the problem of religious liberty as a common human concern and international preoccupation is relatively new. In former times the problem was totally irrelevant. During antiquity all felt that it was natural to worship the deities of their city. It was the task of these deities to protect the house, look after the family, and ensure the welfare of the state. Along with their worshippers they took the rough with the smooth. The deities of Carthage, for example, were by nature the enemies of the deities of Rome. In that context the refusal to worship the deities of the city was felt essentially as an act of disloyalty toward the state.

In the beginning the situation was almost the same in the biblical tradition. In the Bible Yahweh acts as the Hebrews' God. God constantly warns the people not to worship any other deity and to follow the Torah. This people with its one God is also an association of an ethnic entity – the twelve tribes descended from Abraham via Isaac and Jacob – with a land, Israel. The Hebrew community is an ideal prototype of unity: it obeys at one and the same time the *ius sanguinis, loci, et religionis*, the law of blood, place, and religion. It is the perfect prototype of an ethnically homogeneous

---

* In Leonard Swidler, ed., *Religious Liberty and Human Rights in Nations and in Religions* (Philadelphia/New York: Ecumenical Press/Hippocrene Books, 1986), pp. 175-187.

** Mohamed Talbi (Muslim), see above, p. 111.

community rooted in religion and a land, shaped into a state. In a way, to speak of religious liberty in such a case is literally absurd. There was no choice other than adhering to the state-community, or leaving it. Concretely, Jews who converted to another religion *ipso facto* ceased to belong to their state-community. Thus their conversions were felt as betrayals, and as such they warranted the penalty of death.[1] If we dwell on the case of the Jewish community as a prototype, it is because that case is not without some similarities to the classical Islamic *Ummah* as it has been shaped by traditional theology.

For historical reasons the situation changed completely with the appearance of Christian preaching and the destruction of the Jewish state in 70 C.E. From the beginning Christian preaching was not linked with a state: Jesus ordered his disciples "to render unto Caesar the things which are Caesar's, and unto God the things which are God's" (Mt. 22:21). This revolutionary attempt to dissociate the state and the religion and to ensure the freedom of the individual conscience failed. The time was not yet ripe. Consequently the early Christians and the Jews after 70 C.E. were often considered disloyal subjects by the Roman Empire because of their refusal to pay homage to the deities of their city and of their social group. Accordingly they were often treated as rebels, were even called atheists – because they were monotheists! The right to self-determination and religious liberty was denied to them as individuals acting freely in accordance with their consciences.

To make a long story short, let us say that political power and religion preserved more or less, or resumed, their old relations. They needed each other too much. The intolerance of the dominant social group asserted itself everywhere in the world with internal and external wars and many forms of more or less severe discrimination. Of course the Islamic world, though relatively tolerant, was no exception. As everywhere else in the world, human rights have been violated in this area, and it still happens that they are, here and there, more or less overridden. That does not mean, however,

---

[1] See Dt. 13:2-19; and Lev. 24:10-23.

as we shall see, that Islam as such authorizes the violation of these fundamental rights.

Now, to avoid looking only on the dark side of things, we should note that our common past was not entirely so sombre and so ugly. We can also cite some brilliant periods of tolerance, respect, comprehension, and dialogue.[2] Nevertheless, we had to wait until the nineteenth century to see freedom of conscience clearly claimed. Political and philosophical liberalism were then in vogue, but in fact what was claimed was not so much the right of freedom of conscience as the right not to believe. Thus the concept of religious liberty unfortunately became synonymous with secularism, agnosticism, and atheism. As a result, a stubborn fight was launched against it as such. For us to deal with the subject honestly and with equanimity, we need to free ourselves of this false identification.

It must be granted that today religious liberty is, as a matter of fact, definitively rooted in our social life. Since the Declaration of Human Rights in 1948, this concept is henceforth an essential part of international law. Moreover, we already live in a pluralistic world, and our world is going to be more and more pluralistic in the near future. I have written elsewhere[3] that each person has the right to be different and that at the same time our planet is already too small for all our ambitions and dreams. In this new world which is expanding rapidly before our eyes there is no longer room for exclusiveness. We have to accept each other as we are. Diversity is the law of our time. Today, by virtue of an increasingly comprehensive and sophisticated mass media, every person is truly the neighbor of every other person.

In our Islamic countries we have since the beginning been in the habit of living side by side with communities of different faiths. It has not been always easy, as some recent events again make painfully clear. However, it is only recently that we have begun to be confronted with secularism. It is now

---

[2] See, e.g., R. Caspar, "Les versions arabes du dialogue entre le Catholicos Timothée I et le Calife al-Mahdi (IIe/VIIIe siècle)," *Islamochristiana*, vol. 3 (1977), pp. 107-175.

[3] M. Talbi, "Une Communauté de Communautés: Le droit à la différence et les voies de l'harmonie," *Islamochristiana*, vol. 4 (1978), p. 11.

our turn to experience from inside the growth of agnosticism and atheism.[4] We have to be conscious of this overwhelming change in our societies, and accordingly we have to exercise our theological thinking in this new and unprecedented context.

Before going further we must first ask more precisely what religious liberty is. Is it only the right to be an unbeliever? One may indeed say that religious liberty has very often been exclusively identified with atheism. However, this is only one aspect of the question, and from my point of view, a negative one. In fact, religious liberty is basically the right to decide for oneself, without any kind of pressure, fear, or anxiety, whether to believe or not to believe, the right to assume with full consciousness one's destiny – the right, of course, to jettison every kind of faith as superstitions inherited from the Dark Ages, but also the right to espouse the faith of one's choice, to worship, and to bear witness freely. Is this definition in harmony with the Qur'an's basic teachings?

II. The Qur'an's Basic Principles

In my opinion religious liberty is basically grounded, from a Qur'anic perspective, first and foremost on the divinely ordered nature of humanity. A human is not just another being among many others. Among the whole range of creatures only humans have duties and obligations. They are exceptional beings. They cannot be reduced to their bodies because, above everything else, humans are spirits, spirits which have been given the power to conceive the Absolute and to ascend to God. If humans have this exceptional power, this privileged position in creation, it is because God "breathed into him something of His spirit" (Qur'an, XXXII, 9). Of course humans, like all living animals, are material. They have bodies created "from sounding clay, from mud moulded into shape" (Qur'an, XV, 28). But they received the Spirit. They have two sides: a lower side – their clay – and a higher side – the Spirit of God. This higher side, comments A. Yusuf Ali, "if

---

[4] See M. Talbi, "Islam et Occident: Au-delà des affrontements, des ambiguités et des complexes," *Islamochristiana*, vol. 7 (1981), pp. 57-77. A sociological inquiry held recently in Tunisia shows that 5% of the population declare openly that they are atheists, and 15% are indifferent. See A. Hermassi, "*al-Mutaccaf wa-l-faqih*," *Tunisian Review* 15-21, no. 8 (1984), p. 46.

rightly used, would give man superiority over other creatures."[5] Humanity's privileged position in the order of creation is strikingly illustrated in the Qur'an in the scene where the angels are ordered to prostrate themselves before Adam (Qur'an, XV, 29; XXXVIII, 72), the heavenly prototype of humanity. In a way, and provided we keep humanity in its proper place as creature, we may as Muslims, along with the other members of Abraham's spiritual descendants, Jews and Christians, say that humanity was created in God's image. A *hadith* (a saying of the Prophet), although questioned, authorizes this statement. So we can say that on the level of the Spirit all persons, whatever their physical or intellectual abilities and aptitudes may be, are truly equal. They have the same "Breath" of God in them, and by virtue of this "Breath" they have the ability to ascend to God and to respond freely to God's call. Consequently, they have the same dignity and sacredness, and because of this dignity and sacredness they are fully and equally entitled to enjoy the same right to self-determination on earth and for the hereafter. Thus, from a Qur'anic perspective we may say that human rights are rooted in what every human is by nature, and this is by virtue of God's plan and creation. Now it goes without saying that the cornerstone of all human rights is religious liberty, for religion, which is the "explanation of the meaning of life and how to live accordingly," is the most fundamental and comprehensive of human institutions.

It is evident from a Muslim perspective that humanity is not the fruit of mere "chance and necessity."[6] Its creation follows a plan and purpose. Through the "Breath" humanity has received the faculty to be at one with God, and its response, to have a meaning, must be free. The teachings of the Qur'an are clear: humans are privileged beings with "spiritual favours" (Qur'an, XVII, 70); they have not been "created in jest" (Qur'an, XXIII, 115); they have a mission and they are God's "vicegerents on earth" (Qur'an, II, 30). Proceeding from God, with a mission to fulfill, human destiny is ultimately to return to God. "Whoso does right, does it for his own soul; and

---

[5] A. Yusuf Ali, *The Holy Qur'an: Text, Translation, and Commentary* (Leicester, U.K.: The Islamic Foundation, 1975), p. 643, n. 1968.

[6] See Jacques Monod, *Le hasard et la nécessité* (Paris: éd. du Seuil, 1970), wherein the famous biologist develops a materialist point of view.

whoso does wrong, does so to its detriment. Then to your Lord will you all be brought back" (Qur'an, XLV, 15).

For that to happen it is absolutely necessary that each person be able to choose freely and without any kind of coercion. Every person ought in full consciousness to build his or her own destiny. The Qur'an states clearly that compulsion is incompatible with religion: "There should be no compulsion in religion. Truth stands out clear from Error. Whosoever rejects Evil and believes in God hath grasped the most trustworthy hand-hold, that never breaks. God is All-Hearing, All-Knowing" (Qur'an, II, 256).

To the best of my knowledge, among all the revealed texts, only the Qur'an stresses religious liberty in such a precise and unambiguous way: faith, to be true and reliable faith, absolutely needs to be a free and voluntary act. In this connection it is worth stressing that the quoted verse was aimed at reproving and condemning the attitude of some Jews and Christians who, being newly converted to Islam in Madina, were willing to convert their children with them to their new faith.[7] Thus, it is clearly emphasized that faith is an individual concern and commitment and that even parents must refrain from interfering with it. The very nature of faith, as is stressed in the basic text of Islam in clear and indisputable words, is to be a voluntary act born out of conviction and freedom.

In fact, even God refrains from overpowering humans to the point of subduing them against their will. This too is clearly expressed in the Qur'an.[8] Faith is then a free gift, God's gift. Humanity can accept or refuse it. It has the capacity to open its heart and its reason to God's gift. A guidance (*hudan*[9]) has been sent it. It is warmly invited to listen to God's call. God warns it in clear and unambiguous terms. As it is underlined in the cited verse stressing human freedom, "Truth stands out clear from Error." It is up to humanity to make its choice. The human condition – and that is the

---

[7] See Cheikh Si Boubakeur Hamza, *Le Coran: traduction nouvelle et commentaire* (Paris: éd. Fayard-Denoël, 1972), vol. 1, p. 97, who quotes Tabari, Razi, and Ibn Kathir.

[8] See Qur'an, XXVI, 4, and the commentary of Mahmud Shaltut, *al-Islam 'aqidatan wa shari'atan*, 2nd ed. (Cairo, n.d.), p. 33. See also Ali, *The Holy Qur'an*, p. 946 and n. 3140.

[9] See, e.g., Qur'an, II, 38; III, 4; V, 44, 46; VI, 157; IV, 33; XVI, 89, 102; XX, 123; XXVII, 2; XXXI, 3; XLVIII, 28; LXI, 9.

ransom of humanity's dignity and sacredness – is not without something tragic about it. Humans can be misled. They are able to make the wrong choice and to stray from the right path. In a word, they have the capacity to resist God's call, and this capacity is the criterion of their true freedom.

Even the Messenger, whose mission properly is to convey God's call and message, is helpless in such a situation. He is clearly and firmly warned to respect human freedom and God's mystery. "If it had been thy Lord's will, all who are on the earth would have believed, all of them. Wilt thou then compel mankind, against their will, to believe!" (Qur'an, X, 99). A. Yusuf Ali, in his translation of the Qur'an, comments on that verse in this way:

> ...men of faith must not be impatient or angry if they have to contend against Unfaith, and most important of all, they must guard against the temptation of forcing Faith, i.e., imposing it on others by physical compulsion, or any other forms of compulsion such as social pressure, or inducements held out by wealth or position, or other adventitious advantages. Forced Faith is no faith.[10]

The Apostle's mission – and all the more ours – is stringently restricted to advise, warn, convey a message, and admonish without compelling. He is ordered: "Admonish, for thou art but an admonisher. Thou hast no authority to compel them" (Qur'an, LXXXVIII, 21-22). In other words, God has set humanity truly and tragically free. What God wants is, in full consciousness and freedom, a willing and obedient response to the divine call, and that is the very meaning of the Arabic word "Islam."

Now we must emphasize that this does not mean that we have to adopt an attitude of abandon and indifference. We must in fact avoid both Scylla and Charybdis. First, we must, of course, refrain from interfering in the inner life of others, and we have already stressed this aspect of the problem enough. It is time to add that, secondly, we must also avoid being indifferent to every thing, being careless about others. We need to remember that the other is our neighbor. We must bear witness to and convey God's message. This too needs stressing.

We are too tempted today to shut ourselves up and to live comfortably wrapped in our own thoughts. But this is not God's purpose.

---

[10] Ali, *The Holy Qur'an*, p. 510, n. 1480.

Respectfulness is not indifference. God sets the example, for God is nearer to humanity "than the man's own jugular vein" (Qur'an, L, 16), and God knows better than we do our inmost desires, and what these desires "whisper (*tuwaswisu*)" to us (Qur'an, L, 16). Thus, God stands by us and speaks unceasingly to each one of us, warning and promising with a divine pedagogy that fits all persons of different social and intellectual classes, at all times, using images, symbols, and words that only God may use with a total sovereignty.

And God urges us to follow the divine example and to turn our steps toward all our sisters and brothers in humanity, beyond all kinds of frontiers, religious ones included. "O mankind! We created you from a male and a female; and we have made you into nations and tribes that you may know each other. Verily, the most honourable among you, in the sight of God, is he who is the most righteous of you. And God is All-Knowing, All-Aware" (Qur'an, XLIX, 13). A. Yusuf Ali comments on that verse in this way.

> This is addressed to all mankind, and not only to the Muslim brotherhood, though it is understood that in a perfect world the two would be synonymous. As it is, mankind is descended from one pair of parents. Their tribes, races, and nations are convenient labels by which we may know certain differing characteristics. Before God they are all one, and he gets most honour who is most righteous.[11]

In other words, humans are not created for solitariness and impervious individuality. They are created for community, relationship, and dialogue. Their fulfillment is in their reconciliation at once to God and to persons. We have to find the way, in each case, to realize this double reconciliation, without betraying God and without damaging the inner life of the other. To do so we have to listen to God's advice: "Do not argue with the People of the Book unless it is in the most courteous manner, except for those of them who do wrong. And say: We believe in the Revelation which has come down to us and in that which came down to you. Our God and your God is one, and to Him we submit" (Qur'an, XXIX, 46). Let us note that the Arabic word used in the verse and rendered in the translation by the verb "to submit" is "*muslimun*" (= Muslims). So, to be a true Muslim is to

---

[11] *Ibid.*, p. 1407, n. 4933. We generally follow his translation of the Qur'an.

live in a courteous dialogue with all peoples of other faiths and ideologies, and ultimately to submit to God. We must show concern to our neighbors. We have duties toward them; we are not isles of loneliness. The attitude of respectful courtesy recommended by the Qur'an must of course be enlarged to the whole of humankind, believers and unbelievers, except for those who "do wrong," that is to say, those who are unjust and violent and resort deliberately to the argument of the fist, physically or in words. In such a case it is much better to avoid a so-called dialogue in order to avoid the worse.

In short, from the Muslim perspective that is mine, our duty is simply to bear witness in the most courteous way that is most respectful of the inner liberty of our neighbors and their sacredness. We must also be ready at the same time to listen to them in truthfulness. We have to remember, as Muslims, that a hadith of our Prophet states: "The believer is unceasingly in search of wisdom, wherever he finds it he grasps it." Another saying adds: "Look for knowledge everywhere, even as far as in China." And finally, it is up to God to judge, for we, as limited human beings, know only in part. Let me quote: "To each among you have We prescribed a Law and an Open Way. And if God had enforced His Will, He would have made of you all one people. But His plan is to test you in what He hath given you. So strive as in a race in all virtues. The goal of you all is to God. Then will He inform you of that wherein you differed" (Qur'an, V, 51). "Say: O God! Creator of the heavens and the earth! Knower of all that is hidden and open! It is thou that wilt judge between Thy Servants in those matters about which they have differed" (Qur'an, XXXIX, 46).

III. Beyond the Limits Imposed by Traditional Theology

Though all Muslims are bound by the Qur'an's basic teachings, Muslim traditional theology developed in a way that, for historical reasons, does not, in my opinion, always fit in with the spirit of the Qur'an. Let us briefly recall two important cases: on the one hand, the *dhimmis* case – that is to say, the situation of the religious minorities inside the Islamic empire during medieval times – and, on the other hand, the apostate case.

Let us start with the *dhimmis*.[12] First, we must emphasize that, although the doors of many countries (not all of them, however) were opened (*fath*) by force or *jihad*[13] – as it was the general custom then – to pave the way for Islam, in practice Islam itself has almost never been imposed by compulsion. On this point the Qur'anic teachings have been followed. They provided the *dhimmis* with a sound protection against the most unbearable forms of religious intolerance. In particular, with two or three historical exceptions, the *dhimmis* have never been prevented from following the religion of their choice, from worshipping, or from organizing their communities in accordance with their own law. We can even say that in the beginning their situation was often greatly improved by Islamic conquest. They enjoyed long periods of tolerance and real prosperity,[14] very often holding high positions in the administrative, court, and economic activities.

But it is a fact that at certain times and places they suffered from discrimination. Roughly speaking, things began seriously to worsen for them from the reign of al-Mutawakkii (847-861 C.E.). The discrimination, especially in matters of dress, took an openly humiliating shape. The oppression culminated in Egypt during the reign of al-Hakim (996-1021 C.E.), who perhaps was not mentally sane.

In the medieval context of wars, hostilities, and treacheries, this policy of discrimination or open oppression was always prompted, or strongly

---

[12] There is a large bibliography about that question. Cl. Cahen's article in the *Encyclopaedia of Islam* on "*dhimma*" gives the most important references. The basic book is still A. Fattal's, *Le statut légal des non-musulmans en pays d'Islam* (Beirut, 1958). See also B. Lewis' article, "L'Islam et les non-musulmans," *Annales* (Paris), no. 3-4 (1980), pp. 784-800. Bat Yé Or's book, *Le dhimmi, profil de l'opprimé en Orient et en Afrique du Nord* (Paris, 1980), is partial.

[13] It is not unimportant to recall that, from a Muslim perspective, *jihad* is neither war nor holy war. This is an orientalist's conception. The arabic word "*jihad*" literally means "effort." The *jihad* consists in striving to fulfill God's purpose. Its highest form consists in fighting against our inner evil inclinations. It is for historical and contingent reasons that the wars fought by Muslims have more often than not been improperly called *jihad*. It is impossible to give a bibliography; the more recent book on this question is A. Morabia's doctoral thesis, *La notion de jihad dans l'Islam médiéval, des origines à al-Gazali* (Université de Lille III, 1975). See also M. Arkoun, M. Borrmans, and M. Arosio, *L'Islam religion et société* (Paris, 1982), pp. 60-62.

[14] See S. D. Goitein, *A Mediterranean Society*, vol. 1, *Economic Foundations* (Berkeley and Los Angeles: University of California Press, 1968); vol. 2, *The Community* (1971); vol. 3, *The Family* (1978). See also *idem*, *Letters of Medieval Jewish Traders* (Princeton, 1974).

backed, by the theologians. To understand that, we have to remember that it was not then a virtue – according to the medieval mentality everywhere in the world, and within all communities – to consider all human beings as equal. How could one consider as equal Truth and Error, true believers and heretics!

Thus, in our appraisal of the past we must always take the circumstances into account, but above all we must strive to avoid the recurrence of the same situations and errors. In any case, the Qur'an's basic teachings, whose inner meaning we tried to put into relief, lay down for us a clear line of conduct. They teach us to respect the dignity of the other and his/her total freedom. In a world where giant holocausts have been perpetrated, where human rights are still at stake, manipulated or totally ignored, our modern Muslim theologians must denounce loudly all kinds of discriminations as crimes strictly and explicitly condemned by the Qur'an's basic teachings.

However, we must consider the apostate case. In this field, too, traditional theology did not follow the spirit of the Qur'an. This theology abridged seriously the liberty of choice of one's religion. According to this theology, though the conversion to Islam must be, and is in fact, without coercion,[15] it is practically impossible, once inside Islam, to get out of it. The conversion from Islam to another religion is considered treason, and the apostate is liable to the penalty of death.[16] The traditional theologians in their elaboration rely on the one hand on the precedent of the first calif of Islam, Abu Bakr (632-634 C.E.), who energetically fought the tribes who

---

[15] In the formulae of conversion to Islam it is explicitly mentioned that the convert has "freely chosen Islam, without fear, in complete security against danger, and without any kind of coercion." See Muhammad b. Ahmad al-Umawi al-ma'ruf bi-Ibn al-'Attar, *Kitab al-watha'iq wa-l-sigillat* (Madrid: ed. P. Chalmeta and F. Corriente, 1983), p. 405; see also pp. 409-410, 414, 415-416.

[16] See 'Abd al-Rahman al-Gazari, *Kitab al-Fiqh 'ala al-madhahib al-arba'a* (Beirut, 1972), vol. 5, pp. 422-426. It has not been possible for us to have access to Dr. Nu'man 'Abd al-Razzaq al-Samarra'i's book, *Ahkam al-murtadd fi al-sari'a al-islamiya, dirasa muqarana* (The Apostate Status in Islam: A Comparative Study) (Ryad, Saudi Arabia, 1983). According to the Hanbalits, the apostate must immediately be put to death; according to the three other schools of fiqh, s/he is given three days to think it over, and it is only if s/he refuses to retract that s/he must be put to death. See also the formulae of conversion of Ibn al-'Attar, *Kitab al-watha'iq*, p. 407.

rejected his authority after the Prophet's death and refused to pay him the alms taxes, likening their rebellion to apostasy. On the other hand they mainly put forward the authority of this hadith: "Anyone who changes his religion must be put to death."[17]

I know of no implementation throughout the history of Islam of the law condemning the apostate to death – until the hanging of Mahmoud Taha in the Sudan in 1985.[18] This law has remained mostly theoretical, but it is not irrelevant to draw attention to the fact that during the 1970's, in Egypt, the Islamic conservatives narrowly missed enforcing this law against Copts[19] who, without due consideration, converted to Islam, generally to marry Muslim women, and who, in case of the failure of the marriage, returned to their former religion. Recently, too, some Tunisian atheists expressed their concern.[20] So, the case of the apostate in Islam, though mostly theoretical, needs to be cleared up.

Let us first point out that the hadith upon which the penalty of death essentially rests is always more or less mixed with rebellion and highway robbery in the Tradition books. The cited cases of "apostates" killed during the Prophet's life or shortly after his death are all without exception of persons who as consequence of their "apostasy" turned their weapons against the Muslims, whose community at that time was still small and vulnerable. The penalty of death appears in these circumstances as an act of self-defense

---

[17] For this hadith see, e.g., Buhari, *Sahih* (Cairo: ed. al-Sa'b, n.d.), IX, 19; Abu Dawud, *Sunan* (Cairo, 1952), II, p. 440. See also Buhari, *Sahih*, VIII, 201-202, and IX, 18-20; Abu Dawud, *Sunan*, II, pp. 440-442.

[18] Mahmud Taha was hanged by General Numeiri in Khartoum, Sudan, on January 18, 1985, at 10 a.m. as an apostate. Dr. 'Abd al-Hanrid 'Uways supported this enforcement of the law (see *al-Muslimun*, a Saudi weekly paper specializing in Islamic studies, March 23-29, 1985, p. 15).

[19] See Mohamed Charfi, "Islam et droits de l'homme," *Islamochristiana*, vol. 9 (1983), p. 15. See also Claire Brière and Oliver Carré, *Islam, Guerre à l'Occident?* (Paris: éd. Autrement, 1983), where we read: "Ainsi en 1977, une proposition de loi de peine de mort contre l'"apostat manifeste' est présentée au Parlement. Grosse affaire! Une telle loi, en effet, toucherait notamment les communistes militants. En effet, nous l'avons vu, ces derniers sont déclarés athées et apostats. Elle toucherait également les nombreux coptes qui, pour se marier avec une musulmane ou pour divorcer, se déclarent musulmans, puis represent publiquement leur pratique religieuse copte plus tard" (p. 185).

[20] See Talbi, "Islam et Occident," pp. 68-69.

in a war situation. It is undoubtedly for that reason that the Hanafit school of *fich* does not condemn a woman apostate to death, "because women, contrary to men, are not fit for war."[21]

Further, the hadith authorizing the death penalty is not, technically, *mutawatir*,[22] and consequently it is not, according to the traditional system of hadith, binding. Above all, from a modern point of view, this hadith can and must be questioned. In my opinion, there are many persuasive reasons to consider it undoubtedly forged. It may have been forged under the influence of Leviticus (24:16) and Deuteronomy (13:2-19) – where the stoning of the apostate to death is ordered – if not directly, then perhaps indirectly through the Jews and Christians converted to Islam.

In any case, the hadith in question is as a matter of fact at variance with the teachings of the Qur'an, where there is no mention of a required death penalty against the apostate. Even during the life of the Prophet, the case presented itself at various times, and several verses of the Qur'an deal with it.[23] In all these verses, without a single exception, the punishment of the apostate who persists in rejection of Islam after having embraced it is left to God's judgment and to the afterlife. In all the cases mentioned in the Qur'an, and by the commentators, it is a question on the one hand of time-servers – individuals or tribes, who, according to the circumstances, became turncoats[24] – and on the other hand of hesitating persons attracted to the faith of the "People of the Book" (Qur'an, II, 109; III, 99-100), Jews and Christians. Always taking into account the special situation, the Qur'an argues, warns, or recommends the proper attitude to be adopted, without ever threatening death.

---

[21] A. al-Gazari, *Kitab al-Fiqh*, V, 426.

[22] A hadith is called *mutawatir* when it is transmitted by several driving chains of reliable warrantors.

[23] Qur'an, II, 109, 217; III, 85-89, 91, 99-100, 106, 149; V, 57-59; XLVII, 25, 32, 34, 38.

[24] See Hamza, *Le Coran*, commentary on verses III, 85, 88, 91, 101, 106; IV, 31, 91, 106; V, 54; XLIX, 14.

1.   The Qur'an Argues

From a Muslim perspective the Qur'an recognizes all the previous revelations and authenticates and perfects them: "Say: We believe in God, and in what has been revealed to us, and what was revealed to Abraham, Ishmael, Isaac, Jacob and the Tribes, and in that which was given to Moses, Jesus, and the Prophets, from their Lord. We make no distinction between any one of them, and to God we submit (*muslimun*)" (Qur'an, III, 84).

It does not follow that all are permitted, at the convenience of the moment, to change their religion as they change their coats. Such a behavior denotes in fact a lack of true faith. It is for this reason that the following verse insists on the universal significance of Islam, as a call directed to the whole of humankind:[25] "If anyone desires a religion other than Islam, never will it be accepted of him; and in the Hereafter he will be among the losers" (Qur'an, III, 85).

Accordingly the apostates are warned: those who choose apostasy, after being convinced in their inmost thoughts that Islam is the truth, are unjust, and as such they are bereft of God's guidance, with all the consequences that follow for their salvation. "How shall God guide those who reject faith after they accepted it, and bore witness that the Apostle was true, and that clear signs had come to them? But God guides not a people unjust" (Qur'an, III, 86; see also the following verses: 87-91).

Nevertheless, the Qur'an denounces the attitude of "the People of the Book," who exerted pressure on the newly converted to Islam to induce them to retract. There is no doubt that the polemics between the dawning Islam and the old religions were sharp. In this atmosphere the Qur'an urges the persons who espoused Islam to adhere firmly to their new faith, till their death, to close their ranks, to refuse to listen to those who strive to lure them to apostasy, and to avoid their snares. They are also reminded of their former state of disunion when they were "on the brink of the Pit of Fire," and they are exhorted to be a people "inviting to all that is good" in order to ensure their final salvation. Let us quote:

---

[25] See M. Talbi, *Islam et Dialogue* (Tunis: ed. MTE, 1972), pp. 28-33; Arabic tr. in *Islamochristiana*, vol. 4 (1978), pp. 12-16.

> Say: O People of the Book: Why obstruct ye those who believe from the Path of God, seeking to make it crooked, while ye were yourselves witness thereof? But God is not unmindful of all that ye do.
>
> O ye who believe! If you obey a faction of those who have been given the Book, they will turn you back into disbelievers after you have believed.
>
> And how would you disbelieve, while to you are rehearsed the signs of God, and His Messenger is among you? And he who holds fast to God is indeed guided to the Right Path.
>
> O ye who believe! Fear God as He should be feared, and die not except in a state of Islam.
>
> And hold fast, all together, by the Rope of God, and be not divided, and remember God's favour on you: for ye were enemies, and He joined your Hearts in love, so that by His Grace, ye became brethren; and ye were on the brink of the Pit of Fire, and He saved you from it. Thus doth God make His Signs clear to you, that ye may be guided.
>
> Let there arise out of you a Community inviting to all that is good, enjoining what is right, and forbidding what is wrong. They are the ones to attain felicity. (Qur'an, III, 99-104)

Thus, unceasingly and by all means, the Qur'an strives to raise the new Muslims' spirit, in order to prevent them from falling into apostasy. The argumentation is only moral, however. The Qur'an goes on: It is "from selfish envy" (Qur'an, II, 109) that "quite a number of the People of the Book wish they could turn you back to infidelity" (Qur'an, II, 109; see also III, 149); you have not to fear them, "God is your Protector, and He is the best of helpers, soon shall He cast terror into the hearts of the unbelievers" (Qur'an, III, 150-151); "your real friends are God, His Messenger, and the believers...it is the party of God that must certainly triumph...therefore take not for friends those who take your religion for a mockery or sport..." (Qur'an, V, 58-60). And finally, those who, in spite of all that, allow themselves to be tempted by apostasy, are forewarned: if they desert the cause, the cause nevertheless will not fail. Others will carry it forward:

> O ye who believe! If any from among you turn back from his faith, soon will God produce a people whom He will love as they will love Him, – lowly with the Believers, mighty against the Rejecters, striving in the way of God, and never afraid of the reproaches of a fault finder. That is the grace of God, which He will bestow on whom He pleaseth. And God is bountiful, All-Knowing. (Qur'an, V, 57; see also XLVII, 38)

Finally the apostates are given this notice: they "will not injure God in the least, but He will make their deeds of no effect" (Qur'an XLVII, 32).

2. The Qur'an Warns

The young Muslim community is thus given many reasons to adhere to its new religion. The members of this community are also warned that for their salvation they should not depart from their faith. They are urged to follow the true spirit of Islam, and this spirit is defined in two ways: first they will love God and God will love them; secondly they will be humble among their brothers and sisters, but they will not fear the wrongdoers, and they will not join with them. If by fear, weakness, or time-serving, they depart from this line of conduct and fall into apostasy, the loss will be their own, and the punishment will be hard in the hereafter. "And if any of them turn back from their faith, and die in unbelief, their works will bear no fruit in this life. And in the Hereafter they will be companions of the Fire, and will abide therein" (Qur'an, II, 217). The apostates lay themselves open to "the curse of God, of His angels, and of all mankind" (Qur'an, III, 87), "except for those who repent thereafter, and amend, for God is Oft-Forgiving, Most Merciful" (Qur'an, III, 89). But there is no hope for those who persist in their apostasy (Qur'an, III, 90-91). These obstinate apostates will "taste the penalty for rejecting faith" (Qur'an, III, 106; see also III, 140). Such persons are entirely in the hands of evil (Qur'an, XLVII, 25). They secretly plot with the enemies (Qur'an, XLVII, 26-27), and "they obstruct the way to God" (Qur'an, XLVII, 32, 34). As a result "God will not forgive them" (Qur'an, XLVII, 34).

3. The Qur'an Advises

How should such obstinate and ill-disposed apostates be dealt with? How should those be treated who try to draw others into their camp or to manipulate others? Let us underline once more that there is no mention in the Qur'an of any kind of penalty, neither death nor any other one. To use the technical Arab word, we would say that there is no specified *hadd*[26] in this matter. On the contrary, the Muslims are advised to "forgive and overlook till God accomplishes His purpose, for God hath power over all

---

[26] *Hadd* = legal penalty explicitly specified in the Qur'an.

things" (Qur'an, II, 109). In other words, there is no punishment on earth. The case is not answerable to the Law. The debate is between God and the apostate's conscience, and it is not our role to interfere in it.

Muslims are authorized to take up arms only in one case, the case of self-defense, when they are attacked, and their faith is seriously jeopardized. In such a case "fighting" (*al-qital*) is "prescribed" (*kutiba*) for them, even if they "dislike it" (*kurhun lakum*) (Qur'an, II, 216), and it is so even during the sacred month of Pilgrimage (Qur'an, II, 217; II, 194).[27] To summarize, Muslims are urged not to yield, when their conscience is at stake, and to rise up in arms against "those who will not cease fighting you until they turn you back from your faith, if they can" (Qur'an, II, 217).

It is thus evident that the problem of religious liberty, with all its ramifications, is not new within Islam. The Qur'an deals at length with it. At the heart of this problem we meet the ticklish subject of apostasy, and we have seen that with regard to this subject the Qur'an argues, warns, and advises, but it never resorts to the argument of the sword. This is because that argument is meaningless in the matter of faith. In our pluralistic world our modern theologians must take that into account.

We can never stress too much that religious liberty is not an act of charity or a tolerant concession toward misled persons. It is, rather, a fundamental right of everyone. To claim it for myself implies *ipso facto* that I am disposed to claim it for my neighbor, too. But religious liberty is not reduced to the equivalent of atheism. My right, and my duty also, is to bear witness, by fair means, to my own faith and to convey God's call. Ultimately, however, it is up to each person to respond to this call or not, freely and in full consciousness.

From a Muslim perspective, and on the basis of the Qur'an's basic teachings, whose letter and spirit we have tried to adduce, religious liberty is fundamentally and ultimately an act of respect for God's sovereignty and for the mystery of God's plan for humanity, which has been given the terrible privilege of shaping entirely on its own responsibility its destiny on earth and hereafter. Ultimately, to respect humanity's freedom is to respect God's

---

[27] See Ali, *The Hony Qur'an*, p. 77, n. 209, commentary on II, 194.

plan. To be a true Muslim is to submit to this plan. It is to put one's self, voluntarily and freely, with confidence and love, into the hands of God.

A BUDDHIST RESPONSE TO MOHAMED TALBI[*]

Masao Abe[**]

My first impression of Mohamed Talbi's essay, "Religious Liberty: A Muslim Perspective," is that Islam has two sharply contrasting aspects within itself: an aspect of respecting the liberty of choosing one's faith, and an aspect of discrimination and punishment of the apostate that includes the death penalty. As for the first aspect, by quoting the Qur'an, "There should be no compulsion in religion" (II, 256), Talbi states that, "The very nature of faith, as is stressed in the basic text of Islam in clear and indisputable words, is to be a voluntary act born out of conviction and freedom." He also emphasizes, "In fact, even God refrains from overpowering humans to the point of subduing them against their will. This too is clearly expressed in the

---

[*] In Leonard Swidler, ed., *Religious Liberty and Human Rights in Nations and Religions* (Philadelphia/New York: Ecumenical Press/Hippocrene Books, 1986), pp. 189-191.

[**] Masao Abe (Buddhist) is Margaret Gest Visiting Professor at Haverford (PA) College, 1985-87. He is Professor Emeritus of Nara (Japan) University of Education, where he taught philosophy from 1952 to 1980. A graduate of Kyoto (Japan) University, he studied and practiced Buddhism, especially Zen, with Sin'ichi Hisamatsu, as well as Western philosophy. As a Rockefeller Foundation Research Fellow, he studied Christian theology at Union Theological Seminary and Columbia University, 1955-57. He has been a visiting professor at several U.S. schools, including Columbia and Princeton Universities, the Universities of Chicago and Hawaii, and Claremont Graduate School. Since the death of D. T. Suzuki, he has been the leading exponent of Zen and Japanese Buddhism in the West. As a member of the Kyoto School of Philosophy, he is deeply involved in the comparative study of Buddhism and Western thought and in Buddhist-Christian dialogue. His recent book, *Zen and Western Thought* (University of Hawaii Press, 1985), collects his important essays on Zen in relation to Western thought. He has published in a wide variety of Japanese and Western journals, as well as serving on the advisory boards of five journals.

Qur'an." At the same time, however, we are told "In the medieval context of wars, hostilities, and treacheries, this policy of discrimination or open oppression was always prompted...by the theologians." And, according to traditional theology, "The conversion from Islam to another religion is considered treason, and the apostate is liable to the penalty of death." Further, "the punishment of the apostate who persists in rejection of Islam after having embraced it is left to God's judgment and to the afterlife." However, "The apostates lay themselves open to 'the curse of God, of His angels, and of all mankind' (Qur'an, III, 87)...[and] 'God will not forgive them' (Qur'an, XLVII, 34)."

I thus see in Islam two sharply contrasting aspects: the aspect of *the freedom to choose one's faith* and the aspect of *oppression* with regard to faith. Of course, we should not overlook that Talbi emphasizes the first aspect, the freedom to choose one's faith, as the basic teaching of the Qur'an, whereas he discusses the second aspect, the open oppression of faith and the death penalty, as a deviation from the basic teaching of the Qur'an in such a case as the *dhimmis* (the situation of the religious minorities inside the Islamic empire during medieval times) and the apostate (the conversion from Islam to another faith). While I understand that such deviations have taken place for certain historical reasons in special social or international situations, nevertheless, these two aspects are so diametrically opposed that I can hardly reconcile them in a single living religion, Islam.

If a basic teaching of the Qur'an is that faith should not be forced but is a voluntary act based on conviction and freedom, how are such contrary deviations as open oppression and the death penalty of the apostate possible – even under special historical and social situations? If such a serious deviation from the basic teachings of the Qur'an is possible due to particular historical reasons and social situations, I am afraid there is no absolute authority for the Qur'an's basic teachings of the freedom of faith. If, as Talbi emphasizes, God refrains from overpowering humans to the point of subduing them against their will, why does God curse and not forgive apostates?

After a careful rereading of Talbi's essay, I came to understand that the Qur'an emphasizes the free choice of faith without compulsion in religion with regard to the conversion to Islam, but it does not emphasize the free choice of faith to leave and/or reject Islam. In fact, such rejection is seriously judged as treason, and the apostate is liable to the penalty of death. If I am not mistaken in this regard, then I understand the nature of God in Islam as follows: God created all human beings equally by inspiring into them God's "breath," and by virtue of this "breath" they have the ability to be at one with God and to respond freely to God's call. God is full of mercy and charity. At the same time, as the Qur'an clearly states, "God guides not a people unjust" (III, 86), because "How shall God guide those who reject faith after they accept it, and bore witness that the Apostle was true, and that clear signs had come to them?" (*ibid.*). Why is God in Islam so ambivalent? I understand that God has two hands: a hand of mercy and a hand of justice. As the one absolute God, God can use these two hands freely. My question, however, remains: When it is stated, "God guides not a people unjust," why does a merciful God *not* guide a people unjust? Why does an all-loving God *not* forgive an apostate? And what does "unjust" mean? To what is one "unjust"?

God is merciful and quite tolerant with regard to conversion to Islam, whereas God is severe and intolerant with regard to conversion from Islam to another religion. The term "unjust," it seems to me, indicates "unjust" against God's authority as the one absolute God – or at least "unjust" against God's own righteousness as the sole standard of judgment. If this is the case, at least two problems may emerge: First, although God has two hands, namely, a hand of mercy and a hand of justice, the hand of justice often overwhelms the hand of mercy. As a result, discrimination, oppression, and the condemnation of the apostate to death take place. Second, such discrimination, oppression, and condemnation will provoke resentment, hatred, and revenge; such a negative and inimical reaction will create still further negative and inimical reactions, and this reciprocal relation will develop endlessly. With Talbi, I sincerely hope "modern Muslim theologians must denounce loudly all kinds of discriminations as crimes strictly and explicitly condemned by the Qur'an's basic teachings." I also wholeheartedly pray that God's hand of mercy will overwhelm the hand of justice, rather than vice versa.

The Buddhist attitude toward the problem of heresy and apostasy is significantly different from that of Islam. Gautama Buddha, the founder of Buddhism, says:

> To an enemy intent on ill you are a good friend intent on good. To one who constantly seeks for faults you respond by seeking your virtues. Revilers you conquered by patience, plotters by blessings, slanderers by the truth, the malicious by friendliness.

Buddhism does not advocate the notion of one absolute God but, rather, the "law of dependent co-origination," which indicates that everything in and beyond the universe is interdependent and mutually related. Not only human beings (in the universe) are interdependent, but also the divine (which is beyond the universe) and the human are interdependent. To the Buddhist, God who is transcendent, self-existing, and commanding is an unreal entity. Just as without the divine there is no human, so without the human there is no divine. Accordingly, in Buddhism there is no idea of an apostate. A stock Buddhist phrase in this regard is:

> Not rejecting those who come; not running after those who leave.

Buddhism emphasizes wisdom and compassion rather than justice and charity. Just as in Islam charity without justice is not true charity, so in Buddhism compassion without wisdom is not true compassion. Like justice, wisdom makes distinctions clear, but, unlike justice, wisdom neither judges between the just and the unjust nor accepts the just alone while punishing the unjust. Rather, wisdom admits different things in their distinctiveness and acknowledges the different values of the things which are distinguished. While "justice" provokes resentment, hatred, and revenge, and thus creates an endless process of vengeful reactions, "wisdom" inspires understanding, acknowledgement, and mutual appreciation, and thus entails peace and harmony.

Islam is not lacking in the notion of wisdom; as Talbi emphasized, "a hadith of our Prophet states: 'The believer is unceasingly in search of wisdom; wherever he finds it he grasps it.' Another saying adds: 'Look for knowledge everywhere, even as far as in China.'" In this connection, I would like to say to my Islamic friends: As your *hadith* states, please look for wisdom! However, it is not necessary to look as far away as China; rather, Islam can look to India, the birthplace of Buddhism.

RELIGIOUS FREEDOM IN EGYPT: UNDER THE SHADOW OF THE ISLAMIC *DHIMMA* SYSTEM[*]

Abdullahi Ahmed An-Na'im[**]

The existence of religious conflict and strife in Egypt today cannot be denied. Feelings of animosity and distrust between Muslims and non-Muslims often erupt in riots and communal violence. Muslim-Coptic clashes in 1972 resulted in the death of forty-eight people. Similar clashes in 1981 led to the death of eight and the detention of more than 1,500 political and religious personalities, including Pope Shenouda III, the head of the Coptic Church.

The state of religious freedom and tolerance in Egypt reflects centuries of conflict, tension, and interaction among the main religious communities in the area, namely, Muslims, Christians, and Jews. The Islamic-Jewish dimension, however, has both been complicated and alleviated by the rise of Zionism and the establishment of the State of Israel.

[*] In Leonard Swidler, ed., *Religious Liberty and Human Rights in Nations and Religions* (Philadelphia/New York: Ecumenical Press/Hippocrene Books, 1986), pp. 43-59.

[**] Abdullahi Ahmed An-Na'im (Muslim) was from 1979 Professor of Law at the University of Khartoum till his detention in May, 1983, because of his opposition to the implementation of *Shari'a* in the Sudan. After the fall of President Numeiri (April, 1985), he received a Ford Foundation grant to do research on human rights in Islam. A leading member of the Sudanese Islamic reform movement, *jumhoryon*, started by the late Mahmoud M. Taha (executed in January, 1985, by President Numeiri), he has published in Arabic and English on Sudanese law and human rights, and has translated Taha's major work into English. He is at present doing a major study of religious tolerance in Muslim countries and communities. For further details see above, p. 59.

While the social isolation and economic and political difficulties of Egyptian Jews were intensified with charges of allegiance to an alien entity and doubts as to their loyalty to the Egyptian polity, post-World War II conditions and the establishment of the State of Israel encouraged Jewish migration to Israel as well as to other parts of the world. The current official peace between Egypt and Israel is too recent and too uncertain to have had a significant impact on Muslim-Jewish relations in Egypt.

Christians, mainly Copts, constitute the main religious minority in Egypt today. Exact figures are hard to come by in this field, but reliable estimates put the Copts at about 9,000,000, which is about twenty percent of the total population. There also are, of course, some non-Coptic Christians, Jews, Baha'is, and adherents of other religions, as well as atheists and agnostics. Current discussions of the problems of religious freedom and tolerance in Egypt, however, tend to concentrate on Muslim-Coptic relations in view of the size and relative importance of these two communities. From the point of view of religious freedom as a fundamental human right, however, the issues are the same with regard to any religious or nonreligious belief. The illustration and discussion of the problem in terms of Muslim-Coptic relations may be dictated by the availability of current information, but it does not indicate indifference to the problems faced by other groups.

To put the subsequent discussion in context, there is a brief outline of the present Egyptian legal and constitutional system, followed by a brief survey of relevant sources in order to outline a working definition of the concept of religious freedom as established by current international standards. Examples of violation of religious freedom and instances of intolerance are then cited as background for a discussion of some of the underlying causes. Finally, suggestions on remedial action that may be undertaken in Egypt, and possibly in other parts of the Muslim world, are offered.

Legal and Constitutional System

The present Egyptian legal and constitutional system is the outcome of intellectual and political developments going back to the beginning of the nineteenth century.[1] Following the invasion of Egypt by Napoleon in 1798, French civilization and political ideology acquired a strong hold on Egyptian elite classes. Although the General Council, a consultative body, and the Institute of Egypt, a scholarly/scientific body, established by the brief French administration, were disbanded following the expulsion of the French by an Anglo-Turkish expedition, French intellectual and legal traditions endured. Mohamed Ali, the ruler of Egypt from 1805 to 1848, undertook an extensive modernization program, including the introduction of a state school system to supplement the preexisting religious education. He also started the practice of sending Egyptians abroad for education.

As a result of the policies of Mohamed Ali and his successors, Egypt gradually moved to adopt a Western-style legal system, along the lines of the French continental model. There was first the concession to demands by the consuls of Western powers to have jurisdiction over disputes affecting their own nationals living in Egypt. The system was then regularized within the framework of the general legal system by replacing consular jurisdiction with courts staffed by European and Egyptian judges who applied a code derived from European sources. The jurisdiction of these "Mixed Tribunals," as they came to be called, was extended to cover most civil and commercial law matters, leaving the Islamic Shari'a Courts with jurisdiction over only family law and inheritance for Muslims. The civil code applied by the Mixed Tribunals was formally promulgated when the British occupied Egypt in 1882. Mixed Tribunals were gradually abolished in the 1930's and 1940's, and a revised civil code was enacted in 1949, combining Islamic law principles with the French continental concepts of the previous code. Specialized Shari'a Courts were abolished in 1956 as ordinary judges who received training in Islamic Shari'a law as part of their regular legal training

---

[1] The following survey is based on John H. Barton *et al.*, *Law in Radically Different Cultures* (St. Paul, MN: West Publishing Co., 1983), pp. 16-36, and various Arabic sources.

assumed jurisdiction over family law and inheritance for Muslims, together with their general territorial jurisdiction.

On the constitutional and political plane, there were first the developments leading to what may be called constitutional monarchy early in this twentieth century, specially since the adoption of the 1923 Constitution. Britain continued to occupy Egypt from 1882 to 1922, and it exercised considerable influence in Egypt's internal affairs until after the Army's Revolution of 1952 and the final evacuation of all British forces in 1956.

The Egyptian Army took over from King Farouq and his liberal parliamentary system on July 23, 1952. A brief power struggle within the "Free Officers Organization" which led the coup followed before Jamal Abdel Nasser emerged as the undisputed leader of the new regime. He continued in power, under several constitutional instruments, until his death in 1970. The single-party state established by Nasser was taken over by his successor, Anwar Sadat, who promulgated the current Egyptian Constitution in 1971 and undertook some political reform in the mid 1970's by introducing a limited measure of democratic liberties within the Arab Socialist Union, the only legal political organization in post-revolution Egypt until 1983.

Under the 1971 Constitution, the president, who is elected to office by popular vote after nomination by the Peoples Assembly, dominated the political process, with powers to appoint vice-presidents, the prime minister, and the cabinet, in addition to having veto power and emergency powers to issue binding decrees when authorized to do so by the Peoples Assembly. President Sadat consolidated and utilized these powers in his economic and political reforms of the mid-1970's. From the point of view of the present essay, however, it is important to note that the extensive powers of the president, combined with some domestic political considerations, tempted President Sadat to try to manipulate the support of Muslim fundamentalist groups in Egypt against opposition forces. When he realized the dangers of the encouragement he gave the Muslim fundamentalists and attempted to check them following the religious riots of June, 1981, it was too late for him personally. President Sadat was assassinated by a Muslim fundamentalist group on October 5, 1981.

The next president of Egypt, Husny Mubarak, went further in trying to accommodate all factions of political opposition by allowing multi-party politics for the first time since 1952. Several political parties, including the Muslim Brothers, a fundamentalist group advocating the immediate and total implementation of Islamic Shari'a law, contested the elections of 1984. Through an alliance with the Wafd moderate traditional political party, the Muslim Brothers have now gained an influential voice in the mainstream of legitimate Egyptian politics. They are currently employing peaceful political pressure in the advocacy of the implementation of Shari'a law. Other factions of the fundamentalist movement may even be prepared to use force in support of their demands for Islamization.

In relation to religious freedom, it is interesting to note that all Egyptian constitutions since 1923 have had explicit provisions on the matter.[2] Article 3 of the 1923 Constitution provided that all Egyptians are equal before the law, and that they are equal in the enjoyment of civil and political rights and public obligation, without discrimination on grounds of origin or language or religion. Article 13 of the same Constitution added the specific obligation of the state to protect freedom of worship "in accordance with customs observed in Egyptian territory, provided that such observance does not violate public order and is not inconsistent with morals." This proviso seems to have been designed to preserve the traditional relative status of the major religions in the region at the time, namely, Islam, Christianity, and Judaism. There was supposed to be equality before the law, but religious observance had to conform with preexisting custom, even if that custom, as seems to have been the case, sanctioned inequality between Muslims and non-Muslims. The 1930 Egyptian Constitution reiterated the same provisions of the 1923 Constitution, presumably with the same implications noted above. Similar language was also used by the Constitutional Declaration of the Commander-General of the Armed Forces and Leader of

---

[2] All modern Egyptian constitutions and organic documents since 1805 and up to 1971 are published in Arabic, with an analytical table of contents, in *Ad-Dasatir al-Masrya, 1805-1971* (Markaz At-tanzim wa Al-microfilm, 1977). In the following section, I have tried to present the contents of the relevant provisions in English without the benefit of an official translation.

the Army's Revolution on February 10, 1953, following the July 23, 1952, Revolution, and the Constitutions of 1956 and 1964.

President Sadat's Constitution of 1971, however, introduced two elements into his formula. Having dropped, for the first time, the limitation of observance with reference to custom, this Constitution complicated the issue of religious freedom in Egypt by making Islamic Shari'a law a main source of legislation. The provision that Islam was the state religion and that Arabic was its official language was first introduced by Article 3 of the 1956 Constitution. The 1971 Constitution added to this provision the clause that "the principles of Islamic Shari'a law shall be a main source of legislation." This clause was subsequently amended in 1980 to read, "the principles of Islamic Shari'a law shall be *the* main source of legislation."[3] The change from "a main" to "the main" was clearly intended to emphasize the role of Shari'a, thereby giving constitutional support to demands for immediate and total implementation of Shari'a. As we shall see below, this is detrimental to the cause of religious freedom and tolerance. Muslim fundamentalists are now seeking the actual revision of existing legislation in order to provide for the immediate and total implementation of Shari'a. They seemed to have suffered a temporary setback on May 4, 1985, when the Peoples Assembly voted to review the Egyptian legal system "gradually and scientifically" and revise aspects found to be inconsistent with Shari'a.[4] This formula may allow some time for the debate on reform of Shari'a in order to provide for, *inter alia*, a greater religious freedom, as suggested in this essay. To appreciate the need for reform, it is proposed first to establish some working definition of religious freedom before trying to assess the position in Egypt in light of that definition.

Scope and Necessary Implications of Religious Freedom

There is growing support now for the view that basic international documents such as the Universal Declaration of Human Rights are legally binding on all nations as customary international law, regardless of

---

[3] *1985 Facts on File, Inc.,* August 2, 1985, p. 578E1.

[4] *Ibid.*

membership in the United Nations or expression of support for the Declaration. Membership in an international treaty such as the United Nations Charter and specialized human-rights instruments would, of course, create a positive obligation under international law as treaties, without need to invoke the principles of customary international law. In the present context, this means that Egypt is bound by the customary international-law principles of religious freedom as defined in the Universal Declaration, which Egypt supported at its inception in 1948.[5] However, since Egypt is not yet a party to the International Covenant on Civil and Political Rights, with its more specific provisions on religious freedom, treaty obligation can only be derived from the general treaty of which Egypt is a member, namely, the Charter of the United Nations. Respect for religious freedom as defined in international documents may, therefore, be a legal obligation.

These and other documents, moreover, may have a powerful moral and political impact on popular attitudes and official policies even when not legally binding. The practice of other nations, as reflected in their own constitutions and regional documents to which leading states are parties, may also have some influence on attitudes and policies. It is in light of these considerations that we refer to the provisions of international documents in relation to religious freedom.[6]

The history of international concern with religious freedom is the history of the international human-rights movement itself. One of the earliest challenges to the notion that a state has exclusive sovereignty over its own citizens was based on the principles of humanitarian intervention on behalf of religious and religio-ethnic minorities. It is true that at the beginning these were efforts by members of one religion on behalf of their

---

[5] Egypt was one of the few Muslim countries which was independent and a full member of the United Nations in 1948, when the Universal Declaration of Human Rights was adopted. It voted in support of the Declaration, which was adopted without dissenting vote by the General Assembly on December 10, 1948.

[6] Space here does not permit the detailed discussion of the historical background and the description of the nature of the legal system needed for meaningful comparative reference to religious freedom under other legal systems. For a comprehensive treatment of the issues under English law, e.g., see St. John A. Robilliard, *Religion and the Law: Religious Liberty in Modern English Law* (Dover, NH: Longwood Publishing Group, 1984).

co-religionists elsewhere. But the movement gradually shifted into genuine international humanitarian concern regardless of narrow national or religious interest.[7] Thus, Britain was strongly critical of Turkey, its own ally, for the latter's treatment of Armenians in the late nineteenth century. International protests against Russian pogroms against Jews in 1891 and 1905 were at least partially motivated by genuine concern for the principle of religious freedom. The need to provide for religious freedom ranked high in many international treaties until the concept was consolidated and developed by the peace treaties of 1919 and the efforts of the League of Nations. It is very significant to note here the close relationship between regional and international peace on the one hand, and religious freedom on the other, in recognition, no doubt, of the historical fact that religious tension and conflict has always been a major cause of war and armed conflict. Viewed from this angle, the need to protect religious freedom and promote tolerance would be part and parcel of the obligation of all states under the Charter of the United Nations. This is particularly so for Egypt, on whose suggestion the positive state obligation to respect human rights received specific mention in the Charter back in 1945.[8]

The Universal Declaration of Human Rights was designed to specify and elaborate upon the human-rights provisions of the United Nations' Charter. Besides the general Provisions of Article 1 for freedom and equality in dignity and rights for all human beings, and the prohibition of discrimination on grounds of religion under Article 2, both of which are relevant to questions of religious freedom, Article 18 of the Universal Declaration reads as follows: "Everyone has the right to freedom of thought, conscience and religion; this right includes freedom to change his religion or belief, and freedom, either alone or in community of others and in public or

---

[7] Evan Luard, "The Origins of International Concern over Human Rights," in Evan Luard, ed., *The International Protection of Human Rights* (1967), p. 9; and Arthur H. Robertson, *Human Rights in the World*, 2nd ed. (1982), pp. 19-21.

[8] Egypt was one of the countries which suggested the amendment to the Dumbarton Oaks Proposals in 1945 so as to state definitely the United Nations' obligation "to promote respect for human rights and fundamental freedoms" (U.N. Conference on International Organization, vol. 3, pp. 453ff.). See John P. Humphrey, "The U.N. Charter and the Universal Declaration of Human Rights," in Luard, *International Protection*, p. 40.

private, to manifest his religion or belief in teaching, practice, worship and observance." The provisions of the Charter are directly binding on Egypt as treaty obligations. The provisions of the Universal Declaration, moreover, are binding both as the most authoritative interpretation of the Charter's human-rights provisions as customary international law.[9]

The Charter and the Universal Declaration were part of the same process that produced the International Covenant on Civil and Political Rights of 1966.[10] Egypt is not a party to this treaty and may not, therefore, be legally bound by its provisions, but since the Covenant has been signed and ratified by more than seventy states, including many Muslim countries,[11] it can at least be said to have significant persuasive authority in relation to Egypt.

Article 18 of the International Covenant on Civil and Political Rights added three specific implications to the general provisions of Article 18 of the Universal Declaration: freedom from coercion which impairs freedom to have or adopt a religion or belief of one's choice; restriction of limitations on freedom to manifest one's religion or beliefs only to limitations which are prescribed by law and are necessary to protect public safety, order, health, or morals, or the fundamental rights and freedoms of others; and respect for the liberty of parents or legal guardians to ensure the religious and moral education of their children in conformity with their convictions.

Another source of internationally accepted standards of religious freedom is the recent Declaration on the Elimination of Intolerance and Discrimination Based on Religion or Belief, adopted by the General

---

[9] Robertson, *Human Rights*, pp. 27-28.

[10] In accordance with the resolution of the General Assembly of February 12, 1946, the Economic and Social Council directed the Human Rights Commission to prepare the International Bill of Rights, which was later divided into the Universal Declaration of 1948 and the Civil and Political Rights and the Economic, Social, and Cultural Rights Covenants of 1966. See, generally, Louis B. Sohn, "A Short History of the United Nations Documents on Human Rights," in *The United Nations and Human Rights*, 18th report of the Commission to Study the Organization of Peace, pp. 59-60.

[11] Iran, Iraq, Jordan, Lebanon, Libya, Mali, Morocco, Senegal, Syria, and Tunisia are members of the Covenant. Other countries where Muslims constitute a significant proportion of the population, if not the majority, such as Guinea, Tanzania, and Kenya, are also members of the Covenant.

Assembly of the United Nations on November 25, 1981.[12] Article 2 (2) of this Declaration defined intolerance and discrimination based on religion or belief as being any "distinction, exclusion, restriction or preference based on religion or belief and having as its purpose or as its effect nullification or impairment of the recognition, enjoyment or exercise of human rights and fundamental freedoms on an equal basis." Article 3 condemns such discrimination, while Article 4 calls upon states to take effective measures, including enactment and rescindment of legislation, in order to prevent and eliminate such discrimination. Article 5 elaborates upon and regulates the principle of moral education of children in accordance with the wishes of parents or legal guardians. Activities that may be undertaken in exercise of the right to freedom of thought, conscience, or belief mentioned in Article 6 by way of *inter alia* are clearly intended as illustrations of the right, not as an exhaustive list.

Following Article 7 on state obligation to implement through national legislation the rights and freedoms set forth in the Declaration, Article 8 provided that nothing in the Declaration may be construed as restricting or derogating from the rights defined in the Universal Declaration on Human Rights and the International Covenants of Human Rights. This particular Article is important in the Egyptian context because the Declaration does not expressly mention the right to change one's religion, while Article 18 of the Universal Declaration and Article 18 of the International Covenant on Civil and Political Covenant do include this freedom in their formal definition of religious freedom. By endorsing the text of Article 8 of the Declaration on Religious Tolerance, Egypt has reaffirmed its commitment to religious freedom as defined at least in the Universal Declaration, if not also in the Covenant on Civil and Political Rights.

Guarantees against discrimination on grounds of religion or belief and substantive freedoms of religion and belief are also provided for in all three regional human rights instruments, namely, the European Convention for the Protection of Human Rights and Fundamental Freedoms of 1950, the

---

[12] Such a Declaration would not be, in itself, binding, because it is not a treaty, but it may be taken as further evidence in support of an international obligation to maintain standards of religious freedom.

American Convention on Human Rights of 1969, and the African (Banjul) Charter on Human and People's Rights of 1981. Besides the special significance of the African Charter to Egypt as a member of the Organization of African Unity and signatory to the Charter,[13] all three regional documents may be cited in support of the proposition that the protection of religious freedom in these terms has become an established principle of customary international law binding on all states. These documents also add to the moral and political authority in support of this freedom.

When we turn to the available empirical evidence in the case of Egypt, we find that religious freedom has historically been violated and continues to be so violated today. The scale and magnitude of such violation is likely to increase drastically in the near future unless very specific positive steps are taken to guard against this very real possibility.

Religious Freedom and Tolerance in Egypt

Prior to its initial Islamization in the seventh century, Egypt was a predominantly Christian province of the Byzantine Empire. Having adopted the Monophysite doctrine (only one nature in Christ), the Egyptian Church of Alexandria was at odds with the Byzantine Orthodox Church, and Egypt was consequently the scene of bloody religious strife at the time of the Muslim-Arab conquest of 640 C.E.[14] It was not surprising, therefore, that the Egyptians welcomed the Muslim Arabs as liberators – especially since the new administration showed promising signs of religious tolerance and political accommodation for the indigenous Coptic population. Although the system of *dhimma* – the compact between a "tolerated" religious community and the Muslim rulers – clearly violates religious freedom by modern standards, in the context of the seventh century that system was a tremendous relief and significant advancement on then-prevailing standards of religious oppression and intolerance. The majority of Egyptians gradually converted

---

[13] Egypt has fully ratified this Charter, which was adopted by the African Heads of States in Nairobi in June, 1981. The Charter has not yet come into force because, as of July, 1985, it had achieved only fifteen out of the twenty-six necessary ratifications.

[14] Y. Masriya, "A Christian Minority: The Coptics in Egypt," in Willem A. Veenhoven, ed., *Case Studies on Human Rights and Fundamental Freedoms: A World Survey*, vol. 4 (Hingham, MA: Kluwer Academics, 1976), p. 90.

to Islam, but a significant minority of Christians and Jews remained subject to the system of *dhimma* as practiced, and often distorted, by generations of Egyptian rulers, religious leaders, and the general population.

Without going into the controversy of the pros and cons of the *dhimma* system, or trying to apportion blame for excesses in its practice, we can still make the following two remarks which are extremely significant from the point of view of the present realities of religious freedom and tolerance in Egypt. First, we should note that in the field of social attitudes and tolerance of other groups, what often counts is the predominant popular perception, or misconception, of historical experiences, regardless of the "true" or "scientifically" proved historical facts. In the specific Coptic-Muslim situation in Egypt, the Copts seem to perceive their history in Muslim Egypt as "a lengthy tale of persecution, massacres, forced conversions, of devastated and burned churches."[15] The Muslims, on the other hand, appear to resent what they see as favorable treatment accorded the Coptic minority by Western powers, which they perceive as a conspiracy between co-Christians against Islam and the Muslim majority in Egypt. Unable to retaliate against the alien powers, the general Muslim population tended to direct its hostility toward the Copt next door – hence, the periodic instances of religious riots and violence referred to at the beginning of this essay.

The second general remark concerns the nature of the *dhimma* system and principles of Shari'a with regard to non-Muslims in general, and Copts in particular. By citing specific examples of discriminatory and harsh principles of Islamic Shari'a law, especially when considered in the modern context of religious freedom and tolerance, non-Muslims in Egypt achieve the double objective of supporting their claims of historical persecution, while at the same time highlighting present and possible future violations of their religious freedom.

This analysis is supported by the available evidence of recent and contemporary distrust and hostility. When the Wafd political party encouraged Copts to participate in national politics in the 1920's and 1930's, it was accused of being dominated by the Copts. In 1937, for example, King

---

[15] *Ibid.*, p. 84.

Farouq utilized the influential Azhar Islamic University in his bid to discredit the Wafd party as being controlled by the Copts, and therefore unworthy of the confidence of the Muslim majority because the Qur'an provides that a Muslim should not befriend or seek the support of an infidel.[16] In the face of such politically damaging propaganda, the Wafd party, naturally enough, sought to disassociate itself from the Coptic minority.[17]

On the more concrete level, and despite the constitutional provisions noted above guaranteeing equality before the law and freedom of religion in every Egyptian constitution since 1923, Egyptian Copts seem to have faced discrimination at all levels.[18] Not well represented in Abdel Nasser's regime, they suffered serious difficulties as a result of the rise of Muslim fundamentalism, especially during President Sadat's later years.[19] In 1957 the Copts protested against persecution and restrictions in building churches, new laws affecting the personal status of Christians, and discrimination in public office, distribution of land, housing, etc.[20] Again, in the summer of 1972, Coptic religious leaders formally protested to President Sadat against "recent provocations and the planned persecutions publicly announced by the Ministry of WAKFS (supposedly, the Ministry of Religious Affairs).[21] According to a report published in 1983, moreover, with the rise of Muslim fundamentalism and intensive governmental efforts at Islamization, the Copts have suffered.[22] Finally, the exile of Pope Shenouda III and placement of several bishops and priests under house arrest by President Sadat following the 1981 disturbances are seen by Copts as further evidence of persecution and discrimination, because their religious leaders were

---

[16] *Ibid.*, pp. 86-87.

[17] Leland Bowie, "The Copts, the Wafd, and Religious Issues in Egyptian Politics," *Muslim World*, vol. 67 (1977), pp. 106-126.

[18] Edward Watkin, *A Lonely Minority: The Modern History of Egypt's Copts* (1963).

[19] J. D. Pennington, "The Copts in Modern Egypt," *Middle Eastern Studies*, vol. 18 (1982); pp. 158-179.

[20] P. Rondot, *Man, State, and Society in the Contemporary Middle East* (1972), p. 276.

[21] For the text of the official telegram sent by Coptic religious leaders to President Sadat, see Masriya, "A Christian Minority," pp. 91-92.

[22] Shawky F. Karas, "Egypt's Beleaguered Christians," *World Views*, vol. 26 (1983), pp. 53-54.

singled out for harsh retaliation while they were merely defending their community against violence incited by fanatic Muslim fundamentalists.[23]

This sense of continued official as well as popular persecution has led some Coptic leaders to declare that it is necessary for Christians in the Arab world to develop a Muslim identity because it is suicidal for a religious community to isolate itself.[24] The very fact that such a solution is suggested is in itself evidence of the ultimate violation of religious freedom: telling the minority that, in order to live, it has to cease to exist as a community!

This suggestion in fact echoes a previous attempt by Christians in the region, including the Copts in Egypt, to seek reconciliation with the Muslim majority through the concept of Arab nationalism. Copts, like other Christians in the Arab world, did in fact turn to Arab nationalism and sought to establish an Arab identity in order to avoid religious classification with its consequent persecution and discrimination. It has been argued, for example, that, by emphasizing the Coptic contribution to Arab nationalism in Egypt and their patriotism and rejection of domination by any foreign church, it would be possible to support greater liberty and tolerance in Egypt.[25] Coptic apprehensions regarding the development of Arab nationalism and the tensions between Islamic and nationalist revivals are also discussed in the context of a call for reassessment of the basic concepts of the historical background to the relations among Copts, Islam, and Arab nationalism.[26] The need for free and candid democratic dialogue is also seen by other writers who see the problem of sectarian strife in Egypt as a political and

---

[23] *The Reflector* (Essen Coptic Church, Iowa), June, 1982, cited by *Human Rights Internet Reporter*, vol. 7 (1982), p. 970. *The Copts: Christians of Egypt*, vol. 12 (1985), pp. 1-2, complains that Pope Shenouda III, since his release from detention, has been prevented by the authorities from conducting services and delivering his weekly sermon in St. Mark's Cathedral in Cairo, and that he has been barred from visiting Alexandria.

[24] Per Dr. George Bebawi, a deacon in the Coptic Church and former secretary to the Patriarch, reported in an article by Sharon Lefever, "From a Coptic Leader: A Recipe for Moslem Coptic Accord," in *Monday Morning*, vol. 10 (1981), pp. 50-55.

[25] See, e.g., Yusuf Abu-Sayf, "The Copts and the Arab National Movement" (in Arabic), *Al-Mustaqbal Al-'Arabi* 4 (August, 1981), pp. 83-91 and 114-122.

[26] Yusuf Abu-Sayf, et al., "On the Copts and Arab Nationalism" (in Arabic), *Al-Mustaqbal Al-'Arabi* 4 (March, 1982), pp. 121-134.

social problem.[27] The tendency to blame imperialism and Zionism for the problem reflected in some current Arab writings is certainly inconsistent with the spirit of objectivity and candor required for such debate. Foreign influences may have sometimes aggravated the tensions and conflict between Muslims and Copts in Egypt, but they could not have done so if the problem were not there in the first place.

As indicated earlier, it is important to note that the other non-Muslims in Egypt also suffer violations of their religious freedom. Muslims who become Baha'is or atheists have been declared by Egyptian courts and authoritative legal pronouncements (*fatwa*) to be apostates, a status which entails a variety of serious legal consequences even under current Egyptian law.[28] According to a superior Egyptian court, a Baha'i marriage is invalid even if both parties are Baha'is, if either party was previously a Muslim, because, as an apostate from Islam, he or she lacks all capacity to make contracts, including a contract of marriage.[29] With reference to arguments based on religious freedom under the Constitution, the court is reported to have held that the Egyptian Constitution does not protect "fabricated sects which are trying to be elevated to the ranks of heavenly religions."[30] The court was not prepared, it seems, either to explain the source of the competence it granted itself to determine whether beliefs are "fabricated" or to state the criterion by which such determination could be made!

On Underlying Root Causes

The pursuit of causes of human behavior is a hazardous and uncertain endeavor, especially if one purports to identify the most fundamental cause or causes in an exhaustive or exclusive sense. Causes of human behavior are difficult to identify because of the complexity of individual psychic and

---

[27] Foreign forces are accused of forcing issues and trying to exploit the situation by such writers as Jamal Isma'il in his article, "Could What Happened in Lebanon Occur in Egypt?" (in Arabic), *Ad-Dustor* 13 (September 12, 1983), pp. 27-29.

[28] Rudolph Peters and Gert J. J. DeVries, "Apostasy in Islam," *Die Welt des Islam* 17 (1976-1977), p. 11.

[29] *The Human Rights Internet Reporter*, vol. 10 (1985), p. 406.

[30] *Ibid.*

group-dynamics factors that determine motivation for action and reaction within various levels of group interaction. Another source of difficulty is the multiplicity of factors that contribute to the shaping of social and political structures and opportunities for response and accommodation. In relation to the question of religious freedom in Egypt in particular, there is also the lack of independent reliable sources for verification of the various aspects of the historical experience of the various religious groups and communities. This tends to enhance the importance of private perceptions based on unreliable oral traditions which are influenced by such factors as early socialization of individual persons within their families and within other significant groups. All this tends to create a vicious circle of self-fulfilling prophecies as the actions of one side are taken to justify the reaction of the other side which, in turn, is taken into account by the first side in reenforcing initial attitudes and justifying further action.

Despite these difficulties, some hypothesis on underlying causes is necessary for treatment or remedial action. It is useful, nonetheless, to note the difficulties and limitations of causation theorization.

In the context of religious freedom and tolerance in Egypt, there are, on the one hand, Coptic perceptions of historical experience interacting with elements in individual socialization and group dynamics in relation to the Muslim majority. On the other hand, there are Muslim perceptions of historical experience interacting with elements of individual socialization and group dynamics not only in relation to the Copts but also in relation to other religious minorities. Out of this complex process of interaction within and across religious boundaries, initial fears and apprehensions of one side are confirmed and used to justify patterns of behavior that confirm the fears and apprehensions of the other side. Coptic prophecies about Muslim attitudes and behavior toward Copts prompt certain Coptic responses that, in turn, confirm Muslim prophecies about Coptic attitudes and behavior toward Muslims and prompt certain Muslim responses. It is obvious that this vicious circle must be broken through candid, objective *dialogue*.

To break the circle, one side must take the first step in bridging the centuries-old credibility gap. It is herein suggested that the Muslims must not only initiate such dialogue but must also do so with such a degree of candor and objectivity as is necessary under all circumstances. There are at least two main reasons why it is imperative that the Muslims initiate this interchange. There is first the tactical factor, namely, that only the dominant majority can afford to take the first step in bridging the credibility gap. The second reason is substantive in that the Muslims have to demonstrate that the repression and persecution of the *dhimma* system are not going to be repeated.

The *dhimma* system and related aspects of Shari'a rules on the status of non-Muslims are obviously fundamental to the whole process described above. Besides its extremely significant historical role, with its impact on current attitudes and responses, the *dhimma* system and related rules will be reintroduced in Egypt today if the Muslim fundamentalists succeed in achieving immediate and total implementation of traditional Shari'a. Major features of this system and other discriminatory rules are bound to apply even if Shari'a is introduced "gradually and scientifically," as planned by the current Egyptian People's Assembly, unless the highly original reform technique suggested at the end of this essay is employed first to revise Shari'a rules before any legislation is undertaken. The following brief survey will show why the *dhimma* system and related rules of Shari'a had that historical role and continue to pose such a grave threat to religious freedom not only in Egypt but also throughout the Muslim world.

Categorization and discrimination on grounds of religion or belief is fundamental to traditional Shari'a law. As stated by Majid Khadduri forty years ago, "Human Rights in Islam, as prescribed by the Divine law, are the privilege only of persons of full legal capacity. A person with full legal capacity is a living human of mature age, free, and of Moslem faith. It follows, accordingly, that non-Moslems and slaves who lived in the Islamic states were only partially protected by law or had no legal capacity at all."[31] According to Shari'a, a person's status, legal rights, and capacity are determined by one's religion, whether he or she is a Muslim, a *Kitabi* who is a

---

[31] "Human Rights in Islam," *Annals of the American Academy of Political and Social Science*, vol. 243 (1946), p. 79. Reference to slaves is not of historical interest only, because the legal principles governing the status of slaves remain valid within Islamic jurisprudence, although slavery has ceased to exist in practice.

believer in one of the heavenly revealed scriptures, mainly Christians and Jews, or a non-*Kitabi* non-Muslim. Only the first group, Muslim, are full citizens of an Islamic state enjoying all the rights and liberties of a citizen. *Kitabis* may be tolerated as a community enjoying a limited degree of independence under a compact of *dhimma* with the Muslim rulers. A non-*Kitabi* non-Muslim has no rights whatsoever under traditional Shari'a law, except under a license of *aman*, a license or safe-conduct allowed to foreign emissaries and merchants. Polytheists and other unbelievers are not supposed to be tolerated at all as permanent residents of an Islamic state governed by traditional Shari'a law. Their historical or contemporary existence in Muslim countries may be dictated by political expediency or other considerations in violation of strict rules of Shari'a.

This approach to personal status and legal rights is obviously highly objectionable from the point of view of human rights in general and religious freedom in particular. This is clearly illustrated by the briefest review of the relevant rules of Shari'a. A Muslim who abandons Islam, whether or not he or she subsequently embraces another faith, is guilty of the crime of apostasy, which is punishable by death under Shari'a law. Apostasy also involves several civil-law consequences. Besides losing the capacity to conclude any contract, whether in disposition of property or in relation to personal status such as a contract of marriage, an apostate loses all his or her property to the state. If married to a Muslim, his or her marriage is immediately dissolved.[32]

Personal status and legal rights of *Kitabis* are determined by the particular compact of *dhimma* the community concluded with the Muslim rulers, subject to the general rules of Shari'a. In other words, the degree of communal autonomy and range of individual legal rights granted to the particular community of believers in one of the heavenly revealed scriptures are determined by the terms of their compact with the Muslim rulers within the framework of Shari'a law.[33] Originally modeled on the example of the

---

[32] On the meaning and consequences of apostasy, see Peters and DeVries, "Apostasy in Islam."

[33] The following survey is based on the great wealth of detail and documentation provided by Bat Ye'or in her book, *The Dhimmi Jews and Christians under Islam*, tr. David Maisel, Paul Fenton, and David Littman (Rutherford, Madison, Teaneck, NJ: Fairleigh Dickinson University Press; London and Toronto: Associated University Presses, 1985).

compacts concluded during the first decade after Hijra (622 to 632 C.E.) between the Prophet and the Jewish and Christian tribes of Arabia, the compacts of *dhimma* drawn up by generations of Muslim rulers varied with geopolitical conditions – and sometimes with the temperament and personal inclination of the particular ruler. At best, the compact granted the religious minority the "right to collect taxes for their own communal institutions, the right to administer justice in matters of personal law, freedom of religious education and worship, and recognized the official status of the head of each community."[34] Often, unfortunately, the *dhimma* lost its original character and became "the formal expression of a legalized persecution."[35] All compacts of *dhimma* are subject to general Shari'a rules that provide for the imposition of the humiliating personal tax (*jizia*), exclusion from public office, inequality before the law, and other measures designed to segregate and humiliate the tolerated unbelievers in Islam.

Unbelievers in God, as identified by Shari'a, are not tolerated at all within a Muslim state except under temporary license. Hindus and Buddhists, as well as adherents of all "fabricated sects which are trying to be elevated to the ranks of heavenly religions," according to the formula used by the Egyptian court quoted above, are never to be tolerated except under temporary license. They have no rights whatsoever outside the terms of that license.

In the light of this brief survey, one can hardly fail to appreciate the deep resentment and grave apprehensions of Copts and other non-Muslims in Egypt. Historical controversy aside, the best *dhimma* system in conception and implementation would still discriminate against Christians and Jews and violate their religious freedom. Further, the violation of the fundamental rights of other non-Muslims is even much more objectionable in the context of a modern national state.

---

[34] *Ibid.*, p. 49.

[35] *Ibid.*, p. 48.

Toward Greater Religious Freedom

Given that Muslims are the dominant majority which oppresses – or is at least perceived as oppressing – Copts and other non-Muslims in Egypt, the credibility of any proposal to increase and enhance religious freedom depends on the willingness of the Muslims to discuss all aspects of the problem. In particular, Muslims must be prepared to see the full implications of *dhimma* and other Shari'a rules on non-Muslims from the point of view of Egyptian non-Muslims who are the victims of these rules.

However sympathetic a modern Muslim may be, little can be done within the framework of existing Shari'a law. The rules discriminating against non-Muslims and subjecting them to the various limitations outlined above are the necessary product of Shari'a rules of *'usol al-fiqh*, which are the techniques by which detailed Shari'a rules on any given question are determined. Given the sources of Shari'a and the techniques by which rules are derived from those sources, discrimination against some non-Muslims and the total intoleration of others are unavoidable. The only way out is to revise the rules of *'usol al-fiqh* themselves so that alternative Islamic Shari'a rules may be derived from the basic sources of Islam, albeit at variance with some Shari'a principles as known to Muslims today. In other words, to develop modern Islamic Shari'a law, Muslims need to revise the rules that govern the making of rules.

The basic sources of Islam are the Qur'an and Sunna, the first being the literal word of God as revealed to the Prophet, while the second is the example set by the Prophet through his utterances and other traditions. The traditions of his leading companions (*sahaba*) also enjoy varying degrees of authority according to the relative status of the particular companion because the Prophet himself said that his companions are capable of offering guidance to Muslims. With the growth of the Muslim domain and the development of Islamic civilization, learned scholars and jurists turned to the task of the articulation and tabulation of legally binding principles of Shari'a law out of the basic sources indicated above. This involved a highly technical process of authentication of traditions, determination of the relative weight of sources, reconciliation of apparently contradictory authorities and the general rationalization of the emerging body of jurisprudence as a whole.

Of particular significance to the proposed reform of Shari'a rules on *dhimma* and non-Muslims are the rules of abrogation (*naskh*) which determined those parts of the Qur'an and Sunna that were operative as sources of legally binding rules and others which were not so operative, although remaining part of the Qur'an and Sunna. According to these rules, the verses of the Qur'an advocating freedom of choice in religion, for example, do not mean what they appear to say; they should rather be read in the light of the legally operative verses of *jihad* and the status of non-Muslims. Thus, Chapter 18, verse 29 of the Qur'an, which instructs the Prophet to tell people that he is bringing forth the truth as he received it from the Lord and that they are free to believe or disbelieve does not mean that one can remain an unbeliever in Islam without suffering adverse consequences or that a Muslim is free to repudiate his or her faith in Islam. By citing other sources, the early Muslim jurists have determined that the verses of the Qur'an advocating freedom of choice in religion are subject to abrogation or repeal (*naskh*), thereby becoming not legally binding. This is the current position under Shari'a – hence, the rules on *dhimma* and non-Muslims referred to above.

The techniques by which general principles and rules were to be derived from the basic sources came to be known as the science of *'usol al-fiqh*, largely attributed to Imam Ash-shaf'y, the founder of one of the four major Sunni schools of Islamic jurisprudence. The substantive part of Shari'a dealt with rules governing every aspect of public and private, communal and individual, domestic and international life. Sunni and Shii'te schools of jurisprudence differ on many points of detail, but they all agree on the broad principles of *dhimma* and discrimination against non-Muslims outlined above. It is futile, therefore, to seek the abolition of these principles through research into differences between the various schools of jurisprudence or differences between the various jurists and scholars. As indicated above, given the sources and the established techniques for deriving detailed principles and rules from those sources, no Muslim jurist or scholar can possibly reach different conclusions.

It is not possible to change the source of the law and remain within Islam, because Islam, by definition, is the norms, ethical principles, worship

510

practices, etc., to be derived from the Qur'an and Sunna. It may be possible, however, it is suggested, to revise the techniques for deriving detailed rules. In other words, it may be possible to develop a modern version of the science of *'usol al-fiqh*, because it was the work of ordinary men of piety and learning who applied themselves to the sources of Islam in order to meet the needs and expectations of their society in its particular historical and geographical context. What is to prevent pious and learned Muslims of today from applying themselves to the same sources, but with a fresh modern perspective?

One pious and learned Muslim who did precisely that was the late Sudanese scholar Ustadh Mahmoud Mohmed Taha.[36] Space does not permit a full exposition of the thought of Ustadh Mahmoud, but the main implications of his thinking in relation to religious freedom may be summarized as follows.[37] He conceded that the technique of abrogation (*naskh*) mentioned above was necessary and desirable to enact the body of law suited to that stage of human development. Such abrogation, however, was not designed to be a permanent and final abrogation of the verses of freedom of choice in religion, but rather a postponement until such time when the exercise of that freedom of choice and its full implications were the proper norm of the day. In this way, abrogation may now be reversed to enact the verses supporting religious freedom and repeal or abrogate the legal effect of verses restricting such freedom.

To avoid any misunderstanding of the position of Ustadh Mahmoud, it should be emphasized that he did not propose to discard any part of the Qur'an or undermine its divine nature. What he did suggest, however, was that Muslims should undertake modern legislation to enact those verses of

---

[36] Ustadh Mahmoud was executed by former President Numeiri of Sudan on January 18, 1985, because he opposed the immediate total implementation of Islamic Shari'a law without undertaking the reform process he advocated. Numeiri had suddenly undertaken a policy of total Islamization in 1983, until his overthrow on April 6, 1985, three months after he executed Ustadh Mahmoud. For a detailed presentation of Taha's ideas, see above, pp. 59ff.

[37] Ustadh Mahmoud published about twenty books in Arabic and many essays and articles in daily newspapers and magazines in the Sudan. The present author has translated Ustadh Mahmoud's main book, *The Second Message of Islam*, into English, (Syracuse University Press, 1987).

the Qur'an which were previously deemed to be abrogated in the sense that they were not made the source of legally binding rules (*ayat al-ahkam*). In relation to religious liberty, for example, he argued that the verses emphasizing freedom of choice and individual responsibility for such choice before God should be the bases of modern Islamic law. To do that, Muslims need to abrogate the verses of compulsion and discrimination against non-Muslims, in the sense of denying them legal efficacy in modern Islamic law. Such verses shall remain part of the holy Qur'an for all purposes except the purpose of legally binding rules. In other words, in the same way that early Muslim jurists employed the technique of abrogation (*naskh*) to rationalize and develop a body of law for their time, modern Muslims should undertake a similar process in order to develop a body of law for modern society. The only difference is that some of the verses of the Qur'an which were not deemed to be legally binding in the past are to be legally enacted into law today, with the necessary consequence that some of the hitherto-enacted verses are to be rendered unbinding in the legal sense. The resultant law would be modern Islamic law because it is derived from the Qur'an to satisfy the needs and aspirations of modern women and men.

This is one way – and in the view of the present author a very promising way – for reforming Shari'a rules to abolish *dhimma* and all discrimination against non-Muslims under Shari'a. Unless these are abolished, there is no prospect for religious freedom in Egypt or anywhere else in the Muslim world which purports to apply any part of Shari'a. The immediate and total implementation of Shari'a demanded by Muslim fundamentalists would make a difficult situation completely intolerable.

RELIGIOUS LIBERTY AND HUMAN RIGHTS IN THE SUDAN[*]

Khalid Duran[**]

The Sudanese case might be a particularly apt example to illustrate the interrelatedness of the various categories determining the present conference project. Protest movements against the violation of human rights have assumed the form of civil war – patent in the South and simmering in the North. The focal point of this struggle for human rights is the question of religious liberties. The conflict is (a) one within a religion, namely, Islam, involving the cardinal issue of (alleged) apostasy, for which capital punishment was no longer held just as a threat but was actually meted out. It is (b) a conflict within a nation, inasmuch as religious intolerance is largely responsible for the civil war between the North and the South of the country – a civil war that once lasted for some seventeen years and, after an interval of a decade of comparative peace, has been ravaging the Sudan again for over a year now, with ever-increasing intensity. In a way, it is also (c) a conflict between nations, a conflict within the international community; at least it is perceived as such in many parts of Africa. Black Africans tend to view the war in the Sudan as one between an Arab nation in the North and an African nation in the South, with the North occupying the South by way of an age-old expansionism in the name of the Islamic religion. This opinion is

[*] In Leonard Swidler, ed., *Religious Liberty and Human Rights in Nations and in Religions* (Philadelphia/New York: Ecumenical Press/Hippocrene Books, 1986), pp. 61-77.

[**] Khalid Duran (Muslim), see above, p. 49.

held not only by Christians but also by many Muslims in such neighboring countries as Uganda and Kenya. The domination by the North of the South is a cultural-linguistic and an economic-political one. As such it has all the trappings of a national conflict, especially since there is a growing tendency among non-Arab Muslims to side with their non-Muslim compatriots against Arab Northerners. This may seem paradoxical, but it is not without parallels in other parts of the world; for example, black Muslims in Mauritania might occasionally be more sympathetic to Senegalese Christians than to white Mauritanian Muslims.

Much of what is to be said here about religious intolerance in the Sudan might, at the moment, be more potential than real. The fall of the Numeiri-Turabi dictatorship as the result of a popular uprising in March and April, 1985, led to a considerable improvement of the situation. Yet, the same forces of intolerance that backed the ousted regime's controversial "Islamization" program are still very much at work. Not only do they enjoy moral and material support from abroad, but their concepts of religiocultural domination over the rest of the population have also found acceptance with a vocal, though small, section of the educated class. In October, 1985, it was demonstrated on the streets of the capital that this type of highly motivated, well-funded, well-organized religious fanaticism, along with its paramilitary forces, is bent on blocking the process of democratization in order to enforce its ideological notions, regardless of the majority opinion among both Muslim and non-Muslim Sudanese. The rule of the "Muslim Brotherhood" ("National Islamic Front") in the name of Shari'a (Islamic law) from 1983 to 1985 is, therefore, not a matter of past history; rather, it is still an unresolved issue, boding ill for the future of the Sudan.

The antagonism between Northern and Southern Sudan, or between Arabic-speaking Muslims and Christian-led Animists, has its roots in the large-scale slave trade that was common practice till near the end of the nineteenth century. Even after independence in 1956, Southerners used to be called 'abid (slaves) in common Northern parlance. Accordingly, the government had to appeal to the public to desist from the use of such derogatory terms if national unity was not to be jeopardized.

The responsibility for the slave-trade continues to be a hotly debated issue. Northerners refer to the abolition of slavery by order of Ottoman viceroy Mehmet Ali, under whom Egypt was made into an independent power of its own and expanded its hold over the Sudan and even into parts of what is now Uganda. Actually, however, under Mehmet Ali's absolutist rule even sections of the Egyptian population were made to live in a state of semi-slavery. This was especially apparent in the way peasants were forcibly recruited into the army. Some of the Christian missions in Southern Sudan may not have given full priority to the abolition of slavery in the regions under their sway, but it hardly seems tenable to accuse them of having abetted slavery, as some Northern Sudanese and Egyptian authors are fond of alleging. This is not the place to apportion the blame for slavery. The major problem today is that even highly educated Sudanese from the South have valid reasons to complain about a condescending attitude toward them among sections of the Northern Sudanese population, the root cause being that they are regarded as people just emancipated from slavery. A Northern Sudanese professor of political science betrayed this state of mind – perhaps unwittingly – when he was asked about the acceptability of a Southerner as president of the country (instead of their being confined to the role of vice-president, if anything at all). Despite his otherwise progressive stance, he felt that this would be out of the question – just as most people believe a Black could not possibly become president of the United States.

What makes things worse – and is relevant in the present context – is that the way out of this predicament might be conversion to Islam. Some Muslims tend to view this as Islam's emancipationist force. To non-Muslims, however, this is discrimination and religious coercion. Past attempts by Northern administrators to impose Arabic (Muslim) names on Southern school students were regarded by non-Muslims not as a readiness to integrate them but as a first step toward a more-or-less forced conversion.

Language is another issue. The requirement of Arabic – or at least its official or semi-official promotion – is not just a nationalist concern of Northern Sudanese Muslims. It has a religious dimension insofar as Arabic is regarded as a holy language – a belief that is totally unacceptable to non-Muslims. It can safely be said that Southerners would have resisted

Arabization less had there not been this religious dimension to the issue. As a secular language with a purely functional purpose, Arabic might be welcomed by many, because it is an admirable language and a useful instrument.

Muslim Sudanese certainly have a point in charging British colonialism with having deepened the antagonism by virtually cutting off the South from the North, in order to Christianize it. This is not based on historical conjecture, because there is too much evidence to prove that colonial policy aimed to create a "Christian belt" to halt the southward advance of Islam into black Africa. Pent-up resentments caused Southerners in the post-independence Sudan to rise in revolt against the central government, with the result that hundreds of Muslim army officers, administrators, and civilians from the North were killed. The Northern side blamed Christian missionaries from abroad – which was not entirely without foundation – and took strong action against them, at least over a number of years. Keeping in view the fact that the origin of the conflict goes back to the ruthless expeditions of Northern slave traders, it is surprising that the South did not embrace Christianity *en bloc* or *en masse*. The Southern Sudan is still predominantly Animist, and there is also a sizable number of Muslims among the tribespeople – people who embraced Islam freely, not through forced conversion or coercion. Despite the gigantic efforts by European missionaries, Christianity remains restricted to a fairly small minority of Southerners, though they are certainly influential because of the education provided by the mission schools.

The Addis Ababa Agreement of 1972 that ended the first Sudanese civil war provided the South some degree of autonomy. For a number of years it seemed that the Christian-Muslim conflict was amicably resolved. During that period the central government did not go out of its way to integrate Southerners, but instead it made a number of efforts to counter Southern suspicions. The system of government was fairly secularist (politically, not philosophically). There was open confrontation with those Northern forces that had always clamored for the introduction of an Islamic constitution and the conversion of the Sudan into an Islamic state. The one-party system, with the S.S.U. (Sudanese Socialist Union) as the all-embracing political institution, was certainly defective in many ways, but in the particular and peculiar circumstances of the Sudan it was meant to fulfill a specific role – to bridge the gap between North and South, between Muslims and non-Muslims. (Such categorization always implies a degree of generalization!) The Sudan was a member-state of the Arab League even then, but its official designation was the "Democratic Republic of the Sudan," not the "Arab Republic of the Sudan."

Much as the dictatorship of the ousted President Numeiri is now blamed for all the ills of Sudan, and rightly so, it is also true that during the first seven or eight years it held the country together on what was, at least, a semi-secularist basis. The long duration of this dictatorship – altogether sixteen years – cannot be understood if this erstwhile positive aspect is not taken cognizance of. Things began to take a turn for the worse with the policy of "national reconciliation" ushered in by President Numeiri in 1977. This meant reconciliation of the regime with the forces of Muslim totalitarianism, who are usually subsumed under the term "Islamism," that is, believing in Islam as a primarily political ideology, one superior to all other -isms such as capitalism or communism, nationalism or socialism, liberalism or secularism, etc.

As soon as the leaders of political parties with a Muslim fundamentalist or Islamist outlook had returned to their country – with some in important government positions – they made every effort to erode the secularist system from within, seeking gradually to carry through their old design of introducing in the Sudan what they call the "Islamic system." This rekindled fears in the South, causing increasing unrest, and leading eventually to the outbreak of another civil war. The "national reconciliation" – that actually meant the reintegration of the Islamist forces into the political mainstream – was accompanied by economic deterioration, culminating in the disastrous starvation of 1985. In the late 1970's this had already caused fresh resentment in the South. Although the North suffered no less from abject poverty (in fact, the worst-affected regions are in the North), the South felt that its sufferings were due primarily to Northern neglect and economic discrimination.

Islamist ideas – the concept of Islam as a political ideology – are promoted chiefly by two parties in the Sudan. First and foremost is the traditional Umma Party as the political arm of the *ansar* sect, which is probably the strongest Sudanese sect in its number of adherents, although it is only one among many contending forces on the religiopolitical battlefield. The *ansar* sect is of special historical significance, since it enshrines the legacy of the Sudanese Mahdi (Messiah) who died almost exactly 100 years ago, in 1885. He enjoys a special prestige as a kind of national liberator, because he succeeded in driving out – at least temporarily – the Turko-Egyptian occupation forces. His aim, however, was not nationalistic in the sense that we would understand it today. He aimed to establish a theocratic rule not only over the Sudan but also over the entire Muslim world and, ultimately, beyond.

From the viewpoint of human rights, the Mahdi's record was negative with regard to both Muslims and non-Muslims. For the Mahdi, and even more so for his successor, the Khalifa 'Abdallahi, there was simply no question of tolerating Christianity – or any other religion, for that matter. Hundreds of Levantine Christians, who constituted the bulk of the business community in the Sudan in those days, could save their lives only by converting to Islam. Those who wished to return to their faith could do so only after the British had conquered the country and put an end to Mahdist rule. Muslims fared even worse than did Christians under Mahdist rule, because those who did not accept the Mahdi as the "Promised Messiah" were put to the sword, and their wives and children were enslaved. No reading material was allowed except for the Qur'an and the one treatise the Mahdi had written. In order to control the population of the capital, even mosques were pulled down so as to have everyone appear five times a day at the one remaining mosque. Especially the thirteen years of the Khalifa's reign were extremely bleak if examined from the viewpoint of human rights, particularly those concerning religious liberties.

Here one might argue that this is no longer fully relevant because the Mahdi's successors (his offspring) became increasingly moderate, and the Umma Party proved to be pro-British, with all that this entailed in terms of benign conservatism. The best known among the present leaders, a great-grandson of the Mahdi and a former prime minister, is a highly sophisticated graduate of British universities, who is very much at home in the international corridors of political life. Among the Islamists, Sadiq al-Mahdi is comparatively moderate, in some sense almost reformist. He is at loggerheads with his brother-in-law, Dr. Hasan A. al-Turabi, who heads the more radical party, the "Muslim Brotherhood." After a recent split of the "Muslim Brothers," he combined several radical Islamist factions into the "National Islamic Front" (N.I.F.). Sadiq al-Mahdi took a bold stand against Turabi, when the latter was the chief propagandist of the repressive "Islamization" policy under Numeiri. The rank and file of the *ansar* sect, however, still adhere to the fanatic notions of Muslim supremacy over the rest of the population and seek to establish an Islamic state. There is little to distinguish them from the "Muslim Brothers," whose members are often of *ansar* origin. Among the *ansar* elite, too, there has been no critical assessment of their own history, no "revision" of history or coming to terms with the past on the pattern of what the Germans would call "*Vergangenheitsbewältigung.*" Instead of a self-critique or a genuinely religious introspection, even Sadiq al-Mahdi himself frequently indulges in untenable apologetics and Islamist slogan-mongering that put his intellectual stability in doubt.

For both non-Muslims and non-Mahdist Muslims the memories of those theocratic atrocities are still vivid. One century is not that long a time span, and there are still a few grandparents around who can relate stories from their childhood under the Mahdi's successor. This would be enough of a psychological burden even if the present *ansar* leadership were to dissociate itself clearly from that past and proffer a new interpretation of Islam. Since this has not been the case, or only so in a minimal way, the majority of Sudanese (who are not Mahdists) have every reason to fear the influence of this force in politics. In the Sudan it is less a question of "experimenting" with Islam as, for example, in Pakistan. In Khartoum, the "Islamic system" is not projected as an alternative to be implemented for the first time in history, as the Khomeini regime purports to do in Iran. The Sudan, or at least sections of the Sudanese population, celebrated in 1985 the centenary of "Islamization." Even without the tragic events of 1983-1985, we are faced here with the gigantic task of undoing a century-old legacy, with all that this entails in terms of fears and suspicions, of ingrained attitudes and prejudices.

The "Muslim Brotherhood" or N.I.F. as a more modern manifestation of these theocratic ambitions can best be analyzed as fascism in the world of Islam. It bears a close resemblance to the Falange ideology of *nacionalcatolicismo* in Franco Spain. Violent clashes in Khartoum in October, 1985, between "Muslim Brothers" and others, especially non-Muslims from the South, took on an almost racist character, as there were street battles between brown and black. There might be, though, a sad advantage to this aggravation of the situation, inasmuch as people are coming into the open with their real attitudes and true positions. There is no longer any camouflaging of religious intolerance by endless apologetics and untiring rhetorics – with people pointing accusing fingers at others. The N.I.F. now openly demands from the interim central government that the South be crushed with military might and that Shari'a be enforced throughout the country – according to its own narrow interpretation of Shari'a, not according to a consensus of Muslim majority opinion, of course.

Previously, separatist aspirations were largely confined to the Southerners. This trend continues in the full-fledged separatist movement calling for the establishment of a "Savannah Republic" in the southern Sudan. Another idea, however, seems to predominate as a result of the military strength of the insurgent "Sudanese People's Liberation Army" (S.P.L.A.). It advocates an alignment of Southerners with dissident Northerners, be they brown Christians or black Muslims. Together they should subdue Arab-Muslim suprematists and establish a truly secularist order in the Sudan. As a result, Islamists in the North have turned into separatists. Previously, they upheld national unity as the uppermost ideal and wished to exorcise separatism from the South. Now there are voices among the *ansar*, especially among the N.I.F.'s followers, saying that either the South should accept our "Islamic system" or it had better secede, so that we (the Islamists) are no longer blocked. The South, which was seen formerly as easy prey for Islamization, is now regarded as a deadweight encumbering Northern Sudan and preventing it from advancing toward its Islamist destiny.

Beginning with the "national reconciliation" of 1977, the Numeiri regime gradually veered away from its erstwhile secularist stance. Whatever might have been the reasons, personal or political, the dictator came closer and closer to the positions of the Islamists, till he finally made a bid to outpace them by proving to be even more fundamentalist than the "Muslim Brothers." September, 1983, saw the introduction of Shari'a. For most Muslims "Shari'a" has an ethical connotation. They view it less as legal injunctions than as moral precepts. Actually, Shari'a stands for a large variety of religious demands, ranging from rules of cleanliness and a sexual code of behavior to business regulations and questions of social welfare. Modern Islamists have greatly mystified this large mass of precepts as an inexhaustible source of answers to all the questions of life. They have created the myth of a panacea for all the ills of society, a kind of *deus ex machina* on whom Muslims could easily rely. They would then fare much better than by emulating the West.

It may not be without significance that such stalwarts of Muslim orthodoxy as Afghanistan and Morocco, to mention only two, never attached as much importance to the Shari'a as do present-day Islamists who wish for something of their own by which to compete with totalitarian ideologies. In Afghanistan and Morocco, as in most parts of the Muslim world, the mass of the population has mostly followed indigenous law dating from pre-Islamic times. Some sections of the populations integrated a number of elements from the Shari'a into their customary law; others did not do even that. It became something like a standard practice of Islamic religion to have Shari'a and *'urf* (customary law) side by side. The Sudan is no exception to this rule, except that there this organic development, which elsewhere was mostly harmonious, experienced two disturbing interferences – in the nineteenth and in the twentieth centuries. While this made the Sudanese experience differ from that of many other Muslim countries, it is not the only case of this kind. It has a model character for a few other countries. This applies also to the Sudan's having been turned into an experimental field by outsiders. For a new international religious establishment created in Saudi Arabia as a fundamentalist pseudo-church of Islam (in particular, the "Muslim World League" with its enormous network of sub-organizations), the Sudan is of utmost importance. It is regarded as a launching pad for Islamization (in the sense of Shari'a-enforcement) in the rest of Africa. In this poverty-stricken country numerous institutions have been created with impressive funds from oil-rich Gulf states, which are intended to combat popular religion (manifested in the mystic fraternities) and to substitute fundamentalism for it. The next step envisioned is to make this "purified" Islam or, rather, Islamism, spread out from the Sudan into the neighboring countries of black Africa.

Both of the Sudanese experiments with the Shari'a – under the Mahdi 100 years ago, as well as under Numeiri-Turabi till the Spring of 1985 – emphasized the punitive aspects of it, such as the severing of hands and feet, public flogging, and harsh prison terms. The prohibition of alcohol received much publicity, but in essence the entire Shari'a-enforcement boiled down to increased political repression – similar to what had happened under the Mahdi's theocracy. For this reason most people in the post-Numeiri Sudan prefer to speak of the "September Laws." In part, this is expressive of the desire not to blemish the Shari'a with the excesses of a regime generally considered to have been perverse. The term "September Laws" stands symbolically for the worst type of repression witnessed by the country during the twilight of the Numeiri-Turabi government. Important segments of the Sudanese people wish for some kind or other of Shari'a-enactment, but there is a general consensus that it should not be the way the Islamists understand it – and certainly not in the manner in which it was done by the previous regime. The demand for a clear-cut abrogation of the "September Laws" has been voiced in the North even more persuasively than in the South. The South, however, has taken to armed rebellion against them – a desistance from the Shari'a is one of the primary conditions posed by the S.P.L.A. for peaceful negotiations with the central government. This created a dilemma for the interim government, insofar as it found itself unable to do so because of outside pressure, particularly from the oil-rich neighboring Arab states. Therefore, the "September Laws" have been suspended – but not repealed. A democratic government that is to result from the free and general elections announced for April, 1986, will thus be burdened with a pending issue which promises to turn into a major controversy of international proportions. Such

Sudanese developments are bound to have far-reaching effects on large parts of the Muslim world and on other parts of Africa.

Islamists take particular pride in the Shari'a notion of quick justice. Western judicial procedures, with their sheer endless possibilities of appeal and long-lasting lawsuits, are considered decadent if not corrupt. This is a constant theme that is harped upon wherever Islamists are in force, especially in Iran. There might be a grain of truth in this, but the experience in all those countries has been discouraging: overzealous judges, keen on proving the swift effectiveness of Shari'a, committed blunders, and dozens of innocent people were maimed by severe physical punishments. The interim government following upon the Numeiri regime has every good intention of compensating people for the wrongs of the past. However, it could do little to repair the damage done to the victims of rushed justice in the name of the Shari'a. Severed hands and feet cannot be restored to those who proved, at last, to be innocent!

On August 29, 1984, the United Nations Sub-Commission on Prevention of Discrimination and Protection of Minorities adopted a resolution recommending that the United Nations' Commission on Human Rights urge governments which have legislation or practices providing for the penalty of amputation to provide for punishments other than amputation. The resolution cites Art. 5 of the Universal Declaration of Human Rights, which prohibits cruel, inhuman, or degrading punishment. The International Secretariat of Amnesty International reported on "Political Imprisonment in Sudan" (October 31, 1984) that, since September, 1983, at least forty-four amputations had been carried out, including twenty-eight of the right hand upon conviction of theft, and sixteen of the right hand and left foot upon conviction of armed robbery or persistent theft. Several hundred men and women have been flogged with between twenty-five and 100 lashes upon conviction of alcohol offenses, adultery or intended adultery, corruption, and other offenses under Shari'a. After the fall of the dictatorship in 1985, a number of amputated Sudanese, victims of the "September Laws," formed an association, but they were unable to get it registered, and their members continue to suffer much intimidation and a wide variety of discriminations.

Despite all this, one should guard against painting a picture that is nothing but bleak. As in other Third World countries, the experience with colonialism was bitter and left the Sudanese very irritable. They certainly have difficulties in accepting criticism from the "Christian West," which has contributed its own share to exacerbating the country's predicament. Hence, it is especially important to pinpoint exactly where the violations of religious rights takes place, rather than to present too global a case. In this context we stand to benefit from the typology outlined in the preliminary report by Elizabeth Odio-Benito. Examining her points one by one, we discover that the infringement of religious rights is not total. In other words, there is a density of violations at a few points, whereas with regard to other points Sudanese authorities are justified in declaring that there is nothing to complain about. The following comments deal with the Sudanese situation vis-à-vis the nine specific rights enumerated in her report (though not in the same order as she presented them):

1.   "The freedom to worship or assemble in connection with a religion or belief, and to establish and maintain places for these purposes."

A number of Christian sections in Northern Sudan adduce considerable evidence concerning obstruction to the establishment of new churches. In the South, such obstructions are less direct, but indirect obstructions are manifold. The Sudanese Catholic Church has evidence to substantiate its complaint that:

> We were constantly refused the right to build churches or cultural centers; some of our churches were closed, our activities were reduced even though well organized for the profit of Christians as well as Muslims; and in national affairs we were unknown, as if we do not exist.[1]

2.   "The freedom to establish and maintain appropriate charitable or humanitarian institutions."

This is a point of special grievance because the funds for such purposes usually come from abroad. The representatives of foreign missions wishing to aid Christian communities have to go through the central

---

[1] Statement by the Archbishop of Khartoum, Gabriel Zuheir Wako, on behalf of the Sudanese Catholic Church, concerning the introduction of the Shari'a in the Sudan, Khartoum, September 23, 1983. Published in *Mashrek International*, February, 1985.

government. During the sixteen years of Numeiri's rule, even most minor aid operations had to be sanctioned by the president's office. This caused enormous delays, and often nothing came of it at all. Thereby, the impoverished Sudan deprived many of its citizens of substantial foreign assistance because of religious bigotry.

3. "The freedom to solicit and receive voluntary financial and other contributions from individuals and institutions."

Here, much the same situation applies as in the previous point.

4. "The freedom to train, appoint, elect or designate by succession appropriate leaders called for by the requirements and standards of a religion or belief."

Here, obstructions due to individual attitudes have to be distinguished from government policy, which showed some degree of indifference, for the most part.

5. "The freedom to observe days of rest and to celebrate holidays and ceremonies in accordance with the precepts of one's religion or belief."

There has been no obvious obstructionist government policy, except that some authorities did occasionally create hurdles as a result of personal bias. In this case, the behavior of Christians has at times been almost provocative. Khartoum used to witness Christmas processions that assumed the character of para-military marches – something hardly seen elsewhere in the world. It is difficult, indeed, to see any connection between those marches and Christmas. The phenomenon can be understood only as a militant reaction by a Christian minority embittered by all kinds of injuries, past and present.

6. "The freedom to establish and maintain communications with individuals and communities in matters of religion or belief at the national and international levels."

Here, obstructions have been of a more general nature, as a matter of an overall totalitarian government policy, but rarely is it specifically anti-Christian.

7. "The freedom to teach a religion or belief in places suitable for these purposes."

While there has usually been sufficient freedom to do this, it has, nonetheless, been an issue where Christians often felt aggrieved. They are free to teach their religion but find themselves confronted by an educational policy devised by Muslims with a clear bias in favor of the Arab North. Christians in Pakistan would have a very similar complaint (Hindus in Pakistan, even more so!). This observation raises doubts whether this useful nine-point typology is comprehensive enough. It might be necessary to reformulate some of the points or add other ones.

8.   "The freedom to write, issue and disseminate relevant publications in these areas."

This point is somewhat similar to the last one. We should ask what good this freedom is if a poor minority community which is hardly able to produce its own publications is swamped by publications of an opposing majority – moreover, one with government support and sometimes even done through official channels. Islamists such as the "Muslim Brotherhood" and the newly formed N.I.F. receive unlimited funds from the oil-rich Gulf states. Some Islamist factions are heavily financed by Iran, others by Libya. Since this is a question of rivalry, some "Muslim Brothers" look out for who is bidding the most; others cash in from several sources. The net result is that this is by far the richest political party in all the Arab and Muslim states. No matter the sometimes insignificant number of their adherents – the Islamists have the means to produce abundant literature of all kinds and in all languages. They produce direct and indirect propaganda, maintaining dailies and weeklies and monthly and quarterly journals, for old and young, for male and female, for every taste. This literature is beautifully printed and is distributed free of charge or for a nominal price. It makes an impact even at American and European universities, not to speak of one of the poorest countries of the world, like the Sudan, where students are starving for reading matter.

When Russian and Chinese propaganda literature was first permitted on the Pakistani book market, it had an immediate effect and succeeded in stimulating leftism. For one generation, the basic issue was whether to decide for Moscow or Beijing. Later, the Islamists flooded the market with their literature. Leaving aside the question of quality, the "battle of the books" was won by sheer numbers. At present there is nothing that can match Islamist literature in the Muslim world in quantity. Keeping in mind that we are speaking about propaganda, not truly educational or religious materials, we may even call its quality superior. For a new generation of Muslims the question now is whether to decide for Riyadh or for Teheran or perhaps for Tripoli. Non-Muslim minorities, especially in the Sudan, find themselves almost overwhelmed by an aggressive missionary activity, and they have little to counter this spate of publications. The Animist majority in the Southern Sudan suffers most from this onslaught, because Christians at least have their own publications to fall back upon, however disadvantaged those may be.

9.   "The freedom to make, acquire and use to an adequate extent the necessary articles and materials related to the rites or customs of a religion or belief."

This became a major problem under the Numeiri-Turabi dictatorship because of the total prohibition on alcohol, which went so far as to punish Christian clergy for the mere possession of Mass wine. I should like to caution against giving this single issue too much prominence, because it has often diverted attention from other problems that perhaps were more crucial. Nonetheless, it is an issue that bedevils Christian-Muslim relations wherever Islamist rule enforces the prohibition of alcohol. Under the Sudanese "September Laws" it came into the limelight, but it exists elsewhere as well. Moreover, it has a special psychological dimension because of the implied association of Christianity with moral corruption. The public flogging of the Catholic priest, Giuseppe Manara, in 1984, because he was found in possession of sixteen bottles of Mass wine, is to be seen not only as an individual violation of human rights; it was also clearly designed to intimidate the Christian community as a whole and to stimulate prejudice against it.

Significantly, the typology used in the preliminary report does not seem to touch upon the cardinal issue or issues of the Sudanese case. If this is to prove anything, it merely proves the speciality of the Muslim dimension or, rather, its complexity. The cardinal issue is that of non-Muslim citizens' being subjected to a penal law which they have no right to challenge in any way, a law which their elected representatives have no chance of altering, because a dominating class of Muslims declares this evidently human-made law to be divine in origin, and, therefore, unalterable. Manifestly, there is some similarity to the situation in those countries where "democratic people's constitutions" assume a sacrosanct nature comparable to the theocratic system of the Islamists. Both instances stand out for their exceedingly harsh punishments, although the Islamist practice of mutilating ordinary thieves hardly knows any parallel.

The objections of the Sudanese Catholic Church, summarized in the statement by the Archbishop of Khartoum on September 23, 1983, highlight the ramifications of this issue:

> The Christians who do not have the Islamic Shari'a as their behavioral guidance would certainly lack the motivation to obey the law.

> The Islamic Shari'a encourages the Muslims who are in litigation with the Christians and other non-Muslims. The Christians feel that everybody has the same equitable rights.

> An accurate understanding of the law is essential in order to adopt just attitudes toward it. The Christians consider that the adoption of the Islamic Shari'a is a coercive measure imposed by the law to become Muslim.[2]

An application made in 1983 by the president of the Omdurman Bench of Magistrates, Eitidal Muhammad Fadul, and the president of the El Obied Bench of Magistrates, El Rayah Hassan Khalifa, challenged the constitutionality of the new Shari'a legislative provisions, reasoning that:

> Some of the positive duties under the Shari'a violate the rights and liberties of non-Muslims....It therefore follows that this section provides for discrimination on the ground of religious belief in violation of article 38 of the Constitution which states as follows: "All persons in the Democratic Republic of the Sudan are equal before courts of law. The Sudanese have equal rights and duties, irrespective of origin, race, locality, sex, language or religion."

The full implementation of the Shari'a as understood by the Islamists also signifies separate taxation for Muslims and non-Muslims. This does not necessarily imply higher taxes for non-Muslims. In fact, many Muslims might well be more heavily taxed according to the rules of *zakat* (the religious tax), but it does constitute a discriminatory practice. The crucial point is that the

---

[2] *Ibid.*

viewpoint of the non-Muslims be taken into account at all. The Islamist attitude is to point out the advantages their system is supposed to have for non-Muslims. While this is, objectively speaking, sometimes true, it implies a disenfranchisement of the non-Muslims, because they have no choice but to accept what the majority community believes is best for them. An example from India illustrates this point. Under the rule of enlightened Moghul emperors such as Akbar, taxation was secular in nature; Hindus and Muslims were subjected to the same type of government taxes. Later, Emperor Aurangzeb introduced the traditional Shari'a taxation, according to which Muslims had to pay the *zakat* and non-Muslims, a tax called *jizya*. A delegation of Hindu peasants appealed to the authorities to return to the former system; though they had to pay less under Shari'a taxation, they preferred to pay more – as they had done till then – because they did not want to be classified as a kind of citizen different from their Muslim neighbors. In modern parlance we would say they were prepared to pay higher taxes in order not to be declared second-class citizens. The same is the opinion of non-Muslim Sudanese. It would be an important task of human-rights activists to bring this point home to the Islamists who display much insensitivity in this regard.

Under the "September Laws," non-Muslims were not yet exempt from military service. However, should the Shari'a-application be taken to its logical conclusion, the defense of the country would become a preserve of Muslim citizens, with the army closed to Animists and Christians.

In Pakistan, Islamists have developed the concept of a "separate electorate." In this system, Muslims can vote for Muslim candidates; non-Muslims, only for non-Muslims. Again, this is in tune with the ancient Shari'a. In the modern context, however, its primary purpose is to prevent Muslim politicians who are sympathetic to the minorities from gaining votes or being elected with a non-Muslim support. A rule of the "Muslim Brotherhood" or N.I.F. in the Sudan would lead to a similar system.

There is yet another aspect of the application of the Shari'a that does not seem to implicate non-Muslims directly; indirectly, however, it affects them all the more. This is the position of women, which definitely differs from the concept of equal rights for all found in the United Nations' human-rights charter. Whatever arguments the advocates of the traditional Shari'a adduce in favor of its equity, this is certainly one of the most controversial issues. No doubt, in its time (seventh-century Arabia) the Shari'a brought about a revolution and greatly improved the lot of women. This dynamic process, however, came to a halt, and even became retrogressive in part. No wonder, then, that the question of women's rights figures prominently in the literature of contemporary Islam. There is the large apologetic strand endeavoring to prove that true female emancipation can only be found in Islam. On the other side are many Muslim reformers and modernists who are highly conscious that all is not well with the position of women according to the Shari'a as an ossified code of conduct. This issue, more than any other, prompted reformists to demand a further development of the Shari'a in tune with the social developments of the age.

There are numerous Muslim thinkers all over the world, both men and women, who criticize the inferior status of women in the Shari'a handed down to us. At first sight this looks like a headache for Muslim women alone, but the general and detailed restrictions imposed upon women by the Shari'a have their effect on public life as a whole, so that non-Muslim women stand to suffer almost as much as their Muslim sisters. It is not so much the chances for education that diminish as it is the possibilities to put acquired education to use. There is the danger of women being confined to the "classical careers" in education and medicine. Stringent Shari'a interpretations impose restrictions even in those domains, and in some countries women no longer enjoy the professional scope previously achieved. There are some segments among Sudanese Islamists who hold that women teachers can teach only female pupils, that women physicians can treat only female patients, and that female nurses should serve only in women's wards.

According to the traditional Shari'a as it is understood by mainstream Sudanese Islamists, a women's testimony is worth only half that of a man's. So, if two witnesses are needed, but only one male witness is available, there must be two female witnesses to replace the second male. The supposed emotional instability of women is said to render them unfit for most jobs in the legal profession, and this is not the only career becoming taboo if the traditional Shari'a is applied. For non-Muslims this is an altogether unbearable hardship. It closes many careers to female academics. However, this issue also meets with particularly stiff resistance from the bulk of the Muslim community, from most of those believers who do not subscribe to the Islamist ideology. The above-mentioned stipulations became law in Pakistan in 1984. The redeeming feature is that this law was passed only under the aegis of a military dictatorship. There was tremendous opposition to it, and it can safely be said that a parliament emerging out of really free elections is, more likely than not, going to repeal this "law of testimony." Similarly, in the Sudan the overwhelming demand that the "September Laws" be annulled is linked to such justified fears. Muslim women are the vanguard of this protest. The issue of women's rights in the religious context acquired added significance in the Sudan because of the bold stand taken by Mahmoud M. Taha, who was of the opinion that the legal career was a very suitable field to absorb the ever-increasing number of female academics. His writings on this subject throw this issue into bold relief. They constitute both a comprehensive and profound as well as very courageous and conscientious critique of the traditional Shari'a. Moreover, they come from an Islamic perspective and are based on interiorized religious convictions. Significantly, his conclusions are diametrically opposed to those of the Islamists.

It cannot be emphasized enough that imposition of the Shari'a, at least in the shape it assumed as "September Laws," is opposed by Muslims just as much as by Christians and Animists. As a matter of fact, the most sustained effort to rebut the notion of a traditional Shari'a without any further development in light of the present was made by the Northern Sudanese Muslim reformer Mahmoud M. Taha and his movement of the *jumhuriyun* ("Republicans"). In a strictly Islamological perspective, this is certainly a heretical movement, but so were most reform movements in the world of Islam throughout history. Fundamentalists such as the Wahhabis in Saudi Arabia or the Mahdists in Sudan were considered heretical by the majority of Muslims, at least during the initial period. The important fact is that a large segment of educated Sudanese public opinion sympathizes with much of M. Taha's message. In addition, his reform ideas are gaining ground in other parts of the Muslim world.

Sudan's history with the traditional Shari'a as understood by the Mahdist fundamentalists and modern Islamists might explain why such a reformer as M. Taha should rise from that country rather than from neighboring Egypt, with its leading role in Muslim modernism. He was brought to trial with four of his disciples on January 7, 1985. A court, consisting of a single judge with less than two years of judicial experience, took less than two hours to condemn all five to death. He was executed mainly because of his courageous opposition to the "September Laws" and his demand that the civil war be stopped immediately. He insisted, from a purely religious point of view, on the equality of all citizens, regardless of their religion. To this end, he rejected the Islamist concepts of an "Islamic system," an Islamic state, and an Islamic constitution.

The case of M. Taha leads to another issue of special relevance to the typology outlined in the preliminary report to the United Nations. A visitor to the Ministry of Religious Affairs in Khartoum through the years could not help receiving the impression that this seemed to be a Ministry of Islamic Affairs instead. Despite the fact that at least one fourth of the Sudanese population is non-Muslim, there was little indication that this Ministry also catered to the needs of the other religious communities. For this reason, it was criticized by M. Taha, who demanded that it really serve as a Ministry of Religious Affairs, rather than as an Islamic propaganda office or missionary establishment. This greatly upset some Islamists who denounced him for his criticism. Their attacks leave no doubt regarding their inability even to conceive of a joint ministry for the religious affairs of all communities. To them religious liberties cannot assume the characteristics of a pluralist society, only those of a symbiosis of semi-autonomous communities.

M. Taha's self-sacrifice for his convictions brought another cardinal issue to the fore, namely, that of apostasy in Islam – or, to be more precise, the freedom of Muslims to hold different views or interpretations of Islam diverging from those adopted by a given government as the official doctrine. Taha never renounced his faith. On the contrary, all his life was devoted to the cause of Islam as he understood it. The capital punishment prescribed by the traditional Shari'a is, therefore, not merely a threat to those Muslims who choose to abandon their inherited faith, but also is a menace to all who can arbitrarily and all too easily be declared apostates by a religious establishment – while they might actually be fervent believers who do justice according to all the criteria of orthodoxy but differ from others on a few points of interpretation.

What is of special importance in the present context is the convergence between the *jumhuriyun* opposition to the "September Laws" and the objections raised by the Sudanese Catholic Church. M. Taha's teachings correspond to the conclusions of Gabriel Zuheir Wako, Archbishop of Khartoum, when the latter said:

> There are other means to avoid crimes, which are much more harmonious with the nature and dignity of mankind:
> – an effective prevention of crime;
> – an education showing the advantages and the disadvantages of both a criminal and an honest life;
> – a proper religious formation.[3]

The convergence between Christian and Muslim advocacy of human rights is most evident with regard to the public flagellation of women. Thus, Northern Sudanese such as the *jumhuriyun* – but many other Muslims no less – would fully subscribe to the Catholic Church's position as formulated by Wako: "We usually associate women with motherhood. No one could ever bear to see his mother beaten in public or even in private. To beat a woman can raise very strong negative feelings within the community."[4] Finally, the archbishop neatly evoked the tenets of Islam's Holy Scripture, the Qur'an, when he concluded:

> If we follow the retaliation law, "an eye for an eye, and a tooth for a tooth," we would soon be a blind nation. We rarely name God as Just, however; we prefer to call God the Merciful. Our laws should express this splended attribute of God which is mercy.[5]

This tallies with the majority opinion among Sudanese Muslims and has found a forceful restatement in Mahmoud M. Taha's major work, *The Second Message of Islam*.[6] A complaint frequently heard from Muslim

---

[3] *Ibid.*

[4] *Ibid.*

[5] *Ibid.*

[6] The English translation of this work was done, by Abdullahi Ahmed An-Na'im: *The Second Message of Islam* (Syracuse, NY: Syracuse University Press, 1987).

Sudanese during the Numeiri-Turabi years was: Why do outsiders pick up their cudgels on behalf of Christian Sudanese alone? Are we Muslims suffering less? We feel the infringement upon religious liberties not only as dictatorship; for us it also means a perversion of the noble precepts of our religion. Every Muslim prayer is a call to God "the Compassionate, the Merciful."

Appendix

The following excerpts are from *Al Montada*, no. 109-110 (September-October, 1984), pp. 16-18, which carries the full statement, "The Position of the Christian Churches with regard to the Enforcement of the Islamic Shari'a and to the Declaration of the Sudan Being an Islamic State."

We, Christian churches, reaffirm our respect for Islam and for Muslims. We highly regard the spiritual values found in Islam. We profess our loyalty to the Sudan and our commitment to its welfare....We recognize our duty...to contribute to the well-being of our country....It is our right to express this act of loyalty and sincere respect by speaking the truth as we see it, rather than to flatter or keep silent....The road to unity and peace is through understanding, mutual respect, and dialogue. The role of the state is to work for and promote the common good of all citizens without excluding any. The state cannot bring about unity or carry out its role by being discriminatory to the exclusion of a number of citizens, in our case, well over a third....We...once more voice our objection to the enforcement of Islamic Shari'a on all citizens, irrespective of their beliefs, religion, or culture. We also object to...declaring the Sudan an Islamic state when over a third of its citizens are non-Muslims....The oath of loyalty on the Qur'an excludes Christian citizens from participation in the construction and the life of the country; it reduces them to second-class citizens without rights and without freedom. The enforcement fosters divisions in the country [and]...gives rise to religious conflicts....The enforcement would tend to force non-Muslims to become Muslims. Non-Muslims would lose their rights as citizens. It violates the right of any human being to freedom of conscience. Legislation based entirely on Islam cannot in justice bind a nation of diverse religions and cultures....

In spite of the declaration that Islamic Shari'a was not applicable to Christians, we now see that Christians and other non-Muslims have also become the target of these laws...The Christian religion is abused in the public media and in public speeches....Its teaching, legislation, traditions, and practices are ridiculed. The local church leadership, which is 100 per cent Sudanese, has been ignored. They could have been consulted for the common good.

The conflicts within our country have been attributed to Christianity, thus arousing ill-feeling against Christians, and diverting the attention of the nation from the real causes of unrest which are injustice, falsehood, and disregard for other human beings. Christians are being treated as foreigners, when in fact they are real and full citizens of the country. Muslims must live by the dictates of their religion, but they have no right to impose their convictions on others who have different beliefs. In the name of peace, justice, and unity, in the name of the well-being of our country, we make an urgent appeal to the legislators to reaffirm the present and permanent constitution which takes into account the diversity of races, beliefs, religions, and cultures in our country.

Signed by the following church leaders:

Butrus T. Shukai, Bishop of Khartoum

Clement Janda, S.C.C. General Secretary

Daniel M. Zindo, Bishop of Yambio

Rev. Samwiil Jangul Angollo, the Sudanese Church of Christ, Omdurman

Rev. Matthew McChiening, Presbyterian Church in the Sudan, Khartoum

Ephraim A. Natena, Provost, All Saint's Cathedral, Khartoum

Gabriel Zuheir Wako, Archbishop of Khartoum

Joseph Pellerino, Bishop of the Catholic Church, Rumbek

Joseph Nyekindi, Bishop of the Catholic Church, Wau

Paride Taban, Bishop of the Catholic Church, Torit

Vincent Majwok, Bishop of the Catholic Church, Malakal

Joseph Gasi Abangite, Bishop of the Catholic Church, Tombura

Paolino Lukudu Loro, Archbishop of the Catholic Church, Juba

RELIGIONS IN DIALOGUE

1. Leonard Swidler and Paul Mojzes (eds), **Attitudes of Religions and Ideologies Toward the Outsider: The Other**

2. Arlene Anderson Swidler (ed), **Marriage Among the Religions in the World**

3. Leonard Swidler, **Muslims in Dialogue**

4. Paul Mojzes and Leonard Swidler, **Christian Mission and Interreligious Dialogue**

5. Peter K. H. Lee, **Confucian-Christian Encounters in Historical and Contemporary Perspective**